# PROCESSES AND MATERIALS OF MANUFACTURE

## ROY A. LINDBERG

Associate Professor of Production Processes
Mechanical Engineering Department
University of Wisconsin

Allyn and Bacon, Inc.

Boston

Seventh Printing . . November, 1969

© Copyright 1964 by Allyn and Bacon, Inc.

470 Atlantic Avenue, Boston

Library of Congress Catalog Card Number 64–14558

Printed in the United States of America

# PREFACE

Recent years have brought the most rapid technological advance the world has ever seen. It becomes increasingly difficult to be informed in all the important areas of manufacture. This book leads the reader from an understanding of basic operations to a discussion of recent developments in numerical control as applied to machines; metal fabricating with structural adhesives; the application of ultrasonics for cleaning, welding, and cutting metal; high-energy-rate forming methods such as explosive, spark, and magnetic forming.

It is the purpose of this book not only to give the reader a knowledge of important areas of production processes that deal with metal and plastics, but also to help him understand some of the basic principles and theory.

Those who are unfamiliar with this field will be introduced, in rapid succession, to many new concepts. Every effort has been made to clarify each of these concepts by carefully selected schematic diagrams, line drawings, and meaningful photographs.

The subjects have been carefully organized to present a brief overview of the items covered before the more detailed discussion is given. Careful study of this book will aid in making process and equipment selection. Wherever feasible, advantages and disadvantages are pointed out. Summary charts are used not only as an aid in organizing the material but also for process comparison and selection.

The writer gratefully acknowledges the constructive criticism of his colleagues and the cooperation of the publishers and industrial firms that have made this book possible.

R. A. L.

# CONTENTS

v

# THE CHALLENGE
# OF MANUFACTURING

**M**ANUFACTURING PROCESSES have undergone great changes since the days of the Industrial Revolution. Much of the impetus for that revolution was provided by the steam power made available through the inventive genius of James Watt, Newcomen, and others. Our present civilization has experienced the benefits of man's creative genius since that time. However, even at this advanced stage we look forward to exploring the yet uncharted field of science and space, much as Columbus looked for new trade routes in his day.

Even now, vast changes are taking place in our mode of manufacture. As the event of mass production or repetitive manufacture went almost unnoticed when introduced in this country by Eli Whitney in 1796, so today the far-reaching results of technological advance are hard to evaluate fully. Nevertheless, the seeds have been planted, and some of the results are already being realized. Steps in the scientific and technological revolution taking place in the manufacturing field are numerical control, computor technology, and improved materials and processes.

## PRESSURES FOR SCIENTIFIC ADVANCEMENT IN MANUFACTURING

Several factors are at work in fostering the growth of this modern technological and scientific revolution.

The first of these is the upsurge in population. (See Fig. 1-1.) This, coupled with the demand for a higher standard of living, has created huge markets into which working capital could be invested. It is estimated that 70 billion dollars for new tools will be needed annually in the next 10 years.

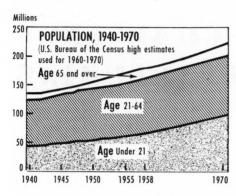

**Fig. I-I.** United States population has grown explosively—9 million added in the 1930's, 19 million added in the 1940's, 30 million in the 1950's. That rate will add 45 million in the 1960's—to a total of 219 million by 1970.

The pressures of foreign and domestic competition are powerful incentives to keep the price of manufactured goods competitive.

The importance of the manufacturing industries to the American economy is being given greater attention, and the result is a more favorable political and social climate for further real advances in manufacturing.

These built-in pressures, then, make the growth of American industry almost inevitable. The rate of growth, and particularly the improvement of production in terms of labor and facility dollars invested, depends on the type and training of the personnel in the manufacturing industries. If they are aware of the technological advances that are available and if they contribute to this development, the rate of growth will be explosive.

One factor that has inhibited industrial growth in the past and may impede future manufacturing progress is the time lag between the development of a new manufacturing process, new machine, or new type of manufacturing equipment or control, and its general adoption by industry. It is doubtful whether this time lag will be acceptable in the rapidly expanding economy of the future.

## NEED FOR INNOVATIONS

Historically, the growth of American productivity has been a gradual one. The emphasis has been on the improvement of existing machines, processes and equipment, and manufacturing techniques rather than on innovation. Innovation is, in itself, a powerful means of overcoming the technological time lag. A company may not care to reequip its plant on the basis of a 10 to 20 percent improvement in productivity. A 100 percent improvement is, however, another matter, and technological innovations of this magnitude are almost irresistible.

There is no strong incentive to replace machines that are technologically obsolete but still reasonably productive and in good condition. The difference between the productivity of the older machine and a newer one designed along the same lines simply may not be great enough to warrant the investment. Only machines based on new concepts, machines with revolutionary new performance, can be economically irresistible in most plants. The development of such machines and methods is one of the challenges which lie within the province of the design and process engineer; it can open up avenues that are explosive in nature in contrast to the usual gradual technological progress.

## THE HIGH COST OF COMMON SENSE

By any standards, manufacturing plants in this country have achieved an extremely high rate of output per worker per dollar of equipment invested. There is, however, a strong limitation on further advances. Until the present, emphasis has been placed on the solution of manufacturing problems by empirical means; indeed, nearly all American industry is committed to the empirical approach.

An economy based on trial-and-error technology must necessarily progress slowly. American industry has reached the point of diminishing returns as far as trial-and-error engineering is concerned. The production challenges of the next 25 years—the development of real innovations that can cause American industry to run, rather than crawl, toward a truly significant increase in productivity and efficiency—must be met through the application of science and sound engineering, thus attaining manufacture on a broad scale.

Many engineers sincerely believe that almost any manufacturing problem can be solved by what they refer to as "common sense." And yet, beyond a certain point, common sense—which usually involves taking a practical, empirical look at the problem—has severe limitations. For example, the fact that all matter is composed ultimately of subatomic particles defies common sense, yet studies of those particles are fundamental to a real understanding of engineering materials.

Similarly, many of the breakthroughs in manufacturing technology are not all common sense. It is only common sense to think that, as material is cut at higher and higher speeds, the cutting tool will become hotter and hotter. Yet, to take an example, experiments at Lockheed, in which materials were cut at speeds up to 200,000 fpm, have conclusively demonstrated that, beyond a certain speed, tool temperatures decrease rather than increase. This phenomenon can be predicted mathematically, as can many other aspects of the machining process. Such work, which is based on general scientific principles rather than empirical or cut-and-try findings, is capable of casting new light on manufacturing problems—a light which common sense tends to obscure. Science, then, is a pathway to industrial progress.

## ROADBLOCKS TO MANUFACTURING PROGRESS

There are several roadblocks to manufacturing progress through science. One of these is the relatively small number of engineers who have applied their knowledge and skill to the manufacturing field. In the past, young people with analytic or scientific minds have not been attracted in sufficient numbers to the manufacturing field. Perhaps this is because manufacturing has traditionally been looked upon as "practical" rather than scientific. Fortunately, the challenges of today's manufacturing have caused a change in this attitude.

Neither industry itself nor educational institutions have shown a great amount of interest in manufacturing engineering. This type of thinking has not been limited to the processing of materials. An excellent example can be found in the electronics field. Except for some work on the electronic properties of vacuum tubes in physics departments, electronics was largely ignored by most universities prior to World War II. Before this time improved electronic circuits were developed, often by radio amateurs, as a result of experiments, but few formal efforts were made to develop scientific theories in the field of electronics. Progress was slow.

When professors in engineering colleges began to apply mathematical principles to the operation of electronic circuits, they could explain, by analysis, some of the "strange" responses that were observed in the field. Analysis provided understanding, and understanding made it possible to develop more efficient circuits and circuits that could do entirely new things. The frequencies in use increased from a few million cycles to 10,000 megacycles, during World War II, as a consequence of new theories developed in engineering schools. During World War II, frequencies in use have increased to 200,000 megacycles, and tomorrow the gap will be closed between today's frequencies and the visible spectrum.

Success in this field was made possible because university-trained scholars saw in the problems a real challenge and a chance to make a major contribution to engineering science. A similar historical sketch could be given for the mining and petroleum sciences. In each case, once the scholar was convinced that the problems were within his province, significant and accelerated progress was made. Something similar can be expected to happen in the manufacturing field.

It was not until after World War II that university scholars turned their attention to metal-cutting research. The increased horsepower and improved cutting-tool materials attracted their attention. The problems that became apparent could not all be solved by the empirical approach. More scientific instruments were brought to focus on metal-cutting forces and chip formation. Grinding, welding, and forming processes were also investigated from a scientific point of view.

European universities have been ahead of American universities in formally recognizing the need for courses related to manufacturing technology. All German technical universities have chairs and institutes for machine-tool engineering and for production engineering. Some of the English universities have similar chairs, but they are still rare in American universities.

European universities are engaged in teaching and research in the field of machine-tool design and operation. Courses are taught in the theory of metal cutting. These include the study of machinability of materials, tool wear, lubrication, cooling, and servomechanisms. The influence of friction and temperature is studied. Certain aspects of solid state, as well as the metallography and crystallography of workpiece materials, are investigated.

Some educators maintain that extremely broad engineering training, perhaps in mechanical engineering, best qualifies a man to enter the manufacturing field. Certainly the range of manufacturing problems is broad, and a wide acquaintance with various engineering disciplines is helpful. At the same time, it should be recognized that manufacturing engineering is a highly specialized field having the same relationship to the engineering sciences as, say, medicine has to the biological sciences. Carrying the parallel a step further, a supply of fully qualified tool and manufacturing engineers is as important to the future economic health of America as a supply of trained physicians is to the physical health of its inhabitants.

## NEED FOR RESEARCH

Ultimately, the degree of innovation—or, manufacturing progress —depends on basic scientific research in the manufacturing area. Traditionally, the relationship of manufacturing industries to science has been a somewhat parasitic one. Although industry has applied the findings of science, it has not, to any great degree, sponsored basic scientific research that is applicable to manufacturing.

With few exceptions, recent breakthroughs in manufacturing technology, breakthroughs that can be exploited by most of industry, have been made as a result of research sponsored by the military services. Numerical control (Fig. 1-2), possibly the leading breakthrough of recent years, was, from its inception, developed and applied with Air Force funds.

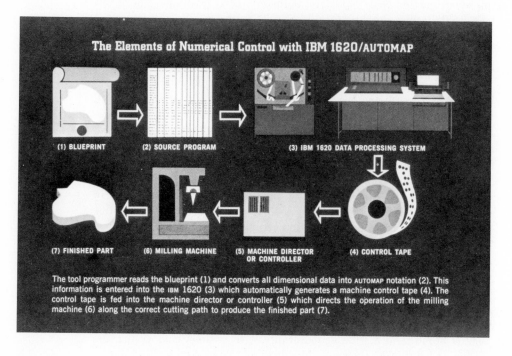

**Fig. 1-2.** The elements of numerical control (courtesy International Business Machines Corp.).

Explosive forming and ultrahigh-velocity machining, two other recent breakthroughs, are primarily the result of Air Force-sponsored research and development. Much of the research and development associated with grinding and shaping of the super alloys and, for that matter, the development of the super alloys themselves, has been financed by the government.

Military necessity was the impetus behind this work, pushing these new developments along at a fast rate, but it is entirely possible that they would have been conceived and put into action years earlier if engineers in private industries had turned their attention to basic research both in their own plants and through the medium of industry-wide programs.

Military-sponsored manufacturing research has had an effect that goes beyond its direct contribution to technology. It has shown what can be accomplished when sufficient funds and scientific and engineering talent are put to work on specific problems. It is doubtful, however, if industry can advance along a broad front on the basis of military-sponsored research alone.

Small companies are able to benefit from research performed by larger companies. A new machining process developed by a machine-tool builder, for example, or a new control developed by a control maker, can be applied by any company, large or small. With respect to basic research, the smaller company may be at a disadvantage. Still, it is surprising how many innovations in manufacturing could be, and sometimes are, performed with a minimum amount of investment and manpower. The basic equipment for explosive-forming research is, after all, merely a concrete-lined tank of water and a stick of dynamite. The raw material of research is ideas. Large companies or the military have no monopoly on ideas. Basic research, whether it is in the manufacturing field or any other, is an investment in qualified personnel.

## TODAY'S CHALLENGES

Recently, a General Motors executive stated:

As stylists and design engineers continue to apply the advances of science and technology in the accomplishment of their objectives, the manufacturing process becomes increasingly complex. This result is inevitable; therefore, successful manufacturing depends more and more on trained minds for the solution of daily problems which face the production supervisor.

Our products, whether they be automotive or other, are no longer a combination of relatively simple mechanical components but are rather a combination of electrical, hydraulic and electronic, as well as mechanical units each of which requires more than a smattering of education to understand their composite functioning.

Today, with the advent of the space age, industry is faced with the challenge of developing new engineering materials. In order to do this, scientists are eagerly trying to understand the nature of materials. As yet, little is known as to what mechanism within a piece of material provides the properties of strength. Several theories have been offered, and the testing of them has begun.

Not only is the prospect of creating new materials fascinating to engineers, but equally challenging is the processing of these new materials.

It is imperative to the economy of a country to develop better materials and more efficient production methods. It will be necessary to produce more reliable parts and assemblies, to closer tolerances, and with lower labor time per unit. This will be necessary not only to meet domestic competition but to meet competition from other countries.

## THE EXPANDING ROLE OF THE COMPUTER

The manufacturing plant of tomorrow will greatly extend the use of the computer. Even now it is possible to design on a computer, then have the same computer process the tape that will be used to direct the machines for the manufacture of the product. The time lag between design and finished product is cut materially. Even more important, the use of computers in manufacturing has freed engineers from tedious routine computations and given them more time for creative work.

Along with computer technology in today's manufacturing plant has come improved instrumentation that can take the place of human senses. Ultrasonic and magnetic crack detectors, infrared analyzers of all kinds, electronic gages that amplify and record sizes and finishes within tolerances of millionths of an inch are only a few of these. This instrumentation, coupled with the ability of the computer to make decisions almost instantaneously on the basis of input data, makes possible the fully automatic control of manufacturing operations.

Not all computers used in manufacturing need be large. Small, simple computers designed for specific purposes are used. An example is a computer used with a numerically controlled machine to detect variations in work-material hardness or thickness. Such computers can be made to override taped instructions to permit the job at hand to be performed more efficiently. Similarly, a computer can be used to detect variations in part size and make necessary machine corrections.

Large computers are now being used to control entire manufacturing lines, regulating the flow of parts and materials and monitoring quality and output. With their ability to process and record large amounts of data, as well as control production, these computers can be an important management tool. Reports on production, inventories, and similar matters can be produced by a computer in seconds, when that computer is linked to stations in the manufacturing area. Thus management will have literally up-to-the-minute information whenever it is needed for decision making.

Some plants are now using computers to simulate production lines. A mathematical model of a line is established, and this model is transmitted to a computer. Mathematical "parts" are then run through the line by means of a computer program. The equivalent of several years' actual production operation can be simulated on a computer in just a few minutes. In the future there will be more of this computer simulation for manufacturing planning, because this technique enables the "bugs" to be worked out of proposed lines before the actual line is built.

Computers can also be used to determine the most efficient machine loading, optimum size of inventories, and the like.

Already computers are being used in product design. The output of a computer that designs a product is a tape that controls a machine tool or even an assembly line. There is reason to believe that this technique will become fairly commonplace in the future. Computers will also be used to determine the performance of new products before they are actually built, applying simulation techniques. Computer simulation may be used to determine the impact of planned products on manufacturing facilities and to develop cost estimates for alternate designs as well.

## FUTURE MANUFACTURING TRENDS

There are many ways to shape metals. Machining or metal removal is only one of these. Processes that may grow in importance are precision forging and casting, cold extrusion, powder-metallurgy techniques, explosive forming, magnetic forming ultrasonic operations and the use of laser light beams. The reason for this change will be the desirability of making parts in as few operations as possible. Basic techniques as well as many of the new manufacturing processes are discussed in this book.

## FUTURE MANPOWER REQUIREMENTS

The highly automated and mechanized plant of the future will require fewer production workers per unit of output than does today's plant. There will be a higher proportion of setup and maintenance personnel who will have a greater degree of skill and training than is normally the case today. Also, a broader range of specialized skills— electronics, hydraulics, electrical—will be required. With a heavy investment in automated equipment, downtime will be costly, and emphasis will be placed on getting idle machines back into production in a hurry.

The manufacturing engineer, the man who plans the production line, will find his task increased in scope. His job will demand a higher degree of knowledge and skill. The basic items of tool engineering, tool design, fixture design, and so on will still be there, but, in view of the extensive use of automated machines and automation, a somewhat broader knowledge will be required. A solid academic background, with emphasis on mathematics and manufacturing science, will be mandatory. Continuous study, coupled with experience in the field, will be necessary to keep abreast of the rapidly advancing technology.

Many of the technical personnel needed to fill manufacturing positions will not be graduate engineers; they will come from among the graduates of two-year technological courses and apprentice-training programs. They will be people who, through self-imposed study, tutorship, or management-sponsored training courses, have acquired a technical background that qualifies them for upgrading. With the fast rate of growth in science and technology, the upgrading of trained personnel will help fill the consequent demand for more engineers and engineering technicians.

Released from some of the time-consuming tasks by the aid of computers and technicians, it is expected that more and more manufacturing engineers will enter top management. These engineers will tend to encourage technical innovation, an attitude that will be the strongest impetus to real progress in engineering.

The organization chart (Fig. 1-3) shows how manufacturing processes and the process engineer fit into the overall operation of the plant. In this type of an organization, all engineering is concerned with the end product, but the process or manufacturing engineer is more inti-

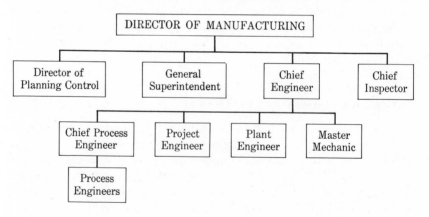

Some duties of the process or manufacturing engineer:
- *a.* Decide on manufacturing feasibility
- *b.* Prepare manufacturing specifications
- *c.* Decide whether to make or buy
- *d.* Prepare tooling estimates
- *e.* Prepare process drawings
- *f.* Prepare machine load charts
- *g.* Specify gauging required

**Fig. 1-3.**  Part of a manufacturing-plant organization chart.

mately associated with seeing it materialize. This chart lists some of the duties that are ordinarily assigned to the process engineer. Duties vary from company to company, depending upon the size and scope of the operation.

The manufacturing engineer must determine feasibility not only of the product designs the company produces, but even those purchased by the company. He must be able to determine whether parts should be purchased or manufactured. Oftentimes, specialty manufacturers can produce parts on a volume basis, thus reducing costs.

In judging the feasibility of manufacture, many things are taken into consideration. The process of manufacture, for example, could involve a choice for a given part between forging, casting, cold forming, or a custom extrusion and weldment. The manufacturing engineer should be able to give detailed information to the purchasing department concerning the selection of products as well as machines and equipment.

The manufacturing engineer must be able to work along with and advise product designers. This requires close cooperation, but it can result in fewer design changes and faster production.

Another area of responsibility is that of following up the use of the specified equipment and tooling for a job to determine if it is being used in accordance with the original plan. If this is not done, it is likely that neither the volume nor the quality of the parts will be as anticipated.

Many items require special tooling in the way of jigs, fixtures, die designs, templates, gages, etc. The tool and manufacturing engineer must be able not only to design them but also to prepare cost estimates.

This brief introduction to the role of the manufacturing engineer and the challenges that lie ahead is not intended to be comprehensive; rather, it is intended to give an idea of the area of work covered. As you study this book, you will see that many new manufacturing processes are constantly being introduced. The manufacturing engineer will be on the alert for methods that can be adapted to help meet the overall objective of *a better product at a lower cost.*

### QUESTIONS

1. What are some contributing factors that can lead to explosive development in manufacturing?
2. Why can technological advances be made faster now than formerly?
3. What factors influence manufacturers to continue operating machines that are obsolete?
4. How will the computer be able to play a larger role in the manufacturing plants of the future?

5. Describe the use of simulation in manufacturing.

6. In what ways will the duties of a manufacturing engineer change in the years ahead?

7. Name some of the specific duties of the manufacturing engineer.

### REFERENCES

Black, T. W., "Revolution in Manufacturing, Part 1—Pathways to Progress," *The Tool and Manufacturing Engineer*, May, 1961.

Black, T. W., "Revolution in Manufacturing, Part 2—The Plant of the Future," *The Tool and Manufacturing Engineer*, June, 1961.

Cronin, F. F., *General Motors Engineering Journal*, Vol. 3, No. 2, May-June, 1956.

# 2

# PROPERTIES
# OF METALS

THE PROPERTIES of metals have been studied ever since man found he could change the hardness of steel by heating it to a bright cherry red and then quenching it in water or other suitable media. What happened to the metal structure was at first theorized, but then, as instruments for study improved, facts replaced theory. The modern-day solid-state physicist is still deeply involved in the complexities of the problem. Some appreciation of the problem can be had when we realize that a piece of matter the size of a pinhead contains roughly 100 billion atoms. Fortunately, nature helps resolve this problem by making the atomic structure of a given solid into a definite pattern. Thus, when atoms are brought together, they tend to arrange themselves in infinitesimal cubes, prisms, and other symmetrical shapes. These geometrical units, joined to each other like perfectly fitted blocks, are embryos of the larger structure known as crystals.

## THE CRYSTAL STRUCTURE OF METAL

Crystals start forming when molten metal begins to solidify. As cooling continues, each tiny crystal grows by adding to itself other crystals in a pine-tree, or dendritic, fashion until each group of crystals touches every other group and the metal becomes solid. After abrasive polishing and etching the metal with an acid, these groups of crystals can be examined with a high-powered microscope.

Each grain consists of millions of tiny unit cells made up of atoms arranged in a definite geometric pattern. Each unit cell may take the form of an imaginary cube, with an atom in each corner and one in the center. This is called a *body-centered cubic* space lattice and is the structure of iron at normal temperatures [Fig. 2-1(*a*)].

If, however, the center of the cube is vacant, and a single atom is contained in the center of each face, it is called a *face-centered cubic structure* [Fig. 2-1(*b*)]. This is the structure of copper, aluminum, and nickel. It is also the structure of iron at elevated temperatures.

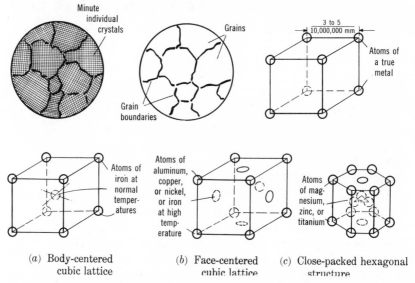

(*a*) Body-centered cubic lattice    (*b*) Face-centered cubic lattice    (*c*) Close-packed hexagonal structure

**Fig. 2-1.**    The various atomic structures found in metals.

When the unit cell takes the form of an imaginary hexagonal prism, having an atom in each corner, another at each of the top and bottom hexagons, and three atoms equally spaced in the center of the prism [Fig. 2-1(*c*)], it is known as a *close-packed hexagonal structure*. This is the structure of magnesium, zinc, and titanium.

The distance between the atoms is extremely small, sometimes only 3 ten-millionths of a millimeter and seldom more than 5 ten-millionths, as determined by X-ray diffraction. These closely spaced atoms have a tremendous attraction for each other. This attraction constitutes the force that resists any attempt to tear the metal apart.

## BASIC NATURE OF METALS UNDER STRESS

Metals in everyday use are subjected to tremendous stresses and strains. When the metal is deformed or cut, certain rows of crystals slip or flow in fixed directions and in one or more parallel planes.

Slippage occurs first in those planes that have the greatest number of atoms. The directions of slip in each plane are along those lines of greatest atom density.

Body-centered structures [Fig. 2-2(a)] have no planes of dense atomic concentration, although they have six planes where concentration is reasonably dense. This is why pure iron is somewhat less ductile than pure aluminum, copper, or nickel.

In face-centered structures, slip occurs readily in four different sets of planes where the concentration of atoms is dense [Fig. 2-2(b)]. There are three different directions of easy slippage in each plane. In pure metals the force that must be exerted to cause slippage is much less than the force that holds the crystals together. This is the reason

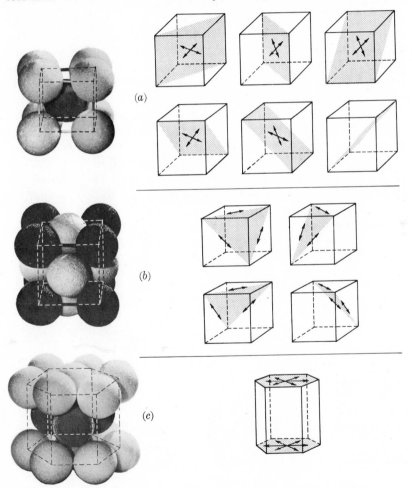

**Fig. 2-2.** The atomic structures of metals are shown as (a) body centered, (b) face centered, and (c) close-packed, hexagonal space lattices. The corresponding number of slip planes is shown for each structure.

why pure aluminum, copper, and nickel flow so readily under stress. This ability of the slipping crystals to hold together makes these metals extremely ductile.

Close-packed hexagonal structures [Fig. 2-2(c)] have only one set of densely packed slip planes, but they have three directions of ready slip in each plane. Generally, the close-packed hexagonal structures are not so ductile as the other two structures.

Although some pure metals are less ductile than others, the resistance to slip among the crystals of all pure metals is much less than the atomic attraction which holds the crystals together. Therefore, unless something happens to slipping crystals to increase their resistance to further slippage, any pure metal under stress would merely bulge out of shape. No breakage would occur; or, in machining, no so-called cutting could be done. However, continued stress on the slipping crystals distorts them until the pressure that must be exerted to produce further slippage is greater than the force that holds the crystals together. The metal no longer bulges out of shape but actually cracks or breaks.

For example, suppose a piece of pure copper is placed on the forming die of a press and subjected to compressive force. This applied force in each grain or crystal is resolved into two stresses, one parallel to the planes of slip and the other perpendicular to them [Fig. 2-3(a)]. If the applied force is great enough, the parallel stress causes the crystals to slip, while the perpendicular stress tries to tear them apart.

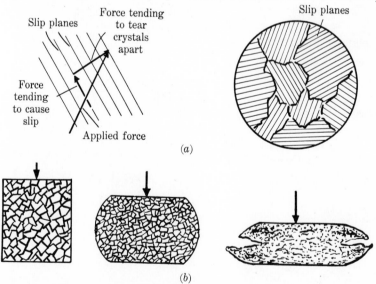

Fig. 2-3. When metal is subjected to continually increasing compressive force, the grains are crushed and distorted. When no further slippage is possible, the metal breaks.

However, the applied force also twists the slipping crystals out of shape until the planes of slip are so distorted that slippage stops. Additional pressure is then needed to cause further slippage. This continues until the crystals are so strained and the planes of slip so warped that no further slippage is possible and the material is fully work hardened. At this stage, the increased perpendicular stress becomes so great that it exceeds the attraction between the atoms of the crystals. The metal is now so highly stressed that it either cracks or breaks if additional pressure is applied [Fig. 2-3(*b*)].

### Dislocations

One of the mysteries surrounding the crystal structure of metals was why they could be deformed by only a fraction of the stress needed to overcome the binding forces between atoms in a crystal lattice. The theory of dislocations was advanced as an answer in 1934, but it was not until 1953 that direct observations could be made with the electron microscope to substantiate this.

Very briefly, the assumption was based on the fact that, under perfect conditions, the crystal structure could be very strong, but tiny imperfections would cause some misalignment of the atoms, and this misalignment tended to weaken the crystalline structure.

There are two main types of dislocation—edge and screw. The edge dislocation occurs at the end of an extra half plane of atoms, while the screw dislocation corresponds to a partial tearing of the crystal planes, much as a stack of papers might be torn (Fig. 2-4). Most dislocations are a combination of both types.

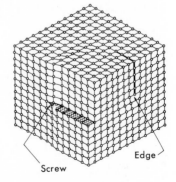

**Fig. 2-4.** Screw dislocations take place as a partial tearing of the crystal plane. Edge dislocations occur at the end of an extra half plane of atoms.

### DEFINING AND MEASURING PROPERTIES OF MATERIALS

Metal properties are so interrelated that it is difficult to talk about one without involving others. For example, one of the most important properties with which we are concerned in manufacturing processes is the hardness of a metal. Hardness, in turn, is closely associated with strength, rigidity, resistance to wear, fatigue, and creep. Some of the more common physical properties of metals and other materials are defined in this chapter, along with a description of how these properties are developed.

## Tensile Properties

**Yield Strength and Yield Point.**   When metals or other materials are subjected to a pulling force, they stretch as the stress increases. The point where the stretch suddenly increases is known as the yield strength. In actual service, the yield strength of most metals and plastics is much more important than their breaking strength.

*Ultimate tensile strength* refers to the force needed to stretch the material beyond its yield point. Oftentimes, when the yield strength of a material is passed, it is considered unsafe for further service.

There is some confusion as to what is meant by yield strength and yield point. The terms may best be explained by the use of stress-elongation diagrams as shown in Fig. 2-5. These curves show how metals stretch, with corresponding increases in tensile stress. The stress is shown in pounds per square inch of cross section and the elongation, or stretch, in percent of the original metal length.

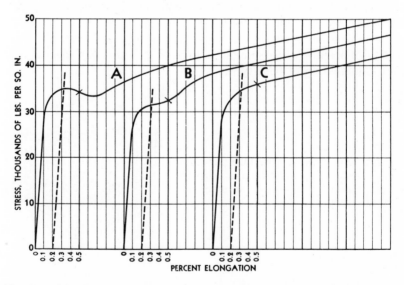

**Fig. 2-5.** Metals *A* and *B* show definite yield points, as indicated by the dip in the stress-strain curve. The yield point for metal *C* is not sharply noticeable. Yield strength is shown at two percent offset (courtesy The International Nickel Co., Inc.).

Curve *A* is for typical mild steel and for almost all soft steels. It shows a distinct dip, indicating that when a certain stress is reached the metal stretches rapidly. Thus the metal has a sharply defined yield point.

Most hard steels and nonferrous metals have yield strengths as indicated by curve *B*.

High nickel alloys such as Monel and other similar nonferrous materials show curves similar to *C*. There is no definite break, which makes it difficult to assign a yield point. Therefore, it is necessary to measure the yield strength.

Yield strength is generally defined as the point where 0.5 percent elongation takes place. It has become common practice to measure yield strength of nonferrous materials as the stress which would produce a certain permanent set. Since this is a little difficult to measure, a simplified version known as the *offset method* is used. It consists of drawing a line parallel to the stress line at a prescribed distance. If the line is drawn at 0.2 percent, as shown, the point at which it crosses the stress line will be known as the yield strength at 0.2 percent offset. Yield strengths at 0.5 percent elongation and at 0.2 percent offset are practically equal in value for many of the nonferrous alloys.

In many applications of materials, it is necessary to know how far the metal can be stressed without taking any permanent set or even varying from a straight-line relation of stress to strain. These applications require a knowledge of proportional and elastic limits.

**Proportional Limit, Elastic Limit, and Proof Stress.** *Proportional limit* is the maximum stress under which a material will maintain a perfectly uniform rate of strain to stress. You will note, in Fig. 2-6, that it is difficult to tell the exact point at which the straight line breaks away from the curve. Even though this value is hard to measure, it is used in important applications such as precision-instrument springs.

Most materials can be stressed slightly above the proportional limit without taking a permanent set. The maximum stress from which a material can recover is called the *elastic limit*. As with yield strength, the elastic limit is somewhat tedious to find, as it consists of a series of slightly increasing loads until the specimen fails to return to the original position. The yield strength is then taken as the equivalent of the last previous load. Because of this difficulty and the inaccuracies of measuring proportional limit, a newer method—that of *proof stress*— has been developed. *Proof stress* is the maximum stress a material can withstand without taking more than a small amount of set. The amount is usually specified as the smallest that can be measured by the extensometer, namely, 0.01 percent in 2 in.

As with yield strength, the preferred method of measuring proof stress is by using a 0.01 percent offset (Fig. 2-6).

In brief summary: Proportional limit is yield strength at 0.00 percent offset. Proof stress is yield strength at 0.01 percent offset. Yield strength is yield strength at 0.20 percent offset.

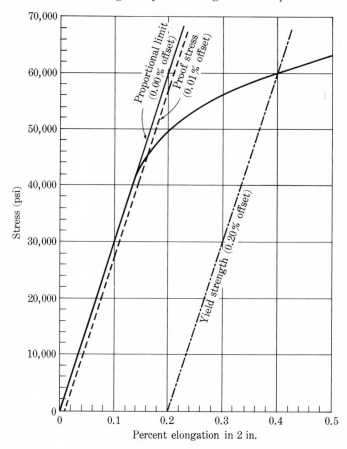

**Fig. 2-6.** Proportional limit is shown as the yield strength at 0.00 percent offset. Proof stress is shown as yield strength at 0.01 percent offset. Yield strength is shown as yield strength at 0.20 percent offset (courtesy International Nickel Co., Inc.).

**Modulus of Elasticity.** The modulus of elasticity refers to stiffness or rigidity. The higher the modulus, the stiffer the material. In many applications this stiffness is more important than strength. It means better performance of closely adjusted parts, less vibration and whipping of shafts, with less tendency to wear unevenly in bearings.

Stainless steel and mild steels have about the same modulus. However, their modulus is twice that of copper-base alloys and three times that of aluminum alloys.

A knowledge of the modulus of various materials may enable the designer to improve the operating effectiveness at minimum cost. As an example, a shaft may be subject to excessive bending, but a shaft of higher modulus might overcome this difficulty without increasing its size or the number of bearing points.

The unit of measurement of modulus of elasticity is pounds per square inch and is determined in either tension, compression, or shear. The values obtained in tension and compression are almost identical. They are known as Young's modulus and denoted by the symbol $E$. Modulus in shear, sometimes called modulus of rigidity, is denoted by $G$ and is usually 40 percent the value of Young's modulus for commonly used materials. Shown in Table 2-1 are various materials with their relative modulus of elasticity in pounds per square inch.

**TABLE 2-1.**

Various Materials, Showing a Comparison of Their Moduli of Elasticity*

Modulus of Elasticity (psi)

| Material | Tension or Compression (Young's Modulus) | Shear or Torsion (Modulus of Rigidity) |
|---|---|---|
| Monel | 26,000,000 | 9,500,000 |
| "K" Monel | 26,000,000 | 9,500,000 |
| "A" nickel | 30,000,000 | 11,000,000 |
| Duranickel | 30,000,000 | 11,000,000 |
| Inconel | 31,000,000 | 11,000,000 |
| Brass | 14,500,000 | 5,000,000 |
| Phosphor bronze | 15,000,000 | 6,500,000 |
| Silicon bronze | 15,000,000 | 5,000,000 |
| Beryllium copper | 18,000,000 | 7,000,000 |
| Nickel silver, 18% | 18,500,000 | 7,000,000 |
| Carbon steel | 30,000,000 | 11,600,000 |
| Chrome-vanadium steel | 30,000,000 | 11,500,000 |
| Type 430, stainless steel | 28,000,000 | 10,000,000 |
| Type 302, stainless steel | 29,000,000 | 10,500,000 |
| Music wire | 30,000,000 | 11,500,000 |

* Courtesy of The International Nickel Co., Inc.

**Ductility.** Ductility is that property of a material which allows it to be deformed without rupture; in other words, it is the ability of a material to be manipulated by cold-working methods such as bending, deep drawing, spinning, and cold heading. The lack of ductility is commonly called *brittleness*.

In order to be suitable for a variety of engineering uses, a good combination of strength and ductility is needed in most metals. Glass, for example, is hard but not ductile. Lead and copper are ductile, but they lack the strength and hardness needed for many applications.

Usually, if two materials have the same strength and hardness, the one that has the higher ductility is the more desirable.

### Hardness

In selecting a metal to withstand wear or erosion, there are three properties to consider—its ductility (already defined), toughness, and hardness. The most important of these is usually hardness.

Hardness is that property of a material that enables it to resist plastic deformation, penetration, indentation, or scratching.

Hardness is important from an engineering standpoint. Resistance to wear by either friction or erosion by steam, oil, and water generally increases with hardness.

**Hardness Testing.** Several methods have been developed for hardness testing. Those most often used are Brinell, Rockwell, Vickers, and Scleroscope. The first three are based on indentation tests and the fourth on the rebound height of a diamond-tipped metallic hammer.

Brinell. In Brinell hardness tests, a tungsten carbide or hardened steel ball, usually 10 mm in diameter, is employed as the indenter (Fig. 2-7). The applied load is 3,000 kg for 15 to 30 sec. for hard materials; 500 or 1,500 kg are applied on the softer nonferrous metals for 30 or 60 sec, respectively. When the load is released, the diameter of the spherical impression is measured with the aid of a Brinell microscope. The Brinell hardness number is derived from the area of the indentation. However, conversion charts based on the diameter of the indentation in millimeters are used to give the hardness numbers directly.

Brinell testing is most useful for larger workpieces such as castings and forgings having section thicknesses of ¼ in. or more. The relatively large indentation is especially good for materials that are coarse-

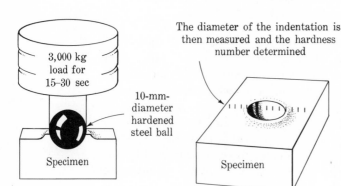

3,000 kg load for 15–30 sec

Specimen

10-mm-diameter hardened steel ball

The diameter of the indentation is then measured and the hardness number determined

Specimen

**Fig. 2-7.** Principles of Brinell hardness testing.

grained, nonhomogeneous, or nonuniform in structure. The indentations produced give a better average reading over a wide variation in hardness.

Brinell testing machines range in size from small portable and bench models to ones weighing a ton or more.

ROCKWELL. The Rockwell hardness tester uses the principle of measuring the difference in penetration between a minor and major load as it is applied to the penetrator. The minor load is 10 kg, and the major load varies with the material being tested. If the material is known to be relatively soft, a 1/16-in.-diameter ball is used with 100 kg as the major load. This is known as the *B scale*. If the material is relatively hard, a sphero-conical diamond Brale penetrator is used with a 150-kg load (Fig. 2-8). The results are read on the *C* scale. Other scales are available and are useful for extremely hard surfaces. Also, very thin sections may be tested by using very small loads on a Rockwell superficial hardness tester. Carefully polished surfaces are required on all parts to be tested.

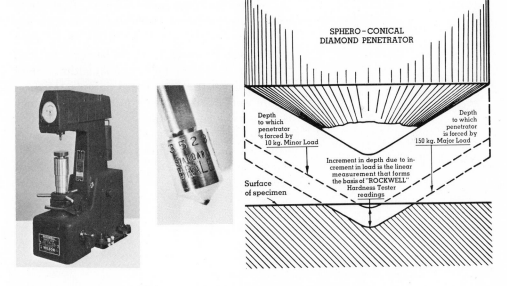

**Fig. 2-8.** Rockwell hardness tester with Brale penetrator used on hard metals (courtesy Wilson Mechanical Instrument Div., American Chain and Cable Co.).

VICKERS. The Vickers hardness tester is very much like the Brinell hardness tester. The main differences are the size and shape of the penetrator and the magnitude of the applied loads. The penetrator used is a square-based diamond pyramid making a point angle of 136 deg. The hardness number is determined by measuring the diagonal across the square-surface impression made by the penetrator. Hardness numbers are identical with those of the Brinell scale up to 300; above this Brinell numbers are progressively lower. The Vickers hardness tester is used for both hard and soft materials and precision testing of thin sheets.

SCLEROSCOPE. The Scleroscope presents one of the fastest and most portable means of checking hardness. The hardness number is based on the height of rebound of a diamond-tipped metallic hammer. The hammer falls free from a given height. The amount of rebound is observed on a scale in the background. The harder the material, the higher the rebound, and vice versa. Thin materials may be checked if a sufficient number of layers are packed together to prevent the hammer from penetrating in the metal to an extent where the rebound is influenced by the steel anvil. This is known as *anvil effect.*

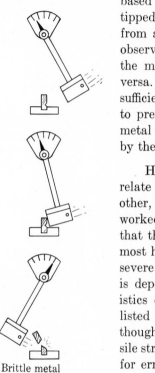

Brittle metal

HARDNESS CONVERSION CHARTS. In order to relate one method of testing hardness with another, hardness conversion charts have been worked out. However, it should be borne in mind that these charts are only approximations. Since most hardness testing is based on indentation or severe work hardening in a localized area, much is dependent on the work-hardening characteristics of the metal. Tensile strengths are often listed on hardness conversion charts also. Although relationships exist between hardness, tensile strength, and yield strength, there are chances for error. It is always better, if possible, to use a tensile testing machine and obtain the values directly.

### Toughness

It is not enough to know only how strong a metal is in tensile strength, or how ductile it is; information as to how it reacts under sudden impact also is of prime importance. This quality is known as toughness. It is measured by the Charpy test or the Izod test.

Both of these tests use a notched specimen. The location and shape of the notch are stan-

Tough metal

**Fig. 2-9.** The principle of the Izod impact test.

dard. The points of support of the specimen, as well as the impact of the hammer, must bear a constant relationship to the location of the notch.

The tests are conducted by mounting the specimens as shown in Fig. 2-9, and then allowing a pendulum of a given weight to fall from a given height. The maximum energy developed by the hammer in the Izod test is 120 ft-lb and in the Charpy test 240 ft-lb.

By properly calibrating the machine, the energy absorbed by the specimen may be measured from the upward swing of the pendulum. The greater the amount of energy absorbed by the specimen, the less will be the upward swing of the pendulum.

### Shear Strength

Shear strength is expressed in the number of pounds per square inch required to produce a fracture when impressed vertically upon the cross section of a material. Methods of testing both single and double shear strength are shown in Fig. 2-10.

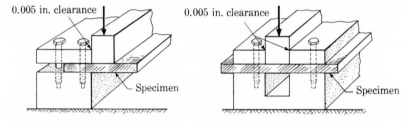

**Fig. 2-10.** Methods used in testing single and double shear.

Shear strength may be calculated as the amount of force needed to make the shear over a given cross-sectional area. For example, in single shear, assuming a required load of 12,300 lb for a bar $\frac{1}{4} \times 1$ in. (area = 0.25 sq in.) the shear strength would be

$$\text{Shear strength} = \frac{\text{applied load}}{\text{area in shear}} \quad \text{or} \quad \frac{12,300}{0.25} = 49,200 \text{ psi}$$

In double shear, the force and the area are doubled, resulting in approximately twice the shear strength in pounds per square inch.

The shear strength of mild steels compared to ultimate tensile strength ranges from about 60 to 80 percent. The lower values are for the harder materials.

Tests made on $\frac{3}{8}$-in.-diameter annealed rods of Monel, steel, naval brass, and bronze containing 1.15 percent tin are shown in Table 2-2.

TABLE 2-2.

### Shear Strength of Soft, ⅜-in.-Diameter Rods†

| Material | Shear Strength (psi)* |
|---|---|
| Monel................ | 58,000 |
| Low-carbon steel....... | 44,500 |
| Naval brass........... | 37,000 |
| Bronze (1.15% tin)..... | 35,500 |

\* Taken in double shear.
Tests conducted by Columbia University, New York.
†Courtesy The International Nickel Co., Inc.

## Creep

Creep is expressed as the plastic behavior of metal or plastics under constant load and at constant temperature. There are three stages of creep. In the first one the material elongates rapidly but at a decreasing rate. In the second stage, ordinarily of long duration, the rate of elongation is constant. In the third stage the rate of elongation increases rapidly until the material fails.

The design engineer is most concerned with second-stage creep, where elongation takes place at a constant specific rate. The percent of elongation and time required are dictated by the requirements of the particular application. An example would be 0.1 percent elongation in 10,000 hr. In rapidly rotating structural members such as rotors and blading of steam and gas turbines, the clearances are extremely small and critical. The designer will be satisfied with nothing short of experimentally determined stress of 1 creep rate unit (CRU) or 1 percent in 100,000 hr.

## THE DEVELOPMENT OF METAL PROPERTIES

The characteristic properties of metals are developed in a number of different ways. The most common methods of developing these properties are by the addition of alloying elements, heat treatment, hot working, and cold working.

## Alloying Elements

Alloying elements are those that are intentionally added to metals to change the physical characteristics of the base metal. Marked changes can be obtained in the base metal through the addition of various alloys; these include the hardness and strength resulting from heat treatment, or an increase in corrosion resistance, ductility, toughness, magnetic properties, etc.

As stated at the beginning of this chapter, the crystal structure of pure metals consists of one characteristic lattice arrangement for a given temperature range. The crystal structure of metals containing alloying elements is much more complicated.

**Types of Alloys.** The alloying elements may exist in the parent metal as solid solutions, intermetallic compounds, or mechanical mixtures.

SOLID SOLUTIONS. When elements combine to form alloys by completely dissolving in each other they are said to be in solid solution. In order to have this occur the atoms of one element must be able to become a part of the space lattice of the other element; for example, when nickel is added to copper in Monel metals the nickel atoms will take the place of some of the copper atoms. Some of the solvent atoms in a space lattice may be replaced by some of the solute or substituted atoms. This is referred to as *substitutional solid* solution. The solute atoms may not always replace the solvent atoms. They may merely occupy positions between the solvent atoms forming what is known as an *interstitial solid* solution. An example of this is carbon in iron at elevated temperatures, or gamma iron.

INTERMETALLIC COMPOUNDS. Compounds are commonly formed between metals and nonmetals; for example, iron oxide. One of the more important intermetallic compounds is that of $Cu_2Zn_3$, or the chief constituent of white brass. Hard metallic compounds, when held in a softer matrix, are used in bearing applications. To be of real value, however, they must be well dispersed throughout the structure.

MECHANICAL MIXTURES. Most metals, when heated to the liquid state, dissolve one another. The reason for this is that many metal atoms have approximately the same size. Composition interfaces disappear quickly, leaving only a homogeneous mixture. Metals that retain their same structural identity and properties are termed mechanical mixtures, or are said to have only partial solubility in the liquid state and complete insolubility in the solid state. Examples of mechanical mixtures are iron and silver, iron and lead, and aluminum and lead.

Alloys of this type have certain constituents that crystallize out first, leaving a solution that freezes at a low fixed temperature. This solution has just the right amount of each constituent for the lowest freezing point of all liquid solutions containing two metals, and is known as a *eutectic mixture*. If the original alloy had the right proportion of the two metals, it would have a lower melting point than either of the metals alone.

### Properties of Alloying Elements.

GENERAL. Each alloying element has a particular job to do. Where a combination of two or more elements exists in a steel, the total result is usually an increase in each of the characteristics that is greater than the sum of their individual effects. The main reason for adding alloying elements to steel is to increase its hardenability. Common alloying elements used in steel are carbon, nickel, chromium, molybdenum, vanadium, tungsten, manganese, copper, sulfur, boron, and aluminum. Although each alloying element may have an individual effect, its main purpose is to change the hardenability of the steel. The effect of each of these elements will be treated from a qualitative rather than a quantitative basis.

CARBON. From the standpoint of its effect upon the base metal, carbon is the most important alloying element. Steels are often designated by their carbon content as being high-, medium-, or low-carbon steels. The general carbon range for each of these categories is 0.05 to 0.30 percent for low-carbon, 0.30 to 0.60 percent for medium-carbon, and 0.60 to 1.3 percent for high-carbon steels. Above this range are the cast irons and below it are the wrought irons.

Carbon affects the hardness, tensile strength, machinability, and melting temperature of steel, as shown graphically in Fig. 2-11. Although actual values are not shown on the graph, it can be seen that tensile strength increases with carbon content up through the high-carbon range. Hardness also increases, but ductility is reduced. The melting point of the steel goes down as the carbon content goes up.

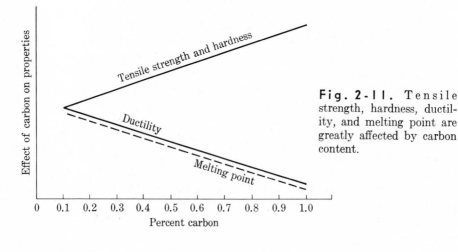

**Fig. 2-11.** Tensile strength, hardness, ductility, and melting point are greatly affected by carbon content.

NICKEL. Nickel increases toughness and resistance to impact, particularly at low temperatures, and lessens distortion in quenching. It lowers the critical temperatures of steel and widens the range of successful heat treatment.

Nickel steels are particularly good for case-hardened parts, such as high-speed gears and roller bearings. Such steels provide strong, tough, wear-resistant cases and also ductile core properties. Case hardening, as explained later, consists of adding carbon to the steel in the outer surface. Nickel does not unite with carbon to contribute to hardness, but it does help provide a tough core.

CHROMIUM. Chromium, unlike nickel, joins with the carbon of the steel to form chromium carbides, thus adding depth hardenability with improved resistance to abrasion and wear. Of the common alloying elements, chromium ranks near the top in hardenability. Chromium steels are relatively stable at high temperatures and are often used where heat is present. Chromium is also helpful in preventing corrosion.

MOLYBDENUM. Molybdenum, like chromium, promotes hardenability of steel. It has a strong tendency to hamper grain growth prior to quenching, thus making the steel fine-grained and unusually tough at the various hardness levels. It is also used to increase tensile and creep strength at high temperatures.

Some familiar items that contain molybdenum are high-speed cutting tools, forged crankshafts and propeller shafts, turbine rotors, high-pressure boiler plate, high-pressure cylinders, gears, and high-quality tubing. Alloys of chromium and molybdenum develop high strength when heat-treated.

VANADIUM. The grain-growth-inhibiting effect of vanadium promotes a fine-grained structure over a fairly broad quenching range, thus imparting strength and toughness to heat-treated steel.

Vanadium is used in constructional steels, not only to refine the grain but also to improve the mechanical-property balance. Generally speaking, the amount of vanadium in constructional steels ranges from approximately 0.03 to 0.25 percent. Larger quantities are required in tool steels. Parts made out of steel containing vanadium would include certain types of spring steel, plates, gears, high-temperature steels, forged axles, shafts, turbine rotors, and other items requiring impact and fatigue resistance.

TUNGSTEN. Tungsten increases the hardness, promotes fine grain, and resists heat. Tungsten has a body-centered lattice and so dissolves in both alpha and gamma iron, forming tungsten carbides. These carbides are very hard and stable. When used in higher percentages (18 percent) and combined with lesser percentages of chromium and vanadium, this metal is referred to as high-speed steel. It has the property of "red hardness"; that is, the cutting-tool edge may become a dull red before the metal softens appreciably or loses its temper.

MANGANESE. Manganese is one of the basic alloying components in steel. In fact, all analyses contain manganese to some extent. Manganese contributes markedly to strength and hardness, but to a lesser degree than does carbon. Actually, the effectiveness of manganese is dependent on the amount of carbon; the higher-carbon-content steels are more affected than the lower-carbon steels. High manganese content with increasing carbon has a tendency to lower both ductility and weldability.

Manganese acts as a deoxidizer in the steel and combines with sulfur to make manganese sulfides which are less harmful than iron sulfides.

Fine-grained manganese steels attain unusual toughness and strength. They are almost impossible to machine except by grinding, but they can be cast and rolled. Although the hardness is comparatively low, they work-harden rapidly. Because of the high rate of work hardening, they develop good wear resistance in such applications as rock-crushing equipment, steam shovels, railroad-switch frogs, and other places where battering actions are encountered.

COPPER. Copper is added to steel in varying amounts, generally from 0.2 to 0.5 percent. It is used primarily to increase resistance to atmospheric corrosion, but it also acts as a strengthening agent.

SULFUR. Sulfur is considered an impurity that unites with steel to form iron sulfides, which contribute to red shortness or cracking while being hot-worked. However, with sufficient manganese, this weakening effect is largely overcome, owing to the formation of manganese sulfides. Sulfur increases the free-cutting action of low-carbon steels because of its embrittling action. Shorter chips are formed instead of long turnings.

BORON. Boron is used in steel for one purpose—to increase its hardenability, or the depth to which the steel will harden when it is quenched. Its use is recommended for steels with carbon contents of 0.60 percent or less.

ALUMINUM. Aluminum has an affinity for oxygen and is therefore used in steel as a reliable deoxidizer. It also helps produce a fine austenitic grain size. When it is present in an amount of approximately 1 percent, it helps promote *nitriding,* a case-hardening process discussed later.

## Heat Treatment

Heat treatment is a term used to denote a process of heating and cooling metals in order to obtain certain desired properties. For example, steels that are to be used for cutting tools must be given the right combination of hardness and toughness in order to be able successfully to machine other metals.

**The Effect of Heating and Cooling Steel.** Carbon is the most important element in determining the ultimate condition of the steel after heat treatment. When heated, carbon chemically combines with iron, forming a carbide of iron called cementite. The carbon in each piece of steel is in the form of cementite, mixed in a matrix of iron, representing a solid solution.

As steel is cooled from an elevated temperature, several types of crystals start to form. They may be ferrite, cementite, pearlite, or others, depending on the carbon content of the steel and the cooling rate. *Ferrite* is practically pure iron; *cementite* is the iron carbide $Fe_3C$ (6.68 percent carbon and 93.32 percent iron). *Pearlite* consists of alternate layers of iron carbide and ferrite (Fig. 2-12). Normally, as the metal cools slowly from a temperature above the upper critical, there is an automatic separation of ferrite and the ferrite-carbide mixture. As the carbon content increases, it unites with greater amounts of ferrite, thus causing an increase in pearlite and a decrease in ferrite. At the point of increase where all of the ferrite is in combination with carbon, the structure will be entirely pearlite. Theoretically, this is at approximately 0.83 percent carbon; actually, it is from 0.75 to 0.85 percent in plain carbon steels. This is called the *eutectoid point*. Eutectoid, taken from the Greek, means "most fusible." The excess carbon above 0.83 percent, as in *hypereutectoid* steels, is rejected by the pearlite

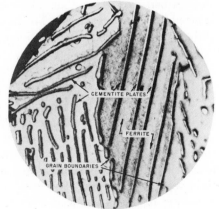

**Fig. 2-12.** Pearlite structure (courtesy The International Nickel Co., Inc.).

crystals and collects at the grain boundaries. Less than 0.83 percent carbon is a *hypoeutectoid* steel whose structure, if cooled slowly, would be pearlite with excess ferrite. Pearlitic steel is generally defined in terms of the eutectoid amount of carbon and the slow cooling rate. However, owing to alloying elements and cooling rates, wide variations of pearlite structure exist.

If a specimen of hypoeutectoid steel is heated uniformly, it will be found that at approximately 1333°F the temperature of the steel will stop rising even though the heat is still being applied. After a short time, the temperature will continue to rise again. Ordinarily, metals expand as they are heated, but it is found that at 1333°F a slight contraction takes place and then, after the pause, expansion again takes place. This indicates the lower critical temperature of the steel, shown on the iron-carbon diagram as $A_1$ (Fig. 2-13). Actually, an atomic change takes place at this point, and the structure changes from a body-centered arrangement (alpha iron) to a face-centered one (beta iron).

As the heating continues, another pause will be noted at $A_3$, at which time there is a transformation of ferrite to austenite. This varies with the carbon content, as shown in the diagram, and is known as the upper critical temperature. At this point the carbon goes completely into solution with the iron, so that it is now evenly distributed.

As the heating continues there is no further important change except that the grains grow larger until the melting point is reached.

**Hardening Steel.** Three requirements are necessary in order successfully to harden a piece of steel: First, the steel must contain enough carbon; second, it must be heated to the correct temperature; third, it must be cooled at a rapid rate (quenched).

CARBON CONTENT. In order to get extreme hardness in a piece of steel, it is necessary that the steel contain 80 points or more of carbon. Low-carbon steels (less than 25 points carbon) will not be materially affected by heat treatment. Medium-carbon steels (30 to 60 points carbon) may be toughened considerably by heat treatment, but they will not be hardened to a very great extent. High-carbon steels (60 to 150 points carbon) may be successfully hardened by simple heat-treating methods.

HEATING. The steel must then be heated to the upper critical point, which is the temperature at which the carbon goes into solution and austenite is formed. Hardening will not occur unless the temperature is high enough to form complete austenite. The proper temperature to which the steel should be heated in all cases is just slightly above the upper critical point. The critical temperature for steel will vary according to the carbon and alloy content. General recommendations

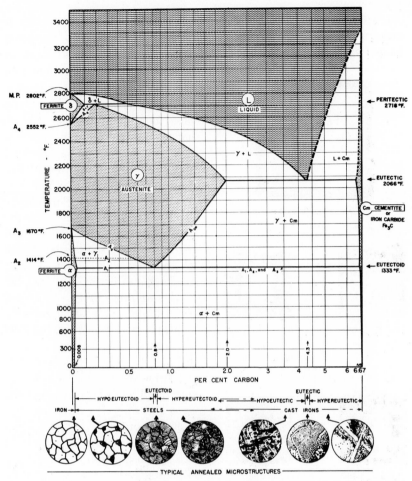

(Revised by Anton Brasunas from diagram in ASM Metals Handbook, 1948 ed.)

Iron–Cementite Phase Diagram.

The critical points for pure iron are shown on the left; the changes in temperatures appear as lines progressing to the right as carbon is added.

**Fig. 2-13.** The iron-carbon equilibrium diagram (courtesy Metals Engineering Institute).

for hardening temperatures of plain carbon steel based on the carbon content are as follows: for steels with 65 to 80 points carbon, 1450° to 1500°F; for steels with 80 to 95 points carbon, 1410° to 1460°F; for steels with 95 to 110 points carbon, 1390° to 1430°F; and for steels with 110 points or more of carbon, 1380° to 1420°F.

QUENCHING. After the steel has been heated to the critical temperature and held at this temperature long enough to become uniformly heated, it should be cooled at a rapid rate. This is known as quenching.

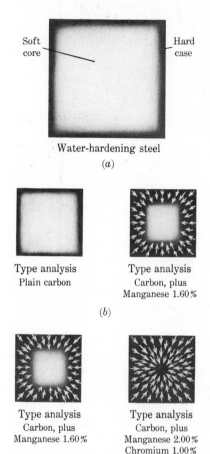

Water-hardening steel
(a)

Type analysis
Plain carbon

Type analysis
Carbon, plus
Manganese 1.60%

(b)

Type analysis
Carbon, plus
Manganese 1.60%

Type analysis
Carbon, plus
Manganese 2.00%
Chromium 1.00%
Molybdenum 1.35%

(c)

**Fig. 2-14.** The effect of alloys on the hardenability of the steel. (a) Hardness does not penetrate far on steels that require a rather severe quench. (b) If manganese is added to plain carbon steel, it can be cooled more slowly, as in oil, and the hardness penetration will be deeper. (c) As more alloys are added, the steel can be cooled still more slowly, as in air, and the hardness will penetrate through the section.

The cooling rate is dependent upon the alloy content. Alloys in steel will not increase the ultimate hardness, but they will increase the hardenability; that is, the ease with which it may be hardened and the depth of hardness (Fig. 2-14). An alloy steel may be cooled at a slower rate than plain carbon steel and still have the same degree of hardness. This slower cooling reduces the stresses developed in the steel and may prevent cracking and breaking during the hardening process.

Different rates of cooling may be attained by immersing the steel in baths of various kinds. These include plain water for fast cooling; brine and caustic solutions for very rapid cooling; oil-water emulsions for slightly slower cooling; and oil, molten salt, or lead baths for slow cooling. Air may be used as a cooling medium for some types of high-speed steel when a very slow cooling rate is desired.

When steel, heated to a temperature slightly above the critical point, is plunged into a cooling bath, the rapidity with which the heat is dissipated by the bath affects the degree of hardness. The alloy content of the material will also affect the degree of hardness obtained with a given cooling rate (Fig. 2-15). When the steel is immersed in the bath, it should be agitated to reduce the tendency of a vapor to form on the surface of the steel, thus preventing uniform cooling. A quenching bath should be used that will give the slowest cooling possible and still give the degree of hardness desired. If a faster rate than necessary is used, terrific stresses, which may break and ruin the work, will be built up in the steel.

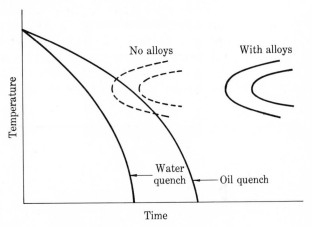

**Fig. 2-15.** The effects of quenching mediums and alloys required for full hardening.

When austenite is immersed in a quenching bath, it changes structure. As solidification takes place, an interlaced needlelike structure forms. This is called *martensite* (Fig. 2-16). The actual transformation from austenite takes place at a low temperature, around 400°F or lower. Martensite is termed an unstable structure, since some of the carbides continue to be ejected from the solution and are dispersed as submicroscopic particles between the unit cells. This results in considerable distortion and strain on the cells. However, theoretically, at least, there is some keying effect of the carbides which limits the plastic flow of the metal, giving it high strength and hardness with a decrease in ductility.

If, instead of quenching from above the upper critical temperature, the metal were cooled slowly and held for a long period of time near

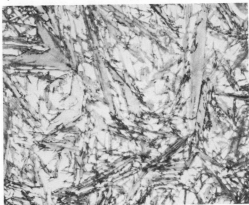

**Fig. 2-16.** Martensite structure.

the temperature of 1,330°F, the result would be ferrite with small spheroidized particles of iron carbide (Fig. 2-17).

Other structures can be obtained by various cooling rates. *Bainite*, a feathery needlelike constituent, is obtained by a pause in the cooling curve at around 800° to 600°F. The advantage of this type of quenching is that it is much less severe, producing less stress and strain on the product. Bainite will have an intermediate hardness around 500 Brinell, as compared to the more slowly cooled pearlite around 200 Brinell, and the rapidly cooled martensite around 650 Brinell.

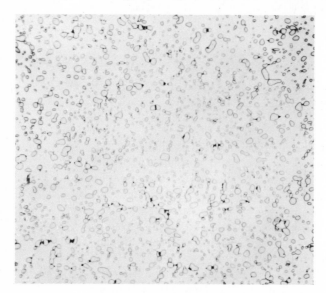

**Fig. 2-17.** Spheroidized iron carbide in annealed steel (courtesy International Nickel Co., Inc.).

**Tempering.** After quenching, the metal is hard, brittle, and unstable in structure. Severe strains caused by the rapid cooling may cause the metal to crack or break. By reheating the metal, some of the locked-up stress may be drawn out and the brittleness may be reduced. The first few hundred degrees of tempering temperature reduce stress, improve toughness, and decrease hardness. Since tempering softens the steel, the relationship of hardness to strength should be known. To find the answer, comparisons should be made of different steels having the same hardness. Shown in Fig. 2-18 is the result of a series of precise tests of a variety of steels. You will note the close relationship of hardness to strength in all of them.

The relationship of tempering temperature and Brinell hardness is shown in Fig. 2-19.

Sometimes, quenching and tempering are combined in one operation, thus avoiding the high internal stresses. These stresses may pro-

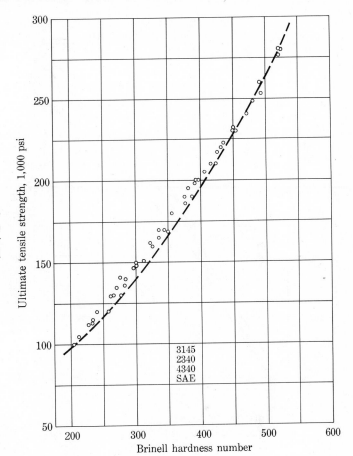

**Fig. 2-18.** Relation between hardness and tensile strength for several alloy steels (courtesy United States Steel Corp.).

duce warping or cracking of the part. To avoid this condition, interrupted quenches are used and are referred to as *marquenching*.

Marquenching consists of quenching the part in oil at 400°F, followed by room-temperature air quenching. The parts are placed in the quenching bath at a temperature just above that at which martensite starts to form. They are kept in the bath long enough to permit the pieces to acquire a uniform temperature throughout, and then are air-cooled to room temperature.

Fairly accurate heat-treating plans can be designed for various steels by combining the three variables—time, temperature, and transformation—into a TTT chart, as shown in Fig. 2-20. The curves in the chart show the different structures and their relationship to time while being quenched. The white line shows the normal cooling curves and reheating to produce the structure termed *tempered martensite*. Tempered martensite is a more stable structure with enlarged carbide part-

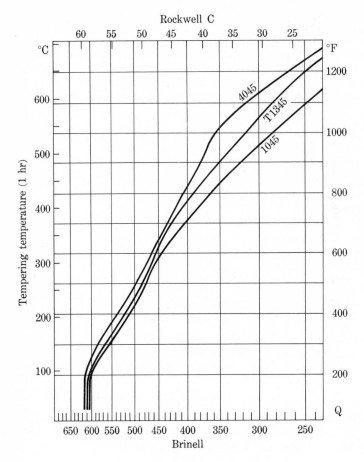

**Fig. 2-19.** Effect of tempering temperature on the hardness of 1045, T1345, and 4045 steels (courtesy United States Steel Corp.).

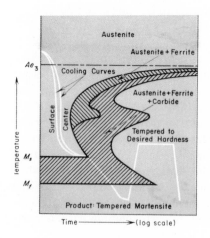

**Fig. 2-20.** A time-temperature-transformation diagram indicating the transformation of austenite to martensite. The letters $M_s$ indicate where martensite starts to form and $M_f$ where the transformation is complete.

icles. The higher the tempering temperature, the larger the carbide particles and the more stable the structure.

Tempering is accomplished either in a furnace, heavy oil, molten lead, or molten salts. The usual tempering temperature ranges from 300° to 1200°F, depending on the type of steel and the hardness required. For most steels the speed of cooling after tempering is of little consequence. In practice, the cooling after tempering is done in air. Some higher-alloy steels are double-tempered to ensure stable structures. During the first tempering, new martensite is formed from some of the retained austenite. The second tempering operation helps temper the newly formed martensite.

**Annealing.** Steel that has been formed, forged, or machined accumulates considerable stress. A *stress-relief anneal* consists of heating the metal to approximately 500°F, allowing a soak period until a uniform temperature is attained, followed by air cooling.

Another annealing method is known as *spheroidize anneal,* and is used in place of the operation described above. The spheroidize anneal is used primarily to improve cold-working operations and machinability of the higher-carbon alloy steels. The process consists of heating the metal high enough (slightly above or slightly below the lower critical temperature) to permit the iron carbide layers to curl up in spherical forms. This allows better slippage of the iron crystals with less force needed to form or machine the metal.

A *full anneal* consists of heating the metal slightly above the $A_3$ line (Fig. 2-13), which allows the grains to recrystallize. It is soaked at this heat until there is a uniform temperature throughout the metal, and then it is furnace-cooled. This allows the metal to break down into ferrite and pearlite structure. The full-anneal process ties up the furnace for a comparatively long time. Therefore, *cyclic annealing* is often used. The cooling phase is done in a molten-salt bath or controlled furnace at a constant temperature within the ferrite-pearlite range until full transformation takes place. Steels treated by this process include alloys of chromium-molybdenum within a carbon range of 0.12 to 0.25 percent.

**Normalizing.** Normalizing is a modified annealing process, the main difference being that the parts are allowed to cool in still air at room temperature. The metal is heated 50° to 100° above the $A_3$ temperature, but in no case high enough or long enough to permit the grains to grow to any considerable size. Forgings that are to be machined are often normalized to restore uniform cutting conditions in the previously distorted crystals. It also allows the metal to recrystallize and form smaller grains. Normalizing produces a harder, less uniform section than does a full anneal. Heavy sections cool slower than thin sections, and therefore they will be softer and have less strength.

Normalizing is often done after machining or hot working to give uniform grain structure. If the parts are to be hardened, there will be less strain and less likelihood of cracking.

**Grain Size.** Metal grains recrystallize at the upper critical temperature. Metals heated to this temperature long enough to become uniform throughout and then quenched have fine grain size. As metals are heated above the upper critical temperature and held there, the grains will merge and become large. The time and temperature above the upper critical will determine the grain size. Large grain size can again be refined by heating metal up to the recrystallization temperature and then allowing it to cool. The rate at which it cools below the upper critical temperature has little or no effect (Fig. 2-21).

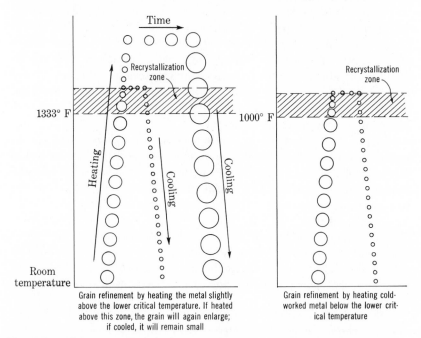

Grain refinement by heating the metal slightly above the lower critical temperature. If heated above this zone, the grain will again enlarge; if cooled, it will remain small

Grain refinement by heating cold-worked metal below the lower critical temperature

**Fig. 2-21.** Schematic diagram of grain growth and refinement.

**Case Hardening.** In order to harden low-carbon or mild steels, it is necessary to add carbon to the outer surface and harden a thin outer case. The process involves two separate operations. The first is a carburizing process, where carbon is added to the outer skin, and the second is to heat-treat the carburized parts so that the outer surface becomes hard. The inside of the part, or the core, does not change materially in structure. The term case hardening includes the entire process of carburizing and hardening.

CARBURIZING. The carburizing process consists of heating low-carbon steel in contact with a carbonaceous compound to a temperature that may vary from 1650° to 1700°F. This temperature is used because, at this heat, the steel is austenitic and absorbs carbon readily. The length of time that the material is kept in contact with the carbonaceous material depends upon the extent of carburizing action desired. The carbon from the carburizing material is absorbed by the steel, and the low-carbon surface is converted to a high-carbon steel. The result is a piece of steel with a low-carbon core and a high-carbon surface. After the material is quenched, the outer surface will be hardened while the inner core remains soft. This gives an ideal structure for many applications.

Many different carburizers may be used. These include wood charcoal, animal charcoal, coal, beans, nuts, bone, leather, or combinations of these materials. The thickness of the cases may be from 0.002 to 0.050 in., depending upon the length of time the steel is heated while in contact with the carbon.

CYANIDE HARDENING. Cyanide may also be used to case-harden steel. It is used to give a very thin but hard outer case. Sodium cyanide or potassium cyanide may be used as the hardening medium. The cyanide is heated until it becomes liquid. When the steel is placed in the cyanide bath, both carbon and nitrogen are added to the outer surface, resulting in a surface harder than that produced by the carburizing process.

NITRIDING. Nitriding is a case-hardening process in which nitrogen, instead of carbon, is added to the skin of the steel. This is used usually only on certain alloys which are susceptible to the formation of chemical nitrides. This forms a very hard case, which has a small amount of distortion, as the entire process is carried out at a relatively low temperature (950°F). No scaling occurs, since the steel is not exposed to air at elevated temperatures, and thus pieces can be finished to size before heat treatment. Ammonia gas is used as the nitrogen-producing material. The case that is produced is very thin (0.001 to 0.005 in. thick).

**Surface Hardening of Medium- and High-Carbon Steels.** Flame and induction hardening are performed on carbon steels containing 0.35 percent carbon or more. This process is also used on cast and malleable irons of suitable composition.

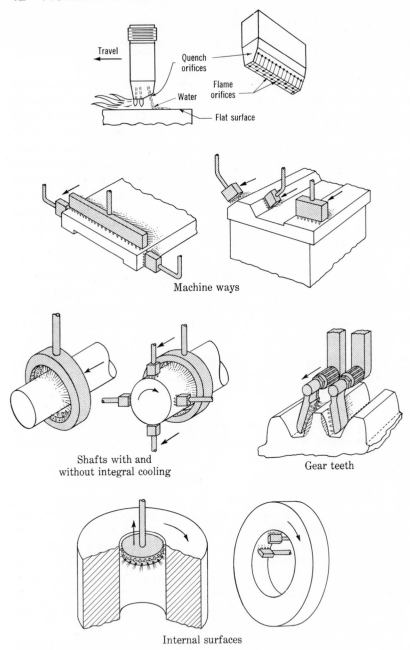

Travel

Quench
orifices

Flame
orifices

Water

Flat surface

Machine ways

Shafts with and
without integral cooling

Gear teeth

Internal surfaces

**Fig. 2-22.** Almost any shape of burner may be obtained for different contours.

FLAME HARDENING. Flame hardening consists of moving an oxyacetylene flame over the part, followed by a quenching spray. The rate at which the flame or *burner* is moved over the work will determine the depth of hardness for a given material. Burners can be obtained for different contours, as shown in Fig. 2-22. Quenching can be built into the burner head or be done as a separate operation after flame heating. The various types of burners vary from the standard torch welding tip to flat, contoured, and ring burners.

In flame hardening there is no sharp line of demarcation between the hardened surface zone and the core, so there is little likelihood that it will chip out or break during service.

The flame is kept at a reasonable distance from sharp corners to prevent overheating, and drilled or tapped holes are normally protected by filling them with wet asbestos or carbonaceous material.

Some advantages of flame hardening are:

1. Large machined parts can be surface-hardened economically.

2. Surfaces can be selectively hardened with minimum warping and with freedom from quench cracking.

3. Scaling is superficial because of the relatively short heating cycle.

4. Electronically controlled equipment provides precise control of case properties.

The disadvantages include:

1. To obtain optimum results, a technique must be established for each design.

2. Overheating can cause cracking or, where thin sections are involved, excessive distortion.

### Induction Hardening

Induction hardening is done by placing the part in a high-frequency alternating magnetic field. Heat is generated by the rapid reversals of polarity. The primary current is carried by a water-cooled copper tube and is induced into the surface layers of the workpiece.

The most commonly used sources of high-frequency current are:

1. Motor-generators with frequencies of 1,000 to 10,000 cycles per second and capacities to 10,000 kw.

2. Spark-gap oscillators with frequencies of 100,000 to 400,000 cycles per second and capacities to 25 kw.

3. Vacuum-tube oscillators operating at 500,000 cycles per second with output capacities of 20 to 50 kw.

The depth of penetration of electrical energy decreases as the frequency increases; for example, the approximate minimum hardness for 3,000 cycles per second is 0.060 in. and for 500,000 cycles per second is 0.020 in.. For this reason, thin-walled sections require high frequencies, and thicker sections must have low frequencies for adequate penetration.

Some advantages of induction hardening are:

1. The operation is fast; comparatively large parts can be processed in a minimum time on automatic machines. Large truck crankshafts can be brought to the proper heat and spray-quenched in 5 sec.

2. It can easily be applied to both external and internal surfaces.

3. A minimum of distortion or oxidation is encountered because of the short cycle time.

### Hot Working

Most metals go through a hot-working process; that is, after the billet has been poured and has cooled sufficiently, it is reduced by rolling, drawing, or extruding. Hot working is done above the recrystallization temperature of the metal and therefore has little or no effect on the hardness of the metal. It may, however, reduce grain size by breaking up the existing crystals into smaller segments. If these crystals are not too distorted in the process, they will permit more planes of slip. Therefore, as a rule, hot-worked metals are relatively ductile.

### Cold Working

When rolling, drawing, pressing, forging, etc., are done below the recrystallization temperature, the process is known as cold working. This treatment generally results in severe distortion of the crystals (Fig. 2-23). Since distorted crystals offer high resistance to slip, cold-worked metals are somewhat brittle, and the compressive force that is necessary to machine or form them is relatively high.

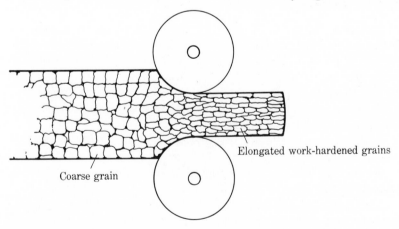

Fig. 2-23. The effect of cold working of metal.

## QUESTIONS

1. Why do the pure metals of aluminum, copper, and nickel flow quite readily under pressure?

2. What explanation can be given for iron being less ductile than aluminum?

3. What theory is used to explain why metals can be deformed with only a fraction of the force needed to overcome the binding forces between the atoms in a crystal lattice?

4. Define each of the following terms: (*a*) yield strength; (*b*) hardness; (*c*) modulus of elasticity.

5. Why may the Brinell hardness test be more accurate than some others when checking castings?

6. What advantages does the Scleroscope hardness tester have?

7. In what forms do alloying elements exist in a parent metal?

8. What chemical compounds add to the machinability of low-carbon steel?

9. (*a*) What is meant by a eutectic mixture? (*b*) What is meant by a eutectoid steel?

10. Name three physical properties affected by the amount of carbon in steel.

11. Name two characteristics of each of the following alloys: (*a*) nickel; (*b*) chromium; (*c*) molybdenum; (*d*) vanadium; (*e*) tungsten; (*f*) manganese.

12. What is the general composition of pearlite?

13. What is the significance of the $A_3$ line shown on the iron-carbon diagram?

14. Three requirements must be fulfilled in order to harden steel properly. What are they?

15. What factors affect the choice of cooling rates for steels?

16. Why is martensite termed an unstable structure?

17. How may a spheroidized structure be obtained in steel?

18. What physical properties are imparted to the steel through the tempering process?

19. What is the advantage of marquenching?

20. Explain the difference between annealing and normalizing, and the need for each.

21. What advantages and disadvantages does cyanide hardening have over carburizing and nitriding?

22. What factors determine the depth of hardness obtained by the flame-hardening method?

## PROBLEMS

1. What is the calculated shear strength of a 3-in.-diameter steel bar that does not fracture until a 450,000-lb shear load is applied?

2. What will the ultimate tensile strength be for the steel bar mentioned in Prob. 1?

3. If a turbine rotor is 20 ft $^{+000}_{-0.005}$ in. in diameter at installation, how much larger could it be after 100,000 hr of use and still be within the specified creep rate?

## REFERENCES

Black, P. H., *Theory of Metal Cutting*, McGraw-Hill Book Company, Inc., New York, 1961.

Dash, W. C., and A. G. Tweet, "Observing Dislocations in Crystals," *Scientific American*, October, 1961.

Holmberg, M. E., "Precipitation-Hardening Stainless Steels," *Machine Design*, October, 1959.

Paret, R. E., "How to Select the Right Stainless," *Machine Design*, June, 1959.

Spencer, L. F., "Surface Hardening of Steels," *Machine Design*, January, 1961.

Ward, B. G., Jr., "Match the Burner to the Job," *American Machinist/Metal Working Manufacturing*, November, 1959.

# 3

# FABRICATING
# CHARACTERISTICS
# OF FERROUS METALS

In THE PRECEDING chapter an explanation was given as to how the various properties of metals, such as hardness, ductility, etc., are developed. This chapter deals with the characteristics that should be observed when fabricating some of the more important ferrous materials. By *fabricating characteristics* is meant how the metal reacts to machining, forming, welding, and casting.

Before considering the fabrication of a metal, it is important to know how it is classified, so that references can be made to a specific type of metal. Therefore, the method of classification will be given for each of the metals before the fabricating characteristics are described.

In this chapter the following common ferrous metals will be discussed as to code-number classification and fabricating characteristics: plain carbon steels; low-alloy steels; tool steels; steel castings; cast iron (ductile, gray, and malleable); and stainless steel, including austenitic, ferritic, and martensitic.

First, however, it will be well to explore more fully the general subjects of classification and fabricating characteristics.

TABLE 3-1.

## AISI-SAE Classification of Steels

| Type of Steel | Numerals (and Digits) |
|---|---|
| Carbon steels | 1XXX |
|    Plain carbon steel | 10XX |
|    Free-cutting (screw stock) | 11XX |
|    Free-cutting, manganese steel | X13XX |
| High-manganese steel | T13XX |
| Nickel steels | 2XXX |
|    3.50% nickel | 23XX |
|    5.00% nickel | 25XX |
| Nickel-chromium steels | 3XXX |
|    1.25% nickel, 0.60% chromium | 31XX |
|    1.75% nickel, 1.00% chromium | 32XX |
|    3.50% nickel, 1.50% chromium | 33XX |
|    3.00% nickel, 0.80% chromium | 34XX |
|    Corrosion- and heat-resisting steels | 30XXX |
| Molybdenum steels | 4XXX |
|    Chromium steel | 41XX |
|    Chromium-nickel steel | 43XX |
|    Nickel steel | 46XX and 48XX |
| Chromium steels | 5XXX |
|    Low-chromium steel | 51XX |
|    Medium-chromium steel | 52XX |
|    Corrosion- and heat-resisting steels | 51XXX |
| Chromium vanadium steels | 6XXX |
| Triple-alloy steels | |
|    30% Ni, 40% Cr, 0.12% Mo | 81XX |
|    55% Ni, 50% Cr, 0.20% Mo | 86XX |
|    55% Ni, 50% Cr, 0.25% Mo | 87XX |
|    55% Ni, 50% Cr, 0.35% Mo | 88XX |
|    3.25% Ni, 1.20% Cr, 0.12% Mo | 93XX |
|    1.00% Ni, 80% Cr, 0.25% Mo | 98XX |
| Tungsten steels | 77XXX and 7XXXX |
| Silicon-manganese steels | 9XXX |

NOTE: The prefix X is used in several instances to denote variations in the range of manganese, sulfur, or chromium. The prefix T is used with the manganese steels (1300 series) to avoid confusion with steels of somewhat different manganese range that have been identified by the same numerals but without the prefix.

**CLASSIFICATION**

The first code-numbering system for steel was made by the Society of Automotive Engineers (SAE). It consists of a four or five-digit system; the first two digits refer to the alloy content and the last two (or three) to the carbon content in *points* carbon, where one point is equal to one one-hundredth of one percent. By referring to Table 3-1, it can be seen that the second digit sometimes represents two elements.

A more recent classification was made by the American Iron and Steel Institute (AISI). This system uses the basic SAE code numbers but adds prefix and suffix letters as follows:

| *Prefix* | *Meaning* |
|---|---|
| B | Acid Bessemer carbon steel |
| C | Basic open-hearth steel; no prefix also stands for basic open-hearth steel |
| CB | May be either Bessemer or open-hearth steel |
| D | Acid open-hearth steel |
| E | Electric-furnace steel when no letter appears |

| *Suffix* (*Limited List*) | *Meaning* |
|---|---|
| a | Restricted chemical composition |
| c | Guaranteed segregation limits |
| h | Guaranteed hardenability |
| i | Guaranteed conformity to nonmetallic inclusions |

Steels are also described as hot-rolled steels (HRS) or cold-rolled steels (CRS). The hot-rolled steels are easily identified as they have the oxide scale that is formed when heating to an elevated temperature. Cold-rolled steels have the scale removed in an acid bath and are then rolled to a finish size.

**FABRICATING CHARACTERISTICS**

Fabricating characteristics of each of the metals that follow will be discussed, where applicable, from the standpoint of machinability, formability, weldability, and castability.

### Machinability

Machinability is an involved term with many ramifications. However, simply stated, it is the ease with which metal can be removed in such operations as turning, drilling, reaming, threading, sawing, etc.

Ease of metal removal implies, among other things, that the forces acting against the cutting tool will be relatively low, that the chips will be easily broken up, that a good finish will result, and that the tool will last a reasonable period of time before it has to be replaced or resharpened. Another way of expressing this is to give each material a *machinability rating*. This has been done for most ferrous metals, using AISI B1112 as the basis of 100 percent machinability. Thus another metal may be said to have a machinability rating of 60 percent, as in the case of one type of stainless steel, or 240 percent for an aluminum alloy. Factors that increase or decrease machinability of a metal are shown in Table 3-2.

### TABLE 3-2.

### Factors Affecting Machinability of Metals

| | Factors That Increase Machinability | Factors That Decrease Machinability |
|---|---|---|
| Structure | Uniform microstructure | Nonuniformity |
| | Small, undistorted grains | Presence of abrasive inclusion |
| | Spheroidal structure in high-carbon steels | Large, distorted grains |
| | Lamellar structure in low- and medium-carbon steels | Spheroidal low- and medium-carbon steels |
| | | Lamellar high-carbon steels |
| Treatment | Hot working of alloys that are hard, such as medium- and high-carbon steels | Hot working of low-carbon steels |
| | Cold working of low-carbon steels | Cold working of higher-carbon steels |
| | Annealing, normalizing, tempering | Quenching |
| Composition | Small amounts of lead, manganese, sulfur, phosphorus | Carbon content below 0.22% or above 0.35% to 0.40% |
| | Absence of abrasive inclusions such as $Al_2O_3$ | High alloy content in steels |

### Formability

The ability of a metal to be formed is based on the ductility of the metal, which, in turn, is based on its crystal structure. As mentioned before, the metal that has a face-centered cubic crystal has the greatest opportunity for slip—four distinct nonparallel planes and three directions of slip in each plane.

Other factors that govern, to a large extent, the flowability or ductility of the material are grain size, hot and cold working, alloying elements, and softening heat treatments, such as annealing and normalizing.

**Grain Size.** If all metals consisted of a single grain or crystal, the tendency to slip in any pure metal would depend solely upon the number of slip planes in the crystal and upon the directions of ready slip in each plane. However, every metal contains many separate grains, and the planes of slip or direction of slip rarely coincide with each other. The tendency to slip in any single grain, therefore, is obstructed, to a certain extent, by the resistance of opposing slip planes in adjacent grains. As will be seen later, small grain sizes are recommended for shallow drawing of copper, and relatively large grains for heavy drawing on the thicker gauges.

**Hot and Cold Working.** The tremendous pressures encountered in hot working tend to reduce the size of the crystals either by preventing the growth of the crystals at elevated temperatures or by breaking up the existing crystals. Generally, the grains are distorted in the process. The amount of distortion will be a determining factor in the ductility of the metal.

Cold working also results in varying degrees of distorted crystals. Generally, cold-worked crystals are more distorted than are the hot-worked, and therefore cold-worked metals are usually less ductile than the hot-worked.

**Alloying Elements.** Most alloying elements in a pure metal reduce its ductility. Whether the alloying element is such that it has replaced atoms of pure metal or has found room for itself in the spaces between the atoms of pure metal, the effect is to reduce the number of slip planes in which ready slippage can occur. For example, steel, which is an alloy of carbon and iron, is less ductile than iron. As steel solidifies, it can hold only an extremely small amount of carbon in solution. The excess carbon being forced out of the individual cells of the atomic structure combines immediately with some iron to form iron carbide. Not only are the slip planes somewhat reduced by the presence of the alloy, but, as in the case of steel, the iron carbides offer increased resistance to slip. Therefore, the ductility of the steel decreases as the amount of carbon in the iron increases.

**Softening Heat Treatments.**  As discussed previously, annealing consists of heating the metal to the recrystallization temperature. At first the grains may be very small, but they grow in size as long as the metal is exposed to this high temperature. When the desired size is obtained, the metal is allowed to cool.

During recrystallization, the ductility of the metal is restored. The warped and distorted crystals are reformed so that the force required to cause slippage is lessened.

## Weldability

It may be said that all metals are weldable by one process or another. However, the real criterion in deciding on the weldability of a metal is *weld quality and the ease with which it can be obtained.*

In deciding on the weldability of a metal, the characteristics commonly considered are the heating and cooling effects on the metal, oxidation, and gas vaporization and solubility.

**Heat and Cooling.**  The effect of heat in determining the weldability of a material is related to the change in microstructure that results. For example, steels are sometimes considered weldable or not weldable on the basis of the hardness of the weld. The deposited weld metal may pick up carbon or other alloys and impurities from the parent metal that make it hard and brittle so that cracks result upon cooling.

The opposite effect may also be considered. A metal may have a certain hardness temper that will be changed by the heat of the weld. Although both of these conditions can be corrected by added precautions and heat treatment, they add to the cost and hinder the simplicity of the weld.

Hot shortness, a characteristic which is indicated by lack of strength at high temperature, may result in weld failures during cooling of certain metals.

**Oxidation.**  Oxidation of the base metal, particularly at elevated temperatures, is an important factor in rating the weldability of a metal. Metals that oxidize rapidly, such as aluminum, interfere with the welding process. The oxide has a higher melting point than the base metal, thus preventing the metal from flowing. It also may become entrapped in the weld metal, resulting in porosity, reduced strength, and brittleness.

**Gas.**  Large volumes of troublesome gas may form in the welding of some metals. These gases may become trapped in the weld because certain elements vaporize at temperatures below those needed for welding. Not only will this cause porosity, but some of the beneficial effects of these elements is lost.

## Castability

The castability of a metal is judged to a large extent on the following factors: solidification rate, shrinkage, segregation, gas porosity, and hot strength.

**Solidification Rate.** The ease at which a metal will continue to flow after it has been poured in the mold depends on its analysis and pouring temperature. Some metals such as gray iron are very fluid and can be poured into thin sections of complex castings.

**Shrinkage.** Shrinkage refers to the reduction in volume of a metal when it goes from a molten to a solid state. For steel, the amount of contraction amounts to about 6.9 to 7.4% by volume, or ¼ in. per ft; gray iron contracts half as much. This shrinkage factor has to be taken into account by the pattern maker and designer, not only to allow for the proper finished size, but also to see that undue strains will not be encountered during shrinkage due to the mold design. Various elements can be added to the alloy to control fluidity and shrinkage as discussed later in this chapter.

**SEGREGATION.** As the metal starts to solidify tiny crystal structures resembling pine trees and referred to as dendrites start to form at the mold edges. As they form they tend to exclude alloying elements. Subsequent crystals that form are progressively richer in alloy content as the metal solidifies. Thus the surface of the casting is not the same quality as that in the center. This is overcome in part at least by subsequent heat treatment, or very slow cooling.

**Gas Porosity.** Some metals in the molten state have a high affinity for oxygen and nitrogen. These gases become trapped as the metal solidifies, creating voids or pinholes.

**Low Hot Strength.** Metals are very low in strength right after solidification. This is especially true of the nonferrous metals. Precautions must be taken at the time of casting to avoid stress concentration that causes flaws and hot tears to develop as the metal solidifies.

## PLAIN CARBON STEELS

### Classification

Steel may be further classified as to carbon content as follows:

| Designation | Meaning |
|---|---|
| Low | 0.05 to approximately 0.30 percent carbon |
| Medium | 0.30 to approximately 0.60 percent carbon |
| High | 0.60 to approximately 0.95 percent carbon |

### Fabricating Characteristics

**Machinability.** The machinability of low-carbon steels is approximately 55 to 60 percent that of B1112. These steels are soft and draggy, generating considerable heat. They have a tendency to build up on the cutting edge, which also makes for inefficient cutting.

The medium-carbon steels cut better, even though the cutting pressures are higher. Both the hot- and cold-rolled steels machine better than the annealed. The machinability ranges between 65 and 70 percent.

High-carbon steels are less machinable than the medium-carbon steels, being at the other extreme—too hard. However, where fine finish and dimensional accuracy are needed, the high-carbon steels are used.

The machining qualities of plain low-carbon steels can be improved by the addition of small amounts of elements such as sulfur and phosphorus. These resulfurized and rephosphorized steels facilitate machining by permitting faster cutting speeds, longer tool life, and better surface finish. Manganese content of 1.00 to 1.90 percent also produces a free-cutting steel in the lower-carbon grades.

Since World War II, a number of grades of lead-bearing steels have taken their place among the free-machining steels. These leaded steels are actually sulfur, phosphorus or manganese free-cutting steels that have 0.15 to 0.35 percent lead added to improve machinability. The addition of lead does not affect the basic mechanical properties of the steel.

**Formability.** Low-carbon steels have good forming qualities, as there is less carbon to interfere with the planes of slip. Steels in this class can be given a class-2 bend, which is a 90-deg bend with a minimum radius of $t$ or the thickness of the metal. Classes of bends have been defined by the American Society for the Testing of Metals (ASTM).

Medium-carbon cold-rolled steels are too low in ductility for any practical degree of cold forming.

The hot-rolled medium-carbon steels are more ductile and can be bent with a 1-$t$ radius up to 0.0090 in. thick.

**Weldability.** Plain carbon steel is the most weldable of all metals. It is only as the carbon percentages increase that there is a tendency of the metal to harden and crack. Fortunately, 90 percent of the welding is done on low-carbon (0.15 percent) steels. This amount of carbon presents no particular difficulties in welding. Near the upper end of the low-carbon range (0.27 to 0.30 percent), there may be some formation of martensite when extremely rapid cooling is used.

Medium- and high-carbon steels will harden when welded if allowed to cool at speeds in excess of the critical cooling rates. Preheating to 500° or 600°F and postheating between 1100° and 1200°F will remove any of the brittle microstructures.

The extra-high-carbon steels, or tool steels, having a carbon range of 1.00 to 1.70 percent, are not recommended for high-temperature welding applications. These metals are usually joined by brazing with a low-temperature silver alloy. Because of the lower temperature of this process, it is possible to repair or fabricate tool-steel parts without affecting their heat-treated condition.

## LOW-ALLOY STEELS

### Classification

The same SAE and AISI classification applies to low-alloy steels as to plain carbon steels.

The low-alloy steels most often used are the chrome-molybdenum, 4130-4140-4150 series; the nickel-chrome-molybdenum, 4320-4337-4340; and the manganese-chrome-nickel 8620-8630-8640-8650 series. The fabricating characteristics of each of these groups will be discussed briefly.

### Fabricating Characteristics

#### Machinability.

CHROME-MOLYBDENUM (4130-4140-4150) SERIES. In general, these steels machine best in their lamellar pearlite condition which can be obtained by normalizing or annealing. Reasonably good tool life can also be produced in the normal hot-rolled condition.

The machinability ratings of steels in this group, when annealed, are as follows:

4130—67%
4140—61%
4150—54%

NICKEL-CHROME-MOLYBDENUM (4320-4337-4340) SERIES. For best tool life, these steels should be machined in the hot-rolled or annealed condition. The Brinell hardness should not be above 207 for good cutting conditions. A suffix letter H is added to the conventional number when the steel is available within a given hardenability band. The following machinability ratings are given for mill-annealed steels in this series:

4320—55%
4340—45%

MANGANESE-CHROME-NICKEL (8620 TO 8650) SERIES.  As with the plain carbon steels, machinability increases with carbon content up to 30 to 35 percent; then it decreases with the increasing carbon content. For best machinability, the steel should be normalized. In this condition the following ratings are applicable:

8620—60%
8630—65%
8640—60%
8650—50%

**Formability.**   Steels in this category are not generally used for forming, other than forging. Here they are employed extensively for gears, bearings, crankshafts, connecting rods, axle shafts, and any other uses where good strength and toughness are necessary. These steels are often case-hardened to provide a surface that can take high compressive loads and still have a core with great toughness.

**Weldability.**   Low-alloy steels can readily be welded by either oxyacetylene or arc methods, as long as certain techniques are applied. For arc welding, a shielded-arc process with special electrodes is used. In gas welding, where strength and corrosion are major factors, the welding rod should be of the same composition as the base material.

The reason for special precautions in welding low-alloy steels is because of their high hardenability. To prevent excessive hardening, preheating and postheating are used. Heat treatment after welding will give the weld and the parent metal similar properties.

For most of these steels, best results can be obtained in arc welding by using a low-hydrogen electrode, as it reduces the hydrogen content of the weld, eliminating brittleness.

**Castability.**   An important characteristic of alloy steels is their ability to air-harden. Thus complicated castings can be hardened when using these alloys, and tensile strengths from 70,000 to 100,000 psi can be obtained without quenching. Nickel and molybdenum with manganese increase the capacity to air-harden.

Combinations of chromium, nickel, manganese, and vanadium are used to produce wear resistance and high strength.

## TOOL STEELS

Tool steels are so named because they have the properties needed in making tools for fixtures; for cutting, shaping, forming, and blanking of materials, either hot or cold; and for precision gages.

## Classification

Tool-steel manufacturers have their own brand names for their products. Since these vary with each manufacturer, to avoid confusion for the consumer, the Joint Industry Conference (JIC) has set up some simple but effective means of identifying tool steels by classes. The system has received wide acceptance.

The JIC symbols are based partly on chemistry, partly on the cooling system required for hardening, and partly on physical characteristics. Some of the symbols adopted are:

| Symbol | Meaning |
|--------|---------|
| T | Tungsten high speed |
| M | Molybdenum high speed |
| D | High carbon, high chromium |
| A | Air hardening |
| O | Oil hardening |
| H | Hot work |
| S | Shock resisting |
| W | Water hardening |

These easily understood symbols are derived from long-standing trade expressions and designations. Numbers following the letters are also used to designate variations of each type. For example, W8 and W12 are water-hardening steels with 0.80 and 1.20 percent carbon, respectively. The AISI and SAE codes are quite similar to the JIC code. A general description of each type of tool steel follows.

**T. and M. Tungsten and Molybdenum High-Speed Steels.** There are three principal types of high-speed steels, classified according to their alloying elements as follows: (1) tungsten (T1); (2) molybdenum (M2); and (3) cobalt (symbol not included in the classification).

The tungsten type has the highest heat resistance. When used in cutting operations, the tools may reach temperatures in excess of 1100°F without softening below 60 $R_c$.

Since tungsten is a critical item and in limited supply, a substitute was developed. Now some tungsten and molybdenum steels can be used interchangeably. Where hardening equipment is limited, the tungsten type is much easier to handle, with less chance of cracking because of decarburization.

In addition to heat resistance, high-speed steels have the desirable properties of high hardness (63 to 66 $R_c$), high compression strength (in excess of 500,000 psi), and outstanding wear resistance. They are close competitors to carbides for metal-cutting-tool material such as drills, reamers, milling cutters, etc.

**D. High-Carbon–High-Chromium Steels.** These steels are second only to the high-speed steels in importance. They are used for all types of die work, including blanking, coining, drawing, forming, and thread rolling, as well as for reamers, gages, and rolls for beading and forming sheet metal. These steels are substantially lower in cost than the high-speed steels.

Depending upon the carbon-to-chromium content, these may be either oil- or air-hardening steels. The oil-hardening type (2 percent carbon) is used for blanking materials up to and including ⅛ in. thick. The air-hardening kind (1.50 percent carbon) is recommended for blanking steels over ⅛ in. thick. This rule is helpful in selecting tool steels for tool and die purposes.

**A. Air-Hardening Die Steels.** The difference between this steel and the one in the preceding category is that it has only 1 percent carbon and 5 percent chromium, compared with over 2 percent carbon and 10 to 12 percent chromium. Some of the air-hardening steels also contain manganese and molybdenum.

Some of the outstanding features of this steel are:

1. It can be air-hardened in large sections. (A comparison of the various depths of hardness obtained with different alloys was shown in the preceding chapter, Fig. 2-14).

2. It is safe to harden in intricate sections.

3. There is little distortion in hardening.

4. It is easier to machine than the high-carbon–high-chromium types.

5. It falls in the intermediate price range.

The air-hardening steels are particularly good for the larger sizes of tools and dies where the oil-hardening nondeforming steels will not harden, or where high-carbon–high-chromium steels are not necessary for the performance required.

**O. Oil-Hardening Nondeforming Die Steels.** This group of steels has a substantially reduced alloy content, compared to the previously mentioned types. Their characteristics include the following:

1. They have a wide range of uses for all types of medium-life tools and dies.

2. They are easy to machine and harden. The hardening temperature is relatively low (1500°F).

3. They harden uniformly where the mass of the section does not exceed the equivalent of a 2½-in.-diameter, 6-in.-long cylinder.

4. They are of moderate cost.

These steels are generally useful where the die sections are of limited mass, and long runs are not required. The oil quench provides a slower cooling action than does water, and there is, therefore, less strain on the workpiece.

**H. Hot-Work Steels.**   Hot-work steels are those that are used for hot-blanking dies, hot-extrusion dies, hot-heading dies, hot-punching dies, and forging and die-casting dies.

Three main types of hot-work steels are available. Two of these are very similar to the high-speed steels described previously—the tungsten and molybdenum types. Both of these have high heat resistance and do not soften until the temperature reaches approximately 1100° to 1200°F.

The third steel in this class is a chrome-molybdenum type. It has 5 percent chromium, 1.3 percent molybdenum, and 0.30 percent carbon. Although this steel does not withstand the high temperatures of the two previously mentioned, there is a wide range of applications.

**S. Shock-Resisting Steels.**   Shock-resisting steels are not only capable of taking a great deal of shock but also have high fatigue resistance and good wearing qualities. The most common type is probably S1 with 0.60 percent carbon and tungsten, chromium, or vanadium. Where shock is severe but heating is intermittent or nominal, a 0.60 percent carbon 2 + percent tungsten with 1.2 percent chromium and 0.20 percent vanadium is often used.

These steels are generally hardened to 58 to 60 $R_c$ by oil quenching. They give extended performance where higher-carbon types of die steels fail.

**W. Water-Hardening Steels.**   Water-hardening steels are often referred to as *straight carbon*. They have some manganese and silicon, but this is not in excess of 0.30 percent. The carbon range is from 0.60 to 1.30 percent; however, 80 percent of all carbon tool steels lie within a carbon range of 0.90 to 1.10 percent.

These steels are particularly useful in a large number of cold-punching and stamping operations where shock is severe. The steel hardens to about a $\frac{1}{8}$-in. depth, which provides a hard outer surface with a tough, shock-dampening core. Many die sections are hardened and tempered to 60 or 62 $R_c$.

Carbon tool steels are low in cost and easy to machine and harden. However, specifying the proper amount of carbon to harden just deep enough to give the desired depth and strength of case, and yet to retain a soft, tough, shock-dampening core, will require considerable experience or advice from the steel supplier.

### Fabricating Characteristics

**Machinability.** Normally, tool steels are purchased in the annealed condition. If they are forged, it may be necessary to normalize and anneal them before machining. Annealed tool steels vary from 160 to 250 Brinell. The main difficulty in machining them is that the alloy content makes them extremely abrasive to machine. If the hardness is too low, these steels tend to become gummy and cause the cutting tool to "hog in" and break. This is especially true of the high-carbon–high-chromium steels. They are easier to machine at 250 Brinell than at 180. It is possible to machine tool steels and die steels in the fully hardened condition when tungsten carbide cutting tools are used.

Rough toolmarks should be removed before hardening tool steels, as they may cause cracks.

Many machinability ratings exist for tool steels, but, since there is such a wide variation in them, they will be listed in order of machining preference, from the most machinable to the least.

1. Water-hardening tool steels
2. Oil-hardening tool steels
3. $\begin{cases}\text{Shock-resisting}\\\text{Hot-work}\\\text{High-speed}\end{cases}$ These tool steels have approximately the same machinability rating

**Formability (Forging).** All steels tend to decarburize when heated to elevated temperatures, but this is more pronounced in the high-alloy steels. To prevent it, tool steels must be heated in atmosphere-controlled furnaces. If these furnaces are not available, the parts should be packed in protective material while being heated. Molybdenum high-speed steels are rolled in borax powder after being heated to 1300° to 1500°F, or dipped hot or cold into a 180°F borax solution.

Preheating or slow uniform heat is recommended to allow penetration to the center of the work. Preheating at 800°F is preferred, since it reduces the time the work must be held at a high temperature. The soak time should be 15 min for each inch of thickness, increased to 20 min for high-chromium steels. It is important to keep tool steels at the proper temperature, as they crack easily when the temperature is too low.

Care must be taken to cool slowly after forging, so that cracks do not develop from the forging strains. Parts may be buried in dry ashes, lime, mica, or other material that retards heat transfer.

**Weldability.** High-alloy steels are welded under the same precautions as described for the low-alloy steels. Special care should be exercised because of the high hardenability of the metals. Generally, welding of these metals is confined to repair work. In order to keep the heat-affected zone as small as possible, arc-welding techniques or silver brazing are recommended.

When arc-welding a heat-treated metal, a stainless-steel filler rod may be used. Sometimes a transition weld is made; that is, the first weld in the break or crack, cut out with a chisel to a **V** form, will be done with a stainless-steel rod and the next pass with a high-strength filler-rod material. The welds should be made in short lengths of 2 in. or less, and lightly peened with the chipping hammer as they cool to help stress-relieve them. Where hardness and toughness are required, the weld may be finished with a layer of hard surfacing material. Although this method will often effect a satisfactory repair, there will still be a narrow heat-affected zone just beyond the weld that will be weaker than the original heat-treated part.

Silver brazing is used to make repairs on tool steels, because the low-melting-point alloys used for bonding can stay below the critical-heat range of the steel. Shown in Fig. 3-1 is a broken high-speed-steel milling cutter that has been silver-brazed and placed back in service. The flow point of the alloys used for this type of brazing may be as low as 1145°F.

**Fig. 3-1.** Silver brazing can be used to effect economical repairs on high-speed and other heat-treated steel (courtesy Handy and Harman).

**Tool-steel Selection**

As a means of summarizing some of the important facts about tool steels, the following points are given as a basis of selection.

1. Always start with the plain carbon steels, since they are the cheapest and easiest to machine. For example, if W8 does not satisfy the requirement in that steel, the hardness may not be deep enough. Then go to W9V, which is not only higher in carbon content but has vanadium for deeper hardness penetration and finer grain structure. This may still be short of some of the requirements needed, so it will be necessary to proceed to the oil- or air-hardening steels.

2. The oil- and air-hardening steels were developed for maximum safety in hardening and minimum dimensional change after heat treatment. They are preferred for dies with adjacent thin and thick sections, sharp corners, or numerous holes. Wear resistance is better than in the W steels, but toughness is not so good. They are generally not suited for elevated-temperature use. The oil-hardening grades are relatively low in cost, whereas the air-hardening ones are rather expensive.

3. The hot-work steels must combine red hardness, wear resistance, and shock resistance. They have relatively low carbon and smaller quantities of alloying elements than do the high-speed steels.

4. The shock-resisting steels are used to withstand cold battering operations where abrasion resistance is of secondary importance.

5. The high-speed steels were developed primarily to provide red hardness and high abrasion resistance along with some shock resistance.

## STEEL CASTINGS

### Classification

The American Society for Testing Metals (ASTM) has formulated the following code for carbon and low-alloy castings.

| ASTM Designation | Meaning |
|---|---|
| 27-55 | Medium-strength carbon-steel castings for general application |
| 148-55 | High-strength steel castings for structural purposes |
| 216-53T | Carbon-steel castings suitable for fusion welding for high-temperature service (tentative) |
| 217-55 | Alloy-steel castings for pressure-containing parts suitable for high-temperature service |
| 351-52T | Ferritic-steel castings for pressure-containing parts suitable for low-temperature service |
| 356-58 | Heavy-walled carbon and low-alloy-steel castings for steam turbines (tentative) |
| 389-59T | Alloy-steel castings specially heat-treated for pressure-containing parts suitable for high-temperature service |

In addition to the listed code numbers, class numbers are given. Class numbers are used to indicate the tensile-strength and yield-point stresses. A class 80–50 cast steel, for example, would be one with a tensile strength of 80,000 psi and a yield point of 50,000 psi.

### Fabricating Characteristics

The mechanical properties of cast steels and wrought steels having the same composition and heat treatment are quite similar. However, there are a few differences. One difference is that wrought products are more ductile in the direction of working and less so in the transverse direction, whereas castings have uniform properties in all directions. The other difference is that there is likely to be more variation in castings than in wrought products, since the equipment, pattern, and even the steel analysis vary from foundry to foundry.

Steel castings stay below the cast-iron range in carbon content. About 60 percent of all steel castings are in the medium-carbon range. They are used extensively in railroads, machine tools, rolling mills, construction equipment, and other applications as shown in Fig. 3-2.

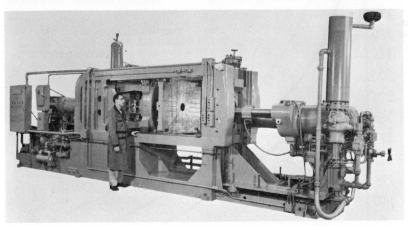

**Fig. 3-2.** Steel castings can be used to fabricate a wide variety of equipment, from small gears for a gearbox to large machine frames.

**Machinability.** Steel castings are often delivered to the customer in the normalized condition, but this does not necessarily produce optimum machinability. Heat treatment to obtain the optimum microstructure for machining is not always employed, because other considerations, such as production requirements, do not warrant it, or because high-impact strength is more important.

The amount of pearlite in carbon steels increases with the carbon content. The laminated pearlite structure is quite rigid and is the most favorable one in steel for optimum machinability, unless too much is present. For cast steels the ideal ratio of ferrite to pearlite is 60:40.

As the pearlite content increases, so does the strength of castings, but machinability goes down. Machinability of cast steels that have an unfavorable distribution of ferrite and pearlite can be improved by spheroidizing.

It is generally accepted that large grain size presents some improvement in machinability. Fine grain size usually adds to the quality of the surface finish but gives less tool life. This is particularly true in the medium-carbon steels.

Alloy-steel castings can be purchased with fine, medium, or coarse grain size, with a variety of microstructures, and with varying degrees of hardness, all of which affect the machinability. Generally, alloy steels are more difficult to machine than carbon steels, because of the carbide-forming elements in the alloys.

Although Brinell hardness cannot be taken as a sole criterion for machinability, it is often used as a rough index. Shown in Fig. 3-3 is a

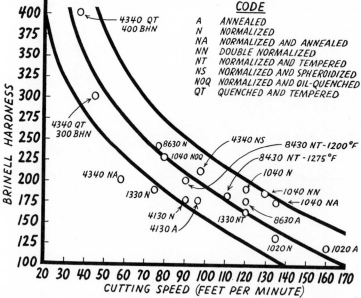

**Fig. 3-3.** Cutting speed for one hr of tool life versus Brinell hardness using high-speed-steel tools (courtesy Steel Founders' Society of America).

relationship that exists for 1 hr. of tool life based on Brinell hardness. The plot indicates that as hardness increases, the cutting speed decreases.

One other main consideration in the machining of steel castings is skin, or outside surface, scale. The oxide surface scale is a result of heat treating and is very detrimental to tool life. It is best to have this removed by pressure blasting before machining. The best results are obtained when the tool is kept well under the skin in the first surface cut. A depth of cut of ¼ to ⅜ in. is recommended as a minimum for the first cut.

The machinability index for cast steels using high-speed cutting tools is given in Table 3-3. It is used in making a quick relative com-

**TABLE 3-3.**

**Machinability Index for Cast Steels with High-Speed-Steel Tools***
**(machining speed: 180 sq ft per min with tool life of 2 to 3 hr)**

| Steel and Heat Treatment | BHN | Machinability Index Number |
|---|---|---|
| B1112 Free-machining steel (wrought) | 179 | 100 |
| 1020 Annealed | 122 | 90 |
| 1020 Normalized | 134 | 75 |
| | | |
| 1040 Double normalized | 185 | 70 |
| 1040 Normalized and annealed | 175 | 75 |
| 1040 Normalized | 190 | 65 |
| 1040 Normalized and oil-quenched | 225 | 45 |
| | | |
| 1330 Normalized | 187 | 40 |
| 1330 Normalized and tempered | 160 | 65 |
| | | |
| 4130 Annealed | 175 | 55 |
| 4130 Normalized and spheroidized | 175 | 50 |
| | | |
| 4340 Normalized and annealed | 200 | 35 |
| 4340 Normalized and spheroidized | 210 | 55 |
| 4340 Quenched and tempered | 300 | 25 |
| 4340 Quenched and tempered | 400 | 20 |
| | | |
| 8430 Normalized and tempered, 1200°F | 200 | 50 |
| 8430 Normalized and tempered, 1275°F | 180 | 60 |
| | | |
| 8630 Normalized | 240 | 40 |
| 8630 Annealed | 175 | 65 |

* Courtesy Steel Founders' Society of America.

parison with B1112 as the base. The base metal was machined at 180 sq ft per min, with a high-speed tool, and gave a tool life of 2 to 3 hr.

**Weldability.** Cast steels are judged weldable by the same methods used in wrought steels. These are manual arc welding with coated electrodes, submerged-arc welding, and inert-gas metal arc welding or metal inert gas (MIG). The shielding gases used are argon, helium, or carbon dioxide.

These methods are discussed in some detail in Chap. 9, but, to differentiate between them, they are shown schematically in Fig. 3-4.

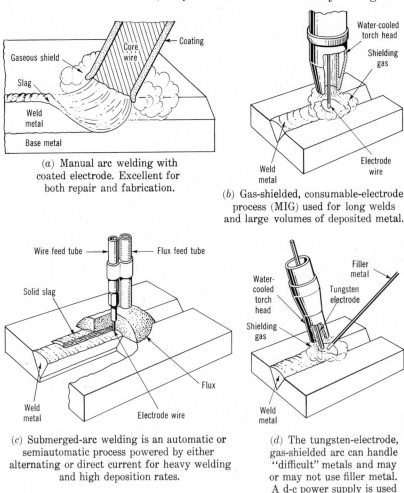

(a) Manual arc welding with coated electrode. Excellent for both repair and fabrication.

(b) Gas-shielded, consumable-electrode process (MIG) used for long welds and large volumes of deposited metal.

(c) Submerged-arc welding is an automatic or semiautomatic process powered by either alternating or direct current for heavy welding and high deposition rates.

(d) The tungsten-electrode, gas-shielded arc can handle "difficult" metals and may or may not use filler metal. A d-c power supply is used except for special jobs (TIG).

**Fig. 3-4.** Welding methods used on cast steel. Both (b) and (c) use bare wires automatically fed from a reel. Shielding is provided by (b) inert gas or (c) flux (courtesy *American Machinist/Metalworking Manufacturing*).

Standard welding procedures used on steel apply to steel castings. With a relatively few exceptions, all castings welded are subsequently stress-relieved or given a full heat treatment (for example, normalized, or quenched and tempered). This eliminates excessive hardness next to the weld as well as severe weld stresses. Another precaution to eliminate both hot and cold cracking of the weld along with permanent deformation of the part is the use of a suitable preheat temperature.

Preheating can be done by placing the casting in a furnace or by localized preheating with a torch. General preheat is preferred, since it minimizes localized stresses. The preheat temperature should be as low as is practical, since too much heat will make welding more difficult. Preheats of 200° to 400°F for the medium-carbon steels are recommended. Preheats over 400°F are recommended for castings containing more carbon and other alloying elements.

Since cast steels are readily weldable, there are times when a combination of casting and welding will prove advantageous. Examples of this are shown in Fig. 3-5. Combination cast-weld construction is used to reduce not only the intricacy of the casting but also high residual stresses.

 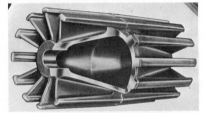

*Original steel casting*    *Redesigned cast-weld construction*

**Fig. 3-5.** It is sometimes advantageous to redesign intricate castings to a cast-weld construction. The half casting eliminated the large center core and, at the same time, afforded better gating and solidification possibilities (courtesy Steel Founders' Society of America).

Steel weldments can often be redesigned as steel castings, and vice versa. Weldments are frequently made up of many separate pieces held in place for fabrication by jigs and fixtures. Unless the separate parts are standard items such as rolled, punched, or extruded shapes, castings will generally be more economical. An example of the redesign of a weldment to a casting is shown in Fig. 3-6. In this case the employment of the tubular form in casting design resulted in greater load-carrying ability for the part.

The wide range of metallurgical qualities with their related physical properties, together with extensive design flexibility, have made steel castings universally accepted for applications throughout industry.

*Weldment* *Casting*

**Fig. 3-6.** The conversion of weldments to castings can be economically feasible when the number of parts requires excessive tooling, or the properties and composition requirements make the welding process difficult or costly (courtesy Steel Founders' Society of America).

## CAST IRON

### Main Types

In order to understand the fabricating characteristics of cast iron, it is necessary to become familiar with each of the main types and how they are obtained.

Cast iron is a rather complex mixture containing 91 to 94 percent metallic iron and varying proportions of other elements, the most important of which are carbon, silicon, manganese, sulfur, and phosphorus. By varying the amount of these elements and the heat treatment, the foundryman is able to produce a multitude of different irons, each with properties adapted to different uses.

The effect of elements other than carbon can be briefly summarized as follows:

1. Up to 3 percent silicon tends to promote the formation of graphitic carbon. It also increases fluidity of the molten metal and lessens casting shrinkage.

2. Sulfur increases shrinkage and acts to prevent the separation of graphitic carbon. To some extent, the harmful effects of sulfur, considered an impurity, may be overcome by the presence of manganese.

3. Considerable phosphorus is used in intricate castings. It increases fluidity and decreases shrinkage. Since these qualities are obtained at the expense of toughness, this element is kept low in important castings.

By varying these elements and the heat treatment, several basic types of cast iron are obtained—gray, malleable, and ductile. Before the classification and fabricating characteristics of each of these metals is discussed, the characteristics developed in each type will be given.

**Gray Iron.** Gray iron and cast iron are often considered to be synonymous terms. The name is derived from the grayish appearance of its fracture, the color being caused by the large amount of visible graphite or carbon. The composition is largely pearlite and flake graphite (Fig. 3-7). The coarse pearlite and coarse graphite are usually associated with slow cooling of an iron that is not highly alloyed. Fine graphite and pearlite are usually the result of more rapid cooling, low silicon content, and such alloying elements as chromium and vanadium.

**Fig. 3-7.** The microstructure of gray cast iron, and space models of flake graphite (courtesy of The International Nickel Co., Inc.).

**Malleable Iron.**    Malleable iron is made from white cast iron, which is a cast iron with virtually all of the carbon in the form of cementite (iron carbide, $Fe_3C$). It is called white iron because of the appearance of the fracture, which is brilliant white, caused by reflection from the facets of the iron carbide. White cast iron is made in the same way as gray iron, except that the graphitizing elements are modified and the cooling rate is considerably increased. It is the rapid cooling rate, often referred to as *chilling*, that produces the iron carbide structure. White cast iron has a hardness between 400 and 550 Brinell and is unmachinable. It is used in wear and abrasion applications such as liners on rock and ore crushers, rolling-mill rolls, plow points, and a variety of road machinery.

When white cast iron is properly annealed, it becomes malleable. The annealing is usually done at two temperatures, the first stage being at 1700°F. It is at this temperature that the coarse primary carbides become graphitized to flake nodules (Fig. 3-8). Then, as the temperature is lowered to about 1325°F, the iron carbide laminations of pearlite that have separated out are graphitized, leaving the final structure ferrite and graphite. The changes in the carbon are shown in Fig. 3-8.

The usual time needed for the two-stage annealing process is anywhere from 30 hr in modern furnaces to 150 hr in older batch-type furnaces.

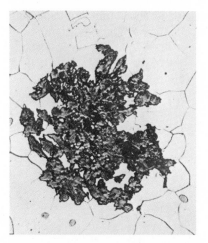 

*Flake aggregate graphite nodule*      *Spheroidal graphite nodule*

**Fig. 3-8.** Photomicrographs showing the development of the graphite nodule in malleable iron (courtesy The International Nickel Co., Inc.).

**Ductile Iron.** For generations, foundrymen and metallurgists have searched for some way to transform brittle cast iron into a tough, strong material. Finally, it was discovered that magnesium could greatly change the properties of cast iron. A small amount of magnesium, about 1 lb/ton of iron, causes the flake graphite to take on a spheroidal shape (Fig. 3-9). Graphite in a spheroidal shape presents the minimum surface for a given volume. Therefore, there are less discontinuities in

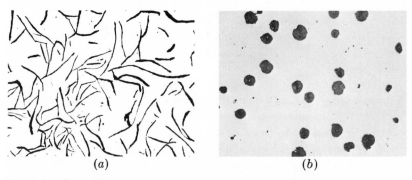

(a)      (b)

**Fig. 3-9.** Comparison of the microstructure of (a) gray cast iron and (b) ductile iron (courtesy The International Nickel Co., Inc.).

the surrounding metal, giving it far more strength and ductility. Thus the processing advantages of steel, including high strength, toughness, ductility, and wear resistance, can be obtained in this readily cast material.

Ductile iron can be heat-treated in a manner similiar to steel. Gray irons can too, but the risk of cracking is much greater.

There has been a rapid growth in the number of foundries licensed to produce this relatively new material that also goes by other names, such as nodular iron and spheroidal iron.

**Inoculated Irons.** Irons can be inoculated, while in the molten state, with certain materials that change their structure without materially changing their composition.

One of the early inoculants was ferrosilicon used on a lower-silicon iron. Addition of the missing silicon in the ladle improved the structure and reduced the tendency of the iron to chill and become hard around the edges. Other inoculants used with silicon are calcium, ferromanganese, and zirconium.

A familiar inoculated iron is Meehanite, which is produced by licensed foundries. It is a specially made white-cast-iron composition which is graphitized in the ladle with calcium silicide. It is produced in a number of grades, including a group for high-temperature service.

## Classification

**Gray Iron.** The most used classification for gray cast iron is that of the American Society for Testing Materials adopted in 1936. These specifications cover seven classes that are numbered in increments of 5, from 20 to 60. The class number refers to its tensile strength; for example, a class 40 cast iron refers to one having a minimum tensile strength of 40,000 psi. The carbon content becomes less as the strength requirement goes up. Alloys in increasing quantities are used to achieve strengths higher than 45,000 psi. Although high-strength cast irons have been developed, they are not widely used because they are still quite brittle.

**Malleable Iron.** About 90 percent of the malleable iron made is classified as 32510, which means that it has a yield point of 32,500 psi and an elongation of 10 percent. Grade 35018 has somewhat lower carbon content, but it has somewhat higher strength and better ductility. Grades 32510 and 35018 are known as standard types of malleable iron. There is an increasing demand for a newer type termed *pearlitic malleable*. Instead of having a ferrite matrix, it is pearlitic, which is stronger and harder than ferrite. These irons are obtained by interrupting the second-stage annealing process, or by introducing larger quantities of manganese which prevents graphitization of the pearlite, or by air cooling followed by tempering.

Pearlitic malleables have strengths up to 90,000 psi, but ductility is low. They are used where higher strengths and wear resistance are needed, along with less resistance to shock.

**Ductile Iron.** The general classification numbers for ductile irons are similar to those for gray cast iron, but a third figure is added which represents the minimum percent of elongation that can be expected. For example, an 80-60-03 has 80,000 psi minimum tensile strength, 60,000 psi minimum yield strength, with 3 percent minimum elongation. There are four regular types of ductile irons: 60-45-10, 80-60-03, 100-70-03, and 120-90-02. In addition, there are two special types, one of which is for heat resistance; the other (Ni-Resist)* has both corrosion and heat resistance.

### Fabricating Characteristics

#### Machinability.

GRAY IRON. The usual range of carbon is between 2.50 and 3.75 percent. The graphite flakes act to cause discontinuities in the ferrite. This helps the chips to break up easily. The graphite also furnishes lubricating qualities to the cutting action of the tool. Although gray cast iron is considered quite machinable, it varies considerably because of the microstructure. The ratings may range from 50 to 125 percent that of B1112.

One of the easiest checks used to determine the machinability of a given piece of material is the Brinell test. The normal hardness range of 130 to 230 Brinell will present no machining difficulties. Beyond this range, however, even a few points will have a large effect on the cutting speed that should be used. Hardnesses above 230 Brinell indicate that the structure contains free carbides which greatly reduce tool life.

Tungsten carbide tools are usually used to machine cast irons because of the abrasive qualities of the material.

Machinability of gray cast irons can be improved through annealing. When this is done, machinability excels that of any other ferrous material.

MALLEABLE IRON. Malleable iron has a machinability rating of 120 percent and is considered one of the most readily machined ferrous metals. The reason for this good machinability is its uniform structure

* Registered trademark of the International Nickel Company, Inc.

and the nodular form of the tempered carbon. The pearlitic malleables, which have a different annealing that leaves some of the carbon content in the form of combined carbides, have machinability ratings of 80 to 90 percent. (The term pearlitic is just a convenient term and does not mean that the microstructure is necessarily in pearlite form.)

DUCTILE IRON. The machinability of ductile iron is similar to that of gray cast iron for equivalent hardnesses and better than that of steel for equivalent strengths. Type 60-45-10 has both maximum machinability and toughness. Although the cutting action is good, the power factor is higher owing to the toughness of the material.

MACHINABILITY COMPARISON. By way of quick review, the following machinability ratings are given for rough approximations:

| Type of Iron | Machinability Index |
|---|---|
| Malleable (standard) | 110–120 |
| Gray iron (flake graphite) | 110 |
| Ductile iron | 90–110 |
| Meehanite | 76 |
| Gray iron (pearlitic) | 68 |

### Weldability.

GRAY IRON. Gray cast iron can be welded with the oxyacetylene torch or with the electric arc. However, owing to its low ductility, special precautions should be taken to avoid cracking in the weld area. Preheating is done, in the case of oxyacetylene welding, to make expansion and contraction more uniform. The opposite effect is used in arc welding, where short welds are made in order to keep the heat at a minimum. Slow cooling is essential to permit the carbon to separate out in the form of graphite flakes. Failure to do this will result in mottled or chilled areas.

Generally, the welding of gray cast iron is limited to repair work rather than fabrication. However, braze welding with bronze or nickel copper is frequently used in fabrication.

MALLEABLE IRONS. Malleable irons are not considered weldable, that is, in the same sense that gray cast iron is weldable. The reason for this is that the heat necessary to melt the edges of the break will completely destroy the malleable properties. Owing to the long-term anneal required to produce these properties originally, a simple annealing process would not restore them. There are times, however, where stresses are low or are in compression only; in this case, successful arc welding can be accomplished. A commercially pure nickel rod or a 10 percent aluminum bronze rod is used.

Since brazing can be done at a temperature of 1700°F or less, it is a preferred method of repair. Silver brazing is also used, since this procedure can be accomplished with even less heat.

DUCTILE IRONS. Ductile iron, being a high-carbon-content material, should be given special consideration, just as in welding gray cast iron. It can be welded by the carbon-arc process and most other fusion processes, either to itself or to other metals such as carbon steel, stainless steel, and nickel. The most easily welded types are 60-45-10 and the high-alloy variety. High-quality welds are made with cored electrodes having 60 percent nickel and 40 percent iron. Noncritical applications may be welded with ordinary steel electrodes.

This material can also be brazed with silver or copper brazing alloys. Crack-free overlays can be made with commercial hard-surfacing rods. This will provide special abrasion and corrosion resistance.

### Castability.

GRAY IRON. From the iron-carbon diagram (Fig. 2-13) it can be seen that carbon markedly lowers the melting point of iron. Many benefits accrue from this fact. The pouring temperature, for example, can be several hundred degrees higher than the melting point, making for excellent fluidity. This makes it possible to produce thin-section castings over a large area. Shrinkage is considerably less than that of steel because the rejection of graphite causes expansion during solidification. The amount of solidification shrinkage differs with the various casting alloys. Class 20 and 25 irons contain sufficient graphite so that there is virtually no shrinkage at all. The higher classes have one half to two thirds the solidification shrinkage of any ferrous alloys.

MALLEABLE IRONS. The molten white irons from which malleable irons are made have high fluidity, allowing complicated shapes to be cast. Good surface finish and close dimensional tolerances are possible. Since malleable irons require a prolonged heat treatment, internal stresses, that may have occurred as the casting solidified and cooled, are removed.

DUCTILE IRONS. Ductile iron is similar to gray cast iron when it somes to casting qualities. It has a low melting point and good fluidity in the molten state. Therefore, it can be poured in intricate shapes and thin sectional parts. The metal will flow several inches in sections as small as 1/16 in. in greensand molds at normal foundry pouring temperatures. Many parts are now being cast from ductile iron that formerly could not be cast, because gray iron did not possess adequate properties and steel could not be cast in such intricate shapes. Some of the advantages of ductile-steel castings are shown in the before-and-after design of a steel wheel (Fig. 3-10).

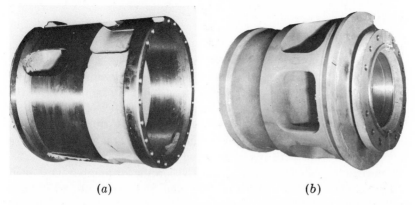

(a)                              (b)

**Fig. 3-10.**  Some of the advantages of ductile iron are shown in the redesign of this heavy-duty wheel from (a) fabrication to (b) casting (courtesy The International Nickel Co., Inc.).

CASTABILITY COMPARISON.  Some of the properties of the cast materials discussed are shown graphically in Fig. 3-11. You will note that, in general, yield strength, tensile strength, elongation, and modulus go progressively up from gray cast iron to malleable iron to cast steel to ductile iron, the exception being higher elongation and modulus for cast steels.

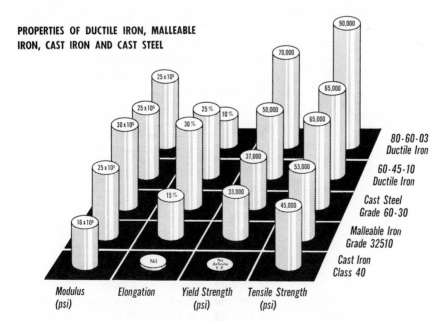

**Fig. 3-11.**  Comparison of the properties of ductile iron, malleable iron, cast iron, and cast steel (courtesy International Nickel Company, Inc.).

STAINLESS STEELS

### Classification

The three main types of stainless steel are *austenitic, ferritic,* and *martensitic.* All of these groups have steels that contain at least 10.5 percent chromium. It is from this element that the excellent corrosion resistance is obtained. Current theory holds that a thin, transparent, and very tough film forms on the chrome surface. It is inert or passive and does not react with many other corrosive materials.

Stainless steels are often grouped according to number. One such system is that of The American Iron and Steel Institute which has the 200, 300, and 400 series. Another system specifies the steel by its chromium or nickel content, such as 18-8, meaning 18 percent chromium and 8 percent nickel. The SAE numbering system, in most cases, merely

**TABLE 3-4.**

#### Numbering Systems for Stainless Steel

| AISI Designation | SAE Designation | General Classification |
|---|---|---|
| 301 | 30301 | |
| 302 | 30302 | |
| 303 | 30303F | Wrought chromium- |
| 304 | 30304 | nickel austenitic |
| 305 | 30305 | steels (not harden- |
| 309 | 30309 | able by thermal treat- |
| 310 | 30310 | ments) |
| 316 | 30316 | |
| 317 | 30317 | |
| 321 | 30321 | |
| | | |
| 410 | 51410 | |
| 414 | 51414 | Wrought stainless |
| 416 | 51416F | martensitic chrom- |
| 420 | 51420 | ium steels |
| 440A | 51440A | (hardenable) |
| 440B | 51440B | |
| 440C | 51440C | |
| | | |
| | | Wrought stainless |
| | | ferritic chromium |
| 430 | 51430 | steels (not hardenable |
| 446 | 51446 | by thermal treat- |
| | | ments) |

adds two digits to the front of the AISI numbers. For example, AISI stainless-steel number 302 is classified as 30302. The SAE stainless steels are listed in Table 3-4, along with the corresponding AISI numbers.

A brief description of each of the three main types of stainless steels follows.

**Austenitic.** Austenitic stainless steels are known as the 300 series. The basic alloy in this series is type 302. It is the 18-8 stainless steel. It is called austenitic because the metal has an austenitic structure at room temperature. It has the highest corrosion resistance of all the stainless alloys. It also claims the greatest strength and scale resistance at elevated temperatures. It also retains ductility at temperatures approaching absolute zero.

The 300 series is generally selected for applications where strength, ductility, and good corrosion resistance are essential.

**Ferritic.** As the name implies, ferritic stainless has a low carbon-to-chromium ratio. This eliminates the effects of thermal transformation and prevents hardening by heat treatment. These steels are magnetic and have good ductility. They do not work-harden to any appreciable degree.

Type 430 is the general-purpose ferritic. It is frequently used as an alternate for 302. It can be easily buffed to a mirror finish and, for this reason, is used extensively for trim molding and other decorative applications.

**Martensitic.** Because of the higher carbon-to-chromium ratio, martensitic steels are the only types hardenable by heat treatment. Hardness, ductility, and ability to hold an edge are characteristics of these alloys. These steels are magnetic in all conditions and possess the best thermal conductivity of the stainless types.

Type 410 is the most widely used steel in this group. It is tough and has good resistance to impact, and it attains a tensile strength of 300,000 psi when hardened.

## Fabricating Characteristics

### Machinability.

AUSTENITIC. Steels in this group tend to work-harden rapidly. The machinability rating is about 50 to 55 percent that of B1112. More power and rigidity are needed in both the tools and the machines. It is especially important to see that the tools have a keen cutting edge, as any rubbing action of a dull tool will work-harden and glaze the surface. For the same reason, all feeding action must be positive. As soon as feeding action is stopped, the tool should be removed from the work, or work hardening will result.

Types 303 and 303Se are the free-machining steels of this group. At least one free-machining steel has been developed for each group. In this case, the high sulfur content or the addition of selenium will help to promote good chip characteristics, with a resulting machinability rating of 70 percent.

FERRITIC. The free-machining steels in this group are 430F and 430Se. With sulfur and selenium added, these steels can provide the highest machinability of all the stainless steels, going as high as 90 to 95 percent. They are used extensively for automatic-screw-machine work and volume production of precision parts that do not require an extremely high level of corrosion resistance.

MARTENSITIC. All grades are suitable for machining, but the free-machining steels are 416 and 416Se. These are rated at approximately 90 percent that of B1112.

### Formability.

GENERAL. The low yield strength and high ductility which are characteristic of stainless steels permit the successful forming of complex shapes. However, stainless steels possess relatively high tensile strength, and they are subject to greater strain hardening than ductile materials; therefore, forming pressures must be greater.

In selecting a stainless alloy for forming, the minimum tensile strength or the maximum ductility (elongation) should not be the main consideration. The alloy, rather, should be chosen by *the rate at which it work-hardens*. For example, parts to be rolled out, such as angles and channels, should have a *high* rate of work hardening, as they are expected to have strength and stiffness when completed. On the other hand, items that are to be deep-drawn must have a *low* rate of work hardening.

Stainless steels can be obtained in various cold-rolled tempers designated as annealed, ¼, ½, ¾, and full hard.

In brief, the various temper designations indicate the following:

| *Temper Designation* | *Meaning* |
| --- | --- |
| Annealed | Best forming condition; unless considerable strain hardening is done, finished part will lack rigidity |
| ¼ hard | Good for parts requiring stretch only; can be used in forming curved parts but must be rigidly held |
| ½ hard | Forming more limited but still satisfactory for some curved sections; especially good for straight bends |
| ¾ and full hard | Used for straight bending or rolling; curved sections can be obtained to a limited extent by stretch forming |

Stainless steels may be obtained in sheet, plate, strip, bar, wire tube, and extruded forms. Sheets vary from 0.005 to 0.172 in. thick. Plates vary from 3/16 in. thick on up.

Sheets and some of the other forms are available in eight standard finishes that range from hot-rolled annealed and descaled to a highly reflective, polished and buffed finish.

AUSTENITIC. Although this group of steels is considered very ductile, they have a high rate of work hardening—higher than desirable for many severe drawing or spinning applications. Nickel and, to a lesser extent, carbon influence the rate of strain hardening. As the nickel-to-chromium ratio is increased, formability increases.

The type of work that can be done on the various tempers of austenitic stainless steels is given in Table 3-5.

**TABLE 3-5.**

### Forming Limitations for Austenitic Stainless Steels*

| Classification of Parts and Operations | Type and Temper | Suitable Methods of Fabrication |
|---|---|---|
| Bending and straight flange forming | Type 301–Up to and including full hard | Roll and bench forming |
| | Types 302, 304, and 305–Up to and including full hard | Power brake forming |
| | Types 302, 304, and 305–Up to and including 1/2 hard | Mechanical press forming |
| Forming of parts with contoured flanges | Type 301–Up to and including 1/4 hard | Mechanical press forming |
| | Types 302, 304, and 305–Up to and including 1/4 hard | Hydropress rubber forming |
| | Types 302, 304, and 305–Up to and including 1/2 hard | Mechanical press forming |
| Forming of deep and shallow parts | Types 302, 304, and 305–Up to and including 1/4 hard | Stretch forming |
| Fabrication of tubular parts | Types 302, 304, and 305–Up to and including 1/4 hard | Hammer forming |
| Forming of cup and box-shaped parts | None of the cold-worked stainless used generally | |

* Courtesy Steel Founders' Society of America.

FERRITIC. In contrast to the austenitic steels, the ferritic do not work-harden to any appreciable extent. They have good ductility, making them suitable for drawing, spinning, bending, and other methods of fabrication.

MARTENSITIC. Steels in this group are seldom used for forming, other than forging. They do, however, possess excellent hot-work properties if slowly cooled and annealed to prevent cracking. Large forgings are reheated to 1,900°F and water-quenched for annealing and full corrosion resistance.

### Weldability.

GENERAL. When welding stainless steel, it is compared to plain carbon steel in important physical properties, as follows:

| Property | Austenitic Stainless | Carbon Steel |
|---|---|---|
| Melting temperature (°F) | 2550–2590 | 2750–2775 |
| Thermal conductivity | 9.4 | 27 |
| Coefficient of thermal expansion | $9.6 \times 10^{-6}$ | $8.4 \times 10^{-6}$ |

The expansion and contraction of metals must be considered in all fabricating processes, but especially so in welding. The coefficients of expansion are given as a means of comparing one metal with another. The coefficient $8.4 \times 10^{-6}$ means that a piece of steel will expand 0.0000084 in. in length when its temperature is raised 1°F.

A number is also assigned to the coefficient of thermal conductivity. The number 27 for plain carbon steel means that it absorbs heat at 27 Btu/hr/sq ft/°F/ft. The coefficient of thermal conductivity is used in welding to estimate the amount of heat that will be required, based on the type of metal and thickness, and to determine what area will be heat-affected. Metals with low thermal conductivity, such as the stainless steel listed, tend to localize the stress. The metal that is hot wants to expand but is hemmed in by the cold adjacent metal. When the metal cools and contracts, the cooler metal does not move, with the result that cracks form during solidification. Methods of dealing with these problems are described in the chapters on welding.

Although stainless steels are considered weldable by conventional processes, the best results are obtained when the molten metal is well protected from the atmosphere during welding. The previously described methods of manual arc welding with coated electrodes, submerged-arc welding, tungsten-electrode inert-gas–shielded-arc welding (TIG), and metal inert-gas welding (MIG), all shown in Fig. 3-4, are applicable.

AUSTENITIC. A number of lower-carbon steels in this group have been formulated expressly to minimize the formation of chromium carbides during welding. When the chromium unites with the carbon, referred to as carbide precipitation, the corrosion-resisting qualities of the steel are lost. Types 304, 309S and 310S, each with a maximum carbon content of 0.08 percent, are generally satisfactory for most ordinary service requirements. Where corrosive conditions are likely to be severe, types 304L or 316L are specified. These steels have a maximum carbon content of 0.03 percent.

Stabilized grades of stainless are also used where corrosion is likely to be severe. These are 321, 347, and 348. Titanium or columbium and tantalum are the alloying elements added. They combine with all the carbon present in the steel, leaving chromium free to resist corrosion.

FERRITIC. Type 405 of this class has exceptionally good properties for fusion welding. The addition of aluminum retards hardening and produces a low-chromium alloy specially modified for welding. Type 430 is good for various resistance-welding processes such as spot and seam. It is not recommended for arc or torch welding of heavy sections when there is likely to be grain growth. When filler metal is required, it should match the base material as nearly as possible for most applications.

MARTENSITIC. Owing to the air-hardening qualities of the martensitic steels, it is recommended that, wherever possible, preheating to 350° to 400°F be used to prevent cracking in the weld. Postheating is also used to keep the metal from hardening. When pre- and postheating are impractical, welding can be done with an 18–8 rod to produce a ductile weld.

**Summary.** A brief review of some of the fabricating characteristics of ferrous metals is given in Table 3-6.

## QUESTIONS

1. Identify the following AISI steels: (*a*) 4150; (*b*) 1020; (*c*) 8650; (*d*) 3140; (*e*) B1112.
2. What treatment, often given to low-carbon steels, tends to increase their machinability?
3. What carbon range in steels gives the best machinability?
4. Why are cold-worked metals generally harder to form than hot-worked ones?
5. How can the ductility of a metal be restored?
6. What is meant by the weldability of a metal?
7. What precautions should be exercised in welding medium- and high-carbon steels?

**TABLE 3-6.**

**Properties of Iron and Steel***

| Material | Specification | Chemical Analysis | | Physical Properties | | | |
|---|---|---|---|---|---|---|---|
| | | Carbon | Others | Yield Strength | Tensile Strength | Elongation, percent in 2 in. | Brinell Hardness |
| Cast iron, gray, Grade 20 | ASTM A48-36 | 3.00-4.00 | | ...... | 20,000 | ... | 163 |
| Gray, Grade 30 | ASTM A48-36 | 3.00-4.00 | | ...... | 30,000 | ... | 180 |
| Nickel | | 2.00-3.50 | Ni 0.25-0.50 | ...... | 40,000 | ... | 310 |
| Chrome-nickel | | 2.00-3.50 | Ni 1.00-3.00 Cr 0.50-1.00 | ...... | 53,000 | ... | 510 |
| White | | 2.00-4.00 | Si 0.80-1.50 | ...... | 46,000 | ... | 420 |
| Malleable | ASTM A47-33 | 1.75-2.30 | Si 0.85-1.20 | 35,000 | 53,000 | 18 | 140 |
| Iron, wrought | ASTM A41-30 | 0.08 | Si 0.15 Slag 1.20 | 26,000 | 46,000 | 35 | 105 |
| Ingot | | | Fe 99.45 | 25,000 | 44,000 | 30 | 100 |
| Steel, cast, low carbon | | 0.11 | Mn 0.60 Si 0.40 | 35,000 | 60,000 | 22 | 120 |
| Medium carbon | | 0.25 | Mn 0.68 Si 0.32 | 44,000 | 72,000 | 18 | 140 |
| High carbon | | 0.48 | Mn 0.68 Si 0.41 | 39,000 | 83,000 | 15 | 182 |
| Steel, rolled, carbon | SAE 1010 | 0.05-0.15 | | 28,000 | 56,000 | 35 | 110 |
| Carbon | SAE 1015 | 0.15-0.25 | | 30,000 | 60,000 | 26 | 120 |
| Carbon | SAE 1025 | 0.20-0.30 | | 33,000 | 67,000 | 25 | 135 |
| Carbon | SAE 1035 | 0.30-0.40 | | 52,000 | 87,000 | 24 | 175 |
| Carbon | SAE 1045 | 0.40-0.50 | | 58,000 | 97,000 | 22 | 200 |
| Carbon | SAE 1050 | 0.45-0.55 | | 60,000 | 102,000 | 20 | 207 |
| Carbon | SAE 1095 | 0.90-1.05 | | 100,000 | 150,000 | 15 | 300 |
| Nickel | SAE 2315 | 0.10-0.20 | Ni 3.25-3.75 | 90,000 | 125,000 | 21 | 230 |
| Ni-Cr | SAE 3240 | 0.35-0.45 | Ni 1.50-2.00 Cr 0.90-1.25 | 113,000 | 136,000 | 21 | 280 |
| Moly | SAE 4130 | 0.25-0.35 | Cr 0.50-0.80 Mo 0.15-0.25 | 115,000 | 139,000 | 18 | 280 |
| Cr | SAE 5140 | 0.35-0.45 | Cr 0.80-1.10 | 128,000 | 150,000 | 19 | 300 |
| Cr-Va | SAE 6130 | 0.25-0.35 | Cr 0.80-1.10 Va 0.15-0.18 | 125,000 | 150,000 | 18 | 310 |
| Si-Mn | SAE 9260 | 0.55-0.65 | Ma 0.60-0.90 Si 1.80-2.20 | 180,000 | 200,000 | 12 | 390 |

* From *Introduction to Mechanical Design* by Y. B. Jefferson and W. J. Brooking, Ronald Press, 1951.

8. Name a JIC tool-steel classification for each of the following items: (a) tool used to cut metal on a lathe; (b) blanking die for steel over ⅛ in. thick; (c) moderate-cost, medium-life, *limited-mass* (sections with less than equivalent 2½-in.-diameter) die.

9. What are some characteristics and uses of the JIC W-steel?

10. (a) What is the main difficulty encountered in machining tool steels? (b) What can be done to improve the machinability?

11. If a JIC T-steel were broken, what method could be used to repair it?

12. How do hot-work tool steels compare with high-speed steels in alloy content?

13. What is the significance of the numbers in steel castings classified as 70–40?

14. How does the oxide surface scale on steel castings shorten tool life?

15. What benefit can be obtained from preheating a steel casting before welding it?

16. Describe the structure of gray cast iron.

17. How does the structure of malleable iron differ from that of gray cast iron?

18. (a) What is Meehanite? (b) How does its structure differ from malleable iron?

19. Identify each of the following cast-iron code numbers: (a) 35018; (b) 100–73–03; (c) 40–20.

20. What cutting-tool material is recommended for gray cast iron? Why?

21. What is a preferred welding repair method for malleable irons?

22. What properties of cast iron make it a metal that is more easily cast than steel?

23. (a) Identify the numeral 18–8 in a stainless-steel classification. (b) What other code number stands for the same material?

24. Name three free-machining stainless steels.

25. (a) What problems are encountered in welding stainless steel? (b) How may they be minimized?

26. What is the important consideration in selecting a stainless steel for forming operations?

## PROBLEMS

1. If AISI B1112 steel is used as a base and is assigned a cutting speed of 200 fpm, what will be the cutting speed for: (a) 1020; (b) 1040; (c) 4150; (d) 8650?

2. What will the minimum bend radius be for each of the following: (a) plain low-carbon steel ⅛ in. thick; (b) hot-rolled medium-carbon steel 0.050 in. thick?

3. Find the cutting speed to be used on a steel with a hardness of 300 BHN if a high-speed tool is used and 2 hr of tool life are desired.

4. If B1112 is rated with a cutting speed of 200 fpm, how fast can each of the following be cut: (a) pearlitic gray iron; (b) ductile iron; (c) standard malleable?

## REFERENCES

*Ductile Irons*, The International Nickel Company, Inc., New York, N. Y., 1957.

Editors of *Machine Design*, The, *The Ferrous Metals Book*, Penton Publishing Company, Cleveland, Ohio, 1961.

Gagnebin, A. P., *The Fundamentals of Iron and Steel Castings*, The International Nickel Company, Inc., New York, N. Y., 1957.

Jefferson, T. B., "The Meaning of Weldability," *Welding Engineer*, June, 1958.

Paret, R. E., "How to Select the Right Stainless," *Machine Design*, June, 1959.

*Steel Castings Handbook*, Steel Founders' Society of America, Cleveland, Ohio, 1960.

# 4

# FABRICATING
# CHARACTERISTICS
# OF NONFERROUS
# METALS

NONFERROUS METALS are those in which iron is not present in any appreciable quantity. The total ouput of all the nonferrous metals combined is approximately one tenth that of iron and steel. However, the use of lightweight corrosion-resistant materials, both for consumer goods and for building construction, has advanced rapidly in the past few years. The most commonly used nonferrous metals and their alloys are aluminum, copper, magnesium, and nickel. The newer metals, titanium, zirconium, and beryllium, are used in lesser quantities, but they are becoming increasingly important and are discussed briefly.

## ALUMINUM

### Classification

Aluminum is used extensively in both the wrought and cast forms. The wrought classification uses a four-digit system and the cast three digits, except for alloy 43.

**Wrought Classification.** The four-digit system put into effect in October, 1954, by the Aluminum Association is as follows:

In Table 4-1 the first digit designates the alloy type. The second digit indicates alloy modification. The last two digits indicate the aluminum purity.

For alloys in use before this classification was devised, the last two numbers are the same as the old numbers; for example, 24S becomes 2024.

**TABLE 4-1.**

**Sequence of Aluminum-Alloy Types in the Four-Digit System**

| Type of Aluminum Alloy | Number Group |
|---|---|
| Aluminum — 99.00% purity or greater | 1XXX |
| Copper | 2XXX |
| Manganese | 3XXX |
| Silicon | 4XXX |
| Magnesium | 5XXX |
| Magnesium and silicon | 6XXX |
| Zinc | 7XXX |
| Other element | 8XXX |
| Unused series | 9XXX |

**Temper Designations.** Some aluminum alloys are strengthened by cold working, others by heat treatment. A temper designation of letters and numbers following the four digits and separated by a hyphen is used to indicate the condition or temper of the aluminum, as follows:

| Designation | Meaning |
|---|---|
| O-Annealed | Accomplished by heating to recrystallization temperature and cooling slowly |
| T-Solution Heat Treatment | Usually a hardening and strengthening process consisting of heating high enough to put alloying constituents in solution and then quenching rapidly |

To gain maximum strength the alloys placed in solution must precipitate throughout the solid-solution matrix. In some alloys, this takes place naturally at room temperature when allowed to stand several days; this is called *natural aging*. Other alloys require heat to gain maximum strength; this is termed *artificial aging*. Numbers after the T show various conditions of heat treatment. A partial list is given.

| Designation | Meaning |
|---|---|
| T-2 | Annealed temper of casting materials |
| T-3 | Solution heat treatment followed by strain hardening; different amounts of strain hardening are indicated by a second digit |
| T-4 | Solution heat treatment followed by natural aging |
| T-5 | Artificial aging after an elevated-temperature rapid-cool fabrication process such as casting or extrusion |
| T-6 | Solution heat treatment followed by artificial aging |

| *Designation* | *Meaning* |
|---|---|
| H | Cold-worked temper of the wrought alloys. One digit after the -H series, -H1, indicates cold working; -H2, cold-worked but partially annealed; -H3, strain-hardened and stabilized. A second digit indicates the degree of hardness, as, -H18, full hard; -H19, extra hard; -H14, midway between fully annealed O and full hard -H18. |
| F | As fabricated. |

An example of the use of the aluminum code would be 2024T-4-H2. This is a copper-alloy aluminum, solution heat-treated, aged naturally, followed by cold working and a partial anneal.

**Cast-Alloy Classification.**  The first digit in the cast-alloy designation is the same as in the wrought alloy. It identifies the alloy type, with the exception of alloys 13 and 43. The main alloying elements for cast materials are:

| *Number* | *Meaning* |
|---|---|
| 1 | Copper (Exceptions are A132 and D132 which have silicon as the main alloying element) |
| 2 | Magnesium |
| 3 | Silicon |
| 6 | Zinc |
| 7 | Tin |

## Fabricating Characteristics

**Machinability.**  Pure grades of aluminum are too soft for good machinability. Work or strain hardening helps overcome some of the gumminess. The most easily machined alloy is 2011-T3. This metal is often referred to as the free-cutting aluminum alloy. It is used extensively for a broad range of screw-machine products. Small amounts of lead and bismuth help produce a better finish and easy-to-handle chips.

The softer alloys sometimes build up on the cutting edge of the tool. However, proper cutting oils and a highly polished tool surface will tend to minimize this.

Two important physical properties that should be kept in mind when machining aluminum are modulus of elasticity and thermal expansion. Listed below is a comparison between aluminum and mild steel.

| *Property* | *Aluminum 2017* | *Mild Steel* |
|---|---|---|
| Modulus of elasticity (psi) | $10.5 \times 10^6$ | $30 \times 10^6$ |
| Thermal expansion | $13.1 \times 10^{-6}$ | $8.4 \times 10^{-6}$ |

Owing to the much lower modulus of elasticity (about one third that of steel), there will be much greater deflection under load. Care should be taken, in making heavy cuts and in clamping the work, to avoid distortion.

When dimensional accuracy is necessary, thermal expansion of the metal is an important consideration. Since the thermal expansion of aluminum is almost twice that of steel, care should be exercised in keeping heat down. Overheating can be reduced to a minimum by using sharp, well-designed tools, coolants, and feeds that are not excessive. It may be necessary, on larger parts, to make a thermal allowance in measuring.

Lathe tool angles for cutting aluminum are pretty much the same as those for steel except for those on the top of the tool, which are known as rake angles. The best general machining conditions require a carbide tool with 0- to 10-deg back rake and from 10- to 20-deg side rake. This contrasts with a lathe tool for machining steel of 0- to −7-deg back rake and from +6 to −7-deg side rake, as shown in Fig. 4-1.

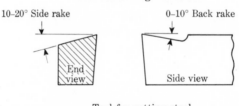

Tool for cutting aluminum

10–20° Side rake    0–10° Back rake

End view    Side view

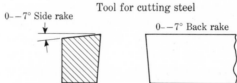

Tool for cutting steel

0–−7° Side rake

0–−7° Back rake

**Fig. 4-1.** The contrast of rake angles used on a single-point tool to cut aluminum and steel.

Surface foot speeds for aluminum range anywhere from 400 to 20,000 fpm.

The chief factors that affect machinability of the various alloys are composition, physical form (cast or wrought), and temper. The copper-containing alloys such as 2011T3, 2017T4, and 2024T4 permit high surface foot speeds, long tool life, and clean cutting.

**Formability.** Most aluminum alloys can be readily formed cold. However, the wide range of alloys and tempers makes for considerable variation in the amount of forming possible.

Generally, depending upon the alloy and temper used, aluminum requires less energy and horsepower than does the forming of heavier metals. Consequently, machine life is increased, power costs are lower, and maintenance is minimized.

As the degree of temper increases, the plastic and elastic ranges decrease, which makes forming more difficult to accomplish and control. Material must be stressed beyond its yield strength in order to form it permanently, or it will tend to return to its original shape. Thus material that is insufficiently stressed will spring back in proportion to the amount of stress applied. Of course, very little springback will be encountered in the soft −O (annealed) plate. The exact amount of springback is difficult to compute. Therefore, tools should be provided with adjustments for overbending, unless preliminary experiments are undertaken to determine the material's springback characteristic.

Each temper (degree of hardness) of an aluminum sheet alloy establishes a specific workability characteristic that must be considered in the planning of operations for bending it. Bending characteristics also vary with the thickness of the sheet.

The non heat-treatable alloys—1100, 3003, 5005, 5050, and 5154—work-harden but have good forming qualities in the softer tempers. In the annealed state they can be bent with O or no radius up to $\frac{1}{4}$ in. thick.

The heat-treatable alloys—2014, 2024, 6061, and 7075—can be formed readily in the annealed temper and are often worked in this state. Work can be done after solution heat treatment and quenching, but it must be done quickly before natural aging starts. Sometimes the solution treatment is performed and the metal is placed in cold storage to delay the aging process until the parts can be formed.

Wrought-aluminum strip sheets and plates are formed by all the conventional forming processes. Special care should be exercised to see that the equipment is kept clean and that, wherever possible, surfaces that the aluminum stock must move over are burr free or have a protective covering to keep them from marring the finished product.

### Weldability.

PHYSICAL PROPERTIES. The physical properties that must be considered in welding aluminum are:

| Property | Aluminum | | Mild Steel |
|---|---|---|---|
| Melting point (°F) | Pure | 1195–1215 | 2750–2775 |
| | Alloy | 995–1190 | |
| Thermal conductivity | Pure | 135 | 27 |
| | Alloy | 109.2 | |
| Thermal expansion | | $13.1 \times 10^{-6}$ | $8.4 \times 10^{-6}$ |

By comparing some of the physical properties of aluminum and steel, it can be seen that the melting point of the aluminum is much lower and the thermal conductivity is much higher. Therefore, more heat will be required to weld a corresponding thickness of aluminum.

The thermal expansion of aluminum is almost twice that of steel. This, coupled with the fact that aluminum weld metal shrinks about 6 percent in volume upon solidification, may put the weld in tension. Some restraint is often necessary to prevent distortion during the welding operation. However, excessive restraint on the component sections during cooling of the weld may result in weld cracking.

The speed at which the weld is made will be one of the determining factors in preventing distortion. A slow rate will cause greater area heating with more expansion and subsequent contraction. For this reason, arc- and resistance-welding methods that make use of highly concentrated heat are the most used.

PREHEATING. Preheating is necessary when welding heavy sections; otherwise the mass of the parent metal will conduct the heat away so fast that the welding arc will not be able to supply heat fast enough for adequate fusion. Preheating helps provide satisfactory fusion, reduces distortion or cracking in the weld, and increases welding speed.

WELDABLE ALLOYS. Either the work-hardenable alloys such as 1100, 3003, 5052, and 5083 or the heat-treatable alloys such as 6061, 6062, and 6063 are weldable. The 2000 and 7000 series are also heat-treatable but are not normally recommended for welding.

Whenever aluminum alloys are heated above 900°F, they lose their heat-treated characteristics or tempers and revert to the annealed condition. Some annealing of the parent metal takes place when a weld is made. With the heat-treatable alloys there is also some loss of ductility in the joint. The desired temper can be restored in the fabricated part by heat treatment after welding.

OXIDE FILM. Aluminum and its alloys rapidly develop an oxide film when exposed to the air. This oxide has a melting point that is in excess of 3600°F, or about 2400°F above the melting point of pure aluminum. Therefore, the aluminum melts before the oxide coating does. When this happens there can be no fusion between the filler metal and the base metal. It is then necessary to remove the oxide film by suitable chemical cleaner, flux, mechanical abrasion, or action of the welding arc. Particles of oxide trapped in the weld will impair its ductility. Thorough brushing with a stainless-steel brush immediately before welding is a recommended procedure. Any grease or oil films remaining in the weld area will cause unsound welds.

GAS ABSORPTION. Molten aluminum readily absorbs available hydrogen from the air. When the weld pool freezes, most of the hydrogen is released because it is practically insoluble in solid aluminum. The released hydrogen may cause porosity in the weld which, in turn, may impair its strength and ductility. Porosity and hydrogen embrittlement can be reduced by having clean surfaces and moisture-free filler rods, and by covering the weld area with an inert gas such as argon. Both TIG and MIG welding are common choices in welding aluminum. These methods provide a protective shield from the atmosphere, and there is no cleaning problem when finished.

If flux is used, as in oxyacetylene welding, it must be removed after welding or it will cause corrosion. Boiling water and a brush can be used. For inaccessible areas 30 min. in cold 10 percent sulfuric acid followed by a cold rinse is a recommended procedure.

**Castability.** The physical properties of aluminum that make it one of the most versatile of all foundry metals are low melting point, low specific gravity, and low density.

Low MELTING POINT. The low melting point makes for minimum of sand burnout; that is, the sand can be used over and over again, only enough being added to take care of mechanical losses. Where metal or permanent molds are used, the low melting temperature of the aluminum promotes long life.

Low SPECIFIC GRAVITY. The light weight of aluminum means that even moderate-sized castings can be efficiently handled manually. Only the largest castings require mechanically transported ladles or crucibles.

Low DENSITY. Low density and low melting point combine to practically eliminate most problems of sand washes that occur when heavier metals are poured. Also, the lower pressures permit more lightly rammed molds with lighter molding equipment.

Special consideration must be given to casting shrinkage, hot shortness, and gas absorption when aluminum castings are made.

CASTING SHRINKAGE. Aluminum always undergoes a large contraction upon solidification, which may range from 3.5 to 8.5 percent by volume. Therefore, it is desirable to have, wherever possible, uniform sections throughout the casting. If section changes are necessary, they should be gradual, or shrinkage cracks will occur. Minimum section thickness in sand castings is generally 3/16 in. and generous fillets should be used.

HOT SHORTNESS. Hot shortness refers to the low strength of aluminum immediately after solidification. The casting design should be made in such a manner as to minimize the occurrence of shrinkage stresses while the metal has comparatively little strength.

GAS ABSORPTION. Molten aluminum readily absorbs hydrogen and oxygen. Since most of the pinholes in aluminum castings are caused by hydrogen, precautions should be taken to reduce it to a minimum. This can be done by having the metal no hotter than necessary for pouring, and by allowing no excessive moisture in the molding sand.

Fortunately, aluminum, while in the molten state, surrounds itself with an envelope of oxide. As long as this envelope remains unbroken, the absorption of gas by the melt is quite low.

## COPPER AND COPPER-BASE ALLOYS

### Classification

**Coppers.** Unlike other common metals, the various types of copper are better known by name than by code number.

Commercially pure copper is available in several grades, all of which have essentially the same mechanical properties: *Electrolytic tough-pitch copper* is susceptible to embrittlement when heated in a reducing atmosphere, but it has high electrical conductivity. *Deoxidized copper* has lower electrical conductivity but improved cold-working characteristics, and it is not subject to embrittlement. It has better welding and brazing characteristics than do other grades of copper. *Oxygen-free copper* has the same electrical conductivity as the tough-pitch copper and is not prone to embrittlement when heated in a reducing atmosphere.

Modified coppers include *tellurium copper,* which contains 0.5 percent tellurium for free-cutting characteristics (selenium or lead is also used for this purpose) and *tellurium-nickel copper,* an age-hardenable alloy that provides high strength, high conductivity, and excellent machinability.

### Copper-Base Alloys.

BRASSES. Brasses are principally alloys of copper and zinc. They are often referred to by the percentage of each, for example 70-30, meaning 70 percent copper and 30 percent zinc. Small amounts of other elements such as lead, tin, or aluminum are added to obtain the desired color, strength, ductility, machinability, corrosion resistance, or a combination of these properties. The main classifications of brasses are:

| *Alloy* | *Meaning* |
|---|---|
| Alpha brasses | Contain less than 36% zinc and are single-phase alloys |
| Alpha-beta brasses | Contain more than 36% zinc and have a two-phase structure |
| Leaded brasses | Contain up to 88.5% copper and up to 3.25% lead |

| *Alloy* | *Meaning* |
|---|---|
| Tin brasses | Known as admiralty and naval brass when the percentage of tin is low, 0.75 to 1.0% |
| Nickel silvers | Brasses containing high percentages of nickel. (The designation 65–18 indicates approximately 65% copper, 18% nickel and the remainder zinc. Nickel is added primarily for its influence on color. When the percentage is high, a silvery-white color is obtained. Nickel also improves mechanical and physical properties.) |

BRONZE. Bronzes are usually thought of as copper-tin alloys. However, there are some types of bronze that contain little or no tin.

| *Alloy* | *Meaning* |
|---|---|
| Phosphor bronze | Most copper-tin alloys are deoxidized with phosphorus; the small amount left in the metal may range from a trace to over 0.35 percent phosphorus, increasing strength, hardness, toughness, and corrosion resistance |
| Aluminum bronze | Contains up to 13.5 percent aluminum and small amounts of manganese and nickel; has good antifrictional properties |
| Silicon bronze | Contains up to 4 percent silicon; has strength similar to mild steel, and excellent corrosion resistance to brine and other nonoxidizing inorganic acids |
| Manganese bronze | Contains up to 3.5 percent manganese that imparts high strength |
| Beryllium bronze | Contains from 2 to 2.75 percent beryllium which makes it respond to precipitation hardening. |

## Fabricating Characteristics

**Machinability.** Because of the wide variety of copper-base alloys, some general information will be given first, followed by machinability ratings according to groups.

GENERAL SPEEDS AND FEEDS. For most copper alloys, it is generally good practice to use the highest practical cutting speed with a relatively light feed and moderate depth of cut. An exception is the machining of sand castings with high-speed tools, in which case low speeds and relatively coarse feeds are used to increase tool life. After the scale has been removed, the higher speeds and lighter feeds can be resumed. Tool life can be considerably increased if the castings are sand-blasted, pickled in acid, or tumbled, to remove the extremely hard abrasive surface scale.

MACHINABILITY RATINGS. Steel and steel alloys have machinability ratings based on B1112 as 100 percent. Copper and copper-base alloys use either free-cutting brass, consisting of 61.50 percent copper,

35.25 percent zinc, and 3.25 percent lead, as the base material, or B1112. The base must be designated.

To classify the relative machinability of copper-base alloys, they can be placed in three groups based on the amount of tool life and amount of power required. The line of demarcation from one group to the other is not sharp but will act as a guide.

*Group I.* The materials in this group are the alpha-beta or two-phase brasses. The beta phase is harder and more brittle, which makes the alloy less ductile, thus permitting heavier feed rates in turning. Lead is added to both single- and double-phase brasses. It is effective in reducing the shear strength of the metal and assists in chip breakage. Alloys and ratings in this group are:

Free-cutting brass—100% (base)
Selenium copper—80%
Leaded naval brass—80%
Leaded commercial bronze—90%

*Group II.* The materials in this group are considered readily machinable, with a rating from 30 to 70 percent. The principal alloys in this group are:

Yellow brass—40%
Manganese bronze—30%
Admiralty brass—50%
Leaded phosphor bronze—50%
Leaded nickel silver—50%
Tin bronze—40%

*Group III.* These materials have a machinability rating up to 30 percent. This group contains the unleaded coppers, nickel silvers, some phosphor bronzes, and beryllium bronze. These alloys usually produce tough stringy chips.

As with aluminum, the main angles to consider for cutting tools are the ones on top of the tool, or the rake angles. Moderate rake is suggested for group I to reduce the tendency of the tool to grab or "hog-in." More pronounced rakes are used on groups II and III to provide free chip flow. The side rake angles in group III exceed those for steel (Fig. 4-2).

Best results are obtained in drilling group I and II materials with straight-fluted drills (Fig. 4-3). These drills have natural zero-degree rake angle and are particularly good for automatic machine work. Group III materials, that produce tough stringy chips, need high-spiral drills as shown in Fig. 4-3. The greater number of twists per inch provides an increased rake angle and assists in ejecting the chips, particularly in deep drilling.

## CARBIDE-TIPPED LATHE TURNING TOOLS

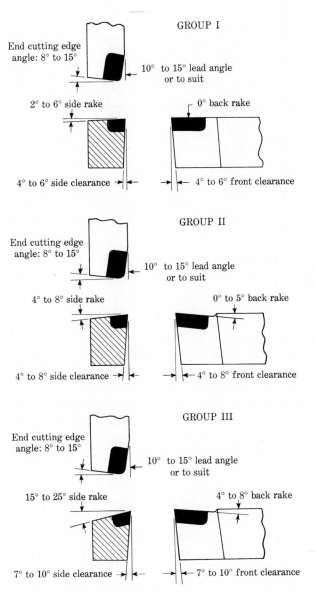

GROUP I

End cutting edge
angle: 8° to 15°

10° to 15° lead angle
or to suit

2° to 6° side rake

0° back rake

4° to 6° side clearance

4° to 6° front clearance

GROUP II

End cutting edge
angle: 8° to 15°

10° to 15° lead angle
or to suit

4° to 8° side rake

0° to 5° back rake

4° to 8° side clearance

4° to 8° front clearance

GROUP III

End cutting edge
angle: 8° to 15°

10° to 15° lead angle
or to suit

15° to 25° side rake

4° to 8° back rake

7° to 10° side clearance

7° to 10° front clearance

**Fig. 4-2.** Suggested angles used on turning tools for the various copper-base alloys.

**Fig. 4-3.** Straight-fluted and slow-spiral drills are used for copper-base alloys of Groups I and II. High-spiral drills are used for Group III alloys. (*a*) Straight-fluted drill, (*b*) standard twist drill, (*c*) slow-spiral or "brass" drill, (*d*) high-spiral drill.

(*a*)    (*b*)    (*c*)    (*d*)

**Formability.** The forming qualities of copper-base alloys are dependent on three main factors; alloy composition, grain size, and temper.

ALLOY COMPOSITION. The most-used alloys for forming are the 70–30 cartridge brasses. However, all brasses from 95–5 to 63–37 are used for pressworking operations. Trouble is encountered when less than 63 percent copper is used, because the beta phase is brittle and may produce fractures or waviness—a surface defect.

Pure coppers such as the electrolytic tough-pitch, oxygen-free, and deoxidized coppers are very ductile, and they work-harden less rapidly than do bronzes or brasses. The deoxidized and oxygen-free coppers can withstand more severe bending and forming than the tough-pitch coppers.

GRAIN SIZE. The grain size of copper alloys is expressed as the average grain diameter in millimeters. Grain structure is related to tensile strength, elongation, hardness, and other properties.

Fine grain or ultrafine grain is material below 0.010-mm grain size. Such material is very smooth after bending, forming, or drawing and can economically be buffed to a high luster. Other grain-size recommendations for cold-working annealed copper alloys are given in Table 4-2.

**TABLE 4-2.**

### Grain Size for Cold-Working Annealed Copper Alloys*

| Nominal Grain Size (mm) | Typical Uses |
|---|---|
| 0.015 | Slight forming operations |
| 0.025 | Shallow drawing |
| 0.035 | For best average surface combined with drawing |
| 0.050 | Deep-drawing operations |
| 0.070 | Heavy drawing on thick gauges |

\* Courtesy American Machinist/Metalworking Manufacturing.

In general, ductility increases with increasing grain size. For very severe draws, particularly of heavy-gauge strip, grain sizes as large as 0.120 mm are not uncommon.

TEMPER. Copper and copper-base alloys may be obtained in the following tempers:

| Temper Designation | Meaning |
|---|---|
| ¼ hard | Extra hard |
| ½ hard | Spring |
| ¾ hard | Extra spring |
| Hard | |

The most common tempers for rods are half hard and hard.

The minimum bend radius varies with alloy and tempers. Annealed copper-base alloys can be bent to a radius equal to the metal thickness, and some of them to one half the metal thickness.

**Weldability.** All four of the commonly employed methods—gas, metal arc, carbon arc, and gas-shielded arc—are in general use for welding copper. It is also joined by brazing and a newer method, discussed later, ultrasonic welding. The gas method, because of the variety of atmospheres obtainable, finds wide use. Its disadvantages are cost and, in some cases, warpage with attendant high-conduction losses into the metal adjacent to the weld.

PHYSICAL PROPERTIES. Physical properties to be considered in welding copper and copper-base alloys are:

| Property | Deoxodized Copper | 70–30 Brass | Mild Steel |
|---|---|---|---|
| Melting temperature (°F) | 1949–1981 | 1680–1750 | 2750–2775 |
| Coefficient of expansion | $9.8 \times 10^{-6}$ | $11.1 \times 10^{-6}$ | $8.4 \times 10^{-6}$ |
| Thermal conductivity | 226 | 70 | 27 |

The physical properties of copper, brass, and steel serve as a comparison and indication of what to expect in the way of heat requirements and possible distortion. Although the melting point of pure copper is lower than that of steel, the thermal conductivity is more than eight times as high. Therefore, much more heat will be needed, and preheating should be used for both gas- and arc-welding methods. Owing to the large amount of heat that is needed for oxyacetylene welding, stresses arising from contraction of the weld in cooling may cause cracking in the hot-short (500°F) range if procedural details are not carefully controlled. The gas-shielded arc is being increasingly used, particularly under humid conditions which cause porosity when using the carbon-arc process. Shielded-arc methods are used on copper up to 3/16 in. thick without preheating.

The most suitable of the coppers to use for welding is the deoxidized type. The fact that the coppers do not contain oxygen, plus the fact that there is some residual deoxidizer in the metal, reduces embrittlement to a minimum.

Resistance welds can be made on all brasses containing 15 or 20 percent zinc or more. The thermal conductivity is sufficiently low in these metals to make spot or seam welding of the lighter gauges practical.

Both soldering and low-temperature brazing are widely employed in joining coppers and brasses.

**Castability.** Copper castings are made almost entirely in sand molds. The technique of casting high-conductivity copper is especially difficult, since considerable skill is required in handling the reducing agents. The molten metal does not flow well, making it difficult to fill molds that are intricate. Copper has the property of being hot short and will break as it solidifies if the design does not permit shrinkage.

The copper-base alloys are more easily cast and handled in the foundry.

## MAGNESIUM

### Classification

Magnesium is a strong, lightweight metal that is not used in its pure state for stressed applications but is alloyed with other metals such as aluminum, zinc, zirconium, manganese, thorium, and rare-earth metals to obtain the strength needed for structural uses. Its light weight is one of its best-known characteristics. Aluminum weighs

1½ times more than manganese, iron and steel 4 times more, and copper and nickel alloys 5 times more.

The ASTM classification designates the principal alloying elements as follows:

| Symbol | Meaning |
|--------|---------|
| A | Aluminum |
| Z | Zinc |
| K | Zirconium |
| M | Manganese |
| H | Thorium |
| E | Rare-earth metals |

The numbers following the alloy types represent approximate percentages of each alloy, respectively. For example, the alloy designation AZ61A is an aluminum-zinc alloy with from 5.8 to 7.2 percent aluminum and 0.4 to 1.5 percent zinc. The letters A, B, or C may follow the number, indicating variations in composition or treatment.

Temper designations similar to those used in aluminum sheet and plate are as follows:

| Temper Designation | Meaning |
|--------------------|---------|
| -F | As fabricated |
| -O | Fully annealed |
| -H1 | Strain-hardened |
| -H2 | Strain-hardened and partially annealed |
| -H24 | The second number represents the degree of hardening in eighths (-H24 is 4/8ths or ½ hard) |
| -T4 | Solution heat-treated |
| -T5 or -T51 | Precipitation heat-treated |
| -T6 or -T61 | Solution heat-treated and artificially aged. |

The tempers listed are for *specification-grade* plates and sheets only. This means that the grade conforms to a majority of standards of the government and nationally recognized societies.

*Standard grade* is identical in composition but is processed in such a manner that it has somewhat lower yield strength, broader tolerances in length, and is supplied in a mill finish. AZ31B is the only material offered in this grade at the present time. The following tempers are offered in this standard-grade sheet and plate.

| Temper Designation | Meaning |
|--------------------|---------|
| -H10 and -H11 | Slightly strain-hardened with good ductility and toughness |
| -H23 | Strain-hardened then partially annealed |

Rolled magnesium alloys are supplied with either a chemical-treatment (chrome pickle) finish, an oil finish, or an acetic nitrate pickle. Plates over ½ in. thick are furnished with a mill finish and oiled, unless otherwise specified. The oil coating is superior to that given by the chrome pickle for normal shipment and storage.

### Fabricating Characteristics

**Machinability.**   Magnesium and its alloys permit machining at extremely high speeds—usually at the maximum obtainable on modern machine tools. Using free-cutting brass as a base, it has a machinability rating of 500. Heavier depths of cut and higher rates of feed are also possible. Excellent surface finish is usually obtained because there is no tendency for the metal to tear or drag. Power requirements for magnesium alloys are about one sixth those for mild steel.

Either high-speed or carbide tools are used, but carbides usually result in better operating economy, especially at the high speeds.

Honing and lapping the tool surfaces ensures free cutting action and reduces the tendency of any particles to adhere to the tool tip.

Tools used for cutting steel or brass can be used for magnesium, but, to take full advantage of the machining characteristics of the material, the tools may be modified as shown in Fig. 4-4. Relief angles are large, with a positive 10-deg. back rake. Milling cutters must provide ample room for the chips.

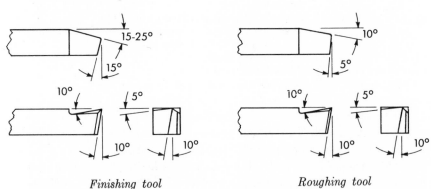

*Finishing tool*                    *Roughing tool*

**Fig. 4-4.**   Typical turning tools for magnesium (courtesy The Dow Chemical Co.).

Much has been said about the fire hazards in machining magnesium, but this becomes a problem only when making very fine cuts or when using dull tools.

Distortion of the machined part may be caused from (1) dull tools, (2) improper tool design, (3) taking cuts that are too fine, (4) dry-cutting of thin small sections, and (5) heavy cutting pressure on thin small parts.

**Formability.** The methods and equipment used for forming magnesium are the same types commonly employed on other metals, the principal difference being that magnesium is best formed at elevated temperatures, except in the case of mild deformations around generous radii. Working is usually done at temperatures between 300 and 700°F. Annealing can be avoided by carefully controlling both time and temperature if a strain-hardened condition is desired in the finished product. Magnesium has a hexagonal crystalline structure which offers fewer planes of slip than the cubic structure found in many other common metals.

For production work it is necessary to heat the forming dies with either gas or electric heaters. Although this is rather expensive and troublesome, the advantages of being able to make parts in one draw that otherwise would require an intermediate anneal may offset it. Hardened dies are not necessary for most types of forming. Generally, hot-formed parts can be made to closer tolerances, as there is less springback.

Some cold drawing can be done. For example, AZ31B-O can stand about a 25 percent reduction. The drawability, or percent reduction, is based on the formula

$$\text{Percent reduction} = \frac{D - d}{D} \times 100$$

where $D$ = blank diameter before drawing
where $d$ = diameter of punch

When hot drawing is used, the amount of reduction may run as high as 68 percent for AZ31B-O.

Bending radii at room temperature for 90-deg. bends is a minimum of 8t but may go as low as 2t when heated to 500°F.

Magnesium can be forged in the temperature range from 550° to 750°F. The dies used to form aluminum can be used. Forging is best done on fairly heavy sections where the radii are large.

**Weldability.** Magnesium can be joined by most of the fusion-welding processes. Since the development of TIG and MIG welding, they have become the most popular joining methods. Electric-resistance welding (spot, seam, and flash) is also used.

The shielded-arc method of welding magnesium is the most common. The blanket of helium or argon gas protects the molten metal from being oxidized. Flux or chemical cleaning is not necessary.

All magnesium alloys can be arc-welded. However, wrought alloy AZ31 and cast alloys AZ63–AZ91 require considerable skill. Filler rods of the same material as the base metal are used, except with AZ31 where an AZ61 rod is used to reduce danger of cracking.

Welds in some magnesium alloys, particularly the magnesium-aluminum-zinc series, are subject to stress corrosion cracking, and thermal treatment must be used to remove the residual stress. This is done by placing the welded part in a jig or clamping plate and heating from 300° to 500°F, according to the alloy. Cooling in air is satisfactory.

Resistance welding is quite satisfactory in all the alloys. Spot welds have excellent static strengths, but fatigue strengths are lower than either riveted or adhesive bonded joints. Spot-welded magnesium assemblies are used mostly for low-stressed applications and occasionally for high-stressed applications not subject to vibration. Joints can be made between magnesium and some dissimilar metals. Such joints, however, are usually quite brittle because of the formation of inter-metallic compounds. Although the structural significance is small, these joints can serve for electrical connections.

Spot welds made in sheet less than 0.040 in. thick usually fail by tearing a button from the sheet. In thicker sheets, weld failures approach more perfect shearing through the weld nugget.

Gas welding, once widely used, is now generally limited to emergency repair because of corrosion difficulties caused by the flux necessary for this type of welding.

Thermal properties compared to aluminum are:

|  | *AZ31* | *Pure Aluminum* |
|---|---|---|
| Melting point (°F) | 1050–1170 | 1195–1215 |
| Thermal conductivity | 44 | 135 |
| Coefficient of thermal expansion | $14 \times 10^{-6}$ | $13.1 \times 10^{-6}$ |

As can be seen, considerably less heat is required for magnesium than for aluminum. The coefficient of expansion is somewhat higher, and adequate jigs and fixtures should be provided.

**Castability.** Magnesium can be sand-cast, die-cast, or cast in permanent molds. The three alloys used for sand casting are magnesium-aluminum-zinc, magnesium-rare earth, and magnesium-thorium.

Magnesium-aluminum-zinc alloys combine good strength and good casting characteristics with stable properties up to 200°F.

For applications requiring high strength at temperatures roughly between 350° and 500°F, casting alloys containing rare earths are employed.

Where properties better than those of the rare-earth-containing alloys are required, thorium compositions are used. Standard alloys

HK31A and HZ32A have been formulated to withstand temperatures in the range of 350° to 700°F.

Generous fillets and radii are important to avoid stress concentrations. Where relatively thin walls join thick walls, a gradually tapered blending should be done. Other principles of good casting design, as discussed in Chap. 5, should be observed.

## NICKEL AND NICKEL ALLOYS

The nickel-base alloys were developed to obtain a nonferrous alloy of increased strength and corrosion resistance. Other properties obtained were ductility and higher hardness. These alloys are classified by name and letter rather than by numbers.

### Classification

| *Wrought Alloys* | *Meaning* |
|---|---|
| A Nickel | Commercially pure nickel; high temperature and corrosion resistance |
| Low-Carbon Nickel | Contains less than 0.02 percent carbon; high-temperature service (above 600°F) |
| Duranickel* | High-strength, spark-erosion-resisting manganese alloy |
| Monel | Nickel-copper alloy for general applications requiring corrosion resistance, toughness, and high strength at high temperatures; at 750°F still has 75 percent of its room-temperature strength |
| "R" Monel | Free-machining nickel-copper alloy |
| "K" Monel | Age-hardenable nickel-copper alloy that can be heat-treated after finishing |

| *Cast Alloys* | *Meaning* |
|---|---|
| Nickel | Cast equivalent of commercially pure wrought |
| A Nickel | 95.6 percent pure, with manganese and silicon added as the principal alloying elements |
| Inconel | Nickel-chromium, heat- and corrosion-resisting alloy, able to withstand temperatures up to 2200°F; has high hot strength, is able to withstand progressive oxidation and fatigue, and is nonmagnetic. |
| "S" Inconel | Nickel-chromium, age-hardenable alloy; *antigalling* or nonsmearing |
| Monel | Similar to wrought form |
| "S" Monel | Age-hardenable nickel-copper cast alloy for valve trim, impellers, pump liners, and similar applications; has 4 percent silicon added to facilitate casting |

* The names Duranickel, Monel, and Inconel are registered trademarks and/or names of The International Nickel Co., Inc.

### Fabricating Characteristics

**Machinability.** The (nickel-copper) Monel alloys have machinability ratings of 25 to 45 percent of B1112, the best being "R" Monel and the poorest "S" Monel, a cast alloy.

The (nickel-chromium) Inconel alloys are still more difficult to machine and have ratings between 30 and 15 percent. Feeds are held below 0.015 in. per revolution and the depth of cut below 0.093 in. These materials are very abrasive.

Like the austenitic stainless steels, these materials also work-harden during machining. Therefore, it is important that the tools be kept sharp and that heavy feeds not be used. The tool must not be allowed to dwell in the cut without positive feed.

Recommended tool angles for machining the high-nickel materials are shown in Fig. 4-5. The tool shown is high-speed steel, but the angles are the same, except that the relief angles may be reduced to 4 deg on the toughest materials in order to give the cutting edge more support.

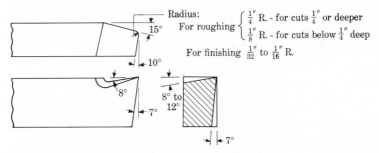

**Fig. 4-5.** A general-purpose, high-speed-steel lathe tool used for cutting high-nickel-alloy materials.

With suitable coolants, cutting speeds can be increased 25 percent. Chemically active soluble oils are used in the ratio of 15 parts of water to 1 of soluble oil. These coolants dissipate heat rapidly. Better finishes can be obtained by using sulfurized oils, but some discoloration may result; this can be removed, however, with a 10 percent solution of sodium cyanide.

**Formability.** Nickel, Monel, and Inconel sheet and strip, in the annealed condition, are practically as ductile as copper, brass, aluminum, and nickel silver. Parts are often deep-drawn to approximate dimensions, annealed, and finished by spinning over a metal form on a lathe.

As with stainless steels, the rate of work hardening is very important because the more the material is deformed, the harder and stronger it becomes.

For pressworking, there are two types of sheets—cold-rolled annealed and cold-rolled annealed deep-drawing quality.

For counter tops, etc., there is a special grade known as "35" Monel. This is a tempered sheet approximately ¼ to ½ hard with a satin finish on one side. The "35" Monel is good for simple bends and lock seams but not for deep drawing.

When nickel, Monel, and Inconel become hardened by either cold or hot working, they can be temper-annealed by heating to moderate temperatures of 1000° to 1300°F. This will relieve internal stresses and produce a partial anneal. If only stress relief is desired, with no annealing effect, the temperature need only be from 525° to 900°F. When further forming or severe drawing is necessary on a partially completed part, full annealing is also necessary. The more the metal has been cold-worked, the lower the annealing temperature. At 1200°F a metal that has had a 40 percent reduction will soften more rapidly than one that has had only 20 percent reduction. In fact, a 20 percent reduction is considered minimum before annealing. Full ductility cannot be restored to parts having less cold working than this.

Nickel, Monel, and Inconel can be either quenched or cooled slowly, since the effect is the same.

"K" Monel and Duranickel are both age- or precipitation-hardening metals and must be quenched rapidly.

**Weldability.** The same processes used to weld steel can be used on nickel and nickel alloys. It is important that the surfaces to be welded are clean, as high-nickel alloys are subject to embrittlement when contaminated at elevated temperatures with lead, sulfur, phosphorus, and some other low-melting-point alloys.

The physical properties to consider are:

|  | A Nickel | Monel | Inconel |
|---|---|---|---|
| Melting temperature (°F) | 2615–2635 | 2370–2460 | 2500–2550 |
| Thermal conductivity | 36 | 15 | 8.7 |
| Coefficient of thermal expansion | $7.4 \times 10^{-6}$ | $7.8 \times 10^{-6}$ | $8.92 \times 10^{-6}$ |

Thermal conductivity is relatively low, except in the case of A nickel, which means that distortion will be concentrated close to the weld. Therefore, it is necessary that jigging and clamping will hold the metal firmly in place. Jigs for welding should provide a grooved backup bar underneath the weld to facilitate cooling the molten metal. The groove will also serve as a mold for the weld metal, allowing uniform penetration.

Metals and alloys that can be joined to nickel, Monel, and Inconel by the metallic-arc process are mild steel, cupronickel and Hastelloy B (a chrome-molybdenum-iron-cobalt alloy used in welding a hard surface on metal).

**Castability.**   The high melting point of the nickel alloys makes pouring similar to that of steel. Although common casting methods are used, care must be taken to control the sulfur, carbon, and silicon. Magnesium is used as a deoxidizer.

## TITANIUM

In its early development, titanium was heralded as the space-age metal. It possessed a high strength-to-weight ratio and good corrosion resistance even in salt water. Its properties lie between aluminum and steel in strength, density, elasticity, and serviceability at elevated temperatures. It is 60 percent heavier than aluminum but only 56 percent as heavy as stainless steel. Titanium also has excellent ductility. Despite all these desirable properties, some of the early enthusiasm for the metal subsided when the difficulties of production and fabrication were encountered.

In the molten state, titanium has an extreme affinity for oxygen and nitrogen, which act to harden and embrittle the metal. Melting must be done in a vacuum or an inert atmosphere. No method has been found to remove any contamination that may be acquired during processing. The special equipment needed and the relatively slow production rate have kept the price of titanium very high, being about 30 to 40 times that of stainless steel. However, extensive research and development are being continued, the goal being titanium alloys that are better and less costly than those in use at the present time.

### Classification

Commercially pure titanium has a close-packed hexagonal (alpha) structure. Titanium alloys may have either close-packed hexagonal structures, body-centered cubic (beta) structures, or a combination of alpha-beta structures. Four groups are made from the foregoing, as follows:

**Commercially Pure Titanium.**   This group consists of 99 percent pure titanium and various percentages of carbon, oxygen, nitrogen, and iron. Designations, such as A-55, Ti-100A, R70, and others are used. The number approximates the tensile strength of the material in thousands of pounds per square inch. Standardization of designations has not progressed far as yet, however, it has been proposed that the letter A for alpha, B for beta, and C for combinations be used.

**All-Alpha Weldable Alloys.** At the present time there is only one commercial alloy, A-110, in this group. It can be obtained in sheet, bar, and wire forms and may be welded with close to 100 percent joint efficiency.

**Alph-Beta, Weldable Alloys.** This group comprises the majority of the titanium alloys. They can be heat-treated and are available in bars, billets, and sheets. The designation may be by composition (for example, Ti-6Al-4V has 6 percent aluminum and 4 percent vanadium) or it may be simply C-120, indicating a combination-phase titanium with 120-130,000 psi tensile strength.

**Alph-Beta, Nonweldable Alloys.** This group contains manganese, molybdenum, aluminum, and chromium as the main alloying elements. Some examples of code designations in this group are MST-4Al-4Mn, MST-3Al-5Cr, and C-110.

### Fabricating Characteristics

**Machinability.** Some of the problems associated with machining titanium are:

1. The chip curls away from the tool at a sharp angle, producing high stress concentration and rapid rise in temperature. The temperature between the chip and tool may be as high as 2000°F.

2. At elevated temperatures titanium has the tendency to dissolve everything in contact with it.

3. Small particles of titanium weld themselves to the cutting tip, causing it to act dull, thus increasing cutting forces and heat.

4. Forgings may have scale on the outside containing titanium carbides, nitrates, and oxides, which are extremely abrasive to the cutting tools. The scale can be removed with a solution of 10 percent hydrofluoric acid, 5 percent nitric acid, and 85 percent water. The soaking time required is 20 to 30 min.

5. When machining the outside diameter of a bar on a lathe, it is found that the slip planes of alpha titanium vary every 90 deg of work rotation. This results in changes in chip thickness and tends to develop pulsating pressures leading to chatter.

Machinability ratings vary with structure. The unalloyed alpha type has a rating of 38 percent of B1112, the alloyed alpha type drops to 29 percent, and combination alpha-beta is from 26 to 20 percent.

Recommendations are for adequate coolant, slow speeds, sharp tools, and proper cutting-tool angles. The suggested tool angles for a high-speed-steel turning tool are shown in Fig. 4-6. High-speed materials containing cobalt and vanadium are probably the best and most economical tools to use on titanium.

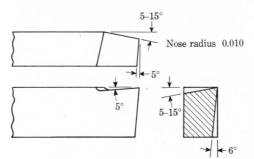

**Fig. 4-6.** High-speed tool geometry used for turning titanium.

Milling titanium is somewhat more difficult than turning because the cutting action is intermittent instead of continuous, as it is on the lathe. The chip becomes welded to the cutter, and, as it enters the work again, it is knocked off along with part of the cutting edge. *Climb milling,* where the cutter rotates in the same direction as the advancing work, is used to minimize welding of the chip. Carbides or cast-alloy materials are preferred for the cutting tool.

In drilling, wear is as likely to take place on the outside margin as on the tip. This is due to the galling or smearing action of the metal. Therefore, the margin should be checked each time the drill is sharpened. The length of the drill should be kept at a minimum.

**Formability.** Cold forming of the close-packed hexagonal structures contained in titanium and magnesium is undesirable. Titanium is formed at 400° to 700°F, while the alloys require 800° to 1000°F. Forging is done at temperatures ranging from 1500° and 1850°F, depending on the section thickness and the alloy used.

Simple bending may be done cold, but the springback is about twice that of stainless steel.

**Weldability.** Resistance welds, because of the close proximity of the surfaces to be welded, can be made without resorting to inert atmosphere.

In fusion welding, air must be prevented from coming in contact with the molten metal. TIG welding is used with either argon or helium. Heavy welding requires a protection of inert gas on the bottom side of the weld also.

The low surface tension of molten titanium makes it desirable to weld it in the horizontal position if at all possible. Because of this low surface tension, more skill is required by the operator than for most other metals.

The physical properties to consider are:

|  | Unalloyed | Ti-6Al-4V |
|---|---|---|
| Melting range (°F) | 3135 | 2822–3002 |
| Thermal conductivity | 9.8 | 4.3 |
| Coefficient of thermal expansion | $5.8 \times 10^{-6}$ | $5.8 \times 10^{-6}$ |

The low thermal conductivity indicates that the heat will be concentrated in the immediate area of the weld. Distortion is not so much of a factor as in most other metals, since the coefficient of expansion is relatively low.

## ZIRCONIUM

Until recently, zirconium was considered one of the rare metals; however, its ores are widely distributed and its occurrence in the earth's crust compares favorably with that of many of the better-known metals. Practically all of the zirconium used in American industry comes from Florida, Australia, and Brazil. It is used principally where extremely high corrosion resistance is necessary. Applications are in chemistry, medicine, electronics, and atomic energy.

### Classification

There are several types of zirconium which are designated by name, such as commercial grade, containing 2 percent hafnium; reactor grade, with 0.001 percent hafnium; and Zircoloy, with 0.02 hafnium, 1.46 tin, 0.12 iron, 0.05 nickel and 0.25 other elements.

### Fabricating Characteristics

The atomic structure of zirconium is much like that of titanium. It is a close-packed hexagonal alpha structure at room temperature, changing to a body-centered beta structure above 1585°F. The hardness varies from 175 to 275 Brinell, which is above aluminum alloys but generally below that of low-alloy steels. The hardness depends greatly on the oxygen and nitrogen in the metal.

Zirconium has no directional properties. Its transverse ductility is as good as the lengthwise direction. The tensile strength of zirconium decreases with rising temperature to 50 percent at temperatures from 600° to 700°F.

**Machinability.**  The difficulties in machining zirconium are:

1.  It work-hardens rapidly.

2.  There is a tendency for it to build up on the cutting edge of the tool.

3.  It is highly abrasive.

4.  When chips are small, there is a fire hazard.

The recommended procedure for machining zirconium is to flood the area with water-soluble coolants to minimize the built-up edge on the tool and to prevent fire. Carbide tools are used to withstand the high abrasive action. Moderate speeds and heavy feeds give the best results. Not only are fine chips a fire hazard, but the work shows a tendency to gall and work-harden if the feed is too small. Excellent surface finishes can be obtained with relatively light horsepower compared to alloy steels. The cutting speeds are slightly less than those used for free-machining steels.

The suggested tool angles for a carbide-tipped tool are shown in Fig. 4-7.

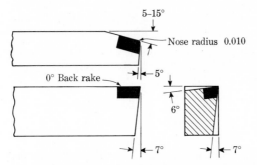

**Fig. 4-7.** Carbide-tool geometry used for turning zirconium.

**Formability.**  The bending of sheets, rods, or strips is best performed at temperatures between 400° and 600°F.

When ingots are heated to 1800°F for forging, a light scale develops. This can be removed by pickling in a solution of nitric-hydrofluoric acid or commercial sodium hydride.

Zirconium sheet can be deep-drawn into cans, using electroplated copper or a commercially available adhesive cement for lubrication. The blanks are heated to 620°F in a 50–50 lithium carbonate-potassium bath, with commercially available waxes as additional lubricants.

**Weldability.**  Owing to the strong tendency of zirconium metal to absorb oxygen and nitrogen, welding must be done in an inert-gas atmosphere. During the welding of thin strip, it is essential to surround the welding area with inert gas, either helium or argon. Argon backing has proved to be preferable to copper or other metallic backing strips.

Tensile tests made on welded zirconium showed that failure usually occurs in the heat-affected zones outside the weld, with ultimate strengths slightly lower than in specimens not welded.

Resistance welding, in which the molten metal is shielded from the atmosphere by the parent metal, has been used successfully on zirconium.

Although it is more expensive, zirconium welding in a vacuum using the electron-beam method has proved highly successful.

The physical properties to consider are:

|  | Commercial Grade | Zircoloy |
|---|---|---|
| Melting point (°F) | 3350 | 3300 |
| Thermal conductivity | 9.6 | 8.1 |
| Coefficient of thermal expansion | $3.1 \times 10^{-6}$ | $3.6 \times 10^{-6}$ |

These properties are very similar to those of titanium and should be given the same consideration.

**Castability.** Zirconium cannot be melted and cast by ordinary methods because of its reaction with the atmosphere and with refractories. It can be successfully melted in a closed, water-cooled copper vessel that is either evacuated or filled with argon. The pouring is then done to an attached mold. *Investment castings* (a process wherein molds are made by surrounding a wax pattern with refractory ceramic material, producing molds that will sustain high temperatures) have been used to make intricate pieces weighing several pounds.

### BERYLLIUM

Beryllium has the highest strength-to-weight ratio of any stable metal, with a weight about that of magnesium and a stiffness greater than steel. The fact that it also has a high elastic modulus, high atomic density, and low atomic weight has earned it the title of "wonder metal of the space age." Although it is of limited quantity, is high in cost (between $70 and $100 per pound), and has associated manufacturing problems, it is becoming a production metal.

The physical properties of beryllium make it possible to achieve and hold extremely close tolerances. Pure beryllium guidance components have been machined to 0.004-in. wall thickness; holes as small as 0.002 in. have been drilled, and deep-hole drilling has been accomplished to a depth of 30 in. with 3/16-in.-diameter drills. Spheres and hemispheres have been generated with sphericity tolerances up to 0.000002 in.

The United States consumption of beryllium is about 8,000 tons per year, which is more than 60 percent of the total world supply. The United States is still dependent on foreign sources because its own large deposits have not been developed.

### Fabricating Characteristics

**Machinability.** Because of the extreme toxicity of beryllium, isolated machining areas are essential. The Atomic Energy Commission recommends that all metal-removal operations be done under high-speed air-exhaust equipment adapted to the operation. For machining operations performed without exhaust, a coolant such as soluble oil should be used to suppress metallic dust and to cool the work.

Various rules for the protection of personnel on the job, including the use of protective clothing, on-site laundering, shower facilities, etc. are also covered by the Defense Metals Information Center (Battelle Memorial Institute).

The machining of beryllium is somewhat similar to that of iron, but the beryllium is more abrasive. Its brittle behavior can cause spalling at the exit cuts and cracking at the surface. During machining, pieces of built-up edge slough off the tool, causing a scuffed, machined appearance.

To prevent rough finishes and edge "breakouts," feeds should not be over 0.015 in. per revolution. Cuts deeper than 1/16 in. can create a safety hazard if the exhaust system is unable to remove the chips efficiently. Usually, no coolant is used.

Carbide tools are used to machine beryllium. The tool life is about equivalent to that of machining steel. However, resharpening costs are higher, because the tools must be resharpened as soon as they become slightly dull. A large side-cutting edge angle is used to ensure that the impact of the load will be taken back of the nose (Fig. 4-8). It will also ease the tool in and out of the cut.

Solid carbide drills are recommended for major drilling operations. When carbide drills are not available, high-speed drills can be used, but the metal tends to seize iron and steel.

The milling of beryllium follows the same pattern as that of turning. Because beryllium tends to break out as the cutter leaves the work, suitable backup material (such as free-cutting steel) should be used.

**Formability.** Rolling, forging, forming, and extrusion of beryllium are generally done hot (1400°F). A mild-steel jacket is used to cover the base metal, thus offering protection from the atmosphere and lubrication, and providing edge restraint to reduce the tendency for cracking.

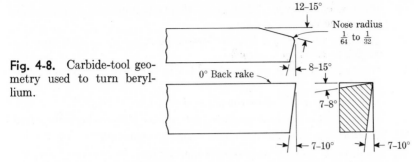

**Fig. 4-8.** Carbide-tool geometry used to turn beryllium.

Beryllium has forging characteristics similar to those of magnesium.

**Weldability.** Most fusion welding of beryllium uses beryllium as the filler metal and a tungsten arc with an inert gas shield, or TIG.

The Battelle Memorial Institute states that fusion welding of beryllium does not yield satisfactory results because of the large grain size and other physical properties of the cast materials. However, with improved knowledge, crack-free welds will soon be possible.

Self-welds are made by placing two pieces of beryllium in close contact from 1 to several hours at temperatures from 1650° to 2280°F (melting point 2345°F). Through a combination of mechanisms, the metals will join. Self-welds can be made in an atmosphere of purified argon, or in a vacuum. To date, the best results have been obtained in a vacuum.

### QUESTIONS

1. Identify each of the following metal code numbers by name and composition: (*a*) 2024 T–3; (*b*) 1100–H18; (*c*) 70–30 brass; (*d*) AZ61A–O; (*e*) Ti–6Al–4V.

2. What takes place in the metal structure during the natural aging of aluminum?

3. How do wrought- and cast-aluminum materials differ from each other in code classification?

4. Why do some aluminum alloys have better machinability than pure wrought aluminum?

5. Explain what consideration should be given to thermal expansion when machining aluminum.

6. What are the two main differences in tool geometry between a tool used for cutting aluminum and one for cutting steel?

7. Is it feasible to form a 2024 aluminum soon after it has been solution heat-treated? Why?

8. What are the properties of aluminum that make it more difficult to weld than plain carbon steel?

9. What are the properties of aluminum that make it one of the most versatile foundry metals?

10. How may the pinholes that are sometimes found on an aluminum sand casting be kept to a minimum?

11. What type of drills are recommended for group I and II copper-base alloys?

12. How does grain size affect the physical properties of copper?

13. What are some problems associated with casting high-conductivity copper?

14. What are the preferred methods of welding magnesium?

15. Name some desirable properties of Inconel.

16. What property of nickel-base alloys causes difficulty in machining?

17. What are two difficulties encountered in machining titanium?

18. What are some properties of beryllium that make it a space-age metal?

19. What is meant by the temper designations of wrought metals?

## PROBLEMS

1. Make a graph plotting the various machinability comparisons of yellow brass, free-cutting brass, magnesium, tin bronze, and unleaded copper.

2. Make a graph plotting the relative machinability ratings of Monel, Inconel, unalloyed alpha-type titanium, zirconium, and magnesium.

3. Compute ratios for the following properties and metals, using mild steel as base 1:

| | Thermal Conductivity | Coefficient of Thermal Expansion |
|---|---|---|
| Steel | 1 | 1 |
| Aluminum | ——— | ——— |
| Copper | ——— | ——— |
| Titanium | ——— | ——— |
| Zirconium | ——— | ——— |
| Nickel alloys | ——— | ——— |

4. What will be the minimum diameter of a punch for cold-drawing magnesium AZ31BO if the blank size is 10 in. in diameter?

## REFERENCES

"How to Work Non-Ferrous Metals," *American Machinist*, Special Report No. 409, 1956.

Materials in Design Engineering, October, 1961.

*Properties and Prices of Zirconium Metal*, Zirconium Metals Corporation of America, New York, N. Y., June, 1954.

Toczko, G. A., and K. Breeze, "A Production Man's Guide to Working Beryllium," *American Machinist and Metal Working*, Special Report No. 498, October, 1960.

*The Tool Engineer's Handbook*, American Society of Tool and Manufacturing Engineers, McGraw-Hill Book Company, Inc., New York, N. Y., 1959.

# 5

# SAND CASTING OF
# METALS AND
# CASTING DESIGN

**A** CASTING can be simply defined as a molten material that has been poured into a prepared cavity and allowed to solidify. Although the principle is simply stated, great skill and long experience are required to gain the knowledge and master the techniques to produce quality castings on difficult jobs.

Many casting processes have been developed over the years to fulfill specific needs of finish, accuracy, speed of production, etc. These processes include sand casting, shell-mold casting, plaster-mold casting, investment casting, permanent-mold casting, centrifugal casting, and die casting.

Sand casting, the most common of these processes, will be discussed in this chapter, along with design considerations. The terminology and basic concepts will carry over into other casting processes discussed in the next chapter.

## SAND CASTING

Sand casting is used primarily for steel and iron, but it can be used for brass, aluminum, bronze, copper, magnesium, and some zinc alloys. There are two principal methods of sand casting. One is known as greensand molding and the other as dry-sand molding.

### Greensand Molding

This is the most widely used molding method. It utilizes a mold made of compressed moist sand. The term *green* tells us that there is moisture in the molding sand and that the mold is not dried out or baked. This method is generally the most expedient but usually is not suitable for large or very heavy castings. It is applicable for castings of rather intricate design, since the greensand does not exert as much resistance to the normal contraction of the casting when it solidifies as does the dry, baked sand. This reduces the formation of hot tears or cracks.

### Dry-Sand Casting

Most large and very heavy castings are made in dry-sand molds. The mold surfaces are given a refractory coating and are dried before the mold is closed for pouring. This hardens the mold and provides the necessary strength to resist large amounts of metal, but it increases the manufacturing time.

Molds which are hardened by a carbon dioxide process, explained later, can also be considered in the dry-sand class.

### Casting Terms and Procedure

A sand casting begins with a wood or metal pattern of the desired shape. It will be larger than the finished part, to allow for shrinkage of the metal, distortion, and machining. The pattern is placed on a *mold board*, which is a board a little larger than the open box, or *flask*, placed over it. Molding sand confined by the flask is then rammed around the pattern. Oftentimes, the sand next to the pattern is sifted or *riddled* to provide a smoother surface. This is called *facing sand*, and the remainder of sand needed to fill up the flask is called *backing sand*.

Patterns of simple design, with one or more flat surfaces, can be molded in one piece. Other patterns may be split into two or more parts to facilitate their removal from the sand. Two-part flasks are needed. The portion of the mold in the lower half of the flask is called the *drag*, and the upper portion is called the *cope* (Fig. 5-1).

Access to the cavity is provided by *sprues*, *runners*, and *gates*, as shown in the diagram. A *pouring basin* can be carved in the sand at the top of the sprue, or a *pour box*, which provides a larger opening, may be laid over the sprue to facilitate pouring.

After the metal is poured, it cools most rapidly where it contacts the sand. Thus the outer surface forms a shell which tends to hold its shape and pull the still-molten metal from the center toward it. The

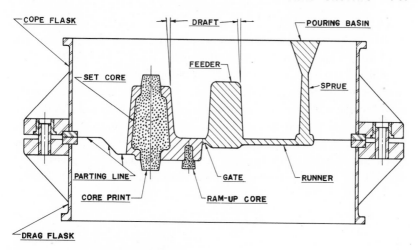

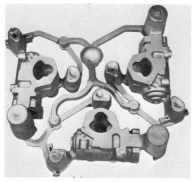

**Fig. 5-1.** Casting-mold terminology.

last bit of metal near the center of the mass may not be of sufficient volume to fill this remaining space, so that a partial void or porous spot will be left in the center of the casting. These porous spots can be avoided by a reservoir or *riser* of molten metal near the cavity.

The size of the gates and runners is very important. It would appear their sole function is to let the metal fill the cavity. However, if they are too large, the molten metal may flow too fast and erode the walls of the runner system. Also, turbulence may result in the mold cavity. If the gates and runners are not large enough, some of the metal may solidify before the section is filled, making an incomplete part. The construction of proper sprues, gates, and risers is achieved by experience, study, and research.

The pattern must be tapered to permit easy removal from the sand. This taper is referred to as the *draft*. The draft for sand molding is generally 1½ to 3 deg.

*Cores* are placed in molds whenever it is necessary to have a hole in the casting. As shown in Fig. 5-1, the core will be left in place after the pattern is removed so that the metal cannot occupy this space. Sometimes the core may be molded integrally with the greensand, and this is referred to as a *greensand core*. Generally, the core is made of sand bonded with core oil, some organic bonding materials, and water. The cores are placed in the mold and, after the pattern is removed, they are located and held in place by the *core prints*, as shown. When cores do not have much support, as shown in Fig. 5-2, support can be supplied by various types of *chaplets* that become part of the casting.

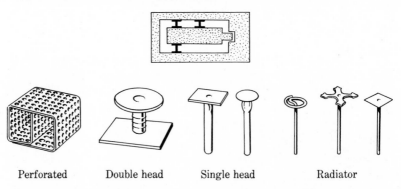

| Perforated | Double head | Single head | Radiator |

**Fig. 5-2.** Various types of chaplets used to support a molding core.

Exterior cores are used to facilitate molding. The small core shown in Fig. 5-1 is of the *ram-up* variety. It is placed in the pattern before the flask is filled with sand so that it rams up as an integral part of the mold.

The *parting line* is the line along which a pattern is divided for molding, or along which the sections of the mold separate. This surface and the pattern are sprinkled with parting dust so that the cope and the drag will separate without rupturing the sand.

Flasks can be made of wood, but they do not stand up under hard usage. Metal flasks are often made of aluminum or magnesium to keep the weight down.

Generally, the flask is removed before the metal is poured, to prevent it from becoming damaged by the hot metal and to speed up its reuse (Fig. 5-3). In its place is put a metal *slip jacket* which prevents the pressure of the molten metal from breaking the mold. Flasks are made in various ways to ease their removal from the mold. Some have a 5-deg inside taper, and others have hinged or quick-locking corners.

**Fig. 5-3.** Metal flask and mold (courtesy Hines Flask Co.).

### Types of Patterns

The selection of the type of pattern, of which there are several, is based largely on the complexity of the piece and the number of parts to be produced. Patterns can be classified as single, loose, solid patterns; split patterns; match-plate patterns; cope-and-drag patterns; loose-piece patterns; and composite patterns.

**Single, Loose, Solid Patterns.** This type of pattern is essentially a duplicate of the part to be cast except, of course, that it is larger, to provide for shrinkage and machining. It also has draft to facilitate its removal from the sand. This pattern is used only where a limited number of parts are to be produced. It contains no gates, sprues, or risers. These must be cut in by hand by the molder, which makes the process slow and comparatively expensive.

**Split Patterns.** Split patterns are made so that one part can be placed in the cope and the other in the drag. This facilitates not only the pattern removal but also the placement of the parting line. Tapered pins hold the two halves together during molding so that the cope half will be accurately located opposite the drag half.

**Match-Plate Patterns.** Match-plate patterns are usually made on an aluminum plate with the cope portion of the pattern on one side and the drag part of the pattern on the other. The cost of making this more elaborate pattern restricts it to cases where medium or large quantities of castings are to be produced. To justify its use, anywhere from a few hundred to a thousand parts should be cast per month. In use, the match plate fits between the cope and the drag, held in place by pins or guides that mate with those on the flask. The match plate is positioned between the two halves of the flask and, after each part has been filled with sand, the match plate is taken out. The mold cavity is then nearly complete, since runners, gates, and risers are included on the match plate (Fig. 5-4).

**Fig. 5-4.** Match-plate pattern (courtesy Central Foundry).

Since runners and gates control the flow of metal to the cavity, having patterns for them mounted on the match plate with the part pattern assures that they will be the same in every mold produced, thus giving more uniform castings. Provision for proper location of the sprue is also provided.

**Cope-and-Drag Patterns.**    To speed up operations so that both the cope and the drag can be "rammed up" at the same time, the match plate is made in two parts. This is sometimes also called a *double match-plate* pattern. In this procedure one workman can fill the cope side with sand while another fills the drag side, or they can both be filled by one man using mechanical equipment, described later.

**Loose-Piece Patterns.**    Loose-piece patterns are needed when the part is such that the pattern cannot be removed as one piece, even though it is split and the parting line is made on more than one plane. In this case the main pattern is usually removed first. Then the separate pieces, which may have to be turned or moved before they can be taken out, are removed. Complicated patterns of this type usually require more maintenance and are slower to mold. However, their cost is sometimes justified by the end product.

**Composite Patterns.**  Large and complicated castings, if in great quantity, are often made with *machine-equipment* patterns. They are similar to the cope-and-drag pattern, but different parts or a *composite* of parts can be made at one time. Each type of part is mounted on a half insert which is interchangeable with other half inserts (Fig. 5-5). This practice effects savings in equipment and cost, yet retains the low piece-price characteristic of high-volume equipment.

COPE  DRAG

**Fig. 5-5.** Composite machine-equipment pattern (courtesy Central Foundry).

### Molding-Sand Preparation and Control

The selection and mixing of the molding sand constitute one of the main factors in controlling the quality of the castings. The two types of molding sand are natural and synthetic.

**Natural Molding Sands.** Deposits of natural molding sands are characterized by a clay content of 5 to 15 percent, distributed throughout the sand. Natural sands vary greatly and therefore must often be reconditioned to obtain certain desirable properties, as follows:

1. The sand should present a smooth surface, which is governed by the *grain size* and *clay content*. The grain size can be determined by running it through a series of sieves. The clay content is determined by washing a 50-gm sample through several cycles in a solution of sodium hydroxide. After the clay is removed, the sand is dried and weighed to see what percent it is of the original.

2. After tempering or moistening the sand with water, its characteristics should be such that it may easily be worked in around the pattern. This is termed *flowability*. The moisture content of sand is determined by weighing the sand before and after drying it in an oven. It can also be found by a commercial "moisture teller," an instrument that registers the moisture in terms of electrical conductivity between two electrodes placed in the sample.

3. After the sand has been rammed in place around the pattern, it should not break out along the edges when the pattern is removed. This is known as *green strength*.

4. The sand should be sufficiently open in structure to permit gas and steam, formed by the molten metal, to escape. This quality is known as *permeability*, and it can be checked with various instruments. One method is to use a standard rammed specimen and see how long it takes 2,000 cc of air to pass through it at a given air pressure. The molder frequently increases the permeability of the sand, after the cope half has been rammed, by inserting a *vent pin* several times to within ¼ in. of the pattern. The vent pin is a 1/16-in. pointed steel wire.

5. The sand must be sufficiently strong to withstand the flow of the molten metal but still weak enough to crumble as the casting starts to solidify and shrink. This quality is determined with a hardness checker on a standard rammed specimen. The hardness checker, when placed on the specimen, measures the penetration depth of a standard steel ball, and registers the distance on a dial.

**Synthetic Sands.**  Synthetic sands have as their base the purer silica sands, such as are found in dune sand. *Bentonite,* a clay derivative of volcanic ash, is added to give the right consistency to the sand.

**Sand Mixing.**  To ensure proper mixing of sand, bonding clay, and water, a mechanical mixer, or *muller,* is used.

## Cores and Coremaking

As stated previously, a core is used to form internal passages in a casting. The characteristics of core materials are similar to those for molding sand. The core must withstand normal handling yet should not prevent the metal in contact with it from contracting normally. A good core will break down or crumble after it has performed its primary function of displacing metal.

**Core Construction.**  Cores are made of fine sand mixed with core oil, some bonding material (usually natural or synthetic resins), and water. After these materials are thoroughly blended, the mixture is placed in molds or coreboxes. Coremaking machines blow the core sand in the corebox. Vents allow the air to escape but trap the sand. By this process, cores can be made in a matter of seconds.

The cores are removed from the corebox and placed in metal coreboxes or on trays and baked at 350° to 450°F. After the cores are baked and cooled, those that consist of two or more parts are pasted together with a synthetic binder.

A newer method of curing cores is with carbon dioxide. When sand is mixed with sodium silicate binder, each grain of sand is coated with a thin film of this viscous liquid. After this coated sand has been packed in the corebox or mold, tiny liquid bridges of binder connect the grains of sand. When carbon dioxide gas is passed through the sand mass, the liquid binder thickens or sets so that the sand grains are bound together, making the sand rigid. The carbon dioxide reacts with the sodium oxide constituent of the binder to produce sodium carbonate. The silicic acid constituent deposits insoluble silica ($SiO_2$) which cements the sand grains together.

Small cores are easily gassed through a small rubber cup held over one end of the corebox. The other end must be vented or supported to allow free passage of gas through the core. Gassing coreboxes from the bottom allows the carbon dioxide to displace more easily the air in the core. Large cores and molds may be gassed by using manifold lids or covers on the coreboxes or mold flasks. In the case of very large cores or molds, direct injection of carbon dioxide gas with a lance is convenient. Cup, manifold, and lance gassing are shown in Fig. 5-6.

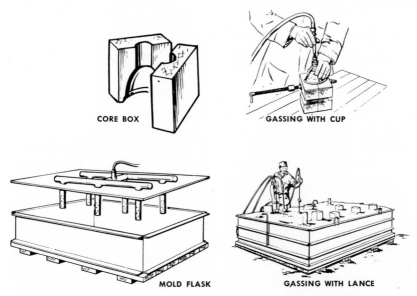

**Fig. 5-6.** Various methods of gassing cores and molds with carbon dioxide. Cup gassing (small core), manifold gassing (mold flask), and lance gassing (large mold) are shown (courtesy Liquid Carbonic division of General Dynamics).

Gassing time will vary, depending upon the size and shape of the core or mold and the method of venting. Either under- or over-gassing will cause the structure to be weak. However, undergassing is preferred to overgassing, because cores will air-harden to some degree. Trial and error must be used to determine gassing times.

About 75 percent of the core sand hardened by carbon dioxide can be reclaimed after use by a pneumatic method. The broken-up core sand is mixed with a high-speed airstream and blown against an impact plate which breaks it down into the individual grains again. Reclaimed sand will require less binder than new sand.

This method of making cores has the advantage of being complete as soon as the cores are removed from the corebox. It also has less distortion as there is no curing time. Less draft is needed, since the cores develop high strength before they are removed from the corebox.

At high temperatures there is a partial fusion of the bond into silicate glass, causing the sand mass to become brittle and easily crushed to powder.

The carbon dioxide process has been extended so that molds can be made by the same process. These molds are produced quickly and have sufficient strength to withstand pouring without an outer slip jacket.

### Types of Molds and Size Classification

**Bench Molds.** Small molds are conveniently made on a bench, hence the name.

**Floor Molds.** Floor molds are for the larger flasks that cannot be easily handled on a bench. This does not necessarily mean that the parts are large; it means that many similar small parts are made at the same time (Fig. 5-7).

**Fig. 5-7.** Pouring a large floor mold (courtesy Allis Chalmers).

**Pit Molding.** Pit molding is done, as the name implies, in a pit or cavity cut in the floor to accommodate very large castings. The pit acts as the drag.

### Molding Equipment

Much of the handwork has been taken out of the modern foundry. Sand is distributed through pneumatic tubes to the molding stations, mechanical means are used to ram it in place, and conveyors transport the finished flask to the pouring floor. The mechanical operations used in filling a mold consist of pneumatic ramming, jolting, squeezing, and sand slinging.

**Pneumatic Rammers.** The simplest aid in making a mold is a pneumatic rammer. It is used in both bench- and floor-molding operations to eliminate hand ramming (Fig. 5-8).

**Fig. 5-8.** Sand ramming of cope with a pneumatic rammer (courtesy Ingersoll-Rand).

**Jolt Machines.**    Another way of packing the sand around the pattern is to give it a series of jolts. This is done by placing the flask with a match-plate pattern on the jolt machine (Fig. 5-9). The top half is filled with sand and subjected to a jolting action. This consists of raising the flask a short distance and allowing it to fall by

**Fig. 5-9.** Large jolt machine used in packing sand around a match-plate pattern (courtesy Osborn Manufacturing Co.).

gravity. The sudden action causes the sand to pack evenly around the pattern. The sand near the top, being less dense, gets very little packing. Sometimes weights are laid on top of the sand to add to the compacting action, thus eliminating any hand ramming.

**Jolt-Squeeze Machine.** Many mold-making machines combine a squeezing action with a jolting action. The assembled flask is placed on the machine with a match-plate pattern between the cope and drag. The drag half is filled with sand and leveled off, and the jolting action rams the sand around the pattern. The flask is then turned over, and the cope is filled with sand and leveled off. A pressure board (Fig. 5-10) is placed on top of the cope, and squeezing action is brought about by the top platen of the machine. After the squeezing action, the platen is swung out of the way. The match-plate pattern is vibrated as the cope is lifted off and as it is drawn from the drag. With the pattern removed, cores can be put in place and the cope returned to position. After stripping off the flask, the mold is moved to the pouring floor.

**Fig. 5-10.** Jolt-squeeze machine eliminates hand ramming of the sand (courtesy Osborn Manufacturing Co.).

**Jolt-Squeeze Rollover Machine.** This machine is similar to the one just described. After the drag half of the flask is filled and jolted and a bottom board is placed over the drag, two arms lift the flask while the operator pivots it over. The cope is filled with sand and squeezed on the pattern plate. As the cope is lifted off, the pattern plate is vibrated to facilitate its withdrawal from the mold. Cores are then put in place, and the cope is returned to position. The flask is stripped off, and the finished mold, ready for pouring, is lowered to the floor by a jib crane (Fig. 5-11). Mold production rates are high with this type of equipment. Only 2 min are required to complete the entire operation.

(a)                                             (b)

**Fig. 5-11.** Jolt-squeeze rollover machine (courtesy Osborn Manufacturing Co.). After the drag has been filled, jolted, and rammed, and the bottom board clamped in place, the operator hits a knee valve which causes arms to raise the flask so it can be turned over easily (*a*). The cope is then filled and rammed, after which the pattern plate is removed (*b*). The cope and drag are then reassembled for pouring.

**Diaphragm Molding Machines.** The automatic diaphragm molding machine uses air pressure on a diaphragm to squeeze the sand into the mold. After the flask has been filled with a measured amount of sand, the diaphragm unit is moved into place. A measured amount of air is pumped into the chamber behind the pad, and the hydraulic cylinder raises the pattern to squeeze the mold. Pressures up to 450 psi are applied evenly to the mold, making possible uniform hardness ratings even in deep pockets (Fig. 5-12).

Because of its uniform pressure, this method has been used to make precision engine-block castings in greensand. A variation of less

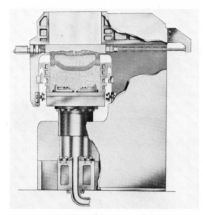
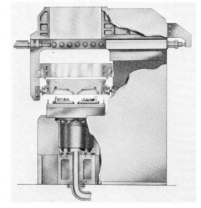

**Fig. 5-12.** Hydropneumatic high-density molding machine makes molds of uniformly high density throughout (courtesy Taccone Corporation).

than 0.5 percent by weight in castings weighing 236 lb has been reported when the mold was made by this method.

**Sand Slingers.** Large floor and pit molds are filled with sand by overhead sand slingers (Fig. 5-13). The operator rides on a traveling boom, directing the sand to the proper places. The sand is delivered to an impeller head by means of conveyor buckets. The impeller head throws the sand down at a rate ranging from 1,000 to 4,000 lb per min. The density of the sand can be controlled by the speed of the impeller head.

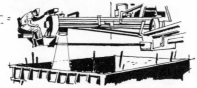

**Fig. 5-13.** A sand slinger can be used to fill a pit mold or a number of smaller molds in a relatively short time (courtesy Gisholt Machine Co.).

**Sandslinger — medium and large castings.**

**Melting the Metal**

The metal is melted in one of several types of furnaces, some of which are shown in Fig. 5-14.

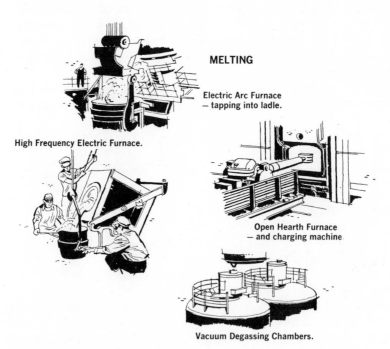

MELTING

Electric Arc Furnace
— tapping into ladle.

High Frequency Electric Furnace.

Open Hearth Furnace
— and charging machine.

Vacuum Degassing Chambers.

**Fig. 5-14.** Some furnaces used to melt steel.

The choice of furnace is based on several factors listed briefly as follows:

1. Economy, including the cost of fuel per pound of melted metal, and the initial cost of the equipment, plus installation and maintenance expenses
2. Temperatures required
3. Quantity of metal required per shift and per hour
4. Ability of the melting mediums to absorb impurities
5. Method of pouring

**Crucible, or Pot-Tilting, Furnaces.** Crucible furnaces, as the name indicates, consist simply of a crucible to hold the metal while it is being melted by a gas or oil flame. It is so arranged that it can be easily tilted when the metal is ready for pouring (Fig. 5-15). The capacity is generally limited to 1,000 lb. Also shown is a twin crucible furnace that utilizes the heat that leaves the firing chamber and passes over the heating crucible to the preheat crucible.

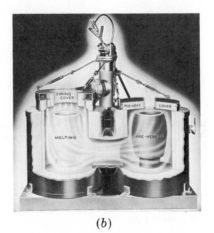

(a)                           (b)

**Fig. 5-15.** (a) A crucible, or pot-tilting, furnace; (b) a twin-crucible furnace (courtesy Randall Foundry Corp.).

**Cupolas.** Cupolas are an outgrowth of the blast furnace. They are designed more specifically for cast-iron melting, and they do handle by far the greatest percentage of this metal. The cupola's wide usage stems from several advantages:

1. Like a blast furnace, it can be tapped at regular intervals, as required, under continuous production.
2. The operating cost is lower than other foundry furnaces producing equivalent tonnages.
3. The chemical composition of the melt can be controlled even under continuous use. Since the molten metal comes in contact with

the carbonaceous coke, the carbon content of the melt tends to be high (Fig. 5-16). It is sometimes necessary to transfer the molten metal to another furnace, such as an air furnace, where some of the carbon can be burned out.

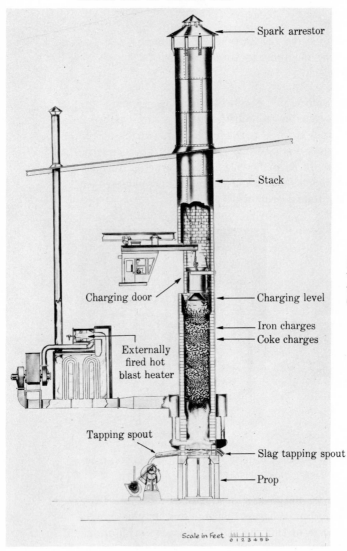

Spark arrestor

Stack

Charging door

Charging level

Iron charges

Coke charges

Externally fired hot blast heater

Tapping spout

Slag tapping spout

Prop

Scale in Feet
0 1 2 3 4 5 6

**Fig. 5-16.** Sectional view of cupola construction (courtesy Whiting Co.).

You will notice, in Fig. 5-16, that the cupola construction is essentially a steel shaft or cylinder lined with firebrick. A wind box and tuyeres are placed near the bottom to supply draft when connected to the blower. The bottom is covered with green foundry sand, rammed in place and tapered toward the taphole. Kindling wood is carefully placed on the sand and then a layer of coke. After the coke is burning well, more coke is gradually added until the bed is of the desired height, depending somewhat on the burning period. When the original coke bed is "burned in," additional coke is added and the cupola is ready for charging.

Charging is done through the charge door located about halfway up the side of the cupola. The charge consists of layers of pig iron or scrap alternated with coke. Small amounts of limestone are added as a flux for the metal. The flux increases the fluidity of the slag (formed from coke ash, metal oxidation, and some of the brick lining) so that it can be tapped off at the slag spout. It is also possible to add alloy-rich materials to the charge or to the ladle at the time the cupola is tapped.

When sufficient charges have been placed in the cupola, melting is started. Usually, ½ hr is required to preheat the stack contents. The blowers are then started, and the metal begins to melt in a matter of minutes. The melting can be observed through peepholes in the side. As the molten metal collects in the bottom of the cupola, the taphole can be opened to deliver the iron to the pouring ladles. When the ladle is full, the wedge-shaped clay plug is returned to the taphole. The forced air is temporarily turned off during the tapping operation.

To shut down the cupola, the stack contents are melted down until about one or two charges are left above the bed. The air blast is reduced, and the bottom doors are opened to allow the contents to be emptied out. Water is sprayed on the white-hot discharge to prevent damage to the cupola. Metal and coke from the charge can be reused gradually in succeeding charges.

**Arc Furnaces.** To produce steel castings of exacting chemical compositions, electric arc furnaces are used. These furnaces provide close control over the melting and refining processes.

The furnace consists of a shell lined with refractory brick. Three carbon electrodes are inserted in the top and extend down close to the metal (Fig. 5-17). When the current is turned on, electric arcs are struck between the electrodes and the charge of metal, providing the heat. Flux is added through a side door to form a protective cover for

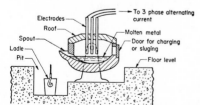

**Fig. 5-17.** Cutaway diagram of electric furnace for melting steel (courtesy American Iron and Steel Institute).

the metal. High temperatures, high melting rates, and close control can be maintained by these furnaces.

**Electric Induction Furnaces.** The high-frequency electric furnace shown in cross-sectional view (Fig. 5-18) is essentially an air transformer in which the primary is a coil of water-cooled copper tubing and the secondary is a metal charge. As the high-frequency electric current is passed through the primary coil, it induces a rapidly alternating magnetic field in the metal. This much heavier secondary current heats the metal very rapidly to the desired temperature. Cooling water in the copper tubing prevents the primary circuit from overheating.

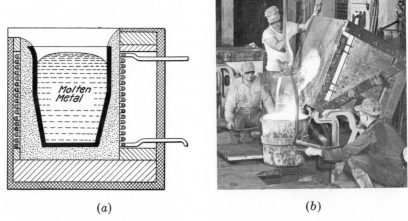

(a)  (b)

**Fig. 5-18.** (a) Cross-sectional view of a high-frequency induction furnace. (b) Pouring steel from a high-frequency electric furnace (courtesy Lebanon Steel Foundry).

Since melting conditions are obtained quickly, very little oxidation of the metal takes place, and no flux is used.

The induction furnace is proving valuable in foundries that do small-lot pouring of various alloys. It is also valuable in melting low-carbon steels, as there is no "pickup" of carbon, such as occurs in electric arc furnaces.

**Pouring the Metal**

After the mold is made and the cores are set in place, the work is checked to see that all has been properly done. The mold is then closed and sent to the pouring floor. Several types of containers are used to move the molten metal from the furnace to the pouring area.

**Ladles.** Large castings of the floor and pit type are poured with a *bottom-pouring* ladle. When the casting is very large, two or three of these ladles are used at one time. For smaller or medium-sized molds, the *teapot ladle* is used (Fig. 5-19). The teapot ladle has a built-in spout which allows the metal to be taken from the bottom and does not disturb the slag that forms on top.

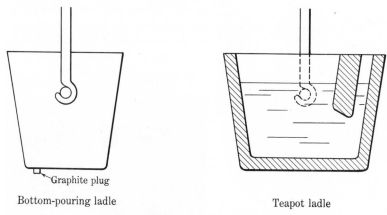

Bottom-pouring ladle          Teapot ladle

**Fig. 5-19.** Ladles used in pouring castings.

Plain ladles are referred to as *lip-pouring* ladles. These receive the metal from the furnace and are placed on the pouring floor to fill the smaller ladles that are handled by monorail conveyors or by hand.

**Pouring.** Pouring the metal must be as carefully controlled as any part of the casting process. The temperature of the metal must be just right. If it is too hot, the hot gases will produce blowholes; if it is too cold, the metal will solidify prematurely and will not fill the entire cavity.

A newer pressure-pouring method now being used by some manufacturers has been developed to ensure sound castings. It consists of forcing molten metal through a refractory tube to the bottom of the cavity by means of compressed air.

**Automatic Equipment.** Foundry processes have become considerably automated. Shown in Fig. 5-20 is a semiautomated foundry process line using a hydropneumatic molding machine. Only the core setting and pouring need be done manually.

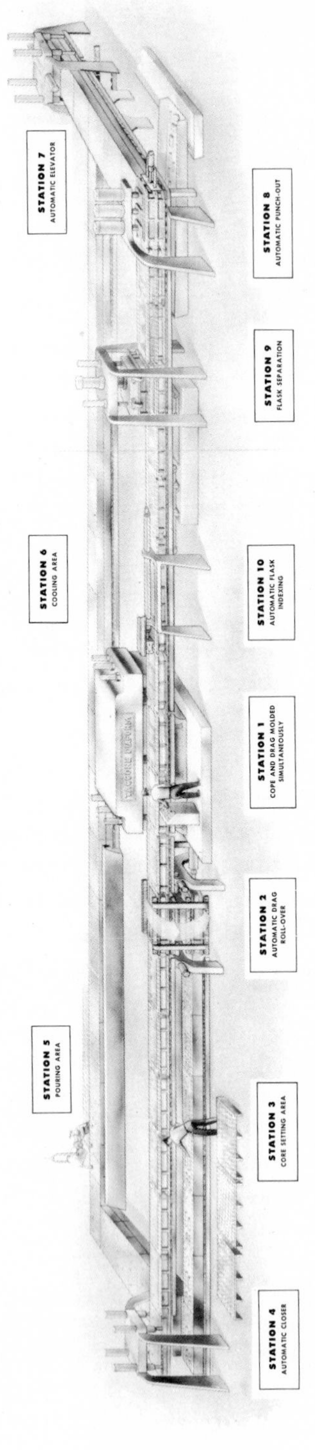

**Fig. 5-20.** Semiautomated molding line using a hydropneumatic molding machine (courtesy Taccone Corp.).

STATION 7
AUTOMATIC ELEVATOR

STATION 8
AUTOMATIC PUNCH-OUT

STATION 9
FLASK SEPARATION

STATION 6
COOLING AREA

STATION 10
AUTOMATIC FLASK INDEXING

STATION 1
COPE AND DRAG MOLDED SIMULTANEOUSLY

STATION 2
AUTOMATIC DRAG ROLL-OVER

STATION 5
POURING AREA

STATION 3
CORE SETTING AREA

STATION 4
AUTOMATIC CLOSER

## Finishing Operations

After the castings have had time to cool below the lower critical temperature, they are separated from the mold and placed on a shakeout table. Here the sand is separated from the casting. It is then taken to the finishing room where the gates and risers are removed. Small gates and risers can be knocked off with a hammer; larger ones require sawing, burning, or shearing. Unwanted metal protrusions, such as fins, bosses, and

**Fig. 5-21.** A battery of swing grinders being used to smooth the casting surfaces where excess metal has been removed (courtesy Lebanon Steel Foundry).

small portions of the gates and risers, need to be smoothed up to blend with the surface of the casting. Most of this work is done with a grinder, and the operation is known as *snag grinding*. On large castings it is easier to move the grinder than the work, so swing-type grinders are used (Fig. 5-21). Smaller castings are brought to stand- or bench-type grinders. Hand and pneumatic chisels are also used to trim castings. A more recent method of removing the excess metal from the casting is by means of a carbon-air torch. This consists of a carbon rod using high-amperage electric current with a stream of compressed air blowing at the base of it. This oxidizes and removes the metal as soon as it is molten. In many foundries this process has replaced all chipping and grinding operations.

Large castings may be taken to a special room where they are subjected to blasting operations of shot, sand, or water.

### Checking and Repairing

The casting is cleaned and inspected for flaws. Surface defects can usually be repaired by welding. More recently, epoxy resins combined with steel or aluminum have been used to fill surface defects. These materials harden quickly and have very low shrinkage values.

Castings are tested both destructively and nondestructively. A destructive test consists of sawing the casting in sections to determine possible porosity locations. Other destructive tests are made by hammer blows and loading to failure. Nondestructive tests are made by X ray, gamma rays, magnaflux, ultrasonics, etc., are discussed in Chap. 28.

### Heat Treatment of the Casting

If heat treatment of the casting is necessary, it is usually done after the preliminary repair and cleaning. If the repair is made with epoxy resins, this would have to be done after heat treatment.

Various materials need different heat treatments. Malleable iron requires a prolonged anneal, steel castings may be quenched and tempered to develop maximum strength, and nonferrous castings may be normalized in preparation for welding or machining.

### Review of the Casting Process

The casting process can become quite involved, especially in its initial presentation. Therefore, by way of brief summary, the important steps are reviewed with a series of line drawings (Fig. 5-22). These pictures will serve to tie the process and terms together.

## CASTING DESIGN

Good casting design usually results from the careful deliberations of the foundry engineer and the product-design engineer. As with almost all engineering, a *good* design is generally a compromise. Shown

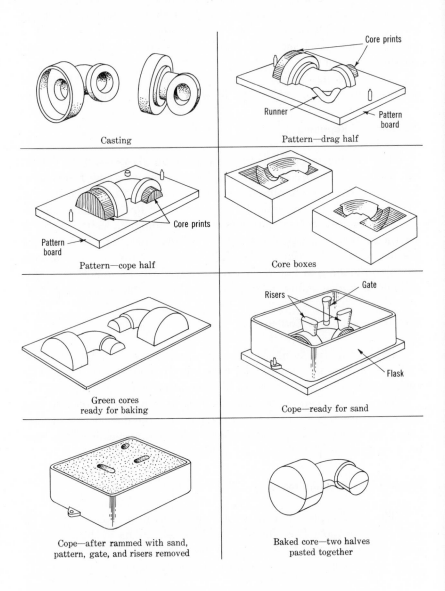

Casting

Pattern—drag half

Pattern—cope half

Core boxes

Green cores
ready for baking

Cope—ready for sand

Cope—after rammed with sand,
pattern, gate, and risers removed

Baked core—two halves
pasted together

**Fig. 5-22.** A summary of the steps involved in producing a steel casting (courtesy Adirondack Steel Casting Co., Inc.).

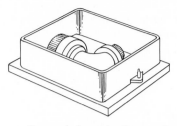

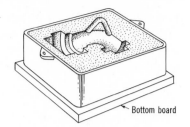

Drag ready for sand—after ramming with sand, bottom board is set on top of flask, flask inverted, and pattern removed

Drag—pattern removed

Bottom board

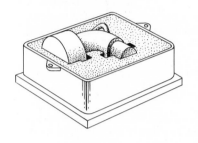

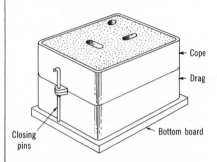

Cope

Drag

Closing pins

Bottom board

Drag with core set in place

Cope and drag assembled, ready for steel

Casting as removed from sand—Risers and gate will be removed, casting chipped and ground where necessary, annealed, inspected, and ready for shipment

**Fig. 5-22.** (*cont.*)

in Fig. 5-23 are two versions of the same fundamental design. The designer's ideal casting would be almost impossible to cast, and the foundryman's ideal would be extremely costly to machine.

For a given part, there is usually an optimum point on the cost curve which represents the "best" design. The curves might look some-

**Fig. 5-23.** The designer's and foundryman's views of an ideal casting (courtesy *Machine Design*).

thing like those in Fig. 5-24, where one curve represents an easy-to-cast hard-to-machine casting, and the other curve the difficult-to-cast easy-to-machine casting. The lowest point of the total-cost curve represents the ultimate goal of the manufacturer.

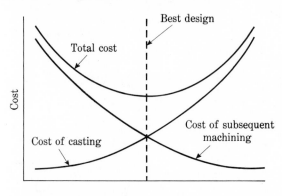

**Fig. 5-24.** The "best" casting design is represented by a summation of the cost of casting and the cost of machining.

### Casting-Design Principles

Although cost reductions are often realized through good casting design, there are other important factors to keep in mind when designing a casting to obtain maximum strength. These include the solidification rate, effect of alloying elements, parting-line placement, avoidance of stress concentration, economic considerations, tolerances expected, and function.

**Solidification Rate.** The rate at which a given metal solidifies largely determines its microstructure. Therefore, in casting design it is important to consider carefully the effect of the size or volume of each cross-sectional area. As an example, normally gray cast iron, when poured in very thin sections, can become white cast iron, and normally white cast iron, poured in heavy sections, can become gray cast iron.

As noted on the iron-carbon equilibrium diagram in Chap. 2, there are two important cooling periods for cast iron. One is at the beginning of solidification, when iron carbides are starting to form and austenite makes its first appearance (about 2,065°F). The other is the transformation to pearlite at 1,333°F. The austenite will have rejected any carbon in excess of a eutectoid mixture (0.83 percent). The excess carbon rejected from the austenite may be dispersed throughout the austenite, or it may migrate and deposit itself on the primary carbide which separated out from the melt. The size and distribution of the graphite flakes are fairly well set at the time of solidification, so that subsequent heat treatment will not have any great effect on them.

To a great extent, the structure of the mold will govern the cooling rate of the metal. For example, a water-cooled mold will have more than twice the cooling action of a regular sand mold. Water cooling is seldom used unless white cast iron is desired.

THE USE OF CHILLS. Where localized cooling of a casting is desired, chills are used. Chills are usually composed of metals of various heat-dissipating capacities, placed in the mold to cause more rapid solidification in localized areas. They may be positioned at an intersection or joint that has a comparatively large volume of metal to cool, thus relieving a hot spot or maintaining a more uniform cooling rate and microstructure. They may also be located at points where it is desirable to have localized hardening, as in the case of bearing or wear surfaces.

In general, it will be well for the casting designer to be aware of the change in solidification rate that accompanies various cross-sectional areas. The sectional area of a casting largely determines its solidification rate, which, in turn, will help determine the microstructure and strength of the casting.

Heavy isolated sections should be avoided. Shown in Fig. 5-25, at the left, are three possible methods of making a small casting with a large central hub. If the hub is solid, as shown in the top section, porosity will occur in the center of the casting. If some of the metal is removed, as shown in the center section, there is some possibility that porosity can be avoided. If the hole is cored entirely through the hub, as indicated in the bottom section, porosity-free castings are assured.

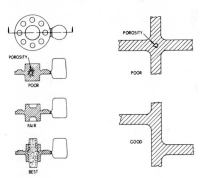

**Fig. 5-25.** Heavy, isolated sections cause porosity in the casting (courtesy Central Foundry).

Wherever possible, wall sections should be staggered to minimize the amount of metal concentrated at the junction, as shown at the right in Fig. 5-25.

Castings with heavy sections can be made if the heavy section is near the outside and is connected with the parting line. They can be gated directly, the metal entrance being increased by means of a gate pad (Fig. 5-26).

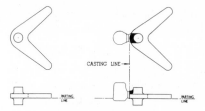

**Fig. 5-26.** The use of a gate pad to facilitate feeding the large hub section (courtesy Central Foundry).

When specifying the desirable strength of a casting, references are often made to a test bar of a size equivalent to the casting cross section in question. One method is to pour a round bar that represents the cross-sectional area of the size that corresponds to the casting cross section. Of course, the cooling rate of a round bar will not be exactly the same as that of the casting area in question, so certain correlations have been worked out. One of these is that the center of a flat plate will cool at the same rate as a round bar whose diameter is twice the thickness of the plate. The edge, which cools at a much faster rate, will require a sample test bar the same diameter as the plate thickness. This variation in cooling rate is well known in the foundry and machine shops, where unmachinable chill is always found first on thin edges.

Even in fairly compact castings, differences in cooling rate will affect the final strength. For example, if a 3-in.-square bar were cast and various sizes of round-bar specimens were taken at the corners and center, as shown in Fig. 5-27, the results would be somewhat as indicated, even in a compact casting such as this. It will be noted that the hardness is higher at the more rapidly cooled corners than in the more slowly cooled center. Tensile strength corresponds closely to hardness and is higher for the harder specimens.

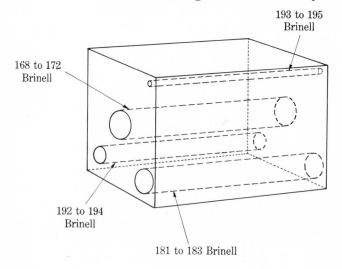

**Fig. 5-27.** The variations in hardness of test rods taken from a 3-in.-square bar of gray cast iron due to differences in cooling rates. Tensile strengths increase from the softest to the hardest bar.

THE USE OF INSCRIBED CIRCLES. The effect of cooling on adjacent portions of a casting is not readily predictable on a useful quantitative basis, but the use of inscribed circles has been worked out by Harold T. Angus of The British Cast Iron Research Association. This method is a help in assessing relative cooling rates of castings at the design stage (Fig. 5-28). The circles are useful in determining chilling tendencies and likely mechanical properties.

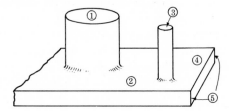

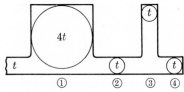

Sectional drawing of casting, showing inscribed circles

**Fig. 5-28.** Crosshatched areas show equivalent cooling rates of various casting sections.

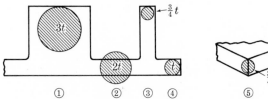

Equivalent diameter of bars which will cool at about the same rate as the particular position on the casting

When an inscribed circle is tangential to three major sides of a section, as in (1), (3), and (4) of Fig. 5-28, the cooling rate can be assumed to be equal to or faster than that of a bar of the same diameter, and the possibility of hard spots, depending on composition and cooling rate, must be considered.

It can be seen that the risk of obtaining hard spots would be greatest at points (3), (4), and (5). It would be necessary to specify iron that would not chill at these points.

Although appreciable variations occur in properties of apparently similar irons, it is possible to make a reasonable assessment of the likely properties of metal when poured into castings or test bars from the same analysis.

The structure and mechanical properties of a cast iron of a given composition depend primarily upon the cooling rate after pouring.

**Effect of Alloying Elements.** Alloys added to cast iron are used to enhance certain properties of a metal, as explained in Chap. 2. Here we are concerned with how alloys can be used to control the solidification rate and, consequently, the properties of the metal.

Silicon is the element normally used in castings to control chill. Nickel, copper, chromium, molybdenum, vanadium, and titanium are also used to affect the cooling rate. Where these elements are added in amounts greater than 0.2 percent, their effect must be considered. For example, 1 percent of nickel is roughly equivalent to 3 percent of silicon and 1 percent of chromium roughly cancels the effect of 1.2 percent of silicon.

**Parting-Line Placement.** With high-production molding techniques, it is desirable to place the gate and feeder at the parting line. In the upper portion of Fig. 5-29, the parting line has been placed at the flange. The heavy boss at the top becomes isolated from the riser, and porosity results. By turning the casting 90 deg and placing the parting line in the other plane, the feeder is permitted to be placed directly on the heavy boss, as shown.

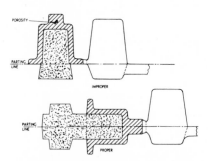

**Fig. 5-29.** Proper placement of the parting line facilitates gating (courtesy Central Foundry).

Some general considerations in regard to the parting line are:

1. Avoid making it at chucking or machining areas that will interfere with locating for other operations.

2. Keep it as even as possible in order to simplify producing the patterns, making the mold, and providing a casting with the minimum of fins.

**Stress Concentrations.** Sharp corners should be avoided in casting design. Stress concentration is developed in any sharp inside corner during cooling, as shown in Fig. 5-30. If the stress exceeds the strength of the material (metal is weak immediately after solidifying), a *heat check* or *hot tear* may form. Very often, such flaws are small, unnoticed, and frequently not harmful, but, since the tendency for them to form is present in any sharp inside corner, better design is accomplished when a proper fillet is utilized. The illustration to the right in Fig. 5-30 shows how this stress is minimized. There is no spot for the concentration of cooling stresses to occur.

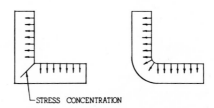

**Fig. 5-30.** Avoid sharp corners in order to minimize stress.

Whenever possible, castings should be designed with uniform thickness. Since this cannot always be done, accepted methods of varying sections are shown in Fig. 5-31. Sharp corners and small radii used to change the thickness of a section are responsible for stress concentrations. A radius of 1 in., or a 15-deg taper, is an acceptable method of design when changes are made on both sides of the section.

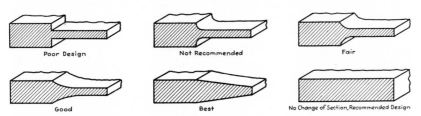

**Fig. 5-31.** Abrupt section changes are not recommended (courtesy Steel Founders' Society of America).

**Economic Considerations.** Good casting design will incorporate savings wherever possible. The designer will consider such factors as multiple-cavity castings, fabrication, the use of cores, subsequent machining operations, and weight reduction.

MULTIPLE-CAVITY CASTING. Substantial savings can be realized by incorporating more than one finished part into a single casting. Molding and handling costs are greatly reduced, since only a fraction of the number of castings need be handled.

An example of this is the single casting of five **V**-8 engine-bearing caps [Fig. 5-32(a)]. The casting is completely machined as a single piece and then cut into separate pieces.

Another example of a single casting for two parts is the front and rear stator-blade carrier which is separated during machining [Fig. 5-32 (b)].

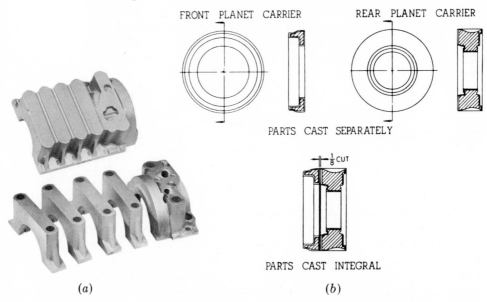

(a)                                           (b)

**Fig. 5-32.** Multiple and integral castings can result in cost reduction. Most of the machining is completed before separation (courtesy Central Foundry).

FABRICATION. Fabricated designs, such as the rear-wheel truck hub shown in Fig. 5-33, can often be simplified. In this case the fabricated version was made by forging the main plate and welding a smaller flange in place. The casting on the right is lighter, stronger, and less costly than the fabricated design.

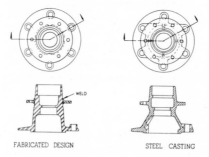

**Fig. 5-33.** Casting at right eliminates an added welding process (courtesy Central Foundry).

CORED HOLES. Engineers are often confronted with the problem of whether to specify cored holes or drilled holes. Sometimes the holes are required as oil passages; others are used to lighten the casting. Cored holes often require boring and reaming. The economics involved in cored holes versus drilled holes must be studied on an individual basis, but generally it is cheaper to core larger holes where appreciable metal can be saved and faster machining results. The universal joint yoke shown in Fig. 5-34 was originally a solid-steel forging. A rather slow drilling operation was required to make the shaft hole. In casting, this hole was cored, followed by a fast core-drilling operation, since most of the metal had already been removed.

**Fig. 5-34.** Cored holes eliminate or reduce secondary operations of drilling and boring (courtesy Central Foundry).

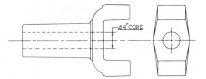

Many times, proper design can combine cores, resulting in a less expensive casting. Figure 5-35 shows the original and the improved design of a truck wheel hub. The original casting could not be formed in greensand. A large *ring core* was necessary, together with a *body core* for the inner portion. The design at the right was considerably improved by eliminating the ribs and backdraft. This made it possible to make the mold in greensand, entirely eliminating the ring core.

**Fig. 5-35.** Redesigning a truck wheel hub for one core instead of two (courtesy Central Foundry).

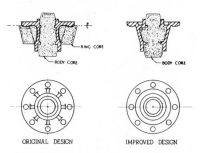

**Subsequent Operations.** Good casting design takes into consideration how parts will be held for machining. The booster body shown in Fig. 5-36, used on several sizes of artillery shells, was originally made from brass bar stock on an automatic screw machine. After extensive testing, it was decided to use malleable iron castings. The manufacturer wished to use the same machines he had used on the brass bar stock. This problem was solved by adding a 1-in.-diameter by 1.25-in.-long lug for holding it in a collet-type chuck. The booster body could then be machined completely during the single chucking, and removed from the lug while machining the back side.

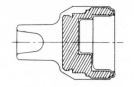
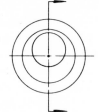

BOOSTER BODY

**Fig. 5-36.** A machining lug added to the booster body allows it to be held in a collet-type chuck for over-all machining. The part was redesigned from brass bar stock to malleable-iron casting (courtesy Central Foundry).

Automotive door hinges have been made from malleable iron for many years. The procedure has been to cast the basic hinge and let the customer drill and countersink the three holes needed to accommodate the flathead screws that fasten the hinges to the body and door. Now, through changed design, the countersink is incorporated in the casting and the hole is punched out at the foundry. Usually, the same fixture used for straightening is used to hold the part for punching. The lock washers grip the cast surface better than the machined surface, and a major cost—that of machining three holes—has been eliminated.

Holes with diameters greater than the thickness of the metal can be punched in malleable cast iron. Two round holes and a square hole are punched simultaneously in an idler arm, as shown in Fig. 5-37.

**Fig. 5-37.** Three holes are punched simultaneously in this malleable-iron casting, eliminating most of the secondary machining operations (courtesy Malleable Castings Council).

WEIGHT REDUCTION. Weight reduction, formerly a problem primarily of aircraft and space engineers, is now also a problem for automotive engineers. Three main methods of reducing weight are:

1. Reduce existing dimensions through stress analysis and related procedures.

2. Convert existing ferrous materials to aluminum or magnesium. This usually results in increased costs, since lightweight metals are higher priced on a volume or strength basis.

3. Convert existing parts from low- or medium-strength ferrous materials to a high-strength ferrous material. This permits reduction in physical size and weight. Often, the greater cost per pound of higher-strength material is offset, because less material is required. Shown in Fig. 5-38 are a gray-iron and a cast-steel differential carrier. By taking advantage of the higher-strength steel, it was possible to design the part 5 lb lighter and still maintain the original, or greater, strength.

**Fig. 5-38.** The gray-iron casting at the left was redesigned for a pearlite malleable-iron casting, with a resultant weight saving of 5 lb. (courtesy Central Foundry).

The seven steps shown in Fig. 5-39 are recommended by the Malleable Founders Society as being basic in creating high-strength lightweight castings.

**Sand-Casting Tolerances.** For ordinary greensand molds, the closest tolerances can be held in one part of the flask. The greatest error is introduced across the parting line. Several other reasons exist for tolerance build-up in greensand castings, as follows:

1. The pattern may deviate from the drawing.

2. Localized casting shrinkage was not fully compensated for by the patternmaker.

3. Warpage may result, owing to restrained cooling of the casting. This is not always predictable, as it is difficult to say which portion of the casting will solidify first.

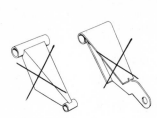 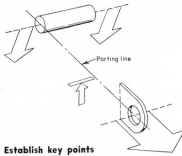

**1** **Start out fresh.**
Erase all preconceptions regarding design of the part. For example, don't limit thinking to straight sections.

**2** **Establish key points on the casting.**
Locate terminal and mating parts. Visualize how the parting line should run for best part design and foundry techniques.

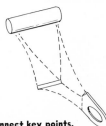  

**4** **Check stresses at critical locations.**
Use experimental stress analysis techniques (brittle lacquer, for example) to refine the casting design.

**3** **Connect key points.**
Consider directions and magnitudes of service stresses when connecting the various terminal points.

 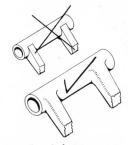

**5** **Strengthen with ribs, corrugations, dimples.**
These simple shapes add greatly to strength, yet cost little in a cast part. Ribs should be used only in compression. Corrugations should be aligned along primary stress direction. Dimples should be oval in shape, with major axis of oval along the direction of stress.

**6** **Smooth out sharp corners.**
Use fillets and radii instead of sharp corners to promote metal flow and avoid stress concentration.

 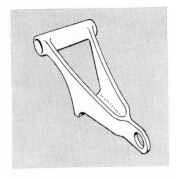

**7** **Make sections uniform.**
Wall thicknesses in a malleable casting are usually from ¼ to 2 in. Sections should be designed to promote directional solidification toward the feeding head, thus insuring proper cooling and heat transfer.

**Fig. 5-39.** Seven steps in creating a high-strength, minimum-weight casting (courtesy *Machine Design*).

4. Pattern rap, core shift, sand pressure, mold growth, and shake-out time may vary.

5. Pouring temperature and rate of pouring will affect tolerance.

The first three items can be corrected by reworking the pattern or by modifying the molding practice. Where the quantity is large, trial-and-error corrections are entirely practical.

When extremely close tolerances are specified, there must be a correspondingly good finish. Since there is no standard specification for surface finish, this should be agreed on by the designer and the foundry-man. The actual tolerances that can be supplied will vary in different foundries and according to the class of work, but Table 5-1 gives typical figures for sand castings.

**TABLE 5-1.**

### Typical Sand-Casting Tolerances

| Approximate Size of Casting (in.) | As-Cast Tolerance (in.) | Additional Machining Allowance per Face (in.) |
|---|---|---|
| Up to 8 | ±1/16 | 1/8 |
| 8 to 18 | ±1/8 | 3/16 |
| 18 to 30 | ±3/16 | 5/16 |
| Above 30 | ±1/4 | 3/8 to 1/2 |

Closer casting tolerances can be obtained with hard molds, as discussed in Chap. 6.

**Functional Design.**   The overriding consideration in casting design is how functional it will be. Function is more important than cost, ease of manufacture, or appearance. The part must perform the job for which it is intended. A comparatively complicated casting should not be rejected on the basis of cost alone. It should be given a fair analysis and compared with other methods of producing the same item. A thorough analysis often leads to design improvements.

### QUESTIONS

1. Explain the term *green* in greensand molding.
2. Why are dry-sand molds used?
3. Explain the terms (*a*) cope and (*b*) drag.
4. What is the function of a riser in a sand casting?
5. Why is it so important that the gates and runners be of the correct size?

6. (*a*) What is the function of the core in sand molding? (*b*) How may cores be held in place? (*c*) How may they be supported?

7. What are the advantages in having a match-plate pattern as compared to a split pattern?

8. How may the sand be tested for permeability?

9. What are the qualities of a good sand core?

10. What is the advantage of using carbon dioxide in making sand cores?

11. What advantages are claimed for the diaphragm molding machine?

12. Why would an induction-type furnace appeal to a small foundry dealing in alloy castings?

13. What steps are involved between the time a casting is poured and the time it has passed inspection?

14. What effect may the cross-sectional area have on the metallurgical structure of a casting?

15. Explain how localized cooling can be accomplished in a sand casting.

16. What is one method used to determine the cooling rate of various cross-sectional areas of the casting?

17. What general statement can be made regarding corners in casting design?

18. What are some methods of dealing with heavy sections in castings to avoid porosity and to obtain a uniform structure?

19. What provisions can be made in the casting design that will aid subsequent operations?

20. What are some principles to bear in mind when designing a casting for minimum weight?

**PROBLEMS**

1. Calculate the amount of metal in lb that would be required to make the casting shown in the accompanying sketch. Add 10 percent for sprues, runners, and risers.

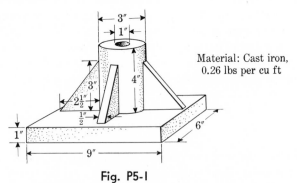

Material: Cast iron, 0.26 lbs per cu ft

Fig. P5-1

2. If 100 castings are made as shown in Fig. P5-1, find the approximate cost per casting. Time required to construct and finish the pattern, 4 hr. Time to make mold, 5 min. Core time, 1 min. Pouring time, 1 min.-45 sec. Shake-

out time, 3 min. Cutting sprues and risers, 2 min. Additional handling time, 8 min. Labor and overhead charge is $10.00 per hr. Cast iron cost is 17 cents per lb. A cooling time of two hours is charged at the overhead rate of $5.00 per hr. Scrap loss is 5 percent.

### REFERENCES

Angus, H. T., *Physical and Engineering Properties of Cast Iron*, The British Cast Iron Research Association, Alvechurch, Birmingham, England, 1960.

Angus, H. T., F. Dunn, and D. Marles, *Transactions of the American Foundrymen's Society*, Vol. 57, 1949.

Hiene, R. W., and P. C. Rosenthal. *Principles of Metal Casting*, McGraw-Hill Book Company, Inc., New York, N. Y., 1955.

Malleable Founders Society, "Seven Steps in Designing Minimum-Weight Castings," *Machine Design*, November, 1961.

Scharf, A., and Charles F. Walton, "Designing Gray Iron Castings," *Machine Design*, January, 1957.

# 6

# OTHER MOLDING PROCESSES

$S$AND-CASTING METHODS have long been a favorite of the foundry because of their low cost and versatility. They may not, however, meet all the more exacting requirements of close tolerances with a minimum of machining and smooth surface finish. Other casting methods have been developed that meet these requirements. These processes are shell-mold casting, plaster-mold casting, investment casting, centrifugal casting, and permanent molding.

## SHELL-MOLD CASTING

The shell-mold method of producing castings is basically a modification of the sand-mold process. It had its early development in Germany during World War II. Instead of using the regular foundry-sand mixture, which has clay and water as binders, a fine dry sand mixed with phenolic resin is applied to a pattern which is heated to approximately 450°F. The resin melts and flows in between the grains of sand, acting as a bond. This feature, plus curing on the pattern, produces a hard, smooth mold which is just as accurate as the pattern itself.

Jolting, squeezing, and ramming of the mold are eliminated in the shell-molding process. In place of the regular sand-molding equipment is an open-faced box mounted on trunnions. A resin-sand mixture is poured into the box to a depth of approximately 10 or 12 in. The pattern plate, which has previously been heated, is clamped face down on top of the box (Fig. 6-1). The box is inverted so that the sand-resin mixture drops directly on the hot pattern face.

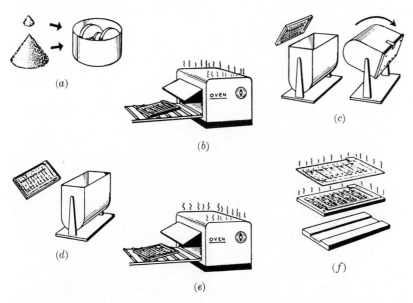

**Fig. 6-1.** The shell-molding process includes (*a*) mixing the resin and sand, (*b*) heating the pattern, (*c*) investing, (*d*) removing the invested pattern, (*e*) curing, and (*f*) stripping.

The length of time during which the mixture is in contact with the hot pattern determines the thickness of the shell. Usually, a **20**- to **35**-sec exposure will result in a shell ⅛ to ⅜ in. thick, which is adequate for most small to medium castings. The box is then returned to its original position, and the pattern, with the soft shell adhering to it, is removed and placed in an oven to cure. An oven temperature of approximately 450°F will require **40** to **60** sec to make the heat-hardening phenolic binder set.

Electric radiant-heat furnaces can be used effectively to direct the heat to the base and sides of projections, as shown in Fig. 6-2.

### Mold Ejection

After the shell has had sufficient curing time, it is removed from the oven. The shell fits rather snugly on the pattern, so some means must be provided for rapid removal. This can be easily accomplished if knockout pins are incorporated into the pattern. These pins can be

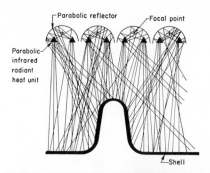

**Fig. 6-2.** Radiant-heat furnaces are used effectively to cure shell molds.

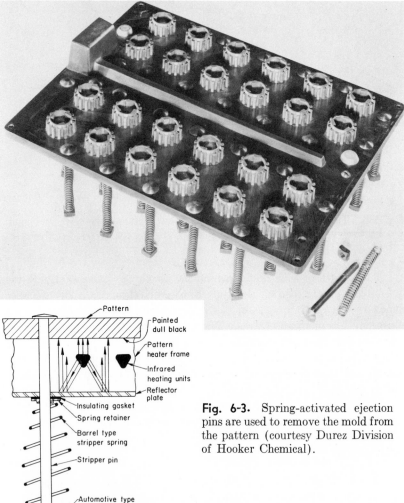

**Fig. 6-3.** Spring-activated ejection pins are used to remove the mold from the pattern (courtesy Durez Division of Hooker Chemical).

spring-activated, as shown in Fig. 6-3, or they can be part of a separately operated mechanical ejection system. In either case, the method of removing the soft shell must be considered at the time the pattern is designed.

It is important to have the ejection pins work together uniformly. If uneven action takes place, broken or distorted molds are likely to result. The pattern also may be subjected to wear or damage.

**Draft.** The amount of draft necessary on shell molds is generally less than on sand molds, as shown in Table 6-1. Only a small amount is necessary to facilitate the removal of the mold from the pattern.

**TABLE 6-1.**

Comparison of Draft Allowances for Greensand and Shell Molds

|  | Greensand (deg) | Shell Mold (deg) |
|---|---|---|
| Normal | 2 | 1 |
| Minimum | 1 | 1/4 |
| In pockets | 3 to 10 | 1 to 2 |

## Mold Assembly

After the shell mold has been stripped from the pattern, it is ready for use, even though it is still warm. Various techniques are used to provide an intimate bond between the mold halves. These include clips, wire staples, tapes, and adhesives (Fig. 6-4). Tongue-and-groove arrangements at the joint help prevent the adhesive from entering the mold cavity and minimize *fins,* or small thin metal protrusions at the parting line of the casting.

**Fig. 6-4.** The two halves of the shell mold can be assembled with clips as shown or, more commonly, with phenolic resin adhesives.

The most satisfactory method of sealing shell halves is with a thermosetting resin of the same general type as the shell-molding resin. The residual heat of the shell is enough to set the phenolic adhesive.

### Pouring

When there is likely to be considerable metalostatic pressure on the mold, it should be supported with backup material such as metal shot, gravel, or molding sand.

### Shake-Out

After the casting has solidified, regular shake-out techniques are used to free the casting from the shell. A series of screens may be used to separate the castings, chunks of mold, and backup materials.

### Sand Recovery

Although it is possible to recover the sand from the sand-resin mixture of the mold, the economics of this procedure is questionable unless the quantity is large.

The resin has to be burned out at high temperature. When this is done, the sand is considered to be the same as new, and it may be used either for greensand molding or recoated with resin for shell molding.

### Patterns and Cores

In order to withstand the heat of curing, the patterns used must be made of metal. Patterns made out of aluminum are satisfactory for short-run production, and gray cast iron, bronze, or steel may be used for high production. Although the pattern expands owing to the curing heat, this can be neglected, since the mold also shrinks after it is removed from the pattern.

Patterns for shell moldings are very accurate and are generally high-cost items. They are made by expert metal patternmakers or tool-and-die makers. They are used in a nearly polished condition.

Whenever possible, the cope and drag sections are placed on the same face of the pattern plate. This facilitates making a complete mold each cycle.

Cores are made by blowing the resin-coated sand into the corebox. The sand mixture is the same as that used for the mold. The corebox can be electrically heated or heated in an oven.

Hollow cores are made by filling the heated corebox with the coated-sand mix. After allowing a sufficient time to build up the proper wall thickness, the unfused sand can be dumped out. Completely hollow cores are made by dumping a predetermined amount of sand-resin mix into the hot corebox and then rotating it. Higher temperatures are used in core production, so curing-cycle times range from 15 to 25 sec, depending upon size.

### Blowing Shell Molds

A more modern approach to shell-mold making than the dump-box method described, is the shell-blowing method. In the dump-box method the sand is not always properly packed (Fig. 6-5). Places where the coated sand is loose or poorly packed lead to weak spots in the mold where the hot metal can break out.

**Fig. 6-5.** The dump-box method of coating the pattern may leave soft spots and areas of unequal density in the mold.

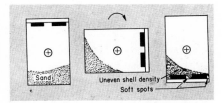

Air disturbances and venthole problems can be eliminated by having the sand-resin mixture fall on the pattern from a height greater than 12 in. rather than by blowing it in. However, most modern shell-molding machines are built on the principle of blowing the sand in place.

### Shell-Mold Machines

High-speed shell-mold-making machines are available that can handle from 30 to 200 full molds per hour, depending upon the pattern plate size and the number of stations available. These machines vary from the hand-operated single-station type to fully automatic multi-station units that combine the investment and curing cycles into a standard mechanized operation.

### Costs

Shell-mold costs are higher than for corresponding greensand molds. This is due primarily to the cost of the resin used. The latter, in turn, is governed by the market cost of the chemicals used to produce the resin. However, owing to the increased volume at which these chemicals are being manufactured, the price has steadily declined.

### Shell-Mold and Greensand Comparisons

Shown in Fig. 6-6 are a greensand mold and a shell mold made to produce the same item. The shell mold weighs one tenth that of the greensand mold, but the cost of the shell mold is greater. In order to cut the ultimate cost of shell-molded parts, weight must be reduced, cores eliminated, and machining reduced or eliminated.

**Fig. 6-6.** Comparison of a greensand mold with a shell mold for the same item. The greensand mold has a total weight of 185 lb, the shell mold 18 lb (courtesy Central Foundry).

The cost of the part shown at the left in Fig. 6-7 increased 40.4 percent when produced by the shell-molding process. The cost of the casting on the right increased 37.5 percent. The cost of the shell material alone amounted to over 2¢ per casting. In these examples, no advantage

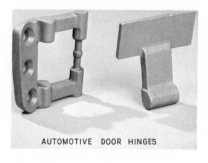

AUTOMOTIVE DOOR HINGES

**Fig. 6-7.** The cost of the casting on the left increased by 40.4 percent when produced by shell molding, that of the casting on the right by 37.5 percent (courtesy of Central Foundry).

was gained by making the parts as shell-mold castings. No machining could be eliminated, and castings produced by either method performed satisfactorily in service. It is obvious that conversion to the shell process was impractical.

The transmission drum shown in Fig. 6-8 was redesigned from the greensand version, shown in the cross-sectional view, to a shell-mold casting. The results were better casting surfaces, longer tool life, less metal that had to be removed by machining. In addition, balance drilling was reduced. The savings in reduced machining alone were enough to justify the use of a shell mold instead of a greensand mold.

**Fig. 6-8.** This transmission drum is a good example of shell-mold casting. Note the deep pocket that can be made with only a small amount of draft.

Some of the advantages of shell molding are summed up in the cross-sectional view of a hub, shown in Fig. 6-9 as cast in sand on the left, compared with the same part cast by the shell-mold process on the right. You will notice, on the greensand casting, that a considerable amount of finish stock must be machined from the inside diameter of the hub because the greensand molding requires a 10-deg draft and a

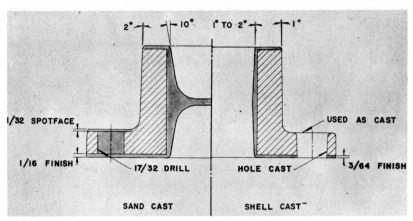

**Fig. 6-9.** Comparison of a greensand casting with a shell-mold casting.

⅛-in. web in the hub. In the shell casting, however, only 1 to 2 deg of draft are needed, and no web is necessary. In the sand casting the flange would be cast solid, and spot-facing and drilling operations would be necessary on the 17/32-in.-diameter holes. In the shell casting, these holes can be cast and the spot-face and drilling operations eliminated. The amount of finish stock allowed on the outside is also reduced. On the basis of these comparisons, it is up to the manufacturer to decide if the advantages gained will be sufficient to offset the increased cost of the shell casting.

The many variables that must be taken into account in casting make it difficult to set casting tolerances accurately. The tolerance chart, Table 6-2, gives a helpful comparison of what can be expected of each process. The figures refer to tolerances on one side of the parting line. It is necessary to add 0.004 in. to the values shown when the dimensions are across the parting line.

**TABLE 6-2.**

**A Comparison of Greensand and Shell-Mold Casting Tolerances**

| General Tolerance Chart | | |
|---|---|---|
| Size of Casting | Greensand | Shell-casting |
| 0 in.- 1 in. | ±0.023 | ±0.006 |
| 1 in.- 2 in. | ±0.030 | ±0.012 |
| 2 in.- 3 in. | ±0.030 | ±0.018 |
| 3 in.- 8 in. | ±0.045 | ±0.030 |
| 8 in.-12 in. | ±0.060 | ±0.041 |

Although greensand is still the most widely used method of producing castings, Fig. 6-10 shows the growing use of the shell-mold process in the automotive field, owing to the increasing emphasis on both reduced machining time and reduced weight. Another area of growth of the shell-molding process is that of core making for rather intricate sand castings such as engine cylinder blocks, heads, etc.

**PLASTER-MOLD CASTING**

Plaster-mold casting is somewhat similar to sand casting in that only one casting is made and then the mold is destroyed. The advantages of plaster are the superior surface finish, good dimensional accuracy, improved metal characteristics, and finer detail.

**Fig. 6-10.** Typical automotive parts produced by the shell-molding process (courtesy Central Foundry).

## Material

Metal-casting plaster is a specially formulated mold material for casting nonferrous alloys. Its main ingredients are 70 to 80 percent gypsum plaster and 20 to 30 percent fibrous strengthener. Water is added to make a creamy slurry.

## Process

The plaster slurry is poured into the flask over the pattern, which is mounted on a match plate. When the plaster reaches its semiset state, the pattern is removed. After both the cope and the drag molds have been made, the match plate is removed, and the mold is put in an oven for drying. It is important that all the moisture be removed so that no gas or steam is formed when the molten metal is poured into it.

Cores, if needed, are made in the same way. Coreboxes are usually highly polished and are made from brass, plastics, white metal, aluminum, or magnesium. The process of pouring a plaster core and the assembly of its parts are shown in Fig. 6-11.

Patterns are usually made out of lightly lacquered plaster, sealed wood, or polished metal. Flexible molded-rubber and plastic-composition materials may also be used for patterns when undercuts are encountered. The patterns are covered with a thin film of soap, lard oil, or paraffin oil to aid in removal from the plaster. Many commercially

(a)        (b)

**Fig. 6-11.** (a) Pouring plaster into corebox to make cores for a tire-mold tread ring. (b) Assembling plaster cores into mold (courtesy Aluminum Company of America).

available waxes, when rubbed down with a soft cloth, make excellent parting compounds.

### Applications

Plaster casting is generally limited to metals whose melting point does not exceed 2,100°F. It is particularly good in achieving fine finishes and close tolerances (32 to 125 micro in.) in aluminum. Other metals regularly cast in plaster molds are beryllium, copper, brasses, and bronzes.

Owing to the fact that plaster has a low thermal conductivity, the metal remains in a fluid state longer and is able to fill very thin (0.040-in.) sections. Heat extraction can be increased by adding other ingredients to the plaster when needed.

Some examples of plaster-cast items in everyday use are a wide variety of gears, handles, levers, household hardware, toys, etc. Little or no machining is required on the finished part. Some plaster-cast parts are shown in Fig. 6-12.

### Expansion Plasters

Plasters are available that expand when they set. The amount of expansion can be controlled by the plaster-to-water ratio. Values of 1/16 to 1/4 in. per ft can be obtained.

Expansion plasters are used in making patterns, match plates, and models. The plaster automatically compensates for the shrink allowance of the cast metal. For example, if a new metal pattern is to be made to replace an old wooden one, the expansion plaster is cast over the wooden pattern. When it sets, the cavity will be larger than the

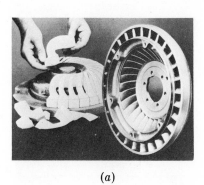

*(a)*

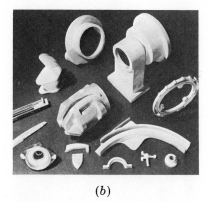

*(b)*

**Fig. 6-12.** (*a*) Plaster casting used to cast aluminum-alloy parts for automatic transmissions. (*b*) Typical casting applications of the plaster process (courtesy Aluminum Company of America).

wooden pattern. However, when the aluminum is cast in the cavity, it will shrink as it cools and be the same size as the original wooden pattern.

## INVESTMENT CASTING

### Lost-Wax Method

Investment casting is a specialized process often called the *lost-wax method*. It was used centuries ago in China and Japan to produce beautiful statuary. Basically, it consists of pressing wax or plastic into a split metal mold. When the material is hard, it is taken out and the fins are removed. Other parts of the assembly may be fastened together at this time, or several assemblies may be gated together. The assembled gated clusters are then dipped in a very-fine-grained slurry of refractory powder and bonding material. This process is referred to as the *investment* of the pattern. After dipping, coarser sand is shaken over the cluster. This sand adheres to the wet slurry and builds up a thicker wall section. The built-up clusters are then placed in metal containers or flasks, and the final investment material is poured around them (Fig. 6-13).

A vibrating table equipped with a vacuum pump is used to eliminate all air from the investment. In some cases a partial vacuum is created around the flasks to assist in this process. After investment, the completed flasks are heated slowly to complete the drying of the mold and then to melt or burn out the wax, plastic, patterns, runners, and sprues. When the molds have reached a temperature of over

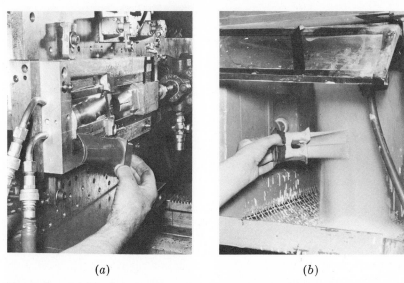

$(a)$                                        $(b)$

**Fig. 6-13.** ($a$) The investment casting process starts with a wax pattern made by injecting a special type of hot wax into a die. ($b$) The wax pattern is covered with ceramic material, which now becomes the mold shell, later to be filled with metal.

1000°F, they are ready for pouring. Vacuum is sometimes applied to the flasks during the pouring operation. In other cases, air pressure or centrifugal methods may be employed to ensure complete filling of the mold cavities. Molds that are not difficult to fill may be poured by gravity, as in greensand molds.

**Fig. 6-14.** Investment-cast parts are checked with care, utilizing contour transcribers, X-ray machines, gages, and ultraviolet light.

When the metal has cooled, the investment material is removed by means of vibrating hammers or by tumbling. As with other castings, the gates and risers are cut off and ground down, and final inspection is performed (Fig. 6-14).

### Frozen-Mercury Process

Frozen mercury may be used for the pattern in place of the wax or plastic mentioned previously. This variation of the investment-casting process offers certain advantages, namely, excellent surface finish, intricate shapes, and high degree of accuracy. The pattern is made by pouring the mercury in precision steel dies and chilling at −100°F. In Fig. 6-15 the frozen-mercury pattern is being removed from the die.

**Fig. 6-15.** Frozen mercury pattern after removal from steel die.

When wax is heated for melting out, it expands with a volumetric increase of about 9 percent. Mercury has a volumetric expansion of 3.5 percent. Thus, the strains imparted to the mold walls are very low compared to the wax. Because of this, large investment castings can be made.

Unlike other investment-casting methods, in the frozen-mercury process the dipping is done in a slurry at −80°F. The shell mold is made by successively dipping in slurries of increasing viscosity until a thickness of about ⅛ in. or more is reached.

After the desired shell has been built up, the mercury is extracted by introducing the mercury at room temperature in the sprue or gate. After most of the mercury is washed out, the mold is allowed to come to room temperature and the remaining mercury is poured out. Recovery of the mercury is almost 100 percent. The remainder of the process is quite similar to the lost-wax method.

A frozen-mercury investment casting has been used to replace as many as 25 assembly operations. The frozen mercury can be welded into intricate shapes merely by bringing the two parts into intimate contact. Shown in Fig. 6-16 is a built-up assembly that has been redesigned for investment casting. In it 20 separate pieces have been replaced by 1.

**Fig. 6-16.** A built-up assembly has been redesigned into a one-piece investment casting (courtesy Kolcast Industries Inc.).

### Applications

Investment castings are used when complex parts are needed or when a complex part is made out of an alloy that is difficult to machine. The parts require no draft, since the pattern is melted out and the mold is destroyed when the part is removed.

Investment castings are most appropriate when:

1. One casting can be redesigned to take the place of several.

2. The part will perform better if made out of tough alloy that may present machining difficulties.

3. Welding, soldering, or mechanical fastening is undesirable.

4. The quantity needed is not large.

5. The design is subject to change after a few hundred pieces or before it is finalized into expensive long-run tooling.

6. Accuracy and reproducibility are needed.

### Tolerance

Tolerances as low as 0.005 in. per in. are obtainable by the investment method, but 0.005 in. or better will result in lower casting charges.

## Materials Cast

Investment casting is applicable to both ferrous and nonferrous metals. It probably is most important for alloys which withstand high stresses, have good oxidation resistance, and are difficult to machine and weld. Various parts made by the investment process are shown in Fig. 6-17.

**Fig. 6-17.** Examples of investment-cast parts (courtesy Arwood Precision Casting Corp.).

## Shaw Process

The newest of the investment-casting techniques is known as the Shaw process. By this process, castings can be made that range in size from a few ounces to 5,000 lb.

The process consists of pouring a slurrylike mixture of refractory aggregate, hydrolized ethyl silicate, and a jelling agent over a pattern. The pattern need not be expendable as in other investment processes. It can be made of wood, plaster, or metal. The mix is allowed to form a flexible jell over the pattern, after which it is easily stripped off. The mold is then ignited with a torch to burn off the volatile portion of the mix. After this, it is brought to a red heat in a furnace, which results in a rigid refractory mold.

Steel castings having ⅛-in. wall thickness and weighing 100 pounds have been cast in molds of this type. On small castings, tolerances may be held within 0.002 in. per in. but on larger pieces the tolerance is generally 0.010 in. per in. The surface finish varies from 80 to 120 $\mu$ in. Parting lines are visible on the casting where the two mold halves are put back together. Pattern-to-finish casting time can be done in 2 hr.

The Shaw process originated in England, but has met with some variations in this country. By using the ceramic slurry to set on a chamotte-type sand mold, it can be baked out in 5 min. (A chamotte-type sand mold is made up of special molding sands containing lime, aluminum, and silicate.) Solid ceramic molds, often used in the Shaw process, require 4 to 5 hr to bake out the trapped gases. The thin ceramic facing allows the Shaw process to be automated. One machine is capable of turning out 120 molds per hour.

Both the Shaw process and the lost-wax method have been combined to gain the special advantages of each. The Shaw process has the advantage of low pattern and tooling costs. However, the pattern contours must be such that the flexible mold can be stripped off. This somewhat limits the angles or curvatures that can be made.

By setting wax-pattern components into the regular pattern or corebox, practically any configuration or complexity can be made. A closeup view of how the combined process operates is shown in Fig. 6-18. In (*a*), all but the curved portion of the blade in the impeller hub is a permanent-type metal pattern. In (*b*), the curved portion of the blade is added, with a consumable-wax pattern. Shown in (*c*) is the cross section of the blade after investment, with the metal portion of the pattern withdrawn and the wax insert still in place. At (*d*) the wax is melted out, leaving a clean, smooth contour.

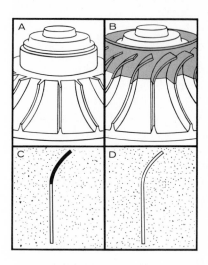

**Fig. 6-18.** A combination of the Shaw process and the lost-wax method was used to produce this impeller hub. (*a*) metal pattern; (*b*) wax pattern added to metal pattern; (*c*) cross-sectional view after investment, metal pattern removed; (*d*) cross section after wax has been melted out (courtesy Lebanon Steel Foundry).

### CENTRIFUGAL CASTING

Most molds are filled with metal simply by the force of gravity; however, methods have been developed that allow pressure to be exerted on the molten metal to provide greater density and more uniform structure. Various centrifugal methods are used to keep the metal under pressure as it is cast. The two principal ones are termed *centrifugal* and *centrifuge*.

## Centrifugal Casting

In true centrifugal casting, the molten metal is poured into a hollow cylindrical mold spinning about either a horizontal or a vertical axis at speeds sufficient to develop 60 to 75 g's (gravities) of centrifugal force. This force causes the liquid metal to flow to the outside of the mold and to remain there in the shape of a hollow cylinder. Heavier components within the metal are thrown outward with greater force than the lighter particles. This helps eliminate light non-metallic particles and impurities, which are congregated inward toward the axis of rotation through flotation (Fig. 6-19). These impurities can then be removed by a light machining operation.

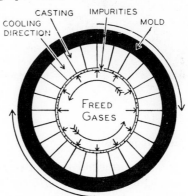

**Fig. 6-19.** The principle of centrifugal casting is to produce a dense high-grade metal by throwing the heavier metal outward and forcing the impurities to congregate inward (courtesy Janney Cylinder Co.).

The mold for centrifugal casting may be made by lining a cylindrical flask with 1 to 2½ in. of sand. The pattern is placed in the center of the mold, and the sand is rammed between the flask wall and the pattern. The pattern is intermittently raised several inches at a time until the top is reached. The sand lining is washed with a mold dressing and baked in a core oven. Cast-iron pipe may be cast directly in cylindrical water-cooled molds with no sand lining.

After pouring the casting, spinning it, and allowing it to cool, it is shaken out, cleaned, and heat-treated to obtain various desired properties.

Some of the largest diameters in the greatest as-cast lengths are shown in Fig. 6-20. Even though only one special application is shown with specifications, the uses are many: rolls, sleeves, rings, bushings, cylinders, liners, tubes, shells, pressure vessels, retorts, pump rotors, and piping. Short lengths are centrifugally cast in diameters up to 62 in. or as small as 2 in.

Although the inner surface is usually round, the outside need not be. It can be any symmetrical shape—hexagonal, octagonal, or square. Occasionally, bosses and flanges are incorporated into the design.

  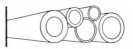 

| up to 33 feet long (depending on diameter or wall thickness) | from 7 to 54 inches in outside diameter | light or heavy walled components | annular parts sectioned from these cylinders |

(a)

(b)

**Fig. 6-20.** (a) Some examples of centrifugal castings that are available in stainless, carbon, and low-alloy steels. (b) A centrifugal casting used in a liquid-air converter machine having very close tolerance (courtesy Sandusky Foundry and Machine Co.).

### Centrifuge Casting

The principal method employed in centrifuge casting consists of arranging the molds on a "wheel." The pouring sprue is at the hub and the gates run down to each of the molds, similar to the spokes on the wheel. This method is particularly adaptable to small intricate castings that would ordinarily be difficult to gate. Risers are usually not necessary.

Molds used for centrifuge casting may be sand (green or dry), plaster, steel, cast iron, or graphite. Cores also may be used. The molds are made very close to tolerance, with little or no allowance for machining.

### PERMANENT MOLDING

One distinct disadvantage of the sand-casting processes is that the mold is destroyed each time it is used. It is natural that attempts would be made to make permanent metal molds. In the Middle Ages, iron molds were used to produce pewterware, such as cups, pitchers, and other utensils. Later, tin soldiers were made by pouring molten metal into iron molds that were hinged together. After a suitable time, the bulk of the still-liquid metal was poured out. The result was a thin-walled casting produced by what is termed *slush molding*.

Permanent molding includes two main types—die casting and permanent-mold casting.

## Die Casting

The search for smoother, more-accurate castings, produced at higher rates, led to applying pressure to the molten metal and the use of die-cut steel molds. By 1904, automobile bearings were being die-cast. Die casting refers to both the process and the product. Today, die casting is used to produce unlimited quantities of parts of such uniformity and accuracy that machining costs are either greatly reduced or eliminated entirely. Die casting is generally considered a one-step process, because molten metal is converted in a matter of seconds from a fluid into a finished or semifinished product.

The process consists of injecting molten metal at high pressures (100 to 100,000 psi) into a split metal die cavity. Within a fraction of a second, the fluid alloy fills the entire die, including all the minute details. Because of the low temperature of the die (it is water-cooled), the casting solidifies quickly, permitting the die halves to be separated and the casting ejected.

If the parts are small, several parts may be cast at one time in what is known as a *multiple-cavity* die.

**Machines.** Two main types of machines are used to produce die castings. The *hot-chamber* machine, shown in sectional view in Fig. 6-21, is used for casting zinc alloys. In this type of machine, a supply of molten metal is kept in a holding pot (*a*) so that, as the plunger (*b*) descends, the required amount of zinc alloy is automatically forced into the die (*c*). As the piston retracts, the cylinder is again filled with the right amount of molten metal.

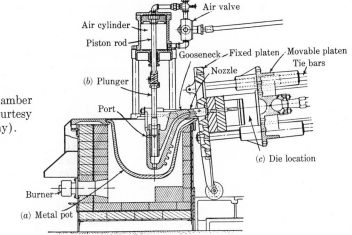

**Fig. 6-21.** The hot-chamber die-casting process (courtesy New Jersey Zinc Company).

The *cold-chamber* machine shown in Fig. 6-22 is used for aluminum, magnesium, and copper alloys. It derives its name from the fact that the metal is ladled into the cold chamber for each shot. This procedure is necessary in die-casting the higher-melting-point alloys, because these metals pick up iron if left in molten form in contact with an iron holding pot or plunger. This iron pickup not only would cause the plunger to freeze in the cylinder but would affect the properties of the die castings produced.

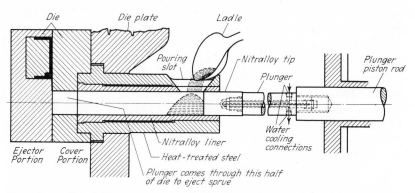

**Fig. 6-22.** Schematic view of the cold-chamber die-casting process (courtesy American Zinc Institute Inc.).

Castings are removed automatically from the die by ejector pins. Most of the castings will have flash where the two die halves come together. This may be removed with trimming dies, or abrasive wheels on larger castings, and by barrel finishing on the smaller sizes.

There are die-casting machines capable of handling over 60 lb of metal per shot. Automobile engine blocks are being made on machines of this type.

**Disadvantages.** The first cost of both the machine and the die is high. Machines cost upwards of $30,000, and dies may run from $1,000 to over $30,000. Die cost is high because of the accuracy to which they are made and the time required to put a high polish on all the cavity surfaces. Dies for zinc castings call for intermediate grades of die steels (heat-treated for long production runs). The higher-melting-point alloys of aluminum, magnesium, and copper require special die steels properly heat-treated.

The sharpest restriction in the use of die castings comes from the limited range of die-casting metals. However, through research and close quality control, maximum physical properties are being secured from the metals being used.

Some difficulty is encountered in getting consistently sound castings, particularly in the larger capacities. Gases tend to be entrapped, which results in small holes in the casting, with a subsequent loss in strength and the annoyance of leaks. Some machines are being modified to put the metal under vacuum to eliminate this source of trouble.

**Advantages.** Castings of extreme smoothness are produced with zinc alloys, and, if the die cavities are properly polished, castings can be plated with little or no additional finishing. This fact, together with the ease and speed of plating the castings with brass, nickel, or chromium, is the primary reason for using zinc die castings for hardware and decorative applications. They are used extensively in automobiles for decorative trim, fuel-system parts, ignition-system parts, window-operating mechanisms, chassis, and grille. The aircraft industry finds wide use for die castings, particularly those made from magnesium, because of the weight factor. Die castings, ranging in size from eight-cylinder engine blocks to tiny instrument parts, are used by almost every industry. A few examples are shown in Fig. 6-23.

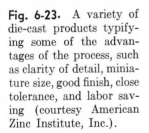

**Fig. 6-23.** A variety of die-cast products typifying some of the advantages of the process, such as clarity of detail, miniature size, good finish, close tolerance, and labor saving (courtesy American Zinc Institute, Inc.).

Probably the greatest single advantage of die casting is the low end cost. Where production runs are long and an appreciable degree of complexity or precision is indicated, die castings are the most economical. The cost per item can be low because of the speed of production and the small amount of labor involved.

Compared with molded plastics, die castings have the advantages of greater strength and stability; they provide more secure anchorage for screws and other fasteners and are generally superior in durability.

Inserts of other materials can be placed in the die cavity and permanently assembled into the casting when the molten metal flows around it. These inserts are usually used to incorporate stiffening or bearing materials. The metallic parts of some zippers are die-cast around the cloth that supports them.

### Metals Used.

ZINC. Zinc alloys account for three fourths of the total tonnage of die castings produced, because they present the most favorable combination of low cost per casting, good physical properties, and ease of casting and finishing. The average melting point of zinc alloys is 716°F. Casting is commonly done at temperatures of 750° to 800°F. Speeds up to 500 casting cycles per hour can be obtained.

ALUMINUM. Aluminum alloys rank second in die-cast use. In some cases they cost no more than zinc castings of the same dimensions. The primary advantage is light weight. Die-casting rates are lower than for zinc, commonly from 80 to 200 die fillings per hour.

COPPER ALLOYS OR BRASS. Brass has the highest physical properties of the die-casting group, but, because of the high melting points of such alloys (ranging up to 1700°F) the die life is short, depending upon the die steels used and the mass volume of the casting sections. Copper alloys have a high specific gravity, and cost per casting is higher than for aluminum or zinc castings. However, this is offset by physical properties of strength, high hardness, and good corrosion resistance. About 150 cycles can be obtained per hour.

### Design Considerations.
As with other casting processes, it is desirable to have as nearly uniform sections as possible. Fillets and radii are preferred to sharp corners. Inserts may justify the higher cost of production due to slower operation, but they must be designed so that they can be positively located and locked in the die. Large flat surfaces should be avoided, especially where appearance in the final assembly is important.

MINIMUM DRAFT REQUIRED
        Outside walls: $\frac{1}{2}$° minimum
        Inside walls: 1° minimum
$\frac{1}{8}$ to $\frac{1}{4}$-in.-diameter cores: 0.020 in. per in. in aluminum
                               0.016 in. per in. in zinc
$\frac{1}{4}$ to 1-in.-diameter cores: 0.016 in. per in. in aluminum
                               0.012 in. per in. in zinc

MINIMUM TOLERANCES REQUIRED

Aluminum ± 0.003 in. for first inch plus ± 0.001 in. per additional linear inch

Zinc: ± 0.002 in. for first inch plus ± 0.001 in. per additional linear inch

MACHINING ALLOWANCE. When machining is necessary, an allowance of 0.010 to 0.020 in. over the final dimension should be left to give a definite cut for the tool. Standard tools and cutters can be used quite satisfactorily, but greater speeds and better finishes can be obtained with larger rake and clearance angles.

The diagram in Fig. 6-24 shows the various stages in the design and production time of an average die casting.

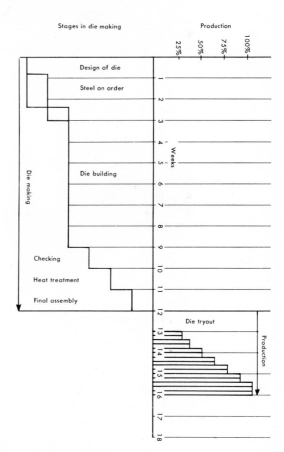

**Fig. 6-24.** Diagram showing the various stages in design and production of an average die casting (courtesy The Hoover Company).

## Permanent-Mold Casting

The permanent-mold process is quite similar to the die-cast process in that the molds are made of metal—usually cast iron, die steels, graphite, copper or aluminum. The cast mold is machined to obtain certain dimensional tolerances and to get proper draft angles. Vent plugs are inserted into the cavity to allow gases to escape when the molten metal is poured into the cavity. Some of the steps used in making the mold are shown in Fig. 6-25.

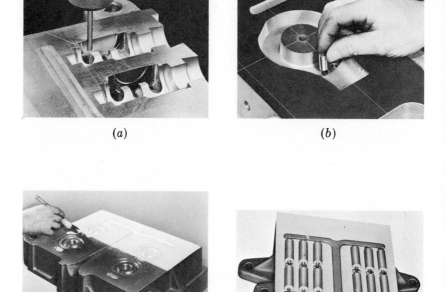

(a)  (b)

(c)  (d)

**Fig. 6-25.** Some steps in producing a cast-iron permanent mold. (a) machining the mold; (b) inserting vent plugs; (c) treating the mold; (d) sample casting (courtesy Eaton Mfg. Co.).

**Pouring Permanent Molds.** Permanent molds may be poured individually or mounted on special turntables (Fig. 6-26). The turntable consists of an actuating mechanism for opening and closing the molds as they continually rotate around a central hub. The complete cycle of the machine can be made in 2 to 6 min, during which time the metal is poured, cooled, and ejected from the mold. Ordinarily, two operators are required, one to pour molten metal into the mold and the other to eject the castings after the molds are mechanically opened. The mold is automatically cleaned, coated with a refractory material,

**Fig. 6-26.** A semiautomatic permanent-mold machine (courtesy Eaton Mfg. Co.).

and closed to protect it from the heat of the molten metal preparatory to another cycle of operation. When cored castings are produced, a third operator is used to set the cores in the molds.

**Disadvantages and Advantages.** The main disadvantage of permanent-mold casting is similar to that of permanent-mold die castings—high initial cost of tooling. The size of the castings is also limited by the mold-making equipment and the mold machine, usually not much over 100 lb.

The advantages of permanent-mold casting over sand castings include generally higher mechanical properties with smoother casting finish, good dimensional uniformity with less finish stock, improved pressure tightness, and ease of adaptability to automatic high production.

The higher mechanical properties stem from the rapid solidification, which improves soundness and microstructure. In the case of cast iron, the minute expansion caused by the conversion of combined carbon to graphite and ferrite is restricted owing to the rigidity of the mold. Thus internal shrinkage and porosity do not occur. The higher cooling rate of permanent-mold castings develops higher strength. For example, regular SAE 110, a fully annealed sand-cast gray iron, has a tensile strength of 20,000 psi, whereas a permanent-mold casting of the same material has a tensile strength of 57,000 psi.

The most frequently used casting processes are summarized in Table 6-3.

TABLE 6-3.

### Review of Principal Casting Processes

| | Advantages | Limitations |
|---|---|---|
| Sand casting | Almost any metal can be used; almost no limit on size and shape of part; extreme complexity possible; low tool cost; most direct route from pattern to mold | Some machining always necessary; castings have rough surfaces; close tolerance difficult to achieve; long thin projections not practical; some alloys develop defects |
| Shell-mold casting | Rapid production rate; high dimensional accuracy; smoother surfaces; uniform grain structure; minimized finishing operations | Some metals cannot be cast; requires expensive patterns, equipment, and resin binder; size of part limited |
| Plaster-mold casting | High dimensional accuracy; smooth surfaces; almost unlimited intricacy; low porosity; plaster mold is easily machined if changes are needed | Limited to nonferrous metals and relatively small parts; mold-making time is relatively long |
| Investment casting | High dimensional accuracy; excellent surface finish; almost unlimited intricacy; almost any metal can be used | Size of part limited; requires expensive patterns and molds; high labor costs |
| Permanent-mold casting | Good surface finish and grain structure; high dimensional accuracy; repeated use of molds (up to 25,000 times); rapid production rate; low scrap loss; low porosity | High initial mold costs; shape size and intricacy limited; high-melting-point metals such as steel unsuitable |
| Die casting | Extremely smooth surfaces; excellent dimensional accuracy; rapid production | High initial die costs; limited to nonferrous metals; size of part limited |

| | Advantages | Limitations |
|---|---|---|
| Centrifugal and centrifuge casting | Centrifugal force helps fill mold completely. Gases and impurities are concentrated nearest center of rotation. Solid good outer surface, gates and risers can be kept to a minimum. | Alloys of separable compounds may not be evenly distributed. Castings must be symmetrical. Centrifuge — generally limited to small intricate castings. |

## QUESTIONS

1. Can the sand used in shell molds be economically recovered?

2. Why are shell-mold patterns generally more expensive than those used in greensand casting?

3. On what basis is it possible for shell molding to compete with sand casting?

4. What general tolerances can be expected in shell molding if taken on both sides of the parting line?

5. What are some advantages of plaster casting?

6. Explain what is meant by investment in the investment-casting process.

7. Why is frozen mercury a good pattern material to use in the investment-casting process?

8. Where does the investment-casting process find its best applications?

9. How does the Shaw process differ from conventional investment-casting procedures?

10. What are some considerations in the use of inserts in die castings?

11. What is the difference between centrifugal casting and centrifuge casting?

12. What materials are most often used for die casting? Why?

13. (a) What are some difficulties encountered in the die casting of comparatively large items such as automobile engine blocks? (b) What is one method of overcoming this difficulty?

14. Why are most die castings not made out of high-strength materials?

15. How do tolerances compare for die casting and investment casting?

16. What are some advantages and limitations of permanent-mold casting?

17. What factors lead to higher product strength in permanent-mold casting than in sand casting?

18. How does the amount of draft used on shell molds compare with that of greensand molds?

19. What are some possible causes of poor shell-mold castings?

20. What are some of the limitations of plaster casting?

## PROBLEMS

1. The hub shown in Fig. 6-9 can be made by sand casting or shell molding. Assume the following savings per part are made by shell molding: Weight reduction, ½ lb. Machining time reduction, 5.2 min. Tooling cost reduction, 1.7 cents. Labor and overhead are calculated at $10.00 per hr. Cast iron cost is figured at 16 cents per lb. Assume the production rate is the same by either method. How much could be added to the shell-molding cost and still show a 10 percent cost reduction over sand casting?

2. Enlarge to full size the one-half scale sketches shown here, and indicate by adding shaded areas and dimensions how machining allowances and draft will differ between the sand cast and the shell-molded part.

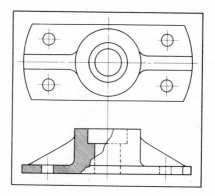

3. How long after the design has been completed for a die casting can it be expected to be in final assembly? When in 50 percent production? When in 100 percent production?

## REFERENCES

*Casting*, Kaiser Aluminum, Kaiser Aluminum and Chemical Sales Inc., Chicago, 1956.

Kramer, Irvin R., "Frozen Mercury Process Increases Scope of Investment Casting," *The Tool Engineer*, May, 1955.

Winter, O. W., "Shell Molding Equipment and Its Use," *The Tool Engineer*, April, 1955.

# 7

# FORGING AND
# HOT WORKING

**F**ORGINGS MAY be defined as metal that has been heated and hammered into shape. The process goes as far back as primitive man, who hammered and shaped his simple tools and weapons while they were still glowing hot from the fire. The men of ancient Greece and Cyprus had exquisite swords and daggers of forged steel. In the United States, forging played an important part in paving the way for interchangeable manufacture. In 1870 John Mahlon Marlin explored the then relatively new technique of the exact duplication of parts by forging the metal between closed dies. The result was the Ballard single-shot rifle which became world-famous not only because of its performance but because replacement parts that actually fit could be obtained.

The advantages of forging parts for the Ballard rifle and other guns were greater strength, lighter weight, and better finish. These same factors are still important contributions of forging today.

In forging, greater strength is obtained largely through the kneading action on the hot metal as it is shaped between the dies. By repeated blows, the hot metal is made to fill the die cavities. In this process of kneading the metal, a very beneficial grain flow takes place. The grain flow changes from a straight flow pattern, obtained in the original rolling process, into the exact repetition of the part contours (Fig. 7-1). The fact that the flow lines remain unbroken and that a tough, fibrous structure results is one of the greatest values of forging.

Because of the density of the metal, obtained by kneading and the fibrous grain flow, forgings are generally the strongest form in which metals can be used.

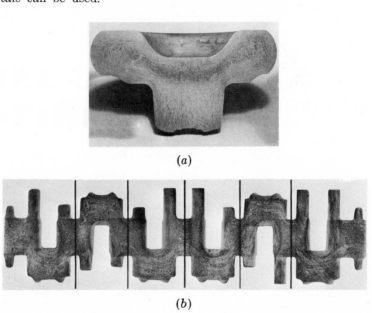

(a)

(b)

**Fig. 7-1.** The grain flow of the metal follows the part contour, contributing to the tough, fibrous structure of the forging. (a) courtesy The Ajax Manufacturing Co. (b) courtesy Drop Forging Association.

### Methods and Equipment

The basic methods of forging hot metal are drop forging, automatic closed die forging, machine or upset forging, press forging, hand forging, and heavy forging.

**Drop Forging.** Drop forgings get their name from the fact that the upper half of a die is raised and allowed to drop on the heated metal placed over the lower half of the die. It is estimated that at least 90 percent of the total tonnage of forgings produced commercially are of the drop-forging type. Drop hammers are generally of either the gravity or the steam type.

Gravity hammers. The most common kind of gravity hammer utilizes a hardwood board which is made to pass vertically between a pair of rotating rolls. The operator allows the rolls to press against the board which raises it quickly to the top of its stroke where it is held by dogs. As the operator releases the holding dogs, the board, with the ram and die fastened to the end of it, falls directly on the hot metal.

Single-acting steam or air cylinders are also used to raise the ram in place of the board and rollers. Air-lift hammers allow variations in the length of the stroke, and consequently the force of the blow can be varied. This is particularly useful in the first few forming operations where the metal has to be rolled and gathered. After that, the full force of the hammer can be used for the finishing operations.

STEAM DROP HAMMERS. Steam drop hammers allow the operator to have constant control of the forging action. The motion of the ram is usually controlled by a foot treadle so that the upper die may be brought down with the force of a few pounds or of several hundred tons.

DROP-FORGING STEPS. After the dies have been made and placed in the hammer, the metal must be selected and cut to the proper length. The proper length may be enough to complete one or several parts. It is then heated thoroughly in a furnace until it is in a plastic condition. Controlled-atmosphere furnaces will keep down decarburization and scaling of the metal. The heating furnaces are usually located in close proximity to the forging presses. It is important that the proper temperature for the particular metal and the specific job be maintained throughout the various forging stages.

(1)

(2)

**Fig. 7-2.** The main forging steps are shown as fullering and edging (1, 2); blocking (3); finishing (4); and trimming (5) (courtesy The Drop Forging Association).

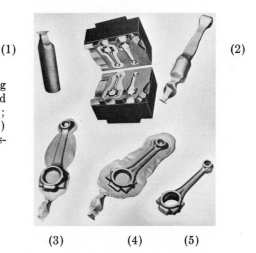

(3)          (4)          (5)

The first forging operations consist of preliminary shaping of the metal, referred to as *fullering* and *edging* (Fig. 7-2). In these preliminary steps the dies are made to reduce the cross-sectional area in one place and gather it in another which not only saves material but starts the fibrous grain flow of the metal.

The shape of the connecting rod shown as an example of forging is further obtained by several successive blows of the hammer in the blocking cavity. In this operation the *flash,* or excess metal, begins to appear. Next, the metal is brought to the finishing impression dies. Here heavy blows compel the plastic metal to fill completely every part of the cavity.

Following the forming operation comes the trimming. This is usually done on a separate trimming press with special trimming dies. In this case, both holes of the connecting rod are punched out at the same time.

**Automatic Closed-Die Forging.** Automation in the forging industry is comparatively new. The difficulties involved in synchronizing feeds and hammer blows seemed to present a problem not easily solved. Now, however, machines have been built that do automatically all the operations connected with this closed-die forging.

The process consists of taking the precut parts from a hopper through a conveyor-type furnace and then through part orientation to the preform and forging operations. The parts are then hot-trimmed, inspected, heat-treated, coined, cleaned, inspected again, and made ready for shipment (Fig. 7-3).

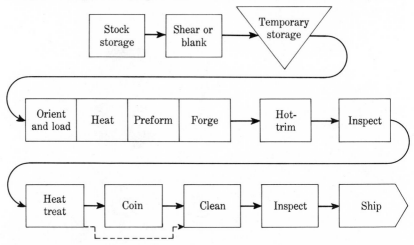

**Fig. 7-3.** Steps in layout for automated forging. From hot-trim on, the series represents optional operations that can be done to complete the product.

A schematic drawing of the type of machine used for automatic forging is shown in Fig. 7-4. You will note the two halves of the die are mounted on air-actuated impellers. The plane of impact is maintained in the center of the machine by means of an electronic compensator employing sensing heads that detect blow eccentricity. The impacter, as it is called, is rated by a number which represents its maximum blow energy expressed in thousandths of foot-pounds.

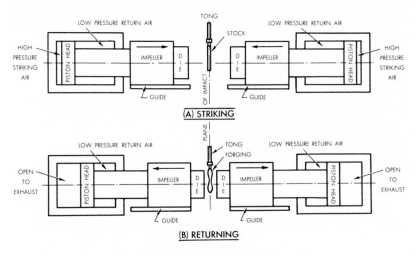

OPERATION OF THE IMPACTER

**Fig. 7-4.** The automatic-forging machine and schematic diagram of operation (courtesy Chambersburg Eng. Co.).

The average number of pounds of steel handled per hour is used in Table 7-1 as a basis for comparing automatic forging with conventional drop forging.

Overall controls can incorporate automatic shutdown of stock movement in the event of any mechanical failures. Warning devices signaling such things as low stock supply or any malfunctioning can also be included.

**TABLE 7-1.**

### Comparison of Automatic Forging with Conventional Drop-Hammer Operations*

| Size Impacter | Average Pounds of Steel/Hour | Comparable Gravity Drop Hammer | Average Pounds of Steel/Hour |
|---|---|---|---|
| #3 | 480 | 1,000 lb | 170 |
| #8 | 1,340 | 2,000 lb | 495 |
| #15 | 2,880 | ——— | — |

\* Chambersberg Eng. Co.

**Machine or Upset Forging.** Machine or upset forging consists of gripping heated bar stock between two dies and striking the protruding end with another die. The material can be increased considerably in diameter, and the final blow can be used to make the metal conform to the die cavities (Fig. 7-5).

**Fig. 7-5.** Dies and punches used in upset forging of a small cluster gear blank (courtesy The Ajax Mfg. Co.).

This process lends itself to the forging of pinion-gear blanks, flanges on axles, drawbars, valve stems, and many other parts that need a larger volume of metal on the end. Careful gathering of the metal results in controlled grain structure, with dense fiber for maximum strength.

Pierced parts may be made by the upset-forging method also. In this method the metal is displaced from the interior and made to flow around the outside, for the full length of the blank when necessary (Fig. 7-6).

**Press Forging.** In press forging, the plastic deformation of the metal is accomplished by a squeezing action. Both hydraulic and mechanical presses are used. The mechanical press is used for high-speed forging production. The hydraulic press is more versatile from the standpoint of varying the stroke length and the amount of pressure

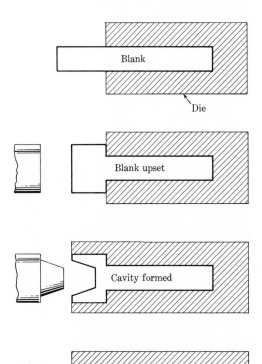

**Fig. 7-6.** Machine forging of a recessed cavity.

applied. Unlike forging with hammers using repeated impact blows, hydraulic presses operate entirely with squeezing force. It is applied continuously, with increasing intensity as the metal continues to flow.

Slugs of metal of the right size are prepared for the die cavity. As with drop forging, the metal may have to be shifted through a series of two or three dies before the finished part is produced.

Press forging is sometimes used in combination with drop-hammer forging. After the part has been forged in a drop-hammer press, it may be transferred to a mechanical press for sizing. A press forge may also be used for *coining,* which causes the metal to flow in a relatively small area by virtue of the heavy pressure exerted.

The structural characteristics of press forgings are generally equal to those of drop forgings. The process is generally limited to small parts and nonferrous-alloy pieces under 30 lb. The largest presses are the hydraulic type used in press forging. Mechanical presses generally range from about 500 to 8,000 tons in capacity, and hydraulic presses from about 250 to 5,000 tons in capacity for drop forging. Recently, however, under government subsidy, the process was expanded to use presses of 50,000-ton capacity for press forging.

**Hand Forging.** Hand forging is a process of forming metal between flat dies. Since it is similar to the village blacksmiths' methods, except that steam or hydraulic power is used, it is also called *smith forging*.

Hand forging requires a skilled operator to form metal parts without the aid of a die. The process is slow and is used only when the number of parts does not justify the use of a die. The size may range from less than 1 lb to parts weighing 200 tons or more. The larger sizes are handled by electric-hydraulic controls.

Die costs can be kept down on short runs by combining hand forging with press or drop forging. An example of this is shown in Fig. 7-7, where dies are used only for the last forming operation and for trimming.

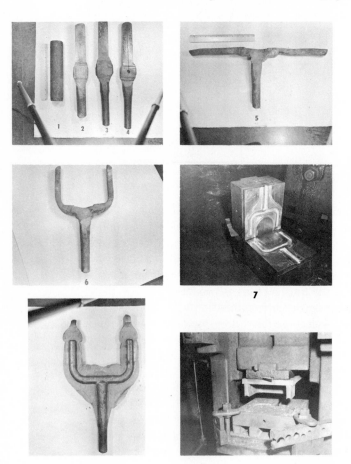

**Fig. 7-7.** An example of combining hand forging with drop forging to keep die costs down. (1) billet, (2) first forging, (3) second forging, (4) drilling and slotting, (5) bending to spread forks, (6) bending to fit yoke into die, (7) drop forging die, (8) untrimmed drop forging, (9) press with trimming die (courtesy Merrill Brothers)

The part is started as a round bar, using flat dies to rough-shape the ends. A hole is drilled through the center section and a saw cut made to separate the tines. A *bulldozer* is used to spread the tines and bend them to shape. (A bulldozer is a horizontal-type press especially adapted for bending and forming operations to prepare a forging for closed dies.) The completed blank is then put in the drop-forging die, after which it is trimmed to make the completed forging.

**Heavy Forging.**　The biggest forgings are produced by steel mills. They include rotors for turbines and generators, propulsion shafts for big ships, anvil bases, and columns for big presses.

A heavy forging made to order for a particular job starts out as an outsize hot-top ingot. It may measure 110 in. in diameter and weigh 500,000 pounds. Working with cranes and heavy chains, experienced forging crews squeeze the heavy shape under a hydraulic press that exerts up to 50,000 lb pressure. With this tremendous pressure, the hot steel can be worked or subjected to a kneading action all the way to the center. This removes some internal stresses and gives a dense tough structure.

A turbine roller like that shown in Fig. 7-8 may take several weeks in the furnace and, with machining and testing, may require 3 to 4 months to complete.

**Fig. 7-8.**　Forging a 100,000 lb steel ingot in a hydraulic forging press (courtesy *Steelways,* published by American Iron and Steel Institute).

After the forging crew get in their initial strikes, the ingot goes back to the reheating furnace in preparation for further forging to shape. The forging is alternately reheated 24 hr and forged 1 hr for about 1 week.

Before machining, the rotor is given a rough sonic test along its entire longitudinal axis. After machining, the forging is sent back to the furnace, where it is heated slowly to about 1,100°F and held at that temperature for 20 to 30 hr for stress relieving. The heat is then turned off and the forging is left to cool. This process is repeated for from several days to 1 week.

The forging is again brought back to the lathe, and an asbestos oven is built around it. Rods are placed at predetermined points on the circumference to check for warpage.

After three constant readings at 1,000°F, the furnace ends are removed and the rotor is allowed to cool. More readings are taken, and, if the rotor has failed to come within 0.002 in. runout tolerance, it is scraped.

**Auxiliary Forging Equipment.** In addition to the equipment already described, various other machines are needed for preliminary or small forging operations. These machines are helve hammers and forging rolls. The bulldozer, as previously described, is also considered an adjunct to the regular forging process.

HELVE HAMMERS. Helve hammers are high-speed hammers used in preparatory shaping of the metal or in *planishing*. Planishing is a term used to denote metalworking by short fast strokes for the purpose of smoothing the surface and obtaining greater overall accuracy.

FORGING ROLLS. Forging rolls are used primarily for reducing short thick sections of stock into long slender sections. The operator places the heated bar stock between semicylindrical rolls, where it is reduced in size by the half revolution of the roll. As the rolls reverse, the operator removes the stock and on the succeeding forward stroke inserts it between another set of rollers with smaller grooves. The process can be repeated between rolls with successively tighter clearance until the material is of the desired size and shape. Roll forging is used for making such parts as axle blanks, gear-shift levers, drive shafts, and leaf springs.

### Forging Practice

#### Materials.

FORGING-QUALITY METALS. Almost all the commonly used metals and alloys can be used for forging. When forging-quality metals are specified, this term refers to the special care used in selecting the metals, thus eliminating defects. As shown in Fig. 7-9, the ingot that will be rolled out and used for forging operations is poured in a hot-top mold so that more of the gases escape during solidification. Also, a little more of the top and bottom of the ingot are cropped to ensure high quality.

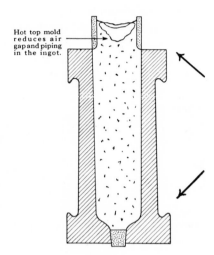

Hot top mold reduces air gap and piping in the ingot.

**Fig. 7-9.** Forging steels have a greater amount of cropping at both the top and the bottom of the ingot. In addition a hot top may be placed on the ingot to keep the pipe or hollow area from forming in the metal that will be used for forging.

VACUUM-DEGASSED STEEL. Another method developed to ensure high-quality steel is by vacuum degassing. Simply stated, the process consists of air-melted steel that is poured through a vacuum. During the process, much of the hydrogen, the major contributing factor to embrittlement and flaking in forgings, is removed. The steel produced is more ductile than air-poured steel.

Originally, the steel ladle was placed in an airtight chamber which was subjected to a vacuum. At the same time, helium gas was injected into the melt to increase the boiling action and expose more steel to the surface. A further protection was given the molten steel by pouring it into ingot molds filled with argon and protecting the pouring process with a blanket of argon.

VACUUM-ARC STEEL. Where exceptionally high-quality steel is required, vacuum-arc steel is made. The process consists of using air-melted steel to make an electrode. The electrode is then arc-melted into a water-cooled crucible under vacuum.

There is an increasing demand for large arc-melted ingots. As production facilities grow, it is expected that the price will drop. Most of the steel processed by vacuum has been of aircraft bearing quality. A major exception is the manufacture of hardened-steel rolls. Several of the major steel producers make such rolls at no premium to the user.

**Heat Treatment of Forgings.** After the forging has been formed, it may have large grains in one portion, where little or no forming is done, and fine grains where the metal is reduced. There is also some strain in the metal from the forging process. Therefore, *before* machining, the metal is generally normalized to produce uniform grain size and relieve some of the stresses, (Fig. 7-10).

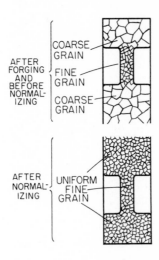

**Fig. 7-10.** In forged gear blanks, the crushing action reduces the grains in the web to a smaller size than the grains in the thicker sections. Normalizing refines this structure and produces grains of a more uniform size throughout the forging.

When steel forgings are to be hardened *after* machining, they are again normalized. This further refines the grain, takes out machining stresses, and helps eliminate cracking or distortion during quenching.

### Quantity and Cost

Parts that are to be made in closed dies generally require high production quantities to offset the high cost. Normally, these quantities will run from 10,000 to 100,000 pieces or more. As stated previously, this picture can be changed by using ingenuity in combining hand flat die forgings with closed dies. There are times, however, when limited quantities of forgings are produced simply because no other process can give the desired strength with the corresponding bulk.

In drop-hammer forging, as in casting, preliminary costs vary considerably, according to the complexity of the item. A rough approximation for small forgings of 1 lb or less would probably run from $1,000 to $2,000. Corresponding initial pattern costs for a casting would probably run between $100 and $200. However, differences to be considered will be the strength that can be obtained from a given weight of material, and secondary machining and finishing costs.

### Design Considerations

Most of the same factors that were discussed in sand-casting design apply also to forgings. Several factors which may call for slightly different design, include draft, angles, fillets, corners, shrinkages, cavities, and dimensional tolerances. Many of these terms are clarified by referring to Fig. 7-11.

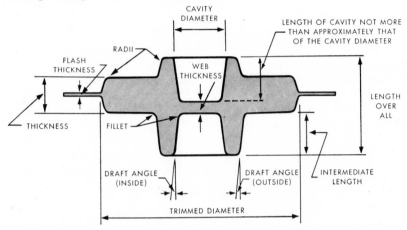

**Fig. 7-11.** The general design considerations shown are flash thickness, 0.040 in.; radii, a minimum of ⅟₁₆ in.; web thickness, ³⁄₁₆ in. minimum; draft angles, 3 to 10 deg for drop forgings and 1 to 5 deg for press forgings. Where possible, the larger part of the impression should be in the upper half so that the scale drops out and is blown away.

**Draft Angles.** Conventional draft angles vary with the type and size of forging. Drop forgings have from 3 to 10 deg, press forgings from 1 to 5 deg of draft. The deeper the cavity the greater the draft.

New tools and techniques have been developed in the forging field that reduce draft and corresponding excess metal. This process, referred to as *precision forging*, can, in many cases, eliminate the draft angle entirely. Because of die-cost considerations, parts have been confined to relatively small sizes ranging in plan area from approximately 25 to 200 sq in.

Some of these forgings have been made in cold dies and others in heated dies. In the cold dies, ejection mechanisms are used. Also, a number of different protective coatings have been used on various materials to permit linear movement in the plastic condition without detracting from the surface finish.

Remarkable features have been produced in some precision forgings. Web thicknesses have been forged as thin as 0.094 in. with pocket depths of 1¼ in. with "no draft" walls.

**Fillets and Corners.** Sharp corners must be avoided because they not only tend to decrease the life of the forging dies, but they require excessive pressures to fill. This may cause stress concentrations in the work. Fillets and corner-radii tolerances are relative to the size of the forging. If they are not specifically designated, the die engineers alter them to fit conditions in production. In general, the minimum fillets and radii must not be less than 1/16 in., and preferably more.

**Shrinkage Factor.** Shrinkage factors are primarily considerations for the die designer. Thus, unless specifically stated, the die designers make the necessary allowances which take into consideration the type of material, forging method, and finishing temperatures.

**Cavities.** In general, cavities should not be specified that are deeper than their diameter.

**Tolerances.** Tolerances on dimensions vary according to the size of the part. For example, a 1-in. part may have a tolerance of $\pm 0.008$ to 0.015 in., depending upon the type of material used and the forging process. On parts 6 in. and over, the tolerance range is usually $\pm 0.015$ to 0.031 in. Closer tolerances are obtained by coining the forging. This consists of restriking the parts in a heavy-duty mechanical press. It is possible to obtain tolerances on thickness dimensions within $\pm 0.005$ and sometimes $\pm 0.002$ in. The process of coining often results in eliminating machining operations.

**Machining Allowance.** Machining allowance is generally a minimum of 1/32 in. per surface. This increases if the surface is large, because it becomes more difficult to hold it true.

**Web Thickness.** The minimum web thickness should be approximately 3/16 in. with a $\pm 1/64$-in. tolerance. The approximate flash thickness will generally range from 0.040 to 0.080 in.

**Finishing.** Removal of ferrous oxide scale formed during forging and heat treatment can be done in several ways—sandblasting, tumbling with various abrasive materials, or pickling in sulfuric acid solutions.

**Summary of Conventional Forging Design.** The drawing (Fig. 7-12) will serve to summarize some of the most important forging-design principles, as follows:

1. Keep the parting line on one plane, if possible.

2. Design all radii as large as possible. Small radii cause die checking and may be difficult to machine in the forging die.

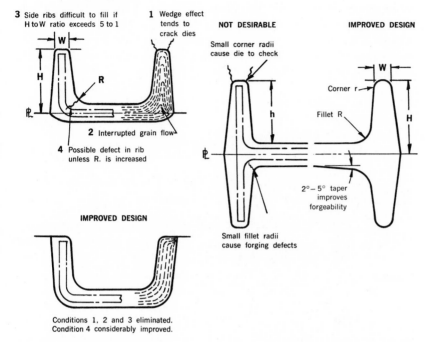

**NOT DESIRABLE**

**3** Side ribs difficult to fill if H to W ratio exceeds 5 to 1

**1** Wedge effect tends to crack dies

**NOT DESIRABLE**

**IMPROVED DESIGN**

Small corner radii cause die to check

Corner r

Fillet R

**2** Interrupted grain flow

**4** Possible defect in rib unless R. is increased

2°– 5° taper improves forgeability

**IMPROVED DESIGN**

Small fillet radii cause forging defects

Conditions 1, 2 and 3 eliminated. Condition 4 considerably improved.

**Fig. 7-12.** Desirable and undesirable features in forging design (courtesy *Metalworking*).

3. Make generous fillets. Small fillets often cause forging defects.

4. Make draft angles as large as possible. Small draft angles cause rapid die wear and may also cause the forging to stick in the die.

5. For economy in large complex objects, forge in two or more parts and then combine the assembly by welding or other fastening methods. This is especially important for short-run jobs where the cost of tooling may be prohibitive.

Careful observance of these principles will result in better forgings at less expense.

## HOT WORKING

### Hot Rolling

Hot rolling consists of taking the hot ingot from a soaking pit, where it has been kept at an elevated temperature, and rolling it first into *blooms* (large oblong squares) and then through a series of other rollers into structural shapes, pipe, and tubing.

**Structural Shapes.** The familiar structural shapes such as channels, H-beams, angles, and rails are produced between various types of forming rolls (Fig. 7-13). The blooms are heated to 2200°F in a continuous-type reheating furnace before being rolled into structural-steel shapes. A single pass between the rolls may reduce the cross section as much as 25 percent. However, it may take as many as 26 passes to produce a structural shape such as an I-beam.

3-high reversing mill

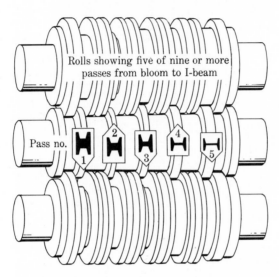

Rolls showing five of nine or more passes from bloom to I-beam

Pass no.

**Fig. 7-13.** Hot-rolling structural shapes (courtesy *Steelways,* published by American Iron and Steel Institute).

**Pipe and Tube Rolling.** Pipe and tubing are hot-rolled by several different methods. They may be made out of flat sheet stock, in which case the seam is either made as a lap or a butt weld.

BUTT-WELDED PIPE. Pipe that is to be butt-welded starts out as flat semifinished steel that is referred to as *skelp.* Grooved rollers bevel the edges so that, when they come together, they exactly match. The ends of the skelp are also cut so that they can easily enter the welding bell used to bend the edges of the heated (2600°F) skelp into a round form (Fig. 7-14).

Pipe size is designated by its nominal inside diameter up to 12 in. and its outside nominal diameter over 12 in. It is, however, the outside diameter of all sizes that is standardized so that lengths of any size will fit when they are coupled together.

Pipe is purposely drawn oversize and reduced by sizing rolls. Then, while the pipe is still soft, the very hard scale on the surface is removed by additional rolling.

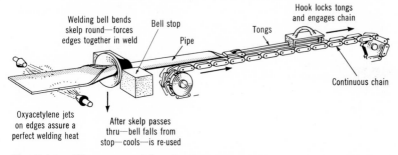

Welding bell bends skelp round—forces edges together in weld

Bell stop

Pipe

Tongs

Hook locks tongs and engages chain

Continuous chain

Oxyacetylene jets on edges assure a perfect welding heat

After skelp passes thru—bell falls from stop—cools—is re-used

**Fig. 7-14.** The process of forming butt-welded pipe (courtesy *Steelways*, published by American Iron and Steel Institute).

LAP-WELDED PIPE. The lap-welding process used in making pipe is quite similar to that used in making butt-welded pipe. The skelp is tapered at opposite edges so that they overlap where they are drawn through the die. The skelp is heated to a cherry-red color before entering the die and is reheated again to 2600°F after leaving the die. It is then rolled between forming rolls with a mandrel inside the pipe to press the lapped edges together, completing the weld. Additional rolling is done, as shown in Fig. 7-15, until the pipe is of the desired size and straightness.

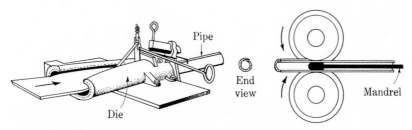

Pipe

End view

Mandrel

Die

**Fig. 7-15.** The process of forming lap-welded pipe.

RESISTANCE BUTT-WELDED TUBING. Resistance butt-welded tubing is another type of tubing closely associated with butt- and lap-welded pipe. However, since heat is required only for the welding, this process will be discussed in Chapter 16.

SEAMLESS TUBING. Seamless tubing can be made by either piercing or drawing.

*Piercing.* The process of making hot-pierced tubing consists of passing a hot-rolled billet between two biconical rollers and over a plug held on a support bar, often referred to as a mandrel (Fig. 7-16).

The biconical rolls serve to spin the round heated billet and force it forward. The piercing action is actually started previous to placing

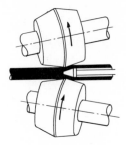

**Fig. 7-16.** Piercing of the hot billet is done between two biconical rollers and over a plug held on a support bar.

it between the rolls, by drilling, punching, or piercing with oxygen. The rolling, kneading action then moves the tube forward at high speed. The first pass makes a rather thick-walled tube, which is again rolled over a plug where it is converted into a longer tube with specified wall thickness. While it is still up to working temperature, it is passed onto a reeling machine which further straightens and sizes it (Fig. 7-17).

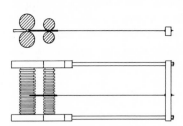

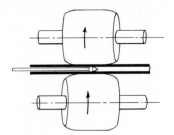

*Rolling over a plug to thinner wall and greater length in an automatic rolling mill*

*Burnishing the surface in a reeling machine*

**Fig. 7-17.** Specified wall thicknesses are obtained by further plug rolling and reeling.

If more accuracy and better finish are desired, the tube may be run through sizing dies. Smaller sizes are obtained by reheating the tubing in a furnace and running the tube through reducing rolls followed by straightening rolls. After cooling, the tubes are usually placed in a pickling bath of dilute sulfuric acid to remove the scale and oxide. If still greater accuracy and fine finish are desired, as is often the case in small-diameter tubing, the process is continued by cold drawing, as described in Chapter 16.

*Drawing.* Tubing and cylinders can be hot-drawn from relatively thick plate stock. The heated blank is placed in position over the die or cavity. The punch descends and pushes the metal through the die to form a cup (Fig. 7-18).

The process may be continued through a series of successively smaller dies and punches to obtain cylinders of the desired size and wall thickness. Oftentimes, a series of successively smaller dies is set up on a bench known as a *hot-draw bench.*

Seamless tubing and cylinders made in this way are used primarily for thick-walled cylindrical tanks.

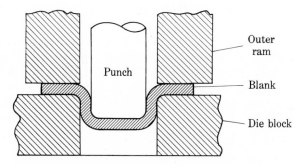

**Fig. 7-18.** Drawing a heavy plate into a cup shape. Successive draws can be made to make a deep cylinder or tubing.

## Extrusions

Extruding is a process in which a billet or slug of metal is forced by high pressure through an orifice that is shaped to provide the desired form to the finished part.

The process, in universal use in the aluminum industry, is represented diagrammatically in Fig. 7-19. The billet is heated to a temperature of 650° to 900°F and is placed in the hollow cylinder, normally 50° colder than the billet. Pressure anywhere from 30 to 70 tons per sq in. is applied by hydraulic pumps.

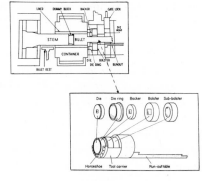

**Fig. 7-19.** Schematic diagram of the extrusion process.

Close temperature control for extruding is essential. A billet that is too cold will require extreme pressures, and an overheated billet will be hot short or weakened.

Commercial extruding is usually carried out with 5- to 7-in.-diameter billets cut 12 to 27 in. long. The billets may be either hot-rolled or cast. They usually have the outer surface removed or are peeled to eliminate surface defects in the billet.

Steel extrusions require a lubricant during the forming process. This is taken care of by carefully coating the hot billet with finely powdered glass. The glass becomes viscous when in contact with the hot billet and provides lubrication to the die and material.

**Materials.** Extrusions are most common among the nonferrous alloys of aluminum-, magnesium-, and copper-base alloys. However, various alloy steels such as AISI 4130, 4340, and 8360 are readily extrudable in rather intricate shapes. The regular 18-8 stainless steel also can be extruded, but tool life is somewhat shorter.

**Use.** Extruded shapes are exceptionally well suited to track and rail applications used extensively for materials handling. They are also used extensively in building hardware, automotive and aircraft parts, flooring strips, and many hardware items such as window sash, door trim, storm sash and doors, etc.

**Advantages.** Extrusions have to compete with similar shapes produced by rolling, casting, or forging. Therefore, they must offer certain advantages:

1. Because of the high reduction ratio (the cross-sectional area of the billet to the cross-sectional area of the shape produced) the metal has excellent transverse flow lines. Structurally speaking, this condition not only adds to the strength of the part but makes easier any secondary operations that may be needed.

2. Shapes can be extruded that are costly to produce by other means (Fig. 7-20).

3. New experiments have indicated that thinner walls can be obtained if the forming pressure is increased. With 200,000 to 240,000 psi pressure, the present wall thicknesses may be decreased 30 to 60 percent. This will offer new design and application possibilities for aluminum extrusions.

4. The cost of extrusion dies is relatively low, so, moderately short runs are practical. Dies are generally made from a chrome-molybdenum steel and heat-treated to a $R_c$ 47-50. More intricate dies can be cut out of hardened steel or carbide by electric-spark or ultrasonic machining.

Extruded shapes can often replace weldments and members previously machined from bar stock. The tonnage figure must, of course,

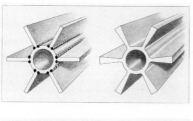
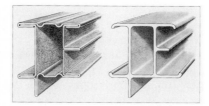

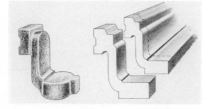

**Fig. 7-20.** Extrusions to facilitate design and eliminate steps in fabrication can be made in a wide variety of shapes (courtesy Reynolds Metals Company).

be considered. Where one or two special lengths are required, it is usually more economical to machine, weld, or fabricate by some other method. However, a small quantity such as 500 lb can sometimes be economically extruded.

A structural member, such as a special channel or angle, will carry a tooling charge of $180 to $200, and special shapes will rarely be more than $250. This is a small cost compared with mill roll charges. Also, the extrusion process allows low cost in-process redesign.

5. There is more flexibility in design for adjacent thin and heavy sections as well as for difficult reentrant angles. Sharp corners, not practical in other processes, can readily be obtained by extrusion.

**Limitations.** There are some limitations to the extrusion process that should be considered:

1. The size of the dies and presses that can be economically built is a limiting factor. The maximum size, at the present time, is about 60 in. wide.

2. Extruding speed is slow compared to roll forming. Roll forming may run several thousand feet per minute, compared with about 700 fpm for extruding.

3. Although the accuracy is good and entirely adequate for most applications, it is not so close as a machined part would be.

**Impact Extrusions.** Extrusions are also made by striking slugs of metal and forming them by high impact. Since this is essentially a cold-working operation, it is discussed in Chapter 16.

## QUESTIONS

1. Why is a forged-steel product stronger than a comparable item made of cast steel?
2. How did drop forgings obtain this name?
3. What are the main types of drop hammers?
4. What purposes are served by (a) fullering; (b) edging?
5. How does upset forging differ from drop forging?
6. State the advantages of both mechanical and hydraulic presses for press-forging applications.
7. When may hand forging be justified?
8. What accounts for a great share of the time used in preparing a large (200,000-lb) forging?
9. What purpose does planishing serve in forging?
10. How does forging metal differ from ordinary hot-rolled metal of the same general composition?
11. (a) What is meant by vacuum-arc steel? (b) What is its principal use?
12. Why is it usually necessary to normalize a forging before machining?
13. Name some considerations in deciding whether the forging process should or should not be used.
14. How is it possible to eliminate practically all draft on a forging?
15. What factors have a bearing on the tolerance that can be achieved in forging?
16. What process can be used to improve the tolerances of the forging?
17. How may costs often be reduced on large, complex forgings?
18. What is the difference in pipe-size designation for small and large diameters?
19. What methods are used to make seamless tubing?
20. What are some advantages that can be gained by using extrusions in fabrication?
21. How do extrusion dies compare in cost with forming rolls?

## PROBLEMS

1. A 2,000-lb gravity-type drop hammer can forge an average of 99 five-lb castings per hr. How long would it take to handle a comparable number of parts on a No. 8 automatic impacter?
2. Assume the casting in Fig. 5-38 is drawn one quarter size and it is to be redesigned as a forging. Sketch a full-size drawing of how the forging should appear before machining. Label draft angles, desirable radii, and machining allowances.

3. Estimate how many more feet of aluminum channel could be roll formed in an eight-hour day than could be extruded.

4. If the extrusion that eliminates the forging shown in Fig. 7-20 weighs 2.2 lbs per ft, what would be the minimum number of feet required before an extrusion die would be considered for this operation?

## REFERENCES

Daniels, H. R., "Forgings That Will Not Fail," *Metalworking*, October, 1961.

Flannagan, B. J., "Forgings—Sure Path to Quality," *Metalworking*, August, 1961.

Gardner, E. M., "Drop Forgings Can Be Used for Short Runs," *American Machinist and Metal Working*, December, 1958.

Kyle, P. E., *The Closed Die Forging Process*, The Macmillan Company, New York, 1954.

Stevenson, J. A., "Tough Shape? Try Extrusions," *Metalworking*, July, 1960.

Technical Committee of Drop Forging Association, *Metal Quality*, 3rd ed., New York, 1954.

# 8

# WELDING PRINCIPLES

**W**ELDING CONSISTS of fusing metals together while they are in the plastic or molten state. Heat for welding metals is most often obtained by gas flame, electric arc, or electrical resistance. Additional metal for filling in and reinforcement is generally obtained from the electrode or filler wire available for that purpose. Some applications require no additional metal to make the weld.

Welding has grown from oxyacetylene and arc welding to over 30 different processes. One or more of these processes can be successfully used to make a given weld. However, after considering costs, quality of weld, quantities to be welded, type of metal, etc., there is usually one process that is better than all others.

In the previous chapters, metal properties were discussed. The evolution of metal from the crystal to the solid state was shown. How stresses come about and how they can be relieved were also described. In welding, we apply these fundamental principles. Most welding processes are, in effect, relatively small-scale, high-quality casting operations. Here we must deal not only with the high heat and metallurgical aspects of the cast metal but also with those of the parent metal, and particularly of the transition zone from the weld metal to the base metal. Thus the knowledge gained from the previous chapters will help in understanding the heat effects of welding and how they can be used in controlling grain size, microstructure, internal stresses, corrosion resistance, and contraction and expansion. After learning about the metallurgical structure of the weld, attention can be turned to the mechanical aspects of welding design and, finally, to how welding standards are enforced through various codes and the process of certifying qualified operators.

## THERMAL EFFECTS OF WELDING

### Grain-Size Control

From the molten metal of the weld to the edge of the heat-affected zone, there will be a wide variation of temperature. Some of the metal has been heated far above the upper critical temperature, some just at critical, some not up to critical, and all the way down to the unaffected base metal. Therefore, as can be expected, the grain size of the weld will be rather large, becoming gradually smaller until the recrystallization temperature is reached. Here the grain size will be at a minimum and then will advance gradually larger again until it blends with the unaffected parent metal (Fig. 8-1). For metals and alloys that do not have a transformation zone, there is only a gradual reduction of grain size from the weld metal to the parent metal.

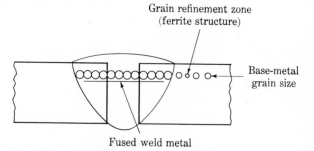

Grain refinement zone (ferrite structure)

Base-metal grain size

Fused weld metal

**Fig. 8-1.** The grain size of the weld metal and the adjacent metal will be affected by both the heat and the speed of the weld in a ferrite structure.

In heavy welds where several passes are required, the heat of each succeeding pass can be used to refine the grain of the previous pass. Care must be exercised to see that the metal has had an opportunity to cool below the lower critical temperature between successive passes. This will prevent overheating, with its resultant excessive grain size. Low-carbon steels can be quenched in water to shorten the time exposed to high temperature. High-carbon steels and alloy steels should not be quenched because of the danger of setting up excessive strains and embrittlement.

### Microstructure Control

The rate at which cooling takes place in the weld area will largely determine its microstructure. If the cooling rate is slow, as in the case of low-carbon steels, the structure will be pearlitic. However, if the cooling is fast and the steel is medium- or high-carbon, the structure is likely to be martensitic. Therefore, in welding hardenable steels and alloys, care should be taken to avoid rapid cooling.

The first pass in thick materials, where multiple-pass welds are required, receives a quenching action from the parent metal. Preheating the joint area to 300° or 400°F minimizes this effect. Of course, the preheat temperature will vary with the type of metal and the cross-sectional area.

The principal drawback of a hardened heat-affected zone is that it makes machining difficult. It may also be sensitive to failures caused by nicks or relatively small flaws.

### nternal-Stress Control

The rapid heating and cooling of the weld can produce thermal stresses that are quite large. During heating there is rapid expansion of the base metal around the weld. If there is enough unaffected metal surrounding the weld zone, or if it is rigidly clamped, the expanding metal in the weld zone will be upset (Fig. 8-2). Upon cooling, the upset section will not return to its original dimensions, and internal stresses will be set up. Shrinkage of the solidifying weld metal will cause internal stresses in the same way. Therefore, in metals with low ductility, provision should be made for expansion and contraction during the welding operation.

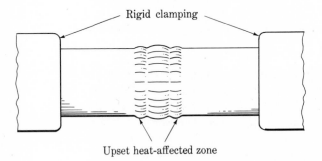

Rigid clamping

**Fig. 8-2.** The upset area adjacent to the weld will become a stress point, particularly in the less ductile metals that are rigidly clamped for welding.

Upset heat-affected zone

When the heat-affected base metal or the solidified weld metal is still at a high temperature, it cannot withstand even relatively low internal stresses. If stress is developed in this weak condition, it tears instead of deforming, as it would at a slightly lower temperature.

Hot cracks are more apt to occur in the weld metal than in the base metal, the reason being that the weld metal is hotter than the base metal and cools last. A second reason is that weld metal is essentially a cast metal with columnar grains, as compared to the rolled and somewhat distorted grains of the base metal. Hot cracks may appear adjacent to the weld zone if the weld is made with ductile metal. For example, high-chromium steels may be welded with a combination chromium-nickel rod. The extra ductility furnished by the nickel content will make it possible to withstand the cooling stress. There is, however, a disadvantage in not using a rod of the same material as the base metal. In this case, chrome-nickel deposit will not have the same corrosion-resistant qualities as the base metal. Therefore, it may be necessary to go over the weld with a light deposit of high-chromium-content electrode.

### Corrosion Control

Steels most often fabricated for corrosion-resistance purposes are the stainless steels. Shown in Fig. 8-3 are the various heat-affected zones of a chromium-nickel steel. The metal on the left side of the weld bead represents a modified chromium-nickel steel with columbium or titanium added to reduce harmful carbide precipitation. On the right side is shown the carbide-precipitation zone. The longer this zone is held in the 1500° to 800°F range, the more pronounced will be the carbide precipitation.

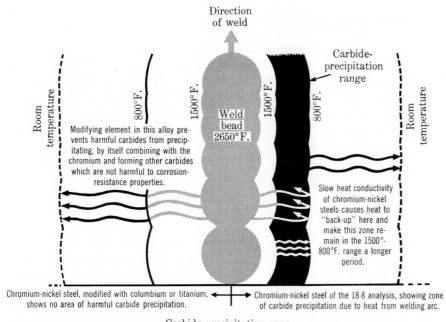

**Fig. 8-3.** The carbide precipitation zone of conventional 18–8 stainless steel compared with a modified chromium-nickel steel (courtesy Allegheny Ludlum Steel Corp.).

It is obvious that if something could be done to reduce the temporary accumulation of heat in the nonmodified stainless steels, they would be more corrosion-resistant. Since copper has a high thermal conductivity, it can be used as a chill bar for the weld, as shown in Fig. 8-4. In this case, the copper bar underneath helps protect the metal from the atmosphere and aids in cooling. The two copper-faced steel hold-down bars on top help dissipate heat and control distortion.

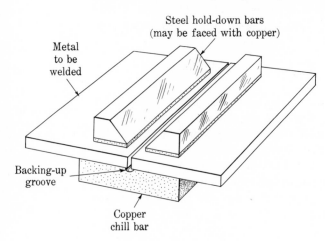

**Fig. 8-4.** Typical chill-bar setup.

### Contraction and Expansion

The rate at which metal contracts and expands is an important factor in knowing what to expect in the way of distortion. If metals that have a high rate of thermal expansion, such as aluminum (approximately twice that of steel), are clamped rigidly, there will be buckling in the weld area. Then, as cooling takes place, contraction results, putting the weld in tension. Many nonferrous metals are weak when hot (hot-short) resulting in cracks as the metal shrinks and cools.

The speed at which the weld is made will determine, to a large extent, the amount of contraction and expansion. Slow speeds will cause greater area heating with greater expansion and, later, more contraction.

**Distortion.** The fact that most metals expand upon heating and contract upon cooling causes distortion in welded assemblies. Much of this can be overcome by planning ahead to make the heat work for you rather than against you.

There are three simple rules that can be used to control distortion:
1. Reduce the effective shrinkage force.
2. Make shrinkage forces work for you.
3. Balance shrinkage forces with other forces.

REDUCE EFFECTIVE SHRINKAGE FORCES. Use only the proper amount of weld material. In order to understand some of the terminology used in connection with the control of distortion, two common welded joints are shown in Fig. 8-5. Study these figures to become familiar with the nomenclature.

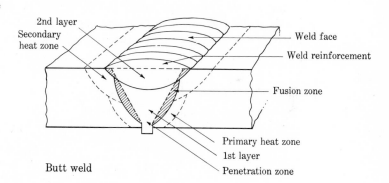

**Fig. 8-5.** Nomenclature of fillet and butt welds. The heat-affected zone of the butt weld is shown.

If the reinforcement shown in either joint were much thicker and wider, it would not add to the strength of the joint but, rather, would increase the distortion. The butt weld shown in Fig. 8-6 is an example of overwelding. Less weld metal means not only less distortion but less expense.

**Fig. 8-6.** Excess metal (shaded area) cools, contracts, and distorts the metal joint.

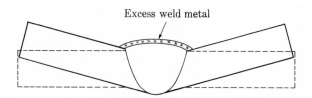

*Use Proper Joint Preparation.* Without proper joint preparation, it will be difficult to make a good weld. The tendency will be to add additional metal to compensate for poor fit-up. To make a proper butt weld without excess metal, it is best to consult a welding handbook.

*Use the Proper Number of Passes.* Heavy sections should be welded with large electrodes, with correspondingly higher heat. This will cause less distortion than a large number of small passes. The amount of lateral distortion (the type shown in Fig. 8-6) is generally 1 deg for each additional pass.

*Place Welds Near the Neutral Axis.* Shrinkage forces will be less effective if the weld does not have unequal leverage by being offset to one side or the other.

*Reduce the Amount of Weld Deposit.* Oftentimes, a continuous weld bead is not needed. Sufficient strength can be obtained by *skip welding.* That is, short distances of the joint can be skipped, reducing the overall heat and weld deposit.

MAKE SHRINKAGE FORCES WORK FOR YOU.

*Allow Shrinkage Forces to Pull Parts into Alignment.* By planning for the shrinkage force, the parts can be offset so that, as the weld metal cools, it will have just enough force to bring the parts into proper position. The before-and-after positions of a T-joint are shown in Fig. 8-7.

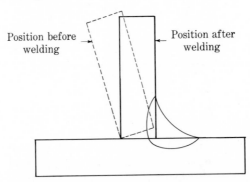

Position before welding

Position after welding

**Fig. 8-7.** Offsetting one of the members to be welded to allow for shrinkage forces.

*Space Parts to Allow for Shrinkage.* To gain the proper alignment of two parts after welding, spacing must be allowed, as shown in Fig. 8-8. The amount to be allowed is often based on experience. As the weld cools, shrinkage forces will pull the two parts to the desired dimension.

BALANCE SHRINKAGE FORCES WITH OTHER FORCES. Heavy metal parts often have enough rigidity to withstand shrinkage forces. How-

**Fig. 8-8.** Correct spacing of the arms allows them to be pulled into correct position by shrinkage forces (courtesy The Lincoln Electric Co.).

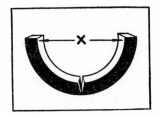

ever, on lighter-gauge metals shrinkage forces should be balanced with other forces.

*Balance Shrinkage Forces with Opposing Welds.* In the previous example of a welded T-joint, allowance was made for shrinkage of the weld metal by offsetting the vertical member. In balanced shrinkage forces, equal welds are made on both sides so that the weld deposits pull against each other (Fig. 8-9).

**Fig. 8-9.** Misalignment and distortion caused by one weld can often be overcome with an opposing weld to balance the shrinkage forces.

Starting position after being tack-welded. Also finished position after bead *B* has been deposited

Position after bead *A* has been deposited

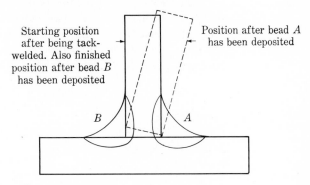

Another example is that of a butt weld in heavy material. If all the passes are made from one side, the contraction of the weld metal as it cools will pull the two plates up. Alternating the weld passes, first one pass on the top and the next on the bottom, etc., until the joint is completed, will balance shrinkage forces.

*Use of Restraining Forces.* By clamping the parts to be welded either with jigs and fixtures, regular clamps, or tack welds, the parts will not be able to move out of alignment as the weld metal cools. In this case, the weld metal is forced to stretch as it cools.

*Peening.* Another method of helping the weld metal stretch as it cools is by lightly peening it with the rounded end of a ball peen hammer or chipping hammer. Care should be exercised to avoid excessive peening, as this will act to impart stresses to the weld or work-harden it, causing it to become brittle.

## JOINT DESIGN

### General

The properties of a welded joint depend largely upon the correct preparation of the metal edges being welded. All mill scale, rust, oxides, and other impurities should be removed from the surfaces to be joined so as to prevent their inclusion in the weld metal. Proper preparation will reduce the amount of heat needed and minimize distortion caused by expansion and contraction.

Five basic types of joints are used in welding; these are butt, lap, T-, corner, and edge joints. There are also several variations of each of these joints.

**Butt Joint.** The butt joint is used to join the ends or edges of two plates or surfaces located approximately in the same plane with each other. Preparation of the edge varies according to the thickness of the metal and the welding process. Light-gauge sections require only 90-deg sheared edges with no spacing, as shown in Fig. 8-10.

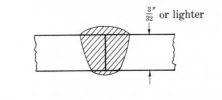

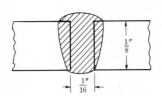 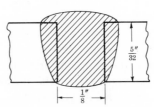

**Fig. 8-10.** Butt weld spacing for light-gauge metals.

Metals ranging from $\frac{3}{8}$ to $\frac{1}{2}$ in. thick, that can be welded only from one side, should be reduced either as a single V- or a single U-joint, as shown in Fig. 8-11. Heavier plates are prepared from both sides. The U-shaped type of joint is more satisfactory and requires less filler rod than the V-type groove. However, it is generally more expensive to prepare than the straight bevel.

A double-bevel V-joint requires approximately one half the amount of filler metal that a single bevel joint would require in the same thickness of material.

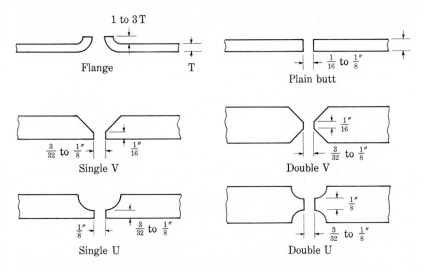

**Fig. 8-11.** Various types of preparation for welded butt joints.

**Lap Joint.** As the name implies, the lap joint is used in joining two overlapping plates so that the edge of each plate is welded to the surface of the other. Common lap joints, as shown in Fig. 8-12, are single lap, double lap, and offset or "joggled" lap joints. The single-welded lap does not develop full strength, but it is preferred to the butt joint for some applications. A good example of this is in tubular construction where one tube telescopes into the other and is lap-welded.

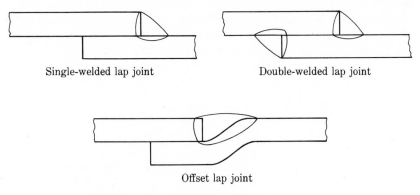

**Fig. 8-12.** Common types of welded lap joints.

**T-Joints.** T-joints are used to weld two plates or sections whose surfaces are at approximately right angles to each other. The various types of T-joints are shown in Fig. 8-13. The included angle of bevel used for T-joints is approximately one half the included angle used for butt joints. Plates on surfaces should have good fit-up in order to ensure uniform penetration and fusion. Edge preparation of the vertical member is the same as that of the butt joint, given previously, in regard to thickness and bevel.

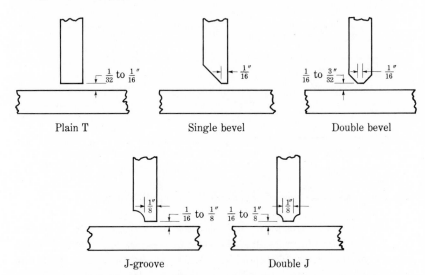

Plain T         Single bevel         Double bevel

J-groove         Double J

**Fig. 8-13.** Various types of T-joint preparation.

**Corner Joint.** The corner joint is used to join the edges of two sheets or plates whose surfaces are at an angle of approximately 90 deg to each other. It is common in the construction of boxes, tanks, frames, and other similar items. Welding can be done on one or both sides, depending on the position and type of corner joint used. Shown in Fig. 8-14 are the more common corner-joint designs.

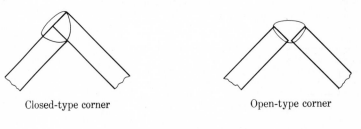

Closed-type corner         Open-type corner

**Fig. 8-14.** Various types of welded corner joints.

Open-type corner welded from both sides

The closed-corner joint is used on lighter sheets where the strength required is not too high. Little or no filler metal is needed, and the edges are just melted together. If it becomes necessary to make a closed-corner joint with heavier plate, the lapped plate is V-beveled or U-grooved to permit penetration to the root of the joint.

The open-corner joint is the type used for heavier plate. The two edges of the plate are melted down, and sufficient filler metal is added to round out the corner. The joint may be welded on the outside and then reinforced by adding a bead on the inside.

**Edge Joint.**   The edge joint consists of joining two parallel plates by means of a weld. This joint (Fig. 8-15) is often used in sheet metal work. The two edges can be easily and quickly melted down, eliminating the need for any filler metal. Other applications are also shown in the figure. In heavy plates, where beveling the edges is done to get deeper penetration, some filler rod is needed.

Sheet metal preparation for edge butt joint

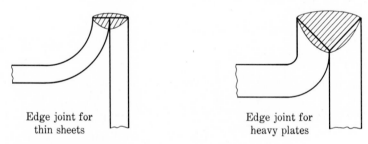

Edge joint for thin sheets   Edge joint for heavy plates

**Fig. 8-15.**   Two common types of edge joints.

No special preparation is necessary for thin sheets except to clean the edges, bend them up on a press brake, and tack-weld them into position for welding. Heavy plates require beveled edges in order to secure good depth of penetration and fusion in the sidewalls.

### Principles in Applying Joint Designs

**Economy.**   Most of the time the structure that is to be fabricated will dictate the type of joint to be used. However, there are several methods of reducing costs of a given type of welded joint:

1. A joint of the type that will require the minimum amount of weld metal should be chosen. The use of automatic welding, with its

deeper penetration, will reduce the beveling required on many hand-welded joints [Fig. 8-16(a)].

2. Double V joints are more economical, from the standpoint of weld metal required, than single V [Fig. 8-16(b)].

3. Make the maximum use of the welded joint. Several parts can be joined with one pass [Fig. 8-16(c)].

4. Flat 45-deg fillet welds are more economical than concave fillet welds, as the strength is still dependent on the actual throat distance [Fig. 8-16(d)].

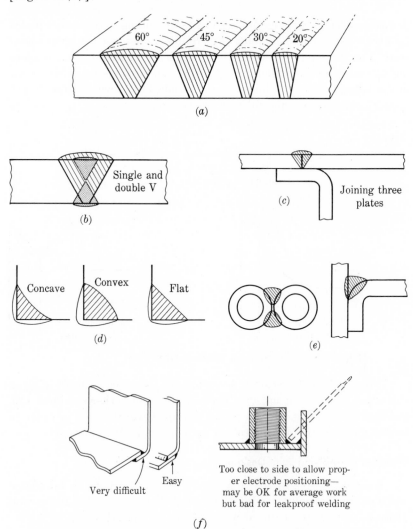

**Fig. 8-16.** Various methods of economizing on welded joints.

5. Curved intersections, such as welding two round bars side by side or the V between two bent sections, should be avoided if possible, since they are more difficult to make and often take a considerable amount of weld metal [Fig. 8-16(e)].

6. When plate planers are available, the U-groove is preferred for thicker plates as it requires less weld metal than conventional bevel-type preparation.

7. The joint can be made better, faster, and more economically if it is easily accessible [Fig. 8-16(f)].

8. Joints should be made with the best possible fit-up. Joints with gaps larger than necessary are costly to fill.

9. The weld size should be correct. The leg size of a fillet weld should be three fourths of the plate thickness if full strength is required [Fig. 8-17(a)]. If rigidity is the main requirement, 50 percent of the full strength of the weld is sufficient.

10. Where intermittent fillet welds are satisfactory, they can be used as a means of reducing costs in hand-welding operations [Fig. 8-17(b)].

11. Large fillets require more than one pass for manual welding. For example, a ⅜-in. fillet instead of a 5/16-in. fillet requires at least two passes, with a 44 percent increase in costs [Fig. 8-17(c)]. Distortion, internal stresses, and the need for subsequent stress relieving can be reduced by keeping the weld material to a minimum.

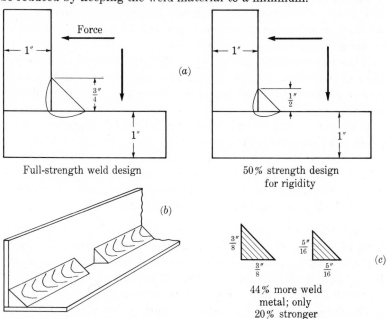

**Fig. 8-17.** The cost of welded joints can often be reduced by not overwelding.

### Stresses in Joint Design

**Weld Contour.** Wherever possible, welded joints should be made with smooth-flowing lines that blend gradually with the parent metal. Any abrupt change in the surface causes it to be a point of stress concentration. An example of this is a fillet weld shown in Fig. 8–18. The stress lines tend to concentrate at the toe of the weld when a convex bead is used, but they flow smoothly when a concave bead is used.

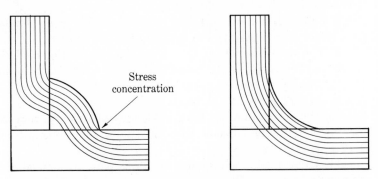

**Fig. 8-18.** Stress concentrations are caused in welded joints where there is an abrupt change in contour, as in the fillet weld on the left.

**Determining Stress Distribution.** Many engineered parts fail in service because of the stress concentrations in a particular area. In fact, most failures in high-duty equipment are caused by fatigue, which, in turn, is influenced by stress concentrations.

A recent aircraft manual cites over 50 failures which originated in regions of stress concentration, and most of them were fatigue failures. Stress concentrations are almost always traceable to improper design, fabrication, or maintenance.

Stress concentration tends to produce failure by fatigue even when the regions of stress concentration are very small. Several methods exist for the study of true stresses; these include mathematical theory of elasticity, strain gages, brittle lacquers, X-ray diffraction, and photoelasticity. The latter is still one of the most precise methods available in the analysis of two-dimensional stress systems.

PHOTOELASTICITY. In the photoelastic method, the joint contour is cut out of clear acrylic plastic material. This model is placed in a field of polarized light produced by a polariscope. The interaction of the polarized light with the model produces stress patterns [Fig. 8–19(a)] from which the stress distribution can be determined.

The basic phenomenon of photoelasticity is that points of increasing stress produce cyclical variations in intensity of the observed light

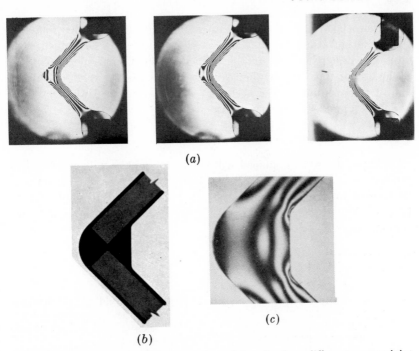

**Fig. 8-19.** Photoelastic stress patterns as determined on different corner-joint designs, but with the same loading, in upper group. Lower pictures show an unloaded and loaded model (courtesy Steel Founders' Society of America).

patterns. At zero stress, the image is black (*b*). Monochromatic light stress in the transparent model produces alternate bright and dark bands called interference fringes. Examination of the photoelastic patterns developed shows a tendency of the fringe lines to group together in regions of stress concentration. The model can be gradually loaded so that the fringe lines can be distinguished and counted. The oval-shaped white dots in the knee of the specimen are known as *isotropic points* or points of equal stress in all directions. On this picture [Fig. 8-19(*c*)] there are six orders (white bars) and a half order (black spot) to the two stress-concentration points on the inside fillet. This gives a fringe order of $N = 6.5$ for a known load of 6.3 lb. The fringe order at the middle of the inside fillet is observed to be equal to $N = 4$. Therefore, the stress-concentration point is about 60 percent greater than in the region of the fillet.

$$\text{Stress concentration factor} = \frac{6.5}{4} = 1.625$$

Any discontinuity on the specimen-fillet surface which has a stress-concentration effect can initiate a fatigue crack in that region.

Photoelastic studies are not only useful for determining points of stress concentration, but they also can be used to show how much more stress one design has over another for a given load. For a more complete discussion of this subject, the reader is referred to the reference at the end of this chapter on the design of steel castings and weldments by the Steel Founders' Society of America.

### Weld Joint Placement

Where the weld is placed will determine how it will be loaded in tension or shear. For those placed in shear, the type of shear—transverse or longitudinal—is also important. For example, welds placed in transverse shear (Fig. 8–20) are stronger than those in longitudinal shear.

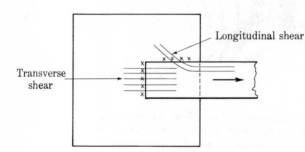

**Fig. 8-20.** Welds placed in transverse shear are 30 percent stronger than those placed in longitudinal shear.

The proper placement of welds will take into consideration the center of gravity or the axis of the applied load [Fig. 8–21(a)]. Joints subjected to turning and tearing effects are shown in the lap-joint examples in Fig. 8–21(b).

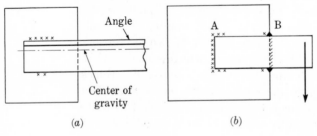

**Fig. 8-21.** (a) The length of the weld should be according to the applied load. (b) Welds are placed to resist turning effect. Welding around the corner also helps resist tearing action.

### Welding Symbols

Many of the standard welding symbols used in making up weld specifications are shown in Fig. 8-22. These symbols have been standardized and adopted by the American Welding Society. Further clarification is given by the supplementary material furnished by the Lincoln Electric Company (Fig. 8-23). For a complete set of welding symbols and their placement, refer to the AWS Handbook.

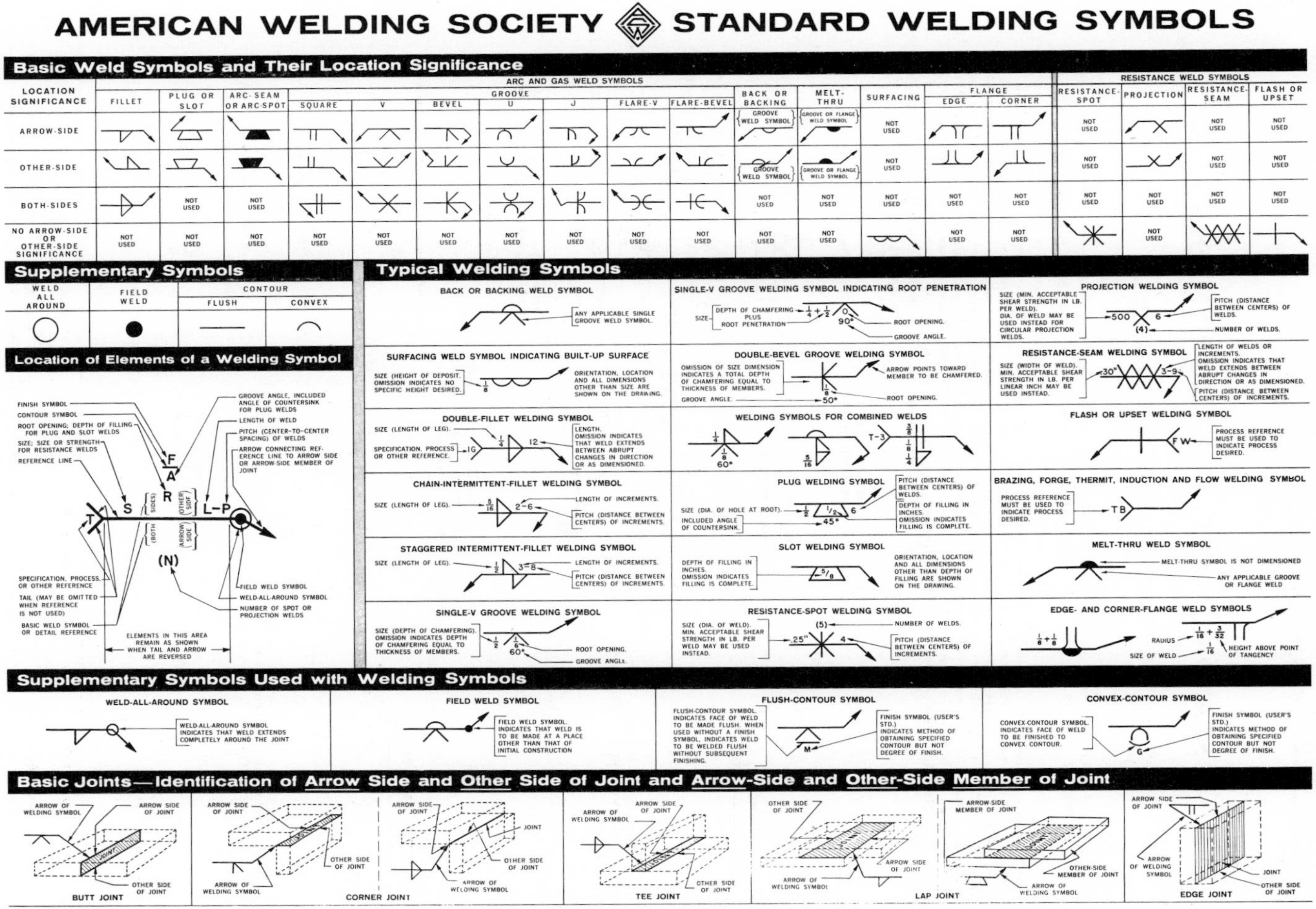
AMERICAN WELDING SOCIETY STANDARD WELDING SYMBOLS
Basic Weld Symbols and Their Location Significance
LOCATION SIGNIFICANCE
ARC AND GAS WELD SYMBOLS
FILLET
PLUG OR SLOT
ARC-SEAM OR ARC-SPOT
GROOVE
SQUARE
V
BEVEL
U
J
FLARE-V
FLARE-BEVEL
BACK OR BACKING
MELT-THRU
SURFACING
FLANGE
EDGE
CORNER
RESISTANCE WELD SYMBOLS
RESISTANCE-SPOT
PROJECTION
RESISTANCE-SEAM
FLASH OR UPSET
ARROW-SIDE
OTHER-SIDE
BOTH-SIDES
NO ARROW-SIDE OR OTHER-SIDE SIGNIFICANCE
GROOVE WELD SYMBOL
GROOVE OR FLANGE WELD SYMBOL
NOT USED
Supplementary Symbols
WELD ALL AROUND
FIELD WELD
CONTOUR
FLUSH
CONVEX
Location of Elements of a Welding Symbol
FINISH SYMBOL
CONTOUR SYMBOL
ROOT OPENING; DEPTH OF FILLING FOR PLUG AND SLOT WELDS
SIZE; SIZE OR STRENGTH FOR RESISTANCE WELDS
REFERENCE LINE
SPECIFICATION, PROCESS, OR OTHER REFERENCE
TAIL (MAY BE OMITTED WHEN REFERENCE IS NOT USED)
BASIC WELD SYMBOL OR DETAIL REFERENCE
ELEMENTS IN THIS AREA REMAIN AS SHOWN WHEN TAIL AND ARROW ARE REVERSED
GROOVE ANGLE, INCLUDED ANGLE OF COUNTERSINK FOR PLUG WELDS
LENGTH OF WELD
PITCH (CENTER-TO-CENTER SPACING) OF WELDS
ARROW CONNECTING REFERENCE LINE TO ARROW SIDE OR ARROW-SIDE MEMBER OF JOINT
FIELD WELD SYMBOL
WELD-ALL-AROUND SYMBOL
NUMBER OF SPOT OR PROJECTION WELDS
F
A
R
S
T
L-P
(N)
(BOTH SIDES)
(OTHER SIDE)
(ARROW SIDE)
Typical Welding Symbols
BACK OR BACKING WELD SYMBOL
ANY APPLICABLE SINGLE GROOVE WELD SYMBOL.
SURFACING WELD SYMBOL INDICATING BUILT-UP SURFACE
SIZE (HEIGHT OF DEPOSIT. OMISSION INDICATES NO SPECIFIC HEIGHT DESIRED.
ORIENTATION, LOCATION AND ALL DIMENSIONS OTHER THAN SIZE ARE SHOWN ON THE DRAWING.
DOUBLE-FILLET WELDING SYMBOL
SIZE (LENGTH OF LEG).
SPECIFICATION, PROCESS OR OTHER REFERENCE.
LENGTH. OMISSION INDICATES THAT WELD EXTENDS BETWEEN ABRUPT CHANGES IN DIRECTION OR AS DIMENSIONED.
CHAIN-INTERMITTENT-FILLET WELDING SYMBOL
LENGTH OF INCREMENTS.
PITCH (DISTANCE BETWEEN CENTERS) OF INCREMENTS.
STAGGERED INTERMITTENT-FILLET WELDING SYMBOL
SINGLE-V GROOVE WELDING SYMBOL
SIZE (DEPTH OF CHAMFERING). OMISSION INDICATES DEPTH OF CHAMFERING EQUAL TO THICKNESS OF MEMBERS.
ROOT OPENING.
GROOVE ANGLE.
SINGLE-V GROOVE WELDING SYMBOL INDICATING ROOT PENETRATION
DEPTH OF CHAMFERING PLUS ROOT PENETRATION
DOUBLE-BEVEL GROOVE WELDING SYMBOL
OMISSION OF SIZE DIMENSION INDICATES A TOTAL DEPTH OF CHAMFERING EQUAL TO THICKNESS OF MEMBERS.
ARROW POINTS TOWARD MEMBER TO BE CHAMFERED.
WELDING SYMBOLS FOR COMBINED WELDS
PLUG WELDING SYMBOL
SIZE (DIA. OF HOLE AT ROOT).
INCLUDED ANGLE OF COUNTERSINK.
PITCH (DISTANCE BETWEEN CENTERS) OF WELDS.
DEPTH OF FILLING IN INCHES. OMISSION INDICATES FILLING IS COMPLETE.
SLOT WELDING SYMBOL
ORIENTATION, LOCATION AND ALL DIMENSIONS OTHER THAN DEPTH OF FILLING ARE SHOWN ON THE DRAWING.
RESISTANCE-SPOT WELDING SYMBOL
SIZE (DIA. OF WELD). MIN. ACCEPTABLE SHEAR STRENGTH IN LB. PER WELD MAY BE USED INSTEAD.
NUMBER OF WELDS.
PITCH (DISTANCE BETWEEN CENTERS) OF INCREMENTS.
PROJECTION WELDING SYMBOL
SIZE (MIN. ACCEPTABLE SHEAR STRENGTH IN LB. PER WELD). DIA. OF WELD MAY BE USED INSTEAD FOR CIRCULAR PROJECTION WELDS.
PITCH (DISTANCE BETWEEN CENTERS) OF WELDS.
RESISTANCE-SEAM WELDING SYMBOL
SIZE (WIDTH OF WELD). MIN. ACCEPTABLE SHEAR STRENGTH IN LB. PER LINEAR INCH MAY BE USED INSTEAD.
LENGTH OF WELDS OR INCREMENTS. OMISSION INDICATES THAT WELD EXTENDS BETWEEN ABRUPT CHANGES IN DIRECTION OR AS DIMENSIONED.
FLASH OR UPSET WELDING SYMBOL
PROCESS REFERENCE MUST BE USED TO INDICATE PROCESS DESIRED.
BRAZING, FORGE, THERMIT, INDUCTION AND FLOW WELDING SYMBOL
MELT-THRU WELD SYMBOL
MELT-THRU SYMBOL IS NOT DIMENSIONED
ANY APPLICABLE GROOVE OR FLANGE WELD
EDGE- AND CORNER-FLANGE WELD SYMBOLS
RADIUS
SIZE OF WELD
HEIGHT ABOVE POINT OF TANGENCY
Supplementary Symbols Used with Welding Symbols
WELD-ALL-AROUND SYMBOL
WELD-ALL-AROUND SYMBOL INDICATES THAT WELD EXTENDS COMPLETELY AROUND THE JOINT
FIELD WELD SYMBOL
FIELD WELD SYMBOL. INDICATES THAT WELD IS TO BE MADE AT A PLACE OTHER THAN THAT OF INITIAL CONSTRUCTION
FLUSH-CONTOUR SYMBOL
FLUSH-CONTOUR SYMBOL. INDICATES FACE OF WELD TO BE MADE FLUSH. WHEN USED WITHOUT A FINISH SYMBOL, INDICATES WELD TO BE WELDED FLUSH WITHOUT SUBSEQUENT FINISHING.
FINISH SYMBOL (USER'S STD.) INDICATES METHOD OF OBTAINING SPECIFIED CONTOUR BUT NOT DEGREE OF FINISH.
CONVEX-CONTOUR SYMBOL
CONVEX-CONTOUR SYMBOL. INDICATES FACE OF WELD TO BE FINISHED TO CONVEX CONTOUR.
Basic Joints—Identification of Arrow Side and Other Side of Joint and Arrow-Side and Other-Side Member of Joint
ARROW OF WELDING SYMBOL
ARROW SIDE OF JOINT
OTHER SIDE OF JOINT
JOINT
ARROW-SIDE MEMBER OF JOINT
OTHER-SIDE MEMBER OF JOINT
BUTT JOINT
CORNER JOINT
TEE JOINT
LAP JOINT
EDGE JOINT



Fig. 8-22.

# STANDARD ARC WELDING SYMBOLS

## IN ORDER OF THEIR MAXIMUM USE

### 1. FILLET WELDS

Fillet welds are used on lap and tee joints for ordinary plate sizes. Good for static load (stress allowable, 13,600 PSI through throat of weld. Leg size x .707 = theoretical throat). Use with caution when joint subjected to high impact and fatigue.

Fraction indicates leg size. Shown only on one weld when both sides are the same.

Indicates welds are intermittent and staggered 2 inches long on 4 inch centers.

### 2. BUTT (GROOVE) WELDS

Butt welds are the most efficient way of transferring all types of stresses (static, fatigue, impact) from one member to another. (Stress allowable is the same as the plate for mild steel or 20,000 PSI in tension and compression and 13,000 PSI in shear for static loading.)

Square butt used on plates up to 3/8″ welded from both sides.

Single vee, welded from one side. Figures indicate a 60° bevel and root opening of 1/16″. Used up to 1/2″ plate.

Double vee, welded from both sides. Figures in tail indicates reference to specification.

Single bevel.

### 3. SPECIAL (GROOVE) WELDS

A tee joint may be welded with complete penetration by using combined single bevel or double bevel groove and fillet welds on both sides. This is preferred for structures subjected to fatigue and impact. (Such welds are indicated by a welding symbol combining the individual weld symbols of the types of weld used.)

"U" and "J" groove welds are used for 3/4″ plate and thicker as this results in less welding when compared to Vee Butt Welds.

Corner flange weld is used for sheet metal and loads that are not severe.

Corner welds not for severe loads.

Corner weld with bead weld on the inside for high strength.

| FILLET | PLUG OR SLOT | ARC-SPOT OR ARC-SEAM | GROOVE | | | | | | | BACK OR BACKING | MELT-THRU | SUR-FACING | FLANGE | |
|---|---|---|---|---|---|---|---|---|---|---|---|---|---|---|
| | | | SQUARE | V | BEVEL | U | J | FLARE-V | FLARE-BEVEL | | | | EDGE | CORNER |

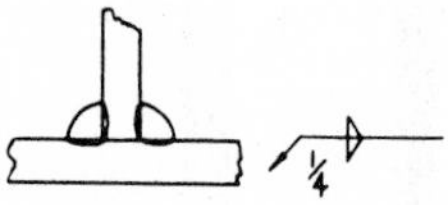

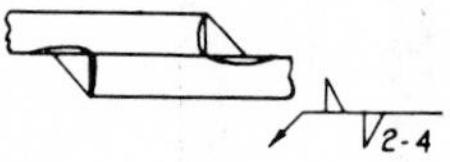

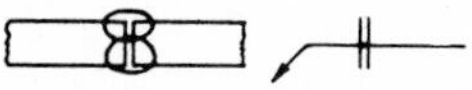

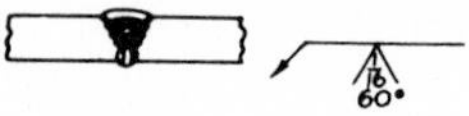

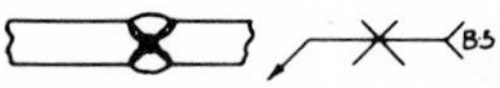

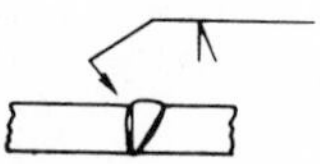

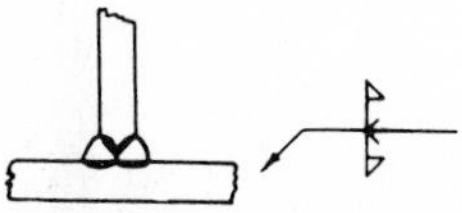

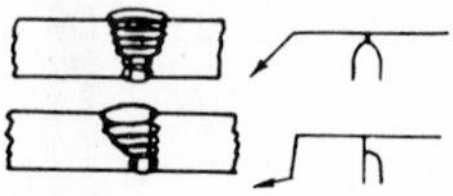

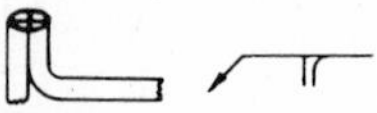

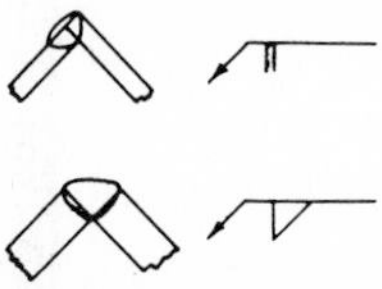

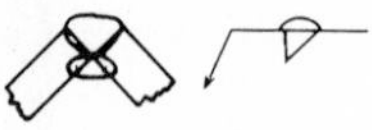

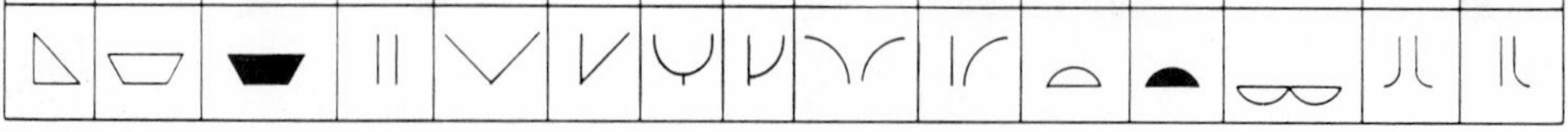

Fig. 8-23

These symbols are necessary for the designer to transfer exact information from the drawing to the point of fabrication. The mere notation "weld all around" is not only transferring the design function to the shop but subjecting the part to excessive cost. Many shops prefer to "play it safe" and overweld; others may not weld enough.

## Load-Carrying Capacity of Welded Joints

Estimated safe loads on arc-welded joints may be obtained, without tedious calculations, from the nomograph shown in Fig. 8-24. It is based on the accepted stress of 13,000 psi for tension, 15,000 psi for compression, and 11,300 psi for shear, with all loads acting through the center of gravity of the section. Eccentricity increases the stresses beyond the uniformly distributed stresses assumed.

In shear calculations the cross-sectional area is taken through the throat of the fillet weld; this assumes the fillet to be an isosceles triangle of 45 deg so that the throat distance is 0.707 percent of the leg, reducing the allowable stress to 8,000 psi for the area of the fused surface — usually the length of the weld times the plate thickness.

The chart is also useful in estimating the allowable loads on arc-welded connections for fillet welds, intermittent fillet welds, butt welds, and slot welds. For example, to find the length of weld necessary to hold a certain load, if the width and the kind of weld to be used are known, we connect the values on scale 5 with scale 4, intersecting the reference line; then we connect the intersection point with the width on scale 1 and find the length required on scale 2.

## Destructive Testing of Welded Joints

When welded construction first started to become a popular method of fabricating metal parts, elaborate testing methods were devised to analyze both the joints and the weld deposits. Today, work done by a qualified welder is often not subjected to testing in any way.

There are, however, various federal, state, and city codes that require certain tests of weld metal and welded joints. To eliminate useless variations between testing agencies and various codes, the American Welding Society has organized a general specification, "Standard Methods for Mechanical Testing of Welds." Some of these test specifications and methods will be discussed briefly.

**Density.**   Generally, weld deposit should be the same as that of the parent metal.

**Etch Test.**   Welds are sectioned, polished, and etched to examine the microstructure of the metal.

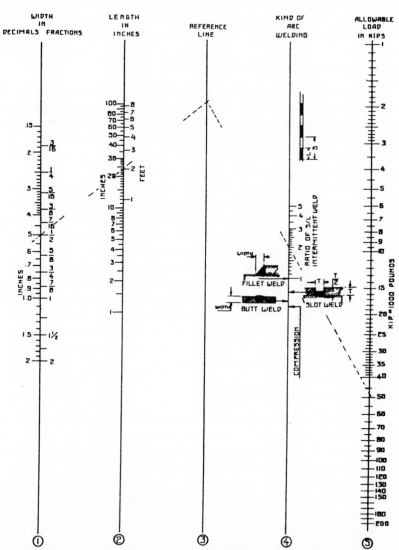

EXAMPLE: INTERMITTENT FILLET WELD, TWO ½" PLATES 24" LONG - FILLETS 2" LONG SPACED 4"  S/L = 4/2 = 2
CONNECT ½ ON SCALE №1 WITH 24 ON SCALE №2 INTERSECTING REFERENCE LINE №3. THEN CONNECT
INTERSECTION POINT ON LINE №3 WITH 2 ON SCALE №4 INTERSECTING SCALE №5 THRU 48 KIPS
THE ALLOWABLE LOAD IS 48 KIPS OR 48.000 POUNDS.

**Fig. 8-24.** A nomograph used in finding safe loading for various welded joints (courtesy *Welding Engr.*).

**Tensile Test.** Tensile-test specimens must be prepared according to specifications. One type is shown in Fig. 8-25. It is placed on a testing machine and tested for yield point, tensile strength, and elongation. Reduction of area can also be calculated by measuring the average cross-sectional area at the break and comparing it with the original area.

**Fig. 8-25.** Typical tensile test specimen of shielded arc-weld metal showed tensile strength of 76,100 lb. per sq. in., elongation in 2 in. of 25.8 percent, reduction in area of 48 percent (courtesy Lincoln Electric Company).

**Guided Bend Test for Soundness.** The guided bend testing machine, shown in Fig. 8-26, is a design recommended by the United States Office of Education and the Committee on Minimum Requirements for Instruction of Welding Operators.

**Fig. 8-26.** Guided bend testing machine (courtesy Lincoln Electric Company).

This test consists of bending a joint 180 deg around a pin which is 1½ in. in diameter. In the case of steel, the test specimen is ⅜ in. thick by 1½ in. wide (the length is not important, usually 4 to 8 in.). Root, face, and side bend tests are made.

**Nick Break Test.** The nick break test consists of welding two plates together, cutting out a section of the weld, and nicking it on opposite sides with a saw. When it is struck with sufficient force, the specimen will break at the nick, exposing the weld metal for examination. Nicks are made so as to leave a cross-sectional area two thirds of the original metal thickness. Machines for testing are quite similar to those used in the guided bend test. Nick break tests may also be done by the Izod method described later.

Information obtained by the nick break test includes brittleness or ductility, grain size, gas holes, inclusions, fisheyes, and lack of penetration. By systematic comparison of several test samples, the quality of the weld can be quite accurately judged. This test, along with the guided bend test, is usually sufficient to ensure the quality of the work.

**Free Bend Test.**   The free bend test is designed to indicate the ductility of the weld metal. The free bend specimen shown in Fig. 8-27 was made in V'd plate by the shielded-arc method. The stretch in weld metal of the specimen shown is equivalent to an elongation of 54 percent.

**Fig. 8-27.** Free bend test specimen showing stretch in outer fibers of shielded arc weld (courtesy Lincoln Electric Company).

**Fillet-Weld Break Test.**   This is a simple low-cost test that consists of hammering the vertical member of a T-joint and testing it for soundness and penetration of the weld.

**Shear-Strength Tests.**   Shear-strength tests can be easily made on lap joints, using a tensile-test machine.

**Notched-Bar Tests.**   Notched-bar tests are somewhat similar to the nick break test but on a more scientific basis and for a different purpose. The notched bar test can be either a Charpy or an Izod type. Specimens of each type are shown in Fig. 8-28. In Charpy tests, the specimens are supported on both ends and are broken by a blow opposite the notch. Izod specimens are mounted in a vise and broken by a single blow of the swinging pendulum. The two tests are not directly related, although correlations can be drawn from a series of tests made by each method. Izod values are usually higher because of the greater cross-sectional area used.

The test is designed to show the notch sensitivity of a material and is measured by the machine in terms of foot-pounds.

**Endurance Tests.**   Endurance tests are of several different types, but all embody the principle of subjecting the material to unlimited

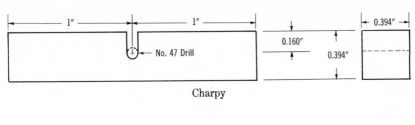

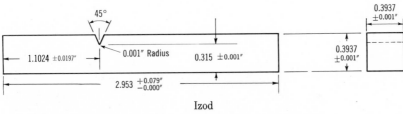

Charpy

Izod

**Fig. 8-28.** Specifications for Charpy and Izod test specimens.

numbers of stress cycles, alternately reversing from tension to compression, until failure. Methods of accomplishing this are: (1) repeated bending back and forth, (2) rotating a suitably loaded beam, or (3) rotating a cantilever beam. For each test the stress range is determined, and a record is made of the number of cycles before failure. The endurance limit for sound ferrous metals is approximately 45 percent of the ultimate tensile strength.

Usually, steels subjected to 10,000,000 cycles are considered to have passed the endurance limit. The reason for this is that any increase in the number of cycles does not produce failure. Shown in Fig. 8-29 is a specimen welded by the shielded-arc method that has passed the 10,000,000-cycle test at 30,000 psi stress in the outside fibers.

**Fig. 8-29.** Typical fatigue test specimen of shielded arc-weld metal after ten million reversals with 30,000 lb per sq in. stress in outside fibers (courtesy Lincoln Electric Company).

**Hardness Tests.** Welds are frequently tested for hardness, because this relates to microstructure, tensile strength, brittleness, and other properties. The methods used are the same as described previously in Chap. 2.

### Nondestructive Testing of Welded Joints

Welds are also checked by nondestructive methods such as magnetic testing, X rays and gamma rays, dye penetrants, and ultrasonic means. These and other tests are described in Chap. 28.

### Qualifications of Welding Operators

The term *certified welder* does not mean that the individual is qualified to weld any material anywhere. On the contrary, he may be able to weld only one material in one position for one company on one particular job. [The four standard positions are flat, horizontal, vertical, and overhead (Fig. 8-30).]

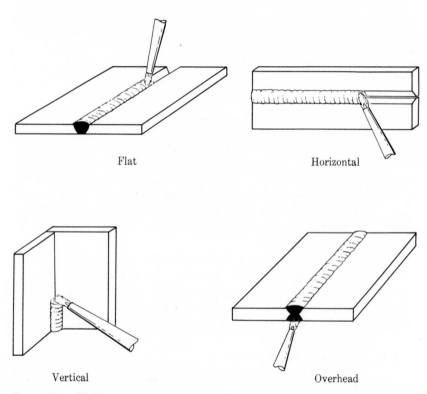

Flat   Horizontal

Vertical   Overhead

**Fig. 8-30.** Welding positions.

Since no standard set of tests can be made for qualifying welding operators for all types of work and conditions, most cities of any size have laboratories where tests can be taken to qualify for welding under various codes.

As an example, a man qualified to weld small underground storage tanks would not have to pass the rigid tests set up by standard codes for welding high-pressure vessels. Operators are tested in making the welds they will encounter in their employment. These tests, although taken in a laboratory, should simulate field conditions as nearly as possible.

## WELD STANDARDS

A question that is frequently asked is: "How good does a weld have to be?" To answer this we must first know what the weld is to be used for and the service conditions it is likely to encounter.

To help answer this question, three classes of weldments have been set up, based primarily upon stresses likely to be encountered in service. In general, these standards are the same for steel, stainless steel, aluminum, and magnesium.

*Class I.* Welds in this class are highly stressed, and the joint is oriented within 45 deg of *normal* to the principal stress. The design factor is 2.0 or less.

*Class II.* These welds are moderately stressed, and the joint is oriented within 45 deg of *parallel* to the principal stress. The design factor is greater than 2.0.

*Class III.* Welds in this class are lightly stressed and have a design factor of 3.0 or more.

Cast- and wrought-steel weldments are further subdivided, depending on the strength level obtained when they were heat-treated. This applies to Classes I and II as follows:

> Class 1A: 150,000 psi and up
> Class 1B: under 150,000 psi

Moderately stressed:

> Class IIA: 150,000 psi and up
> Class IIB: under 150,000 psi

A partial list of inspection requirements is shown in Table 8-1 to acquaint the reader with differences looked for in the visual inspection of the various classes of welds. In addition to the visual-inspection table shown, others are used for magnetic-particle or penetrant inspection and radiographic inspection.

**TABLE 8-1.**

**Visual Inspection Requirements for Various Classes of Welds***

| VISUAL INSPECTION | Steel Class IA Stainless Steel Class I Aluminum & Magnesium Class I | Group B Steel Class IB & IIA Stainless Steel Class II | Group D Steel Class IIB & III Stainless Steel Class III Aluminum & Magnesium Class II & III |
|---|---|---|---|
| *Undercut* | 5% reduction in T, max (T = minimum parent-metal thickness) | | |
| Contour | | must be smoothly rounded | NS (NS = Not Specified) |
| Dist. from end of weld | | 20% of bead length but not less than 1.0 in. | NS |
| Length, each | | 0.25 in. max | 0.20 in. max |
| Length, cumulative | | Group B: 10%; Group D: 20% of weld length, max | NS |
| Distance between undercuts | | 0.06 in. min | 3.0 in. min |
| Depth | | 10% of T, but not to exceed 0.025 in. | 25% of T, max |
| *Scratch or burn marks* | 5% reduction in T, max | NS | 25% of T, max |
| *Cracks* | None accepted | NS | NS |
| *Crater* or depression below level of either parent metal surface | None accepted, face or root bead | NS | NS |
| *End-of-bead crater* | None accepted | 20% of T, but not to exceed 0.025 in. | 0.10 in. max in last 10% of weld bead |

| | | | |
|---|---|---|---|
| Underfill (depression of face or root bead below level of either parent metal surface) | None accepted | | |
|   Depth | | 0.02 in. max | 25% of T max |
|   Length, each | | 1.5 in. max | 1.0 in. max |
|   Length, cumulative | | 3.0 in. max in any 12 in. of weld | 3.0 in. max in any 12 in. of weld |
| Reinforcement of face of root bead | 0.050 in. max | Group B: 0.06 in. max<br>Group D: 0.08 in. max | NS |
| Drop-through beyond root | 0.050 in. max | 0.12 in. max | NS |
| Overlap beyond fusion limits, edge or toe | None accepted | NS | NS |
| Included slag exposed by machining after welding | None accepted | None accepted | NS |
| Burn-through | None accepted | 0.12 in. max | NS |
| Shrinkage on side opposite weld (lap and fillet welds): | | | |
|   Length, each | NS | 0.31 in. max | NS |
|   Length, cumulative | NS | 2 areas max in any 12 in. | NS |
|   Distance between shrinkage areas | NS | 3 in. min | NS |
| Porous areas | NS | NS | 0.10 in. max dimension |
| Fillet weld throat concavity or convexity | NS | NS | 20% of theoretical throat, max |

\* Courtesy *American Machinist/Metalworking Manufacturing.*

### QUESTIONS

1. What effect does welding have on the grain size of the metal in the heat-affected zone of the parent metal?
2. In what way do several passes affect the grain size of the weld?
3. What effect will preheating have on the microstructure of the weld area in medium- and high-carbon steels?
4. Explain why stresses are set up in a rigidly clamped welded structure as it cools.
5. Why are hot cracks more apt to occur in the weld metal than in the base metal?
6. How may stainless steels be modified to keep carbide precipitation to a minimum?
7. In referring to metals, what is meant by hot short?
8. Explain the effect of speed or rate of welding on distortion.
9. Why is it generally better to make one or two passes with large electrodes than three or four passes with small electrodes?
10. How can shrinkage forces be made to work for you?
11. Why is edge preparation normally necessary when welding heavy plate stock?
12. When can intermittent welding be used to advantage?
13. Why is overwelding poor practice?
14. What are some methods used to study stress concentrations?
15. How do fringe lines on photoelastic studies indicate stress concentration?
16. Why is a weld placed in transverse shear stronger than one in longitudinal shear?
17. What information can be obtained from a nick break test?
18. What units are used in reporting the Charpy and Izod tests?
19. What relationship is there between an endurance test and a tensile test?
20. Why is only a certified welder allowed to weld certain materials under certain conditions?
21. What is the difference between a class I and a class II weld?

### PROBLEMS

1. A model weld is constructed and tested by a photoelastic method and is found to have 3.2 fringe lines; a modified design is found to have 5.5 fringe lines in the same area. How much stronger (percent) is the original weld?
2. If a low-carbon steel bar $3/4$ by 2 in. is butt-welded to a similar steel bar and the welds are not reinforced, what is the maximum load the welded bar will be able to carry when subjected to a direct tension load?
3. If the safe allowable load per lineal inch of a 5/16-in. fillet weld in longitudinal shear is 3,000 lb, how much will a $3/8$- by 4-in. low-carbon steel bar have to be lapped to the main structure if it must support a 50,000-lb load?

4. If two ½-in. mild-steel plates are joined by a butt weld 6 in. long, what will be the total allowable tensile load of the joint in pounds per square inch?

5. If the joint given in Prob. 4 were a double lap weld, how many pounds per square inch could it support in shear?

6. (a) A bar of mild steel is required to support a normal tension loading of 90,000 lbs. What size round bar should be used, and what should be the cross-sectional area of the weld in the middle of the member? The normal tensile loading is 40,000 psi. (b) If a square bar is used, what size will be needed?

## REFERENCES

*American Welding Society Standard Welding Symbols*, A2.0-58 American Welding Society, New York 18, N. Y.

*Arc Welding in Machinery Design and Manufacture*, James F. Lincoln Arc Welding Foundation, Cleveland, 1958.

*Designer's Guide for Welded Construction*, The Lincoln Electric Company, Cleveland, 1955.

Hoffman, R. J., "What Load Will a Welded Joint Carry Safely," reprinted from *Welding Engineer*.

Jakobowski, J. W., "Weld Quality Standards," *American Machinist/Metalworking Manufacturing*, April, 1960.

*Procedure Handbook of Arc Welding Design and Practice*, The Lincoln Electric Company, Cleveland, 1957.

*Studies of the Design of Steel Castings and Steel Weldments as Related to Methods of Their Manufacture*, Steel Founders' Society of America, Cleveland, 1959.

*The Tool Engineers Handbook*, American Society of Tool and Manufacturing Engineers, McGraw-Hill Book Company, New York, 1959.

*Welding Handbook*, American Welding Society, New York, 4th Edition 1957.

# 9

# ARC
# WELDING

**B**Y EXAMINING the Master Chart of Welding Processes compiled by the American Welding Society (Fig. 9-1), you can see that arc welding is divided into two main types—metal-electrode and carbon-electrode—with several subtypes under each one. The major emphasis in this chapter will be on the principal kinds of metal arc welding, with only a brief description of carbon-arc welding, since it is not extensively used.

## METAL-ELECTRODE WELDING

The metallic arc-welding process is termed a *nonpressure fusion process*. The heat is developed in an arc produced between a metal electrode or wire and the work to be welded. Under the intense heat developed by the arc, ranging from 5000° to 10,000°F, a small part of the base metal, or work to be welded, is brought to the melting point almost instantaneously. At the same time, the end of the metal electrode is melted, and tiny globules or drops of molten metal pass through the arc to the base metal, as shown by high-speed photography in Fig. 9-2.

One must become familiar with several pieces of equipment and some operating variables in order to understand arc welding. These include welding current sources; welding current characteristics; the types, classification, and selection of electrodes: other equipment; etc.

## MASTER CHART OF WELDING PROCESSES

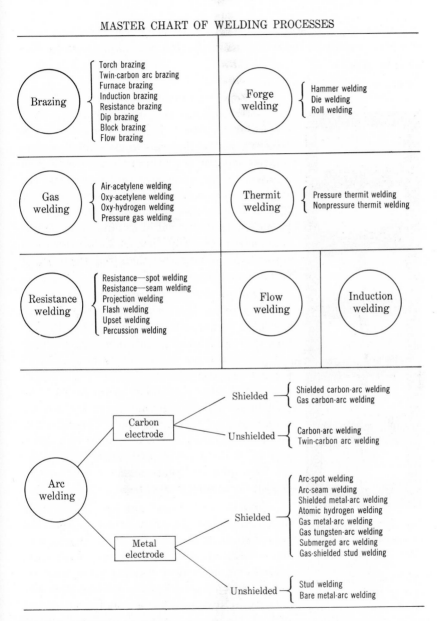

**Fig. 9-1.** Welding processes.

## Current Sources for Manual Arc Welding

**Alternating-Current Machines.** Alternating-current welding machines are mostly of the transformer type, but a-c motor-generator sets are also made.

ALTERNATING-CURRENT TRANSFORMERS. In the a-c transformer the primary coil is hooked directly to the power line. The secondary coil is either tapped at intervals to give different current settings, or the primary coil is moved in relation to the secondary so as to vary the strength of the electrical field (Fig. 9-3). Many light-duty machines depend on a shunt that can be mechanically moved in or out of the central transformer core. The current can be made to go through this shunt rather than from the primary to the secondary coil.

*Transformer advantages.* The principal advantages of the transformer over the generator are lower initial cost—generally about 40 percent less—and lower maintenance costs. There are practically no moving parts in the transformer and, consequently, there is very little wear. It is also very quiet in operation. One particular operating advantage of the a-c arc is that there is no *arc blow.* This is a phenomenon that sometimes occurs when welding with direct current. A distorted magnetic field deflects the arc from its normal path, making it difficult to deposit the metal properly.

*Transformer disadvantages.* The main disadvantage of the transformer is that the *polarity* cannot be changed. Polarity refers to the directional flow of the current. In *straight polarity* the electrode or welding rod is negative, and in *reversed polarity* it is positive. Reversed polarity is recommended for nonferrous metals such as aluminum, bronze, Monel, and nickel, and also for making welds in the vertical and overhead positions. Reversed polarity generally gives a greater digging action, resulting in deeper penetration. Straight polarity is used in mild steel for greater speed and smoother beads.

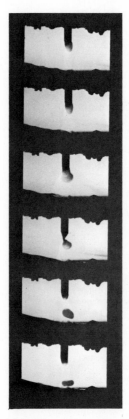

**Fig. 9-2.** High-speed photography is used to show how the metal is pinched off from the electrode as it passes through the arc in globular form. Photos were made at 3,600 frames per sec.

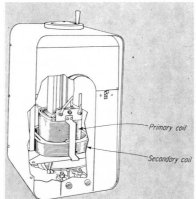

**Fig. 9-3.** The a-c transformer used for arc welding.

**Direct-Current Machines.** Direct current machines are of the motor-generator type or the a-c–d-c rectifier type.

MOTOR-GENERATOR SETS. The Motor-generator set consists of a heavy-duty d-c generator driven by a suitable motor or engine. The voltage of such a generator will usually range from 15 to 45 volts across the arc, although any setting is subject to constant variation owing to changes in the arc conditions. Current output will vary from 20 to 1,000 amp, depending upon the type of unit. Most generators are made of the variable-voltage type, so that the voltage automatically responds to the demands of the arc. However, the voltage can be set to the desired range by means of a rheostat mounted on the control panel of the machine. A change in amperage is obtained by tapping into the field coils of the generator at different points, to increase or decrease its strength. This is taken care of by a selector switch on the control panel. This machine is referred to as a *dual-control* type (Fig. 9-4). Other machines have one control for proportionately adjusting both voltage and amperage.

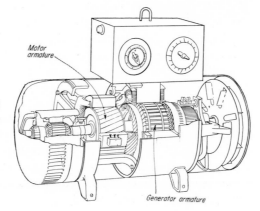

**Fig. 9-4.** A dual-control motor-generator-type welding machine.

*Motor-generator advantages.* The motor-generator machine is versatile and is regarded as the general-purpose welder in industry. As explained previously, it can be used on either straight or reverse polarity. Thus it can be employed on nearly all ferrous and nonferrous materials. It is also used for all positions of welding.

Gasoline- or diesel-driven generators provide compact self-contained units that can be used even in remote areas.

The motor-generator set has an advantage over both the a-c transformer and the d-c rectifier in that its output is not affected by normal variations in power-line voltage.

*Motor-generator disadvantages.* The disadvantage of these machines are the higher initial cost and higher maintenance costs, and the fact that the machine is quite noisy in operation.

**Alternating-Current–Direct-Current Rectifiers.** The transformer rectifier unit consists of a three-phase transformer that adjusts line voltage to the proper level (Fig. 9-5). The rectifier plates that change the alternating current to direct current are usually made from selenium, but silicon now seems to be gaining favor.

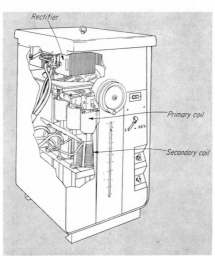

**Fig. 9-5.** Direct current can be supplied for welding through a rectifier.

ADVANTAGES OF AC–DC RECTIFIERS. The a-c–d-c rectifier has the advantage of being able to supply any type of current needed, although, some are made to supply only direct current. Other than that, the advantages are similar to those given for the a-c transformer, with one exception—this machine has good performance even at low welding currents.

DISADVANTAGES OF A-C–D-C RECTIFIERS.  Perhaps the main disadvantage of the a-c–d-c rectifier is that the life of the selenium plates is limited to about 7 years under normal usage.

### Welding Current Characteristics

Before any decision can be made as to what type of equipment is best suited to a given welding operation, it is necessary to understand the electrical characteristics of the power sources used. These are constant current, constant potential, open-circuit voltage, arc voltage, duty cycle, efficiency, and power factor.

**Constant Current.**  When an arc is struck, the electrode is shorted to the work. If a constant-current power source is used, at the moment of contact (short circuit) the amperage shoots up to maximum level and the voltage automatically drops off to a minimum level. As the electrode moves away from the work, the voltage rises to maintain the arc while the amperage drops to working levels. During welding, the voltage varies directly and the amperage inversely with the arc length.

Stating it another way, when the welding electrode is moved closer to the weld puddle, the voltage decreases, the amperage increases, and the metal is deposited more rapidly. When the electrode is moved away, the deposition rate is reduced. The drooping arc-voltage characteristic is necessary for the proper operation of a manual arc, since it will tolerate a wide variation of arc lengths with relatively minor changes in arc current.

**Constant Potential.**  The constant-potential type of machine is designed to maintain a preset voltage level throughout its range. With this type of current arrangement, tap switches and vernier controls are provided so that the voltage can be reduced to almost zero, but the original slope of the curve does not change. The volt-ampere curves for both the constant current and the constant potential are shown in Fig. 9-6.

This type of machine does not tolerate a short-circuit condition. It provides, in effect, unlimited amperage to melt a consumable wire electrode at the instant of contact. This is ideal for automatic machines but is not suited to manual welding.

The control on a constant-current machine reads in amperes, but the constant-potential machine reads in volts. The operator sets a desired voltage level at the power source. Amperage, on the other hand, is automatically determined and maintained by the setting of the wire feed speed on the machine's automatic feeder unit. An increase in wire speed, for example, automatically increases the amperage necessary to melt the wire at a rate that maintains the preset voltage.

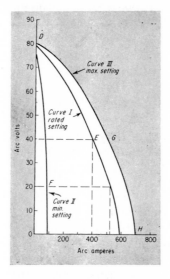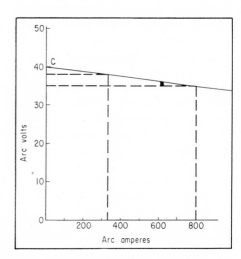

**Fig. 9-6.** The constant-current, drooping arc voltage is compared to a constant-potential, flat, volt-ampere characteristic.

**Open-Circuit Voltage.** Open-circuit voltage refers to the potential voltage of the machine when the circuit is open or the machine is idling. These voltages vary with the type of machine and manufacturer, but they generally range from 65 to 100 volts. Open-circuit voltage has little relationship to arc voltage, which is largely a function of arc length, but it does have an influence on arc stability. It may be said that high open-circuit voltages generally provide better arc stability. However, for the sake of safety, the open-circuit voltages of transformers are generally limited to 80 volts and motor generators to 100 volts.

**Arc Voltage.** Arc voltage refers to the voltage required between the electrode and the work. Once the arc has been established this value drops down to about 18 v and usually does not exceed 34 v. The variation is accounted for by the changes in arc length. Long arc lengths require higher voltages with correspondingly less current and vice versa. The total amount of current change, however, must be governed by the open-circuit voltage setting on the machine.

When it is desirable to deposit a comparatively large amount of metal, as in flat position or downhand welding, the high open-circuit voltage is used since it produces a constant hot arc despite minor variations in arc length.

In overhead welding the current at the electrode end must be reduced. After a small amount of metal is deposited, the weldor lengthens the arc, thus reducing the current so the metal can solidify. Then as the electrode is brought back with a short arc the voltage goes down and the amperage up so the metal can be deposited quickly. Arc voltage is very important in determining the various rates of metal deposit.

**Duty Cycle.** All welders show three ratings—amperes, volts, and duty cycle— on the nameplate. Duty cycle is the percentage of a 10-min period that a welder can operate at rated power output without overheating or suffering other damage. A welder rated at 300 amp, 40 volts, 60 percent duty cycle can supply its rated power (300 amp at a 40-volt load) when operated 60 percent of the time, or 6 min out of every 10.

A machine can be operated at 100 percent duty cycle by reducing the current setting to $77\frac{1}{2}$ percent of the nameplate rating, or 230 amp in the case of a 300-amp welder. To operate at maximum current (above rated capacity) the duty cycle should be reduced to half that of the rated value, or, in this case, to 3 min out of every 10.

**Efficiency.** Efficiency is used as an important point of comparison in evaluating welding power sources, because high efficiency means low-cost power. Although electric power accounts for less than 10 percent of the total direct welding costs, it can still be a sizable amount.

On this point the motor generator is at a disadvantage, since it has a large mass that must be running at high speeds regardless of whether power is being delivered or not. Alternating-current transformers and d-c rectifier units have no moving parts other than a cooling fan, and so can operate at much higher efficiencies on light loads with negligible no-load power losses. This is important when operating at low duty cycles. Even at normal loads the motor generator does not match the efficiency of other units.

**Power-Factor Correction.** When a-c machines are used for welding, not all the useful power supplied by the incoming line is usable unless the power factor is at what is known as *unity;* that is, when the amperes drawn from the line are in phase with the line voltage. Since this seldom occurs, a power-factor correction is needed. Power factor (PF) then stands for the ratio of the usable current to the total current (kw to kva).

This correction is taken care of on individual machines, or on the incoming line, by installing static condensers. These condensers are out of phase with the line voltage in the opposite direction to the welding equipment. One is said to be a *lagging current* and the other a *leading current.* The formula for finding the PF correction is the cosine of the numbers of degrees the amperes are out of phase with the volts.

Welding characteristics are not affected by power factor. Its main effect is on the cost of the incoming power and other equipment in the plant. Some plants have large synchronous motors operating air compressors and other equipment. These motors have a favorable influence on power factor and may be able to keep it within acceptable limits.

### Electrodes—Types, Classification, and Selection

**Electrode Types.** Shielded-arc or heavily coated electrodes consist of wires of a definite composition over which a coating is formed, by dipping, extrusion, or winding. This coating, of cellulosic, minerals or iron powder materials, may amount to 10 percent or more of the total weight of the electrode. Combinations of both cellulosic and mineral types are also used.

CELLULOSIC COATING. The cellulosic coatings derive their name from wood pulp, sawdust, cotton, and various other cellulosic compositions obtained in the manufacture of rayon. This coating forms a gaseous shield for protection around the arc stream during the welding operation and a light slag covering for the deposited metal (Fig. 9-7).

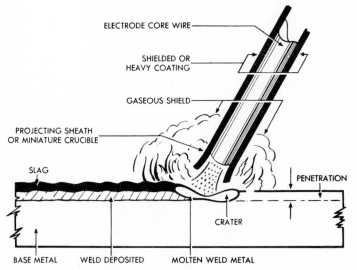

ELECTRODE CORE WIRE

SHIELDED OR HEAVY COATING

GASEOUS SHIELD

PROJECTING SHEATH OR MINIATURE CRUCIBLE

SLAG

PENETRATION

CRATER

BASE METAL     WELD DEPOSITED     MOLTEN WELD METAL

**Fig. 9-7.** The welding action of a cellulosic-coated metal electrode.

*Use.* The expanding gas furnished by the burning cellulosic material acts to give a forceful digging action to the weld. It can be used in any position but is particularly useful in vertical, horizontal, and overhead positions.

MINERAL COATING. Mineral coatings are manufactured from natural silicates such as asbestos and clay. By adding oxides of certain refractory metals such as titanium, the harsh digging action of the arc is modified to give an arc that is softer and less penetrating. This type of action is desirable in making welds where the fit-up is poor and on sheet metal parts where shallow penetration is desired. The mineral-coated rod depends on the heavy slag for protection and control of the chemistry of the deposited metal.

The heavy slag acts to slow the cooling rate of the metal, allowing gas to escape and slag particles to rise to the top. Cooling stresses are reduced, and a more homogeneous microstructure results.

*Use.* The burn-off rate of mineral-coated electrodes is much higher than the cellulosic type, resulting in a larger molten pool and faster deposition rate. Because of this and the large amount of slag produced, they are more advantageously used for *downhand* welding. Downhand welding is used in making flat welds and those inclined up to 45 deg.

IRON-POWDER COATINGS. The use of iron powder in the electrode coating is comparatively new. The addition of iron powder brought about several desirable effects; particularly, the welding speed increased, and the appearance of the bead improved. The iron powder in the coating not only helps to form an effective crucible at the end of the rod, which is longer than that formed with other coatings, but it more effectively concentrates the heat and gives an automatically consistent arc length. Welding is made considerably easier since the electrode can be dragged upon the work without having to hold it a certain height above the work. Slag is often self-removing. There is less sticking of the electrode, which often occurs in the small sizes. Finally, it furnishes more inches of weld per electrode because the iron in the coating goes into the weld. Iron-powder electrodes require about 25 percent higher current setting than for equal-sized conventional rods. Also, because of the heavy coating, there are about half as many rods per pound.

**Electrode Classification.** The American Welding Society and the American Society for Testing Materials have jointly established a code for welding electrodes based on tensile strength, position, current supply, and application.

The code is based on an "E" prefix with four or five digits following it. The first two digits of four-digit numbers refer to minimum ultimate tensile strength. The third digit refers to the welding position in which the electrode can be used, as follows:

| *Digit* | *Meaning* |
|---------|-----------|
| 1 | All positions |
| 2 | Horizontal and flat positions |
| 3 | Flat position |

The fourth digit refers to current, and indirectly to coating, as follows:

| Digit | Meaning |
|---|---|
| 0 | Direct-current reverse when third digit is 1 |
| 0 | Direct-current reverse and alternating current when third digit is 2 or 3 |
| 1 | Alternating-current or direct-current reverse |
| 2 | Straight polarity or alternating current |
| 3 | Alternating- or direct-current straight |
| 5 | Direct-current reverse (lime or titania sodium, low hydrogen) |
| 6 | Alternating- or direct-current reverse (titania or lime potassium, low hydrogen) |
| 8 | Alternating- or direct-current reverse (titania, calcium carbonate, fluorspar, and iron powder) |

NOTE. Hydrogen in a weld is a source of porosity and embrittlement. It has a tendency to harden on cooling and to cause *underbead cracking* (cracking of the previously deposited layer). Low-hydrogen electrodes have been designed expressly to keep these harmful effects to a minimum.

Suffix letters are now being added to the standard code. The letters A, B, and C are used to designate the chemical composition of the weld deposit. The number following this letter further classifies the deposit.

| Letter | Meaning |
|---|---|
| A | Carbon-molybdenum deposit |
| B | Chrome-molybdenum deposit |
| C | Nickel deposit |

As the numbers following the letters increase from 1 to 3, so do the alloying elements. For example XXXX-B-1 is 0.5 Cr–0.5 Mo; XXXX-B-2 is 1.0 Cr–0.5 Mo; XXXXB-3 is 2.25 Cr– 1.0 Mo.

An example of one of the standard code numbers now used will help clarify some of the preceding information.

| Code | Meaning |
|---|---|
| E70XX | 70,000 psi minimum tensile strength |
| E7016 | Can be used in all positions |
| E7016 | Designed for use with alternating current or d-c reverse polarity because the third digit is 1. |

Table 9-1 (pages 246–247) contains a list of commonly used electrodes, positions of use, general description, and test requirements.

**Basic Steps in Selecting Proper Electrodes.** Much of the information needed in selecting an electrode for a certain job is contained in the code just described. These include tensile properties, position of the weld, and the type of current source. All these factors are important, but the position of the weld bears further discussion. (Additional factors will be discussed in following pages.)

WELD POSITIONING. The main advantage of being able to position a joint is to increase the speed of welding. Therefore, in selecting the electrode, if the weld is normally other than flat, repositioning it for welding should be considered. Positioning can be accomplished manually, but there are so many universal positioning devices on the market that manual positioning can seldom be justified.

To make weld beads in either the vertical or the overhead position requires fast-freezing electrodes with lower deposition rates and special techniques to help overcome the force of gravity. An example of the advantage of positioning a fillet weld from vertical to horizontal is shown in Fig. 9-8. You will note that the speed increased from 4.5 ipm to 19.2 ipm.

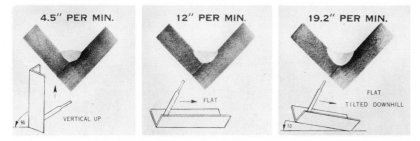

**Fig. 9-8.** Effect of position on speed of welding fillet welds in plate ⅜ in. or thinner (courtesy Lincoln Electric Company).

Good positioning is important not only in respect to the weld direction but in respect to improving the *operating factor*. By operating factor is meant the percentage of time that the arc is actually welding. Here the convenience of the supplies, machine controls, and accessibility is important. A 50 percent factor means that only half the number of feet per hour have been welded as would be done with a 100 percent operating factor.

**Fig. 9-9.** This large welding positioner is able to put all welds on this 12½-ton rotor housing in the downhand position (courtesy Harnishfeger Corp.).

**TABLE 9-1.**

## Classification of Commonly Used Electrodes*

| AWS-ASTM Classification | Type of Coating or Covering | Capable of Producing Satisfactory Welds in Positions Shown^a | Type of Current |
|---|---|---|---|
| | | E45 SERIES. — MINIMUM TENSILE STRENGTH OF DEPOSITED METAL IN AS-WELDED CONDITION 45,000 PSI. | |
| E4510......... E4520......... | {Sulcoated or light} {coated} | F, V, OH, H H-Fillets, F | Not specified but generally dc, straight polarity (electrode negative) |
| | | E60 SERIES. — MINIMUM TENSILE STRENGTH OF DEPOSITED METAL IN AS-WELDED CONDITION 60,000 PSI. | |
| E6010......... | High cellulose sodium | F, V, OH, H | For use with dc, reverse polarity (electrode positive) only. |
| E6011......... | High cellulose potassium | F, V, OH, H | For use with ac or dc reverse polarity (electrode positive). |
| E6012......... | High titania sodium | F, V, OH, H | For use with dc, straight polarity (electrode negative), or ac. |
| E6013......... | High titania potassium | F, V, OH, H | For use with ac or dc, straight polarity (electrode negative). |
| E6014......... | Iron powder, titania | F, V, OH, H | For use with dc, either polarity or ac. |
| E6015......... | Low hydrogen sodium | F, V, OH, H | For use with dc, reverse polarity (electrode positive) only. |
| E6016......... | Low hydrogen potassium | F, V, OH, H | For use with ac or dc reverse polarity (electrode positive). |

| | | | |
|---|---|---|---|
| E6018 ........... | Iron powder, low hydrogen | F, V, OH, H | For use with ac or dc, reverse polarity. |
| E6020 ........... | High iron oxide | H-Fillets, F | For use with dc, straight polarity (electrode negative), or ac for horizontal fillet welds; and dc, either polarity, or ac, for flat-position welding. |
| E6024 ........... | Iron powder, titania | H-Fillets, F | For use with dc, either polarity, or ac. |
| E6027 ........... | Iron powder, iron oxide | H-Fillets, F | For use with dc, straight polarity (electrode negative), or ac for horizontal fillet welds; and dc, either polarity, or ac, for flat-position welding. |
| E6028 ........... | Iron powder, low hydrogen | H-Fillets, F | For use with ac or dc, reverse polarity. |
| E6030 ........... | High iron oxide | F | For use with dc, either polarity, or ac. |

E70 SERIES. — MINIMUM TENSILE STRENGTH OF DEPOSITED METAL IN AS-WELDED CONDITION 70,000 PSI.

| | | | |
|---|---|---|---|
| E7014 ........... | Iron powder, titania | F, V, OH, H | For use with dc, either polarity, or ac. |
| E7015 ........... | Low hydrogen sodium | F, V, OH, H | For use with dc, reverse polarity (electrode positive) only. |
| E7016 ........... | Low hydrogen potassium | F, V, OH, H | For use with ac or dc reverse polarity (electrode positive). |
| E7018 ........... | Iron powder, low hydrogen | F, V, OH, H | For use with ac or dc, reverse polarity. |
| E7024 ........... | Iron powder, titania | H-Fillets, F | For use with dc, either polarity, or ac. |
| E7028 ........... | Iron powder, low hydrogen | H-Fillets, F | For use with ac or dc, reverse polarity. |

[a] The abbreviations F, H, V, OH, and H-Fillets indicate welding positions as follows:

F = Flat
H = Horizontal
V = Vertical
OH = Overhead } For electrodes 3/16 in. and under, except 5/32 in. and under for classifications EXX14, EXX15, EXX16 and EXX18.
H-Fillets = Horizontal Fillets

* ASTM and AWS Classification A233-58.

SPEED. A second question that is important in the selection of an electrode for a given job is, "Which one can meet the weld specifications and yet achieve the greatest speed?" In this consideration there are three classifications of electrodes: fast fill, fast follow, and fast freeze.

*Fast fill.* Fast-fill electrodes are used for joints that require a given amount of metal to bring them to the required size, as in the case of a large fillet or deep grooves. In order to deposit a large amount of metal quickly, electrodes with high-deposition ratings are chosen, such as E6012 or E6013 for fillets and lap joints and the E6020's for the deep grooves.

The electrodes listed are standard, but the newer iron-powder electrode is also considered an excellent fast-fill type. The E6024 iron-powder electrode was the first one to come out in this group and is still considered very good, but E6018 is now becoming more popular.

*Fast follow.* Fast follow consists of using an electrode to spread the weld deposit thinly over a long length of joint in a very short time. In order to do this the molten-metal crater must be able to follow the electrode at relatively high travel speeds (20 in. or more per min). Fast-follow electrodes are used in manually lap-welding automobile frames. This is accomplished at rates up to 60 ipm. It is not uncommon to weld 48 in. of joint with one electrode. Many of the fast-follow applications are in sheet metal, and the best electrode to use for this is the E6012 in the smaller sizes (3/16 in. or less).

*Fast freeze.* Vertical and overhead welds require the fast-freeze electrode, as mentioned previously. The best one for this purpose is E6010.

WELDABILITY. A third important factor to consider in choosing the proper electrode is the weldability of the metal.

The weldability of various metals was discussed in Chaps. 3 and 4, but, in brief review, it refers to being able to make a good sound weld that is not sensitive to cracking. Some steels, for example, are high in carbon, phosphorus, sulfur, or special alloys, and require careful consideration in selecting the proper electrode to produce a crack-free weld. Heavy sections, if not preheated, tend to produce a quenching action on the weld that can, in turn, result in cracks. The first consideration in welding these materials, then, is not speed or ease of welding, but which electrode will produce a crack-free weld. The best choices here are the low-hydrogen-type electrodes classified as E6015 and E6016.

Low-hydrogen electrode is the name given to a mineral-type coating that was at first called "lime ferritic." It is now called "basic low hydrogen," since it is the basic or alkaline property of the slag and its low hydrogen content that provide the unique qualities for welding difficult-to-weld steels. Low-hydrogen electrodes developed from the idea that the basic calcium carbonate–calcium fluoride covering used on stainless-steel-core wire might work well on a mild-steel-core wire alloyed with manganese and molybdenum. It proved to be satisfactory in welding armor plate that had been so prone to cracking. However, the welding of heavy armor plate was still erratic, and it was found that this was because some hydrogen was contained in the coating. Consequently, the hydrogen was reduced to a minimum.

In 1956 iron powder was added to the coating. There are now three main types of low-hydrogen iron-powder electrodes—conventional E7016; E7018, containing approximately 30 percent iron powder; E7028, containing approximately 50 percent iron powder. The iron-powder addition increases the burn-off or deposition rate of the metal.

In use, there may be some porosity each time the arc is struck unless a special effort is made to keep the arc short. The shielding carbon dioxide gas is largely produced from the decomposition of the calcium carbonate, which constitutes the largest amount of any ingredient in the covering. Since it requires only a fraction of a second for the electrode covering to reach this decomposition temperature, a short arc must be maintained or the metal will not be adequately protected from the atmosphere.

Moisture in the coating of low-hydrogen electrodes has a detrimental effect on the quality of the weld if it is over 0.5 percent. A general recommendation is that these electrodes be stored where the temperature is at least 10°F above the outdoor temperature. This is not always adequate. The best results are obtained by keeping the electrodes in a dry-rod storage oven at 250° to 350°F.

ELECTRODE SIZE.   A general rule in selecting electrode size is never to use one that is larger in diameter than the thickness of the metal to be welded. For vertical and overhead welding, 3/16 in. is the largest diameter you should use, regardless of the plate thickness. Larger electrodes make it too difficult to control the deposited metal.

### Other Equipment

**Arc-Welding Helmets.**   In order to protect the eyes and face of a welder from the dangerous ultraviolet and infrared rays of the arc, welding helmets are necessary. The ultraviolet rays can burn the skin, with the same effect as severe sunburn, while the infrared rays can cause temporary painful injury to the eyes. Helmets should be inspected to see that they are leakproof against the rays of the arc. The colored glass of the helmet filters out most of the harmful effects of the infrared and ultraviolet rays, as well as some of the visible rays. A plain cover glass is used outside of the colored glass for inexpensive protection. It should be replaced from time to time, as it becomes badly pitted and spattered.

**Protective Clothing.** Gloves must be worn by the welder to protect his hands from the harmful rays of the arc and from being burned by molten metal, spatter, and sparks. Flexible leather-gauntlet gloves should be heavy enough so that they will not shrivel up or burn through easily.

Other protective clothing usually worn consists of a leather apron, leather capes and sleeves (for overhead welding), and a cap. Welders should wear high-cuff shoes and should turn the cuffs of their trousers down to prevent molten metal from being caught in them.

**Cables.** The welding current is conducted from the power source through the electrode holder, the arc, the metal, and back to the machine by means of insulated copper or aluminum cables. A flexible cable is needed for the electrode holder. This is achieved by having many thousands of strands of fine wire enclosed in insulating materials with a rubber covering.

The size of the cables required varies with the size of the machine and the distance from the work. For example, a 200-amp machine with a 60 percent duty cycle can use a No. 2 cable for distances up to 150 ft. From 150 to 200 ft, a No. 1 cable would be required.

**Electrode Holders and Ground Clamps.** The electrode holder is an insulated clamping device for holding the electrode. The electrode jaws are made to hold the bare end of the electrode in either a vertical or an angular position. Ground clamps furnish a quick means of attaching the ground lead to the work.

### Basic Types of Automatic and Semiautomatic Arc Welding

One of the main types of arc welding, shielded-metal arc, has already been introduced along with the current sources used. Referring to the welding-processes chart (Fig. 9-1), you will see many other processes given for metal-electrode welding, such as submerged-arc, inert-gas (MIG and TIG) $CO_2$, atomic hydrogen, and stud welding. These will be discussed briefly, pointing out some of the uses and advantages of each.

**Submerged-Arc Welding.** Submerged-arc welding derives its name from the fact the entire welding action is submerged beneath a mineral material known as flux (Fig. 9-10). The arc is started by a short initial contact with the work, by a steel-wool fuse ball, or by a high-frequency spark. As the flow of current starts, the welding arc becomes submerged in a sea of molten flux which shields the arc and the molten metal from oxidation and covers the hot weld deposit, allowing it to cool more slowly.

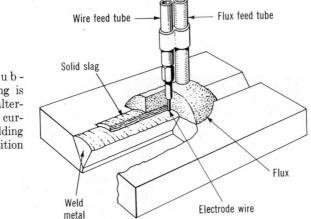

**Fig. 9-10.** Submerged-arc welding is used with either alternating or direct current for heavy welding and high deposition rates.

The bare wire electrode, ranging in size from 5/64 to ¼ in. and occasionally to 3/8 in., is held on a coiled reel and fed mechanically by means of continuously rotating drive rolls. The speed is varied according to the travel of the machine and the needs of the job.

Automatic heads are available for either alternating or direct current. The a-c transformers are better suited to heavy plate work and where continuous seams are used. The low current settings required for light-gauge work make the a-c arc difficult to control.

The d-c type head on reversed polarity can be used to advantage on higher-gauge metal. (A minimum of 14-gauge metal is recommended.) Direct current has superior arc-striking qualities and generally better arc control. However, it is still subject to arc blow. Welding voltage control used on this equipment helps make the process automatic.

ADVANTAGES.  The submerged arc can handle extremely high current densities. For example, currents as high as 600 amp can be used with 5/64-in.-diameter electrode wire. This creates a current density of 10,000 amp per sq in., or 6 to 10 times that carried by a manual electrode of equivalent size. The advantage of high current density is, of course, the high *melt-off* rate that can be obtained. Speeds can be obtained that range from 15 ipm on heavy fillet welds in 1-in. plate to 150 ipm on ¼-in. material.

The high speeds and high current densities result in deep penetration. Butt welds can be made in steel plate up to 5/8 in. thick without any edge preparation. Because of the deep penetration, the use of smaller V's is practical. Shown in Fig. 9-11 is an example of a weld made in heavy plate with only a 15-deg U-groove-type preparation. This weld was made by using two electrodes at once in tandem position, or one in back of the other. A side-by-side or transverse position is also used. By the use of multiple electrodes, speeds can be increased from 1½ to 2 times that of the single electrode.

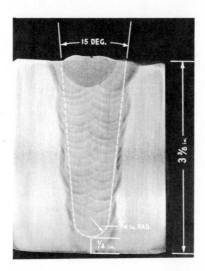

**Fig. 9-11.** A cross section of a multipass weld made with submerged arc (courtesy Linde Co., division of Union Carbide Corp.).

The quality of the weld is excellent and uniform. There is no spatter, and the fused flux on top of the weld pops off by itself, revealing a weld that needs little or no finishing.

Use.   Metals welded by the submerged-arc process are low-carbon steels, low-alloy steels, stainless steels, and high-alloy steels. Special precautions, such as preheat and postheat, must be taken in welding the high-alloy steels. Common nonferrous metals are also welded by this process.

Because of the large amount of molten metal, most of the welding is limited to the flat position.

**Inert-Gas-Shielded Arc Welding.**   As explained briefly in Chap. 3, inert gas can be used with a metal electrode, metal inert gas (MIG), or tungsten inert gas (TIG). The inert shielding gases used are helium or argon. Carbon dioxide and various mixtures of oxygen and argon, though not necessarily inert, come under the inert process.

MIG WELDING. Metal inert-gas-shielded arc welding is somewhat similar to submerged-arc welding in that the bare wire electrode is fed from a reel through powered feed rolls into the arc (Fig. 9-12). It differs in the fact that the shielding is done by an inert gas and the arc is clearly visible at all times. Whereas the submerged arc lends itself to mechanized control more than to manual welding, the opposite is true of MIG.

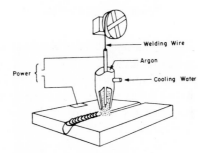

**Fig. 9-12.** Shielded metal inert-gas welding (MIG) (courtesy Linde Co., division of Union Carbide Corp.).

These welders are primarily designed as constant-potential machines, since the arc is self-regulating. This simplifies voltage control and requires only that the machine be equipped with a constant-speed wire feeder. Direct-current reversed polarity is often used, but it can be changed to straight for welding mild steel by changing the leads or the polarity switch.

Two arc lengths are used, as shown in Fig. 9-13. The short circuit produces a small "cold" weld puddle effective for light-gauge metals. The long or spray-type arc provides intense heat used for welding thicker plates.

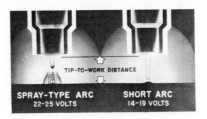

**Fig. 9-13.** Two types of arc in MIG welding, the spray type or conventional being used for heavy plate and the short arc for light-gauge metals (courtesy Linde Co., division of Union Carbide Corp.).

Two types of welding action—continuous fusion welding and spot welding—are provided. In spot welding, the operator holds the torch against the work and pulls the trigger; the machine starts the flow of shielding gas, establishes the arc, feeds the wire at the preselected rate, and times the weld duration. The equipment used is shown in Fig. 9-14.

**Fig. 9-14.** A combination metal inert-gas machine used for both manual spot welds and continuous fusion welds (courtesy Linde Co., division of Union Carbide Corp.).

*Advantages.* Inert gas provides a shielding medium that requires no flux removal, thus eliminating postwelding cleaning or finishing. The high welding speeds (up to 785 ipm using 0.030-in. wire on 3/64-in. carbon steel) minimize distortion of the base metal, leaving its properties relatively undisturbed. Loss of alloying elements is practically negligible, so wire of the same composition as the base metal can be used.

*Uses.* This method can be used on practically all commercially available metals. It can be used for deep-groove welding of plates and castings, just as the submerged-arc process can, but it is more advantageous on light-gauge metals where high speeds are possible. Continuous-duty machines generally range from 200 to 500 amp.

TIG WELDING. Tungsten inert-gas welding differs from the previously described metal inert-gas process primarily in the fact that it has what is considered a nonconsumable electrode. Actually, the tungsten electrode is consumed at a very slow rate and must occasionally be replaced. It is vaporized very slowly and does not become part of the weld. Filler metal can be added manually or mechanically by the operator for joints that require it. The *torch*, as the electrode holder is called, can be either air- or water-cooled (Fig. 9-15). Water-cooled torches are used for heavier work (200 to 500-amp continuous-duty machines) and the air-cooled for capacities up to this range. The torches are extremely light and easy to handle, weighing less than 1 lb in most cases.

Either direct or alternating current can be used for TIG welding. The selection of current is generally based on the metal to be welded. Direct-current straight polarity is best suited for automatic welding of ferrous metals, since maintaining the correct arc length is critical. For nonferrous metals, particularly aluminum and magnesium, alternating current is best because it helps clean the oxide coating from the metal as it is being welded. The a-c arc is stabilized by superimposing a high-frequency current of high voltage and low power on the regular welding current.

*Advantages.* The chief advantage of the TIG process over the MIG process is that it can be used with or without filler rod.

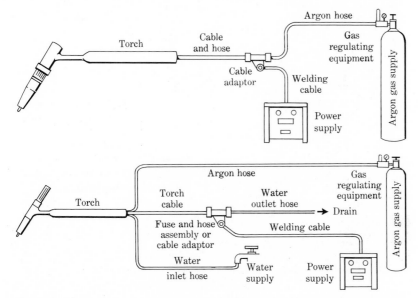

**Fig. 9-15.** A comparison of the setup for TIG welding using either the light-duty air-cooled torch or the heavy-duty water-cooled torch (courtesy Linde Co., division of Union Carbide Corp.).

*Use.* This method finds its greatest application in welding aluminum, stainless steels, and magnesium. It is used, however, on nearly all other types of metals—brass, copper, cast iron, and low- and high-alloy steels, including pure nickel, Monel, and Inconel. Of particular interest has been the work in welding commercially pure titanium, for which welding speeds and feeds have been developed that compare with those of other metals. Postheat treatment is required to obtain acceptable weld ductility. This process has also found wide acceptance in applying hard facing and surfacing materials, discussed in a later chapter.

CARBON DIOXIDE WELDING. Carbon dioxide welding embodies the same principles as MIG welding but makes use of a lower-cost shielding gas. This process is comparatively new, but it is fast becoming one of the most versatile methods available today for welding mild- and low-alloy steels. It employs a rapidly consumable bare electrode wire that is automatically fed into the weld puddle at speeds up to 1,500 ipm.

Although low-alloy steels can be welded with straight carbon dioxide gas shielding, better results are generally obtained by mixing it with 20 percent argon.

Shown in Fig. 9-16 is typical application of carbon dioxide welding on mild steel, complete with process data.

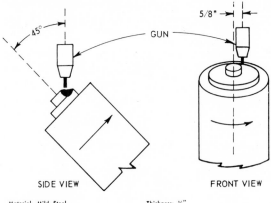

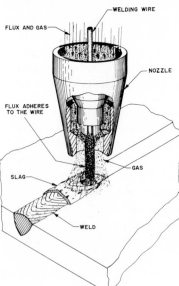

**Fig. 9-16.** An example of the use of carbon dioxide welding on mild steel (courtesy Pure Carbonic Company, division of Air Reduction Co., Inc.).

Material: Mild Steel
Filler Wire: .045" A-675
Gas: Carbon Dioxide
Lineal Weld Speed: 40 Inches Per Minute
Welding Position: Down-Hand Fillet (Automatic Head)
Current:     320 amps                          Arc Voltage: 30 Volts
Backing:     None
Fixture:     Simple Rotation
Remarks:     Cylinder rotated at 45° angle in counter-clockwise direction. Head ⅜" to
             right of center. Arc directed 1/32" up into spud. Weld overlapped 1".

Thickness: ¼"
Wire Feed: 420 IPM    No. of Passes: 1
Flow: 45 Cubic Feet Per Hour

MAGNETIC-FLUX, GAS-SHIELDED ARC WELDING. Another type of shielding was developed in 1957 for what was essentially MIG welding. As in the previously described process, carbon dioxide used as the shielding gas, but a powdered flux is mixed with it. The flux becomes magnetized while passing through the arc and is attracted to the welding wire (Fig. 9-17). The flux coating stabilizes the arc and produces a slag

**Fig. 9-17.** The magnetic-flux process has an automatically fed consumable electrode shielded by carbon dioxide and a magnetic flux (courtesy the Linde Co., division of Union Carbide Corp.).

which metallurgically refines and protects the weld pool. Thus the weld contour and the period of coalescence have the beneficial effects of the light slag covering.

On 3/8-in.-size fillet welds where high currents can be used, the increased speed obtained over carbon dioxide welding was found to be 15 percent. It also resulted in better weld quality with no undercutting. A comparison is also made of welding speed with covered electrodes (Fig. 9-18).

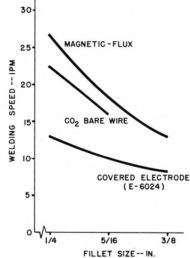

**Fig. 9-18.** A comparison of the speed of welding for various-sized fillet welds made by the processes shown (courtesy the Linde Co., division of Union Carbide Corp.).

The processes discussed—submerged-arc, metal inert gas, tungsten inert gas, carbon dioxide, and magnetic flux—have all given industry increased weld penetration. Accordingly, designers can design joints with smaller welds. Studies have shown that these wire-fed processes may safely employ welds which are two and three sizes smaller than those made by the conventional coated-stick electrode. You will note, in Fig. 9-19, that the welds are the same size, but the one made by the magnetic-flux process has much deeper penetration.

**Fig. 9-19.** A comparison of the amount of penetration obtained with the same size welds made by the magnetic-flux process (on the left) and the coated-stick electrode (on the right) (courtesy the Linde Co., division of Union Carbide Corp.).

ATOMIC-HYDROGEN WELDING. The main differences between this process and TIG are that the arc is maintained between two tungsten electrodes, instead of between the work and the electrode, and the shielding gas is hydrogen. The temperature of the arc is sufficient to break down the molecular hydrogen that passes between the two electrodes into atomic hydrogen. The atoms of hydrogen thus formed recombine at the surface of the metal being welded to form molecules of hydrogen, releasing the heat energy that was previously absorbed in the arc.

*Advantage.* This method of heat transfer, plus the protection of the hydrogen gas, makes this process advantageous for welding thin sheets of chrome, nickel, and molybdenum steels when high finish is needed.

**Stud Welding.** Stud welding consists of placing a *stud* (usually a threaded bolt without a head) into a spring-type chuck on the end of a welding gun. In the end of the stud is a recess, filled and capped, that contains the flux which acts as a chemical cleaner of the surface before the weld metal is deposited. A ceramic ferrule, placed over the end of the stud, confines the arc to a limited space, making a neat-appearing joint with some shielding for the molten metal (Fig. 9-20). The stud, with the ferrule over the end, is placed against the base plate in the desired position, and the trigger is pulled. This sets off a series of reactions. First the stud is retracted from the base plate about 1/16 in. The arc causes the flux, held in the capped stud recess, to be released for chemical cleaning, and a pool of metal forms which is confined and protected by the ceramic ferrule. After a preset time the current is automatically turned off, and the stud is instantly plunged into the pool of metal by the spring action of the gun. After the weld cools, the ceramic ferrule is easily broken and removed.

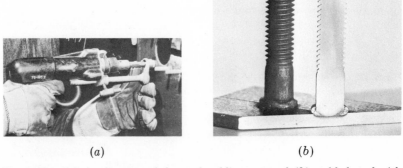

(a)                                    (b)

**Fig. 9-20.** (a) Application of the stud welding gun and (b) welded stud with sectional view (courtesy Nelson Stud Welding, division of Gregory Industries Inc.).

The current source was, at one time, a problem, since the guns require a high short-interval amperage. Workers in the construction field used to hook up two 400-amp generators in parallel, since they needed a much greater source of power. Now, however, ultrahigh-speed generators that can turn out the necessary current are available. Studs 1½ in. in diameter, for example, require about 4,500 amp at 65 to 70 volts for 2 sec.

ADVANTAGES.   Considerable saving in time and money can be realized by being able to place studs almost instantaneously where needed rather than having to pursue the conventional steps of drilling a hole and using a conventional bolt. Another advantage is that studs can be placed for fastening surfaces not otherwise accessible by conventional methods. In addition, no surface preparation is necessary; the interior surface can remain smooth.

USE.   Studs are available in a wide range of lengths, diameters, and shapes. As an example, both J-bolts and I-bolts are standard items in a variety of sizes and threads. Still another example is an aluminum-insert steel stud that can be used to attach aluminum sheet to steel support members. Since the steel is attached to steel and the aluminum to aluminum, there is little danger of electrolytic action. Generally, stud welding is limited to a minimum of 20-gauge (0.035-in.) steel to prevent excessive burnthrough.

This method can be used on practically all carbon steels and alloy steels. High-carbon and high-alloy steels require the usual precautions of pre- and postheating. Procedures have been worked out for stud-welding copper and nickel alloys. Some types of aluminum need protective gas shielding. Heat-treatable aluminum alloys are not recommended for stud welding.

## CARBON-ELECTRODE WELDING

Carbon-electrode welding differs from shielded metal arc welding in that the arc is maintained between a carbon electrode and the base metal or between two carbon electrodes. The latter is referred to as a carbon-arc torch. Filler metal may or may not be added, depending upon the requirements of the joint. Alternating current is usually used, but straight polarity can be used if an electrode one size larger is used on the positive side. Reverse polarity causes the electrode to give off a black sooty smoke.

The carbon-electrode process can be used for welding aluminum, copper, nickel, and Monel. It is also used for brazing, braze welding, soldering, and metal heating for bending, tempering, annealing, etc.

A summary of newer semiautomatic welding processes, showing the principal applications, advantages, and limitations, is given in Fig. 9-21.

| | Submerged Arc | Inert Arc | $CO_2$ | $CO_2$ (flux coated) | Open Arc |
|---|---|---|---|---|---|
| Principal Applications | For welding mild, alloy, and stainless steels, 16 gauge and thicker; for surfacing. | For all weldable metals, including aluminum, copper, stainless steel, titanium, cast iron, high-temperature alloys, and hard-to-weld metals. For depositing aluminum-bronze, stainless, or copper on mild steel. For 12 gauge and thicker. | For welding low- and medium-carbon, low-alloy high-tensile, and high-strength steels, and some stainless-steel grades. For 10 gauge and thicker. | For welding carbon steels. | For hard-surfacing and build-up work and plate fabrication. |
| Advantages | High deposition rate and welding speed. Good penetration. Flat contoured bead has excellent appearance. Low hydrogen deposits of X-ray quality. | High heat permits fast, all-position welding on metals 1/8" and thicker. Little distortion. | Visible arc. High deposition rate; low cost per pound of weld. High operator factor. Inexpensive shielding gas. Deep penetration reduces weld size and amount of filler wire | High-quality welds at high speeds. High deposition rate. Visible arc. Unaffected by moderate amounts of rust, scale, dirt, or moisture. | High speed. Good penetration. Good bead appearance. |

| | | | | |
|---|---|---|---|---|
| **Advantages** | Combination of wires and fluxes gives variety of weld chemistry. Easy slag removal. Little plate preparation. Minimum grinding or finishing. Spatter-free welds. Hidden arc. | High production; high-operator factor. X-ray quality welds. Convex, good looking welds. No weld cleaning. Visible arc. | required; smaller bevels on plate; little distortion. No slag cleaning. X-ray quality, smooth welds. Wide range of thicknesses can be welded; no limitation to number of passes with proper wire. | Little operator training needed. For all-position welding. Good for poor fit-up. Little tendency for undercutting. Good bead appearance. | Simple equipment. High hardness and smooth weld. Visible arc. |
| **Limitations** | For flat and horizontal welding. Hidden arc. Flux feeding, removing, and reclaiming. Possible flux entrapment. | Not used on metals under 1/8″ thick. Wire and gas costs relatively high. Equipment is bulkier than TIG. Some spatter. | Deep penetration is not good on thin sections or poor fit-up. Some spatter. Limited to flat and horizontal position. Slightly more operator training. Bead not as smooth as with tubular wire or submerged arc. Narrow weld bead requires good tracking. | Wire cost higher than solid $CO_2$ wire. Slag removal. | Lower quality weld. Flat welding position. Not for thin metal. |

**Fig. 9-21.**  Summary chart of semiautomatic arc-welding processes (courtesy *Welding Design and Fabrication*).

1. What is the effect of arc blow?

2. Compare the effects of straight and reverse polarity.

3. What are some advantages of an a-c–d-c rectifier for supplying welding current?

4. Why is a constant-current-type welding machine referred to by this name, since the amperage and voltage vary with the arc length?

5. Why is a constant-potential-type machine not suited for manual welding?

6. Of what interest to a potential customer is the open-circuit voltage of a machine?

7. What is meant by duty cycle, as listed on the nameplate of a welding machine?

8. How do a-c–d-c generators compare with rectifiers or transformers as to efficiency?

9. What is meant by power-factor correction?

10. What purpose does the cellulosic coating on the electrode serve during the welding operation?

11. Where may mineral-coated electrodes be used to advantage?

12. Why are mineral-coated electrodes recommended for downhand welding?

13. What are some advantages of the iron-powder electrode?

14. Identify the following code numbers used in designating various electrodes: (a) E6010; (b) E7015; (c) E8011; (d) E9013; (e) E9015; (f) E9016.

15. How may the operating factor often be improved in welding?

16. What is meant by a fast-follow type of electrode?

17. In selecting an electrode for welding an alloy steel, what should be the first consideration?

18. Why was iron powder added to the coating of the low-hydrogen-type electrode?

19. Why is it especially important to have a short arc when starting a weld with a low-hydrogen electrode?

20. What kind of storage is recommended for low-hydrogen electrodes?

21. What is meant by submerged arc?

22. What is the advantage of a welding process that can handle high current densities?

23. Explain the difference between TIG and MIG welding processes.

24. Why are two different arc lengths used in MIG welding?

25. Of what advantage is alternating current in TIG welding on nonferrous metals?

26. What is the main difference between MIG welding and carbon dioxide welding?

27. What is the difference between carbon dioxide welding and magnetic-flux welding?

28. Of what significance have the welding developments discussed in this chapter been to design engineers?

## PROBLEMS

1. A welder is rated at 200 amp and 49 volts. It has an 80 percent duty cycle. How long will this machine be able to operate at full capacity? How long can it safely operate above its rated capacity?

2. A certain 300-amp a-c transformer welder is considered 85 percent efficient over most of its operating range, whereas a d-c generator of similar capacity is 55 percent efficient over the higher part of its range. If both are operated on a 60 percent duty cycle for a 9-hr shift at 1.5¢ per kwhr, what is the saving in using the more efficient machine? The average closed circuit voltage is 20v. Electrodes used are 5/32-in. dia.

3. The following comparisons are made between hand welding with 14-in. E6012 electrodes and a fully automatic process using a 5/32-in. wire.

| | Hand-Welding Method | Automatic Method |
|---|---|---|
| Arc speed, ft per hr | 25 | 60 |
| Electrode used, lb per ft | 0.30 | 0.20 |
| Electrode cost, lb | 13¢ | 20¢ |
| Labor and overhead, hr | $9.00 | $9.00 |

What is the relative cost per foot of each method?

4. What will be the approximate cost of hand welding a 60-deg single-V butt joint made in ½-in. plate 30 in. long? Use the information given in Prob. 3. The weld is made in two passes.

## REFERENCES

Johnson, A., and K. F. Dudey, "How to Choose Arc Welding Power Sources," *American Machinist/Metalworking Manufacturing*, August, 1958.

*Procedure Handbook of Arc Welding Design and Practice*, The Lincoln Electric Company, Cleveland, 1957.

"Production Fasteners Find New Markets," *Business Week*, September, 1950.

Semi-Automatic Welding Equipment Guide Selector, *Welding Design and Fabrication*, August, 1961.

Shutt, R., "New Iron Powder Electrodes and Their Application," *The Welding Journal*, 1956.

Smith, D. C., "Development, Properties and Usability of Low-Hydrogen Electrodes," *The Welding Journal*, Welding Research Supplement, September, 1959.

Telford, R. T., and F. T. Stanchus, "Industrial Applications of Magnetic Flux Gas-Shielded Arc Welding," *The Welding Journal*, August, 1958.

*The Tool Engineers Handbook*, American Society of Tool and Manufacturing Engineers, McGraw-Hill Book Company, Inc., New York, 1959.

*Welding Handbook*, American Welding Society, New York, 4th Edition 1958.

Wilson, J. L., G. E. Claussen, and C. E. Jackson, "The Effect of I²R Heating on Electrode Melting Rate," *The Welding Journal*, January, 1956.

# 10

# GAS WELDING, BRAZING, SOFT SOLDERING, AND HARD SURFACING

**G**AS WELDING generally refers to heating metal for both fusion- and braze-welding purposes with an oxyacetylene flame. As shown on the welding-processes chart, (Fig. 9-1), oxygen and hydrogen are also used.

Scientists knew as early as 1895 that a mixture of oxygen and acetylene would burn at a very high temperature, but there was no suitable means of mixing and controlling them. It was not until 1903 that a welding torch was developed which could mix and control oxygen and acetylene to produce a flame of about 6000°F.

## Oxygen

Oxygen can be obtained by either a liquid-air or an electrolytic process.

**Liquid-Air Process.** Most of the oxygen used for welding is obtained by the liquid-air process. Air is compressed and cooled to a point where the gases become liquid. Then, as the liquid air is allowed to rise in temperature, the various gases can be taken off separately. Nitrogen is given off first at −321°F. Oxygen is given off next at −297°F. These gases, having been thus separated, are further purified and compressed into cylinders for use as needed.

**Electrolytic Process.** In the electrolytic process, oxygen is obtained by passing a direct current through water, to which an acid alkali has been added. The electric current breaks the water down into its chemical elements of hydrogen and oxygen. The oxygen collects at the positive terminal, while hydrogen is collected at the negative terminal.

### Acetylene

Acetylene is a fuel gas composed of carbon and hydrogen, $C_2H_2$. It is obtained from the chemical reaction of water and calcium carbide:

$$CaC_2 + 2H_2O \rightarrow C_2H_2 + Ca(OH)_2$$

The reaction provides acetylene gas and hydrated (or slaked) lime as a sludge. A special hopper for dropping the calcium carbide into a tank of water at controlled rates is referred to as an *acetylene generator*. A 300-lb generator is one into which 300 lb of calcium carbide are loaded and slowly dropped into 300 gal of water. Since calcium carbide generates 4.5 cu ft of acetylene per pound, a generator of this type could operate at full load for a period of 4.5 hr.

### Oxyacetylene Welding Equipment

The principal items of equipment needed for gas welding are oxygen and acetylene cylinders, regulators, torches, and hose (Fig. 10-1).

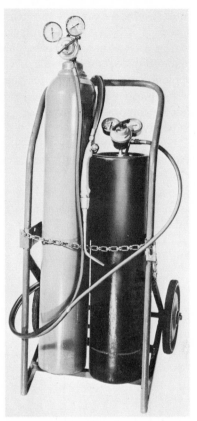

**Fig. 10-1.** A portable oxyacetylene welding outfit, complete with carrying cart (courtesy Linde Co., division of Union Carbide Corp.).

#### Cylinders.

OXYGEN CYLINDERS. Oxygen is contained in seamless steel cylinders ranging in capacity from 80 to 224 cu ft. The cylinders are charged with oxygen at 2,200 psi at 70°F. To guard against tank explosion, which might occur in case of fire, each cylinder is provided with a safety device such as a metal bursting disk that releases the pressure when it gets too high.

The present trend is to use oxygen in its liquid state, referred to as LOX, rather than in cylinders. The cost of transportation alone is one eleventh as much.

ACETYLENE CYLINDERS. Acetylene can be compressed into cylinders at pressures up to 250 psi, or it may be used directly from the generator.

When compressed into cylinders, the acetylene is dissolved in acetone, which, in turn, is absorbed by a porous filler material in the tank. The filler consists of such things as balsa wood, charcoal, finely shredded asbestos, infusorial earth, corn pith, and silicon. The filler material is necessary because acetylene stored in a free state can be made to dissociate or break down by heat or shock and possibly would explode at pressures greater than 15 psi. Above 29.4 psi, it becomes self-explosive if shocked or jarred. Dissolved in acetone, however, it can be compressed to 250 psi — a safe pressure set by the Bureau of Explosives.

To prevent the acetone from being drawn off with the acetylene, the volume used should not exceed 50 cu ft per hr from a standard 275-cu-ft cylinder.

Acetylene valves also have steel safety plugs, with a small hole in the center filled with a low-melting-point metal alloy that will melt out at from 212° to 220°F.

Cutaway views of oxygen and acetylene cylinders are shown in Fig. 10-2.

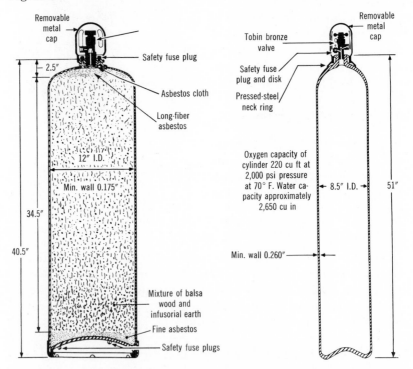

**Fig. 10-2.** Cutaway views of oxygen and acetylene cylinders (courtesy Linde Co., division of Union Carbide Corp.).

**Regulators.** The gases compressed into the oxygen and acetylene cylinders are at pressures too high for welding. Regulators are used to reduce these pressures and to control the flow of gases from the cylinders. Most regulators are of either single-stage or two-stage construction (Fig. 10-3). Single-stage regulators reduce the pressure of the gases to working pressure in one step or stage, whereas two-stage regulators do the same work in two steps or stages. Less readjustment is needed when cylinders are fitted with two-stage regulators.

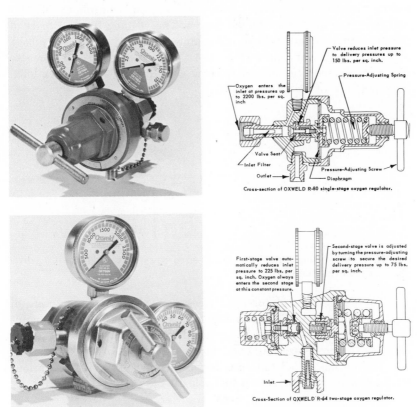

**Fig. 10-3.** Single- and two-stage regulators (courtesy Linde Co., division of Union Carbide Corp.).

Acetylene regulators are of the same general design as oxygen regulators, although they are not made to withstand such high pressures.

Two gages are mounted on the regulator to indicate tank pressure and line pressure. High-pressure oxygen gages read in pounds per square inch from 0 to 3,000, although oxygen pressures do not exceed 2,200 psi. The gage also is graduated to indicate the number of cubic feet of oxygen left in the tank. The high-pressure acetylene gage is graduated to 275 psi and the working gage to 15 psi.

When several torches are used in stationary welding installations, the oxygen and acetylene are obtained from a number of cylinders manifolded or connected together and equipped with master regulators to control the pressure and flow of the gases to each of the welding stations.

**Torches.** The welding torch is used to mix the gases in the right proportions, to control the volume of gases burned at the welding tip, and to direct the flow. Two valves are used; one controls the flow of acetylene, the other the flow of oxygen. The welding tip, that part of the torch that extends beyond the chamber where the gases are mixed, is made from drawn copper (Fig. 10-4). Tip sizes are based on the size of the orifice diameter and are selected according to the cross-sectional area and type of metal being welded.

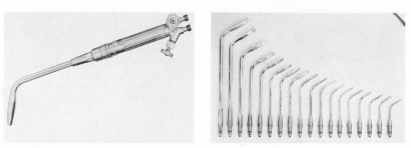

**Fig. 10-4.** A welding torch and various-sized tips (courtesy Linde Co., division of Union Carbide Corp.).

The designation of torch-tip sizes varies with manufacturers of welding equipment. The torch-tip numbers assigned by the manufacturer refer to the size of the orifice provided for the flame — small numbers for small-sized tips, and vice versa.

The recommended rod sizes for oxyacetylene welding of various thicknesses of steel are shown in Table 10-1.

**TABLE 10-1.**

**Recommended Rod Sizes for Oxyacetylene Welding***

| Thickness of Metal | Rod Diameter (Inches) |
|---|---|
| 18 gauge and lighter | 1/16 |
| 18 to 16 gauge | 1/16 to 3/32 |
| 16 to 10 gauge | 3/32 to 1/8 |
| 10 gauge to 3/16″ | 1/8 to 5/32 |
| 1/4″ and heavier | 3/16 to 1/4 |

* Courtesy Linde Co.

There are two general types of torches — low-pressure, or injector type, and medium-pressure, or balanced type. In the low-pressure type the acetylene pressure is less than 1 psi. The high-pressure oxygen draws the required amount of acetylene with it, operating on the well-known Venturi principle. Medium-pressure torches operate on equal pressures of both gases.

**Hose.** The hose that connects the torch and the regulator is specially manufactured for welding use. It is made of light, flexible, strong, nonporous, cord-reinforced rubber. It is available in a range of sizes and is designated by inside diameters and number of plies of fabric desired. Single hose is furnished in sizes from $\frac{1}{8}$ to $\frac{1}{2}$ in. inside diameter and is available in standard lengths of $12\frac{1}{2}$ and 25 ft, or in 100-ft reels. The acetylene and oxygen hoses are the same in grade but differ in color; the oxygen hose is green and the acetylene hose is red. Also, the swivel nuts on the end of the hose used in connecting to the torch or regulator have right-hand threads for the oxygen and left-hand threads for the acetylene. The acetylene connection nuts are grooved to simplify further their identification. Single- or twinned-type hoses are available; that is, the oxygen and acetylene hoses are molded or bonded together. This design helps prevent the hose from kinking or becoming entangled while welding.

### Flame Types and Adjustment

When the torch is first lighted, only the acetylene is turned on, producing a long, bushy, yellowish-colored flame. This flame is smoky and soot-producing. As soon as the oxygen valve is opened, the acetylene flame is shortened, changing to a three-part flame. It consists of an inner cone and a secondary flame surrounded by an outer flame envelope. When the right amount of oxygen is turned on, the secondary, or reducing flame, draws back even with the inner cone. It is out from this inner cone about 1/16 in. that the heat for welding is developed. The reaction that supports the flame is

$$C_2H_2 = 2C + H_2 + 86,600 \text{ Btu}$$
$$2C + 2O_2 = 2CO_2 + 352,000 \text{ Btu}$$
$$H_2 + 1/2O_2 = H_2O + 104,100 \text{ Btu}$$
$$\text{Total heat/mole} = 542,700 \text{ Btu}$$

The three types of flames are (1) neutral, (2) reducing or carburizing, and (3) oxidizing.

**Neutral Flame.** The neutral flame [Fig. 10-5(a)] has two clearly defined zones. The inner portion consists of a luminous cone surrounded by the flame envelope. It is also spoken of as a *balanced flame* because it is produced when equal volumes of oxygen and acetylene are drawn from the cylinders. However, $1\frac{1}{2}$ parts of oxygen are taken from the atmosphere. This flame is the one most often used, as it allows the weld-metal pool to remain quiet and clear, flowing along easily.

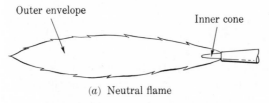

(*a*) Neutral flame

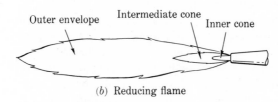

(*b*) Reducing flame

**Fig. 10-5.** The three types of oxyacetylene flames.

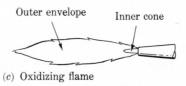

(*c*) Oxidizing flame

**Reducing Flame.**   The reducing or carburizing flame [Fig. 10-5(*b*)] is produced by mixing less than 1 part of oxygen to 1 part acetylene. There are three distinct zones in the flame — a bluish-white inner cone, a white intermediate cone, and an outer envelope with reddish feathers. When this reducing flame is used to weld steel, the metal boils and is not clear. However, the flame can be used to advantage for hard-facing operations and for welding nonferrous alloys such as nickel and Monel. It is sometimes used in silver-brazing operations to give a low-temperature soaking heat to the parts being joined.

**Oxidizing Flame.**   The oxidizing flame [Fig. 10-5(*c*)] is produced when slightly more than 1 volume of oxygen is mixed with 1 volume of acetylene. The inner cone of the flame is short, bluish in color, and pointed. This flame is also distinguishable by its hissing sound. When applied to steel, an oxidizing flame causes the molten metal to foam and give off sparks.

This flame is useful for welding brasses, bronzes, and cast iron because it helps make an oxide scum on the surface of the metal, thus forming a protective shield.

In ordinary gas welding with the neutral flame, the hot gas serves to protect the molten metal of the weld and the end of the filler rod from the atmosphere.

### Manual Oxyacetylene Welding

There are two distinct methods of employing the torch to make a weld — forehand and backhand — (Fig. 10-6). In forehand welding the torch tip is held at approximately 60 deg to the plates being welded. Forehand welding allows preheating of the plate edges immediately ahead of the molten pool, and this is the method more commonly used. By moving the tip and welding rod in opposite directions perpendicular to the weld, the heat can be carefully balanced so as to melt the end of the welding rod and sidewalls of the plates in a uniformly distributed molten puddle.

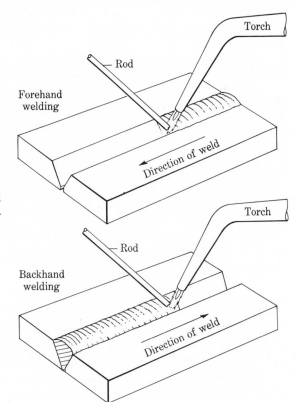

**Fig. 10-6.** Forehand and backhand welding.

Backhand welding is done with the torch pointing back at the molten puddle at approximately 60 deg to the plates being welded. This method is used principally for heavy sections, as it permits a narrower V at the joint. In general, it requires less puddling of the molten metal, and less welding rod is used.

### Advantages and Disadvantages of Gas Welding

**Advantages.** The oxyacetylene flame is generally more easily controlled and not as piercing as metallic arc welding. Therefore, it is used extensively for sheet metal fabrication and repairs.

The oxyacetylene torch is versatile. It can be used for brazing, braze welding, soldering, preheating, postheating, heating for bending, heat treatment, metal cutting, metal cleaning, etc.

It is very portable; small-sized units are comparatively light, weighing only 150 lb complete with carrying truck. In this size the oxygen cylinder contains 80 cu ft and the acetylene cylinder 60 cu ft. This, and even larger units, can be moved almost anywhere for needed repairs or fabrication.

**Disadvantages.** The disadvantages of oxyacetylene welding are as follows:

1. It takes considerably longer for the metal to heat up than in arc welding. There is no almost instantaneous pool.

2. Harmful thermal effects are aggravated by prolonged heat, and there will, in most cases, be a larger heat-affected area. This often results in increased grain growth, more distortion, and, in some cases, loss of corrosion resistance.

3. Oxyacetylene tanks are leased, and when they are kept beyond a specified period, demurrage charges are incurred.

4. Oxygen and acetylene gases are rather expensive.

5. There are safety problems involved in handling and storing the gases.

6. Flux applications and the shielding provided by the oxyacetylene flame are not nearly so positive as those supplied by the inert gas in TIG, MIG, or carbon dioxide welding.

### Oxyacetylene Welding Safety

The following points are not intended to be comprehensive, but they do indicate some of the basic safety precautions to be observed when using or storing oxyacetylene welding equipment.

1. Never allow oil or grease to come in contact with oxygen under pressure, as it can become explosive.

2. Do not use matches to light a torch. Use friction lighters, pilot flames, or other ignition sources. Do not attempt to light the torch from hot metal in a confined space. The accumulated gases may cause an explosion.

3. Always wear goggles when working with a lighted torch. The dark glass helps filter out the ultraviolet light of the flame. Use a clear cover glass on the outside of the colored glass to protect it from spatter.

4. Store acetylene cylinders in an upright position, away from highly cumbustible materials and heat. Keep oxygen cylinders separated from the acetylene cylinders, preferably by fire-resistant material.

5. Always reduce the acetylene pressure to 15 psi or less before attempting to use it.

6. Do not open acetylene cylinder valves more than 1½ turns. Always leave in place the special T-wrench used for opening the cylinder, so that the acetylene can be quickly turned off in emergencies.

7. Do not open acetylene cylinders near sparks or flame.

8. Never interchange oxygen and acetylene equipment.

9. If an acetylene tank should catch fire, extinguish it with a fire extinguisher or a wet blanket.

10. Before attaching regulators, bleed the cylinders for an instant to blow out any dirt that may be in the nozzle connection.

11. Do not attempt to repair leaky cylinder valves. Notify the supplier and, in the meantime, place the tanks in a safe place, preferably out of doors.

12. Do not use oxygen as a substitute for compressed air.

13. Open the oxygen cylinder valve all the way when in use, to prevent leakage around the double-seated valve.

14. Use care with the welding hose so that it does not become injured or punctured.

15. To test for leaks on oxyacetylene equipment, apply a soapy-water solution to the areas in question.

16. Be sure that proper ventilation (usually exhaust fans) is provided in the welding area.

17. Do not allow oxyacetylene tanks to stand exposed in the hot sun.

18. Do not attempt to move an oxyacetylene cylinder without a protective cap over the valve.

## BRAZING AND BRAZE WELDING

### Brazing

Brazing differs from welding in that the metals to be joined are not melted and deeply fused with the filler metal. Instead, brazing employs a filler metal which melts at a temperature below the melting point of the metals to be joined, and is drawn into the close-fitting joint by capillary action. The surfaces must be clean so that a *wetting* action can take place. *Wetting* refers to the attraction that occurs between the molecules of the alloy and the base metal on properly cleaned surfaces at the right temperature.

**Brazing Procedure.** In order to develop adequate strength by means of the brazing process, the following steps should be used:
1. Design the joint.
2. Clean the metal.
3. Choose the proper filler material, flux, and brazing process.
4. Postclean and inspect.
5. Heat-treat.

Joint design. The two main types of joints used in brazing are the butt joint and lap joint. The scarf joint is a compromise between these two. The joint should be selected on the basis of service requirements, such as mechanical strength, electrical conductivity, and pressure tightness. Other considerations are the brazing process to be used, fabricating techniques, and production quantities.

*Lap joints.* Lap joints should be used, in preference to other types of joints, where strength is a primary consideration. An overlap of three times the thickness of the thinnest member will usually give maximum efficiency [Fig. 10-7(a)]. Overlaps greater than this lead to poor

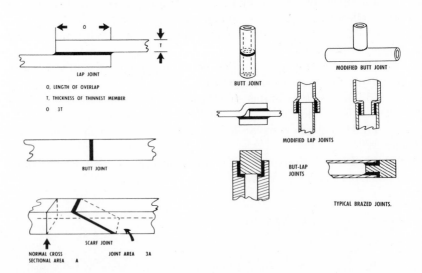

**Fig. 10-7.** Basic types of brazed joints (courtesy Air Reduction Sales Co.).

brazing owing to insufficient penetration, inclusions, etc. This joint is also recommended when leak tightness and good electrical conductivity are required.

*Butt joints.* The butt joint can provide a smooth joint of minimum thickness. Since the butt joint is more difficult to fit up and to preserve alignment and the necessary clearances, its strength will not generally be as reliable as the lap joint [Fig. 10-7(b)].

*Scarf joints.* The scarf joint is an attempt to maintain the smooth contour of the butt joint and, at the same time, provide the large joint area of the lap joint [Fig. 10-7(c)]. The scarf joint is stronger than the butt joint, but it requires considerable preparation. Both scarf and butt joints, when properly made with silver-brazing alloys, are considerably stronger than the parent material.

*Stress distribution.* The brazed joint should be designed to minimize stress concentrations that may tear the joint. Two approaches are used: one is to increase the flexibility of the joint; the other is the opposite — to stiffen the flexible members. Shown in Fig. 10-8 are illustrations of joint design.

*Joint clearance.* Joint clearance is the distance between the surfaces of the joint into which the brazing filler metal must flow. The clearance varies greatly with conditions. It is entirely different at room temperature from what it is at brazing temperature. In general practice, the clearance at room temperature is specified. For any given combination of base and filler metals there is a *best* joint clearance, as indicated by the curve in Fig. 10-9. Values below the minimum clearance are weak because the alloy does not flow into the joint, and clearances beyond maximum result in greatly lowered strength.

Sometimes, when one member surrounds another and the internal member has a greater expansion rate than the outside member, the clearance will be lost and capillary action will be prevented. In this case, clearance near maximum should be used. Another factor to consider is when an internal member has greater contraction than the outer member. When this occurs the braze may be fractured, but the right braze material — one with a long temperature range between solidus and liquidus and with a sluggish flow — may be able to bridge large gaps and preserve sufficient strength to resist cracking or cooling.

*Introduction of brazing alloys into the joint.* Brazing alloys may be introduced into the joint by *face* feeding or *preplacement*. Face feeding consists of holding the alloy in the hand and applying it when the joint has reached the proper temperature, as indicated by the flux becoming liquid. In preplacement the alloy is placed in or near the fluxed joint, and at brazing temperature it melts and flows into the joint. Pre-

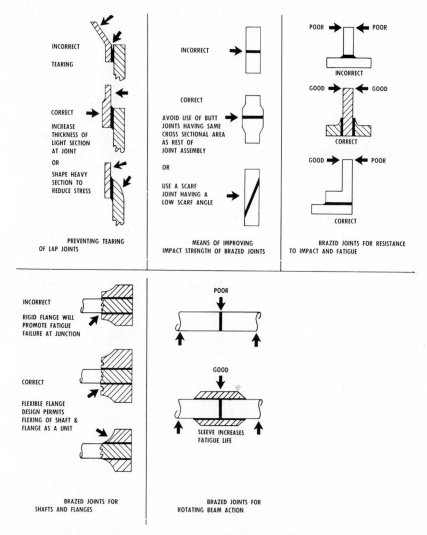

**Fig. 10-8.** The brazed joint should be designed to utilize to full advantage the contact area available. Other principles mentioned in the text are also shown (courtesy Air Reduction Sales Co.).

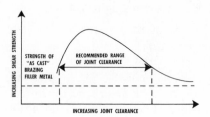

**Fig. 10-9.** Joint clearances generally vary from 0.002 to 0.010 in. The curve shows the relationship between too little, the right amount, and too much clearance as it affects shear strength (courtesy Air Reduction Sales Co.).

placed filler metal may be in the form of rings, washers, shims, slugs, powder, or sprayed-on coatings.

In designing joints for preplaced alloy, it is best to arrange for the alloy to flow with the aid of gravity and to provide for inspection (Fig. 10-10). When a groove is used for the wire, as shown, it must be deducted from the joint area in determining the amount of overlap needed.

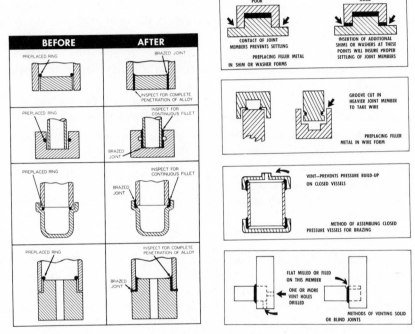

**Fig. 10-10.** Joints with preplaced filler material (courtesy Air Reduction Sales Co.).

CLEANING METAL. The parts to be joined must be free of all oil, dirt, grease, and oxides, or capillary action will not take place. Cleaning may be done either chemically or mechanically. Chemical cleaning usually gives the best results.

*Chemical cleaning.* Chemical cleaners used to remove grease are carbon tetrachloride, trichloroethylene, or trisodiumphosphate. Oxides can be removed with nitric or sulfuric acids. Other proprietary cleaners are available. The choice of a cleaner depends on the particular surfaces to be joined, and on their condition.

*Mechanical cleaning.* Mechanical cleaning consists of grinding, filing, brushing, cleaning with steel wool, and machining. When cutting fluids are used in machining, they must be removed by chemical cleaning.

SELECTING THE BRAZING FILLER MATERIAL. Brazing filler materials have been referred to as *hard solders* or *brazing alloys*. However, these terms are becoming obsolete, and brazing filler material is preferred.

Brazing filler metals are divided into seven classifications. In order of popularity these are: silver, copper and copper-zinc, copper-phosphorus, aluminum-silicon, heat-resisting materials, copper-gold, and magnesium.

Abbreviations are often used in identifying these filler materials— B represents brazing and RB indicates that the filler material can be used for either welding or brazing. Thus, in the classification RBCuZN-A, the Cu and Zn refer to the filler composition of copper and zinc and the suffix A is used further to identify members of the same family.

Without question, the most popular filler metals for brazing are the silver alloys which are often inaccurately called *silver solders*.

*Heat-resisting filler materials.* Recently, great interest has been built up in brazing high nickel and stainless steels for high-temperature service.

BAgMn remains strong in the temperature range from 500° to 900°F. It is usually deposited by furnace brazing with a reducing atmosphere.

BNiCr retains its strength up to 2000°F.

FLUX.  Most brazing operations require a flux to maintain thorough cleanliness of the areas to be brazed. Flux is a mixture of chemical compounds and is usually obtained in paste or powder form from the manufacturer. A number of types to suit the particular alloys used have been developed. Immediately after cleaning, the flux is applied to the surface where the brazing is to take place. During the brazing process, it acts to break up the oxide film that forms on the metal, allowing the filler metal to make a proper bond with the base metal (Fig. 10-11).

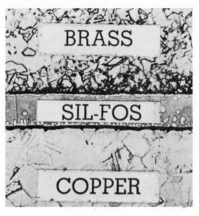

**Fig. 10-11.** This photomicrograph shows the penetration made by capillary action of the filler metal between the metals being joined (courtesy Handy and Harman).

Inert atmospheres are used to help prevent oxidation of the metal surface during the brazing process. Some atmospheres eliminate the need for flux; others do not. Controlled atmospheres are used primarily in furnace brazing but they may be used in induction and resistance brazing.

BRAZING PROCESSES. Although the AWS master chart of welding processes lists eight methods for the application of brazing alloys, only four are of extensive commercial importance; these are torch, induction, furnace, and dip.

Other less-used methods are block brazing, two-carbon-arc brazing, and ultrasonic brazing, all of which are described in the *American Welding Society Handbook*.

*Torch brazing.* Torch brazing is normally thought of as being done with the regular oxyacetylene welding torch, but natural gas and oxygen, or air and acetylene, butane, or propane are also used. The choice depends on the mass of the parts to be joined, production requirements, accessibility, etc. The oxyacetylene flame is the hottest and, with multiflame tips, can usually do the work faster and more uniformly.

The flame used should be neutral or slightly reducing; the oxidizing flame should be avoided. The filler metal is touched to the joint when the flux becomes liquid and clear as water. It is the parent metal, not the flame, that transfers the heat to the brazing alloy.

*Induction brazing.* In induction brazing the heat is derived by electrically inducing a high-frequency (500 to 10,000 cycles per second and higher) eddy current into the work from a coil that surrounds the part. The depth of heating can be determined by the frequencies used; lower frequencies produce deeper heating, and vice versa. Thus the heat can be carefully controlled to go no deeper than is required by the joint. The process is fast, minimizing the time the parts must remain at an elevated temperature.

*Furnace brazing.* Furnace brazing is best suited to parts that are of quite uniform mass. Preplaced filler material is used. The joint must be designed for this operation, as stated previously, or clearances will not be correct. The joints should be made, as far as possible, to be self-aligning and self-jigging. The use of jigs usually makes for slower heating and increased costs. Argon, hydrogen, or helium are the gases used for the furnace's nonoxidizing atmosphere.

Furnace brazing can be done with a conveyor-type belt, the speed of which will regulate the heating time.

*Dip brazing.* There are two methods of dip brazing. In one, the parts to be brazed are dipped into a bath of molten filler material. The bath is usually covered with a layer of molten flux. In the other method, the filler metal is preplaced, and the parts to be joined are dipped in a bath of flux. In both, the work is supported in jigs. Dip brazing is well adapted to parts of irregular shape.

POSTBRAZE CLEANING AND INSPECTION.

*Cleaning.* After brazing, it is necessary to remove *all* flux residue inside and out. In most cases the flux can be removed by hot running water. If this is not sufficient, low-pressure live steam is used. If the parts have been overheated during brazing, then a chemical bath, with a neutralizing water rinse afterward, is needed.

*Inspection.* A large part of braze inspection can be visual. In this case it is best to have a standard sample to go by so as to know what is acceptable.

Other inspection methods used are pressure testing, die penetrants, radiography, etc. These methods are described in Chapter **28**. Destructive tests are also used on the first few parts, and spot checks are made as often as needed.

HEAT TREATMENT OF BRAZED PARTS.   Heat treatment may be accomplished concurrently with brazing or after brazing. In the first instance the filler metal is such that it solidifies above the required heat-treating temperature. In the second situation the filler material will be such that it solidifies at the same temperature as required for heat treatment.

## Braze Welding

Braze welding is somewhat similar to brazing in that the base metals are not melted but are joined by an alloy of lower melting point. The main difference is that capillary action is not used to draw the filler material into the joint. A braze-welded joint is designed very much like a welded joint, but an effort should be made to avoid sharp corners that are easily overheated, or ones that become points of stress concentration (Fig. 10-12).

Braze welding is used extensively for repair work and some fabrication on such metals as cast iron, malleable iron, wrought iron, and steel. It is also used, although to a lesser extent, on copper, nickel, and high-melting-point brasses and bronzes. Some of the brasses and bronzes melt at a point so near that of the filler metal that fusion welding, rather than brazing, is done.

Braze welding is not recommended on parts that will be subjected to temperatures higher than 650°F.

**Strength.**   The strength of a braze-welded joint is similar to that of fusion welding. It is, however, dependent on the quality of the bond

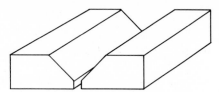

Butt joint prepared for fusion welding

**Fig. 10-12.** A comparison of butt joints prepared for fusion welding and braze welding.

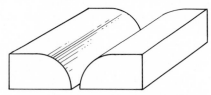

Butt joint prepared for braze welding

between the filler metal and the base metal. It also depends on the quality of the filler metal after it is deposited. It is important that it be free from blowholes, slag inclusions, and other physical defects. Some of the same forces used in brazing—namely, interalloying and intergranular penetration—are at work in braze welding.

INTERALLOYING. The metal surface must be cleaned, usually by mechanical means or solvents, so that the filler metal will wet the surface. Commercial flux is used to remove the oxide film at the time of brazing. In a narrow zone at the interface of the two alloys—the base metal and the filler metal—there will be some diffusion of both materials. This is especially true in such metals as copper, zinc, and tin.

INTERGRANULAR PENETRATION. The brazing heat, usually dull red in the case of ferrous materials, is enough to open up the crystal grain structure to allow the brass filler material to penetrate along the grain boundaries. It is this action that gives braze welding its great strength.

## SOFT SOLDERING

Soft solders are composed chiefly of tin and lead, along with small amounts of other elements such as antimony, bismuth, or silver. Soldering, as a method of joining metal parts, has been used for centuries. Wiped joints were made as early as the 15th century. The alloys used contained about one third tin and two thirds lead, which is very close to the lowest-melting-point soft solder available today. Pure tin melts at 450°F, lead at 620°F; surprisingly enough, when these two metals are mixed together, at 63 parts tin and 37 parts lead by weight, a eutectic mixture occurs, and the melting point drops to 361°F. Tin mixes with lead in all proportions, the most common compositions being 40/60, 50/50, and 60/40. The first-mentioned number is always tin. Tin, contrary to popular belief, is an expensive metal. It is obtained from Asia, Africa, and South America. Lead on the other hand, sells for about one sixth the price of tin.

A good all-around solder is 40/60. It starts to melt at 361°F and is completely molten at 460°F. A somewhat more popular but more expensive solder is the 50/50 type which is a little easier to use because it has a narrower plastic range, becoming completely molten at 414°F.

The 60/40 composition is more expensive, but it is also very fluid and is used where a low-melting solder is required. It is plastic at 361°F and liquid at 370°F.

### Soldering Procedure

The steps involved in joining two metals with solder are similar to those in brazing. These include cleaning, fitting the parts, applying flux, heating the work where the solder is to be applied, applying the solder, allowing the part to cool without disturbance, and final cleaning.

**Cleaning.**   Cleaning of the metal is usually done with a wire brush, steel wool, emery cloth, and files (Fig. 10-13).

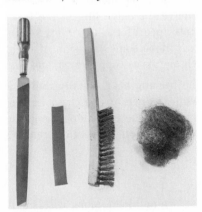

**Fig. 10-13.**  Materials used in cleaning work before soldering are file, emery cloth, wire brush, and steel wool.

**Fitting.**  It is of the utmost importance that the parts fit closely together. Parts that do not fit closely will be weak.

**Applying Flux.**  Flux may be contained in the solder, as in rosin-core or acid-core solder. Rosin-core solder is a *must* for electrical wiring, because the residue of the flux is inert, noncorrosive, and electrically nonconductive. It does not attract dust or moisture and will not corrode delicate wiring.

Acid-core solder is considered an all-purpose solder wherever a more active flux is desired and electrical work is not involved.

Flux for bar- or solid-type solders is applied to the joint as a paste in the case of the rosin type, or by brushing the liquid on for the acid type. A common acid flux is made by dropping zinc strips in hydrochloric acid until the bubbling action ceases. Another method is to dissolve about 12 oz of fused zinc chloride in a quart of water.

A lower-melting-point flux can be made by combining 1 part sal ammoniac ($NH_4Cl$) with 3 parts zinc chloride and then dissolving in the desired quantity (according to strength needed) of warm water. This combination melts at about 356°F and is suitable for use with all solders in applications where a corrosive flux is permissible.

**Heating.** There are many ways of transmitting heat to the joint area. These include soldering irons, torches, electrical resistance, hot plates, ovens, induction heating, and dip soldering. Some of these methods have been discussed in connection with brazing and, because of the similarity, will not be repeated here.

TORCHES. In addition to the air-acetylene torch, the disposable-tank propane torches are very popular. They furnish an easily portable, instantaneous heat source. Various types of interchangeable tips are used to control the flame, from a "pencil point" for fine work to the flared tip used in preheating.

SOLDERING COPPERS. The most-used method of applying heat in hand soldering is with the soldering iron. Soldering coppers, as they are often called, are sold by weight—½ lb for light work, 1 lb for medium soldering, and 1½ lb for heavier work. The irons, usually sold in pairs, are heated in small gas or charcoal furnaces. Electric-iron size recommendations are 100 watts for general work, 200 watts for medium to heavy soldering, and 350 watts for rugged work. Correct and incorrect methods of holding the soldering iron are shown in Fig. 10-14.

The soldering iron must be able to transfer the heat quickly into the base metal. In order to do this, it must be "tinned"; that is, all oxidation (black spots) must be removed. This can best be done with

**Fig. 10-14.** The correct and incorrect methods of holding the soldering copper. Very little heat transfer results when only the point touches the metal as shown at the right.

a file. After filing down to the base metal, it should be heated until the copper turns yellow, brown, and purple. A flux-core solder is then applied to all faces, using a dry rag to wipe off any excess solder. When irons become overheated, the tinning is destroyed and must be repeated.

RESISTANCE SOLDERING. In resistance soldering the work is heated by its own resistance to an applied current. It quickly produces a high heat. A resistance unit works with approximately 6 volts, stepped down from regular plant voltage for reasons of safety and to prevent arcing. Often, most of the heat for soldering comes from the internal resistance of probes which, in turn, conduct it to the work.

OVEN SOLDERING. Oven soldering is an old high-production technique that has been used on automobile radiator cores and other parts where it is desirable to make a number of joints at one time. The parts are held in fixtures. This method demands close tolerances and the usual cleaning and fluxing.

**Applying the Solder.** The pieces to be soldered must be firmly held together to prevent their moving while the soldering operation is going on. Where flux-core solder is used, it should be applied only to the joint, not to the soldering tip. If the joint is hot enough, the solder will flow into it by capillary action.

**Cooling and Cleaning.** Once the heat has been removed, the parts must remain undisturbed until the solder has had an opportunity to solidify. Any disturbance at this time can set up tiny fractures inside the joint that may cause failure later on.

Clean warm water should be used to remove the flux residue. Wiping with a dry rag is an extra insurance against flux streaks and water stains.

### Aluminum Soldering

Aluminum is often thought of as being very difficult to solder. One of the reasons for this is that an oxide film forms over the metal rather quickly after cleaning. Now, however, there are several methods of removing this oxide as the soldering is being done. These methods are flux soldering [Fig. 10-15(a)], in which a chemical action removes the oxide; friction soldering [Fig. 10-15(b)], where abrasive action removes the oxide; and ultrasonic soldering [Fig. 10-15(c)], which uses cavitation produced in the molten solder pool to break up the oxide film.

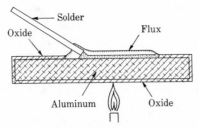

(a) Removing aluminum oxide by fluxing. Chemical action of the flux removes the oxide.

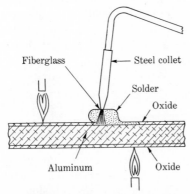

(b) Abrasive removal of oxide. Brushing action abrades oxide from the aluminum surface, allowing solder to tin the surface.

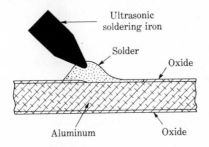

(c) Ultrasonic soldering. Ultrasonic waves cause cavitation, breaking up the oxide and floating it to the top of the solder puddle. A frequency of 20 kc is often used to cause active cavitation.

**Fig. 10-15.**  Various methods of removing the oxide film from aluminum during the soldering operation (courtesy Reynolds Metals Company).

The solders used are shown in Table 10-2. Of the low-temperature solders, the best is a tin-zinc eutectic which melts at 400°F. A low-temperature solder has an advantage over brazing because there is less heat, with a minimum loss of strength and hardness and the least warpage. This is particularly important in complex structures.

Intermediate-heat solders wet aluminum more readily than do the low-temperature solders. They also form large fillets with stronger and more corrosion-resistant joints.

The high-temperature solders contain from 90 to 100 percent zinc. They are the strongest and cheapest of all the aluminum solders.

Corrosion in the soldered joint may be either chemical or galvanic. In either case, moisture must be present before corrosive action can take place. By coating the joint with a waterproof coating, moisture is eliminated, and the joint remains free of corrosion.

In brief summary it may be pointed out that soft soldering offers only a small amount of strength and is used primarily for making good electrical bonds or for sealing fabricated joints held together by rivets, spot welds, or other mechanical means.

### HARD SURFACING—METAL AND CERAMIC APPLICATIONS

Hard surfacing or hard facing generally consists of applying alloys or ceramic materials to a metal surface. The purposes of the application are to increase resistance to wear, abrasion, cavitation, corrosion, heat, or impact. In most cases the hard-facing alloys can be applied by means of the various electric-arc methods already discussed, or by the use of oxyacetylene, oxypropane, or oxyhydrogen flames. Sometimes a combination of both electric arc and gas is used, as in the more recent *plasma* method.

Since the welding processes already discussed can be used for depositing hard-surfacing materials, the use of each will be pointed out briefly, and then an explanation of the newer flame-spray methods will be given.

### Welding-Process Selection for Hard Facing

**Oxyacetylene Process.** The oxyacetylene process is generally used to apply hard-facing materials where it is necessary to achieve a surface with the minimum of required finishing. It is especially good in applying crack-free applications of nonferrous alloys.

Tungsten carbide is often used as the hard-surfacing material. It is handled by having small particles of it in a mild-steel tube; as the tube is melted, the tungsten carbide particles become fused to the surface in a matrix of mild steel.

**TABLE 10-2.**

## Aluminum-Solder Characteristics*

| Solder Type | Melting Range (°F) | Common Constituents | Ease of Application | Wetting of Aluminum | Joint Strength | Corrosion Resistance | Effect on Aluminum |
|---|---|---|---|---|---|---|---|
| Low melting point | 300–500 | Cadmium Tin Bismuth Lead Zinc | Best | Poor to fair | Low | Low | Negligible |
| Intermediate melting point | 500–700 | Cadmium Tin Zinc | Moderate | Good to excellent | Moderate | Moderate | Moderate |
| High melting point | 700–800 | Zinc Tin Aluminum Copper | Most difficult | Good to excellent | High | Good | Reduces strength at joint |

* Courtesy *The Tool and Manufacturing Engineer.*

**Inert-Gas Process.** The inert-gas process is particularly adaptable where a flawless deposit is required, mainly on new construction rather than building up a worn surface for repair. Shown in Fig. 10-16 is a schematic view of how tungsten carbide particles are fed down from a vibratory hopper to the base metal, where they are fused on by the addition of a wire that flows in around the particles. This composite surface is very abrasive-resistant yet is not brittle.

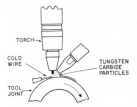

**Fig. 10-16.** Schematic view of an inert-gas tungsten-arc hard-surfacing machine used to apply tungsten carbide particles in a steel matrix (courtesy Linde Co., division of Union Carbide Corp.).

**Atomic-Hydrogen Process.** This process is essentially the same as ordinary atomic hydrogen welding, except the filler rod is of a hard-surfacing type. It is best where a large mass of metal requires a small overlay of hard surface.

**Submerged-Arc Process.** The submerged-arc process is of most value in large runs of similar work. Multiple electrodes and oscillation techniques have made this method a very fast one. The welding head can be made to oscillate back and forth up to 3 in. A forward speed of 3 to 5 ipm can be maintained with a 2-in.-wide oscillation. The pellet rolls shown in Fig. 10-17 have been hard-surfaced using the

**Fig. 10-17.** Pellet rolls before and after hard surfacing with the submerged-arc process and oscillation (courtesy Linde Co., division of Union Carbide Corp.).

oscillating technique. A mild-steel wire was used in conjunction with a submerged-arc hard-surfacing composition which produced a deposit hardness of $R_c58$. The main disadvantage is the high heat input that may cause cracking of the hardened overlays.

**Manual Metal Arc Process.** This process is the one most frequently used. It is usually more adaptable to position and location than are the other methods. It is quick and economical for short jobs, and a wider range of alloys may be used.

Hard-surfaced rods are divided into five groups, according to the alloy content. The groups are arranged in order of increasing hardness, starting with group I, which has less than 20 percent alloying element. The alloys used are mainly chromium, tungsten, manganese, silicon, and carbon. Group V consists of crushed tungsten carbides. These particles may be fused to strips of mild steel, embedded in a high-strength rod, or packed in a mild-steel tube.

## Flame Spraying

The principle of flame spraying consists of feeding a suitable wire or powder through a gun, where it is heated and vaporized by an oxyacetylene or oxypropane flame and then propelled by compressed air, or other means, to become embedded on the surface of the workpiece. There are several variations of this method, and these will be discussed later.

**Surface Preparation.** Surfaces to be sprayed must be absolutely clean and sufficiently roughened to offer the maximum amount of mechanical anchorage for the coating. The methods employed are blasting, machining, or the use of a bond coat.

BLASTING. The use of clean, sharp, crushed steel grit or aluminum oxide blasted against the surface by compressed air will provide reentrant angles for mechanical bonding.

MACHINING. Surfaces that are to be machined after spraying or hard surfacing need an exceptionally strong bond. If a heavy coating or built-up surface is required, an undercut will first have to be made to provide room. These undercuts should be made as shown in Fig. 10-18.

The grooves are made with a standard $\frac{1}{8}$-in. cutoff tool ground down to 0.045 or 0.050 in. wide, and rounded on the end. The grooves are cut about 0.025 in. deep and about 0.015 in. apart. If an exceptionally strong bond is not required, grooving at the ends may be sufficient.

Undercut

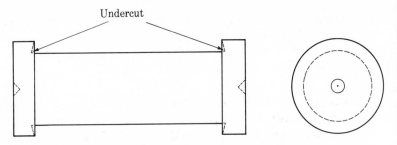

**Fig. 10-18.** Undercuts are made to provide additional anchorage for the spray metals when exceptionally strong bonds are needed.

The holding power of this grooved surface is greatly increased by rolling down the ridges with a knurling tool (Fig. 10-19).

A faster method is to cut threads on the undercut surface. The threads are also rolled down with the rotary tool until they are only partly open. This method is entirely satisfactory for applications that do not require exceptionally high bond strengths.

**Fig. 10-19.** The holding power of the grooved surface can be enhanced by knurling.

*Preparation of internal surfaces.* Metallizing on shafts has the advantage of being hot when applied and then shrinking or contracting like a shrink-fit sleeve. However, greater care must be exercised in applying coatings of this type on internal surfaces where contraction would tend to pull the metallized surface away from the base metal as it cools. To overcome this difficulty, it is recommended that, after the internal surface has been prepared, the part be heated up to 350°F so that the stress may be reduced in the coating after cooling. The inside-diameter preparation can be made by going over the surface with a boring tool, using a fairly coarse feed so that the bore is not too smooth.

*Preparation of flat surfaces.* Shrinkage stresses that tend to lift the coating away from flat surfaces may be overcome either by spraying over the edge, to give a clamping action, or by cutting short slots, near the edge, that taper inward (Fig. 10-20). The base metal may also be heated to 350°F to equalize cooling stresses.

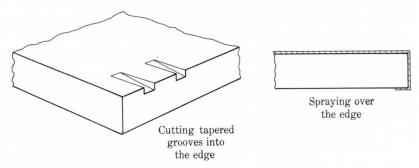

Cutting tapered grooves into the edge

Spraying over the edge

**Fig. 10-20.** Methods of treating flat stock to keep the sprayed coating from lifting as it shrinks.

It is important that these operations be done dry, as oil of any kind would impair the bond. The surface should not be handled until after metallizing. If this is not possible, the part should be wrapped in paper or a clean cloth before it is removed from the lathe. Any oil or grease that may come in contact with the work surface must be removed by vapor degreasing or other chemical cleaning methods.

BOND COAT. Molybdenum is used as bond coat because it can adhere to a smooth surface. When it is applied, surfaces that are not to be coated must be masked or oiled. Care must be taken that oil does not run into the undercut. The oil moisture can be boiled off by running the flame of the gun over the area. With the exception of copper or copper-base alloys, molybdenum bonds well to most metals.

**Selection of Metal and Ceramic Coatings.** Materials used as sprays are selected on the basis of their various characteristics such as hardness, strength, wearing quality, shrink, corrosion resistance, etc.

Light coatings up to 1/16 in. are easily applied and present no special problems. Heavy coatings up to ⅛ in. or more should be given special consideration, and, wherever possible, low-shrink metals should be used.

Ceramic coatings are applied in rod or powder form. They consist of aluminum oxide, zirconium oxide, zirconium silicate, chromium oxide, and magnesium aluminate. These coatings are extremely hard and erosion-resistant. Their melting points range between 3000° and 4500°F.

Composite coatings of ceramics and plastic impregnates are integrated with metals to supply useful properties beyond those possible with the coating alone. *Laminar* coatings—alternate layers of sprayed metal and ceramic materials—have been used with good results in rocket-blast shielding structures.

Ceramics and metals may be mixed in continuously varying proportions to achieve graduations from all metal to all ceramic. This is known as *gradated construction*.

Aluminum oxides are very hard and erosion-resistant even at high temperatures. They have good insulating properties and are economical.

Zirconia has a higher melting point than aluminum oxide and offers good resistance to thermal and mechanical shock. It is used to protect rocket components from hot, high-velocity, corrosive gases. It has also been successfully used to extend the life of annealing and normalizing rolls in steel mills and furnace tubes.

**Methods of Flame Spraying.** There are four main methods of applying flame-sprayed metallic and ceramic coatings. These are the rod-and-wire method, detonation-gun method, powder method, and plasma method.

Rod-and-wire method. The rod-and-wire method of flame spraying is based on the theory that coating materials must become

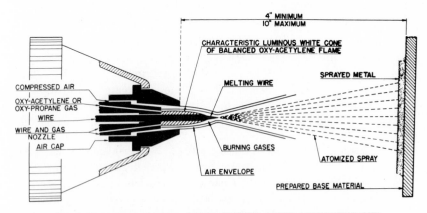

WIRE NOZZLE AND AIR CAP CROSS SECTION—METCO METALLIZING GUN

**Fig. 10-21.** This type of equipment is used for wire-type metallizing or rod-type application of ceramic coatings (courtesy Metco Inc.).

fully molten by means of a flame before they are released. The process uses compressed air to atomize fully the molten metal or oxides and project them against a prepared surface where they are embedded, assuring good mechanical adhesions (Fig. 10-21).

The compressed air helps cool the work parts, so the coatings may be applied successfully not only to metals but also to glass, wood, asbestos, and certain plastics.

DETONATION-GUN METHOD. The detonation-gun method of applying both metallic and ceramic coatings consists of using a specially constructed gun (Fig. 10-22). Measured quantities of fuel and particles of coating material are detonated in a manner somewhat like the operation of a machine gun. The small molten particles are blasted from the gun and embedded into the workpiece surface, where microscopic welding action takes place, producing a tenacious bond. Successive detonations build up the coating material to the required thickness.

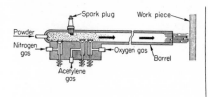

Controlled quantities of oxygen, acetylene, and suspended particles of coating material are admitted into the gun chamber. Detonation of the mixture by a spark heats the particles to a plastic condition and propels them at a supersonic velocity toward the workpiece.

Formulations of tungsten carbide with cobalt, nickel, or chromium-carbide additives, chromium carbide with a nickel-chromium additive, and aluminum oxide.

**Fig. 10-22.** Detonation-gun method (courtesy Linde Co., division of Union Carbide Corp.).

Because of the noise of the process, the gun is isolated by double concrete walls insulated with sound-absorbing materials. Aiming and firing are remotely controlled from a panel outside the firing chamber.

Although temperatures within the gun may reach 6000°F, the parts being sprayed do not exceed 400°F. Therefore, distortion of precision parts is minimized. The detonation gun can be used to apply steel, cast iron, aluminum, nickel, copper, titanium, magnesium, various alloys, and tungsten. However, the base material must be able to resist permanent deformation encountered under the load and stress.

Detonation-gun coatings are used in many industries where tungsten carbide coatings are needed to solve wear problems. Some examples of use are detonation-gun-plated plug and ring gages, and cutting edges that are subjected to intense wear, such as skiving knives for rubber and plastic or tubular drills for cutting acoustical tile and paper. It is not uncommon to get four times more wear out of carbide-plated parts over the uncoated parts.

The detonation gun is a process patented and operated by the Linde Air Products Company. The services are sold, but the equipment is not.

POWDER METHOD. The powder-spray method uses an oxyacetylene welding torch with a modified tip which permits the powdered metal to be sprayed through the flame. A carrier gas—argon, helium, nitrogen, carbon dioxide, or compressed air—conveys the powdered metal to the torch tip. The fuel gas can be acetylene or hydrogen (Fig. 10-23).

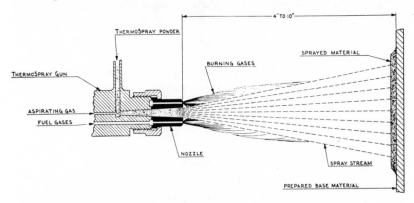

METCO ThermoSpray Gun

**Fig. 10-23.** Powder-spray methods.

Powdered alloys used for fused coatings are hard-facing metals—basically chromium-nickel compositions to which boron or silicon and phosphorus are added. The screen-mesh size of the powder metals must be within the limits of 100 to 150. The surfaces to be overlaid should be thoroughly cleaned and roughened by machining or grit blasting, as described previously.

Powdered-metal sprays can be deposited in narrow bands, making thin edges possible. The coating is deposited just ahead of the torch flame, which immediately fuses the coating to the surface. Deposits as thin as 0.003 or as thick as 0.070 in. can be made in one pass. If heavier deposits are needed, a second pass is made. The bond is a true weld and, as such, will withstand the same conditions as rod surfacing, including abrasion, erosion, corrosion, impact, and heat.

PLASMA METHOD. In plasma plating, a jet of air goes through an electric arc. The heat of the arc ionizes the gas. When this ionized conducting gas, called plasma, is forced through a nozzle, the gas becomes a plasma jet (Fig. 10-24). The high concentration of energy that results from squeezing an arc through a nozzle produces extremely high temperatures and voltages. The nozzle is water-cooled. The gases used are argon, helium, nitrogen, hydrogen, or a mixture to suit the application.

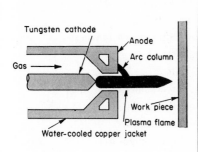

Tungsten cathode

Anode

Arc column

Gas →

Work piece

Plasma flame

Water-cooled copper jacket

A high-current electric arc is concentrated and stabilized in the controlled atmosphere of a special nozzle. Some of the gas (usually argon) flows through the arc where it is heated as high as 30,000 F and accelerated to supersonic speed. The gas forms a highly ionized plasma jet. Particles of coating material, in powder or wire form, are introduced into the plasma where they are melted, then accelerated to a high velocity toward the workpiece. The work is cooled by jets of $CO_2$ or air.

Tungsten, tantalum, molybdenum, aluminum oxide, and zirconium oxide.

**Fig. 10-24.** Plasma method.

The plasma gun can be used for metal spraying with either solids or powders. When fine powder is used, the individual particles are melted and accelerated to velocities near the gas-stream velocity. The molten particles are propelled against the workpiece, where they flatten out, solidify, and form a coating.

The ability to reach high temperatures—20,000 to 30,000°F—is significant for many of the refractory metals and ceramic compounds.

### QUESTIONS

1. How is most of the oxygen that is used for welding obtained?
2. How is acetylene gas obtained?
3. What is meant by LOX?

4. Why can acetylene be compressed in cylinders at 250 psi and not be explosive?

5. What is the advantage of a two-stage regulator?

6. Why are two gages mounted on an oxygen tank that is used for welding?

7. What is the principal difference in the two main types of welding torches?

8. How do the hose fittings for oxygen and acetylene differ?

9. How is a neutral flame obtained?

10. When can a reducing flame be used to advantage?

11. Explain the difference between forehand and backhand welding.

12. Briefly summarize the principal advantages and disadvantages of gas welding.

13. What is the fundamental difference between brazing and welding?

14. What is the meaning of wetting, as applied to brazing?

15. What is the preferred type of joint for brazing when strength is a primary consideration?

16. What are the factors to keep in mind when designing a joint for brazing?

17. Identify the brazing filter material given as RBCuZn-A.

18. Why is flux necessary in the brazing operation?

19. What are the advantages of heating by induction for brazing?

20. Why is it important to clean the parts after brazing?

21. How does braze welding differ from brazing?

22. What parts of tin and lead comprise a eutectic mixture?

23. Why is rosin-core solder specified for electrical wiring?

24. What is the result of overheating a soldering copper?

25. Why is aluminum considered a rather difficult metal to solder?

26. How may chemical or galvanic corrosion be eliminated in an aluminum soldered joint?

27. Describe the composition of one type of hard-facing deposit.

28. What method is used in preparing a surface for metal spraying if the surface will later need to be machined?

29. What is the composition of a sprayed ceramic coating?

30. Describe a gradated construction in metallic-ceramic spraying.

31. What are some advantages of the powder-spray process?

32. How is the extremely high temperature of a plasma jet obtained?

**PROBLEMS**

1. Compare the operating cost of welding 100 ft of 16-gauge sheet stock by oxyacetylene welding and by manual arc welding:

         *Oxacetylene Method*                        *Arc Method*

    (a) Gas consumption—equal parts of oxygen and acetylene—3 cu ft per hr

(b)  0.016 lb rod per ft of weld       0.022 lb electrode per ft of weld
(c)  Welding speed, 25 ft per hr       Welding speed, 30 in. per min
(d)  Oxygen cost, 3.5¢ per cu ft       Welding-current cost, 0.008¢ per ft
(e)  Acetylene cost, 1.5¢ per cu ft
(f)  Rod cost, 30¢ per lb              Electrode cost, 18¢ per lb

Assume that labor and overhead costs are $6.00 per hr for both types of welding.

2. In establishing an oxyacetylene welding division, the question arose as to whether to buy the acetylene in tanks or to generate it. It was determined that five No. 3 Airco tips would be the maximum consumption at any one time. These would be used on the average of 6 hr per day. The following cost information was obtained: carbide in 100-lb cans, $6.80; acetylene in 275-cu-ft cylinders, $11.50 (No. 3 Airco uses 8.8 cu ft per hr); 50-lb acetylene generators, $275; 150-lb generators, $600; 300-lb generators, $850. It was decided that the generator could be conveniently recharged 3 times per week. Each pound of calcium carbide generates 4.5 cu ft of acetylene gas. It was also decided to add 0.002¢ per cu ft to the cost of acetylene generated, for extra maintenance, separate room, etc. The generator will be depreciated in equal amounts over a ten-year period.

State which system should be used, according to cost figures.

3. A properly made ¼-in. fillet weld contains 0.031 cu in. of weld metal per inch of weld. When overwelded so that the legs are 5/16 in., the weld metal increases to 0.049 cu in. of metal per inch of weld. What is the weight of weld-metal increase in 15 lineal feet of weld? Steel weighs 489 lb/cu ft. What would the electrode cost be for this much metal at current prices?

## REFERENCES

"Brazing Processes," *Welding Engineer*, August, 1958.

"The Basics of Soldering," *American Machinist/Metalworking Manufacturing*, Special Report No. 502, February, 1961.

Bruno, C., "Soldering Aluminum," *The Tool and Manufacturing Engineer*, November, 1960.

Hackman, R. L., "Putting Plasma Jets to Work," *The Tool and Manufacturing Engineer*, March, 1961.

*The Oxyacetylene Handbook*, Linde Company, Division of Union Carbide Corporation, New York, 1943.

Richardson, L. D., "Fundamentals of Wear Resistant Overlay," *Welding Engineer*, June, 1960.

*The Tool Engineer's Handbook*, American Society of Tool and Manufacturing Engineers, McGraw-Hill Book Company, New York, 1959.

*Welding Handbook*, American Welding Society, 4th ed., New York, 1960.

Westerhold, R. J., T. C. McGeary, H. A. Huff, and R. L. Wolfe, "Flame Sprayed Coatings," *Machine Design*, August, 1961.

Zuchowski, R. S., and J. H. Neely, "Mechanized Surfacing with Alloy Materials," *The Welding Journal*, January, 1958.

# 11

# FLAME- AND
# ARC-CUTTING
# PROCESSES

**F**LAME CUTTING is a term used to describe the process of separating metals by the use of an oxy-fuel flame. It refers almost exclusively to ferrous metals. In fact, plain carbon steels are the only metals that oxidize before they melt. When steel is brought up to a temperature of between 1400° and 1600°F, it reacts rapidly with oxygen to form iron oxides ($Fe_3O_4$). The melting point of the oxide is somewhat lower than that of the steel. The heat generated by the burning iron is sufficient to melt the iron oxide and some free iron which runs off as molten slag, exposing more iron to the oxygen jet.

Theoretically, 1 cu ft of oxygen is required to oxidize about 3/4 cu in. of iron. Actually, the *kerf*, or cut, is not entirely oxidized, but 30 to 40 percent of the metal is washed out as metallic iron.

Once the cut is started, there should be enough heat to continue it without the use of preheating flames, using only the oxygen, but in practice, this does not work out. Excessive radiation at the surface, small pieces of dirt, and paint scale make it necessary that the oxygen be surrounded with preheating flames throughout the cutting operation.

Although acetylene is widely used as the fuel gas, other gases that can be used are hydrogen, natural gas, and propane—often at considerable savings.

### Flame-Cutting Equipment

**Manual Cutting.** The cutting torch somewhat resembles the welding torch, but it has provision for several neutral flames and a jet of high-pressure oxygen in the center (Fig. 11-1). The neutral preheating flames are adjusted and controlled as described previously in gas welding. The oxygen needed for cutting is controlled by a quick-acting trigger or lever-type valve.

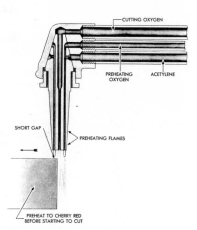

**Fig. 11-1.** The cutting torch has an oxygen jet surrounded by preheating flames.

The thickness and type of material to be cut will determine the tip size. Best results are obtained when the cutting oxygen pressure, cutting speed, tip size, and preheating flames are controlled to give a narrow, clean cut. Cuts that are improperly made will produce ragged and irregular edges, with slag adhering at the bottom of the plates. One indication of the proper speed is the drag lines. The faster the rate of traverse, the more the bottom of the cut lags behind. This is evidenced by a series of curved lines (Fig. 11-2). Fine, fairly vertical lines left on the side of the metal indicate a good-quality cut. Faults to avoid in torch cutting are shown in Figs. 11-2 and 11-3.

**Machine Cutting.** Although manual flame cutting is entirely satisfactory for a wide range of cutting operations, machine flame cutting is finding increased application. Machine flame cutting provides greater speed, accuracy, and economy. The machines can be used for straight-line cutting, circle cutting, plate-edge preparation, and shape cutting.

STRAIGHT-LINE AND CIRCLE CUTTING. Machine flame cutting consists, in its simpler form, of mounting the cutting torch on a carriage driven by a variable-speed motor. This unit is mounted on a track for straight cutting. Mechanized flame cutting often replaces machine

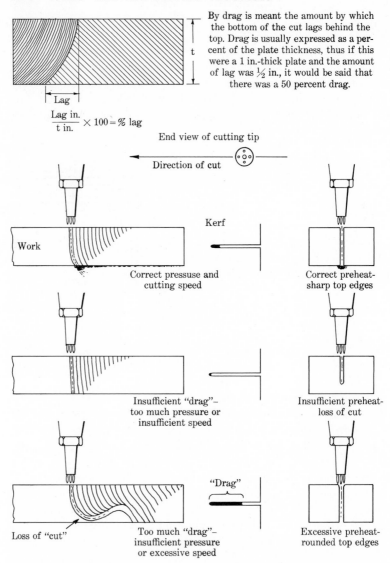

By drag is meant the amount by which the bottom of the cut lags behind the top. Drag is usually expressed as a per-cent of the plate thickness, thus if this were a 1 in.-thick plate and the amount of lag was $\frac{1}{2}$ in., it would be said that there was a 50 percent drag.

$$\frac{\text{Lag in.}}{\text{t in.}} \times 100 = \% \text{ lag}$$

End view of cutting tip

Direction of cut

Kerf

Work

Correct pressuse and cutting speed

Correct preheat- sharp top edges

Insufficient "drag"– too much pressure or insufficient speed

Insufficient preheat- loss of cut

"Drag"

Loss of "cut"

Too much "drag"– insufficient pressure or excessive speed

Excessive preheat- rounded top edges

Sight method for determining correct cutting procedure.

**Fig. 11-2.** Correct cutting conditions are indicated by the correct amount of drag.

cutting. Where extreme accuracy demands machine-tool finishing, the cut can be made to remove all but a small finishing cut.

Most portable cutting machines are made to work both on a straight-line track or in a circular path. Various sized circles can be cut by the setting made on a radius-rod attachment.

When cutting plate with the hand torch, faulty work-manship may arise from a variety of causes. These defects are explained below in connection with examples in Fig. 11-3. For comparison, a correctly made cut in 1-in. plate is shown in 1. Here the edge is square and the drag lines are vertical and not pronounced.

## Defects

2—Gouging at bottom, because preheat flames were too short—only about ⅛ in. long—and cutting speed was too slow.

3—Top surface melted over, cut edge irregular, and too much slag. The preheat flames were too long—about ½ in.

4—Top edge melted over because the cutting speed was too slow. Too low an oxygen pressure was used.

5—No control of the cut because oxygen pressure was too high and nozzle size too small.

6—Irregular kerf lines produced because the cutting speed was too slow.

7—The cut edge is irregular and there is rake or lag to the cut lines from using excessive cutting speed.

8—A wavy and irregular cut edge was produced by un-steady blow-pipe travel.

9—Gouges were caused where the cut was restarted, be-cause the cut was lost and not carefully recommenced.

## Good and Bad Kerfs

10—A good kerf made by correct procedure.

11—Top edge melted over by too much preheat and nozzle too close to plate.

12—Tapered kerf resulting from holding the nozzle too high above the plate, so the heat and oxygen stream could spread.

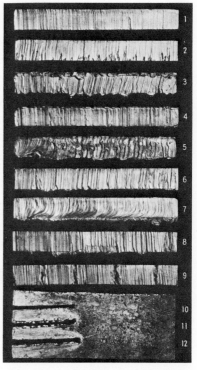

**Fig. 11-3.** Faults to avoid in torch cutting (courtesy Linde Co., division of Union Carbide Corp.).

PLATE-EDGE PREPARATION. Plate edges usually need beveling or grooving in preparation for welding. Bevel cuts are easily made by inclining the torch at the desired angle, just as in making a vertical cut. Usually, if the plate edge calls for a J or U preparation, a gouging tip is used. This nozzle is designed to deliver a relatively large jet of oxygen at low velocity. The torch is held at a low angle, approximately 20 deg to the horizontal as the cut is started and then lowered to about 5 deg when it is moving along.

SHAPE CUTTING. Shape cutting refers to any contour cutting of metal. It can be accomplished by freehand manipulation of the torch, but this is not generally satisfactory, except for very rough work. The newest development in this field is the *photocell,* or *photoelectric, tracer;* other methods of template tracing are also used.

*Photoelectric tracers.* A photocell tracer (Fig. 11-4), is, in essence, an electric eye that guides the motorized unit used to control the path of the cutting torch. It is possible to trace simple pencil or ink sketches of intricate shapes. Kerf width is provided for so that it does not have to be considered in the drawing. The kerf dial can be set so that the part produced is the exact size, is smaller, or is larger than the drawing. This kerf adjustment can be as wide as ¼ in. Dimensional tolerances held by the photocell method are as close as $+ 0$ and $- 1/32$ in.

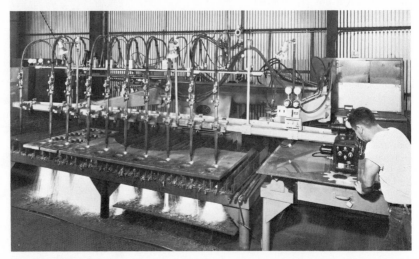

**Fig. 11-4.** A photoelectric tracer used for a multiple-shape cutting operation (courtesy Air Reduction Sales Company).

*Template tracers.* Although not quite so easy to use as a photocell, templates are still widely employed as a means of guiding the cutting torch. Strip templates can be easily formed and used, with a special tracing head to guide the cutting torch. Magnetic-type tracer heads are used on solid ferrous metal-type templates (Fig. 11-5). Simple templates for hand guiding of the tracer head can be cut out of plywood.

**Fig. 11-5.** Automatic tracing is done with a strip-type tracer or a magnetic-head tracer (courtesy Linde Co., division of Union Carbide Corp.).

STACK CUTTING. Considerable time can be saved in cutting a number of identical parts by stacking them and cutting them all in one pass (Fig. 11-6).

**Fig. 11-6.** Twelve ¾-in. steel plates are tightly clamped together for stack cutting (courtesy Air Reduction Sales Company).

The plates should be tightly clamped as any air space may cause the cut to be lost. If a high preheat flame is used for a thick stack, a "waster plate" can be used to protect the top plate.

### Physical and Metallurgical Effects of Torch Cutting

Flame cutting of mild steel has very little effect on the metal adjacent to the cut. However, as the carbon content or alloys are increased, there will be some hardening of the edge due to the quenching action of the adjacent metal and the atmosphere. The hard edges may be difficult to machine, and the lowered ductility of this hard layer may cause cracking under load. The best method of avoiding this condition is to preheat the metal. Medium-carbon steels should be heated from 350° to 700°F, and low-alloy high-tensile-strength steels from 600° to 900°F.

Heavy plates do not warp when flame-cut, but plates ½ in. or less in thickness may have to be clamped or the amount of cutting done at one time be restricted. Judicious postheating with a torch can be effective in reducing or eliminating warpage.

### Cutting Alloy Steels, Concrete, and Cast Iron

**Alloy Steels.** As stated previously, steel is readily cut by the oxy-acetylene flame because the oxide film that forms over the molten metal is of a lower melting point than the base metal. This is not true in cutting some alloy steels. For example, stainless steel, when molten, forms a chromium oxide slag that hampers further cutting. Full-oxygen methods used to cut stainless steel or other high-melting-point oxide materials are flux-injection cutting and powder cutting.

FLUX-INJECTION CUTTING. This process consists of feeding a nonmetallic flux into the hose line carrying the oxygen. The powder disposes of the viscous chromium oxide slag that would otherwise cling to the heated metal surface.

This method is applicable to most stainless steels, but it is not recommended for the high-nickel types such as Type 330 (15 percent chromium and 35 percent nickel).

Another method used to cut stainless steels, if the flux-injection attachment is not available, is to lay a steel welding rod or steel plate along the line of cut. The heat developed by the oxygen with the steel rod or plate will generally be sufficient to melt a slot in the stainless steel. The cutting of stainless steel is actually more of a melting process than an oxidation process.

POWDER CUTTING. The powder-cutting method, first introduced in 1943, employs a cutting torch with a tube feed unit. The tube contains iron-rich powder which is fed to the torch tip under either compressed air or nitrogen. When the powder reaches the oxygen cutting stream, it burns with considerable heat. With this increased heat, the oxygen's flame-cutting action is speeded up, and the number of materials to which it can be applied is substantially increased.

The powder-cutting process was originally introduced to cut stainless steel, but since then it has been successfully used on other alloy steels, cast iron, bronze, nickel, aluminum, certain refractories, and concrete. Nonferrous materials require that a mixture of aluminum and iron powder be used instead of the straight iron powder.

Both flux-injection and powder-cutting methods are still being used, but they are rapidly being replaced by the plasma arc discussed later in this chapter.

**Concrete Cutting.** Concrete and reinforced concrete can be efficiently cut with a powder-cutting torch in thicknesses up to 18 in. This is a mechanized operation, and average cutting speeds range from 1 to $2\frac{1}{2}$ ipm. For concrete thicker than 18 in., the powder lance is used.

**Cast-Iron Cutting.** Cast iron also has a higher-melting-point oxide than the base metal. When the cast iron melts, the oxides and impurities mix together, making it very difficult to cut. It must have a much higher preheat temperature and an oxygen pressure from 25 to 100 percent greater than for steel. The preheating flames should be adjusted to have an excess of acetylene. The motion used in cutting is to swing the torch from side to side in a small arc. The diameter of the arc is equal to the width of the kerf, which is determined by the thickness and quality of the metal. Thick or poor-quality metals require cuts to permit some working of the molten metal with a steel rod.

**Lance Cutting.**  An oxygen lance is a simple device consisting essentially of a length of steel pipe, (usually 1/8- or 1/4-in. size), a length of hose, some couplings, a control valve, and an oxygen tank, complete with regulator. With this equipment no preheating flame is provided, so an auxiliary torch is needed. After heating the metal to the kindling temperature, the lance is brought over to start the cut. Other methods are also used to obtain the heat necessary to start the cut, such as placing a red-hot piece of steel on the starting point or heating the end of the lance until it is red hot. When it is brought in contact with metal and the oxygen is turned on, the end of the pipe will burn brilliantly, furnishing enough heat to start the cut.

The oxygen lance is an excellent tool for piercing holes in steel. For example, a hole 2½ in. in diameter can be cut in 1-ft-thick steel in a matter of 2 min. It is routinely used in tapping blast and open-hearth furnaces.

In making continuous cuts, the lance and cutting torch are frequently used together. The torch furnishes the heat needed to keep the cut going along the top surface, and the lance carries the cut through the piece. When the lance reaches the bottom of the metal, it is brought back to the top and again lowered, each time making an advance. Masses of steel 8 ft thick have been cut by this method.

Powder cutting is also done with lance equipment. This consists of a lance handle with one or more lengths of black-iron pipe attached. Iron and aluminum powders are mixed with oxygen in the lance handle, and they burn at the end of the pipe.

The powder-cutting lance has proved successful in cutting firebrick, aluminum billets, bronze, both steel and cast iron containing inclusions, and concrete.

It is particularly good for cutting thick concrete. One example of this work is cited to give an understanding of the method's usefulness. The powder lance was called on to cut a hole for a pipeline in a concrete wall 12 ft thick. A clean 8-in.-diameter hole was pierced in a matter of 1¼ hr.

Powder cutting of concrete has become very important. Concrete walls 4 ft thick have been cut at the rate of 1½ ft per hr.

## ARC-CUTTING METHODS

Originally, electric arc cutting was confined to using the heat of the arc produced between a coated electrode or a carbon electrode and the work. With a high-current setting and straight polarity (electrode negative) the metal was separated by melting rather than by oxidation. Although this process is applicable to both ferrous and nonferrous metals, the surface finish and accuracy are not good. It is used mostly for rough work such as cutting up scrap, rivet cutting, and hole piercing. For most of these operations the coated electrode is preferred. The coating acts as an insulator, thus preventing the arc from shorting against the sidewalls of the hole being cut.

Arc-cutting methods have now been improved to include arc-air, oxygen-arc, tungsten-arc, and plasma-flame.

### Arc-Air Cutting

The arc-air method of cutting metals consists of melting the metal with an electric arc and then removing the molten metal by means of a high-velocity air jet.

The equipment consists of a torch or electrode holder with a concentric cable which carries both air and current. A lever at the bottom of the holder controls the air that passes through a hole adjacent to the electrode (Fig. 11-7). The electrode usually is a combination of carbon and graphite, either plain or copper-coated.

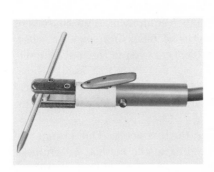

**Fig. 11-7.** Manual- and machine-type arc-air torches used in cutting, gouging, and beveling metals. The metal is melted and simultaneously removed with compressed air (courtesy Arcair Company).

The arc-air process is not only used for cutting both ferrous and nonferrous metals, but also as an effective grooving tool. As an example, grooves 3/8 in. wide and 1/4 in. deep are usually cut at about 3 fpm.

The arc-air torch is relatively inexpensive to operate. Costs run roughly $1.50 per hr, exclusive of labor, using 3/8 in. electrodes.

### Oxygen-Arc Cutting

The oxygen arc consists of a coated electrode with a small-diameter hole down through the center through which oxygen is blown. This method is quite similar to the oxyacetylene process, except the heat is now supplied by the arc.

### Tungsten-Arc Cutting

As stated previously, metals that form a high-melting-point oxide present problems in cutting. Although flux-injection and powder-cutting methods are used, they still have some objectionable features. Powder cutting raises quite a bit of smoke that may interfere with other operations in the area. Additional work is sometimes needed in the way of grinding to offset powder contamination of the cut surface.

The tungsten arc used for cutting is no different from TIG described previously. Cutting is accomplished by increasing the current density above good welding conditions. Typical speeds for cutting are 40 to 60 ipm on 1/8-in. aluminum and 20 to 40 ipm on 1/8-in. stainless steel. A shielding gas of 65 percent argon and 35 percent hydrogen is used. Nitrogen can be used, but it is more hazardous to operators because it forms toxic fumes.

The quality of cut along the kerf wall is smooth and, in most cases, needs no further machining or grinding on metal thicknesses up to 3/4 in. The process is limited to 2-in.-thick stainless steel. The thicker the metal, the greater must be the tolerance allowed.

An example of production tolerance obtainable is a 30-in.-diameter wheel cut from 3/4-in.-thick stainless steel, using the tungsten-arc torch in combination with a photoelectric tracing head. The specified tolerance was ±1/16 in., however, the actual tolerance was less than that.

### Plasma-Flame Cutting

Plasma-flame cutting is also referred to as constricted-tungsten-arc cutting. The difference between tungsten-arc cutting and constricted-tungsten-arc cutting is shown in Fig. 11-8.

The nozzle of the plasma torch has a relatively small opening to constrict the arc, and the tip of the electrode is located within the nozzle instead of protruding, as it does on the TIG torch.

The welding arc, as commonly used in the open air, also produces a plasma gas. Air molecules are first dissociated and then ionized by collisions with the electron flow within the arc. Open-arc plasma temperatures are relatively low (10,000°F) owing to the freedom with which the heated air can expand laterally.

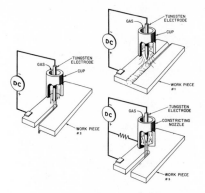

**Fig. 11-8.** A comparison of tungsten-arc cutting with constricted-tungsten-arc cutting. Ordinary TIG welding is also shown (courtesy Linde Co., division of Union Carbide Corp.).

When the arc current is constricted to a small cross-sectional area, the current density is significantly increased. The gas, which protects the nozzle walls, is heated to temperatures calculated at as high as 60,000°F. Each gas molecule is subject to many collisions with high-energy electrons, and ionization occurs (Fig. 11-9).

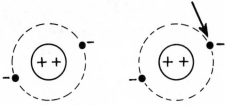

1. Neutral atom of gas in which electrons (-) balance nucleus (+)

2. An electron is knocked off the atom by bombardment.

**Fig. 11-9.** Ionization of gas.

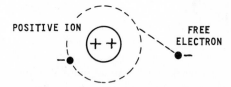

3. Upon losing the electron, the atom becomes a charged particle called an ion. Energy is absorbed during this process. The partially ionized gas is called plasma.

The transferred type of arc is used in plasma-flame cutting. In this, the workpiece is part of the electrical circuit. The electric arc strikes the anode, bombarding it with electrons and adding to the heat transferred by the plasma. The two account for the high treat-transfer rate of the plasma flame—20 times that of an oxyacetylene flame. The arc is stabilized by means of a gas vortex within the orifice. Thus the metal walls are protected, and the arc is kept in the center of the orifice (Fig. 11-10).

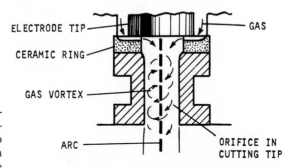

ELECTRODE TIP
CERAMIC RING
GAS VORTEX
ARC
GAS
ORIFICE IN CUTTING TIP

**Fig. 11-10.** The plasma arc uses a vortex-type stabilization to keep the arc centered in the orifice and at the same time protect the sidewalls of the torch.

Gas-sheath stabilization is used in the plasma flame cutter. Grooves in the ceramic ring cause the incoming gas to swirl, forming a vortex within the orifice. The velocity is greatest at the walls, less at the center. This velocity distribution produces an insulating gas sheath to keep the arc centered in the orifice.

The plasma flame is used on 1/4- to 5-in.-thick aluminum and 1/4- to 4-in.-thick stainless steel. Dross free cuts can be made on stainless steel up to 2 in. thick. By *dross* is meant the slag that adheres to the bottom side of the cut. Chipping and grinding are necessary to remove it.

The plasma torch has several advantages over the fuel oxygen torch:

1. It can cut faster and leave a narrower kerf. Mild steel 3/4 in. thick can be cut at 70 ipm, compared to oxygen cutting of 20 ipm.

2. Operating costs are less. Figure 11-11 shows comparative operating costs between the two methods. The ratio of savings in favor of the arc is now about 3:1. This figure is exclusive of labor rates.

3. The plasma flame can be used to cut any metal, since it is primarily a melting process.

4. Plasma-flame energy seems to be unlimited. The greater the power used, the greater the volume of kerf material that can be removed. Oxy-fuel cutting is limited to the maximum temperature of the chemical reaction (burning).

The main disadvantage of the process is the high initial cost of the equipment. Thus only those who do quantity cutting will be able to amortize the cost in a reasonable time.

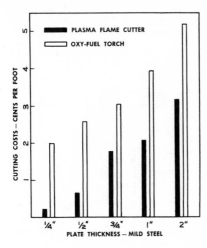

**Fig. 11-11.** Comparative cutting costs between the plasma flame cutter and the oxy-fuel torch (courtesy Thermal Dynamics).

## QUESTIONS

1. Why is plain carbon steel a relatively easy metal to flame cut?
2. What other gases may be used instead of acetylene for the fuel gas?
3. How do drag lines indicate the proper speed of flame cutting?
4. What type of tip is needed to produce J- or V-grooves on the edges of plate?
5. What tolerance can be expected in flame cutting when the photoelectric tracer is used?
6. How can hard edges be avoided on flame-cut alloy steels?
7. Why are stainless steel and cast iron considered difficult to flame cut?
8. In what way does iron powder aid the flame-cutting action for some materials?
9. What is the essential difference between a cutting torch and an oxygen lance?
10. How does the arc-air method of cutting differ from the oxygen arc?
11. What change is made to convert TIG welding equipment from a torch to a welder?
12. Explain what is meant by *plasma* in plasma-flame cutting?
13. What is meant by the transfer-type arc?
14. Compare the cutting characteristics of a plasma torch with an oxyacetylene torch.

## PROBLEMS

1. Approximately how much oxygen would it take to make four cuts 18 in. wide across a steel plate 1 in. thick and 4 ft wide? Assume 30 percent of the metal in the cut is washed out as metallic iron and not oxidized, and that the operation is 85 percent efficient.

2. What would the approximate time be for cutting a 10-in.-diameter hole through a 10-in.-thick concrete wall? Assume an average speed for the powder-cutting torch.

3. What would be the approximate cost of cutting a groove ¼ in. deep and ⅜ in. wide in fifteen pieces of steel 10 ft long with the Arcair process? The labor and overhead charge is $10.00 per hr.

4. Compare the time required to cut 200 3-ft-diameter blanks from mild steel plate ¾ in. thick with a plasma torch and with a conventional oxyacetylene cutting torch. What will the direct costs of each method be, calculated on a per-foot basis?

**REFERENCES**

Berg, R. E., "Plasma Cutting Torches—What They Can Do, What They Can't Do," *American Machinist/Metalworking Manufacturing*, November, 1961.

"Constricted Tungsten—Arc Cutting of Aluminum," *The Welding Journal*, May, 1956.

*The Oxyacetylene Handbook*, Linde Company, Division of Union Carbide Corporation, New York, 1943.

Stepath, M. D., "The Arc Air Process," *The Welding Journal*, September, 1954.

Wait, J. D., and S. H. Resh, "Tungsten Arc Cutting," *The Welding Journal*, June, 1959.

# 12

# RESISTANCE WELDING

**R**ESISTANCE WELDING is based on the well-known principle that heat is generated by the resistance offered to the flow of electrical current. The amount of heat generated in the workpiece depends on the magnitude of the welding current, the resistance of the current-conducting path, and the time the current is allowed to flow. This is expressed by the formula

$$H = I^2RT$$

where

$H =$ heat generated, in joules
$I =$ current, in rms amperes
$R =$ resistance, in ohms
$T =$ time of current flow, in seconds

The heat generation is directly proportional to the resistance offered by any point in the circuit. Since the interface of two joining surfaces is the point of greatest resistance, it is also the point of greatest heat. In simple resistance welding a high-amperage low-voltage current is passed from one adjoining plate to the other until the metal becomes heated to a temperature that is high enough to cause localized fusion and the formation of a weld nugget. Additional pressure is applied, after the current is turned off, to squeeze the two parts into a localized homogeneous mass.

The principle types of resistance welding can be divided into two groups: Lap welds, including spot, Seam, and Projection; and butt welds, including upset butt and flash butt.

## SPOT WELDING

Spot welding is the basic type of resistance welding. Therefore, points covered in explaining it will not be repeated for the other processes. The fundamental circuit components are shown in Fig. 12-1.

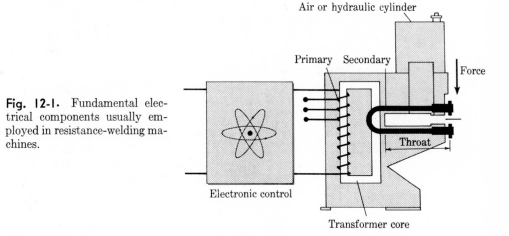

**Fig. 12-1.** Fundamental electrical components usually employed in resistance-welding machines.

Current, time, and pressure are recognized as the fundamental variables of spot welding. For welding most metals, these must be kept within very close limits. Therefore, they will be discussed from the standpoint of their relation to current control.

### Current Control

Electronic tubes are used as the switching devices for stopping and starting the primary circuit. Thyratron tubes are used for currents up to 40 amp, ignitrons for currents above 40 amp. Electronic contactors eliminate most of the noise and maintenance common to mechanical-type contactors.

Magnetic contactors can also be used as a switching device. They are made to open the power circuit when the a-c wave approaches zero. Magnetic contactors have the advantage of low initial cost, but maintenance cost is higher, and they are not able to function consistently in rapid welding cycles.

### Time Control

The time involved in spot welding is relatively short. Usually, the duration of current flow is a fraction of a second. For example, a spot weld can be made in two 1/16-in.-thick pieces of mild steel in 15 cycles or $\frac{1}{4}$ sec when using 60-cycle current.

Low-carbon steels offer little or no metallurgical problems when spot-welded. Once the nugget is formed, the metal passes from austenite back to pearlite. If medium- and high-carbon steels were to be treated in the same manner, the rapid cooling of the spot would result in brittle martensite. This does not mean that medium- or high-carbon steels cannot be resistance-welded, but other processes, such as quench and postheat, are needed to permit the proper heat treatment of the spot immediately after it is made.

The normal timing sequence consists of *squeeze time*—the interval between application of the tip pressure to the work and application of welding current; *weld time*—the time for current flow; *hold time*—the interval after the current is shut off but during which the electrodes are held in place to forge the metal while it is cooling and to draw off the heat; and *off time*—the interval allowed for the work to be transferred to a new location before the cycle repeats (Fig. 12-2).

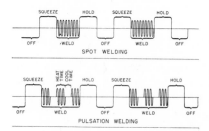

**Fig. 12-2.** The normal timing sequence for spot welding compared with pulsation welding.

Also shown in Fig. 12-2 is the *pulsation-welding* cycle. The main difference between this and the conventional cycle is that, instead of the weld period being one period of current flow, there is an intermittent flow with cooling no-current intervals between current-flow periods. This method is frequently used on multiple-layer welds, projection welds, and welds on two pieces of steel thicker than $\frac{1}{8}$ in. It also has the advantage of increased electrode life.

When more precise current control is needed, as in welding aluminum or magnesium, a three-phase welder is often used. These machines can provide a slowly rising rather than a rapidly rising wave front. Also, a modulated delay of a secondary current can be obtained, thus eliminating the formation of cooling cracks (Fig. 12-3).

Timers are *synchronous* or *nonsynchronous*. The nonsynchronous ones are those that start and stop the flow of welding current at any time with respect to the voltage wave form. The opening and closing of the contactor is not necessarily synchronized with the line-voltage

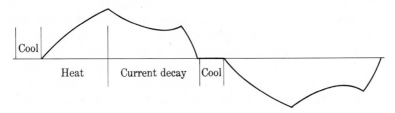

**Fig. 12-3.** Added current control obtainable with three-phase machines.

wave form. This can affect the a-c frequency as much as ±1 cycle. There are many noncritical conditions that this small deviation will not affect.

## Pressure Control

Most ferrous metals are welded with constant pressure, but high-conductivity low-resistivity metals need variable pressure. During the weld or heating time, a higher forging pressure may be introduced in order to obtain a sound, rather than a superficial, weld. It is necessary for the parts to be forced together under high pressure after the metals have reached the fusion temperature.

The amount of pressure that can be exerted depends on the metals being joined. If the metals are quite soft, they may flatten or distort under the electrode, which would, at best, be a deterrent to good appearance and more frequently would result in an unsatisfactory weld. Thus not only the welding current but also the clamping and squeezing pressures must be selected on the basis of the base metal, the thickness, and the type of welding used.

Accurate control is the essence of success in resistance welding. To repeat, controls must regulate the magnitude of the current, its wave shape, the timing, and the rest of the welding cycle. The more accurately these are controlled, the better and more consistent the welds will be.

## Single-Phase and Three-Phase Welders

**Single-Phase System.** Basically, single-phase resistance welders are transformers that change line voltages to lower values in order to intensify the current. Since resistance welding must be done with current flowing in one direction through the materials, pulsed direct current is used. This is obtained by placing ignition tubes in the primary supply line to the transformer.

Welding heat is controlled by a tap selection on the welding-transformer primary, and by a phase-shift control that varies the ignitron-contactor induction period.

Heat is generated in the material in half-cycle pulses. Between these, there is no current in the weld area. As a result, when the electrical conductivity of the material is high, as in aluminum, the amount of heat loss in the interpulse period generally results in unsatisfactory welds. However, single-phase machines are still considered the "work-horses" when welding under less critical conditions, as in mild steel, high-nickel alloys, titanium, etc.

**Three-Phase System.** The three-phase system has the advantage of better distribution of the electrical load, since it uses high power factor on all three phases. Thus the kilovolt-ampere demand and the primary demand for three-phase machines may be one half and one third, respectively, of that required by a single-phase machine. Single and three-phase control circuits are shown in Fig. 12-4.

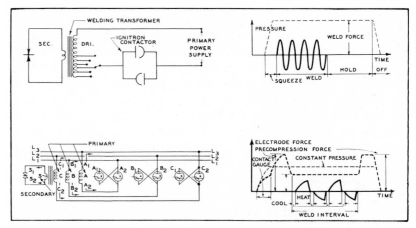

**Fig. 12-4.** Basic types of control circuits for resistance welders, and the typical welding cycle they provide: single phase, direct energy (top) and three phase, direct energy (below) (courtesy Modern Assembly Practice).

All these machines are direct-energy types. There are also stored-energy types. The latter, either electromechanically or electrostatically, accumulate sufficient current and then discharge it across the electrodes. Although these machines have some distinct advantages, such as almost instantaneous discharge of current and a good power factor, their wave shape is not suitable for welding low-conductivity materials.

The newest approach to precise control is a Dekatron electronic counter which consists, in part, of a multicathode tube that actually counts the cycles of power-line frequency as well as the impulses of welding current to ensure absolute consistency from cycle to cycle. Timing-control dials, under this arrangement, are calibrated in *cycles*, and current dials in *impulses* of secondary current.

### Design Considerations

There is a direct relationship between the weld strength of a given joint and its design. The factors that must be considered in each joint design are the amount of overlap, the spot spacing, the spot strength, and the accessibility.

**Overlap.** The amount of overlap required for a good spot weld in lap joints is determined by the weld size, which, in turn, is determined by the metal thickness. An acceptable weld size for a thickness range of from 0.032 to 0.188 in. is roughly estimated at 0.10 in. plus two times the thickness of the thinnest member. The overlap should be equal to two times the weld size plus ⅛ in. The ⅛ in. is for the tolerance in positioning the weld. If fixturing is used so that the spot will be made exactly in the center of the overlap, the ⅛ in. can be disregarded.

Welds placed too close to the edge will often squirt molten metal from the joint. This edge expulsion, or "spitting," will cause unsound and weak welds.

**Spot Spacing.** Spot spacing should never shunt current to the previous weld, thus reducing the size of the weld being made. A general rule is to allow 16t, t = the thickness of the material. However, if distortion is more important than strength, the figure should be increased to 48t. When it is necessary to place spot welds where there is apt to be current shunting, the current must be increased to compensate.

**Spot Strength.** Spot strength varies directly with area. It is generally safe to assume that the strength will be equal to the weld area times the tensile strength of the metal in the annealed state.

**Accessibility.** Offset electrodes can be used (Fig. 12-5), to make spot welds in places that are inaccessible by the conventional type. If the offset is great, excessive tip deflection, skidding, and surface deformation are likely. When the size of the electrode must be restricted to accommodate the joint, it will tend to overheat.

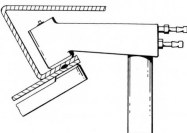

**Fig. 12-5.** An offset electrode is needed for the less accessible areas.

## Surface Preparation

Preweld surface preparation is necessary to minimize variations in contact resistance between the metals being joined as well as between the weld material and the electrodes. Dirt and oxide surfaces that come in contact with the electrodes must be removed or reduced to ensure good welds with good surface appearance. This practice also minimizes the tendency of the electrode to pick up some of the metal. A uniform oxide surface can be tolerated, but rusty material should not be spot-welded. Oil will not affect weld quality as such, but the particles and dirt in the oil will cause erratic welding. Oil in contact with the electrodes causes carbonization of the tips, decreasing their life.

Metal cleaning is done by vapor degreasers, chemical cleaning, and various mechanical methods. Sandblasting should not be used, because the silica that becomes embedded on the surface produces very undependable results.

## Equipment

Spot welders are of several types, ranging from small manually controlled machines to large three-phase and stored-energy machines with electronic controls.

**Rocker-Arm Type.** The pressure for welding is transferred to the electrodes by means of a lever arm which can be operated manually or by a pneumatic circuit.

**Press Type.** The press-type machine exerts pressure on the electrodes by means of a ram that is activated by air or electric motors. Hydraulic cylinders are used for welding heavy-gauge work.

**Portable Guns.** It is not always convenient to move equipment that is being fabricated by spot welding into many different positions, nor would the places be accessible for standard equipment; thus portable guns are now extensively used, for example on truck- and auto-body construction.

The guns are mechanically, pneumatically, or hydraulically operated. An example of the kind of work performed by welding guns is shown in Fig. 12-6.

Portable welding equipment requires the same cooling and controls as are used on stationary machines for equivalent work. Air-operated guns are usually equipped with remote solenoid-valve controls.

**Spot-Welding Electrodes.** The welding electrodes are made of copper alloys, and, when the duty cycle is high, they are constructed so

**Fig. 12-6.** Portable spot welders are used where assemblies are too large or awkward to be done on a stationary machine. On this assembly, 42 welds are made in one position in approximately 1¾ min. A swivel-joint electrode is used on the outside surface to eliminate surface indentation (courtesy Sciaky).

as to provide for water cooling. This is necessary to prevent spreading or mushrooming of the tips (Fig. 12-7). As a general rule, the harder the copper alloy, the better life it will have but the less conductive it will be. Consequently, hard alloys are restricted to uses where they can be adequately cooled.

Pointed tips are widely used, since, with continued wear, they mushroom uniformly. Domed tips, used for welding many nonferrous

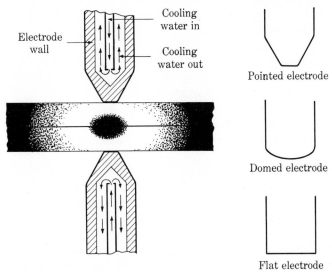

**Fig. 12-7.** Electrode tips must provide passageway for cooling water when high currents or high duty cycles are required.

materials, are characterized by their ability to withstand heavy pressure and severe heating without mushrooming. The radius of the dome varies, but a 2- to 4-in. radius is most commonly used. Filing of electrodes while on the machine should not be permitted, because it is too difficult to restore the original contour.

When invisible or inconspicuous welds are desired, or where the weld indentation is to be at a minimum, a flat tip is used. A domed tip is used for the mating electrode.

Offset electrodes are made for corner welds, for parts with overhanging flanges, and for the less-accessible areas. Their limitations were mentioned previously.

Normally, the opposing electrodes will be of similar size and shape. In certain cases, however, it is necessary to have unequal-sized electrodes. This is true in welding dissimilar metals or in welding similar materials of unequal thickness. A larger electrode will be needed on the side of the thicker material, or the material with the least resistivity, in order to center the spot between the two materials.

### Testing

The appearance of spot welds can be very deceiving. A weld may appear good even though, in essence, there is no weld. Nondestructive methods of testing are not satisfactory. Destructive tests for spot welds are numerous and are described in American Welding Society Recommended Practices for Resistance Welds C1. 1-50.

Three common destructive tests are shown in Fig. 12-8 and are described in the following paragraphs.

**Peel Test.**  The test that is probably the simplest to execute and yet give effective results is the peel test. All that is required is a sample strip containing welds and a means of pulling it apart.

If the penetration is good, the weld nugget will pull a hole in either piece. This is particularly true in materials up to 0.094 in. thick. Greater thicknesses may only pull out a slug of metal, leaving a crater in both pieces.

**Tensile Test.**  Portable tensile testing machines are available for testing spot welds. These machines are of 10,000-psi capacity and will pull single spot welds in mild steel up to 0.094 in. thick.

**Cross-sectional Test.**  Cross-sectional tests consist of cutting through the middle of the weld, polishing, etching it in a suitable acid, and inspecting it under a microscope. The penetration of the weld nugget into the base sheet should be between 40 and 70 percent of the sheet

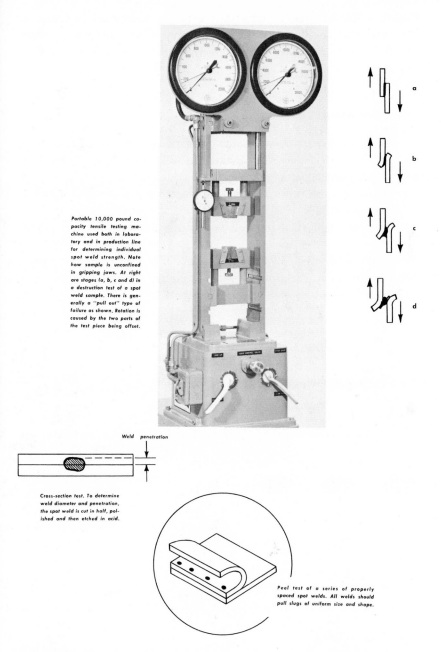

Portable 10,000 pound capacity tensile testing machine used both in laboratory and in production line for determining individual spot weld strength. Note how sample is unconfined in gripping jaws. At right are stages (a, b, c and d) in a destruction test of a spot weld sample. There is generally a "pull out" type of failure as shown. Rotation is caused by the two parts of the test piece being offset.

Weld penetration

Cross-section test. To determine weld diameter and penetration, the spot weld is cut in half, polished and then etched in acid.

Peel test of a series of properly spaced spot welds. All welds should pull slugs of uniform size and shape.

**Fig. 12-8.** Three common destructive tests (courtesy Riehle Testing Machines).

thickness. In addition to penetration, the metallurgical structure of the weld can be identified for grain size, microstructure, and any harmful effects, such as carbide precipitation which occurs in stainless steel.

## SEAM WELDING

Seam welding is a continuous type of spot welding. Instead of using pointed electrodes that make one weld at a time, the work is passed between copper wheels or rollers which act as electrodes. Thyratron and ignitron tubes are used to "make and break" the circuit.

The appearance of the completed weld is that of a series of overlapping spot welds which resemble stitches, hence the name *stitch welding*.

Seam welding can be used to produce highly efficient water- and gastight joints. A variation of seam welding, called *roll welding,* is used to produce a series of intermittent spots (Fig. 12-9).

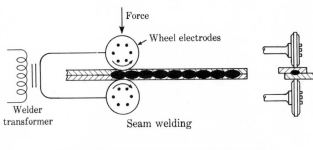

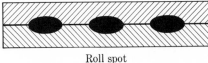

Roll spot

**Fig. 12-9.** Seam and roll spot welding. Seam welding can be done as shown, or one of the wheels can be replaced with a flat backing electrode that supports the work for the entire length of the seam.

Most seam welding can be done on two types of standard machines. In one machine the rotation of the wheels is at right angles to the throat; in the other, the rotation is parallel to the throat.

### Cooling Electrodes

Some seam welders use an external flow of water over the rotating electrode, but other machine manufacturers eliminate this inconvenience by cooling the rolls with refrigerant. Cooling reduces distortion of the work and lowers the maintenance costs of the welding wheels.

## Testing

The most common method of testing seam welds is to cut a sample of the area and pull to destruction. A satisfactory weld will generally show a failure in the metal rather than in the seam.

Seam welds can also be tested by "pillow tests." Two rectangular or square sheets are joined together by welding a seam all around the edges. A pipe connection is welded to the center of one sheet. Hydraulic pressure is applied through the pipe until the sheets expand, looking like pillows. The bursting pressure is recorded, as is the length of the weld line. Failure should occur in the parent metal rather than in the weld.

## PROJECTION WELDING

Projection welding is another variation of spot welding. Small projections are raised on one side of the sheet or plate where it is to be welded to another. The projections act to localize the heat of the welding circuit. During the welding process, the projections collapse, owing to heat and pressure, and the parts to be joined are brought in close contact (Fig. 12-10).

**Fig. 12-10.** In projection welding the current is concentrated in the areas of the raised projections. During the welding process the projections are flattened by heat and pressure. Several projections can be welded at one time.

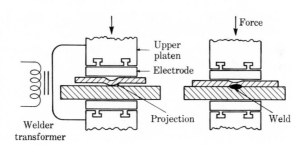

## Advantages

This method of welding gives longer electrode life, since the electrodes can be made of harder material, with less wear and maintenance resulting from fusing and overheating. The prelocated spots permit welds that would be impractical by other resistance methods. Outer or top surfaces can be produced with no electrode marks, making it possible to paint or plate them without grinding or polishing.

## Limitations

One of the main limitations of projection welding is the fact that it can be used on a comparatively small group of metals and alloys.

These are low-carbon steels, high-carbon and low-alloy steels, stainless and high-alloy steels, zinc die castings, terneplate, and some dissimilar and refractory metals. With brasses and coppers the method has not been too satisfactory. Aluminum applications are rare, although they have been practical in special cases.

### Applications

One of the most common applications of projection welding is for attaching small fasteners, nuts, special bolts, studs, and similar parts to larger components. A wide variety of these parts are available with preformed projections.

Projection-welded joints are not generally water- or gastight but can be made so by sweating solder into the seam. This is usually satisfactory unless the parts are exposed to substances that will attack the solder.

### UPSET BUTT WELDING

The material to be welded is clamped in suitable electrode clamps. The ends to be welded touch each other as the current is turned on. The high resistance of the joint causes fusion at the interface. Just enough pressure is applied to keep the joint from arcing. As the metal becomes plastic, the force is enough to make a large, symmetrical upset that eliminates oxidized metal from the joint area. The excess metal is then removed by machining.

### Flash Butt Welding

In flash butt welding, the ends of the stock are held in very light contact. As the current is turned on, it causes flashing and great heat. The metal burns away, and the pieces move together in an accelerated motion, maintaining uniform flashing action. When the inner faces reach the proper temperature, they are forced together under high pressure, and the current is cut off (Fig. 12-11).

Although quite similar in equipment to the flash method, upset butt welding uses a different control system.

**Advantages and Use.** Flash butt welding offers strength factors up to 100 percent. No extra material, such as welding rod or flux, is required. Generally, no special preparation of the weld surface is required.

Dissimilar metals with varying melting temperatures can be flash butt welded. The size and shape of the parts should be similar, but

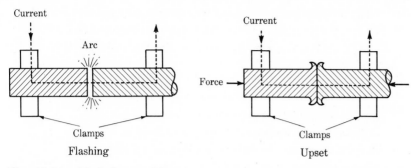

**Fig. 12-11.** Flash butt welding.

a 15 percent variation in end dimensions is permissible for commercial use.

The process is regularly used for end joining of rods, tubes, bars, forgings, fittings, etc. Heavy forgings can sometimes be eliminated by welding small forgings to bar stock.

### Percussion Welding

In percussion welding, two workpieces are brought together at a rapid rate. Just before they meet, a flash of arc melts both of the colliding surfaces. The molten surfaces are then squeezed together by the collision, and some of the metal is forced out to the sides of the joint.

Percussion welding is particularly good for joining small-diameter wires, for example, welding 0.002- and 0.015-in.-diameter wires in electronic applications, and for materials of widely differing properties. Wires can be joined by soldering or other processes, but the advantage of percussion welding is that it is almost instantaneous.

The welds are produced either by stored-energy type machines or by rapid dissipation of current from a standard 60-cycle-per-second a-c source.

Parts other than fine wires have pinpoint-type projections that are formed or coined into the part. These localize the heat so that the small area is instantaneously vaporized upon contact.

Some metal combinations that have been welded by this process, with excellent results, are copper to Nichrome, copper wire to type 304 stainless plate, thorium to thorium, and thorium to Zircaloy.

### QUESTIONS

1. Upon what principle is resistance welding based?
2. What are the fundamental variables of resistance welding?
3. How can heavy currents be switched off and on quickly without arcing?

4. What are the advantages offered by a three-phase resistance welder?

5. What is the principle of the stored-energy-type resistance welder?

6. What are the determining factors in deciding how much overlap is needed in a spot weld?

7. Why are spot welds generally spaced 16t or more apart?

8. What surface preparation is needed for spot welding?

9. When is it necessary to have unequal-size electrodes?

10. Describe a common destructive test for spot welds?

11. How can seam welds be tested other than by pulling?

12. What is meant by projection welding?

13. What are some advantages and limitations of projection welding?

14. What is the difference between upset butt welding and flash butt welding?

15. What is the principle of percussion welding?

### PROBLEMS

1. What should the overlap be for two pieces of 16-gauge mild steel when making a spot-welded joint? What should the size of the electrode tip be?

2. What should the spot spacing ordinarily be for two pieces of $\frac{1}{8}$-in.-thick mild steel?

3. What could the spot spacing be on two pieces of 1/16-in. stainless steel if distortion became a factor?

4. What should the tensile strength be of a single spot-welded joint made between two $\frac{1}{8}$-in.-thick pieces of 1100–0 aluminum?

5. What are the minimum and maximum sizes of a rod that could be flash butt welded to a 1-in.-diameter bar?

### REFERENCES

Eshelman, R. H., "Projection Welding—Growing Importance for Automatic Assembly," *The Tool and Manufacturing Engineer*, May, 1955.

Johnson, I. W., "Spot Welding of Carbon Steel," Welding Research Council Report, *The Welding Journal*, Supplement, March, 1960.

Owczarski, W. A., and A. J. Palmer, "Percussion Welding," *American Machinist/Metal working Manufacturing*, June, 1961.

"Putting Resistance Welding To Work," *Modern Assembly Practice*, November, 1958.

*Resistance Welding Manual*, Resistance Welder Manufacturers' Association, Philadelphia, 1948.

Spencer, L. F., "Spot Welding Procedures and Design," *Welding Engineer*, September, 1959.

*Welding Handbook*, American Welding Society, 4th ed., New York, 1960.

*Welding and Soldering of Armco Stainless Steels*, Armco Steel Corporation, Middletown, Ohio, 1953.

# 13

# NEWER
# WELDING
# PROCESSES

**T**HE NEWER developments in welding have been separated here from the more basic processes so that the reader will have a better picture of the technological advances made in the past few years. These have come in response to the increasing demand for speed in fabrication and for better methods of dealing with reactive materials. Some of the processes can be considered new; others are modifications of older ones. These developments are here arranged under the headings of fusion processes, brazing and soldering, resistance welding, and solid-state processes.

## FUSION PROCESSES

Fusion processes involve actual melting of the components that compose the weldment. Newer developments in this field include electroslag welding, the Dip-Transfer or Short-Arc process, electron-beam welding, plasma arc, and Innershield welding.

### Electroslag Welding

This unique process was first developed in Russia. Granular flux is placed in the gap between the plates being welded, and, as the current is turned on, submerged-arc welding takes place in a U-shaped starting block, tack-welded to the bottom of the joint. As the flux melts, a slag blanket from 1 to 1½ in. thick is formed. At this point the arc goes out, and current is conducted directly from the electrode wire through the slag (Fig. 13-1). The high resistance of the slag causes most of the heating for the remainder of the weld. When the arc goes out, the operator switches the transformer from constant current to constant potential.

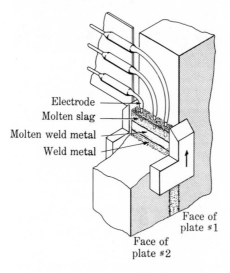

Electrode
Molten slag
Molten weld metal
Weld metal
Face of plate #1
Face of plate #2

**Fig. 13-1.** Schematic view of the main elements of electroslag welding. More than one electrode can be used, as shown.

This process is used to weld metals from 1½ to 15 in. thick, the maximum reported thickness being 40 in. Welding is done with the joint positioned vertically, starting at the bottom and progressing upward. The molten metal and slag are retained between the work parts by means of copper shoes. The water-cooled copper bar helps the metal at the bottom of the pool to solidify, thus forming the weld. Temperature sensors on the water-cooled copper shoes sense the build-up of weld metal and cause the whole mechanism to move upward as needed. Two other probes control the addition of granular flux from the hopper over the weld zone. As solidification occurs, the electrode wire is fed vertically into the slag pool at a rate somewhat less than it is used, thus maintaining the end of the wire at a constant distance from the molten metal pool. Single stationary electrodes are used for metals in the 2-in. range. By moving the electrode back and forth horizontally, welds can be made in metals 6 to 8 in. thick. When multiple electrodes are used, welds of almost unlimited thickness can be made.

**Applications.** The most common use thus far has been for butt welds in heavy forging and plate. Other uses have been for T-joints, corner joints, and reinforcing surface welds.

**Advantages.** No joint preparation is required other than tacking the U-channel starting plate at the bottom. Thick steel can be welded economically.

**Disadvantages.** There is some tendency toward hot cracking and notch sensitivity in the heat-affected zone. Also, it is difficult to close cylindrical welds.

### Dip-Transfer or Short-Arc Process

In some cases of high-speed welding, certain disadvantages are inherent in the carbon dioxide welding process, especially when welding low-carbon steel. The highly oxidizing nature of carbon dioxide may sometimes cause a loss in critical electrode alloy constituents. Unless a short length of arc is maintained, excessive spatter results. Also, the large fluid pool, characteristic of the carbon dioxide process, is sometimes difficult to control.

Two trademarked processes have been marketed to overcome these difficulties. One, called Dip Transfer, is by Airco; the other, Short Arc, is by The Linde Company.

These processes differ from other arc-welding processes in that the welding wire short-circuits during part of the cycle, or as many as 200 times per sec.

The short circuit puts a high load on the power; however, before the surge reaches its maximum peak, overheating at the point where the electrode is in contact with the weld pool causes it to be wiped off. Then, with an assist from the electromagnetic pinch effect, the current is broken, a relatively high-current arc is established, and the process is ready to repeat (Fig. 13-2).

**Fig. 13-2.** Schematic representation of metal transfer by the Dip-Transfer process (courtesy Air Reduction Sales Co.).

Owing to this cycling and method of transfer, the weld pool remains small, and there is no spatter. Of course, if the circuit current is too low, spatter will result, or if too high, there will be too much fluctuation, making it difficult to control.

**Advantages.** The advantages of this process may be enumerated as follows:

1. The current heat input is low.

2. Thin sheets can be manually welded with semiautomatic equipment. In fact, it is particularly well adapted to sheets 0.253 in. thick or thinner.

3. Skill requirements are lower than for regular stick-type manual welding.

4. Spatter loss is low.

5. Distortion is low.

6. Little or no postweld cleanup is required.

7. Deposition rates are high for out-of-position welding (other than flat or downhand). Deposition rates as high as 6 lb per hr have been achieved in the vertical position. Small-diameter wires are used, with an average current setting to 200 amp.

**Disadvantages.** The limitations are as follows:

1. Small-diameter wire must be used; wires larger than 0.045 in. result in arc difficulties.

2. Penetration and heat input are limited.

3. The deposition rate is low for flat-position welding.

4. The most common type of power source, that of high starting potential, cannot be used. This also makes for cold starts.

Many jobs that have been regularly assigned to TIG welding can now be done faster by the Dip-Transfer or Short-Arc methods.

### Electron-Beam Welding

Electron-beam welding is, perhaps, the most spectacular of the recent welding developments that have become commercially feasible. Heat to melt and fuse the metal is generated not by a flame or an electric arc but by a stream of highly accelerated electrons. These electrons are accelerated to about one tenth the speed of light, at which velocity they attain a potential temperature of millions of degrees. This energy does not appear as heat, however, until the electrons hit the work. The beam can be easily controlled in intensity, and can be focused to a pinpoint or broadened to cover a wide track. Either electrostatic or electromagnetic focusing is used (Fig. 13-3).

**Electrostatic Focusing.** In this method, the electrons are emitted through a small hole in a plate. Owing to electrical lines of force around the hole, the stream of electrons is focused into a narrow beam as it passes through the hole.

**Electromagnetic Focusing.** This method employs a series of magnetic lenses to concentrate the beam.

Electrostatic focusing is simpler, but electromagnetic focusing results in a narrower beam and a higher concentration of energy. Sharp focus is desirable for most welding. The out-of-focus broad circle can be extremely useful in scouring contaminants from the face of the work prior to welding. With the beam out of focus and the power reduced,

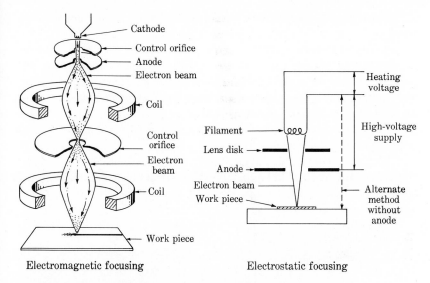

Electromagnetic focusing          Electrostatic focusing

**Fig. 13-3.** Two methods used in electron-beam focusing.

the operator can track the weld seam beforehand to vaporize oxides and other surface impurities. These are drawn off, since the entire operation is done under a high vacuum.

The vacuum required is 1 ten-millionth of an atmosphere, or $0.1\mu$ (micron) Hg. In this vacuum, gaseous impurities total less than 1 ppm, as opposed to at least 20 ppm as the best level attainable with inert-gas-shielded methods.

**Electron Acceleration.** The source of energy for electron-beam welding is the tungsten cathode filament which, when heated to about 2,000°C, emits a cloud of electrons. The electrons are pulled or accelerated toward the workpiece by an accelerating anode. The cathode potential at the filament is fixed at 15,000 volts. The accelerating anode varies between 0 and 10,000 volts. It is normally set at about 5,000 volts to maintain a 10,000-volt potential between the cathode and the accelerating anode. The enclosure for the beam or "electron gun" is not water-cooled because the beams are prevented from striking the gun walls by the field near the anode.

The X rays produced by the 15,000 volts are soft and can be shielded by the steel and glass in the welding chamber. At higher voltages, lead shielding of the weld box and auxiliary equipment may be required.

**Advantages.** The high vacuum makes it possible to weld such highly reactive vacuum-melted materials as titanium, zirconium, and hafnium with the same control of purity as in the original material.

Since the environment is free of gases, voids cannot form in the weld.

A 10-in. vacuum system can be operated for less than 50¢ per hr, including ordinary maintenance. A 16-in. system for a 50- by 100-in. chamber can be operated for about 75¢ per hr. Inert-gas, operating, and maintenance costs for comparable sizes of weld dry boxes run about $10 and $25 per hr, respectively.

The welded joint is usually cleaner and brighter than the parent metal. Surface cleanup is eliminated.

Electron-beam welds have a highly desirable depth-to-width ratio. Because of the small weld puddle, the heat-affected zone is substantially smaller than with TIG welds (Fig. 13-4).

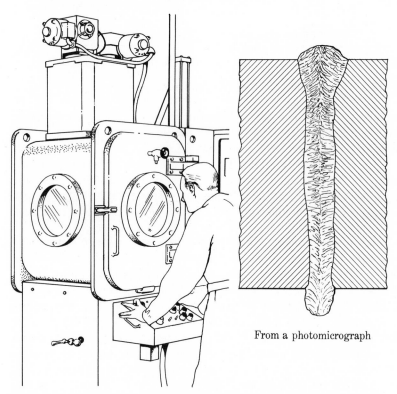

From a photomicrograph

**Fig. 13-4.** Electron-beam welding equipment and a photomicrograph of a weld made by the process in ½-in.-thick 304 stainless steel.

Precise heat control is obtainable. When welding one-of-a-kind assemblies, the operator can gradually increase beam energy to obtain proper welding conditions. If fusion is incomplete the first time, an additional pass can be made at a slightly higher input.

Owing to the close control of the heat input, the chance of burn-through is greatly reduced. Section thickness in the joint area need not be beefed up to provide the margin of safety needed with stick arc welding.

Edge and butt welds can be made in metals as thin as 0.001 in. Also, small thin parts can be welded to heavy sections. Butt joints can be made in plates up to ¼ in. without edge preparation.

**Disadvantages.** The electron beam travels on a line of sight. Therefore, obstructed joints cannot be welded.

The work must be manipulated through vacuum seals. The work is thus generally limited to either straight-line or rotary motions (Fig. 13-5). Joints with compound curvatures cannot be welded conveniently.

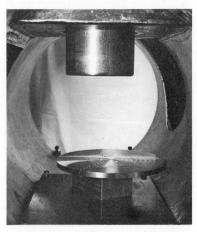

**Fig. 13-5.** A turntable is placed inside the electron-beam welder for circular welding. A carriage may be substituted for linear and transverse movements (courtesy Air Reduction Sales Co.).

Electron-beam welding is operated on high vacuum and high voltages, thus making the initial cost of the equipment high.

Although the welding process is not difficult, the complexity of the circuitry requires very competent personnel.

### Plasma Arc

The principle of the plasma arc was explained in connection with metal spraying in Chap. 10. It is presented here because it is also considered one of the newer fusion-welding processes.

The two main types of plasma arcs, transferred and nontransferred, are shown in Fig. 13-6. In the transferred-arc type of equipment, the arc moves from the cathode to the work, which is the anode. In non-transferred equipment, the arc is struck between the tungsten electrode and a water-cooled electrode. Since no exterior electrode is required, this flame may be used for any application where conventional oxy-fuel flames are applicable.

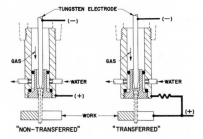

**Fig. 13-6.** Schematic cross sections of nontransferred- and transferred-arc torches (courtesy the Linde Co., division of Union Carbide Corp.).

In welding, the transferred arc moves along over the joint, and the plasma, shielded from the air by the outer annular shielding gas stream, melts the seam. As the torch moves away from the joint, the metal cools and solidifies. The plasma produces a remarkably small variance in weld-bead dimensions even over a wide range of torch-to-work distances. The plasma torch is well suited to flange-welding sheet metal parts at high speed.

A small arc torch has been used to weld 0.007-in.-thick stainless sheet at 25 ipm using a 15-amp current.

### Innershield Welding*

Innershield welding is a new fusion process in which a tubular electrode provides both the filler metal and the arc shielding. When welding, the core ingredients at the tip of the electrode generate a vapor that expands until it reaches the cooler atmosphere surrounding the arc. It then condenses to form a chemically inert shield around the molten metal.

The process is available for either semi- or full-automatic use. The semiautomatic arrangement is referred to as *squirt welding* by its manufacturer, The Lincoln Electric Company. The welding gun used is shown in Fig. 13-7.

The big advantage of the Innershield process is the speed at which it can be used. Sheet metal and plate in thicknesses up to ⅜ in. can be welded in one pass. Some comparisons of speed between Innershield, submerged-arc, and manual electrode welding are given in Table 13-1.

Power sources used are 600-amp constant-potential machines for the semiautomatic Innershield squirt welding and 1,100-amp machines for full-automatic Innershield welding.

* Trade name of The Lincoln Electric Co.

**Fig. 13-7.** The welding gun used for semiautomatic Innershield welding or squirt welding (courtesy The Lincoln Electric Co.).

**TABLE 13-1.**

Comparison of Welding Speeds by Innershield, submerged-Arc, and Manual Welding*

|  |  | Innershield Full-Automatic | Submerged-Arc Full-Automatic | Manual Electrodes |
|---|---|---|---|---|
| *Butt welds* | 16-gauge sheet | 300 ipm | difficult | 30 ipm |
|  | 3/16″ plate | 130 ipm | 75 ipm | 18 ipm |
| *Fillet welds* | 14-gauge sheet | 160 ipm | difficult | 24 ipm |
|  | 1/4″ leg size | 90 ipm | 40 ipm | 15 ipm |
| *Lap welds* | 14-gauge sheet | 170 ipm | 120 ipm | 30 ipm |
|  | 3/16″ leg size | 90 ipm | 42 ipm | 16 ipm |

\* courtesy of The Lincoln Electric Company.

## BRAZING AND SOLDERING

**Brazing.** One of the newer developments in brazing has to do with the sandwich-type and honeycomb core construction that is widely used in aircraft and missile construction. The component parts to be brazed are enclosed in a metal envelope hermetically sealed around the edges, and the entire assembly is placed in a furnace to heat to the proper temperature.

New methods of heating, such as radiant heating and the use of high-intensity quartz lamps, have been investigated lately with satisfactory results. Electric-blanket heating for brazing has also been developed as a commercial method.

With respect to brazing alloys, advances have been made in the use of silver alloys containing small amounts of lithium for improved wettability. Small amounts of ceramic materials such as alumina, ($Al_2O_3$) in the brazing alloy have materially helped in the formation of uniform fillets.

**Soldering.** A new development in soldering is an ultrasonic soldering head. Parts to be soldered are heated to a temperature slightly above the melting point of the solder being used. As the solder is applied to the heated surface, the tip of the ultrasonic head is brought into contact with the molten solder. This creates intense vibration within the solder, forming cavitations and removing metal oxide films, thus permitting the solder to alloy with the base metal. No flux is required. This method can be used in the usual soldering applications but is especially useful in joining silicon, germanium, aluminum, silver, and magnesium.

### RESISTANCE WELDING

Resistance-welding processes depend on resistance-heating effects in the parts being joined. New developments include foil-seam welding, magnetic-force welding, and high-frequency resistance welding.

### Foil-Seam Welding

The foil-butt-seam welding process was developed in Europe. In the United States it is the exclusive license of Precision Welder and Flexopress Corporation. It is similar to conventional seam welding, except that a narrow strip of metal is introduced between the parent metal and one or both of the welding electrodes (Fig. 13-8). The strip is usually 0.010 in. thick and ⅛ to 5/32 in. wide. The function of the foil is to distribute welding current to both sheets and prevent too rapid withdrawal of heat from the joint area. The foil may or may not provide filler metal.

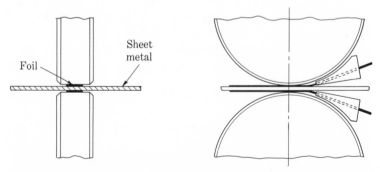

**Fig. 13-8.** Arrangement of roller electrodes, foil guide, and workpieces in foil-seam welding (courtesy Precision Welder and Flexopress Corp.).

**Advantages.**   Strong leakproof joints are made at high speed. Little, if any, final dressing of the weld is needed, and very little distortion occurs. Since these welded sheets can be used as stock in a punch press without dressing, small scrap sheets can be reclaimed economically.

### Magnetic-Force Welding

The prime consideration in resistance welding is the follow-up time. A means of synchronizing the electrode force with current duration and magnitude has been achieved with the development of a magnetic-force welder by Precision Welder and Flexopress Corporation. The work is positioned in the welder and held with a slight pressure exerted by means of an air cylinder. The forging pressure is accomplished not with conventional air or hydraulic pressure but by electromagnets in the welding circuit. The forging stroke can be delayed for welding some combinations of metal which need a longer time to reach forging temperature.

**Advantages.**   More heat is generated by a given current because of the higher contact resistance that accompanies low electrode force. The resulting heat is concentrated near the weld forging plane and permits welding vinyl-coated steels and other prefinished material with no damage to the surface. The process has also been used to make large-area welds with shallow heat penetration.

### High-Frequency Resistance Welding

High-frequency electricity has long been used in heating metals but only recently has it been employed for welding purposes. As developed by the New Rochelle Thermatool Corporation, the equipment operates at 450,000 cycles per second, compared with 60 cycles per second for most a-c resistance welding.

It is a high-speed process and is best suited for high-production use, as shown schematically in Fig. 13-9. Welding speeds range from 200 to 1,000 fpm.

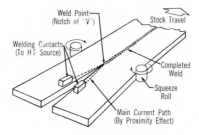

**Fig. 13-9.**  Schematic view of high-frequency resistance welding.

The process is based on several "peculiarities" of high-frequency current. One is the proximity effect, in which the current follows a path of low inductance rather than low resistance.

Normally the low-inductance path is the one closest to the return conductor of the circuit. In welding tubing or strip, the two contacts are placed on opposite sides of the V-shaped gap, and each edge alternately acts as the return conductor during each half cycle. This causes the current to flow in a V-shaped path between the contacts, and to concentrate almost entirely at the edges of the metal.

**Advantages.** The advantages of high-frequency resistance welding can be briefly enumerated as follows:

1. Joining can be done at high speed—up to 1,000 fpm in light-gauge materials up to 0.012 in. thick.

2. The power required is a fraction of that needed for standard resistance welding, the reason being that the effective resistance of the metal is so much higher at 450 kc that, by the $I^2R$ law, the amperage required for a given amount of heat input is sharply reduced.

3. The heat-affected zone is very shallow, resulting in welds of high tensile strength and good ductility.

4. Most of the process variables that affect normal resistance welding, such as contact resistance, contact pressure, surface condition, the amount of squeeze applied to the joint, etc., do not apply to high-frequency welding because the joint faces are heated without actually touching each other.

High-frequency resistance welding is now being used on aluminum, copper and copper alloys, nickel alloys, zirconium, and many types of steel. Besides tubing and pipe, the process is being used to butt-seam-weld strip.

## SOLID-STATE PROCESSES

### Solid-State Theory

Theoretically, it is possible to place two clean metallic surfaces into such intimate contact that the cohesive forces between the atoms would be sufficient to hold them together. This condition is approached when sliding two precision blocks together, as explained in Chap. 27. We say that the blocks are *wrung* together and develop a resistance to being pulled apart of 250 psi. As good as this is, it does not approach a perfect bond. If each block were composed of but a single crystal, and if they were perfectly clean and smooth and oriented in the proper plane, then, when joined, the strength should be that of the parent metal. No force would be required to effect this perfect joint. Of course, this type of joint is only theory, since perfect planarity of cleavage faces in the crystals is impossible to obtain. Also, the degree of cleanliness required is attainable only under the most stringent laboratory conditions. In addition, the polycrystalline structure of most materials cannot be readily matched between opposed surfaces in materials of any type.

Despite the difficulties mentioned, there have been some important developments in what may be the beginning of solid-state bonding. These processes are: ultrasonic welding, friction welding, diffusion-bond welding, and explosive welding.

### Ultrasonic Welding

In ultrasonic welding, the surfaces to be joined are made to slide in contact under a compressive force (Fig. 13-10). Shear vibrations are introduced which produce what is termed a *solid-state metallurgical bond* over half the surface width. The remainder is a mechanical bond.

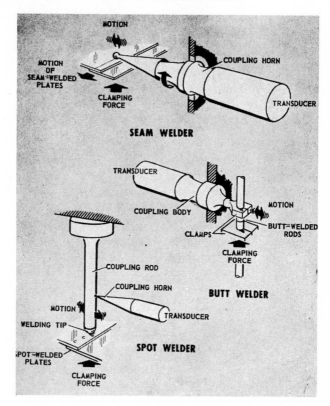

**Fig. 13-10.** Basic arrangements in ultrasonic welding (courtesy *American Machinist/Metalworking Manufacturing*).

As shown schematically in Fig. 13-10, a solid metal conical horn serves as a mechanical step-up transformer to amplify small vibrations and to transfer them through a coupling system to a vibratory element which is in contact with the metal to be welded. The contact is at very light pressure—only 25 psi.

For most applications the tips are either spherical or cylindrical in shape. They can be mounted on conventional machines, or they may be portable (Fig. 13-11).

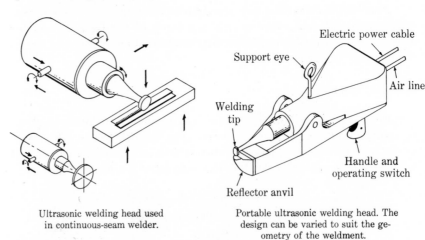

Ultrasonic welding head used in continuous-seam welder.

Portable ultrasonic welding head. The design can be varied to suit the geometry of the weldment.

**Fig. 13-11.** Ultrasonic welding tips, whether for continuous or for spot welding, are cylindrical or spherical in shape and can be portable or mounted in conventional spot and seam welders (courtesy *The Tool and Manufacturing Engineer*).

Recent progress in ultrasonic welding has resulted in new and improved transducer-coupling systems which permit more energy to be delivered to the weld zone. Spot-type welding equipment, with capacities ranging up to 8,000 watts, has been developed, enabling aluminum sheets in excess of 0.090 in. thick to be spot-welded with strengths that exceed military specifications.

Equipment for continuous welding has been developed in various sizes and power capacities for handling the thinnest foil as well as light-gauge sheets.

**Advantages.** The advantages of ultrasonic welding are:
1. Very-thin-gauge materials can be welded.
2. Surface preparation is not critical.
3. Minimum surface deformation results.
4. No contamination occurs from gases and arcs.

5. Thin sections can be welded to thick sections.
6. Dissimilar metals can be joined.
7. The heat-affected zone is minimized.

**Disadvantages.**   The disadvantages are:
1. Heavy-gauge materials are not weldable.
2. Materials being welded tend to weld to the coupling and anvil.
3. Equipment life is short, owing to fatigue.
4. Very ductile materials will yield under ultrasonic strain without sliding.
5. Hard materials will fatigue under the stresses necessary for welding.

The most extensive use of ultrasonic welding has been in joining foil and sheet-gauge aluminum.

### Friction Welding

Friction welding is done by rotating one piece against another at speeds up to 12,000 rpm. This gives a gradual build-up of pressure until the contact surfaces become molten. At this point the rotation is suddenly stopped, and the pressure is increased until the weld is made.

The parts are then held in this position until the temperature drops to normal. The total time may range from 5 to 25 sec.

Friction welding has been used on a variety of materials such as low-carbon steel, free-machining and stainless steels, cast iron, brass, aluminum, and titanium. In addition, dissimilar metals such as brass to steel, brass to cast iron, and cast iron to copper have been welded.

**Advantages.**   The main advantages of friction welding are simplicity of operation and low power requirements. One part is mounted in a chuck and rotated against the stationary piece. The process lends itself to production welding and automation. Surface impurities and oxide films are broken up and thrown off during the friction-heating process.

**Disadvantages.**   So far, the process has been applied only to the joining of small pieces in the form of bar stock.

### Diffusion-Bond Welding

Diffusion-bond welding consists of placing the parts to be welded under pressure. Heat below the solidus temperature of the metal is usually applied to speed the rate of diffusion and to decrease the time required to make the joint. The width of the diffusion zone is dependent on time and temperature factors.

There are three common joint systems for diffusion bonding: metal-to-metal without intermediate materials, metal-to-metal with intermediate materials, and metal-to-ceramic materials.

The intermediate materials are usually plated on. Sometimes, combinations of two or three metals are plated so that there is a barrier metal to prevent diffusion within the plated areas. For example, in joining beryllium-copper to Monel, the beryllium-copper is first plated with nickel, then with gold. The Monel is plated with copper. The two parts are then diffusion-bonded with pressures ranging between 4,000 and 8,000 psi and temperatures below 1000°F. The length of time needed for the weld varies from about 20 min to 3 hr. It is sometimes necessary to use inert gas to prevent oxidation at the bonding surfaces.

Diffusion-bond welding has been used on relatively few metals so far; however, it looks promising for joining many dissimilar metals.

### Explosive Welding

Explosives received their initial start in the manufacturing field by forming metals that could be done only with difficulty in presswork-ing. It is now possible to use this same energy for welding and joining metals.

Explosive welding can be done in two ways—either by a very high normal force or by causing a sudden shear between two surfaces under pressure. Shown in Fig. 13-12 is an example of high impact that virtually assures the deformation of the metal needed at the weld zone and a controlled shear. The shear is controlled by the geometric aspects of the collision. Appropriate amounts of shear explosive are placed on the outside surfaces of each strip and detonated simultaneously. The two strips are projected toward each other and collide. Factors of spacing

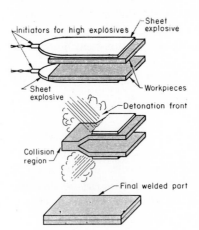

**Fig. 13-12.** Schematic drawing of the explosively driven impact-welding process. The strength of the weld depends on the angle of the detonation front (courtesy *The Tool and Manufacturing Engineer*).

and explosive conditions are critical; if not correct, there will be spalling of the metal.

An interesting phenomenon that occurs in explosive welding is the eruption of microscopic swirls on the interface surfaces (Fig. 13-13). These are called jets, and they contribute greatly to the strength of the weld by their interlocking action. Surface jetting is dependent on the angle at which the plates come together. The various angles that have been reported are 1 to 15 deg for welding aluminum, and anywhere from 7 to 50 deg for welding steel, provided both plates are covered by explosives.

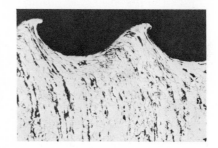

**Fig. 13-13.** Eruption of surface jets on a steel projectile. These increase the weld strength by interlocking with similar jets on the opposing surface (courtesy *The Tool and Manufacturing Engineer*).

Explosive welding can be considered a cold-welding process, since only the local interface region reaches welding temperature. The effects of heat treatment should not be lost.

Since this process is still in its early research stages, very little quantitative data are available. Enough is known, however, to indicate that the process is practical.

So far, most of the explosive welding has been done on aluminum and mild steel, but successful welds have been reported in aluminum to Inconel, aluminum to stainless steel, stainless steel to itself, and aluminum sandwiched between stainless steel.

### Explosive Joining

In explosive welding there is a fused, interlocking bond; in explosive joining there is a *frictional* or *mechanical bond* (Fig. 13-14). In joints

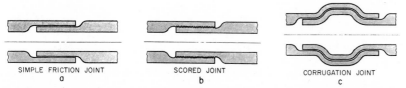

SIMPLE FRICTION JOINT            SCORED JOINT            CORRUGATION JOINT
a                                      b                            c

**Fig. 13-14.** Three types of explosively formed joints. Corrugation eliminates friction as a primary holding force.

of this type, an elastic strain in the mating area puts the fibers of the outer cylinder in compression and those of the inner cylinder in tension. The coefficient of friction between the surfaces can be increased by appropriate preparation such as scoring and knurling.

An improvement on frictional keying is the mating corrugation technique shown in Fig. 13-15.

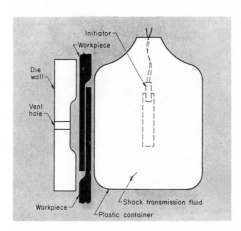

**Fig. 13-15.** Schematic drawing of the materials required to explosively form a corrugation joint (courtesy *The Tool and Manufacturing Engineer*).

A relatively simple die for forming the corrugated parts is shown in Fig. 13-16. The die is of segmented design to facilitate loading and unloading.

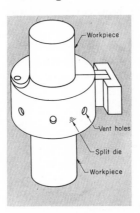

**Fig. 13-16.** Simple segmented die for forming corrugated joint. Hinged die blocks are necessary for part removal.

## FUTURE WELDING PROCESSES

This chapter has described some of the newer welding processes, but it is safe to say that, before the ink is dry on this page, other newer techniques will have been developed, descriptions of which will be found in current scientific literature and trade journals. This only points up the fact that nothing is static in the field of manufacturing processes. The reader should keep abreast of what is being developed by regularly checking current literature in the field.

Even at this writing, pending developments include low-hydrogen electrodes that will require no special storage precautions, and a square-wave a-c power source with distinct applications for welding aluminum. Other improved power sources are ion-beam welding, self-correcting resistance-welding control circuits, and automatic guiding of the arc in high-speed welding operations.

## QUESTIONS

1. How is it possible to keep a large amount of heat in the weld area when using the electroslag method?

2. For what type of welding is Dip-Transfer or Short-Arc-type welding particularly suited?

3. What is the principle of electron-beam welding?

4. Why doesn't the electron gun in electron-beam welding require water cooling?

5. What are two advantages and two disadvantages of electron-beam welding?

6. What is the nature of the electrode in innershield welding?

7. How does an ultrasonic head aid the soldering operation?

8. How does foil-butt-seam welding differ from conventional seam welding?

9. What is the advantage of using magnetic force in resistance welding rather than conventional air or hydraulic force?

10. Explain what is meant by the proximity effect of high-frequency current when used in butt welding.

11. Name some limitations of ultrasonic welding?

12. What are some of the advantages of friction welding?

13. Name the principal ways bonding is accomplished in explosive welding?

14. What is the difference between explosive welding and explosive joining?

## PROBLEMS

1. What would the approximate weld time be for lap welding two 14-gauge sheets of mild steel 8 ft long using the manual stick electrode? The leg size required is $\frac{1}{4}$ in. Compare this speed with submerged-arc time and Innershield time for the same work.

2. Approximately how long would the weld time be for seam butt-welding 10,000 ft of 20-gauge tubing by the high-frequency resistance method?

**REFERENCES**

Chyle, J. J., "New Welding Developments," *Machine Design*, July, 1959.

Crane, T. H., "Electron Beam Welding," *Metalworking*, December, 1959.

Greene, W. J., R. R. Banks, and R. M. Niedzielski, "A New Electron-Beam Welding Unit," *The Welding Journal*, August, 1960.

Hackman, R. L., "Putting Plasma Jets to Work," *The Tool and Manufacturing Engineer*, March, 1961.

Jones, B. J., and W. C. Pothoff, "Ultrasonic Welding Comes of Age," *The Tool and Manufacturing Engineer*, September, 1958.

Miller, B. S., "How H-F Resistance Heating Welds Metals," *Metalworking*, January, 1962.

Parr, F. J., "Welding Developments, New Tools for Production," *The Tool and Manufacturing Engineer*, January, 1960.

Rieppel, P. J., "New Developments in Metal Joining Processes," *Machine Design*, June, 1960.

*Welding Handbook*, American Welding Society, 4th ed., New York, 1960.

Zernow, L., I. Lieberman, and W. L. Kincheloe, "Welding and Joining, New Applications of Explosives," *The Tool and Manufacturing Engineer*, July, 1961.

# 14

# PLASTICS

**T**HE WIDESPREAD USE of plastics covers the comparatively brief span of about 30 years. These materials are still in infancy when compared to other common ones such as steel, copper, and brass, which were known and used in ancient times. Nevertheless, plastics now rank second to steel as an industrial material. The cubic-foot production of plastics is 50 percent greater than that of all nonferrous metals combined.

Prior to World War II, plastics usage was restricted to areas where no other material was suitable. Today, by contrast, they are considered, in many cases, a superior replacement. As an example, the average modern car contains 22 lb of plastics which have replaced 150 lb of steel and other metals.

Plastics are not cheap; pound for pound, they cost more than most natural materials, but they are chosen because of their favorable weight ratios, ease of fabrication, service life, etc.

## COMPOSITION OF PLASTICS

Plastics have their origin in the chemical synthesis of materials from five different sources: agriculture, agriculture and petroleum, petroleum and coal, petroleum and mineral, and mineral. Of these, the coal-and-petroleum source is the most used (Fig. 14-1).

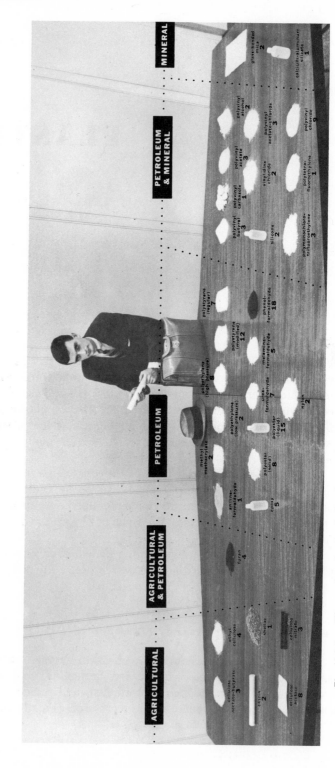

Fig. 14-1. The main plastic derivatives and their family groups (courtesy E. I. du Pont de Nemours & Co., Inc.).

The development of plastics is a chemical achievement brought about through the study of molecular segments. For example, methyl methacrylate, a crystal-clear material with optical properties superior to all but the finest glass, was developed by du Pont chemists after 7 years of research.

They linked 1,000 polymethyl methacrylate molecular segments together to form a giant molecule. Its crystallike property was so dramatic that, during its first public showing in 1936, guards watched it—and an almost priceless rock crystal—with equal zeal.

Another petroleum-coal derivative is the well-known polystyrene. Benzene, driven off from coal by a distillation process, is linked with ethylene gas derived from petroleum. The new combination forms ethyl benzene which is dehydrogenated to styrene. With the aid of catalysts, heat, and pressure, thousands of styrene molecules are made to link together to form long-chain-line molecules that clump into small granules of crude polystyrene. These grains are hot-worked and cut into small pellets called *molding powder,* the most common form in which plastics are supplied.

New plastics are continually being produced because so many thousands of molecular combinations can be made. If, for example, the ethylene gas used in producing polystyrene were combined with chlorine (from salt) and *polymerized,* the result would be polyvinyl chloride, a plastic with properties very much different from those of polystyrene (Fig. 14-2). *Polymerized* means that the new compound formed has a weight that is a multiple of the original substance.

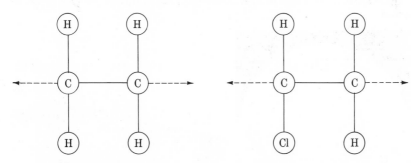

The polyethylene building block          The polyvinyl building block

**Fig. 14-2.**  A new plastic product is developed with essentially the same molecular segments, but with the addition of chlorine in the polyvinyl building block.

## MAIN TYPES OF PLASTIC MATERIALS

For purposes of simplification, most plastics can be classified under 1 of 14 recognized family groups. These groups generally can be further classified as thermosetting plastics or thermoplastics. A few plastics are in between. They can be formulated to be either thermosetting or thermoplastic.

A brief description of some of the principal plastic resins, their properties, and their applications is given under the headings Thermosetting Plastics and Thermoplastics.

### Thermosetting Plastics

Thermosetting plastics are those that cure with the application of heat. An irreversible chemical reaction, called *cross-linking*, occurs. This reaction links the resin chains so that the molded piece is essentially one giant, three-dimensional molecule. Subsequent heating may soften the structure somewhat but will not restore its former flowability.

**Aminos: Urea and Melamine.**  Urea formaldehyde resin is derived from the reaction of urea (carbamide) with formaldehyde or its polymers. It is widely used in making ball-point pen barrels, electric-mixer housings, cosmetic cases, distributor heads, etc. The ureas are resistant to many solvents, oil, grease, and temperatures up to 210°F. Urea is also used in liquid form as an adhesive for plywoods, as a textile- and paper-treating resin, and as a surface coat to provide a marproof finish.

The melamines are probably most familiar in the form of colorful tableware (Fig. 14-3). They are derived from a reaction of dicyandiamide with formaldehyde. They are also used as a laminating resin for shockproof plastic laminates. When the resin is used with asbestos or glass fibers as filler material, its heat resistance is in the range of 400°F.

*Melamine*

*Urea*

**Fig. 14-3.**  Examples of melamine and urea plastics (courtesy American Cyanamid Co., Plastics and Resins Division).

**Polyesters.** Polyesters get their name from the fact they are derived from polymeric esters. They are used primarily as binders for low-pressure laminates in such products as boat hulls, automobile bodies, aircraft parts, chairs, luggage, awnings, laundry tubs, etc. The liquid polyester resin is used to impregnate sheets of glass fiber which are then pressed over molds or dies to make the desired form. The polyesters are easily handled and, when used with fiber glass, can be molded with or without pressure and with or without heat. Products of reinforced polyester resins are characterized by high-impact strength, light weight, good dimensional stability, and good dielectric properties. Polyester resins cost about half as much as epoxy resins.

**Alkyds.** Alkyds are described as oil-modified polyester resins. They were originally used only for synthetic enamels and lacquers. As such, they provide a tough, versatile, uniform, and economical finish. Alkyds now are also used in the solid form, particularly as electronic-tube bases, in automotive ignition parts, and in places where electrical insulation and high-temperature resistance are important.

**Phenolics.** Phenolics are made by a reaction between phenol and formaldehyde. They are probably the most widely used and cheapest of the thermosetting plastics, and sometimes are referred to as the "workhorse" of this group. Phenolics are strong, rigid, dimensionally stable, heat- and solvent-resistant, and, most important, are non-conductors of electricity. They are molded into television and radio cabinets, telephones, appliance handles, clock cases, electrical sockets, and thousands of other items familiar in our everyday lives (Fig. 14-4).

**Fig. 14-4.** Some applications of phenolic resins (courtesy Union Carbide Plastics Company).

Some of the phenolics are brittle, but high-impact types are also available. In liquid form, phenolics are used in making industrial and decorative laminates, protective coatings, and adhesives. They are applied as a resin on paper or fabric to form the sheet material used in modern-day printed electrical circuits. The plywood industry uses almost 10 percent of all the phenolic resins manufactured. Cast phenolic resins are available in many colors.

Another application of phenolic resins is as a binder for the sand in the shell-molding process discussed in Chap. 6. These shell molds are able to retain their shape while the molten metal is poured into them, even though the temperature of the metal is far above the working temperature of the plastic.

**Silicones.** Although silicones were prepared in the latter part of the 19th century, they were not accepted for industrial use until 1943. The basic ingredients consist of silica and coke which are mixed and placed in an electric furnace. The silica is reduced to silicon, which is one of the starting materials. The other reactant is methyl chloride, prepared by chlorinating methane gas. The two reactants are mixed in a reaction at a high temperature and moderate pressure, using copper as a catalyst. The desired products are then hydrolyzed and condensed to form silicon polymers.

To the engineer, the silicones represent a new class of engineering materials with a most unusual combination of properties. They are a chemical hybrid, a cross between organic and inorganic materials. They have both the stability of inorganic products and the versatility of organics. As a molding compound they have good dielectric qualities, plus the ability to withstand high heat (up to 500°F). The only other plastic able to stand this heat is Teflon, which is also a poor heat conductor and is often used where thermal barriers are needed. It too is lighter than aluminum and superior to most metals in corrosion resistance.

In liquid form, silicones are used as a water-repellent treatment for natural and synthetic fibers. They may also be used as release agents when molding many and varied materials, such as glass, rubber, metals, and plastics. Silicone greases are manufactured for both high- and low-temperature lubrication. Another product, Silastic, developed by Dow Corning, looks and feels like rubber, but it is able to survive where organic rubber fails at −130°F. Other uses of silicone include paint additives, mold material, antifoaming compounds, and cosmetic ingredients (Fig. 14-5).

**Epoxy Resins.** Epoxy resin is one of the newcomers to the plastic field, being first introduced as a molding plastic in 1952. It is basically

**Fig. 14-5.** Silicones used both as liquids and as solids (courtesy Dow-Corning Corporation).

a polymer of epichlorhydrin and bisphenol. The plastic develops good strength either with or without reinforcement. Epoxies are quite versatile. They can be used as laminated resins, casting resins, or bonding resins. It is as a bonding or adhesive agent that they are best known However, since their cost has dropped, they are being used more and more for making dies and other tooling. They hold extreme accuracy, as close as 0.002 in. per in. on large tools.

Epoxies can be filled with a variety of materials ranging from glass fibers to steel and aluminum powders. When filled with the steel or aluminum powders, they are often used to make dies simply by casting the filled plastic over the pattern. Accuracy is good, since the shrinkage factor is very low. They are also used as patching compound for both metal and plastic parts.

**Polyurethanes.** Polyurethane is a foam-type plastic material, used primarily for cushions, insulation purposes, and packaging electronic equipment. It is especially good for this latter application because it can be made to foam in place; that is, the electronic components are set in their respective positions, and a liquid mixture of urethane is poured into the spaces between the components and allowed to expand and fill them completely. Foaming is caused by a dispersion of gas throughout the resin, thus increasing its volume while maintaining its weight. By special formulation and controls, volume can be increased from 2 to 250 times. Densities can be varied from 2 to 30 lb per cu ft.

A similar product consists of polystyrene beads that can be expanded either by heat or by a catalyst (Fig. 14-6).

**Fig. 14-6.** Polystyrene beads, shown at the right, can be expanded by applying heat. They can be molded into many shapes.

## Thermoplastics

Thermoplastics are those that soften with the application of heat and harden upon cooling. They are sometimes referred to as "plastics with a memory," since they will return to their original shape when heated.

**The Cellulosics.** The family of cellulosics comprises such a wide variety of materials that only the main ones will be discussed briefly.

The name cellulose stems from the cellulose agricultural products — cotton linters and wood pulp — from which it is derived. It was first turned into fiber by a 19th-century French chemist. However, it remained a laboratory sample until about 1929. Since then, research and development have made cellulose acetate a commercial fiber that has many of the characteristics of silk. It is widely used in the clothing industry because of its easy maintenance and low cost. Cellulose acetate can also be made in solid form for molded parts such as toys, beads, cutlery handles, electrical parts, knobs, blister packaging, etc. It is known for its toughness and high impact strength. It is the most easily worked of all plastics. In sheet form cellulose acetate has become the household term cellophane. It is also made as an electrical-insulating tape.

Cellulose nitrate is probably one of the first well-known plastics. It was called by its trade name of Celluloid. It is tough and can be made in a wide variety of beautiful colors. It is still familiar in spectacle frames, heel covers, and fabric coatings.

**Methyl Methacrylate.**    Methyl methacrylate is well known under its trade names of Lucite and Plexiglas. It is the clearest of the plastics and has the best light transmission. It is also used to pipe light around corners, and, in this capacity, is used in surgical instruments. It is also employed for *edge lighting* instrument panels, etc. (Edge lighting means that the light will travel through a sheet of plastic and cause the far edge, or any edge not covered, to produce light.) Methyl methacrylate can be formed easily at temperatures around 250°F. It first became popular as a nose section for bombers, then as a canopy, and then as various other aircraft domes. It is now widely used for outdoor signs, contact lenses, brush backs, transparent bowls, drink dispensers, etc. (Fig. 14-7).

**Fig. 14-7.**    Clear methyl methacrylate, Plexiglass, used as a transparent bowl and lid for a cold-drink dispenser (courtesy Rohm & Haas Co.).

**Polystyrene.**    As explained previously, polystyrene is made from ethylene and benzene, petroleum, and coal derivatives. It is an easily molded thermoplastic which may be either crystal clear or colored. It

**Fig. 14-8.**    Some applications of polystyrene (courtesy Union Carbide Plastics Co. division of Union Carbide Corp.).

has found wide acceptance as wall tile, tableware, food containers, and formed displays. It can be molded as a high-impact-type plastic. Some uses of polystyrene are shown in Fig. 14-8.

**Polyethylene.** Polyethylene is made from the petroleum derivative ethylene. It is probably best known for its flexibility and waxy feel. It is used for refrigerator containers, pipe and tubing, wire insulation, bags, squeeze bottles, and tumblers (Fig. 14-9). Its usual color is milky white.

**Fig. 14-9.** Polyethylene molded products (courtesy Monsanto Chemical Co., Plastics Division).

**Polyvinyl Chloride.** The vinyl chlorides are formed from hydrochloric acid, limestone, and natural gas or coal. The forms of vinyl chloride are almost unlimited. Some popular uses are for wading pools, shower curtains, floor tile, garden hose, and as a thin vinyl film. It can be processed in many different ways, by extruding, casting, spread-coating, spraying, and molding by several different processes. It can be made either rigid or nonrigid. The rigid type is used mainly for pipe and ducting to handle corrosive liquids and vapors.

One of the newer applications is *vinyl-coated steel.* This versatile construction material combines the color, texture, and protection of plastics with the strength of steel. Vinyl-coated steel is produced by a roller coating process that produces superior adhesion because of the inclusion of a thermosetting plastic adhesive that is applied, in coil or sheet form, to a clean, electrochemically treated surface. As a result, the vinyl coatings can stand severe deformation involving up to 30 to 35 percent elongation. This material has not been used extensively as an outdoor building material, but it has found wide acceptance in automotive interiors and decorative paneling inside commercial buildings.

**Nylon.** Nylon has been important as a textile for some time. It is also used for brush bristles, molded gears, bushings, cams, and aerosol bottles. Its outstanding features are a low coefficient of friction and its resistance to heat, abrasion, and chemicals. It is strong, tough, and lightweight. It is usually milky white in color and is still quite expensive.

**Teflon.** Teflon is a du Pont trade name for a fluorinated ethylene-propylene (FEP) resin material that has outstanding qualities as a high-frequency current insulator, for gasket and packing material, valve seats, diaphragms, and bearings, and in locations where there is a need for high resistance to heat (550°F) and chemical corrosion. Teflon has an oily surface that will not adhere to most sticky materials. For this reason it is used as a coating for bakery equipment and other parts that contact tacky materials. Perhaps its outstanding use is as a self-lubricating bearing. The lubrication principle of Teflon is inherent in its molecular form; the lubricant cannot be "squeezed out" like that of metallic bearings. Some uses of Teflon and Nylon are shown in Fig. 14-10.

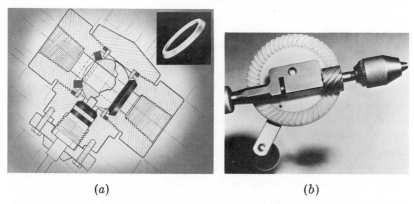

(a)            (b)

**Fig. 14-10.** (a) Teflon gaskets are used for tight-sealing, no-stick operation (courtesy E. I. du Pont de Nemours & Co., Inc.). (b) Nylon-molded gears are quiet and self-lubricating (courtesy Illinois Tool Works).

## Future Types

At the present time the plastics that make up most of the market are the ureas, phenolics, vinyls, styrenes, and alkyds. However, with new materials being developed, this situation can change easily. Already, alloys of plastics have brought forth new materials with some intermediate physical and chemical properties. Plastics have also been combined with other materials to create new end products having the advantages of both components. Mixtures of styrene or phenolics with rubber are now in use, and they exhibit properties of outstanding toughness and shock resistance.

## PLASTICS COSTS

Except for the epoxy resins, most of the thermosetting plastics range in price from about 20 to 50¢ per lb. Epoxy-resin costs are about twice this amount.

The thermoplastic materials are generally somewhat higher in price than the thermosetting plastics, but molding rates are faster, so the overall cost of the manufactured part may well be less than with the thermoset.

Thermoplastic sheet materials may range from about 50¢ per lb for methyl methacrylate up to about $1.15 per lb for cellulose acetate. The relative prices are subject to fluctuation and will vary with the quantity purchased, color desired, amount and type of filler, etc.

After compounding, the various plastic materials are supplied to the manufacturer in liquid, granular, and powdered forms for further processing and forming into finished products.

## MATERIALS FOR PROCESSING PLASTICS

Most plastic resins have to be combined, compounded, or otherwise chemically treated before they are ready for processing. Such additions take the form of plasticizers (which soften the plastic and make it more flexible), stabilizers (which prevent degradation in the plastic when exposed to heat or light), fillers (which add bulk and reduce overall costs), colorants (which add integral color to the processed plastic end product), and reinforcing fibers (which improve impact strength, electrical properties, etc., of the finished products). Solvents are used to give the degree of temporary fluidity necessary to such operations as dipping, brushing, spraying, etc., and catalysts are often added to speed up the curing of a compound.

### Newer Plastic Materials

**Polypropylenes.** This group of relatively new plastics offers a balance of properties rather than any one outstanding characteristic. It has high resistance to heat and chemicals, and high rigidity even at elevated temperatures. It has practically no post-mold shrinkage, and has a high resilience which permits undercut parts to be stripped from the mold without permanent distortion. Standard grades have low impact strength at low temperatures, but can be modified with rubber blends to increase this value. However, an increase in impact strength is usually accomplished with the sacrifice of some rigidity and ease of processing. Although it can be fabricated by different methods, the most common is injection molding.

**Polycarbonates.** This is a new plastic material that is probably better known by its General Electric trade name Lexan. It has extremely high resistance to impact and temperature variation. These resins can be hammered, exposed to temperatures well above 212°F or below 32°F, immersed in water or dilute acids, and subjected to strong electrical fields. Some examples of uses are electronic components, pressure vessels, safety helmets, pump impellers, and light lenses. It is injection molded, but techniques are being developed for extruding it.

**Acetal Resins.** Another relatively new plastic is perhaps better known by its du Pont trade name of Derlin. It is available as homopolymers or copolymers derived from formaldehyde. The primary advantages of acetal resins are high tensile strength and stiffness, high fatigue endurance, toughness under repeated impact, good resistance to creep, and low coefficient of friction. Acetal resins are used in making gears, conveyor parts, bearings, plumbing components, pump components, electrical components, and for many other applications.

### Reinforcement Materials

Fiberglas* materials are added to the various plastics to give a high strength-to-weight ratio. A strength-to-weight comparison is made between the various Fiberglas-reinforced plastics and various metals (Fig. 14-11).

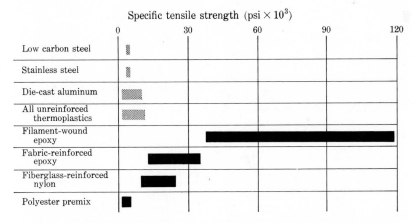

**Fig. 14-11.** Strength-to-weight comparison between Fiberglas-reinforced plastics and some common metals (courtesy Owens-Corning Fiberglas Corporation).

Other properties that are improved are stiffness (about 50 percent) and impact strength. The thermal coefficient of linear expansion is reduced much below that of unreinforced plastics.

* Fiberglas is a trademark of Owens-Corning Fiberglas Corporation.

Fiberglas, used as the reinforcing material, is supplied in several basic forms. These allow for flexibility in cost, strength, and choice of manufacturing process. The basic forms, shown in Figs. 14-12 and 14-13, are continuous-strand, fabric, woven rovings, chopped strands, reinforcing mats, and surfacing mat.

**Fig. 14-12.** Basic forms of Fiberglas used in reinforcing plastics (courtesy Owens-Corning Fiberglas Corporation).

(a)

(b)

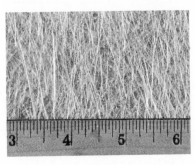

(c)

**Fig. 14-13.** (a) Continuous-strand Fiberglas chopped into short lengths to facilitate molding complex structures; (b) reinforcing mat used for medium-strength structures with uniform cross section; (c) surfacing mat used, with other reinforcements, for appearance and weathering (courtesy Owens-Corning Fiberglas Corporation).

Resins used with the glass reinforcement are polyesters, phenolics, silicones, melamines, acrylics, and polyesters modified with acrylics and epoxies. Of these, polyester resins are used about 85 percent of the time because they do a good job and are the most economical. Some thermoplastic materials are also used, including nylon, polystyrene, polycarbonate, and fluorocarbon, or Teflon.

## MOLDING METHODS

The methods of manufacturing, as applied to plastic powders (both reinforced and unreinforced), include injection molding, jet molding, compression molding, transfer molding, extrusion molding, cast molding, and slush molding. All these processes are based on the fact that when the plastic is heated it will soften to a viscous liquid that can be forced into a mold of the desired shape, where it solidifies.

### Injection Molding

Injection molding is the method most commonly used for the production of thermoplastic parts.

The process consists of feeding plastic pellets into the hopper above the heating cylinder of the machine. With successive strokes of the injection ram, the material is compacted and forced forward through the thin annular space between a heated "torpedo" in the center of the cylinder and the cylinder walls. There the material is softened. It passes through the cylinder nozzle and is forced into the cold mold (Fig. 14-14).

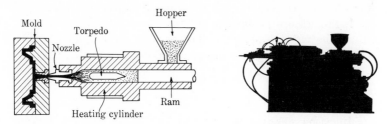

**Fig. 14-14.** Injection molding process and a 4½-oz-capacity Fellows machine.

The fluid plastic completely fills the mold cavity, which is shaped to the contours of the finished product. When the plastic has cooled and solidified, the mold is opened and the finished piece, an exact image of the mold cavity, is ejected. Ejection is aided by knockout or ejector pins.

The temperature to which the material is raised in the heating cylinder is between 350° and 525°F. Every type of material has a characteristic molding temperature, depending on the plasticizer content.

The mold is kept cool so that the injected plastic material will cool quickly and can be removed without distortion. Cooling is done by circulating water through the mold frame.

To speed up molding cycles and facilitate production, a pre-plasticating chamber is included on many machines. It consists of an auxiliary heating cylinder which melts the plastic granules and transfers the melt to the injection cylinder, where it is further heated and held ready for injection.

**Machine Size.**   Injection-machine size is usually designated by the maximum amount of material the heating cylinder will deliver in one stroke of the injection ram. This amount is expressed in ounces and may range from a fraction of an ounce, on small hand-operated machines, up to 500 oz. The most popular size is from 8- to 16-oz capacity.

**Advantages and Disadvantages.**   Injection molding provides the highest production rate of producing plastic parts. The time required per shot will vary with the material and the size of the mold, but 300 to 400 shots per hr are not uncommon. Metal inserts such as bearings, screws, clamps, etc., can be put into the mold and cast integrally with the plastic. The initial mold cost is usually high, because of the accuracy and high degree of surface finish required.

**Material Handling.**   Various methods are employed to keep the larger-volume machines supplied with material. These methods consist of mechanical conveyors such as screws, paddles, and chains; both low- and high-pressure pneumatic systems; and the newest method, which utilizes the vacuum principle. The vacuum method has the advantage of efficiently handling even dusty materials.

### Jet Molding

Injection molding is generally limited to forming thermoplastic materials, but some thermosetting materials and rubber compounds are *jet-molded* on the same machines. This, however, requires a change. The torpedo spreader in the heater is taken out so that the main heating takes place at the nozzle passage to the sprue.

### Compression Molding

Compression molding is the process most widely used for the forming of thermosetting plastic parts. It consists of placing the right amount of plastic compound in an open heated mold. The upper part of the die is brought down to compress the material into the required shape and density. When the mold is closed, the material undergoes a chemical change, or polymerization, that hardens it (Fig. 14-15).

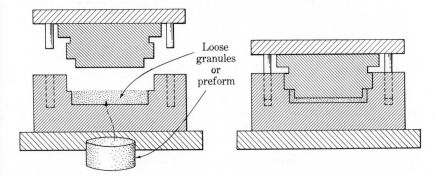

Loose granules or preform

**Fig. 14-15.** Compression molding.

Compression molds may be of the positive or the flash type. In the latter, some of the material is allowed to escape over a land. As the mold closes completely, the material on the land becomes very thin. This is the *flash*, or *fin* (Fig. 14-16). Since the fin solidifies first, it prevents any more material from escaping.

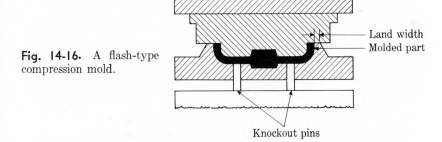

**Fig. 14-16.** A flash-type compression mold.

Land width
Molded part

Knockout pins

Molding pressures vary from 2,000 to 10,000 psi. A basic figure is 2,000 to 3,000 psi on the mold land. The curing time in the mold may vary from 30 sec on some hard materials to 135 sec on soft materials.

### Transfer Molding

Transfer molding is a variation of compression molding, in which heat and pressure are applied to the molding materials outside of the mold until they become fluid. The fluid material is then forced through a series of channels from the external chamber to the mold cavity, where final cure takes place.

When complex parts are molded, it may be necessary for the mold to open in several directions in order to remove the part, cores, and insert supports. In ordinary compression molding these parts must be quite substantial, or they will be damaged before the resin reaches its plastic state. In transfer molding this problem is largely eliminated, and more intricate and fragile pieces can be produced.

### Extrusion Molding

The extrusion of plastics consists of feeding plastic material, in powder or granular form, from a hopper to a heated cylinder. A rotating screw carries the heated plastic forward and forces it through a heated die orifice of the required shape (Fig. 14-17). As it leaves the die it can be cooled by running through water or by air blasts, or it can be allowed

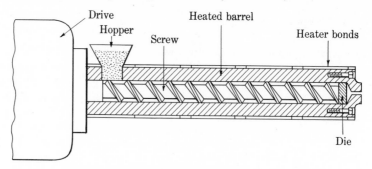

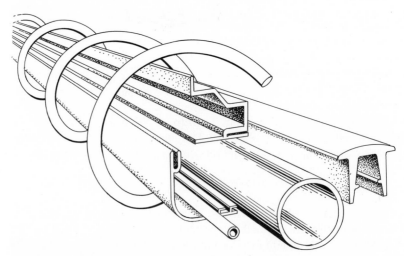

**Fig. 14-17.**  Schematic arrangement of a machine for extrusion molding. Also shown are plastic extrusions.

to cool at room temperature. The cooling period must be carefully controlled, because either too fast or too slow cooling can cause distortion.

**Applications.**  Extrusions are applicable to the continuous production of tubes, rods, sheets, films, pipe, rope, and a wide variety of profiles. Extrusions can be used to coat wire by having it pass through the center of the die, with the plastic extruded around it. Extrusions are thermoplastics and are not recommended for structural members bearing heavy loads.

## Casting Molding

All the methods described thus far use heat and pressure, but *casting* of plastics involves heat without pressure. The plastic, either thermoplastic or thermosetting in granular or powdered form, is liquefied either by heating or with solvents. The liquid is then poured in the mold and cured at room temperature by the addition of catalysts.

Cast acrylic sheets are the highest grade of plastic sheets available. They are superior to other plastic sheets prepared by molding or extrusion because of the optical quality of the surface, freedom from internal stress, and excellent outdoor aging characteristics. Plastic film (sheeting 0.010 in. and under) can be produced by casting it on a moving belt or by precipitation in a chemical bath.

## Slush Molding

Slush molding is somewhat similar to cast molding in that no pressure is used. In this process a thermoplastic-resin slurry or "slush" is poured into a preheated mold. The heat causes the slurry to set in a viscous layer of the desired wall thickness, after which the excess slurry is poured out. The resin left in the mold is cured by additional heat and then chilled. In its final flexible form it is simply stripped out of the mold.

Slush molding is applicable for flexible toys, insulated overshoes, artificial flowers, squeeze bulbs, and other products where difficulty is experienced in removing the part from the mold.

## CALENDERING

An important method of making film and sheet is known as calendering. In this process the plastics compound, usually in the form of a warm doughy mass, is passed between a series of heated rollers where it is thoroughly worked. It emerges from the rolls squeezed into flat film or sheet. The thickness of the sheet is determined by the gap between the last pair of rolls—the gauging rolls. It is cooled on a chill roll (Fig. 14-18).

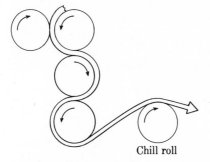

Chill roll

**Fig. 14-18.** Calendering—a method of producing sheet and film plastics.

Calendering can also be used to apply a plastic covering to such backing materials as paper, fabric, etc. The film and backing material are simply squeezed together in the heated rollers.

## FABRICATING METHODS

Plastic films, sheets, extrusions, and molded shapes often need other fabricating processes before they are ready for market. Fabricating includes sheet-forming methods, blow molding, laminating and reinforcing (both low-pressure and high-pressure methods), machining, and welding.

### Sheet-Forming Methods

One of the most important fabricating operations — and one that has virtually grown into an entire industry of its own — is that of heat-forming film or sheeting. The basic principle is this: The heat-softened film or sheet is forced against a cold mold, permanently taking on the contours of the mold. A wide range of forming methods has been developed. In addition to mechanical pressure, air and vacuum are used. (Fig. 14-19).

**New Developments in Sheet Forming.** New developments point the way to higher production through completely automated machines. For example, new double-heater machines heat from both top and bottom to form heavy-gauge sheets up to 0.250 in. thick in half the time previously required. The heaters are independently operated so that the bottom heater can be withdrawn automatically at the moment the material begins to sag, while the top heater continues heating to the exact temperature needed.

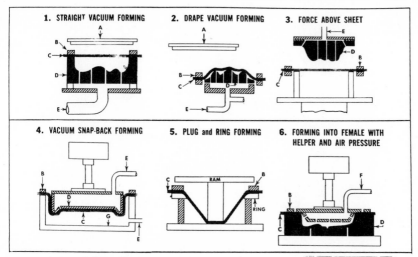

IN THESE SIMPLIFIED schematics of seven basic methods of sheet forming, letters indicate the following: A = Heater; B = Clamp; C = Plastic Sheet; D = Mold; E = Vacuum Line; and F = Air-Pressure Line.

THE methods sketched here are as follows:

(1) STRAIGHT VACUUM FORMING. Clamped in a stationary frame, the heated sheet is vacuum-drawn into the mold.

(2) DRAPE VACUUM FORMING. Moveable frame or clamp drapes the sheet, softened by heat, over male mold before vacuum is applied.

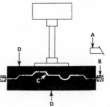

(3) FORCE ABOVE SHEET. Mold descends onto heated sheet, partially forming it; then the vacuum is applied.

(4) VACUUM SNAP-BACK FORMING. Vacuum is applied, drawing preheated sheet into cavity G. Male plug moves down until it reaches a predetermined position. Vacuum is then applied through male plug.

(5) PLUG AND RING FORMING. Heated sheet is placed over a ring and clamped down. Mold mounted on ram is forced into it.

(6) FORMING INTO FEMALE WITH HELPER AND AIR PRESSURE. As press closes, cored plug pushes heated sheet into cavity. Air pressure, introduced through plug, pushes sheet into female mold. Holes in mold let air escape.

(7) PRESSURE FORMING. After heating, framed sheet is formed between matched male and female dies.

**Fig. 14-19.** Basic methods for forming thermoplastic sheets (courtesy Modern Plastics Encyclopedia).

### Blow Molding

Blow molding is a simple process of placing a softened thermoplastic closed-end tube in a cavity and applying air pressure to inflate it (Fig. 14-20). After allowing sufficient time for the plastic to cool, the mold is opened and the part is removed.

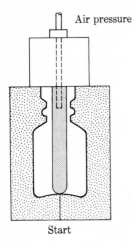
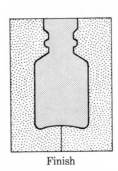

Start    Finish

**Fig. 14-20.** Blow molding used to form thermoplastic bottles.

### Laminating and Reinforcing

Laminates, in the plastic industry, refer to a variety of materials bonded together. These range from vinyl sheets to reinforced Fiberglas. The basic process consists of saturating the materials to be laminated in a plastic resin, and then subjecting them to heat and pressure, which fuses them into a solid mass. The amount of heat and pressure varies; hence we have the terms *high-pressure* and *low-pressure* laminates. Generally, the low-pressure laminates are those that require from 0 to 400 psi pressure, the high-pressure ones from 1,000 to 2,000 psi. Low-pressure laminating lends itself to either open molds or closed matched-die molds (Fig. 14-21).

**Fig. 14-21.** The principles of the open mold and the closed mold are schematically shown.

**Open Molds.** Open molds are single-cavity molds, either male or female, with the following characteristics:

1. The initial investment is low. (Cost mounts up when molds have to match. Since little pressure is exerted, the mold can be made of plaster, wood, or reinforced plastics.

2. The labor cost per part is relatively high.

3. Molds can be made quickly, and design changes are relatively simple.

4. The production rate is low.

Parts can be made in open molds by a number of different methods, including contact molding, pressure-bag, vacuum-bag, and autoclave (Fig. 14-22).

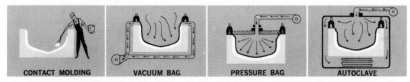

| CONTACT MOLDING | VACUUM BAG | PRESSURE BAG | AUTOCLAVE |

**Fig. 14-22.** Open mold methods used in fabricating reinforced plastic parts (courtesy Owens-Corning Fiberglas Corporation).

CONTACT MOLDING. Layers of reinforcing material, in the form of glass fabric, mat, chopped strands, etc., are coated with catalyzed resin and placed in layers on the prepared form. The number of layers depends on the strength required in the finished product. The reinforcing material acts like steel in concrete, adding to the mechanical strength, impact resistance, and dimensional stability.

To speed up output of boats and other products, and to make possible on-the-site fabricating, the reinforced-plastics industry developed the *spray-up molding* method. It utilizes the same types of molds used in hand lay-up, but the reinforcing material and plastic are applied with spray guns. Several types of guns are used. Some are made to spray both resin and reinforcement simultaneously; others alternate streams of resin and reinforcement (Fig. 14-23).

**Fig. 14-23.** A spray gun used to apply both fiber glass and resin (courtesy Spray-bilt).

The resins used are epoxies or polyesters. The guns that deposit reinforcement use continuous-filament glass fibers that are chopped into short lengths as they are applied.

The major advantages of contact molding are the short time it takes to get into production and the relatively low-cost molds. Another factor is that large-size moldings, such as boats, tanks, trucking bodies, and chemical equipment, can be formed.

PRESSURE-BAG FORMING. A lay-up of resin-impregnated material is placed on the mold and covered with a tailored bag of rubber sheeting. Air or steam pressure up to 50 psi is used between the bag and a pressure plate secured to the top of the mold.

VACUUM-BAG FORMING. The mold and lay-up are prepared as described in pressure-bag forming. A cellophane or polyvinyl film is placed over the lay-up and secured to the mold. Following this, a vacuum is drawn through the ports provided, and the resulting atmospheric pressure exerted on the film forces the layers to conform to the mold contours.

AUTOCLAVE FORMING. Autoclave forming is a modification of the pressure-bag method, the main difference being that, after the lay-up has been made and covered with a plastic film, the entire assembly is placed in a steam autoclave at 50 to 100 psi. The additional pressure permits higher glass content and improved air removal.

OPEN-MOLD SUMMARY. The advantages and disadvantages of the various open-mold methods are given in Table 14-1.

### Closed, or Matched-Die, Molding.

MANUFACTURE. Where fully automatic production at rapid cycling rates is desired, matched metal dies give the best performance. The tooling usually used is solid steel for small products, and cast Meehanite or semisteel for larger parts. The dies are made by machining on duplicating mills or other equipment until they are within close tolerance. After machining, they are filed, polished, and flame-hardened. The surface is again polished and buffed to a high luster. A large percentage of the die-manufacturing time is allotted to developing a high surface finish. The molded product will show any small defect left on the die surface.

Matched dies can also be made from reinforced plastics for medium- and short-run production. A wood or plastic pattern is first sealed, waxed, and coated with parting material. A box is built around it, and the surface of the pattern is covered with layers of resin-saturated glass fabric. After the lay-up has had time to set, a mass casting of epoxy resin and filler can be poured in to make up bulk for the remainder of the die. After the die has had time to cure, the pattern is removed, and the process is repeated to make the matching punch. This time, the die serves as the pattern. Sheet wax or felt is placed in the die before the punch is poured to take the place of the material that will be molded.

MOLDING METHODS. Matched-die molding can be done with either reinforced or unreinforced materials. The processes used are quite

**TABLE 14-1.**

**Advantages and Disadvantages of Various Open-mold Fabricating Methods***

| | Contact Molding | Vacuum Bag | Pressure Bag | Autoclave |
|---|---|---|---|---|
| Advantages | 1. Simplest process.<br>2. Low cost molds.<br>3. No size restrictions.<br>4. Max. design flexibility.<br>5. Design changes readily made.<br>6. Min. equipment needed.<br>7. Gel-coats possible. | 1. Higher glass loading.<br>2. Better unfinished side.<br>3. Less air and voids.<br>4. Better adhesion in sandwich constructions possible.<br>5. Retains advantages of contact molding. | 1. Cylindrical shapes can be made.<br>2. Higher glass loading.<br>3. Dense, void-free moldings.<br>4. Undercuts possible.<br>5. Cores and inserts used.<br>6. Retains advantages of contact molding. | 1. Undercuts possible.<br>2. 65 percent glass loading.<br>3. Dense, void-free moldings.<br>4. Cores and inserts used.<br>5. Retains advantages of contact molding. |
| Limitations | 1. Labor per unit is high.<br>2. One finished surface.<br>3. Quality depends on operator. | 1. More labor.<br>2. Surface next to bag not as good as surface next to mold.<br>3. Quality depends on operator. | 1. Only female molds.<br>2. More labor.<br>3. Surface next to bag not as good as surface next to mold.<br>4. Quality depends on operator. | 1. Extra labor to load autoclave.<br>2. Autoclave is expensive.<br>3. Size of autoclave limits size of parts that can be made.<br>4. Quality depends on operator. |
| Output† | 1 boat hull (25 feet).<br>4 tanks (2 x 4 x 2 feet).<br>† Based on one mold for eight hours. | Slightly slower than contact molding. | Slightly slower than contact molding. | Slightly slower than contact molding. |
| Mold‡ | Wood, plaster, sheet metal, reinforced plastics.<br>‡ Usual mold materials. | Wood, plaster, sheet metal, reinforced plastics, castings. | Reinforced plastics, sometimes heated castings. | Sheet metal, castings. |

* Courtesy Owens-Corning Fiberglas Corporation.

similar, but the reinforced type, described here, is more comprehensive. These processes are preform molding, mat and fabric molding, and premix molding.

*Preform molding.* In reinforced preform molding, the mat or fabric is shaped to conform to the mold in which it will be placed. This is done in three different ways, as shown in Fig. 14-24.

DIRECTED FIBER    PLENUM CHAMBER    WATER SLURRY

**Fig. 14-24.** When complex cross sections are molded, fabric preforms are made by these methods (courtesy Owens-Corning Fiberglas Corporation).

The preform, made by one of the described processes, is combined with a resin mix either just prior to or just after placing it in the matched-die mold cavity (Fig. 14-25). The heated metal molds form and cure the part at 100 to 300 psi. Molding temperatures usually range from 225° to 300°F. The cure cycle varies from slightly under 1 min to 5 min, depending on thickness, size, and shape.

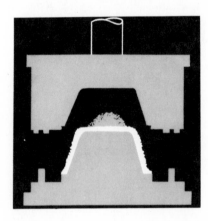

**Fig. 14-25.** The resin mix may be added just prior to or just after the mat fabric or preform is placed in the mold (courtesy Owens-Corning Fiberglas Corporation).

*Mat and fabric molding.* This process is similar to preform molding, except that the material is placed in the mold in chopped-strand mat or fabrics that have been tailored to the die. The resin may be poured on it, as described previously, or the material may be purchased with the resin already in it. This is known as *pre-preg* material. The synthetic resins are partly polymerized. Pre-pregs are made in a variety of materials, from epoxy paper to asbestos phenolic. Pre-preg fabrics facilitate molding many high-strength containers and structural components (Fig. 14-26).

**Fig. 14-26.** Pre-preg plastic materials are being used to form missile containers, access doors for reentry vehicles, structural components for aircraft, etc.

*Premix molding.* In premix molding, the resin, reinforcement, fillers, catalysts, and pigments are mixed together to form a doughy mass that can be molded by compression or transfer techniques.

Resins generally used are polyesters, epoxies, and phenolics. The most common reinforcement is of chopped glass fibers, but others, such as sisal, asbestos, and synthetic fibers can be used.

The premix is often made in rope form, as shown in Fig. 14-27. This form can be tailored to meet many specific end-use requirements at the lowest possible cost per pound. It is used in molding housings, tote-boxes, laundry tubs, sleds, etc.

**Fig. 14-27.** Premix plastics placed in the closed-die mold.

ADVANTAGES. Matched-die molding is a comparatively high-speed process. The parts have high strength, uniform appearance, and good surface finish. The automobile industry is now one of the large-volume users of matched-die plastic products. Preform molding and mat, and fabric molding are compared in Table 14-2.

**Filament Winding.** One of the newer methods of building lightweight, high-strength, reinforced plastic structures is by filament winding. This consists of impregnating strands of reinforcing material, usually glass fibers, with epoxy resin. These strands are then wound directly on the basic structure or on a mandrel, which is later removed.

Originally "wet winding" or impregnating the strand just before it was applied, was the only method used. Now, pre-preg material is available; this not only simplifies the process but also makes possible the use of a wider variety of resins.

The filament can be applied in any one of three standard patterns — circumferential, helical, and longitudinal (Fig. 14-28). These methods may be used alone or in combination to give the most effective ratio of loop to longitudinal stress.

Helical pattern is generated on winding machine that rotates the part and traverses the filament feed back and forth

Longitudinal winding will be overlaid with circumferential winding, as filament strength is high along axis, low in shear

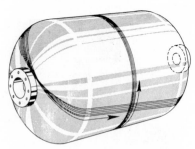

-Two types of filament windings on a pressure vessel.

**Fig. 14-28.** Three types of filament winding.

The outstanding property of filament-wound structures is their high strength-to-weight ratio — even better than high-strength steel or titanium.

The cost is usually much lower than metal fabricated parts, often only 10 percent of the cost of titanium fabrications. The tooling cost is only a fraction of that associated with fabricating high-strength-to-density metals. Also, the same tooling can be used to produce structures of varying wall thickness.

Other advantages of filament-wound structures are extremely good corrosion resistance, low thermal conductivity, high dielectric properties, and shatterproof construction.

There are no size limitations on parts that can be made by filament winding. Structures 15 ft in diameter and 65 ft long have been made. Uniformity of structure is assured by numerically controlled winding. As the process becomes automated, filament-wound parts will be found not only in defense applications but in those of everyday use, such as water heaters, large storage tanks, and sports equipment.

### Machining

The following brief description of the machining of plastics is intended only to point out some of the more general cutting characteristics of these materials. For this purpose, plastics will be divided into two broad groups — cast and extruded plastics, and laminated plastics.

**Cast and Extruded Plastics.** Nearly all plastics are considered poor heat conductors, although the thermosetting ones give less trouble than do the thermoplastics. Since the workpiece cannot conduct the heat away, heat must localize in the tool. This leads to short tool life and to eventual gumming or burning of the plastic. Coolants that do not discolor the plastic or do not present a cleaning problem can be used. Water or soluble oil and water are the most often used; more specifically, soap solutions are recommended for nylon, and a mixture of 10 parts of water to 1 part of 40 percent sodium silicate for polystyrene.

Acrylic and polystyrene plastics can be machined to tolerances of ±0.001 in. However, to maintain close tolerances, it is necessary to anneal at the time of machining. This is especially true when considerable material is to be removed and there is likelihood of stress build-up. Annealing can be accomplished by heating the plastic to about 10°F below the practical heat-distortion temperature. Because of the poor heat conductivity, the time required for the anneal may be as long as 24 hr.

In general, tool angles can be similar to those used in machining copper and brass. Twist drills cut better when the cutting lip is "dubbed off" to make a zero-degree rake with about a 1/16-in. land (Fig. 14-29). This causes a scraping rather than a cutting action that will keep the material from chipping out.

**TABLE 14-2.**

## A Comparison Between Various Closed-die Molding Processes*

| Process | Resin | Fiberglas | Normal Percent Fiberglas By Weight | Maximum Filler Percent By Weight | Molding Temperature °F | Molding Pressure psi | Molding Cycles | Finished Surfaces | Size of Products To Date |
|---|---|---|---|---|---|---|---|---|---|
| Matched-die Molding Preform: directed fiber, plenum chamber, water slurry | Polyester | chopped strands | 30 | 40 | 225 to 300 | 100 to 300 | 1 to 5 min. | 2 | from safety helmets to 17-foot boat hulls (directed fiber); from safety helmets to chairs (plenum chamber and water slurry) |
| Mat | Polyester Phenolic Melamine Silicone Epoxy | mat | 30 | 40 | 225 to 350 | 100 to 3,000 | 1 to 10 min. | 2 | from small trays to 4 foot by 8 foot panels |

| Process | Material | Reinforcement | % | % | Pressure | Temp. | Rate | Cycle | No. | Applications |
|---|---|---|---|---|---|---|---|---|---|---|
| Fabric | Polyester Phenolic Melamine Silicone Epoxy | fabrics, prepreg woven and non-wovens | 60 | | none | 225 to 350 | 100 to 3,000 | 1 to 30 min. | 2 | panels up to 5 inches thick, 4 feet by 8 feet |
| Compression Molding of Premix/ Molding Compound | Polyester Epoxy All molding compounds | spun roving continuous roving | 25 | 25 | 65 | 250 to 350 | 250 to 2,000 | 0.5 to 5 min. | 2 | housings; electrical switch gear to laundry tubs; objects to 200 pounds |
| Transfer Molding of Premix/ Molding Compound | Polyester Epoxy All molding compounds | chopped strands chopped spun roving | 25 | 25 | 65 | 250 to 350 | 1,000 to 5,000 | 0.5 to 5 min. | 2 | electronic components 4″ pipe fittings |
| Injection Molding | Thermo- plastics: nylon, Teflon, polystyrene etc. | continuous roving milled fibers | 40 | 10 | 5 | 275 to 750 | 10,000 to 25,000 | 0.25 to 1.5 min. | 2 | under 0.5 pounds to 2 pounds |
| Continuous Laminating | Acrylic Polyester | mat fabric | 25 | 35 | none | 190 to 250 | 5 to 20 | 40 sq. ft. to 50 sq. ft./min. | 2 | 4 foot-wide panels, unlimited length |

* Courtesy Owens-Corning Fiberglas Corporation.

Drill "dubbed off" to a $\frac{1}{16}$"-wide land

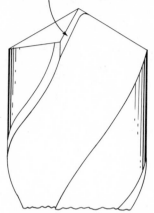

**Fig. 14-29.** Ordinary twist drill ground for drilling plastics.

Speeds of 100 to 300 fpm are ordinarily used for machining. If abrasive fillers are used in the plastics, the speed should be cut to about one half this figure.

**Laminated Plastics.** Laminated plastics are very abrasive. High-speed tools can be used, but carbides, in most instances, prove to be the most economical. A good exhaust system is recommended as a health precaution when machining laminates.

In general, rotary files and burrs are run at higher speeds when machining plastics than when cutting metals in order to prevent edge chipping. Laminated plastics can be milled with standard tools at speeds and feeds similar to those used with bronze and soft steel. The feed rate is determined by the desired finish. Tolerances closer than 0.002 in. are not practical because of the thermal expansion and spring-back of the material after it is machined.

### Welding

Most thermoplastic materials can be welded by processes similar to those used in welding metals. These include hot-gas welding, heated-tool welding, and friction welding.

**Hot-Gas Welding.** Instead of the oxyacetylene torch, an electrically heated gun is used. Compressed air passes the heating element and strikes the joint area at about 400°F. The gun is held from ⅛ to ½ in. away from the filler rod and joint (Fig. 14-30). Nitrogen gas is used in place of compressed air on oxygen-sensitive plastics such as polyethylene. Filler material, when needed, can be a strip of the parent plastic.

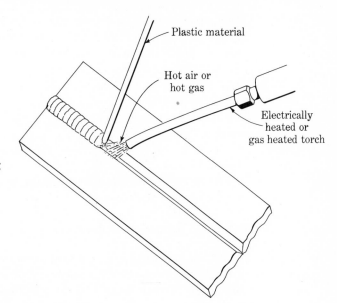

Plastic material

Hot air or
hot gas

Electrically
heated or
gas heated torch

**Fig. 14-30.** Hot-gas welding
of plastics.

**Heated-Tool Welding.** Another welding technique employs a heated plate. The plastic films or sheets are brought in contact with the heated surface until they are sufficiently soft, at which time they are removed from the heat and quickly joined together. They are firmly held together until the melted plastic cools and makes a firm joint.

Gas-heated tubes, electrical strip heaters, and soldering coppers are convenient sources of heat. The time required for fusion to take place varies, but an interval of 4 to 10 sec at 3 to 12 lb pressure generally gives good results. The time interval from the time the two pieces are removed from the heat and until they are joined is the most critical factor and should be kept at 1 sec.

**Friction Welding.** Two plastic parts may be fusion-welded together by frictional heat. The easiest way to accomplish this is to have one part spinning in the lathe and bring the stationary part up against it. All that is required is a pressure ranging from 10 to 200 psi for a few seconds. The whole operation, including chucking, seldom requires more than 30 sec.

The parts to be welded require no special cleaning, since the surface film and dirt are squeezed out in the course of the spinning operation.

## DESIGN CONSIDERATIONS

In designing a part to be made out of some type of plastic, one must first consider all aspects of its proposed use and whether it will serve effectively and economically. A preliminary design can then be made, based on shape limitations, dimensional tolerances, critical dimensions, methods of bonding, etc. At this time the designer makes his final selection of material and process, keeping in mind the advantages and limitations of each. Some principles of material and process selection are as follows:

1. The process of manufacture is based on the material used and on the design.

2. Chemical, electrical, and thermal performance depend on the type of resin used.

3. In reinforced plastics, strength results from the arrangement and the amount of glass used.

### Relationship of Strength to Reinforcement

There is a straight-line relationship between the amount of glass used and the strength of the finished product. For example, a part containing 80 percent glass and 20 percent resin is almost four times stronger than a part containing the opposite proportions.

The arrangement of the reinforcement is just as important as is the amount. There are three standard arrangements: parallel strands, or one-directional; right angle, or two-directional; and random, or in all directions.

One-directional placement of fibers develops maximum strength, but in *one direction*. Example of uses are rocket-motor housings, golf clubs, and fishing rods.

The two-directional arrangement has less strength than the parallel arrangement, but it is in *two directions*. Some applications are for wing tips, boats, and swimming pools.

The random pattern has the least strength, but it is in *all directions*. This pattern is used in safety helmets, chairs, luggage, and machine-tool housings.

The amount of glass that can be loaded into an item is dependent on the arrangement: when strands are placed parallel, the loading possibility ranges from 45 to 90 percent; when they are at right angles, the loading drops to from 55 to 75 percent; a random arrangement permits only 15 to 50 percent loading.

### NEW DEVELOPMENTS

Plastics have had a phenomenal growth. This is due both to the development of the materials and to the processes that take full advantage of them. One of the newer developments is the massive casting of nylon. Generally, the use of nylon has been limited to rather small parts, but a method has been discovered that permits direct conversion from monomeric caprolactam to solid complex shapes at atmospheric pressure. All the precaution necessary is that the liquid monomer be heated to an exact temperature. It is then mixed with a catalyst and poured into a heated mold, where it cures in a matter of minutes (Fig. 14-31). It shrinks slightly during solidification, and this facilitates its

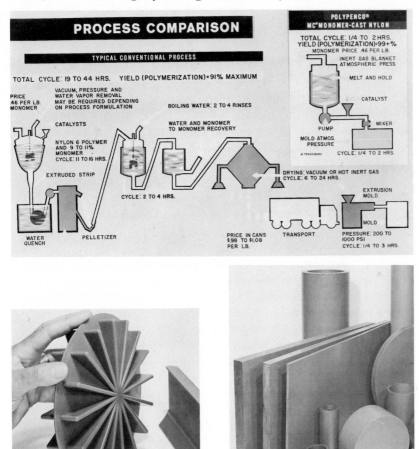

**Fig. 14-31.** The newer streamlined nylon-casting technique, shown schematically, makes massive casting possible and reduces material costs about 50 percent. A variety of mill shapes are shown. The impeller and impeller blades shown are used for handling abrasive material in a wide range of applications. Nylon is light, tough, and abrasion resistant (courtesy The Polymer Corporation).

removal from the mold. This method not only saves considerable time, but the cost is greatly reduced. A conventional mold for the injection molding of 7 lb of nylon might cost $5,000 or more, whereas a mold for monomer casting would cost $300 to $700. The material cost is approximately half that of nylon molding powders.

This process is being used in the production of complex castings ranging from 1 to 100 lb, in a variety of items such as gears, bushings, bearings, valve seats, backup rolls for paper manufacture, etc.

## QUESTIONS

1. What are the source materials for plastics?
2. Define a polymerized plastic.
3. Name the two main types of plastics.
4. Name four common thermosetting plastics and several uses of each.
5. Name four common thermoplastic materials and several uses of each.
6. State the purpose of each of the following materials as it is used with plastics: plasticizers, stabilizers, fillers, solvents, and catalysts.
7. What are the common forms of reinforcing used in plastics?
8. Why are the polyester resins the type most commonly used with reinforcing materials?
9. Describe the injection molding process.
10. Why is injection molding suited to high production?
11. What is meant by a *flash-type* compression mold?
12. Why can more intricate and fragile work be done in transfer molding than in injection molding?
13. What types of items are manufactured by the extrusion process?
14. Describe how vacuum forming of plastic sheets is accomplished?
15. What is the difference between pressure-bag forming and vacuum-bag forming?
16. Why is matched-die molding of reinforced plastics used when the dies are more costly to produce?
17. How do pre-preg materials facilitate molding?
18. What is the outstanding property of filament-wound structures?
19. Why are carbide tools recommended for machining laminated plastics?
20. How can the directional strength of reinforced plastics be controlled?
21. What method is used to make large nylon parts at relatively low cost?

## PROBLEMS

1. What would be the average molding time for a reinforced, polyester chair seat? If the chair area were equivalent to 1/10 the area of the tank mentioned in Table 14-1, how would the molding time compare?

2. If the contact mold used to make the chair in Prob. 14-1 costs $500.00 to construct, and the matched die molds cost $8,000.00, how many chairs will have to be made to warrant the matched dies? Labor and overhead can be figured at $10.00 per hr.

3. What would the approximate production rate be for continuously molded paneling 4 ft wide and 8 ft long if no time needed to be allowed for cutting to length.

4. What would the average range of time be for molding 500 Melamine plates by the injection-molding process if a multiple-cavity die for three parts is used?

## REFERENCES

*Design Plastics Book*, Machine Design, September 20, 1962, The Penton Publishing Co., Cleveland, Ohio.

Gorcey, R., "Filament-Wound Pressure Vessels," *Machine Design*, June, 1961.

Meyer, J. A., and H. Shapiro, "Selection of Urethane Plastic Foams for Packaging Electronic Equipment," *Machine Design*, March, 1958.

*Modern Plastics Encyclopedia*, Plastics Catalogue Corporation, New York, 1961.

Scott, D. D., "Selection and Application of Epoxy Foams," *Machine Design*, June, 1958.

Wason, R. A., "How To Machine Plastics," *The Tool and Manufacturing Engineer*, Part I, November, 1956, and Part II, February, 1957.

# 15

# ADHESIVES AND
# FASTENERS

T HE SEARCH for faster, more efficient bonding methods has focused manufacturers' attention on adhesives.

Adhesives new to industry are chemical compounds that have replaced some of the older protein glues made from animal hides, soybeans, etc. Present-day industrial adhesives, of which there are many, are based primarily on various epoxy and polyester resins and natural and synthetic rubbers.

## ADHESIVE BONDING

Adhesive bonding, instead of the more conventional methods of assembly such as riveting, bolting, soldering, and welding, is being used in the production of railway cars, boats, refrigerators, storage tanks, microwave reflectors, and countless other items of commercial and industrial use. Many of the joints made in fabricating aircraft wing-and-tail assemblies are of the adhesive-bond type. Increased use is also evident in the fabrication of aircraft internal structures. Cost, in many instances, is cut one third, and time 75 percent.

Almost any structure within a reasonable temperature service range can be assembled through adhesive-bonding techniques. Most of these bonded structures will show a favorable weight-to-strength ratio and a decrease in cost compared to conventional fastening and joining methods.

In the aircraft industry, enthusiasm for the technique grew with the discovery that "gluing" provided the needed smooth surfaces for supersonic planes, permitted thinner skins with consequent weight reduction, made more complex designs possible, and avoided local stress concentrations around conventional fasteners.

Adhesive bonding increases damping effect and resistance of the joint to fatigue and reduces corrosion. It is also possible to combine the liquid sealing of joints with the actual joining operation, both so important in wing-tank construction.

Adhesive-bonded sandwich-type construction is used in radar reflectors and space communications, because of the close dimensional tolerances that can be maintained. Reflector "horns" up to 180 ft long have employed adhesive construction. The strength of some adhesives under cryogenic (very-low-temperature) conditions has been very good.

The automotive industry has been slower to accept adhesive bonding. Aside from its well-known application of attaching brake linings to brake shoes, other efforts have been largely experimental. More recent applications have been binding stamped X-members to the underside of front hoods and rear decks. The plastic resin is applied to the stamping on the press line, gaining some strength then, but final cure takes place in the heat of the paint-drying booth.

### Advantages

The advantages gained from this method of joining have made it attractive to the metalworking world. Some of these are as follows:

1. There is no difficulty in bonding dissimilar materials such as ceramic-to-steel, alnico to zinc, copper to steel, or magnesium to cast iron. These are just a few of the combinations that are now possible with an epoxy adhesive. The brazing of an alnico magnet to a zinc die casting would involve considerable skill with a welding torch.

2. Materials can be attached to very thin metal parts, far too thin for any other type of fastening, for example, a motor stack laminate, where a sprayable epoxy is used (Fig. 15-1).

**Fig. l5-l.** Thin motor laminates are successfully bonded together with epoxy-resin adhesives. Excellent dielectric strength is furnished, and there is no metallic corrosion between the dissimilar metals (courtesy Rubber and Asbestos Corp.).

3. In most cases there is no need for high heats in joining.

4. Adhesives automatically provide heat or electrical insulating layers between two joined surfaces. In the motor laminates of Fig. 15-1, adhesives furnish excellent dielectric strength and low power factors. Such dissimilar metals as beryllium, copper, and stainless steel can be joined without metallic corrosion.

5. The bonding load is distributed uniformly over a large area. As in a lap joint, the load is distributed over the entire area of the contacting surfaces.

6. Fewer specialized personnel are needed.

7. In many cases, weight can be reduced and service life increased, as in aluminum honeycomb assemblies.

8. Substantially less afterfinishing is required, as compared with welding, soldering, or brazing methods.

9. Adhesives often permit extensive design simplifications. Laminated wood or metal parts, bent to shape before bonding, require much less machining time than does a part cut from solid stock.

10. The lighter weight of the completed assembly means greater economy in packing and shipping.

Some of the uses and advantages of general adhesive bonding are shown in Fig. 15-2.

### Disadvantages

1. Adhesives are not as stable as metal-joining methods.

2. The joints are difficult to inspect and/or test nondestructively.

3. At the present time, extensive tests for durability and permanence of adhesive joints have not been conducted. Some standard procedures have been specified by the military and by ASTM.

4. Some rather elaborate jigs and fixtures may be needed to supply heat and pressure.

5. Adhesives may be susceptible to high humidity and extremes of temperature.

6. They may have less strength than some other joining methods.

7. Strong reliable joints are produced only on clean surfaces.

### PRINCIPLES OF ADHESIVES

Adhesives, whether applied as a liquid or as a film, are dependent for strength on the following factors: chemical forces between the components, cohesive strength of the components and adhesive, and the effective area of the bond.

As an example, a postage stamp is moistened to make tacky the dextrin film on the back. When it is applied to an envelope, the water

Insulation

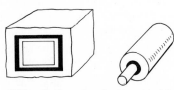

With adhesives, low-density materials can be easily fastened with the stress evenly distributed over the entire joined area. This increases insulation efficiency, avoids wires cutting into or pulling through the insulation.

Sound and vibration damping

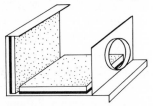

Waffle felt, fibrous glass, asphalt-impregnated materials, and other sound- and vibration-damping materials can be attached with adhesives that resist moisture and normal temperature extremes (—20° to 120°F.). The adhesive also serves as a corrosion-preventive coating on metal.

Upholstery

Flexible upholstery materials are readily bonded, even under light immediate stress, due to the high degree of tack offered by this type of adhesive. Some adhesives are specially compounded to prevent their bleeding through the upholstery materials.

Gasket adhesives

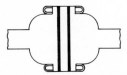

Oil-resistant adhesives can be used effectively for bonding many types of gasket materials in motors, pipe systems, ducts, etc. The adhesive also acts as a secondary seal, ensuring top performance of the gasket.

Desk and counter tops

Flexible sheet materials such as linoleum, vinyl, canvas, rubber, etc. are easily applied to metal, wood, or other subsurfaces with adhesives. Fast-drying and high-strength adhesives allow production-line techniques for most large-area bonding jobs.

**Fig. 15-2.** Adhesives are used in joining a wide variety of materials under widely varying conditions (courtesy Minnesota Mining and Manufacturing Co.).

dries out through the fibers in the paper, and a strong bond results owing to both fibrous entanglement and chemical affinity. If the stamp is applied to glass, there will be no fibrous interlocking; instead, there will be a chemical affinity with the oxygenated materials present. Without this chemical reaction or fibrous interlocking, there will be no effective bond. To illustrate: A crude-rubber cement containing sulfur, accelerators, and carbon black is applied alike to polished steel plate and polished brass. After it is heated for vulcanization to 300°F for 20 min and 300 psi are applied, there is no bond with the steel, but with the brass there is a bond strength of up to 60 psi. This is due to a chemical reaction that took place, forming a strong compatible film of complex sulfides.

Present theory holds that adhesion is primarily due to a chemical affinity of the adhesive for the substrate, and that mechanical action is only incidental. A schematic representation of bonding is shown in Fig. 15-3.

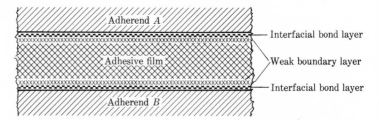

**Fig. 15-3.** Most adhesion is due to molecular attraction between the adhesive and the adherend. Some mechanical bonding is possible in porous materials.

Pressure is generally used with adhesive application to: (1) assure adequate contact between all members of the system; (2) hold the parts together while the solvent is drying, or while a cure is taking place that gives the adhesive its strength; (3) offset the destructive effects of gases and steams evolved during the cure, as in most curing of rubbers, phenolics, elastomers, vinyl-phenolics, and amine-aldehyde; and (4) cause the adhesive to flow over the joint area uniformly and expel entrapped air.

## CLASSIFICATION OF ADHESIVES

Adhesives can be divided into two broad groups—structural and nonstructural. In the first group are those used because of their high load carrying characteristics. In the second group are those, also known as glues or cements, used for low load applications. An example of this type is the waterproof latex adhesive being used to install tile flooring (Fig. 15-4). Other examples of its use were shown previously in Fig. 15-3. Since metal bonding is done primarily with structural adhesives, they will be the main topic of discussion in this chapter.

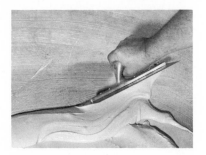

**Fig. 15-4.** Water- or oil-soluble adhesives are used in applying resilient flooring on concrete, terrazzo, or ceramic-tile subflooring (courtesy Armstrong Cork Company).

### Structural Adhesives

Structural adhesives can be further classified as thermoplastic and thermosetting just as plastics are classified. The important difference is that the thermoplastics are reversible; that is, they may be resoftened repeatedly by heat. Of course, any adhesive that is heated to too high a temperature will decompose and lose its bond strength. The too-high temperature is governed by the chemical structure of the adhesive.

**Thermoplastic Adhesives.** The thermoplastic adhesives most commonly used are the polyamides, vinyls, and nonvulcanizing neoprene rubber. In the structural field, the vinyls have proved very versatile. Polyvinyl acetate can be used to form strong bonds with glass, metals, and porous materials.

**Thermosetting Adhesives.** Thermosetting plastics can be formulated as strong, waterproof, mold-resistant, and heat-resistant adhesives. In this class, the phenol-formaldehyde resins have wide usage, forming one of the best bonding materials for waterproof plywood.

Resorcinol-formaldehyde resins are similar to phenolic resins but have the advantage of curing at room temperature.

One of the newer thermosetting adhesives that has been widely acclaimed is epoxy resin. It develops good strength, between 2,000 and 4,000 psi at room temperature, and cures without volatile by-products and with little shrinkage.

Silicone rubbers have also been used as bonding agents for nonstructural applications. They have proved successful in extremely low temperatures.

Other thermosetting adhesives are melamine-formaldehyde, polyurethanes, polyesters, phenolic-rubber, phenolic-vinyl and buna and neoprene rubbers.

Thermosetting adhesives with reinforcing fabrics are best for minimizing *creep* in structural applications. By creep is meant the dimensional change encountered in a material under load, following the initial instantaneous elastic or rapid deformation. Creep at room temperature is sometimes called *cold flow*. Thermosetting adhesives are generally preferred wherever elevated temperatures are encountered.

Structural adhesives are also made from combinations of rubbers and synthetic resins. An example of this is a nitrile-rubber–phenolic-resin combination, which can develop a shear strength of 2,000 to 3,500 psi at room temperature. These adhesives combine the specific adhesion and strength of the phenolic resins with the flexibility and resilience of the rubber. Some structural adhesives used in the lap-joint bonding of aluminum develop 3,000 to 6,000 psi tensile strength at room temperature.

## DEVELOPMENT OF ADHESIVE STRENGTH

There are four basic ways in which adhesives develop strength after application; these are by loss of solvent, cooling of hot melts, pressure sensitivity, and chemical reaction.

### Loss of Solvent

The air-drying adhesives are solutions, emulsions, or dispersions of such bonding agents as thermoplastic resin or rubber in water or organic solvents. In all cases, at least a part of the solvent must be lost from the adhesive film to produce a gelling or hardening by which the final bond strength is achieved. The solvent may be lost to the air before the joint is assembled, as with many rubber-base adhesives, or it may be largely transferred into the porous adherends after assembly. Representing the first type are the water-soluble or oil-soluble elastomers used in applying insulation, floor coverings, upholstery, etc.

Adhesives in this category are also classified as *long-tack* and *short-tack*. The long-tack adhesives are those that remain sticky even after complete evaporation of the solvent vehicle. These adhesives are sometimes referred to as *permanently tacky*. They are usually light in color and will adhere to any clean, dry surface. They are generally low in strength, because permanent tack and high degree of flow go hand in hand.

Short-tack adhesives usually develop an aggressive tack or stickiness while drying and, when dry, are generally firm and tough yet retain a great deal of flexibility.

### Cooling of Hot Melts

Fusible adhesives are predominantly those made from thermoplastic powders. These solids become liquid with the application of heat.

Bond strength is attained after the adhesive solidifies by cooling. Powders are usually applied as liquid by first heating them until they become a thin, easily manipulated paste. Powders offer the advantages of freedom from formulation errors and of ease in handling.

### Pressure Sensitivity

Pressure-sensitive adhesives are basically high-viscosity liquids, generally supplied on a suitable backing, in tape form. They bond instantly upon the application of slight pressure, by virtue of their high degree of initial tackiness. Pressure-sensitive adhesives are available in a wide range of viscosities and can be applied to any surface to which parts are to be temporarily positioned (Fig. 15-5).

**Fig. 15-5.** Pressure-sensitive tapes can be used to perform difficult clamping jobs. Here a double-coated tape is used to hold nonferrous metals for a milling operation (courtesy Minnesota Mining and Manufacturing Company).

Again, because of the relatively low shear strengths obtained, adhesives of this type are not considered structural.

Some pressure-sensitive tapes have polyethylene on both sides to keep the tape from sticking to itself in the roll. Just before use, the polyethylene is stripped off and discarded. An advantage of supported tapes (those applied to a backing material) is that they act to control glue-line thickness. The glass fabric, which is the support or carrier for the resin, not only serves as a stop to prevent glue-line starvation, which can be the result of excess clamping pressure, but also adds significantly to the tensile strength. Other advantages are insurance against formulation error, and lower overall cost, in some instances, since the fabricator need not measure, mix, or spread the material.

### Chemical Reaction

Many adhesives, predominantly thermosetting materials, develop strength by a chemical reaction known as curing. For curing to take place, two reactive components must be present and be intimately mixed. One component is normally called the *adhesive,* the other the curing agent, or *catalyst.* In some cases, the two parts are simply labeled "Part A" and "Part B."

Both components may be obtained, in a premixed form, as either tape or powder. All that is needed for activation is heat.

## SELECTION OF ADHESIVES

Adhesive selection is exacting work. Scores of new adhesive formulations are being developed constantly to answer the need for given applications. For example, there are dozens of formula variations for bonding urethane foams and latex foams to themselves or to rigid material such as wood or rubber.

Shown in Fig. 15-6 is a manufacturer's adhesive request form. You will note that it calls for service conditions of the surfaces to be bonded. It also asks for methods of application, methods of assembly, curing temperature, if any, cured properties, and strength in service.

**1 WHAT MATERIALS ARE BEING JOINED?**

MY APPLICATION IS TO:

☐ BOND ______________
☐ COAT ______________ to
☐ SEAL ______________
☐ POT ______________

Please be specific — say "aluminum to foamed styrene" NOT "metal to plastic." Submit samples if possible.

**2 WHAT ARE THE END-USE SERVICE REQUIREMENTS?**

MY ASSEMBLY WILL BE EXPECTED TO WITHSTAND:

A. Temperature extremes of ________ °F ☐ continuously ☐ intermittently
B. These chemicals or solvents ________ ☐ immersion ☐ vapor
________ ☐ continuously ☐ intermittently
C. These conditions: ☐ moisture ☐ sunlight ☐ outdoor weathering
D. Color requirements: ________
E. These loads: (Describe amount and *type* of strength required. Sketch, if possible)

**3 WHICH PRODUCTION METHOD WILL BE USED?**

A. I prefer the following form of adhesive: ☐ liquid ☐ paste ☐ film ☐ powder
B. This will be ☐ hand ☐ machine application.
C. My equipment makes it desirable to use:
☐ brush ☐ knife or trowel ☐ spray ☐ roll coater
☐ extruder ☐ caulking gun ☐ other________
D. These are my application requirements:
Viscosity desired: ________ Curing time available: ________
Drying time required: ________ Pressure available: ________
Curing temp. available: ________
E. If necessary, we ☐ can ☐ cannot use a 2-part adhesive.

**Fig. 15-6.** Manufacturer's adhesive request form (courtesy Rubber and Asbestos Corp.).

Despite the complexity of the problem, certain points, which should be considered in selecting the proper adhesive, may serve as a general guide. These include the type of adherends, type and design of joints, level of strength required, permanence required, surface preparation, application, and costs.

### Type of Adherends

The surface on which the adhesive is to be used will have a great deal to do with the type chosen. For instance, we must know what chemical reaction will be set up between the adhesive and the substrate material.

Some materials, such as metals and plastics, present a smooth surface, whereas others are quite porous. The adhesive must be formulated so that it will adhere well to the smooth surface, in one case, but not have excessive solvent absorption in another.

Dozens of formulation variations are needed for bonding urethane foams and latex foams, to themselves or to rigid materials such as wood or metal. To speed automated production, formulations incorporating extremely fast-drying solvents are made available. Other formulations are designed to work with tie-coats to hold back *plasticizer* migration from vinyl foams. (A plasticizer is used to increase the flexibility or distensibility of an adhesive.) Some bonds must be rigid, others flexible (Fig. 15-7).

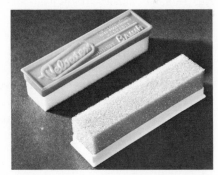

**Fig. 15-7.** Some adhesives are formulated to be flexible, others to be rigid.

### Type and Design of Joints

The most effective use of adhesives presupposes good joint design. The principle types of joints, along with the types of loads they can withstand, are presented here.

The first consideration in joint design for adhesive-bonded parts is the kind of load or stress to which the part will be subjected. Generally, the designer should try to avoid joints that concentrate stresses in a small area or on an edge. The common types of joints used for adhesive application, with their relative stress, are shown in Fig. 15-8.

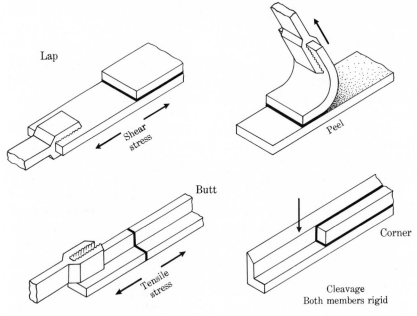

**Fig. 15-8.** Common types of joints and stresses used in adhesive applications.

Most of the adhesives used for bonding metal to metal are comparatively rigid, strong in shear, but not so strong in peel or cleavage. Thus, by designing the joint so that the adhesive is in shear, the effect of peel and cleavage can be minimized.

It is commonly believed that the strongest joints are made with the thinnest films. It has been shown, however, that certain types of adhesives show little difference in shear strength over a relatively wide range of film thicknesses—0.0005 to 0.010 in. Optimum film thicknesses vary, and the manufacturer's recommendation should be consulted.

**Improving Lap Joints.** The strength of a lap joint is directly proportional to its width. Assuming that the depth of the lap remains constant, a 2-in.-wide joint will be twice as strong as a 1-in. joint.

Strength also increases with the depth of the lap, although not proportionately. The reason is that the edges of the lap carry a relatively higher proportion of the load· than does the interior. Thus the unit increase in strength lowers as the depth of the lap increases.

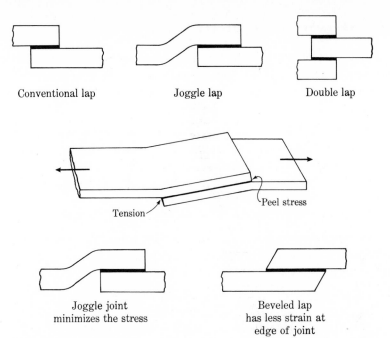

Conventional lap  Joggle lap  Double lap

Tension  Peel stress

Joggle joint
minimizes the stress

Beveled lap
has less strain at
edge of joint

**Fig. 15-9.** Common types of adhesive lap joints and methods used to improve them.

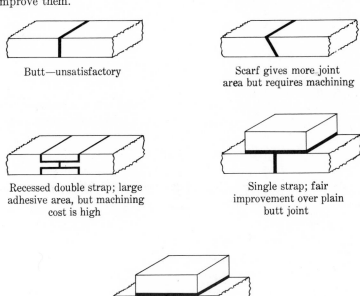

Butt—unsatisfactory

Scarf gives more joint
area but requires machining

Recessed double strap; large
adhesive area, but machining
cost is high

Single strap; fair
improvement over plain
butt joint

Double strap;
considerable surface increase

**Fig. 15-10.** Methods of improving adhesive butt joints.

Lap joints in tension tend to bend and change, so that peel becomes the main stress (Fig. 15-9). Several methods of joint design are recommended that will minimize the stress and peel at the joint edges.

**Improving Butt Joints.**   A plain butt joint is unsatisfactory for adhesive application, since the effective area is relatively small and stress concentrations are high. There are several ways in which the area can be increased. These include half lap, recessed double-strap scarf, single strap, and double strap, as shown in Fig. 15-10.

**Improving Angle Joints.**   As with the butt joint, the common angle joint does not provide very much bonding area. Various methods of improvement are shown in Fig. 15-11.

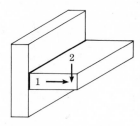

When the angle joint is stressed as shown, its strength is good. However, if the stress is parallel to the joint surface, as shown by arrow 2, the stress becomes a cleavage force.

**Fig. 15-11.** Methods of improving adhesive flanged angle joints.

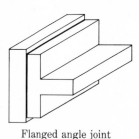

Flanged angle joint

The bonding area is increased.

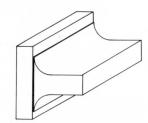

Tapered flange angle joint

Increased bonding area with minimized stress at the weakest point.

**Improving Corner Joints.**   Corner joints are subject to both peel and cleavage stresses. When the load on a corner joint is at right angles to the adhesive, it is relatively weak. Methods of strengthening the joint are shown in Fig. 15-12.

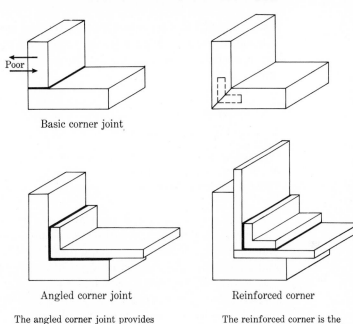

Basic corner joint

**Fig. 15-12.** Methods of improving adhesive corner joints.

Angled corner joint

The angled corner joint provides greater adhesive area plus reinforcement to minimize the weakness of the joint.

Reinforced corner

The reinforced corner is the strongest type, providing the most adhesive area and reinforcement.

**Joints for Sheet Metal Reinforcement.** Sheet metal parts can be reinforced or made rigid with channel-type backing (Fig. 15-13). If the sheet metal flexes, peel can be minimized by having the flanged edges tapered or ribbed, as shown.

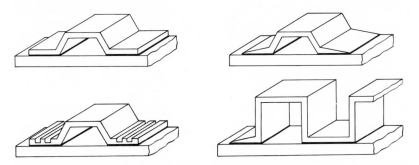

**Fig. 15-13.** Channel-type reinforcement is subject to peel stresses at the edges. Tapering or grooving the edge will help reduce the effect.

## Level of Strength Required

The strength developed in adhesive joining is dependent not only on the inherent strength but on other factors, such as the type of joint used, type of loading, temperature, adherend material, etc. Therefore, it is difficult to give definite figures without citing the environment. The shear-strength ranges given here are intended as a comparative guide only.

| Type of Adhesive | Average Shear Strength, Values at Room Temperature (psi) |
|---|---|
| Reclaimed rubber-type adhesives | 50–300 |
| Oil-soluble elastomers | 30–200 |
| Oil-resistant elastomers | 500–3,000 |
| Modified epoxies (heat cured) | 3,000–5,000 |
| Phenolic-elastomer films | 3,000–4,200 |
| Vinyl phenolic | 2,000–5,000 |

Structural adhesives, developed to produce high strength, are most often composed of synthetic resins or combinations of synthetic resins and elastomers. Common synthetic resins used are epoxy, urea, phenol, and resorcinol. The thermosetting-resin adhesives are generally hard and somewhat rigid when completely cured. The elastomer-resin combinations have high strength but retain a considerable amount of flexibility even after curing. Almost any adhesive can be made more flexible by formulation. Epoxy resins, for example, are made quite flexible by modification with polysulfide rubbers.

### Permanence Required

In considering the permanence of an adhesive, environmental factors, such as the chemicals or solvents it will have to withstand, must be taken into account. Many resins are damaged by water, oil, certain acids, and alkalies. Weathering effects and temperature extremes are very important factors in deciding which adhesive is to be used.

Many adhesives can be formulated to match closely the coefficient of expansion of the adherends. This helps to minimize the stresses due to temperature changes.

### Surface Preparation

The first step in preparing the surfaces to be bonded is to see that they are smooth and well fitted. Next, they should be cleaned. Thorough preparation is of the utmost importance. Even a thumbprint on an otherwise clean surface will impair adhesion.

Some metals are cleaned and given an acid etch to provide greater cohesive strength. Because of the likelihood of contamination of the metal surface during storage, it is desirable to use the etched metal within hours after treatment. If storage is necessary, the metal should be kept tightly wrapped or in airtight containers to minimize contamination. The etched surface must never be touched with bare hands; handlers should wear clean cotton gloves.

### Application

Adhesives are applied in a variety of ways—by hand brushing, spraying, roller coating, knife coating, and dipping. Some of these methods are shown in Fig. 15-14.

Tape-type adhesives are gaining in popularity because there is no need for mixing, and the application will be a known uniform thickness. *Lay-down* refers to the amount of adhesive applied, and *glue-line thick-*

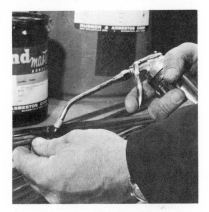
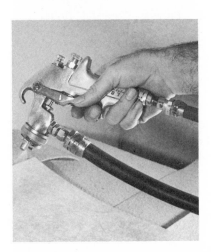

**Fig. 15-14.** Common methods of applying adhesives range from hand application with a brush or trowel to automated spray application. The manufacturer can usually formulate the adhesive to application requirements (courtesy Rubber and Asbestos Corp.).

*ness* refers to the amount of adhesive that remains after pressure has been applied to the lay-down and it has been cured. As an example, to achieve an ultimate glue-line thickness of 1 to 3 mils, anywhere from 5 to 15 mils of 20 percent-solid wet adhesive (lay-down) must be applied.

The actual application of the adhesive to the part can be done either with one thick coat on one of the components or with two thin coats, one on each component. Of the two methods, one thin coat on each of the two surfaces is generally the better. It results in longer tack life and stronger bond.

The best bonding strengths are usually achieved when 1 to 3 mils of solvent-free adhesive remain after two smooth, flat, parallel surfaces are bonded together.

The amount of lay-down depends upon the porosity and smoothness of the surfaces to be bonded, the fit of the joint, and the strength required. If the surface is porous, allowance must be made for the solvent release to achieve the desired glue-line thickness.

Rough surfaces must have enough adhesive applied to fill in all small depressions, plus enough excess adhesive to achieve the desired glue-line thickness. This can usually be done with one coat.

The gap between the two surfaces should not exceed a few thousandths of an inch. The space must be flat and parallel, and within the manufacturer's recommended tolerances, or maximum strength will not be achieved.

**Time Allowed for Bond Development.** Solvent-dispersed liquid adhesives should be assembled when they are *tacky,* or wet enough to adhere to the opposite surface. The amount of *flow* required for good adhesion is very small. Therefore, parts should be assembled when the adhesive is at the optimum consistency. After this, the pressure (and heat) is applied to cure or harden.

**Pressure.** Pressure is required to hold the two parts in intimate contact until sufficient adhesive bond is established to resist the stresses that are likely to be encountered in subsequent processing. The pressure should always be uniformly distributed over the entire joint. Generally, it is desirable to use as high a clamping pressure as the adherends will stand without compressive damage. Some adhesives, such as epoxy resins, can bond under very low pressures, whereas certain phenol-rubber formulations require high pressures to ensure adequate flow.

**Drying the Solvent.** Drying the solvent out of the spread adhesive takes from 1 to more than 60 min. depending on the porosity of the materials involved, thickness of the adhesive coat, strength required of the adhesive immediately after assembly, drying temperature, air flow over the adhesive surface, humidity, and solvents used in the adhesive.

Drying can be done at room temperature in some cases. However, heat hastens the drying and saves time and floor space. Common drying methods include warm air from a unit heater, infrared lamps, and hot plates. Various ways of drying are shown in Fig. 15-15.

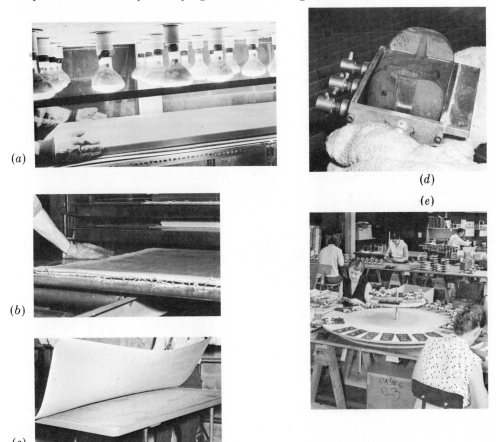

**Fig. 15-15.** Adhesive drying can be speeded up with (*a*) heat from infrared lamps; (*b*) other parts may be heated in ovens; (*c*) some set upon contact; (*d*) others require pressure; and (*e*) some require only air drying (courtesy Rubber and Asbestos Corp.).

It is important that the solvent be allowed to evaporate at a prescribed rate in order to develop full strength. On damp days, moisture may condense on the surface of adhesives drying at room temperature. This may result from using too volatile a solvent that "flashes off" and then cools with a film of condensation. The condensation can sometimes be removed by heating the adhesive-coated surfaces, although this may be detrimental to the surface cure.

**Assembly By Reactivation.**   Certain adhesives are known as a *dry-film* type. The surfaces are prepared in advance, thoroughly dried, and stored for several days. They are then reactivated by one of several methods:

1.   A light coat of liquid adhesive is added to the dry adhesive, or a dilution solvent (a specific one for the dry adhesive) is applied lightly with a rag or sponge.

2.   The dry adhesive can be heated with infrared lamps, hot air, or hot plates to the reactivation temperature of the specific adhesive. These temperatures usually range from 180° to 400°F. Parts may be positioned and then reactivated. Since the tack life is short, it is important to have the parts positioned accurately.

The dry-film adhesive shown in Fig. 15-16 is an example of one that can be reactivated with either solvents or heat. It is used to cut labor costs through minimum handling, yet it ensures a proper bond.

**Fig. 15-16.**   Dry film adhesives are used for ease of assembly and to insure an adequate uniform bond. The film can be reactivated by either solvents or heat. The example shown is an aluminum honeycomb sandwich construction (courtesy Rubber and Asbestos Corp.).

**Safety Precautions.**   Some of the curing agents used in adhesives are alkaline compounds capable of producing caustic burns upon contact with the skin. These materials will also produce dermatitis if proper handling procedures are not observed. The vapors produced by a curing agent such as diethylenetriamine are irritating to the eyes and mucous membranes of the respiratory tract.

In mixing all two-part adhesives good personal cleanliness should be observed to avoid dermatitis. Hands should be washed frequently, and care should be exercised to avoid touching eyes, ears, etc., with dirty hands. Other precautions are:

1.   Mix in an area with adequate ventilation so that fumes will not be injurious.

2. Wear goggles or shields for eye protection.

3. Cure in ovens vented to the outside atmosphere.

Standard regulations regarding flammable materials should be observed. Meticulous housekeeping standards must be maintained.

Strict supervision must be enforced to prevent the inadvertent contamination of nonoperating areas, for example, the contamination of doorknobs, valves, handrails, etc.

## Costs

In judging the cost of adhesives, several factors are pertinent. The small amount of time needed for curing or the ease of assembly may offset an initial high price. For example, a relatively expensive (about $75.00 per lb) adhesive is Eastman 910 cyanocrylate. It has extremely high strength value and rapid curing qualities. Moisture from the air acts as a catalyst. It is generally used in small, difficult-to-bond assembly units. (Probably one of its most interesting applications has been to replace stitches for an appendectomy.) For certain purposes, its advantages may make it more economical in the long run.

Another factor in considering adhesive costs is whether the material is in the solid or the dispersed form. Since the amount of solvent necessary will be difficult to predict, prices should be compared on the basis of the solid material. The following present-day prices, given on this basis, are approximations only, since the quantity purchased can also change the picture.

| Adhesive | Cost per Pound |
|---|---|
| Phenolics | 25¢ |
| Resorcinal phenolics | 45¢ |
| Nitrile rubber | 75¢ |
| Melamine | 45¢ |
| Epoxy | $1.00 |
| Vinyl | 50¢ |
| Urea | 10–12¢ |

## NEW AND FUTURE DEVELOPMENTS

Many commercial jet transport planes are now using adhesive-bonded structures. Military planes, rockets, and satellites also use them. The bonding of parts in the electronics field is advancing rapidly. The feasibility of bonding aluminum engines has been demonstrated, and automobile manufacturers have experimentally built up car and truck bodies with no welding, using adhesive bonding exclusively.

With the advent of newer adhesives which offer good peel strength, fatigue resistance, and simplicity of tooling beyond anything available in the older materials, this method of joining will be increasingly used.

## Epoxy Pellets

A newer method of applying adhesives is in the form of epoxy pellets (Fig. 15-17). The pellets are formulated from powdered epoxies that have been partially reacted and arrested. These powders are then pressed into a wide variety of shapes to suit the job. The size of the pellet will be such that, when heat is applied, the liquid formed will be just enough to fill a particular cavity.

**Fig. 15-17.** Cast-epoxy pellets can be obtained in a variety of sizes and shapes (courtesy Joseph Waldmann and Sons, Epoxy Products Division).

A typical application of an epoxy pellet is shown in Fig. 15-18, where two aluminum tubes are joined. The epoxy pellet has been pre-shaped to fit the flared end of the tube. Brazing could probably have been used, but there might have been danger of melting the thin wall.

Pellets will cure at 300°F or as low as 185°F. Of course, the higher the heat, the faster the cure. A pellet that cures at 300°F requires only

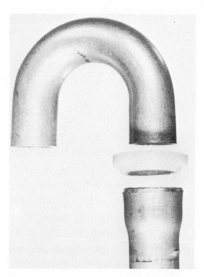

**Fig. 15-18.** An epoxy pellet is used to make a strong bond between two pieces of fitted aluminum tubing. The pellet, shaped to fit the large end, melts under heat and gives just enough liquid to fill the cavity. It then cures to form a bond (courtesy Waldmann and Sons, Epoxy Products Division).

3 hr, whereas at 212°F, 24 hr are required. The heaters most commonly used are induction, dielectric, oven, and infrared types.

The simplicity of handling makes the pellets much more adaptable to large runs and even to automated ones.

## FASTENERS

The dynamic growth of the fastener industry in recent years has made it difficult to keep informed as to what might be available for a given joining operation. The purpose of this brief discussion is not to point out all the various fasteners that are available, but rather to call attention to the main types and to give references where more detailed information can be found.

Fasteners can be classified in five broad categories as follows:

1. Threaded fasteners
2. Small rivets
3. Pin fasteners
4. Retaining rings
5. Quick-operating fasteners

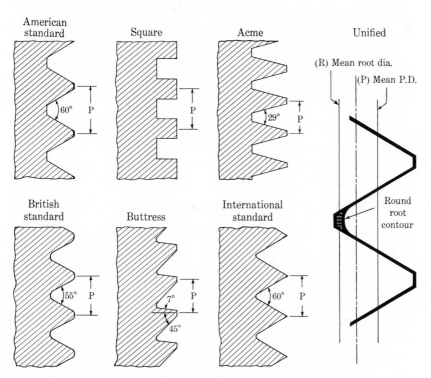

**Fig. 15-19.** Basic thread forms.

### Threaded Fasteners

The most familiar types of mechanical fasteners are screws, nuts, and bolts. Before going into the main types available, it will be well to understand the basic thread nomenclature.

THREAD FORMS. Thread forms refer to the theoretical profiles of the threads. Basic thread forms shown in Fig. 15-19 are: American Standard, Square, Acme, British Standard, Buttress, International, and Unified.

NOMINAL SIZE. The general size identification of the outside diameter of the thread.

MAJOR, MINOR, AND PITCH DIAMETERS. These terms can best be explained by referring to Fig. 15-20.

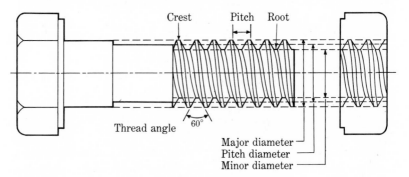

**Fig. 15-20.** Basic thread nomenclature.

PITCH. The distance from a point on one thread to the corresponding point on the adjacent thread measured parallel to the axis.

INCLUDED ANGLE. The included angle of a thread is the angle between the flanks of the thread measured in an axial plane.

LEAD. The distance a screw advances axially in one full turn.

SCREW THREAD DESIGNATION.

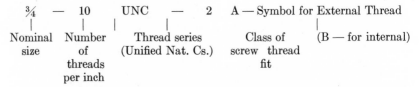

THREAD SERIES. In 1948 the United States, Britain, and Canada reached an agreement as to a Unified thread form, pitch and tolerance of threaded parts $\frac{1}{4}$ in. and larger in the coarse, fine, extra fine, and special thread series. These are designated as UNC, UNF, UNEF, and UNS, respectively. The form of the thread is essentially that of the National form with a 60-deg included angle but with provision for rounding the crest and the root. A flat root is permitted when using unworn tools. The crest of the external thread may be flat or rounded. The Unified thread is interchangeable with the American Standard Series.

**Thread Fits.** Three classes of thread fits are available in the Unified series. They are designated by numbers 1, 2, and 3. When used with a suffix "A" the number refers to the external thread, and with a suffix "B" to the internal thread.

Class 1 is a loose fit, used where quick and easy assembly is necessary and where a considerable amount of shake or play is not objectionable.

Class 2 is a free fit recommended for all general-purpose work. Allowance is provided for normal electroplating. After plating, the fit is almost the same as the American Standard Class 2 fit.

Class 3 is a medium fit intended for precision products where a minimum of shake or play is desired. It is the closest fit that is commercially practical to produce. It increases threading costs and should be specified only when necessary.

**Standard Threaded Fasteners.** The wide variety of threaded fasteners evolved from many specialized applications that have become standard. The common types of screws are machine screws, capscrews, setscrews, selftapping screws, and drive screws (Fig. 15-21). Also shown are standard screw heads.

MACHINE SCREWS. Machine screws are made in all the head styles shown in Fig. 15-21. The points are not finished. They are used for general fastening in tapped holes or with nuts.

CAPSCREWS. Capscrews are made to closer tolerances and have a better finish than machine screws. They are used for fastening automotive parts, machine-tool parts, farm machinery, etc.

SETSCREWS. Setscrews are made in square heads, headless socket, and slotted types. The points made are shown in Fig. 15-21. The cup point, made to dig into soft metals, is the most common type.

SELF-TAPPING SCREWS. These screws, depending on the type used, can either cut or form the thread in the mating part. Thread-forming types are shown in Fig. 15-21 as *(a), (b),* and *(c).* Type *(f)* is one of a variety of thread-cutting screws. They are used for metal and plastics 0.050 to 0.500 in. thick. They are also used for fastening to castings and

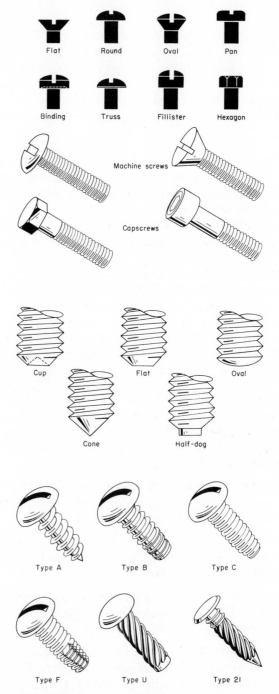

**Fig. 15-21.** Common types of screws (courtesy *American Machinist/Metalworking Manufacturing*).

forgings. Selftapping screws are tightened so as to remain in tension. It is necessary to follow the manufacturer's recommendation closely so that they are tightened properly. In addition to the styles shown, a hexhead type is also made.

DRIVE SCREWS. The type U thread-forming screw is hammered or pressed into a prepared hole. It is used in metals 0.050 in. thick and for fastening to castings, forgings, and plastics. Type 21 is used for fastening fabric, fiber, and leather to sheet metal.

BOLTS. The common types of bolts used are machine, stove, carriage, plow, lag, and hanger, as shown in Fig. 15–22.

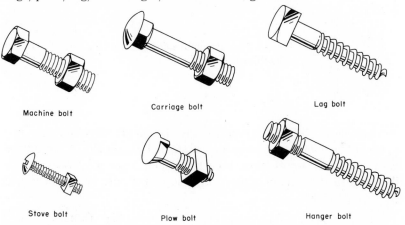

Machine bolt

Carriage bolt

Lag bolt

Stove bolt

Plow bolt

Hanger bolt

**Fig. 15-22.** Common types of bolts (courtesy *American Machinist/Metalworking Manufacturing*).

MACHINE BOLTS. Machine bolts are made with square, hex, rounded, or countersunk heads. Nut styles used are either hex or square.

STOVE BOLTS. Stove bolts are regular machine screws supplied with nuts (usually square).

CARRIAGE BOLTS. The square, oval, ribbed, or finned neck of the carriage bolt keeps it from turning. The heads are usually truss, countersunk, or flat type.

PLOW BOLTS. The plow bolt with its flush-countersunk finned head is widely used for heavy roadbuilding machinery, farm machinery, and railroad equipment.

LAG BOLTS. Lag bolts or lag screws are used in wooden construction or with anchoring devices in concrete.

HANGER BOLTS. A hanger bolt is a stud-type lag screw. A coarse thread and nut is provided in place of the head to facilitate fastening and unfastening equipment against a wooden surface.

**Nuts.** Standard Nuts and Jamb Nuts. In the American Standard, ASA B 18.2-1955, there are two series of standard nuts, referred to as heavy and finished. The heavy type is thick and is for bolt holes that have large clearances. The finished nut refers to the quality of manufacture being of close tolerance rather than the surface being completely finished. It is designed for common all-round usage.

Jam nuts are thinner than the finished nut and are usually used with either the standard finished nut or heavy nut to lock it in place. The jamb nut is placed at the bottom as shown in Fig. 15-23.

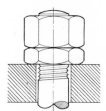

**Fig. 15-23.** Recommended practice for assembly of jam nuts to provide a locking action.

**Lock Nuts.** Wherever there is any danger of vibration that may cause bolted joints to loosen, some type of lock should be considered. Many different types have been developed, most of which can be classified in three main types: insert type, pressure type and washer type (Fig. 15-24).

INSERT TYPE. The insert-type lock nut, Fig. 15-24*(a)*, has a resilient material added in the head which is of smaller diameter than the major diameter of the bolt. As the bolt goes through this section the compressive forces developed provide a locking action.

PRESSURE TYPE. The pressure-type lock nuts are usually made in such a way that when the proper torque is applied, the seating action forces the threaded segments radially inward. This is accomplished by relieving and slotting the nut or by spring action as shown in Fig. 15-24*(b)*.

WASHER TYPE. Increasingly popular lock nuts are the nut lock-washer assemblies shown in Fig. 15-24*(c)*. They are designed to spin freely until torque is applied causing the teeth or "funnels" to dig in and lock to the mating surface.

OTHER LOCKING METHODS. There are many ways a bolt and nut assembly may be locked other than the examples given. Some of these methods consist of peening or punching the end of the threaded assembly, the use of set screws, or safety wire. Quite a different approach is a Locktite sealant that is poured between the mating surfaces to form a tough plastic as it hardens. It is reported that no amount of vibration will loosen the assembly, yet it can be removed with ordinary tools.

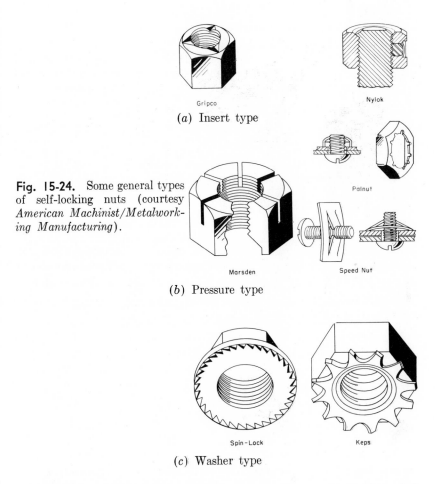

Gripco

Nylok

(*a*) Insert type

**Fig. 15-24.** Some general types of self-locking nuts (courtesy *American Machinist/Metalworking Manufacturing*).

Palnut

Marsden

Speed Nut

(*b*) Pressure type

Spin-Lock

Keps

(*c*) Washer type

An added advantage of this method is that the threaded joint is sealed against fluid pressure and corrosion.

**Threaded Inserts.**   Soft or thin materials cannot always be counted on to give the necessary support needed for threaded fasteners. A solution to this problem has been the development of inserts. The inserts are made so that they can be driven, pressed, or screwed into the base material. Most of the inserts are self-locking and are made of steel, stainless steel, or aluminum alloy.

A variety of threaded inserts has been developed, some of which are shown in Fig. 15-25.

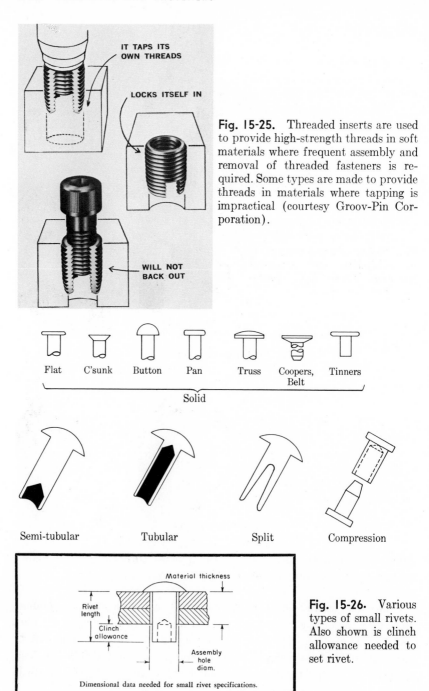

IT TAPS ITS
OWN THREADS

LOCKS ITSELF IN

WILL NOT
BACK OUT

**Fig. 15-25.** Threaded inserts are used to provide high-strength threads in soft materials where frequent assembly and removal of threaded fasteners is required. Some types are made to provide threads in materials where tapping is impractical (courtesy Groov-Pin Corporation).

| Flat | C'sunk | Button | Pan | Truss | Coopers, Belt | Tinners |

Solid

Semi-tubular          Tubular          Split          Compression

Material thickness

Rivet length

Clinch allowance

Assembly hole diam.

Dimensional data needed for small rivet specifications.

**Fig. 15-26.** Various types of small rivets. Also shown is clinch allowance needed to set rivet.

## Small Rivets

Standard rivets have long been a favorite permanent fastening method because of dependability and low cost. Other advantages are the ability to join a wide variety of similar or dissimilar materials, low equipment costs, high production rates, wide choice of rivet types and materials, and no need for skilled labor.

Small rivets (7/16-in. diameter or smaller) are used in the assembly of many industrial products. They are used wherever shear and tensile loadings are high, and permanent, lightweight fasteners are needed. They may be classified as solid, semi-tubular, tubular or split (bifurcated), and compression (Fig. 15-26).

**Solid and Semi-Tubular Rivets.** The semi-tubular rivet when properly set is essentially the same as a solid rivet, since the hole in the end of the rivet is just enough to form the clinch. As with the solid rivet, the semi-tubular rivet is used wherever maximum shear strength is needed.

A special type of solid rivet is shown in Fig. 15-27. Setting is accomplished by forming an aluminum-alloy collar into the grooves of the small end.

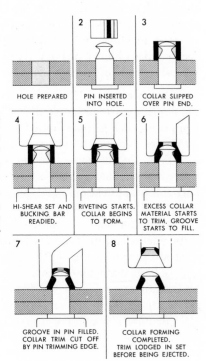

**Fig. 15-27.** Hi-Shear rivets consist of a headed pin and collar. Most of the pins are made from high-strength alloy steel, stainless steel, or titanium. Most of the collars are made of aluminum alloy. A special rivet set tool is used in combination with a standard rivet gun or squeezer to form the collar securely into the pin groove (courtesy Hi-Shear Corporation).

**Split and Compression Rivets.** The split or bifurcated rivet is used to punch its own hole through fiber, wood, or plastic.

The compression rivet consists of two parts: a solid blank and a deep-drilled tubular member. When the two members are pressed together they form an interference fit. The heads of both members can be made the same size for appearance's sake.

**Rivet Length.** Care must be exercised to see that the rivets are of the right length. Too short a rivet results in inadequate clinch, and too long a rivet results in poor set with buckling and excessive wear on tooling. Normally, the allowance for clinch on a full-tubular rivet is about one hundred percent of the shank diameter. As shown in Fig. 15-26 the semi-tubular rivet requires between 50 and 70 percent of the shank diameter for clinching.

**Rivet Spacing.** Standards should be consulted for the proper edge distance and spacing between rivets. The best results can be ascertained, however, by testing an actual assembly under simulated working conditions.

**Rivet Setting.** There are three main methods of setting or forming the shank end of a rivet: (1) upsetting a solid rivet with a penumatic hammer and backing or bucking bar, (2) using a bench or flow-type riveting machine for tubular and bifurcated rivets, and (3) using special rivets known as blind rivets. The third method will be discussed here since it is of a special nature.

BLIND RIVETS. The blind rivet can be used where both sides of the assembly are not accessible. This eliminates the need for fastening equipment such as pneumatic hammers and bucking bars. Some of the most used types of blind rivets are shown in Fig. 15-28.

From the foregoing illustrations one can see there may be a selection problem when it comes to obtaining the right type of rivet for a particular application. The main considerations are the allowable shear load, cost, and whether or not it needs to be fluid tight.

Allowable loads for most rivets have been established by detailed tests. Shear-load limits of semi-tubular rivets in aluminum, brass, and steel are shown in Fig. 15-29 on page 417.

In large diameters aluminum rivets are more easily set with manual tools than are some of the higher-strength materials. All-aluminum rivets are more expensive than those that have aluminum bodies and steel mandrels. Steel rivets have the advantage of high strength and low cost. They are often chemically treated or enameled for corrosion resistance.

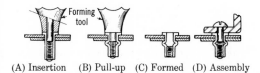

(A) Insertion  (B) Pull-up  (C) Formed  (D) Assembly

RIVNUTS...
have a threaded core which accepts a special pull-up tool. Tool upsets the rivet shank making a tight metal-to-metal fit. Pull-up stud is then disengaged

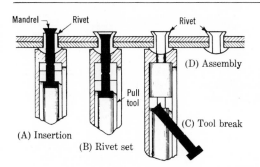

(A) Insertion  (B) Rivet set  (C) Tool break  (D) Assembly

CHERRY RIVETS...
are installed by placing the shank in the hole and pulling the stem with a special tool to form the blind head. These rivets are available in pull-through and self-plugging types

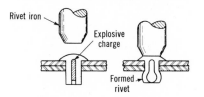

EXPLOSIVE RIVETS...
resemble ordinary solid rivets, but have a small explosive charge in the shank. Charge is detonated by heat from an electric gun, expanding charged end of shank and forming a blind head

(A) Insert rivet  (B) Partially driven  (C) Assembly

DRIVE RIVETS...
have a drilled hole into which a grooved steel pin is placed. Pin is driven with hammer until it is flush with the head, spreading the four sections of shank outward, forming clinch

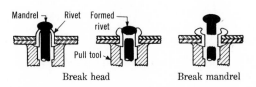

Break head    Break mandrel

POP RIVETS...
consist of two parts, a hollow rivet and a mandrel. Special tool pulls the mandrel into the rivet material. After upsetting the rivet and clinching, the mandrel breaks at the head or at the necked stem. Both types are illustrated

**Fig. 15-28.** Various types of blind rivets (courtesy *American Machinist/ Metalworking Manufacturing*).

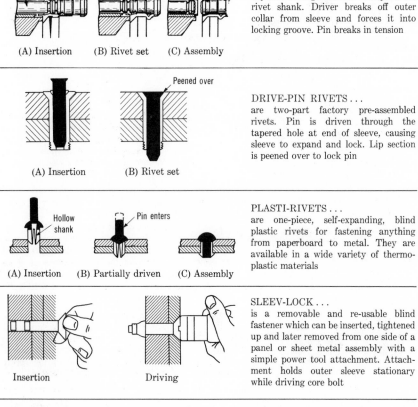

**CHOBERT RIVETS...**
are upset by drawing a mandrel through the tapered hole. These rivets will adjust for slight misalignment of hole while providing tight clinch. Pull-through type (illustrated) and self-plugging type available

**HUCK RIVETS...**
consist of a sleeve and a pin. As the pin is pulled through the sleeve it upsets the rivet shank. Driver breaks off outer collar from sleeve and forces it into locking groove. Pin breaks in tension

**DRIVE-PIN RIVETS...**
are two-part factory pre-assembled rivets. Pin is driven through the tapered hole at end of sleeve, causing sleeve to expand and lock. Lip section is peened over to lock pin

**PLASTI-RIVETS...**
are one-piece, self-expanding, blind plastic rivets for fastening anything from paperboard to metal. They are available in a wide variety of thermoplastic materials

**SLEEV-LOCK...**
is a removable and re-usable blind fastener which can be inserted, tightened up and later removed from one side of a panel or sheet metal assembly with a simple power tool attachment. Attachment holds outer sleeve stationary while driving core bolt

**Fig. 15-28.** *(cont.)*

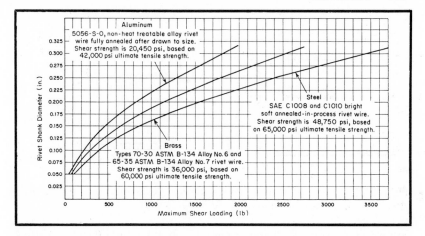

**Fig. 15-29.** Shear load limits for semitubular rivets. Data are based on minimum rivet body diameter and apply only to joints in which the edge distance and hole spacing are great enough to prevent failure in the assembly that is being joined. They do not hold for tubular rivets which have a hole that extends into the load bearing area. Also they do not take into account the offset that results because the shank is not expanded to fill the hole (courtesy *Machine Design*).

A choice of whether the rivet should be a break-stem type or one that makes a tight seal will be dependent on the product. In the break-stem type where the head falls off, a through hole is left making this type unsatisfactory for some products. If the product is subject to high-frequency vibration, the mandrel of the break-stem type may resonate.

The fluid-tight rivet is available for assemblies that must be leak-proof. It consists of an aluminum-alloy solid rivet that has a soft-aluminum head washer. When installed with conventional methods and tools it forms an effective seal.

### Pin Fasteners

Many standard pins have been developed for quick, neat assembly operations where the load is primarily in shear. A number of pins have been standardized as *machine pins* and are discussed in ASA B 5.20-1954. These pins are the straight pin (either chamfered or square end), the dowel pin, the clevis pin, the taper pin, and the cotter pin (Fig. 15-30).

#### Standard Pins.

STRAIGHT PINS AND DOWEL PINS. Common uses of standard, straight, and dowel-type pins are: holding laminated sections together, locking components to a shaft, and as hinge pins. Standard straight pins

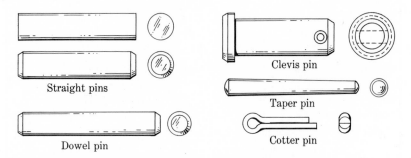

**Fig. 15-30.** Standard type fasteners referred to as machine pins (*courtesy American Machinist/Metalworking Manufacturing*).

are made in twelve diameters ranging from a nominal 0.062 in. through 0.500 in. Dowel pins may be had in either the hardened or unhardened condition and range in size from 0.062 in. to 1.000 in. in mild steel but only up to ⅞ in. in the hardened pin. Although not standard, several manufacturers make a one-inch-diameter dowel pin. Standard pins are 0.0002 in. oversize on the nominal diameter. Oversize pins are 0.001 in. oversize.

CLEVIS PIN. The primary application of the clevis pin is to join two parts together in mobile assembly. A cotter pin inserted through the hole in the clevis pin usually forms the locking device; however, threaded ends may also be obtained. The standard material is either soft or cyanide-hardened steel.

TAPER PINS. Taper pins are made with a taper of ¼ in. per foot measured on the diameter. They are made of mild steel, stainless steel, alloy steels, and brass. Drilled holes are prepared for the tapered pin by reaming with a helically-fluted tapered reamer. The pin is then driven into the hole until it is seated. It is generally recommended for light-duty shear loads since the torque capacity must be determined on the basis of double shear for the average diameter along the pin length.

COTTER PINS. The most common use of the cotter pin is in locking a slotted or castillated nut in position. A variety of points can be obtained both to facilitate insertion and to allow separation of the ends after the pin is in place.

**Nonstandard Pins.** The nonstandard pins are generally those that have not been used for as long a period as those discussed previously. The pins discussed here may be divided into two broad groups: *semipermanent* and *quick release*.

SEMIPERMANENT PINS. The semipermanent pins are of two basic types: solid with grooved surfaces, and tubular (Fig. 15-31).

Grooved pins have a longitudinal groove rolled or pressed into the surface. These grooves act to expand the effective pin diameter so that when the pin is driven or pressed into a drilled hole the displaced material tends to flow back causing a locking effect. The pins are normally made from SAE 1112, but where high shear loads are encountered, heat treated SAE 6150 is recommended. Other materials used include stainless steel type 303, Monel metal, brass, and bronze.

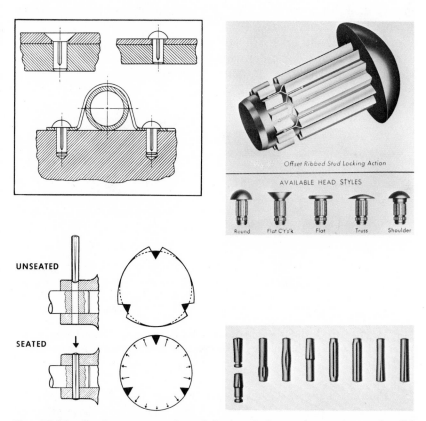

**Fig. 15-31.** Semipermanent pins of both tubular spring action and solid grooved surface types (courtesy Groov-Pin Corp.).

The drive studs are used wherever a headed fastener is needed in such applications as fastening name plates to cast iron or conduit straps to structural material. The offset-ribbed type is designed for any material subject to plastic deformation. It is designed to withstand considerable vibration.

Rollpins® are slotted, chamfered, cylindrical spring pins. The slot allows the spring to compress as it is driven into the hole. The constraining action of the hole wall keeps it in position. Maximum strength is obtained if the pin is assembled so that the direction of the load is 180 deg away from the point of application. Shear loads can be increased considerably when combinations of pins are used one inside the other. As an example, a 3/32-in. pin can be used with a 5/32-in. pin developing a double shear strength of 4,000 psi. The pin lends itself to hand or automatic assembly. It can be used where assembly and disassembly are needed, since neither the hole nor the pin is damaged. A pin somewhat similar in nature is one that is spirally wrapped instead of slotted.

QUICK-RELEASE PINS. Most quick-release pins are made so that a clearance hole must be provided, and locking is achieved by two spring-loaded balls (Fig. 15-32).

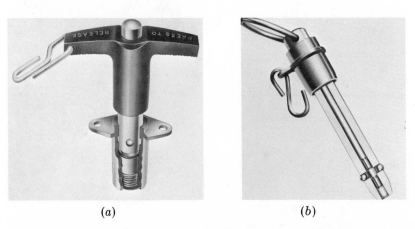

(a)                              (b)

**Fig. 15-32.** (a) A single-acting, quick-release-type pin with flush mounting receptacle; (b) a double-acting, quick-release pin with ring handle (courtesy Audel, Inc.).

Pull-out loads vary, but normally range from 10 to 30 psi, depending on the pin size. Most pins of this type have a chain attached to keep them from becoming mislaid or lodged in the assembly.

### Retaining Rings

Retaining rings perform three basic functions: (1) to locate accurately one component in relation to another by means of providing

® Rollpin is a registered trade name of the Elastic Stop Nut Corporation of America.

a shoulder, (2) to lock or retain the component in place, and (3) to take up end play caused by accumulated tolerances or wear in the parts being retained. Retaining rings can be classified as stamped and bent-wire types, also external and internal.

**Stamped Retaining Rings.** Stamped retaining rings are made on the principle of tapered radial width that decreases symmetrically from the center to the free ends (Fig. 15-33).

Most retaining rings are designed to seat in grooves. Bowed rings are used to take up any objectionable end play, to preload bearings, and to provide spring tension adjustment that eliminates rattle in machine linkages.

Most of the stamped-type rings are made out of high-carbon spring steel with an oil-dipped finish. Rings are also available in aluminum, phosphor, bronze, beryllium, copper, and stainless steel.

Special pliers are required to place most retaining rings in the assembly. The pliers fit into the small holes in the lugs to either expand or contract the ring as needed. Radially-assembled rings can be installed or removed with a screwdriver.

### Quick-Operating Fasteners

The term quick in quick-operating fasteners usually refers to one simple action such as a quarter of a turn or a short, pressing-sliding motion that can be accomplished in a matter of seconds.

Again, the number of fasteners in this category is very large. For simplification they will be divided into three main types: quick-turn fasteners, lever-type fasteners, and slide-action fasteners.

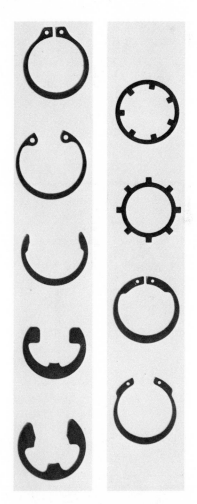

**Fig. 15-33.** Stamped retaining rings for both external and internal assembly. Bowed rings are also used to take up end play or preload bearings (courtesy Industrial Retaining Ring Co.).

**Quick-Turn Fasteners.**   Most of the quick-turn fasteners are designed to open or close by a quarter turn. The locking action is usually dependent on both an axial force, furnished by a spring, and a cam for holding it in place, Fig. 15-34.

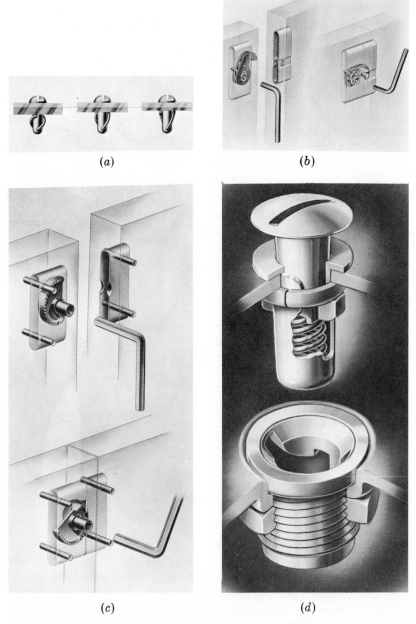

(a)

(b)

(c)

(d)

**Fig. 15-34.**   Examples of quick-turn fasteners. The spring-lock fastener (a) is

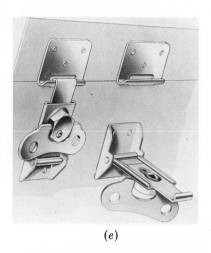

*(e)*                                    *(f)*

secured in place by a quarter turn on the rivet-like pin, causing the wires to flex spirally. A second quarter turn releases it. The quick-lock, two-piece assembly (*b*) is also secured by a quarter turn. Cam surfaces on receptacle cause stud to engage to positive stop. The Dual-lock (*c*) uses an off-center cam to actuate a latch hook. It is built to withstand a tension load of 7,000 lb. The Roto-lock (*d*) uses a tapered serrated cam that meshes with projections on the striker when rotated a partial turn. The Link-lock (*e*) is a quick-operating latching device used where heavy locking pressure is required. The hinge-lock (*f*) acts as a hinge and locking device to bring down a strong seal on gasketed equipment containers (courtesy Simmons Fastener Corporation).

**Lever-Type Fasteners.** An everyday example of the lever-type quick-operating fastener is found on most luggage containers. Two variations of this type of fastener are shown in Fig. 15-35. Other locking devices include cam and latch.

**Slide-Action Fasteners.** A familiar type of slide fastener is the door latch that uses a sliding spring-loaded bolt. A smaller fastener of this type is shown in Fig. 15-36. A spring-loaded locking action is provided to withstand shock and vibration.

### Fastening Plastic Parts

Many common fasteners can be used in joining plastic parts, provided that the properties of the plastics are considered. For example, the coefficient of linear expansion of many plastic materials is ten times that of steel. Also, plastics have a tendency to cold flow or creep under applied loads.

With these properties in mind, general rules can be established.

*Type A*          *Type B*

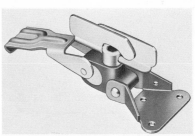

*Type C*

**Fig. 15-35.**   Lever-type quick-operating fasteners. *Type A* provides a recessed base, locking action is by means of a lever and two coil springs. As the lever is depressed on *Type B* the spring force in the strap holds the latch closed. As the lock nut on *Type C* is turned it rotates a worm gear causing the engaging link to catch the strike panel, clamping it in place (courtesy Bassick Co.).

**Fig. 15-36.**   Quick-acting, slide-type fastener (courtesy Dimco Gray Company).

1. Large hole tolerances should be used wherever possible.

2. Large flat washers should be used to help disperse the load to avoid concentrated stress and cold flow.

Screw-type fasteners are generally more suitable for thermosetting and reinforced plastics than the thermoplastic resins. Blind holes tapped into thermosetting plastics should allow bottom clearance beyond the depth of the screw to help prevent loosening.

Both plastic and metal rivets are used for fastening. The compression rivet, shown in Fig. 15-26, is especially good for plastic parts. Plastic parts are usually riveted to metal but seldom to other plastic parts.

The spring-clip-type steel nuts shown in Fig. 15-24 are excellent for holding plastic parts in gentle tension. These fasteners permit lateral movement of the plastic parts but hold them securely together.

Inserts are often molded into the plastic parts. These serve to impart special strength-bearing characteristics and act to retain fastening studs, pins, splines, and bushings.

## Fastening Costs

Fasteners are often selected on the basis of appearance or convenience without due regard to cost, since this can be quite cumbersome to calculate. However, it may prove to be worth the effort needed to set up a standard procedure relating relative installed costs of the various fasteners.

These are the general considerations:

*Machinery*—Need for standard drill presses or special riveting machines, etc. Expected life, maintenance, etc.

*Fasteners*—The cost of the fastener may have little bearing on its final cost in place.

*Labor*—This is easy to determine after the equipment is in operation, but difficult to predict in advance.

*Tooling*—Costs for tools such as jigs and fixtures will vary widely. Is is usually best to base these costs on the basis of 100 or 1,000 parts.

*Other factors*—Such items as handling, assembly preparation, supplementary operations, and overhead must all be considered and added to the overall costs.

**Fastening-cost Calculations.** For every type of fastening operation it is possible to make a simple formula that will give the approximate cost. These formulas are given in Table 15-1.

### QUESTIONS

1. Why have adhesives been accepted as an industrial joining method?
2. What are some of the limitations of adhesive bonding?
3. What is considered to be the principal force in adhesive bonding?
4. What type of adhesive is preferred for structures that must operate at elevated temperatures?

**TABLE 15-1.**

## Fastening Costs*

EQUIPMENT COST

Initial cost . . . . . . . . . . . . . . . . . . . . . . . . . . . . . . . . . . . . . . . $_____

Anticipated useful life . . . . . . . . . . . . . . . . . . . . . . . . . . . _____ years

$$\text{Cost/hr} = \frac{\text{Machine Cost}}{\text{Useful life} \times \text{hrs/year}} \quad \text{. . . . . . . . . . . . . . .} \quad \$\underline{\quad}/\text{hr}$$

$$\text{Cost/unit} = \frac{\text{Cost/hr} \times 100}{\text{Assemblies/hr} \times \text{Fasteners/assembly}} \quad \$\underline{\quad}/100$$

FASTENER COST

$$\text{Unit cost} \frac{\$/1000 \times 100}{1000} \quad \text{. . . . . . . . . . . . . . . . . . . .} \$\underline{\quad}/100$$

TOOLING COST

*Fixtures*

Cost of fixtures . . . . . . . . . . . . . . . . . . . . . . . . . . . . . . . . . $_____

Anticipated useful life . . . . . . . . . . . . . . . . . . . . . . . . . . . _____ years

$$\text{Cost/hr} = \frac{\text{Total cost}}{\text{Life} \times \text{hrs/year}} \quad \text{. . . . . . . . . . . . . . . .} \$\underline{\quad}/\text{hr}$$

$$\text{Cost/fastener} = \frac{\text{Cost/hr} \times 100}{\text{Assemblies/hr} \times \text{Fasteners/assembly}} \text{. . . . . .} \$\underline{\quad}/100$$

*Tools*

$$\text{Cost/fastener} = \frac{\text{Initial cost} \times 100}{\text{Expected number of fastenings}} \text{. . . . . . . . . . .} \$\underline{\quad}/100$$

LABOR COST

Cost/hr . . . . . . . . . . . . . . . . . . . . . . . . . . . . . . . . . . . . . . . $_____

$$\text{Cost/fastener} = \frac{\text{Cost/hr} \times 100}{\text{Assemblies/hr} \times \text{Fasteners/assembly}} \text{. . . . .} \$\underline{\quad}/100$$

HANDLING COSTS (If not part of overhead)

Labor cost of handling to and from machine . . . . . . . $_____/hr

Handling Cost/fastener =

$$\frac{\text{Cost/hr} \times 100}{\text{Assemblies/hr} \times \text{Fasteners/assembly}} \quad \$\underline{\quad}/100$$

MAINTENANCE COSTS

$$\frac{\text{Machine costs} \times \text{Yearly maintenance rate} \times 100}{\text{Hrs/year} \times \text{Assemblies/hr} \times \text{Fasteners/assembly}} \text{. . . . . . . . .} \$\underline{\quad}/100$$

COST OF SUPPLEMENTARY OPERATION (Figured on per 100 fastener basis)

Punching, Drilling, Tapping, Grinding, Cleaning, Polishing,

Other . . . . . . . . . . . . . . . . . . . . . . . . . . . . . . . . . . . . . . . $_____/100

OVERHEAD COSTS . . . . . . . . . . . . . . . . . . . . . . . . . . . . . . . . . . $_____/100

*Total Costs*_____

* Courtesy *Machine Design.*

5. What are the principal methods by which adhesives develop strength after they have been applied.

6. What are some advantages of the pressure-sensitive tape-type adhesives?

7. Is it better to design an adhesive joint so that the load will cause shear or cleavage? Why?

8. How may stress and peel be minimized at the edges of an adhesive lap joint?

9. How can corner joints be made to resist both peel and cleavage?

10. Compare the room-temperature shear strength of vinyl phenolic adhesives with other common adhesives.

11. How is the amount of adhesive needed for a particular joint determined?

12. What are some advantages of a dry-film adhesive?

13. What may be the principal cost considerations in making adhesive joints other than the cost of the adhesive itself?

14. How does an Acme thread differ from a square thread?

15. How does the unified-thread series differ from the American standard?

16. What class of thread fit would you recommend for a screw in a measuring instrument?

17. What type of set-screw point would generally be recommended for fastening a pulley on a shaft?

18. Name the two main types of self-tapping screws.

19. How do stove bolts differ from machine screws?

20. Explain how each of the following lock nuts functions: insert type, pressure type, and washer type.

21. What application do threaded inserts serve?

22. Name some advantages of using small rivets as a fastening method.

23. What application do explosive rivets serve?

24. In what respect is a Rollpin similar to a taper pin?

25. Explain the principle of groove-type pins.

26. What type of retaining ring can be used to help eliminate end play?

27. Describe three different principles used in quick-turn fasteners.

28. How does mechanical fastening of plastic parts differ from fastening metal parts?

29. Name the principal factors involved in calculating fastening costs.

### PROBLEMS

1. What would the maximum shear strength be of a joint having a lap area of 2 sq in. if a vinyl phenolic adhesive were used and tested at room temperature? How would this compare with epoxy resin? What would the cost ratio be for the two adhesives?

2. How long should semi-tubular rivets be for fastening two pieces of 16-gauge metal together? How long would full tubular rivets be for the same job?

3. What would the maximum shear loading be for a $\frac{1}{4}$-in. diameter semi-tubular 5056-S-O aluminum rivet? How does this load compare with that of a SAE C1010 annealed steel rivet?

4. What would the tooling cost be per 100 for a quick-release-type fastener that required a fixture for installation costing $125? The fixture will be used over a period of three years on the average of 20 hrs per week based on a regular 40-hr week. Thirty assemblies are turned out per hour each with two fasteners. The initial cost of the drill press needed for the operation is $350. This cost is shared equally with another operation in the plant.

## ADHESIVE REFERENCES

*The Tool Engineers Handbook*, American Society of Tool and Manufacturing Engineers, McGraw-Hill Book Company, Inc., New York, 1959.

Been, J. L., *Adhesive Bonding*, McGraw-Hill Book Company, Inc., New York, 1955.

Black, J. M., and R. F. Blomquist, "Development of Improved Structural Epoxy-Resin Adhesives and Bonding Processes for Metal," *Forest Products Laboratory Report No. 2008*, Madison, 1954.

Butzlaff, H. R., and K. F. Charter, "Adhesives May Solve Your Bonding Problems," *Welding Engineer*, October, 1961.

*Epon® Adhesives Manual*, Shell Chemical Company, Pittsburg, Cal.

Gould, Bernard, "Guide to Adhesives Selection," *Adhesives Age*, March, 1959.

Humke, R. K., "Choosing and Using Rubber Base Adhesives," *Machine Design*, January, 1959.

Siner, S. J., "Shaped Pellets Aid Epoxy Bonding," *American Machinist/Metalworking Manufacturing*, September, 1961.

*Welding Handbook*, American Welding Society, 4th ed., New York, 1960.

## FASTENER REFERENCES

Dwyer, John J., Jr., "A Production Man's Guide to Fastening Devices," *American Machinist/Metalworking Manufacturing Special Report No. 464*, Sept. 8, 1958.

*The Fasteners Book, Machine Design*, Sept. 29, 1960.

Heilig, Charles E., Jr., "An Engineer's Guide to Blind Riveting Practices." *American Machinist/Metalworking Manufacturing Special Report No. 478*, Sept. 7, 1959.

Laughner, V. H., and A. D. Hargan, *Handbook of Fastening and Joining Metal Parts*, McGraw-Hill Book Co., Inc., 1956.

Parks, J. A., "Quick Operating Fasteners," *Machine Design*, December 25, 1958.

*Society of Automotive Engineers Handbook*, Society of Automotive Engineers Inc. 485 Lexington Ave., New York 17, N.Y.

Soled, Julius P. E., *Fasteners Handbook*, Reinhold Publishing Corporation, New York, 1957.

Wallenbrock, R. E., "Fastening and Joining Plastic Parts," *Machine Design*, February, 1956.

# 16

# COLD
# FORMING

**T**HE COLD FORMING of metal, as practiced today, offers modern industry many advantages in the production of complex parts. The process is generally associated with a variety of methods used in forming sheet and plate, but it is also used in making extrusions and in impact forming of bar stock. Much of the current success of cold forming can be attributed to the development of devices that automatically move the workpiece from one station to another.

## PHYSICAL PROPERTIES AND DESIGN PRINCIPLES

In cold forming, it is important not only to take advantage of modern progressive-feeding equipment but to utilize to full advantage the physical properties gained from the process. From previous chapters we have learned how cold working can increase strength and rigidity. This knowledge is important, since it enables the designer to choose the right gauge of material for a given product. By the *right* gauge is usually meant the thinnest gauge that will give the desired results. Knowing which gauge of metal to use can produce significant savings.

Many design and fabrication techniques are available that add strength and rigidity to simple parts fabricated in sheet metal. For example, strength can be incorporated into the structure by means of flanges, ribs, corrugations, beads, etc. (Fig. 16-1).

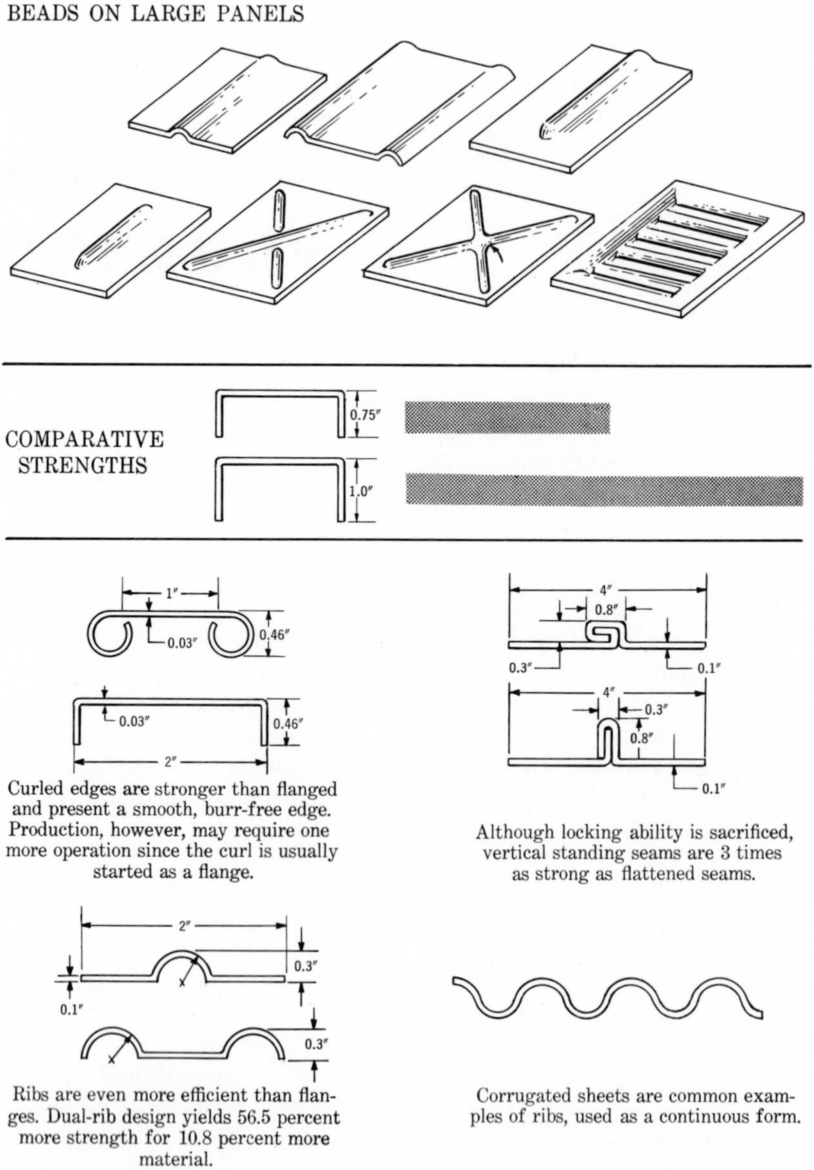
BEADS ON LARGE PANELS
COMPARATIVE STRENGTHS
0.75″
1.0″
1″
0.03″
0.46″
0.03″
0.46″
2″
Curled edges are stronger than flanged and present a smooth, burr-free edge. Production, however, may require one more operation since the curl is usually started as a flange.
4″
0.8″
0.3″
0.1″
4″
0.3″
0.8″
0.1″
Although locking ability is sacrificed, vertical standing seams are 3 times as strong as flattened seams.
2″
0.3″
0.1″
0.3″
Ribs are even more efficient than flanges. Dual-rib design yields 56.5 percent more strength for 10.8 percent more material.
Corrugated sheets are common examples of ribs, used as a continuous form.

**Fig. 16-1.** Methods of increasing strength and rigidity on sheet metal parts (courtesy *Machine Design*).

Although ribs, beads, and flanges are generally thought of in connection with flat stock, they can be equally effective on cylindrical shapes. Sometimes beads serve the dual purpose of adding strength and taking care of excess metal. An example of this is "dishpanning," the bulge normally encountered when fabricating large drawn shells. A number of shallow beads not only eliminate the undesirable bulge but add rigidity and strength (Fig. 16-2).

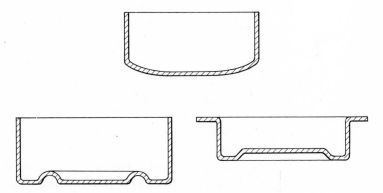

**Fig. 16-2.** Beads used in the bottom of a container add strength and eliminate the "dishpanning" effect of drawing.

A comparison of the physical properties of hot-rolled and cold-drawn steels is given in Table 16-1.

**TABLE 16-1.**

### Comparison of Physical Characteristics of Hot-Rolled and Cold-Drawn Steel

| AISI Number | Condition of Steel | Tensile Strength (psi) | Yield Point (psi) | Brinell Hardness | Machinability Rating (%) |
|---|---|---|---|---|---|
| C1020 | Hot-rolled | 65,000 | 43,000 | 143 | 50 |
| C1020 | Cold-drawn | 78,000 | 66,000 | 156 | 60 |
| 4140 | Hot-rolled | 89,000 | 62,000 | 187 | 57 |
| 4140 | Cold-drawn | 102,000 | 90,000 | 223 | 66 |

You will notice, in comparing the materials listed, that there is considerable increase in tensile strength, yield strength, hardness, and machinability of the cold-drawn as compared to the hot-rolled material. The most marked change is in yield strength, which increases from 43,000 to 66,000 in the case of the low-carbon steel, and from 62,000 to 90,000 for the alloy steel.

Many similar metalworking operations can be done either hot or cold. Hot working is done at a temperature high enough to produce recrystallization. If the metal is worked at the time recrystallization takes place, little or no strain hardening results. Cold forming, on the other hand, is done below the recrystallization temperature of the metal, and considerable strain hardening results. Recrystallization occurs at widely differing temperatures, tin for example recrystallizes at 25°F, aluminum alloys at about 600°F and low-carbon steel at about 1000°F.

The principal methods of cold forming involve dies. As with plastic materials, metals can be formed by closed (matching) dies or by single die-forming methods. Matched-die methods, including manufacture and use, die sets, and die classification, will be described next, and then we shall turn our attention to the various kinds of presses and their use.

## MATCHED-DIE METHODS

### Manufacture and Use

Dies usually represent a considerable investment. This is particularly true if the dies are matched. The term *matched dies* refers to dies in which the punch matches the die to very close tolerances. These dies are used for accurately forming parts in high production, such as household appliances and auto-body parts. They are usually cut out of steel, cast iron, or semisteel on duplicating mills or die-sinking machines (Fig. 16-3). Many hours of filing and polishing are needed to bring them to the desired finish and tolerance.

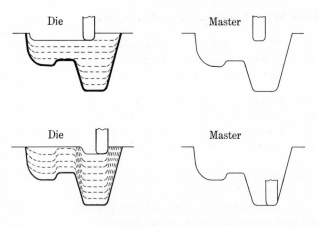

**Fig. 16-3.** The duplicating mill is used to rough- and finish-cut a die cavity, using a master pattern.

Shorter-run matching dies can be made by casting both components. In this process, whether the dies are made out of epoxy resin or low-melting-point zinc alloys, the method is much the same.

The pattern is made of wood or plaster. It is given several protective coatings and is covered with a parting agent. A box is built around it, and the die is cast over it. The pattern is removed, and the punch is then cast into the die. Provision must be made for the material thickness

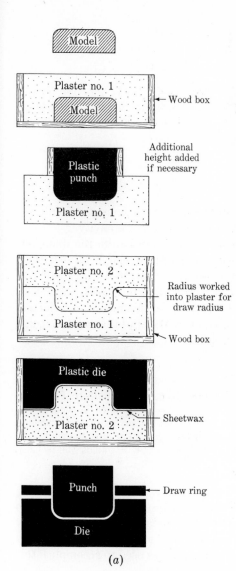

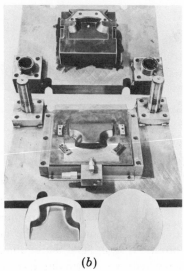

(b)

**Fig. 16-4.** (a) The process of making matched plastic dies. (b) A matched plastic die and formed part (courtesy Ren Plastics Inc.).

between the punch and die. This is taken care of by layers of sheet wax or, in some cases, felt cloth (Fig. 16-4).

If the materials are resilient, as in some epoxy-resin mixtures, no allowance is made for metal thickness between the punch and die. The punch is cast right on the die, with only parting material in between.

An example of an epoxy-resin die formed by this method is shown in Fig. 16-5.

Matched dies are used for drawing operations of forming, embossing, and ironing. They may also be used to restrike formed or partially formed work as in drop-hammer forging of sheet metal parts.

**Fig. 16-5.** Epoxy dies are used to form both large and small parts (courtesy Ren Plastics Inc.).

**Drawing Dies.** Drawing of sheet metal parts consist of pulling a sheet metal blank over a draw ring radius into a die cavity.

Deep draws usually require several redraws before the diameter-to-height proportion can be greatly reduced. A simple drawn shell, produced from 3003-0 aluminum, is shown in Fig. 16-6 with the necessary redraws. Formulas have been worked out for various materials (these may be found in handbooks), and thus the amount of reduction per draw can be quite accurately predicted. Material that work-hardens readily must be annealed between draws.

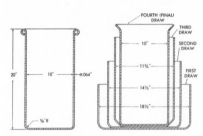

**Fig. 16-6.** The number of redraws necessary to produce a shell 20 in. deep and 10 in. in diameter out of 3003-0 aluminum are shown at the right (courtesy Reynolds Metals Co.).

IRONING. Sometimes it is desirable to produce drawn parts with considerable variation in the thickness of metal. For example, it may be necessary to have a relatively heavy end on a shell casing, or a heavy top to allow for machining. The drawing process used to accomplish this is known as *ironing*.

**Drop-Hammer Forging.** Drop-hammer forging uses matching dies to form sheet metal parts. The metal is not restricted, as it is in drawing. In order to avoid wrinkles, the dies must be carefully designed both for the shape of the blank and for the forming operation. The speed at which the hammer strikes the metal is also important. Air hammers can be closely controlled to apply a slow squeezing action at the start, followed by blows of increasing intensity.

Drop-hammer forging is used extensively in the aircraft industry for forming aluminum parts. The dies used are usually made out of

*Kirksite,* a low-melting-point alloy. These dies can be cast to shape and then touched up by grinding after they are mounted in the press. Dies needed for larger quantities are usually made from cast iron, semisteel, or steel.

## Die Sets

In general practice, when dies are spoken of, both the punch and the die are meant, as shown in Fig. 16-7. Not all dies are mounted in die sets as shown; they may be mounted directly in the press. This requires careful alignment of the punch and die each time they are taken out or put in. Since this can be very time-consuming, die sets are used. The punch and die need only be aligned in the set once. After the run is completed, the entire unit is placed in storage. When it is to be used again, the setup time required will be only a few minutes.

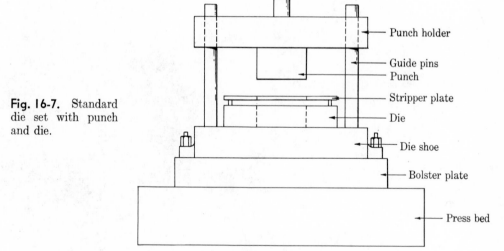

**Fig. 16-7.** Standard die set with punch and die.

Punch holder

Guide pins
Punch

Stripper plate
Die

Die shoe

Bolster plate

Press bed

The function of the stripper shown in Fig. 16-7 is to keep the metal from sticking to the punch as it is withdrawn from the die. Spring-action strippers are often used around the punch rather than the solid-type shown.

## Die Classification

Dies are classified both as to operation and as to their construction.

**Classification as to Operation.** All die work can be classified into four basic types of operations: cutting, bending, drawing, and squeezing. Each of these operations has several subdivisions as follows:

## PRESSWORKING OPERATIONS

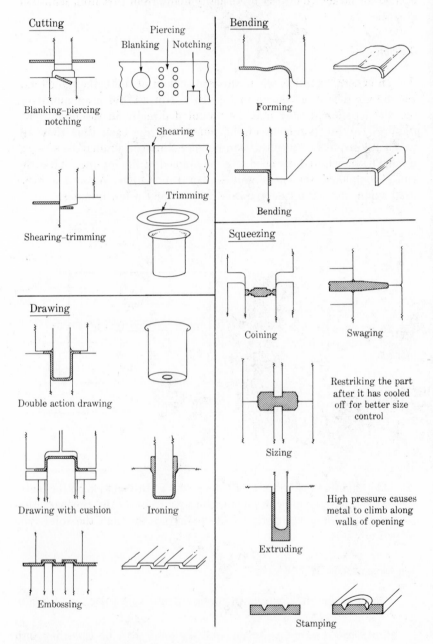

**Fig. 16-8.**  Four main pressworking operations.

Cutting—blanking, piercing, notching, shearing, trimming, and shaving

Bending—folding, seaming, curling, and angle bending

Drawing—forming, embossing, and ironing

Squeezing—coining, sizing, swaging, extruding, and upsetting

The four main types of die operations and some of the variations are shown schematically in Fig. 16-8.

**Classification According to Construction.** The die construction may be such that various operations are performed as the material moves in progressive steps through the die, or that more than one operation can be done at one station in the die. Dies are classified as simple, compound or combination, progressive, transfer, and special.

SIMPLE DIES. Simple dies perform one operation, usually forming or cutting.

COMPOUND OR COMBINATION DIES. These dies perform more than one operation in one location; that is, a part can be blanked and formed in one stroke of the press, as shown in Fig. 16-9.

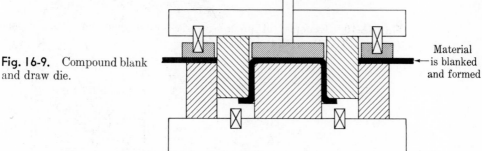

Knockout pin

**Fig. 16-9.** Compound blank and draw die.

Material is blanked and formed

PROGRESSIVE DIES. The combination dies have the disadvantage of crowding too many die elements into a limited area, which makes construction and maintenance costs higher. A progressive die is arranged with two or more stations so that the operations can be spread out over more area to reduce maintenance costs and increase operating speeds. Examples of progressive die work are shown in Fig. 16-10.

TRANSFER DIES. Transfer dies are used where the complexity, shape, or size of the part does not permit it to be fed from station to station. Transfer dies incorporate a mechanism for moving the part from one die to the next (Fig. 16-11). The transfer mechanism is powered by the stroke of the press ram. Also shown in Fig. 16-11 is a "press pacer" used to move parts from one press to another. Feed fingers pick the part out of the die and move it to the next press.

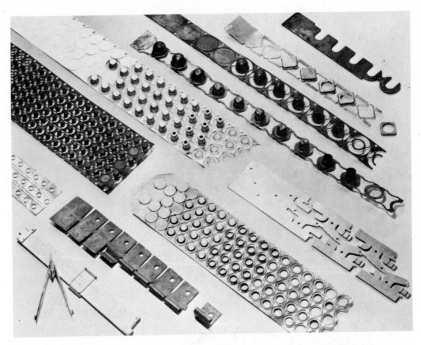

**Fig. 16-10.** Examples of progressive die-forming and cutting operations (courtesy The Brandes Press Inc.).

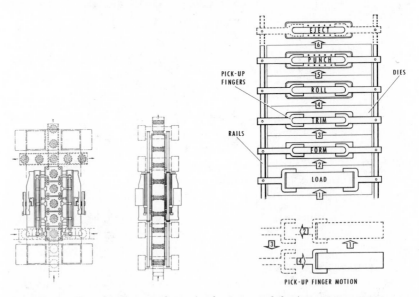

**Fig. 16-11.** Tranfer dies are shown in the press at left. A press-to-press transfer mechanism is shown in the center, with a more detailed view at the right.

## Presses

**Types and Uses.** Press classification is a broad subject, since much of it has resulted from common usage. There are many ways by which a press can be classified; some of these are the drive mechanism, or method of moving the ram; the number of drives; the frame type; the frame position; the action, or number of rams; the size, including tonnage, bolster area, and shut height; and the suspension, or number of connections for the ram.

Each of these points will be covered briefly; more complete information can be obtained by consulting the references at the end of the chapter.

DRIVES. Press drives can be broadly classified as mechanical or hydraulic. There are several types of mechanical drives, such as crank-shaft, eccentric, cam, toggle, rack and pinion, screw, and knuckle. The most widely used of these are the crank, eccentric shafts, and toggle mechanism, as shown in Fig. 16-12.

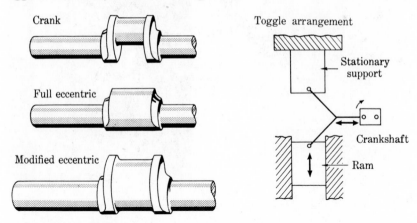

**Fig. 16-12.** The crank and eccentric are among the most commonly used methods of imparting motion to the ram. The eccentric and toggle are used where a slower squeezing action is desired.

The crank method of converting rotary motion to straight thrust provides a variable mechanical advantage between the drive and the ram. Near the bottom of the stroke, a toggle effect is obtained, giving a high mechanical advantage. Presses are rated by the power they develop at or near the bottom of the stroke.

NUMBER OF DRIVES. The number of drives refers to the number of places from which the crankshaft, cam, or whatever driving mechanism is used, is being driven. For example, a small press may be driven from one flywheel, whereas large presses may have as many as four drives and four flywheels.

FRAME TYPE. The most easily distinguished characteristic of a press is its frame. Common types of frames are C-frame and straight-side.

*C-frame presses.* C-frame presses get their name from the C-shaped upright frame (Fig. 16-13). They include open-back inclinable (OBI), gap-frame, adjustable-bed, and horning presses.

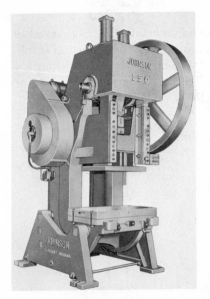 

**Fig. 16-13.** C-frame presses (courtesy Johnson Machine and Press Corp.).

The OBI press is one of industry's most versatile presses. It is usually a low-tonnage press, ranging from a 1-ton bench model to a 200-ton floor press. The fact that it has an open back and can be inclined backward up to 45 deg facilitates the removal of both the manufactured part and the scrap.

The gap-frame press is essentially the same as the OBI but is not inclinable. The frame is of one solid piece, and it may or may not have an open back.

Adjustable-bed presses provide for raising and lowering the bed to suit the required die space. Some of these presses allow the bed to be swung out from under the slide so that a horn can be used in place of the bed (Fig. 16-14).

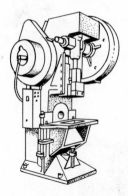 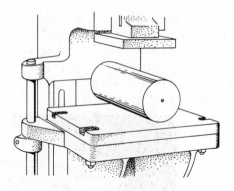

**Fig. 16-14.** Adjustable-bed and horning-press combination.

Horning presses are useful for secondary operations such as punching holes in formed parts. If the holes are made prior to forming, distortion results. Oftentimes, a die on the ram is all that is needed.

*Straight-side Presses.* Straight-side presses are made for larger die areas and higher tonnages than the C-frame presses can accommodate. The straight-side frame gives a strong, rigid construction. Two common types of straight-side presses are shown in Fig. 16-15.

FRAME POSITION. The three common positions of the press frame are vertical, inclined, and horizontal. Vertical is the most common. The OBI is an example of the inclined. Some presses are made with a fixed angle.

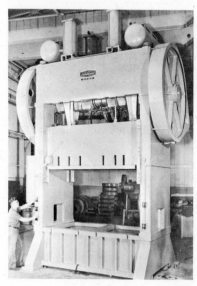 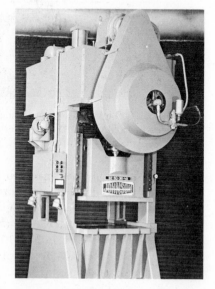

**Fig. 16-15.** Two common types of straight-side-frame presses (courtesy Johnson Machine and Press Corp.).

The horizontal press is usually small and of the high-speed type. Ejection of piece parts and scrap presents little difficulty owing to the free fall of both items. Although horizontal presses can be counted on for high production, there is also more wear on the sliding parts than on a vertical press. A versatile horizontal press is the multislide press shown in (Fig. 16-16).

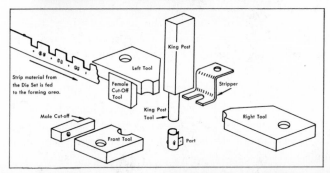

**Fig. 16-16.** A four-slide automatic combination press can be used for forming either wire or ribbon stock. Strip material is fed in and formed by the four tools around the king post (courtesy A. H. Nilson Machine Company).

These machines are made so that several slides can be used to complete the forming operation around a stake. Strip material is fed into the press, progressively stamped, notched, bent, formed around a stake, cut off, and ejected. Examples of the type of work done on strip material are shown in Fig. 16-16. Some rather complicated parts can be made at rates of 125 per min. These machines are also used for wire-forming operations.

ACTION. Press action refers to the number of rams or slides on the press. There may be one, two, or three as follows:

*Single action.* A single-action press is the conventional type, having one ram located in the top, or crown, of the press.

*Double action.* A double-action press has a ram within a ram. The outer ram comes down first, to seat the material and keep the right amount of pressure on it. This is especially important, in deep-drawing or forming operations, to control the rate at which the metal is allowed to flow into the cavity. If the metal is allowed to move in too fast, it will wrinkle; if too slow, it will thin out or may even tear. This type of work is often done on a toggle press. The toggle arrangement is used to operate the outer ram.

*Triple action.* A triple-action press has the arrangement of the double action plus an additional ram that is located in the bed of the press. This third ram can be made to move upward after the other two have completed their action.

SIZE. Press size is expressed by a combination of the following factors: tonnage, bolster area, and shut height.

*Tonnage.* The size of a press is often designated by the number of tons of force that can be exerted by the ram. The tonnage rating on the nameplate of the press usually has a built-in safety factor. However, exceeding the rated capacity leads to excess wear and should not be practiced.

The size of a mechanical crank- or eccentric-drive press is directly proportional to the area of the crank at the bearing. This can be approximated by multiplying the cross-sectional area of the crankshaft at the bearing by the shear strength of the material it is made of. The tonnage rating is made with the stroke in or near its bottom position.

The tonnage rating of hydraulic presses is proportional to the size of the piston diameter and the amount of oil pressure on it. Unlike the mechanical press, the pressure needed can be easily adjusted. Hydraulic presses range in size from small bench models of 50 tons to large 50,000-ton forging presses. The hydraulic press has the advantage over the mechanical-type press of having an easily adjusted stroke length and pressure variation. This makes it an ideal press for experimental work. The mechanical-type press is usually faster in operation.

*Bolster area.* The bolster area refers to the size of the plate (bolster) on the press bed. The bolster plate is bolted to the press bed. Various T-slots and holes are made in the bolster plate to facilitate clamping arrangements for dies and die sets. A standard arrangement of T-slot location and mounting holes has been worked out by the Joint Industry Conference (JIC).

*Shut height.* The shut height of a press refers to the distance between the ram and the bolster when the stroke is in bottom position and the adjustment is up. The shut height of the press determines the height of the dies that can be used, since their height must not be more than the shut-height dimension of the press.

SUSPENSION. Suspension refers to the number of connections between the drive and the ram. On most crank-type presses, the connecting rod serves also as the suspension for the ram. Other presses may have two or more rod arrangements that hold the ram to the drive mechanism and suspend it between slides on the sides of the press.

**Press Identification.** With so many factors used to designate press size and type, an industry standard has been worked out. A JIC standard press designation is as follows:

$OBI - 22 - 12\frac{3}{4} \times 17\frac{1}{2}$

Bed size left to right and front to back<br>Tonnage capacity<br>Type of press

Other designations in place of the OBI shown are: S, single action; T, triple action; D, double action. A number following the letter indicates the points of suspension used. For example, T2 would be the code for a triple-action press with two points of suspension from the drive to the ram.

**Special Presses.** Presses that do not come in the classifications mentioned above, but which are widely used, are automatic presses, turret punch presses, and press brakes.

AUTOMATIC PRESSES. Automatic presses are also referred to as dieing machines. In this type of press the top structure consists of a die set as shown in Fig. 16-17. The crankshaft is below the bed, re-

**Fig. 16-17.** An automatic press or dieing machine (courtesy The Brandes Press Co.).

sulting in a low center of gravity which minimizes vibration, ordinarily a problem on machines operating at speeds up to 240 strokes per minute. These presses range from 15- to 4,000-ton capacity.

Turret punch presses. A turret punch press consists of two cylindrical turrets mounted horizontally on the upper and lower arms of a C-frame (Fig. 16-18). The turrets are synchronized and rotate together to the desired station. An indexing device locks the turrets and assures correct alignment of the punch and die selected for use.

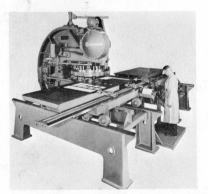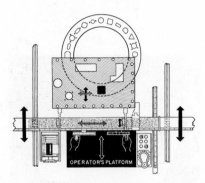

**Fig. 16-18.** Turret-type punch press used to punch holes in sheet and plate stock. This press may be equipped with a tape-controlled unit that automatically positions the work, selects the right tool from the turret station, and trips the press (courtesy Wiedemann Machine Co.).

Mounted in the turrets are numerous punches and dies depending on the job specifications. Complicated hole patterns, including openings of many sizes and shapes, can be located and punched either manually or by tape control. A gaging table facilitates material location and movement. Both in and out dimensions and crosswise dimensions are controlled by graduated handwheels, or by tape, to $\pm 0.007$-in. tolerance.

Press brakes. The press brake is a modified C-frame press used extensively for forming, bending, corrugating, beading, and straightening long sheets. It can also be used for punching, blanking, notching, piercing, and trimming of both small and large parts. With proper dies, rectangular, curved, straight, or tapered work can be produced (Fig. 16-19).

Press-brake dies are of comparatively simple construction. They may be fabricated from combinations of standard square and round bar stock. Several press-brake dies and their applications are shown in Fig. 16-20.

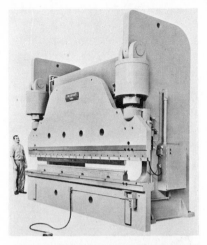

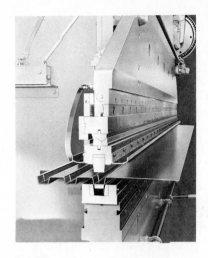

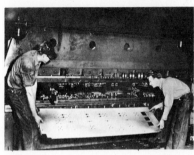

**Fig. 16-19.** The press brake, with two examples of the type of work for which it is used (courtesy Cincinnati Shaper Co.).

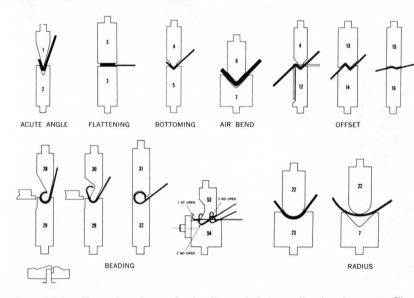

**Fig. 16-20.** Examples of press-brake dies and their application (courtesy Cincinnati Shaper Co.).

## SINGLE-DIE-FORMING METHODS

In order to decrease both the cost and the time involved in making matched dies, several single-die-forming methods have been developed. These methods are generally limited to the lighter-gauge metals, except in the case of explosive forming. Single-die-forming processes include rubber forming, hydroforming, stretch forming, explosive forming, and electromagnetic forming.

### Rubber Forming

Rubber forming is a convenient method of forming nonferrous light-gauge materials. Basically, it consists of having one half of the die made out of metal or plastic and the other half out of rubber. The fact that the rubber changes shape readily makes it a practical forming medium. The rubber used must be of the right hardness, that is, soft enough to cause the metal to flow but not so soft that it fills up the cavities before maximum pressure is applied.

**Guerin Process.** The Guerin process, shown in Fig. 16-21, is used to form sheet metal into relatively shallow parts. The male dies are made of metal, and several layers of rubber, held in a retainer, serve as the female die. The male dies are usually grouped on sliding platens so that they can be easily moved in and out under the press ram. Materials formed by the Guerin process are mostly aluminum and magnesium alloys; however, stainless steel as thick as 0.1875 in. has been used successfully. Holes can be punched in annealed aluminum and stainless up to 0.050 in. thick.

The male dies for rubber forming can be made of steel, Kirksite, Masonite, plastic, or aluminum. It is quite often desirable to "face" plastic or Masonite dies with thin sheet steel.

Sharp corners should not be used in the die design, since the rubber will not flow into them. Where sharp corners are necessary, they can be taken care of by metal die inserts. Locating pins are used to keep the metal from sliding around before it is formed.

**Marforming.** Marforming is similar to the Guerin process except that a pressure pad is used to keep the stock from wrinkling and tearing as the draw takes place. It is used for deeper draws working with correspondingly thicker rubber sections and higher pressure capabilities. Draws up to 8 in. can be made on 8-in.-diameter 1100-0 aluminum cups. Hydraulic stripping action can also be incorporated, as most rubber forming is done on hydraulic-type presses.

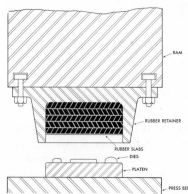

RAM

RUBBER RETAINER

RUBBER SLABS

DIES

PLATEN

PRESS BED

**Fig. 16-21.** Punch and die arrangement for the Guerin process and a large hydraulic press arranged for multiple feeding (courtesy E. W. Bliss Company).

**Bulging.** The process of bulging, or making a cylinder with enlarged diameter, can be readily accomplished on nonferrous metals by the use of a rubber punch and an appropriate die (as shown in Fig. 16-22) or with hydraulic pressure.

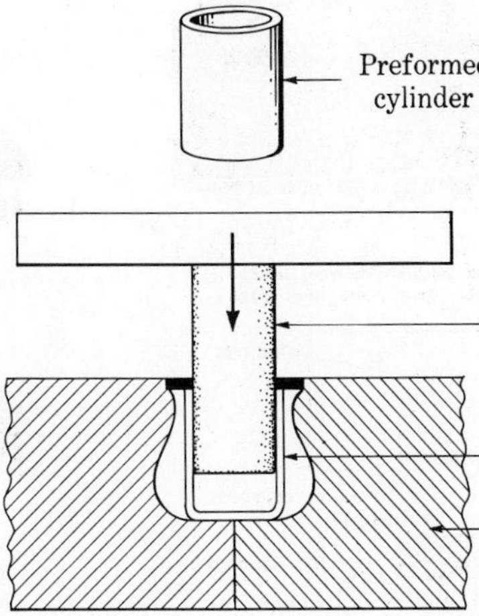

**Fig. 16-22.** The rubber punch is brought down, causing metal to flow out against the walls of the die. The die halves are then separated, and the bulged part is removed.

Preformed cylinder

Rubber punch

Blank

Die

## Hydroforming

Hydroforming, as the name implies, is forming with fluid pressure. In this case the pressure is furnished by hydraulic fluid on one side of a rubber diaphragm, the part to be formed being located on the other side (Fig. 16-23). The diaphragm is sealed to withstand hydraulic pressures up to 15,000 psi when backed up by the workpiece.

In the hydroforming process, the blank is placed on the blank holder and enough pressure is applied to hold it in place. The punch is then moved up against the metal blank. As the punch moves up into the forming-dome cavity, pressure continues to increase, causing the metal to flow evenly around the punch. After forming, the hydraulic pressure is released and the punch is retracted, leaving the formed part on top of the blank holder.

The advantage of hydroforming is that there is very little, if any, thinning of the metal being formed. The reason for this is that the metal is tightly gripped between the punch and the diaphragm, allowing it to ease the metal over the form without slipping. Hydroforming can usually perform, in one or two operations, what would take four or five draws by ordinary pressworking methods, as shown in Fig. 16-24.

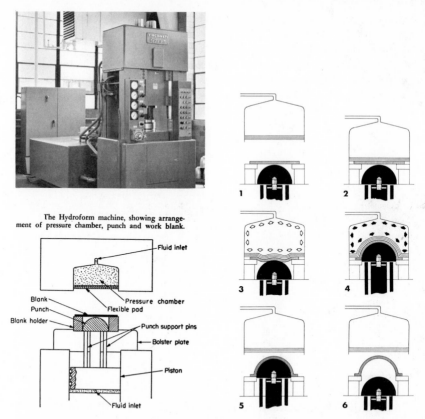

The Hydroform machine, showing arrangement of pressure chamber, punch and work blank.

Fluid inlet

Blank
Punch
Blank holder

Pressure chamber
Flexible pad

Punch support pins

Bolster plate

Piston

Fluid inlet

**Fig. 16-23.** The hydroforming cycle begins with (1) dome raised and the blank in place. (2) The dome is lowered, clamping the blank to the holder, and (3) starting pressure is applied to force the blank against the punch. (4) The punch moves upward, increasing the pressure and forming the part. (5) After the forming pressure is released, the dome rises and (6) the work is stripped from the punch (courtesy the Cincinnati Milling Machine Co.).

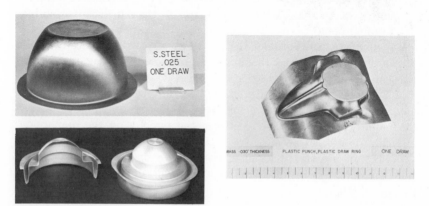

S.STEEL
.025
ONE DRAW

BRASS .030" THICKNESS    PLASTIC PUNCH, PLASTIC DRAW RING    ONE DRAW

**Fig. 16-24.** Parts formed by one or two draws with the hydroforming process (courtesy The Cincinnati Milling Machine Co.).

### Stretch Forming

Stretch forming of metal consists of placing the sheet material in tensile load over a form block. The material is stressed beyond its elastic limit, causing it to take a permanent set.

In bending, fibers on the inside of the neutral axis are compressed and those on the outside are stretched. In stretch forming, all of the fibers are stretched, but those on the inside radius of the bend are stretched less than those on the outside (Fig. 16-25). Since the metal is placed under one type of load in stretch forming, there is no *springback* (attempt to regain some of its former position). However, allowance must be made for dimensional changes that occur in the metal being used; that is, during stretching, the length of the part increases and the width decreases.

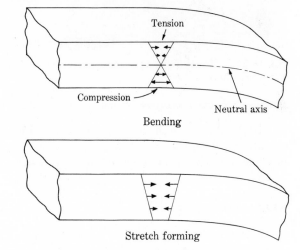

**Fig. 16-25.** Theory of stretch forming.

There are several methods of stretch forming, but only contour-forming types will be discussed here.

**Contour Forming.** Contour stretch forming is used to produce compound curves in sheet stock (Fig. 16-26). The ends of the stock are gripped in hydraulically operated serrated jaws. Stretching is accomplished by one or more hydraulic cylinders moving up under the die. Forming by this method is restricted to parts that do not have sharp edges, which tend to restrict the stretch in local areas that would lead to fractures.

The forming block is usually highly polished and lubricated. Sometimes, a blanket of thin rubber or fiber glass is used to avoid the cost of a highly polished surface or the need of lubricants.

Contour stretch forming is very useful in making preliminary models of aircraft and automotive parts. It is also used on a production basis for forming truck and trailer bodies.

**Fig. 16-26.** Stretch-forming a compound curve in sheet stock (courtesy Sheridan-Gray Inc.).

### Explosive and Electromagnetic Forming

Both explosive and electromagnetic forming are single-die-forming operations. Since they are relatively new processes they are described in Chap. 30, where new manufacturing processes are discussed.

## METAL SPINNING

Spinning is a method of forming symmetrical shapes such as spheres, cones, parabolas, etc., in sheet metal by means of a rotating form or chuck. The forming is done by application of pressure on the metal with a roller or spinning tool that causes it to conform to the shape of the rotating wood or metal chuck. The spinning process can be divided into two main methods—conventional spinning and displacement spinning (often referred to as power roll forming).

### Conventional Spinning

The spinning method originated to fill a need for the small-quantity production of cylindrical shapes, but it now can produce parts in lots of several thousand. This advancement has resulted from the development of semiautomatic and automatic spinning equipment, and from the realization by methods engineers that spinning, combined with other operations such as roll forming, can produce parts that are difficult or impossible to make by any other method. Spinning may be used after drawing as a final operation in perfecting contours, truing diameters, and removing tapers from cylindrical draws. Drawn articles may also be spun to form odd shapes, necks, and flanges.

Hand spinning requires skill and experience. The metal must be made to flow at the proper rate, or wrinkles and tears will result. A blank somewhat larger than the diameter of the finished shell is placed between a live center and the chuck. The tools used consist mainly of steel rods with various-shaped ends and long wooden handles (Fig. 16-27).

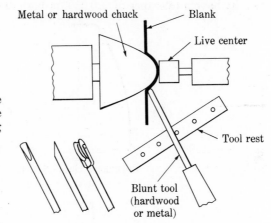

**Fig. 16-27.** Forming the metal to the shape of the chuck on a metal-spinning lathe.

Other tools are used to perform various operations such as trimming the top edge or rolling a bead to give strength and rigidity to the upper edge.

The size of parts that can be spun is limited only by the equipment available. Gap lathes are used for medium-sized jobs, but large jobs (16 ft in diameter or more) require the construction of special equipment (Fig. 16-28).

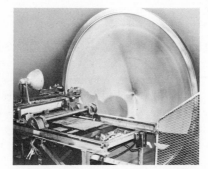

**Fig. 16-28.** Spinning a stainless-steel storage-tank head on a 144-in. maximum diameter spinning machine (courtesy Walker Stainless Equipment Co., Inc.).

Forming operations that are quite severe require several chucks, as shown in Fig. 16-29.

Metals that can be spun at room temperature include aluminum and its alloys, copper, brass, and the lighter gauges of stainless steel. Room-temperature formability of magnesium and titanium is poor, but with the application of heat they can be readily worked.

The tolerances of spun parts are larger than those for parts made with matching dies; however, since many sheet metal parts do not require close tolerances, the spinning process is entirely adequate. Small parts up to 5 in. in diameter usually have a tolerance of ±0.015 on the diameter and ±0.030 on the length. Larger parts, 5 to 20 in. in diameter, usually have a tolerance of ±0.030 for both diameter and length.

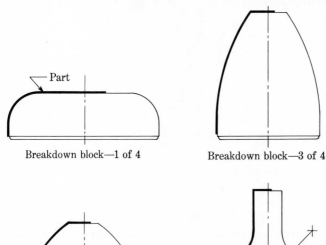

Breakdown block—1 of 4

Breakdown block—3 of 4

Breakdown block—2 of 4

Finishing block—4 of 4

**Fig. 16-29.** Spinning requires several blocks or chucks when the height-to-diameter ratio is high. A relatively large area of metal has to be moved, and several breakdown steps are needed to maintain control of the metal flow.

## Displacement Spinning or Power Roll Forming

Power roll forming is a cold-rolling process in which material in a blank is caused to flow over a rotating mandrel. Forming is accomplished by one or more hardened-steel rollers which travel parallel to and at a preset distance from the surface of the mandrel during the forming operation (Fig. 16-30). As the mandrel and workpiece are revolved, the rollers, which may be either hydraulically or mechanically actuated, displace the blank material in a spiral manner. The contours of the formed piece are identical with those of the mandrel, and the wall thickness can be closely controlled. When precision parts are desired, 0.015 or 0.020 in. can be left for machining.

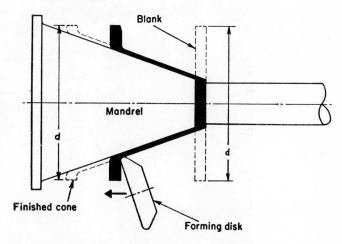

**Fig. 16-30.** Schematic diagram showing the principle of the flow-turning process. Note that the diameter of the blank is the same as that of the finished part.

The control over workpiece contours and wall thickness gives the process significant advantages over drawing and conventional spinning. Springback, encountered in both pressworking and conventional spinning, is eliminated. Rolling the metal increases its strength and hardness. There is also a beneficial effect on the granular structure of the metal. Tests have shown that flow turning can increase the tensile strength of the finished product by as much as 100 percent over that of the original metal.

In roll forming, no calculations as to blank diameter are needed, since the starting blank is the same diameter as the finished part. The workpiece material is drawn from the thickness of the blank rather than from the diameter. Cone-shaped parts are usually produced from flat blanks. Some parts, such as cylinders, require preformed blanks so that a sufficient volume of metal can be maintained for wall thickness. Preformed blanks can be made from partially machined forgings, partially machined centrifugal castings, drawn or machined cups, and welded cylindrical sections.

Generally, flow turning is limited to symmetrical cylindrical or conical shapes. Special setups can be made for elliptical shapes. The metal thickness that can be worked is usually not more than ½ in. The minimum diameter of the mandrel is also ½ in. Flow-turning equipment is shown in Fig. 16-31.

**Fig. 16-31.** A 70 by 72-in. vertical hydrospin machine capable of exerting 70,000 lb of force (courtesy Cincinnati Milling Machine Co.).

## ROLL FORMING

There are two main types of roll forming: one uses continuous-strip material for high-production work; the other uses sheet and plate stock.

### Continuous Roll Forming

Continuous roll forming utilizes a series of rolls to gradually change the shape of the metal. As the metal passes between the rolls in a fast-moving continuous strip, the cross-sectional shape is changed to the desired form. The forms are almost limitless in variation (Fig. 16-32).

The intricacy of the shape, the size of the section, the thickness, and the type of material will determine the number of rolls required. A simple angle or channel with straight web and flanges can usually

**Fig. 16-32.** A wide variety of shapes can be produced in continuous strip by roll forming (courtesy The Yoder Co.).

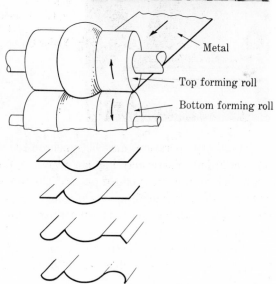

Metal

Top forming roll

Bottom forming roll

**Fig. 16-33.** Progressive rolls needed to form a curtain rail.

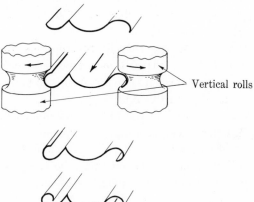

Vertical rolls

be formed with 3 or 4 pairs of rolls, whereas the more complicated shapes require up to 12 or more roll passes (Fig. 16-33). In addition, some straightening rolls and some idle-station rolls may be needed.

Most roll-formed parts require quite accurate stock width. The starting point of cold rolling is, therefore, flat rolled metal, either hot- or cold-rolled, as it comes from the rolling mills, in big coils. It is put through a multiple gang slitter and coiler at high speed, averaging only 2 or 3 min of actual cutting time per coil (Fig. 16-34).

**Fig. 16-34.** Rotary slitting machines can uncoil stock, slit it to a number of equal or unequal widths, and recoil it at a very high speed (courtesy The Yoder Co.).

Auxiliary operations may be synchronized with the cold-roll-forming operations. These may include edge trimming, spot or seam welding to make different types of open or closed seams on tubular shapes, cutting-to-length, notching, perforating, making functional or ornamental cuts, embossing and stenciling, curving, coiling, and ring forming.

In most cases these extra operations are performed automatically, without extra labor or reduction of the normal forming speed, which is about 100 fpm.

Allowing for unavoidable interruptions, the production per 8-hr day is upwards of 30,000 ft per machine, with one operator and one helper. Changeover from one set of rolls to another may, in most cases, be accomplished in 1 or 2 hr.

Materials used for roll forming include hot- and cold-rolled carbon steel, stainless steel, bronze, brass, copper, zinc, and aluminum. Magnesium and titanium can be rolled, but they need moderate amounts of heat. Vinyl-painted steel strip may be successfully formed, eliminating several secondary handling operations.

The size of sections that can be formed by rolling range up to $\frac{3}{4}$ in. thick and from a fraction of an inch up to 80 in. wide.

Tubular shapes are made with a series of rolls, as shown in Fig. 16-35. This cold-roll process can make lock seams, either inside or outside of the tube, and other scarf, lap, and flange seams.

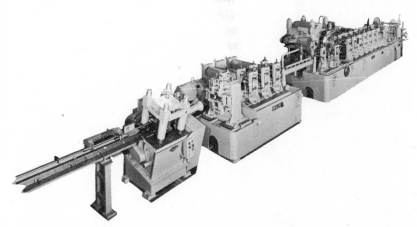

**Fig. 16-35.** A series of rolls is used to make resistance-welded steel tubing. Other tubing may be made with various types of joints of nonwelded construction (courtesy The McKay Machine Company).

Much of present-day tubing is roll-formed cold and then resistance-welded. A small bead or flash is formed on the outside of the tube by the metal being squeezed up from the seam. This weld flash is removed from the outside of the tube by two cutting tools mounted in adjustable tandem right behind the wheel-type welding electrodes. The removal of internal flash is seldom required. Various cold-formed resistance-welded tubes are shown in Fig. 16-36. Roll forming tube mills can produce between 30,000 and 50,000 ft of tubing, from ¼ to 4 in. in diameter, per 8-hr day. Tube wall thickness can vary from 0.020 to 0.156 in. Pipe mills produce sizes from ½ to 24 in. in diameter, with wall thicknesses ranging up to ¾ in.

### Sheet and Plate Bending Rolls

Plain and beaded cylinders, cones, ovals, etc., are fabricated on bending rolls. Bending-roll machines range in size from those that are able to roll heavy steel plate 1 in. thick, to small bench models used for light-gauge sheet metal work. In either case, the bending action takes place between rotating horizontal bending rolls. The most commonly used type is shown in Fig. 16-37. By adjusting the lower front roll up or down, various thicknesses of metal can be accommodated.

Bending rolls are used to fabricate a wide variety of parts, including production quantities of tanks and pipe. In heavy-gauge pipe

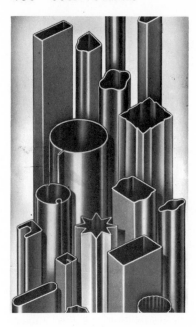

**Fig. 16-36.** Cold-formed resistance-welded tubing (courtesy The Yoder Co.).

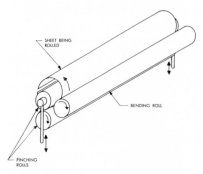

**Fig. 16-37.** Roll forming of sheet metal.

and tank manufacture, no attempt is made to close the circle completely. After the part is removed from the rolls, it is placed in a fixture to close the gap prior to welding.

## OTHER FORMING AND DRAWING METHODS

### Rotary Swaging

Rotary swaging is the process used to reduce the cross-sectional area of rods and tubes (Fig. 16-38).

The operations shown in Fig. 16-38 can be closely controlled, maintaining tolerances within ±0.0005 on small diameters and within ±0.005 on large diameters.

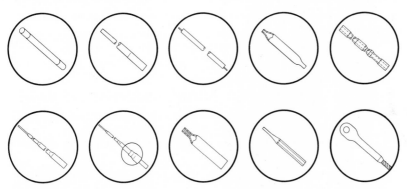

**Fig. 16-38.** Swaging is used to reduce the cross-sectional area of tubes and rods (courtesy The Torrington Co.).

Swaging is often spoken of as a cold-forging operation, because the metal forming takes place under the hammering blows of die sections. The swaging machine consists mainly of a hollow spindle which carries the die sections and rollers (Fig. 16-39).

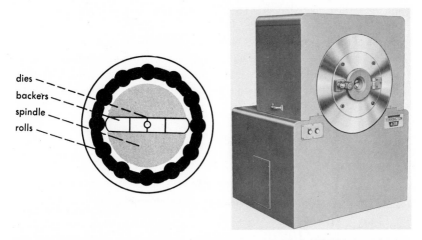

**Fig. 16-39.** The rotary swaging machine reduces the end of stock by a series of rollers that rotate over backer, forcing the dies together (courtesy The Torrington Co.).

As the machine is started, the outer rolls are moved outward by centrifugal force, but, as the hammers contact the opposite rolls, they are forced together, moving the dies together simultaneously. Approximately 1,200 to 6,000 blows per minute are struck by the dies. Under normal conditions the metallurgical qualities of the metal are improved. However, this is dependent on the condition of the metal before starting and on the amount of reduction desired, since too much reduction without proper annealing will result in fractures. The finish also is generally improved.

The material may be fed into the machine by hand, hydraulically, or by air. Power feeding is usually used on the larger, heavier pieces.

Some advantages of swaging are:

1. Swaging machines are relatively inexpensive and simple to operate, maintain, and repair.

2. Metal characteristics are generally improved.

3. Swaging furnishes an excellent means of attaching fittings to tubing or tubing to wire cable.

4. The operation is fast and requires very little setup time.

The main disadvantage of swaging is that the machine tends to be noisy, owing to its hammering, squeezing action. Maintenance problems result from failure to keep the dies clean or from the use of dies that are not suited to the operation involved.

### Cold Drawing

Rods, tubes, and extrusions are often given a cold-finishing operation to reduce the size, increase the strength, improve the finish, and provide better accuracy.

Bars or tubes that have been hot-rolled are prepared for drawing by first removing the oxide scale in a pickling acid. After the scale is removed, the material is washed in lime to remove the acid. The lime, plus soap or oil, acts as a good drawing lubricant. The process is shown schematically in Fig. 16-40.

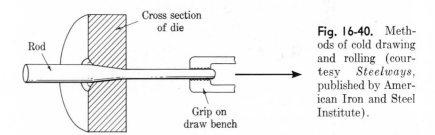

**Fig. 16-40.** Methods of cold drawing and rolling (courtesy *Steelways,* published by American Iron and Steel Institute).

Other methods of finishing bar stock involve turning and grinding. Ground stock is considered the aristocrat of cold-finished steel. It is extremely accurate and straight.

## QUESTIONS

1. What are some methods of adding strength, without additional weight, to fabricated metal parts?
2. Compare hot-rolled and cold-drawn C1020 steels as to tensile strength, yield strength, and machinability.
3. What is meant by the term matched dies?
4. Describe a relatively quick way of making matched dies for short-run operations.
5. What is the difference between drawing and ironing sheet-metal parts?
6. What purpose do die sets serve?
7. Tell the main purpose of each of the following die types: compound, progressive, and transfer.
8. What is the most common type of press drive?
9. What type of press is an OBI?
10. What is the main application of a horning press?
11. For what type of work is the multislide press suited?
12. What is a double-action press used for?
13. How is the shut height of a press determined?
14. Identify the following JIC press designation: D-150-28-32.
15. Describe a dieing machine.
16. To what type of work is the turret punch press well suited?
17. State briefly the applications of each of the following forming processes: Guerin process, hydroforming, and stretch forming.
18. What are some spinning operations that can be used to finish parts formed in a press?
19. How does power roll forming differ from spinning?
20. What may the production rate be on a continuous roll-forming machine in an eight-hour day?
21. Name some applications of swaging.

## PROBLEMS

1. The size press needed for a particular blanking operation can be calculated by the following formula: Blanking force = $(Lt\,S_s)/2000$, where $L$ = length of cutting edge, $t$ = thickness of material in in., and $S_s$ = ultimate shear strength of the material being blanked in psi. A safety factor is added to the answer to allow for die wear and changes in the material. Thus, the calculated blanking force is usually doubled. If shear is provided on the face of the punch or die by grinding at a slight angle, the force required for blanking is greatly reduced and the formula changes to

$$\text{Blanking force} = \frac{\dfrac{Lt\,S_s}{2000} \times t}{t + Sh}$$

where $Sh$ = the amount of shear in inches. The amount of shear used is usually the thickness of the material being blanked or less.

(a) What size press is required for making 6-in.-diameter blanks in 1/16-in.-thick 1100-0 aluminum with a shear strength of 9,500 psi.

(b) What would the blanking pressure be if a 0.0625-in. shear angle were ground on the punch?

2. When a part is to be formed the amount of material to allow for bending is as follows:

$$L = \frac{2\pi a}{360} (r + 0.40t) \text{ where } L = \text{length to allow in in., } a = \text{total number}$$

of degrees of bend, $r$ = inside bend radius in in., and $t$ = material thickness in in.

(a) How wide should the strip material be before forming it into a 2-in. angle iron? The material is $\frac{1}{8}$ in. thick. Angle iron size is given by the outside dimension. Bend radius $= t$.

(b) How wide would strip material have to be before forming 3-in.-wide channel iron $1\frac{1}{2}$ in. high and $\frac{1}{8}$ in. thick? Bend radius $= t$.

3. A 20-in.-diameter aluminum blank is to be drawn into a shell. A 50 percent reduction is made in the first draw; the two succeeding draws each make an additional 15 percent reduction. What is the size of the finished shell?

4. A cover 8 in. in diameter and 2 in. deep is to be formed from mild steel having an ultimate shear strength of 60,000 psi. The inside radius of bend is equal to $2t$. The material is $\frac{1}{8}$ in. thick. (a) What is the size of the blank? (b) What is the size of the press required for the blanking operation?

## REFERENCES

*Aluminum Forming*, Reynolds Metals Company, Louisville, 1958.

*ARDC Production Design Handbook*, United States Department of Commerce, Office of Technical Services, Washington, D.C., 1960.

Bartle, E. W., "Cutting Machine and Material Costs with Power Roll Forming," *The Tool Engineer*, November, 1957.

Coenen, Francis L., "Basic Tooling for Spinning Metals," *The Tool Engineer*, March, 1954.

*Cold Roll Forming*, The Yoder Company, Cleveland, 1956.

Eary, D. F., and E. A. Reed, *Techniques of Pressworking Sheet Metal*, Prentice-Hall, Inc., Englewood Cliffs, N.J., 1958.

*Forming and Bending*, Kaiser Aluminum, 1st ed., 1956.

"How To Select Swaging Equipment and Dies," *Metalworking*, 1959.

Strasser, F., "How Strong Are Stampings?" *Machine Design*, December, 1958.

Strasser, F., "Strengthening Metal Stampings," *Machine Design*, November 1, 1956.

# 17

# POWDER
# METALLURGY

**T**HE MANUFACTURE of parts from powdered metals can be briefly described as a process of placing metal powder in a mold and compressing it. After the compressed powder is removed from the mold, it is heated or sintered to give it strength.

Powder metallurgy is not a discovery of modern times. It had its more notable beginnings in ancient Egypt around 3000 B.C. The Incas of Peru also used it. However, it was a "lost art" until a brief rebirth in 1829, when an Englishman cold-pressed and sintered some platinum powder to produce the first ductile platinum. It was used again in 1916 to produce the first commercial tungsten wire.

During World War II, when new methods for mass production of machine parts were being investigated both here and abroad, the process came into its own. Germany was short of copper. German scientists found that shell driving bands, usually made of copper, could just as well be made of porous iron impregnated with paraffin wax. The good forming qualities of this material soon led to other applications. The past two decades have seen major advances in the use of powder-metal parts in consumer, industrial, and military applications.

## PROCESS DESCRIPTION

The manufacture of parts by the powder-metallurgy process usually involves a series of steps, as follows: the manufacture of metal powders, blending, briquetting, presintering, and sintering, and a number of secondary operations including sizing, coining, machining, impregnation, infiltration, plating, and heat treatment. These processes are shown schematically in Fig. 17-1.

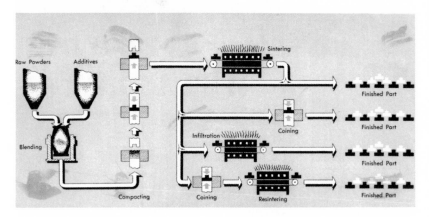

**Fig. 17-I.** Schematic diagram of the powder-metallurgy process (courtesy *Machine Design*).

## Manufacture of Metal Powders

A wide range of metal powders having a nearly infinite range of properties has been developed in recent years. The powders most commonly used are copper-base and iron-base materials. Other powders not used extensively, but supplying a constantly growing need are stainless steel, titanium, nickel, beryllium, chromium, and other refractory and exotic metals. Powder· metallurgy is the only way of making some items that are commonplace today as, for example, tungsten carbide cutting tools. This is the only way of supplying the high demand for certain high-purity metals.

The particle size of powders falls into a range of 1 to $100\mu$ ($1\mu = 10^{-6}$ in.), with the range of 10 to $20\mu$ being predominant. There are various methods of manufacturing powders of this size, but those most commonly used are atomization, reduction, electrolysis, crushing, and milling (Fig. 17-2).

**Atomization.**   In the atomization process, molten metal is forced through a nozzle into a stream of air or water. Upon contact with the stream, the molten metal is solidified into particles of a wide range of sizes. The size is controlled by varying the nozzle size, metal flow rate, and the temperature and pressure of the stream. This process is used mostly for low-melting-point metals because of the corrosive action of the metal on the nozzle at high temperatures.

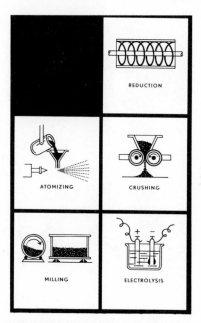

**Fig. 17-2.** Various methods of manufacturing metal powders (courtesy The Hoeganaes Sponge Iron Corp.).

**Reduction.** Sponge-iron powder is a pure, porous iron obtained when iron oxide or iron ore is reduced at temperatures below the melting point of the iron in an atmosphere-controlled furnace. The sponge iron is made into powder by crushing and grinding. The ingredients are shown pictorially in Fig. 17-3.

**Electrolysis.** The electrolytic process is similar to electroplating. In this process the metal plates are placed in a tank of electrolyte. The plates act as anodes, while other metal plates are placed into the electrolyte to act as cathodes. High amperage produces a powdery deposit on the cathodes. After a period of time the cathode plates are removed from the tank and rinsed to remove the electrolyte. After a drying period, the deposit is scraped off and pulverized to produce powder of the desired grain size. An annealing process follows pulverization to remove work-hardening effects.

### Mixing or Blending of Powders

The blend of the powders determines the many different properties that can be obtained. During the blending operation, lubricants are added to reduce friction during the pressing operations. This both reduces die wear and lowers the pressure required for pressing. Through blending, uniform distribution of particle size is obtained, and the different powders are thoroughly mixed. The mixing may be done

Sponge iron

Coke

Iron ore

Lime stone

**Fig. 17-3.** The ingredients for making iron powders and some finished parts (courtesy Hoeganaes Sponge Iron Corp.).

either wet or dry. Wet mixing has the advantage of reducing dust and the danger of explosion which is present with some finely divided powders.

### Briquetting

Briquetting is the art of converting loose powder into a "green" compact of accurately defined size and shape. Owing to interparticle friction, pressure applied from one direction will not be distributed uniformly throughout the part. Metal powders do not *flow* much under pressure, so density variation is kept to a minimum by multiple-action briquetting presses which apply pressure from both the top and bottom of the die (Fig. 17-4). The briquette is considered fairly fragile, but it can be handled.

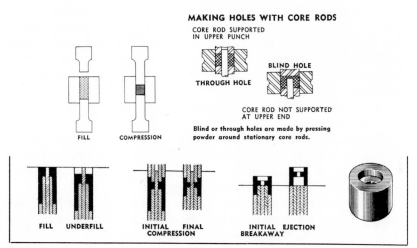

**Fig. 17-4.** Briquetting dies for powdered-metal parts use pressure from both the top and the bottom to achieve more uniform density (courtesy *Metalworking*).

For high-volume parts, tungsten carbide is used for the die material. Although the cost is higher, it will outwear other materials by a ratio of roughly 10:1. Some of these dies can produce a million parts before they become worn beyond tolerance limits. High-carbon–high-chrome vanadium steels are second-choice die materials. High-carbon tool steels can be used for low-volume and light-duty applications. The punches have to be made with some sacrifice of hardness for toughness.

The dies must be highly polished to aid in briquetting and ejection. Clearances between punches, dies, and core rods must be held to a minimum to maintain alignment and concentricities, but they must be large enough to permit free movement under all operating conditions. Figure 17-5 shows how a core rod is used to make a thin-walled bushing.

**Fig. 17-5.** Core rods and a five-step sequence make thin-walled bushings (courtesy *Metalworking*).

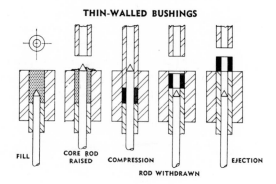

The powder is compressed to approximately one third of its original volume. Slight pressure on the punches results only in denser particle packing. As pressure is increased (up to 200,000 psi maximum), plastic deformation of the particles takes place. Thin sections bend and break. Cold welding and interlocking of adjacent grains takes place, and voids are filled.

The presses used for briquetting may be either mechanical or hydraulic, or a combination of the two.

Mechanical presses usually operate in the lower pressure ranges and rely on fast action for high-production rates. These presses operate on a given stroke length; therefore, the parts produced are of uniform volume, but it is difficult to control density.

Hydraulic presses are slower but can develop high pressures. Since stroke is adjustable, parts of uniform density can be produced. Capacities of these presses range from 150 to 5,000 tons.

### Presintering

Presintering is done at a temperature below the final sintering temperature. Its purpose is to increase the strength of the briquette for handling, or to remove lubricants and binders added to the powders during the blending operation. Some materials, such as tungsten carbide, become very hard after sintering, but they are relatively easy to machine at this stage. If no machining is required, presintering can be eliminated.

### Sintering

Sintering is performed to achieve all possible final strength and hardness needed in the finished product. The three most important variables governing the sintering process are temperature, time, and sintering atmosphere. Other factors that have an influence are the green density, the size composition, and desired properties of the compacts.

By keeping the part at the right temperature for a proper period of time, bonding of the particles is accomplished by the exchange of atoms between the individual particles.

Sintering is accomplished in high-volume, continuous furnaces (Fig. 17-6). Because of the large exposed areas of the briquettes, the sintering furnaces contain controlled atmosphere for protection against oxidation and other chemical reactions.

### Secondary Operations

Many powder-metal parts may be used in the "as sintered" condition. However, when the desired surface finish, tolerance, or metal

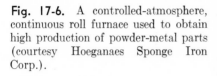

**Fig. 17-6.** A controlled-atmosphere, continuous roll furnace used to obtain high production of powder-metal parts (courtesy Hoeganaes Sponge Iron Corp.).

structures cannot be obtained by briquetting, additional finishing operations must follow. These operations include sizing, coining, machining, impregnation, infiltration, plating, and heat treatment.

**Sizing.** When a part must be dimensionally correct, sintering is followed by a sizing operation. In this, the sintered part is placed in a die, which is designed to meet the required tolerances, and is re-pressed.

**Coining.** The coining operation is very similar to sizing, except that this time the sintered part is re-pressed in the die to reduce the void space and impart the required density. After coining, the part is usually resintered for stress relief. Oftentimes, the sizing and coining operations are combined in the same die.

**Machining.** The principal object of powder metallurgy is to be able to press metal powders directly into dimensionally accurate finished shapes. However, certain features, such as threads, reentrant angles, grooves, side holes, and undercuts, are usually not practical for powder-metallurgy fabrication. These features are generally machined on the semifinished sintered blanks (Fig. 17-7).

Boring, turning, drilling, tapping, and all the conventional machining operations are performed easily on sintered metal parts. Although high-speed tools prove satisfactory for short runs, tungsten carbide cutting tools are recommended because they retain a sharp cutting edge for a much longer time. When finishing, very sharp tools, fine feeds, and high speeds are essential if the open-pore structure necessary for filters and the self-lubricating qualities of bearings are to be preserved.

Ordinary coolants are not recommended for the machining operation, since they cannot be removed easily from the porous structure and

**Fig. 17-7.** Powdered-metal parts shown with required machining. Hubs, as shown, can be made without machining up to ¾-in. diameter and 5/16-in. width (courtesy Amplex Division, Chrysler Corp.).

may cause internal corrosion of the part. Volatile coolants like carbon tetrachloride can be used because they vaporize readily and leave no residue. Coolant oil of the same type used to impregnate a self-lubricating bearing can also be used.

Reaming is not recommended unless the tool is very sharp. The cut should be limited to 0.005 in. in diameter. A better tool for obtaining desired hole diameters is the button-type burnishing tool shown in Fig. 17-8. These tools are recommended for holding bore tolerances of 0.0005 in. or less. Normally the burnishing tool is 0.0003 in. larger than

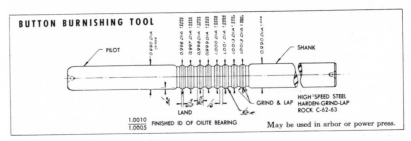

**Fig. 17-8.** A burnishing tool used to finish bearing diameters to close tolerances (courtesy Amplex Division, Chrysler Corp.).

the finished size required, to compensate for springback of the metal. For example, if the bore diameter is to be 1.001 in., the burnishing-tool diameter should be 1.0013 in.

**Impregnation.**   When self-lubricating properties are desired, the sintered parts are impregnated with oil, grease, wax, or other lubricating materials. In this process the parts are placed in tanks of lubricants heated to approximately 200°F. The porous structure is completely impregnated in 10 to 20 min. The lubricant is retained in the part by capillary action, until external pressure or heat of friction draws it to the surface.

**Infiltration.**   An infiltrated part is made by first pressing and sintering iron powder to about 77 percent of theoretical density. A replica or infiltration blank of copper or brass is then placed on the part, which is sent through the furnace a second time. The infiltrant melts and soaks through the porous part, producing close to 100 percent density.

Infiltration provides increased strength, hardness, and density not obtainable by straight sintering.

**Plating.**   Plating of any part usually has two objectives—pleasing appearance and protection from corrosion. The procedures for plating powdered-metal parts are quite different from those used for wrought- or cast-metal parts. Peening, tumbling, or other methods of mechanical smoothing of the part prior to plating provide a more even surface for smoother plating.

These methods, however, do not take care of inner porosity, and any electrolyte which has been entrapped in the porous structure will cause internal corrosion, leading to failure. Therefore, before the part can be plated, porosity must be eliminated. Impregnation with molten metal helps, but, since the pores are not filled completely, galvanic corrosion is likely between the dissimilar metals. Also, the difference in coefficients of expansion and contraction will eventually lift the plating material. Impregnating the part with a plastic resin will overcome most of these difficulties. The resins have low coefficients of expansion, do not react galvanically with the metal part, are low in cost, and have good filling properties. After the porosity has been eliminated, regular plating procedures can be used.

**Heat Treatment.**   Powdered-metal parts are heat-treated to improve grain structure, strength, and hardness. The conventional methods of heat treatment used for wrought metals can also be used for powdered metals but care must be taken in several steps of the process. Porosity decreases the heat conductivity; therefore, longer heating and shorter cooling periods are required. Heat treatment must be carried on in a controlled atmosphere to prevent oxidation of the internal structure.

Carbon, in the form of graphite, added to iron-powder mixtures to produce medium- or high-carbon steel is an inexpensive way of improving the physical properties of a part.

The tensile and yield strengths of iron-graphite compacts are related directly to density. The higher-density materials have higher yield strengths, since a greater volume of material is stressed. To develop high tensile strength, high-density materials must be allowed sufficient time to attain complete diffusion of the carbon.

## PROPERTIES OF METAL POWDERS AND FINISHED PARTS

### Metal Combinations

Powder metallurgy makes it possible to unite materials that cannot be alloyed in the usual sense or would not yield the desired characteristics if they were joined mechanically. Examples of this are lead dispersed in copper to form bearing surfaces, copper and carbon combinations for commutator brushes, steel and copper combined to make a self-brazing alloy, and a combination of ceramics and metals to produce refractory cermets.

### Particle Size and Distribution

Particle size and distribution are important factors in the control of porosity, density, and compressibility. They also control the amount of shrinkage when sintering. If all coarse or all fine particles are used, the overall porosity is greater than with a mixture of different grain sizes. A range of grain sizes makes for a close-fitting pattern. The density of a part is reduced when all large particles are used, owing to the large void space. When all small particles are used, the density is good, but higher briquetting pressures are required because of the large amount of contact area between the particles and the small deformation. Proper particle size and distribution are determined by a series of standard screens. The amount held back by each screen allows the percentage of each size of particle, on a weight basis, to be estimated.

### Density and Flow Rate

The apparent density of the material is determined from the variation in the particle size and is given by the volume-to-weight ratio of a loosely filled mixture. To manufacture a part of a certain density, a metal powder of a corresponding apparent density is used. An increase in density of the product can be obtained, but the power required will also increase.

Through controllable density, one area of a part can be made hard and dense while another portion of the same piece is soft and porous. Porosity can be varied from practically nil to so much that the part can be used as a filter (Fig. 17-9).

**Fig. 17-9.** A wide variation in particle size and density is obtainable in powdered-metal parts (courtesy Amplex Division, Chrysler Corporation).

The flow rate of the powder governs the amount of time required to fill a cavity and is important for equal filling of narrow cavities. The flow rate also helps determine the possible production rate.

## Purity

Impurities in the powder have various effects on the briquetting and sintering operations. Foreign substances cause wear on the die parts and thus reduce the useful life of the die. Oxides and gaseous impurities can be removed from the part during sintering by the use of a reducing atmosphere.

## Green Strength

Green strength refers to the mechanical strength of a compacted part prior to sintering. This factor is very important for convenient handling during mass production.

## DESIGN CONSIDERATIONS

When powdered metals are considered for a new or existing part, a number of factors must be evaluated. These include quantity, tolerances, physical characteristics, shapes, and size.

### Quantity

The quantity must be sufficient to justify the necessary investment in tools and dies. A die may cost from several hundred dollars for a small simple part to several thousand dollars for a larger, more complicated one. Die life varies greatly; it may range from 100,000 parts for a tool-steel die to over a million parts for carbide-lined dies with high-carbon–high-chrome punches.

### Tolerances

Pressed and sintered ferrous parts can be controlled to about ±0.002 in. per in. on diameters and other dimensions formed by the die. Sizing can be used to cut this tolerance in half.

### Physical Characteristics

Most powder-metal parts are produced in the range of 15,000 to 40,000 psi tensile strength. However, tensile strengths up to 100,000 can be obtained with iron powders and additives. Surface hardness greater than $R_c$ 60 can be obtained in iron-powder parts.

### Shapes

Metal powders do not flow easily, even under high pressures. Best results are obtained when narrow and deep passages are avoided. Holes cannot be placed at right angles to the direction of pressing. Inside fillets are preferred to sharp corners, both for ease in fabrication and for strength in the finished part. Sharp points on the punches and dies should be avoided, as they wear quickly.

Substantial economies are frequently realized by revising an original design to adapt it for manufacture by powder metallurgy.

### Size

The size of the part that can be made is limited by the size of the available presses. Practical size limitations, at the present time, are from about ⅛ to 25 sq in. in cross section and from 1/32 to 6 in. in height. By rule of thumb, the ratio of height to effective diameter is never greater than 4:1 for parts less than 1 in. in diameter; as the diameter increases, this ratio decreases considerably.

## APPLICATIONS OF POWDERED METALLURGY

The applications of powdered metals can be divided into two broad categories—those items that are dependent on the unique properties of the materials, and those that are used for structural or machine parts.

### Parts Dependent on Properties of Materials

**Bearings.** Porous oil-impregnated metal is an ideal bearing material. It is especially recommended where positive lubrication is left to the human element. The impregnated oils or greases frequently provide lifetime lubrication. The lubricant is metered to the bearing surface by capillary action when heat or pressure is applied (Fig. 17-10).

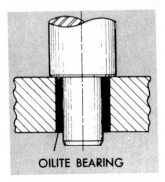

**OILITE BEARING**

**Fig. 17-10.** Self-lubricating, oil-impregnated, powdered-metal bearings and bearing stock. Drawing shows bearing pressed in place (courtesy Amplex).

**Metal Filters.** Powdered-metal filters provide uniform depth filtration of particles as small as $5\mu$. These filters may be cleaned by reversing the flow or by back-flushing with solvent. Other uses include filtering, diffusing, and controlling the flow of gases and liquids; separating liquids having different surface tensions; removing moisture from airstreams; acting as sound deadeners; and serving as wicks for lubricating airstreams (Fig. 17-11).

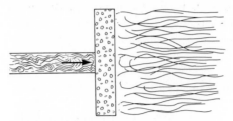

Diffusing air

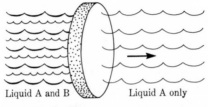

Liquid A and B          Liquid A only

Separating liquids

**Fig. 17-11.** Powdered metals are used as air diffusers, liquid separators, and filters.

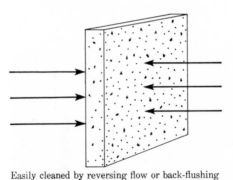

Easily cleaned by reversing flow or back-flushing with a solvent.

Filters

**Welding Electrodes, Flame-Cutting, and Scarfing.** Large quantities of powdered iron are used in the manufacture of electrodes for arc welding. Powdered iron is also used in flame cutting and flame scarfing.

### Structural or Machine Parts

Perhaps the outstanding reasons for using powdered metals for machine parts are the facts that there is no scrap, and very little, if any, machining is required.

Machine parts are produced in a broad range of ferrous and non-ferrous alloys. The physical properties range up to the equivalent of low-carbon steel. Factors in favor of powdered-metal parts are: (1)

elimination of most machining operations, (2) low cost per part in large quantities, (3) quiet operation, (4) low wear because of self-lubrication, and (5) vibration dampening. A group of miscellaneous machine parts is shown in Fig. **17-12**.

**Fig. 17-12.** Miscellaneous machine parts made by the powder-metallurgy process (courtesy Graphite Co., division of the Wickes Corporation).

## ECONOMICS

As stated previously, to be profitable, powdered-metal parts must be made in fairly large quantities. However, if tooling is simple, these may be as low as 500 or 1,000 pieces. In runs of 10,000 parts, powdered-metal applications are likely to have the advantage over conventional processes.

Labor and machine-time costs are low. Semiskilled labor is all that is required, and production rates of 500 to 50,000 pieces per hour can be obtained. Another major economic consideration is the elimination of scrap loss owing to the machining. The cost of manufacturing a powdered-metal bearing, as compared to conventional manufacturing methods, is shown in Fig. **17-13**.

## FUTURE DEVELOPMENT

Sintered metal parts are being made in progressively larger components. At one time the process was confined to ounces; now some parts are being measured in pounds.

New and important advances are being made in materials. New alloy combinations and preblended powder mixes are being introduced on the market.

Continuous compacting and hot-pressing methods are under development.

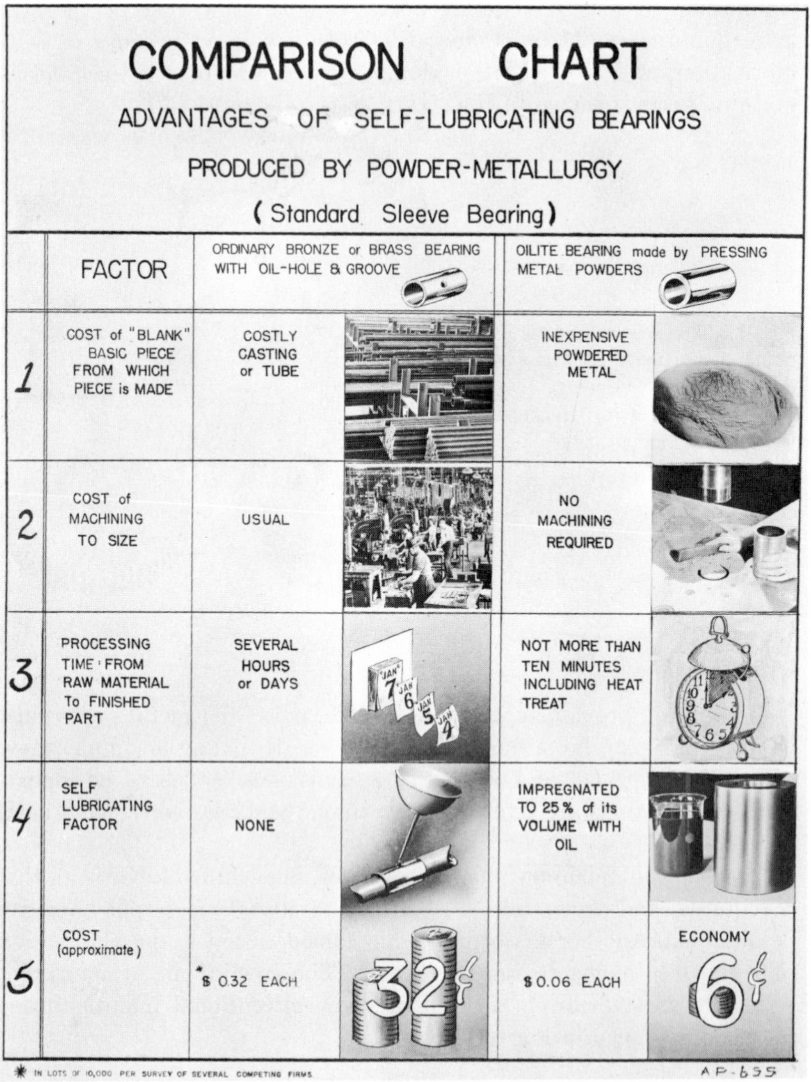

# COMPARISON CHART

## ADVANTAGES OF SELF-LUBRICATING BEARINGS

## PRODUCED BY POWDER-METALLURGY

### ( Standard Sleeve Bearing )

| | FACTOR | ORDINARY BRONZE or BRASS BEARING WITH OIL-HOLE & GROOVE | | OILITE BEARING made by PRESSING METAL POWDERS | |
|---|---|---|---|---|---|
| 1 | COST of "BLANK" BASIC PIECE FROM WHICH PIECE is MADE | COSTLY CASTING or TUBE | | INEXPENSIVE POWDERED METAL | |
| 2 | COST of MACHINING TO SIZE | USUAL | | NO MACHINING REQUIRED | |
| 3 | PROCESSING TIME · FROM RAW MATERIAL To FINISHED PART | SEVERAL HOURS or DAYS | | NOT MORE THAN TEN MINUTES INCLUDING HEAT TREAT | |
| 4 | SELF LUBRICATING FACTOR | NONE | | IMPREGNATED TO 25 % of its VOLUME WITH OIL | |
| 5 | COST (approximate) | $ 0.32 EACH | | $ 0.06 EACH | ECONOMY |

✳ IN LOTS OF 10,000 PER SURVEY OF SEVERAL COMPETING FIRMS                    AP-655

**Fig. 17-13.** Comparison of powdered-metal fabrication costs with those of conventional methods (courtesy American Powdered Metals Inc.).

## CERMETS

Cermets are a combination of metals and ceramics, bonded together in much the same way as are powdered metals alone. These materials represent an attempt to impart the high refractoriness of ceramics along with the toughness and thermal-shock resistance of metals.

## Types of Cermets

The field of cermets is relatively new, and only a few potentially good materials have been able to survive the developmental stage. These may be placed in two categories—oxide-based and carbide-based cermets.

**Oxide-Based Cermets.** The most common of the cermets in this group is the chromium–alumina-based cermet, or, as it is classified, CR-AL203. A chromium content of 98 percent or higher is used with the oxide. The powders are mixed together, placed in a mold, and subjected to 10,000 to 12,000 psi. Higher pressures can be employed if a wax type of binder lubricant is used. Parts pressed at pressures ranging from 25,000 to 40,000 psi will be about as hard as chalk. Light finishing operations can be performed at this stage.

Sintering is done in an atmosphere-controlled furnace at 2800° to 3000°F.

Other cermets of the oxide type are chromium-molybdenum-alumina-titania and the metal-modified oxides. The former is reported to have improved resistance to thermal shock, abrasion, and sliding friction. There is some loss in corrosion resistance owing to the reduced chromium content.

**Carbide-Based Cermets.** As mentioned in Chap. 18, tungsten or titanium and tantalum carbides used cobalt as the principal binder. However, because of its relatively poor resistance to oxidation at elevated temperatures, research was done to find something better. Nickel was the first metal that seemed promising, and other metals have since been added to improve the properties.

## Applications of Cermets

Cermets are being produced under a number of different trade names. They are being used where abrasive power, heat resistance, and impact strengths higher than those found in ceramic materials are necessary. Some specific applications are ramjet nozzles, disk brake inserts, cutting tools, and crucibles for highly reactant materials.

### QUESTIONS

1. What is meant by powder metallurgy?
2. What metals are most commonly made in powder form?
3. Describe two methods used in making powdered metals.

4. Why is pressure applied from both the top and the bottom to produce briquettes?

5. What is the purpose of presintering?

6. What is accomplished during the sintering process?

7. Explain briefly what is accomplished by sizing, coining, impregnation, and infiltration of powder-metal parts.

8. Why must the cutting tools used in machining powder-metal bearings be very sharp?

9. What preparation is necessary before powder-metal parts can be plated?

10. What special precautions are necessary when heat treating powder-metal parts?

11. What is the significance of particle size in compacting the powders?

12. What tolerance can be expected on powder-metal parts?

13. Why is a 25-sq-in. cross section about the largest powder-metal part produced?

14. Why do powder-metal structures make good bearings?

15. Why are powder metals used for machine parts?

16. When is it economically feasible to use powder-metal manufacture?

17. What are cermets?

18. What are some applications of cermets?

## PROBLEMS

1. What volume of powder would be required to make 100 bearings 1 in. long with a 1-in. outside diameter and $\frac{5}{8}$-in. inside diameter if the metal compresses to 77 percent of its theoretical density?

2. What size press would be required to make the bearing mentioned in Prob. 1 if a compacting pressure of 75,000 psi is required? Allow for a 50 percent safety factor.

3. How high could the rotor for a gasoline pump shown in Fig. 17-12 be if it is 2 in. in diameter?

4. What would be the approximate diameter of the largest gear that could be made in powder metals if the inside diameter was 2 in. and the thickness 1 in.?

# 18

# CUTTING-TOOL
# PRINCIPLES

**T**HE ACTION of a single-point tool in cutting metal has often been compared to a knife or wedge, but this analogy is not entirely true. Metal cutting requires a well-supported cutting edge. The metal is severely compressed in the area in front of the cutting tool. This causes high-temperature shear and plastic flow.

Most of the action takes place in the vicinity of the shear plane, as shown in Fig. 18-1. The metal in the shear-plane area is compressed

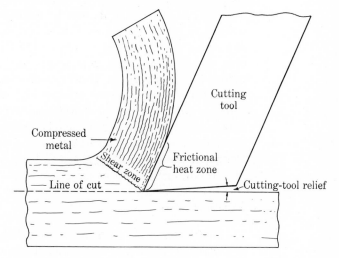

**Fig. 18-1.** The separation action of metal in the shear zone ahead of the cutting point.

Compressed metal

Shear zone

Cutting tool

Frictional heat zone

Line of cut

Cutting-tool relief

and moves up along the face of the tool. Three distinct types of cutting action take place (Fig. 18-2). These get their names from the types of chips produced—continuous, continuous with a built-up edge, and segmented chips.

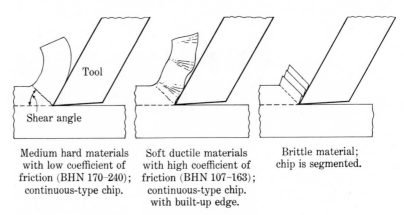

| Medium hard materials with low coefficient of friction (BHN 170–240); continuous-type chip. | Soft ductile materials with high coefficient of friction (BHN 107–163); continuous-type chip. with built-up edge. | Brittle material; chip is segmented. |

**Fig. 18-2.** Cutting tool action on various materials.

### Continuous Chips

Continuous chips are those that do not fracture as the metal moves up across the face of the tool. The back side of the chip that has passed the cutting tool is smooth. Unless some obstruction is placed in its path, the chip will probably not curl but will form a snarl around the cutting-tool point and the work.

### Continuous Chips with a Built-Up Edge

Soft, ductile materials can be strained in shear to a high degree without rupture. The internal shear action is followed by a secondary flow along the base of the chip, at the tool face. Owing to the high heat and pressure being generated, small particles of metal become welded to the cutting tip. This built-up edge changes the cutting action considerably, increasing the friction and therefore the heat generated and thus contributing to a shorter tool life. The built-up edge remains only momentarily. It is then sloughed off on the back side of the chip, leaving an inconsistent finish on the metal surface. Proper tool geometry along with the right cutting speed and cutting fluid can reduce built-up-edge conditions to a minimum.

### Segmented Chips

Brittle materials, such as gray cast iron, are removed by a combination of shear and fracture, causing the chips to come off in segments.

## CUTTING-TOOL GEOMETRY

The basic angles needed on a single-point tool may be best understood by removing the unwanted surfaces from an oblong tool blank of square cross section (Fig. 18-3).

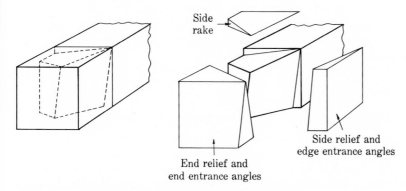

Side rake

End relief and
end entrance angles

Side relief and
edge entrance angles

**Fig. 18-3.** The development of essential tool geometry.

### Relief Angles

Relief on both the side and end of the tool is necessary to keep it from rubbing. These relief angles are usually kept to a minimum to provide good support when machining hard metals. They may be increased to produce a cleaner cut on some soft materials. Secondary clearances are used below the cutting edge to reduce the amount of regrinding needed for touching up the cutting edge.

### End and Side Cutting-Edge Angles

The end of the tool is cut back approximately 15 deg to relieve the amount of surface contact. The side-cutting edge angle serves two purposes: it protects the point from taking the initial shock of the cut, and it serves to thin out the chip. For a given depth of cut, the material will be spread over a greater cutting surface (Fig. 18-4).

**Fig. 18-4.** Relative chip thickness, determined by the edge entrance angle.

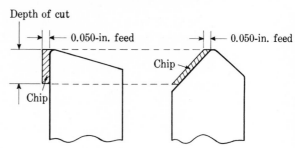

Depth of cut

0.050-in. feed        0.050-in. feed

Chip

Chip

### Back-Rake Angles

Rake angles cause the top surface of the tool to slope. Sloping the top surface back (positive back rake) is necessary in machining soft, ductile, draggy materials if excessive built-up edge is to be avoided. Although too much back rake helps prevent any built-up edge, it also reduces the strength of the tool and its ability to conduct the heat away from the cutting edge. Negative back rake (the top surface slopes toward the cutting edge) is used for heavy intermittent cutting. It is also used in very high-speed machining to lend more area to the included angle of the cutting tip.

### Side-Rake Angles

Positive side rake, as shown in Fig. 18-5, is used to direct the flow of chips and make the cutting edge smaller. The higher the rake angle, the less cutting force is required; however, the cutting edge becomes fragile. Negative side rake is sometimes used to increase the cutting-edge strength, although it also increases the force required for the cut. The added strength needed for making heavy intermittent cuts that severely shock the tool, as in milling or planing, is obtained with negative side rake.

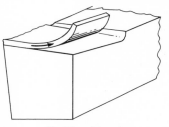

Positive side rake

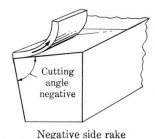

Negative side rake

**Fig. 18-5.** Side rake.

### Nose Radius

The nose radius is the rounded tip of the cutting end. The amount of the radius varies with the general depth of the cut for which the tool is to be used. A large radius provides a strong tool, more contact area, and a smoother cut. Pressures on the cutting tool and the stock being machined are proportionate to the contact area. For example, small-diameter parts require a small nose radius with light cuts to minimize tool pressures and obtain a true surface.

The tool angles of a carbide tool used to cut low-carbon steel are shown in Fig. 18-6.

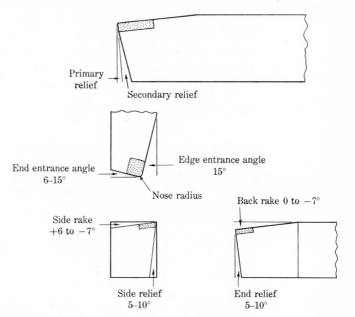

**Fig. 18-6.** Cutting-tool geometry for a carbide tool used to cut mild steel.

Primary relief

Secondary relief

End entrance angle
6–15°

Edge entrance angle
15°

Nose radius

Back rake 0 to −7°

Side rake
+6 to −7°

Side relief
5–10°

End relief
5–10°

## Tool Signatures

The Cutting Tool Manufacturers Association has established a standard system of tool signatures in which various angles that make up a single-point tool appear in a definite order. The order used is back rake, side rake, end relief, end clearance, side relief, side clearance, end cutting edge, side cutting edge, and nose radius. A given tool may be designated as 10, 12, 8(10), 8(10), 6, 6, 3/64. When clearance below the cutting edge is used on relief angles, it is placed in parentheses—the value (10) in this signature. References to clearance angles are often omitted in actual practice.

## Chip Breakers

As the metal is separated from the parent material, it should be broken into comparatively small pieces for ease of handling and to prevent it from becoming a work hazard. A chip breaker forms an obstruction to the metal, as it flows out across the face of the tool, causing it to curl and break. The fact that the metal is already work-hardened helps the chip breaker to perform effectively. Various types of chip breakers are made, but all of them consist mainly of a step ground into the leading edge of the tool or a piece of cutting-tool material clamped on top of the cutting tool (Fig. 18-7). The efficiency of the chip breaker is primarily a function of its width as compared to the feed being used. A light cut with a fine feed allows the chip to travel over a flat surface before it is made to curl. Under these conditions the chip would only be lightly curled or might even cause a snarl. To remedy this situation, adjustable chip breakers are now made to make the width of the breaker setback correspond to the cut.

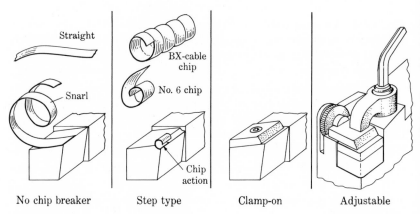

**Fig. 18-7.**   Common chip breakers.

### Chip Forms

The most desirable type of chip is termed a number 6 chip, since it resembles that numeral. A long continuous chip, rather tightly curled, is termed a *BX-cable chip*. These are not too objectionable from the standpoint of safety, but they are harder to remove from the machine. A chip forming no curl at all will usually become entangled with the work or cutting tool and is referred to as a *snarl* (Fig. 18-7).

### CUTTING-TOOL MATERIALS

Much of the rapid growth of modern industry can be attributed to the continuous improvement in cutting tools and cutting-tool materials. This improvement, in turn, has accelerated a demand for better machines having ever-greater cutting capacity owing to speed, horsepower, and rigidity. The cutting-tool materials that have progressively contributed to increased speeds and feeds are high-carbon steel, high-speed steel, cast alloys, cemented carbides, diamonds, and ceramics (cemented oxides).

High-carbon steels as described in Chap. 3, are those that contain 0.90 to 1.10 percent carbon. This type of steel was the only cutting-tool

### High-Carbon Steel

material available for the first 120 years of machine-tool use, but it has now been generally replaced by steels containing alloying elements that are better able to resist wear and heat.

### High-Speed Steel

A big stride forward in metal cutting was made at the turn of the century when Taylor, of the Bethlehem Steel Company, discovered the proper heat treatment for high-speed steel. This discovery led to the development of 18-4-1, the general-purpose high-speed steel composed of 18 percent chromium, 4 percent nickel, and 1 percent vanadium. Other types have been developed and are known by their main alloying elements, such as molybdenum and cobalt. The ability of tungsten to resist heat gives this tool material a quality known as *red hardness*. This means that the cutting edge of the tool may reach a high temperature, approximately 1000°F, before it breaks down rapidly. High-speed tools find their best application in drills, reamers, counterbores, milling cutters, and single-point tools that must be ground for a special job.

### Cast Alloys

Cast-alloy tool materials are composed of cobalt, chromium, and tungsten. These alloys are cast into a mold to form the cutting tool. This combination of alloys gives an increased heat resistance in the range of 1200° to 1400°F. At this temperature, the metal begins to soften, but it will reharden again after cooling.

The cast alloys are capable of taking a high polish, which helps prevent the metal from sticking to the face of the tool and forming a built-up edge. The built-up edge, which is a characteristic result of cutting soft, ductile materials, impairs the cutting efficiency of the tool. These tools are also extremely corrosion-resistant, which makes them desirable in machining chemical-bearing rubbers and plastics. Cast-alloy tools are better known by the trade name of *Stellite*.

### Cemented Carbides

Cemented carbides are so named because they are composed principally of carbon mixed with other elements such as tantalum and titanium. These elements are cemented together, with a cobalt binder, by the powder-metallurgy process. Pure tungsten powder is mixed under high heat with pure carbon (lampblack) in the ratio of 94 percent and 6 percent by weight. The new compound, tungsten carbide, is then mixed with cobalt until the mass is entirely homogeneous. The amount of cobalt used will regulate the toughness of the tool. A high cobalt content will result in greater toughness at the expense of hardness, and vice versa. Tungsten carbide is suitable for machining metals that do not form a continuous chip, as in cast iron, or a weak chip, as in aluminum. Steel, however, has a strong chip that slides across the face of the tool or is curled and broken on the top of the tip. Steel tends to adhere (has a high coefficient of friction) to tungsten carbide. Alloying powders are added to decrease this friction and make the tip more slippery, thereby avoiding excessive wear on the top of the tool.

The alloying elements of tantalum and titanium are added in the form of powders and are mixed in at the time the cobalt is added. The amount of each alloy will determine the cutting characteristics of the tool.

Carbide tools may be classified into two general groups—one for cutting steel and the other for all other materials. A further breakdown may be made according to other properties, as shown in Table 18-1.

### TABLE 18-1.

#### General Classification of Cemented Carbides

| Class | Type | Use |
|---|---|---|
| 1 to 3 | Tungsten (edge-wear resistance) | Rough and finish cuts on cast iron and aluminum; softer grade (3) used for wire-drawing dies |
| 4 to 6 | Titanium (top-wear or crater resistance) | Harder grade (4) used on light cuts on steel; softer grades (5–6) used for medium and roughing cuts on steel |
| 7, 8 | Tantalum (wear and crater resistance) | Light cuts on steel (7)<br>Heavy cuts on steel (8) |
| 9, 10 | Tantalum (wear, heat, and shock resistance) | Machining, gage constructing, and hot flash trimming dies |

### Diamond Tools

Diamond tools are not thought of as a general-production cutting tool because of the expense and care involved in their use, but they may be justified for applications of high finish and close tolerances. Generally, diamonds have proved their effectiveness in maintaining a good finish and a high degree of accuracy on instrument parts and in light boring operations.

The diamond is carefully examined under a polarized light to determine its cleavage planes and cutting surfaces. It is then brazed or clamped into a metal holder (Fig. 18-8). Because of the diamond's brittleness, shock in operation should be avoided by using rigid, vibrationless machines and even surfaces for cutting.

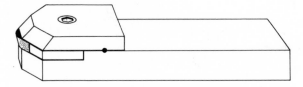

**Fig. 18-8.** Industrial diamond used as a cutting tool.

### Ceramic Tools

The latest development in the metal-cutting tools uses aluminum oxide materials, generally referred to as ceramics. The earliest investigations of aluminum oxide as a cutting tool appear to have been made in Germany in 1905. A United States patent was issued in 1942, but national recognition was not gained until 1954, when a laboratory at the Watertown Arsenal recorded the high-speed machining ability of this material.

Ceramic tools are made by compacting aluminum oxide powder in a mold at about 4,000 psi or more. The part is then sintered at 3,000°F. This method is known as *cold pressing*. Pressure may be applied simultaneously with heat to form a higher-density structure. Hot-pressed ceramics are more expensive owing to higher mold costs.

These tools have very low heat conductivity and extremely high compressive strength, but they are quite brittle. Generally, where shock and vibration are not factors, ceramic tools can outperform carbides. A rule of thumb indicates a cutting speed two to three times that of carbides. Because of their extreme hardness, ceramic tools have proved successful where they are exposed to abrasive wear, such as is encountered when machining cast iron or plastic materials.

Ceramic-tool research has shown that longer tool life can be obtained when sharp cutting edges are honed off at a 30-deg angle to the top edge. The width of this land should be approximately one-half to two-thirds of the feed used (Fig. 18-9).

### TOOLHOLDERS AND INSERTS

The wide variety of toolholders for single-point tools may be classified as the three distinct types shown in Fig. 18-10.

Honed leading edge width is
equal to $\frac{1}{2}$ to $\frac{2}{3}$ of the feed.

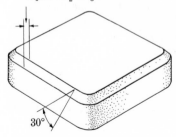

30°

**Fig. 18-9.** Ceramic-tool insert with honed angle on cutting edge.

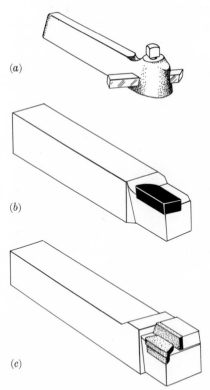

(a)

(b)

(c)

**Fig. 18-10.** Main types of toolholders (a) solid high-speed insert, (b) brazed carbide tip, and (c) clamp-on type.

### High-Speed Inserts

The solid high-speed steel insert is usually ground by hand and placed in the toolholder [Fig. 18-10(a)]. Back rake is usually included in the holder to simplify grinding.

### Brazed-Tip Toolholders

Carbide-tool cost necessitated economizing on material. As a result, high-carbon-steel shanks were milled out and carbide tips were brazed into position [Fig. 18-10(b)]. Brazed-tip tools are used for general turning, drilling, milling, and reaming. As single-point turning tools, they are especially useful when some modification is needed for a special job.

### Clamped Disposable Insert Holders

A more recent development is the clamp-on type of toolholder [Fig. 18-10(c)]. It was developed for two reasons: to get away from brazing strains and to be able to use more of the cutting edges of the tool. By the simple process of unclamping the tool insert, rotating it to the next cutting edge, and reclamping, the machine is ready to cut again. This saves much time over having to take the entire toolholder out, regrind the tip, and reset it. Where negative rake is incorporated into the holder, both sides of the insert may be used. A square insert would thus have eight cutting edges. These inserts are often referred to as "throwaway" inserts, since they are cheaper to replace than to regrind. The most common insert shapes are shown in Fig. 18-11.

**Fig. 18-11.** The most common types of carbide and ceramic cutting-tool inserts.

## TOOL LIFE

After the selection of the right tool geometry and material, our next consideration should be good performance or, as it is termed, good tool life. Obtaining proper tool life poses a complex problem, involving such factors as the machinability of the material being cut, relative speeds and feeds, and the economics of how long the tool must last to get maximum performance out of both the tool and the machine. Common ways in which tools fail are flank or edge wear, top or crater wear, and chipping or spalling (Fig. 18-12).

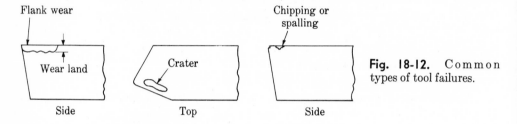

**Fig. 18-12.** Common types of tool failures.

### Flank Abrasion

Materials that are abrasive in nature but produce only short chips cause the leading edge or flank of the tool to wear off. Cast iron is in this category. For most practical purposes, on single-point tools, a 0.030-in. wear land is considered standard for carbide tools before they are indexed to the next cutting edge. The wear-land width is measured accurately with a Brinell microscope, previously described in Chap. 2. In production runs, the number of pieces that can be turned out before this wear land is exceeded is determined and recorded. When this given number of parts or amount of surfaces is reached, the tool is automatically changed to avoid failure, which is rapid beyond 0.030 in.

### Cratering

The curved indented surface on the top of the tool, called a *crater*, is caused by the more ductile materials that curl back as they hit the top of the tool and the chip breaker. Microscopic particles of the tool are picked up on the back side of the passing chip. This condition, if permitted to continue, will weaken the entire cutting edge until it breaks off. Often, this is an indication that the wrong grade of carbide is being used and that it should be replaced by a harder type. Also, the proper coolant or lubricant will tend to minimize this wear.

## Chipping or Spalling

A cutting tool that has improperly ground relief angles will either rub on the material or be weak because of excessive clearance angles. If the cutting edges are not well supported, they will be subject to cracking and spalling. The proper setting of the tool is also an important consideration.

Turning tools are set at center height or slightly above. Too much variation either way will cause the clearance angles to change drastically with respect to the material being cut (Fig. 18-13).

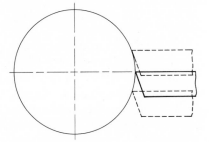

**Fig. 18-13.** The difference in clearance angles with respect to the height of the tool.

You will notice that the end clearance becomes large when the tool is set below center. This weakens the tool and may cause it to chip. Too much above center causes the tool to rub.

Other factors that cause the tool to chip or spall are excessive chip loads, intermittent heating and cooling, and interrupted cutting. Excessive chip loads are caused by too fast a feed or too deep a cut. Intermittent heating and cooling result because the cutting fluid is not able to cover the cutting point constantly, and because the tool keeps entering and leaving the material. Interrupted cutting is caused by a tool entering and leaving the work as in milling or planing. Hard grades of carbide are likely to chip under these conditions.

## CUTTING SPEEDS AND FEEDS

### Cutting Speed

Cutting speed is the number of lineal feet of material to pass the tool bit in 1 min. Optimum cutting speeds have been carefully worked out, based on the type of material being cut and the kind of material in the cutting tool. For example, the cutting speed of 1020 steel with a high-speed tool is listed as 100 fpm. A carbide tool used to cut the same material would be able to run at 400 fpm.

Some of the questions that must be answered in determining the right cutting speed for a given operation are: How long must the tool last? How rigid is the machine? What type of tool is being used? Will coolant be used? What will be the average depth of the cut and rate of feed? Each of these items will be discussed briefly.

### Calculation of Tool Life

Frederick Taylor, who was largely responsible for high-speed steel, also designed a formula that can be used to express tool life in minutes. This is

$$VT^n = C$$

where
  $V$ = velocity or cutting speed
  $T$ = tool life in minutes (0.030) wear land
  $n$ = the slope of the curve on log paper
  $C$ = the constant, dependent on cutting conditions
These conditions may be plotted as shown in Fig. 18-14.

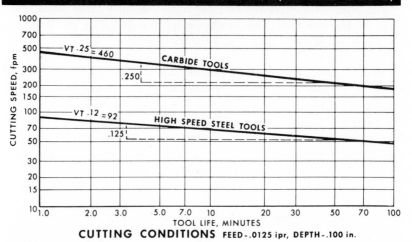

**TYPICAL CURVES OF CUTTING SPEED VS TOOL LIFE (FOR STEELS-350 BHN)**

**CUTTING CONDITIONS** FEED-.0125 ipr, DEPTH-.100 in.

**Fig. 18-14.** The tool-life curve based on Taylor's formula $VT^n = C$ (courtesy Metallurgical Products Department, General Electric Co.).

The points plotted on the curve are obtained by measuring the wear land on the tool. At 400 fpm the tool will last only 1.5 min; at 250 fpm the tool will last 25 min. The plotted lines are referred to as curves, which they would be on ordinary graph paper, but on log-log paper they become straight lines. Once the curves have been drawn for a given set of conditions, the cutting speed for a desired tool life may be chosen; for example, 200 fpm would provide a tool life of **70** min for a carbide tool, Fig. 18-14. The slope of the curve, or $n$ factor, changes as the cutting-tool material and other factors vary.

## Machine Rigidity

Very rigid machines are needed now, more than ever before, to accommodate the higher cutting speeds made possible by the new tool materials. The oxide tools, especially, because of their brittleness, require firm setups and rigid machines.

## Type of Tool

The amount of surface contact is often important in deciding how high the cutting speed can be and still produce a good chatter-free surface. Form tools (Fig. 18-15) have a large amount of contact surface and are usually used at approximately one half the regular surface foot speed.

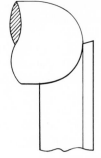

**Fig. 18-15.** Straight and circular form tools. Large surface-contact areas require a reduction in cutting speed to avoid chatter marks on the work.

## Effective Use of Cutting Fluids

Generally, the cutting speeds may be increased without shortening tool life, when the proper type and amount of cutting fluid or coolant is used. The primary purpose of a coolant is to reduce the temperature encountered at the cutting-tool tip. This is accomplished in three ways:

1. Lubrication is provided to reduce friction between the tip and the material (called the interface).

2. The antiweld properties of the cutting fluid provide more effective cutting, with less built-up edge on the tool.

3. Temperature is reduced by the general cooling properties of the fluid, due to its high thermal conductivity.

**Types of Cutting Fluids.** Cutting fluids are classified in five main groups. These include soluble oils; straight oils, both mineral and fatty; chemical-additive oils (sulfurized and chlorinated); chemical compounds; and solid lubricants.

SOLUBLE OILS. The soluble oils are mixed with water by the addition of an emulsifier. Water has excellent cooling properties, and the oil provides lubrication and corrosion resistance. These superior qualities make soluble oils a general choice for drilling, milling, and lathe work. The amount of water used varies with the type of operation. Light cutting operations, as in grinding, require only a small percentage of oils, as low as 100:1.

STRAIGHT OILS. The straight mineral oils are used in some light machining operations; however, their biggest use is in blending with other oils or with water to make soluble oil. The fatty oils, both animal and vegetable, are used in combination with mineral oils. This blend makes an excellent lubricant and coolant for automatic-screw-machine work and other light machining operations where accuracy and good finish are of prime importance. Fatty oils are not chemically active and therefore do not stain either the ferrous or the nonferrous materials.

CHEMICAL-ADDITIVE OIL. Sulfur and chlorine are used to increase both the lubricating and the cooling qualities of the various oils with which they are combined. Sulfur causes a chemical reaction with metal when subjected to heat and pressure. An iron sulfide film is formed between the metal and the face of the tool. Although this film is extremely thin, it protects the tool and provides lubrication. Sulfurized mineral oils are commonly used for machining the tough, stringy, low-carbon steels. These oils minimize tearing and rough finishes caused by built-up edges. Highly sulfurized mineral oils are not satisfactory for machining copper, brass, and bronze, because a reaction takes place which leaves stains on the metal. Chlorinated mineral oils are particularly effective in promoting antiweld characteristics. Their reaction is similar to sulfurized oils, but they become active at a lower temperature.

CHEMICAL COMPOUNDS. In recent years, chemical compounds have grown in favor as coolants, particularly in grinding. These compounds consist mainly of a rust inhibitor, such as sodium nitrate, mixed with a high percentage of water. Since water serves as an excellent coolant and lubricating properties are not important, all that is needed is an ingredient to guard against rust on the machine surfaces and the part produced.

SOLID LUBRICANTS. Stick waxes and bar soaps are sometimes used as a convenient means of applying lubrication to the cutting tool. Some common applications for solid lubricants are shown in Fig. 18-16.

**Fig. 18-16.** Common applications of stick-type lubricant for metal-cutting operations (courtesy S. C. Johnson and Son, Inc.).

ON TAPS

Lubrication to cut smoother threads—increase life of taps.

ON BAND AND CIRCLE SAWS

Lubrication to lengthen blade life—give smoother cuts—reduce burrs.

**Application of Cutting Fluids.** Coolants and lubricants are applied in several ways. Low production requires only hand application. A brush is used to apply coolant to either the material being cut or the cutting tool. Higher production requires more efficient systems of distribution; namely, flood, jet, and mist.

FLOOD METHOD. In the flood system, a large volume of coolant flows over the material and the cutting tool, the principle being to keep the heat down in the whole area of operation. The coolant tank is usually in the base of the machine. A recirculating pump is used to keep pressure on the coolant as it is forced over the work and tool. Most of the cutting fluid is used over and over until a periodic change time. If cutting oil is used, a considerable amount of it may cling to the chips. Centrifugal separators are used to reclaim the oil before the chips are sold as scrap metal.

JET METHOD. The jet system makes use of a small high-speed jet of coolant or cutting oil directed at the point of metal separation from underneath the tool (Fig. 18-17).

Tool-tip pressures of 50,000 psi or more are encountered at the cutting edge. The high-jet method does not overcome this pressure but depends on slight irregularities in both the cutting edge of the tool and the work surface. The tiny passageways thus formed allow space for the now-heated coolant to expand, vaporize, and condense on the cooler tool surface (Fig. 18-18).

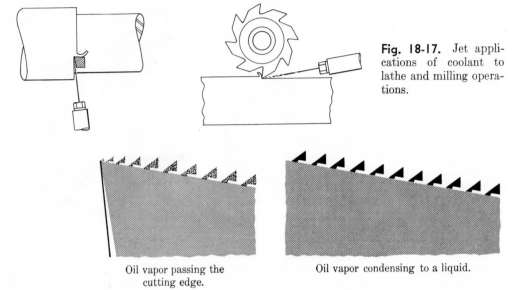

**Fig. 18-17.** Jet applications of coolant to lathe and milling operations.

Oil vapor passing the cutting edge.

Oil vapor condensing to a liquid.

**Fig. 18-18.** The oil vapor is heated to vaporization and condenses on the cutting tool (courtesy Gulf Oil Corporation).

In the process of vaporizing, the cutting oil picks up considerable heat from the cutting edge of the tool and the trapped condensed oil forms a lubricant between the tool and the chip.

The high-speed-jet system uses a gear- or vane-type pump capable of maintaining 400 to 600 psi at a flow of 1 gal per min.

Studies of this method of coolant application, as compared to the conventional flood system, indicate that, at normal cutting speeds, high-speed tools last from 6 to 12 times longer and carbide tools from 3 to 5 times longer.

Although the claims made for this method of coolant application are impressive, one does not find wide adoption of it. The reason seems to lie in the more difficult setup required.

Mist-coolant application.   Coolant is vaporized either by putting pressure on a tank of the proper liquid or by passing compressed air through a nozzle, thus creating a vacuum in the liquid line and siphoning the coolant from the tank. Both systems work on the principle that compressed air expands and absorbs some heat in the process. Also, coolant is forced under pressure into places difficult of access. The volume of mist is controlled by a needle valve in the air line mounted on the coolant container (Fig. 18-19).

The coolant used may vary from a light mixture of soluble oils, waxes, and water to a specially prepared misting compound. The reservoir capacity generally ranges from 1 qt to 5 gal. Several nozzles can be

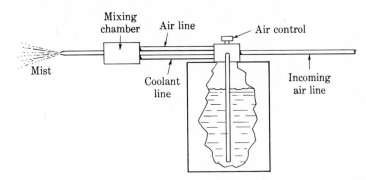

**Fig. 18-19.** Siphon-type mist-coolant system.

attached to one tank so that more than one tool or machine can be serviced at one time, or a centralized system may be used to service a whole production area. The amount of coolant used is small—a matter of a few ounces per hour for each nozzle.

COOLANT-APPLICATION COMPARISON. An appraisal of coolants and the efficiency with which they are applied to the work embraces nearly all of the present knowledge of metal cutting. The effect of coolants on tool life, finish, distortion, horsepower, and tool forces are studied, along with the various microstructures of the metals. The tool forces measured in research tests are tangential, radial, axial, or longitudinal, as shown in Fig. 18-20.

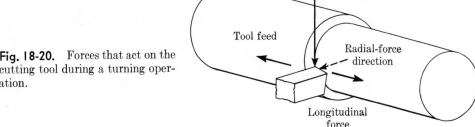

**Fig. 18-20.** Forces that act on the cutting tool during a turning operation.

The primary tool force used in calculating the total power consumption in machining is tangential, as shown in Fig. 18-20. It is the major force that causes the metal to deform into a chip and generate heat at the tool-tip interface. Tangential force is reduced as side rake is increased. Axial force is parallel to the workpiece and is represented as being opposite to the direction of feed. It is the second largest force, about 40 percent of the tangential force.

The radial force tends to push the tool back out of the cut. It is more pronounced when the nose radius is large, or in form tools. Tools that have positive back rake will tend to be drawn into the cut.

Studies indicate that mist cooling provides the best tool life for most cutting speeds. It reduces the tangential force at the lower speeds. Flood cooling systems were found to be second best in improving tool life, and were better than mist cooling in reducing tangential force at higher speeds.

A comparison of the volume of metal removed for each type of coolant application is shown in Fig. 18-21. A 0.030-in. wear land was used as a criterion for judging tool life. The soluble oil was a ratio of 20 parts of water to 1 part of soluble oil flowing at the rate of 2 gpm. The mist coolant was 1 part of mist cooling liquid to 5,000 parts of air at a rate of 0.0022 gpm.

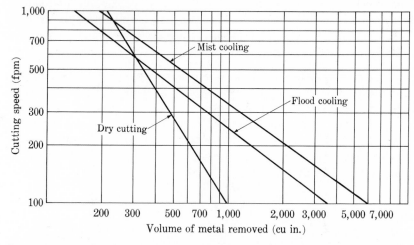

**Fig. 18-21.** Mist, flood, and dry cutting compared on a cubic-inch-removal basis (courtesy *The Tool and Manufacturing Engineer*).

The severity of the metal-cutting operation is also a factor in the choice of coolant. Metal-cutting operations, listed in order of severity, the most severe being given first, are broaching, tapping, threading, gear generation, reaming, milling, boring, drilling, and turning.

**Coolant Choice for Various Metals.**    The following list gives the most commonly used coolants for a few of the best-known metals.

| *Material* | *Coolant* |
|---|---|
| High-carbon steel | Sulfurized fatty oil |
| Low-carbon steel | Sulfurized mineral oil or soluble oil |
| Cast iron | Usually machined dry |
| Copper and copper alloys | Mineral oils or soluble oil |
| Aluminum and aluminum alloys | Dry or light-viscosity oil |
| Magnesium | Dry or light-viscosity inactive oils |

## Machinability

Machinability, referred to in Chaps. **2** and **3**, is described as the ease with which metal can be removed. Some factors that are used to predict and calculate machinability are tensile strength, Brinell hardness, and shear angle. The shear angle of a given material may be calculated by comparing the chip thickness with the depth of cut the tool was set to remove. If the angle of shear is small, the path of shear is long, as shown by the dotted line in Fig. **18-22**.

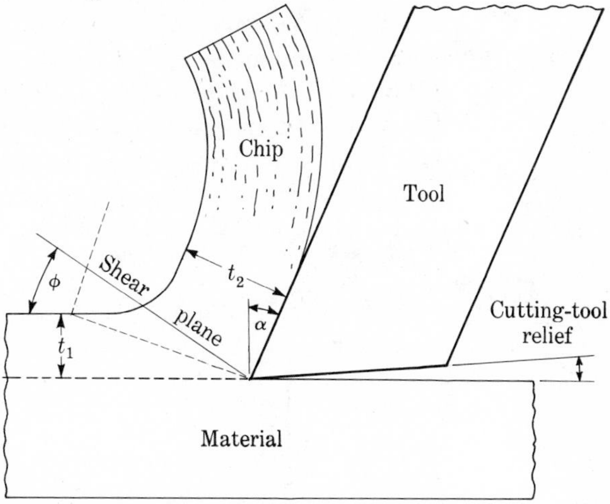

**Fig. 18-22.** Schematic view of tool and shear plane in orthogonal cutting.

The machinability of metal is often expressed in terms of cutting ratio $t_1/t_2$ or in terms of shear angle which is found by the use of the formula

$$\tan \phi = \frac{r_c \cos \alpha}{1 - r_c \sin \alpha}$$

Any change in tool rake angle will be reflected in the calculated shear angle of the material. Figure 18-22 shows the tool in orthogonal cutting; that is, the tool is set perpendicular to the travel, and only a single straight cutting edge is active. When compound rake angles or oblique cutting are involved, other formulas and charts, listed in the reference section at the end of this chapter, are used to calculate the shear angle of the material.

## Depth of Cut Versus Feed and Cutting Speed

When deciding on the best method of maintaining good tool life and at the same time increasing the cubic-inch removal rate, the first choice is to increase the depth of the cut, then the feed, and lastly the surface feet per minute. The cubic-inch removal rate is expressed as

$$\text{Depth of cut} \times \text{feed} \times \text{rpm}$$

The maximum cubic-inch removal rate will be governed by the setup and the horsepower of the machine.

## METAL-CUTTING ECONOMICS

All the foregoing information is of little use unless it is intelligently applied to obtain the *lowest possible unit cost and the highest possible production rate for any given operation.* We know that, at high cutting speeds, we can expect increased tool cost owing to shorter tool life. We can, at the same time, expect the machine cost per piece to go down. Throwaway carbide tips are preferable to brazed-type tooling from the standpoint of downtime. These factors are shown graphically in Fig. 18-23.

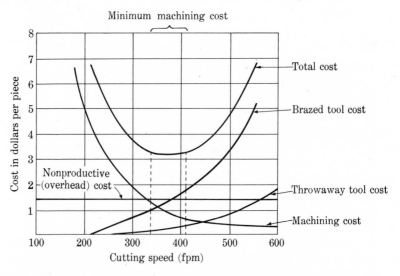

**Fig. 18-23.** Factors used in plotting minimum machining cost.

So much emphasis has been placed on tool life that sometimes other factors, such as the amount of money invested in the machine and its ever-increasing obsolescence, fade into the background. Sometimes the answer has been to work machines that require a large capital outlay continuously in order to make them pay off during their expected life. This, in turn, often requires premium labor rates. An alternative answer may be to make the same machines work harder.

As shown in Fig. 18-23, machine cost goes down rapidly with increase in cutting speed. Although the increased speed causes tool cost to rise, this factor is relatively insignificant when compared to the costs of labor and equipment.

The total cost per piece is based on the machining cost, time, labor, and overhead, plus tool-changing cost, plus regrinding and depreciation cost, plus nonproductive cost. (Nonproductive cost is the total of the labor involved in loading, unloading, placing the tool in position for the cut, etc.) The total cost, as plotted, is a summation of all the costs and represents the surface foot speed that can best be used to produce a part at minimum cost and in minimum time.

## QUESTIONS

1. Describe the three types of cutting actions that are common to various metals?
2. Explain the use of each of the following cutting-tool angles: relief, back-rake, end, and side cutting-edge angles.
3. Explain the effect of varying the side rake from positive to negative.
4. Why do small-diameter parts require tools that have a small nose radius for machining?
5. What is meant by tool signatures?
6. What is the relationship between the distance the chip breaker is back from the cutting edge and the feed used on the machine?
7. What are considered the most and least desirable chip forms?
8. Why are high-carbon steels generally not used for metal cutting?
9. What is the content of 18-4-1 steel?
10. How does high-speed steel compare with cast alloy as a tool material?
11. What are the respective carbide types recommended for steel and cast iron?
12. What are some machining operations that may use diamond cutting tools?
13. What are the chief advantages and disadvantages of ceramic tools?
14. Discuss the advantages of a clamped disposable-insert-type tool.
15. Describe the main types of tool failure?
16. What is meant by the cutting speed of a metal?
17. Explain how tool-life curves are established.
18. Name three ways a cutting fluid is able to reduce the tool-tip temperature.
19. When does it become necessary to use chemical additive oils?
20. Why is the mixture of chemical compounds with water a good coolant for grinding?
21. By what methods are coolants applied to the tool and to the work?
22. What are the forces acting on a single-point tool as it is engaged in the cut?
23. What are some methods used to predict the machinability of a metal?

**PROBLEMS**

1. What would be the sfpm of a 8-in.-diameter cylinder rotating at 250 rpm?
2. Find the cubic-inch removal rate for each of the following: (*a*) 3-in.-diameter stock turning at 200 fpm, using a 0.050 depth of cut and a 0.020 feed. (*b*) 8-in.-diameter stock turning at 200 fpm, using 0.050 depth of cut and a 0.020 feed. Cu in. per min (cim) $= 12 fdV$, where $f =$ feed in in., $d =$ depth in in., and $V =$ fpm.
3. The power required at the motor (hpm) can be calculated in terms of the cubic-inch removal rate: $\text{hpm} = \dfrac{\text{cim} \times \text{hp}_c}{\text{mechanical efficiency}}$ where $\text{hp}_c =$ horsepower constant and mechanical efficiency can usually be figured at 70 to 80 percent. Constants have been worked out for various materials. A few are given as follows: low carbon steels $= 0.6$, medium and high carbon $= 0.8$, most alloy steels $= 0.9$, hard cast irons $= 0.8$, medium and soft $= 0.3$. Most brass, aluminum, and plastics $= 0.1$–$0.3$. Compare the horsepower required at the motor for the following materials:

|  | *1020* | *4150* | *Malleable (soft)* |
|---|---|---|---|
| fpm | 200 | 120 | 220 |
| feed | 0.010 | 0.010 | 0.010 |
| depth | 0.125 | 0.125 | 0.125 |

4. Using Taylor's formula we find the following conditions for normalized 3140 steel cut with a HSS tool: $n = 0.12$, $C = 131$. What would $V$ be if $T$ were 10 min?
5. How much would the horsepower have to be increased if the cut were doubled for the 1020 steel in Prob. 3?
6. After an orthogonal cut, the chip thickness measured was 0.040 in. The actual cut depth was 0.025 in. What is the cutting ratio?
7. What is the shear angle of the cut made in Prob. 6 if the back rake on the tool is 7 deg? What can be said about the relative machinability of this metal?

**REFERENCES**

Black, P. H., *Theory of Metal Cutting*, McGraw-Hill Book Company, Inc., New York, 1961.

Boston, O. W., *Metal Processing*, John Wiley & Sons, Inc., New York, 1951.

*Metal Machining with Cutting Fluids*, Gulf Oil Corporation, Pittsburgh, 1952.

*Speeds and Feeds for Better Turning Results*, The Monarch Machine Tool Company, Sidney, Ohio, 1957.

*Tool Engineers Handbook*, American Society of Tool Manufacturing Engineers, McGraw-Hill Book Company, Inc., New York, 1959.

# 19

# LATHES

IN THE BEGINNINGS of civilization, man realized the value of round objects, in the form of rollers and wheels, to help him transport heavy burdens. Gradually, the wheel was refined, bringing many inventions that changed his way of living. Among these were fine chariots, beautiful pottery, and advanced weapons of war.

The constant search for improved methods of making wheels, shafts, and other cylindrical items led to the development of the lathe. Although the lathe was originally a cylinder-turning machine, it became very versatile, and many other tasks gradually were assigned to it. Henry Maudsley, an Englishman, is credited with making the first screw-cutting engine lathe in about 1797.

Some lathes have only one cutting tool and are generally used for limited or low production. Others have several cutting tools but only one work-holding station, and these are usually considered machines of medium production. Those that have several work-holding stations and many tools are called high-production lathes.

## LOW-PRODUCTION LATHES

Low-production lathes are those that can easily be set up for a few parts. The various types are engine lathe, toolroom lathe, bench lathe, speed lathe, and special-purpose lathes.

### Engine Lathes

The most common metalworking lathe is called an engine lathe. This term dates back to the time when the early lathes were powered by steam engines. The engine lathe (Fig. 19-1) is capable of performing a wide variety of operations.

**Fig. 19-1.** Engine lathe making a cut on stock located between centers (courtesy The Monarch Machine Tool Co.).

A careful study of the operations shown in Fig. 19-2 will help you understand the capabilities of this machine. The setups shown in this figure are for limited quantities.

**Basic Structure of the Engine Lathe.** The five main parts of the modern engine lathe are the headstock, tailstock, bed, carriage, and quick-change gearbox as shown in Fig. 19-3.

HEADSTOCK. The headstock contains the driving mechanism—either pulleys or gears—to turn the work. Provision is made so that 8 or 10 different speeds may be obtained on the smaller-sized lathes, and several times this number on larger ones. The headstock furnishes a means of support for the work, either with a center fitted into the spindle or by a chuck.

TAILSTOCK. The tailstock is the most common means of supporting the outer end of the stock. It may be positioned upon the bed at any point and locked securely in place. It contains the dead center which is held in place by a taper. Adjusting screws in the base of the tailstock are used to shift it laterally on the bed. This provides a means

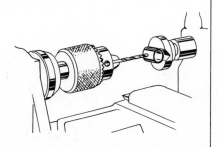

Drilling an oil hole in a bushing with
crotch center in tailstock.

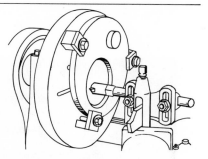

Boring an eccentric hole on the
faceplate of the lathe.

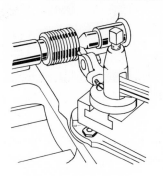

Cutting a screw thread with
compound rest set at 29 deg.

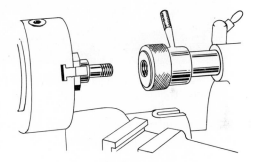

Die mounted in tailstock of lathe
for threading studs.

Knurling a steel piece in the lathe.

Coarse      Medium

Sample of knurling.

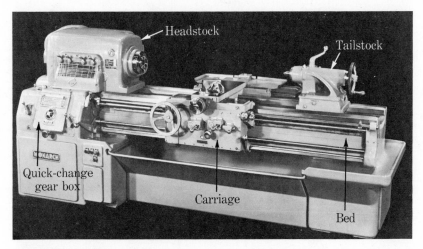

**Fig. 19-3.** The five main parts of an engine lathe (courtesy The Monarch Machine Tool Co.).

of maintaining accurate alignment with the headstock center. It also makes it possible to introduce a small amount of taper into the work (Fig. 19-4).

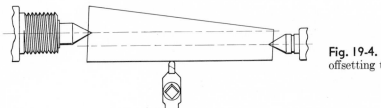

**Fig. 19-4.** Cutting a taper by offsetting the tailstock.

BED. The bed makes up the basic structure of the lathe, on which all other parts are mounted. It is usually made of aged gray cast iron in the smaller-sized lathes, and may be of welded-steel construction in the larger sizes. At the top of the bed are the ways (Fig. 19-5). They act as guides for accurate movement of the carriage and tailstock.

Much of the machine's accuracy is dependent on the preciseness of the ways. They are usually finished by a milling or planing operation followed by grinding and then are hand-scraped for further exactness of the mating parts. Some manufacturers prefer to harden and grind the ways and also make them replaceable.

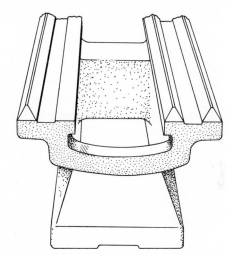

**Fig. 19-5.** Lathe bed section, showing inverted **V** and flat-type ways.

CARRIAGE. The carriage, as the name implies, is used to carry the cutting tool along the bed longitudinally (Fig. 19-6). A cross slide is mounted on top of the carriage. It moves the tool laterally across the bed. Another slide is mounted above the cross slide. This is referred to as the *compound rest*. The compound rest can be swiveled in a hori-

Compound Rest Knob

Cross Feed Knob

Apron Handwheel

Carriage Lock Screw

Feed Change Lever

Half Nut Lever

Automatic Feed Friction Clutch

**Fig. 19-6.** Lathe carriage (courtesy South Bend Lathe, Inc.).

zontal plane at any desired angle with respect to the work, thus furnishing another method of cutting tapers. Since this method is dependent on hand turning of the compound-rest knob, it is generally limited to short, steep tapers. The back side of the carriage is often equipped with a taper attachment which provides still another way of cutting tapers. This is a more convenient method of cutting long tapers than by offsetting the tailstock, since it can be quickly engaged or disengaged so as not to interfere with straight turning.

QUICK-CHANGE GEARBOX.  The quick-change gearbox allows the operator to change the longitudinal or cross-feed quickly. Feed refers to the amount the tool is made to advance per revolution of the work. The quick-change gearbox also provides settings for cutting all the commonly used threads.

### Lathe Size and Accuracy.

LATHE SIZE.  The size of a modern engine lathe is given by the maximum diameter of swing, in inches, and the maximum length of bar that can be turned between centers, in inches. *Swing* refers to twice the distance from the lathe center point to the top of the ways. An engine-lathe size specification may read: swing $12\frac{3}{4}$ in. over bed, $7\frac{5}{8}$ in. over cross slide; length 47 in.

ACCURACY.  Lathe dials are graduated in increments of 0.001 in. Some are made to read directly; that is, for each 0.001-in. depth of cut, a corresponding 0.001 in. will be removed from the stock. Other lathes are made so that the tool moves in the amount registered on the dial. Since the material is removed from both sides of the stock, the amount taken off will be twice the dial reading. Engine-lathe work can, with good equipment, be maintained within 0.001- or 0.002-in. accuracy.

### Work-Holding Methods.

LATHE CENTERS.  The work to be turned is first cut to length, and then center holes are drilled into each end [Fig. 19-7(b)]. A dog is securely fastened to one end of the work, which is then placed between the lathe centers. The tail of the dog fits in a slot of the drive plate for positive rotation.

CHUCKS.  Another common method of mounting work in a lathe is by means of a chuck (Fig. 19-8). The universal chuck shown in the figure is self-centering; all three jaws move toward the center on a scroll arrangement. This permits the operator to load and unload work quickly and easily.

A more versatile chuck is the four-jaw independent type (Fig. 19-9). Loading and unloading the work is slower in this chuck, since

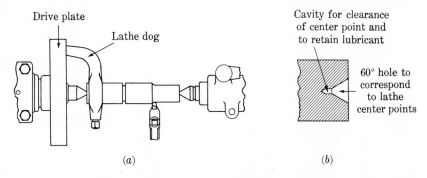

Drive plate

Lathe dog

Cavity for clearance
of center point and
to retain lubricant

60° hole to
correspond
to lathe
center points

(a)

(b)

**Fig. 19-7.** (a) Stock mounted between centers on a lathe. (b) Center holes drilled into each end of the stock.

**Fig. 19-8.** Round work held in a universal chuck (courtesy South Bend Lathe, Inc.).

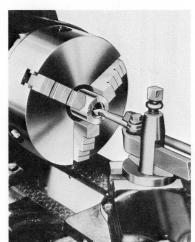

**Fig. 19-9.** Centering work with a dial test indicator using an independent four-jaw chuck (courtesy South Bend Lathe, Inc.).

the jaws must be adjusted separately; however, it has more holding power and can be used for both on- and off-center work. It can also be used to advantage on odd-shaped pieces.

The collet chuck (Fig. 19-10) is the most accurate of all chucks. The collets have split tapers that are made to close by means of a draw-in handwheel which fits through the spindle of the headstock.

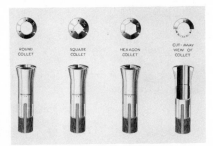

**Fig. 19-10.** Various types of collet chucks and their uses (courtesy South Bend Lathe, Inc.).

**Fig. 19-11.** Rubber-flex collets (courtesy The Jacobs Manufacturing Co.).

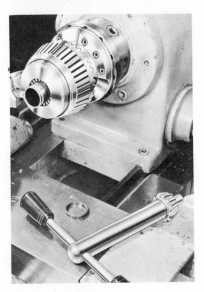

The work mounted in the collet should not be more than a few thousandths of an inch larger or smaller than the size stamped on the collet.

A newer, more versatile collet chuck is the rubber-flex type (Fig. 19-11). The parts to be chucked may vary as much as ⅛ in. in diameter for each collet, except in the smallest size, 1/16 in. The standard range of sizes for collets of this type is 1/16 to 1⅜ in.

FACEPLATE. The faceplate shown in Fig. 19-12 is made with bolt slots so that flat work may be clamped or bolted to it. More elaborate setups may call for angle plates, as shown, or for fixtures attached to the faceplate.

**Fig. 19-12.** Boring a bracket with an angle plate attached to the faceplate (courtesy South Bend Lathe, Inc.).

MANDREL. It is often desirable to machine a surface concentric and true with the inside diameter. This can be accomplished with the aid of a mandrel. Several types of mandrels are shown in Fig. 19-13.

The solid mandrel (*a*) has an 0.008-in.-per-ft taper. The part to be machined is placed on the small end of the mandrel and forced on with an arbor press until it is firmly in place.

### Work-Support Equipment.

CENTER REST. Stock extending from the chuck which is to be drilled or bored will not have the benefit of the tailstock support. If the stock extends from the chuck for a distance equivalent to more than 3 diameters, a center rest (Fig. 19-14) is used. The steady rest may also be used to give support for long stock when it is machined between centers.

FOLLOWER REST. Long, comparatively small-diameter work machined between centers on a lathe cannot be accurately cut. The stock

Large end

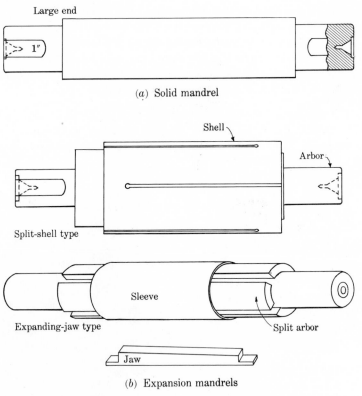

$\gg$ 1"

(a) Solid mandrel

Shell

Arbor

Split-shell type

Sleeve

Split arbor

Expanding-jaw type

Jaw

(b) Expansion mandrels

**Fig. 19-13.** Solid and expansion mandrels used to hold parts for machining so the outside surface is concentric with the bore.

**Fig. 19-14.** Stock supported with a steady rest for a boring operation (courtesy South Bend Lathe, Inc.).

tends to spring away from the cutting tool. A follower rest is used to overcome this difficulty (Fig. 19-15). The rest is bolted to the carriage and is adjusted to follow directly behind the cutting tool.

**Fig. 19-15.** A follower rest used to support slender stock as it is being machined (courtesy South Bend Lathe, Inc.).

### Toolroom Lathe

There is very little difference in appearance between an engine lathe and a toolroom lathe. However, a toolroom lathe is built with greater precision, has a greater range of speeds and feeds, and has more attachments. It is more expensive than the engine lathe and is designed for precision toolroom work.

### Bench Lathe

The bench lathe is a small version of the engine lathe. It is usually mounted on a bench, hence its name. The bed length seldom exceeds 6 ft.

### Speed Lathes

Speed lathes are built to satisfy light-machining operations that require a comparatively high speed (Fig. 19-16). High surface foot speeds are required for buffing, polishing, spinning, and wood turning, and these operations can be done on a lathe of this type.

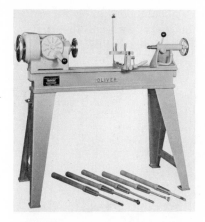

**Fig. 19-16.** A speed-type lathe that can be used for spinning and wood turning (courtesy Oliver Machinery Co.).

## Special Lathes

A number of special lathes are necessary for jobs not conveniently handled on the engine- or toolroom-type lathes. One of these special machines—the gap lathe—is shown in Fig. 19-17.

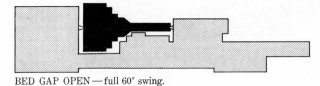

BED GAP OPEN—full 60″ swing.

Gap lathe

**Fig. 19-17.** Gap lathes offer an extra-large swing.

**Duplicating Lathe.** The duplicating lathe is very much like an ordinary engine lathe except that it is equipped with a tracer attachment (Fig. 19-18). A template, which may be cut out on a metal-cut-

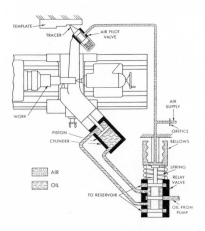

**Fig. 19-18.** An air–oil circuit applied to lathe work (courtesy The Monarch Machine Tool Co.).

ting band saw and then filed for accuracy, is attached to a stand so that a stylus can trace its contour. The stylus, in turn, actuates a pilot valve that is used to control the hydraulic cylinder attached to the cutting tool.

Tracer attachments may be set up for between-center work or facing operations. An application of tracer turning is shown in Fig. 19-19. Timesavings that might be realized by using this method instead of the conventional engine lathe are also shown. Note that the accuracy is indicated to be within 0.0002 in. on some dimensions.

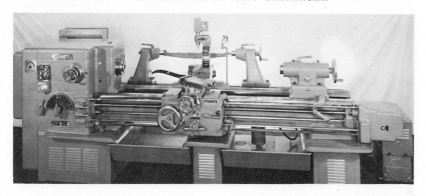

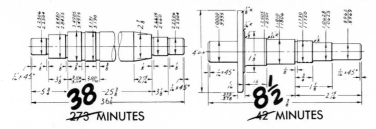

**Fig. 19-19.** A lathe tracer arrangement with typical parts, and the time required compared to the same operation by a standard engine lathe (courtesy Sidney Machine Tool Co.).

## MEDIUM-PRODUCTION LATHES

When the volume of production of certain machine parts is such that it does not warrant the use of fully automatic lathes but is greater than can be handled economically on the standard engine lathes, medium-production lathes are used. These are the automatic tracer lathe, automatic cross-slide lathe, and turret lathe.

Unless equipped with stock-feeding mechanisms, each of these machines requires an operator.

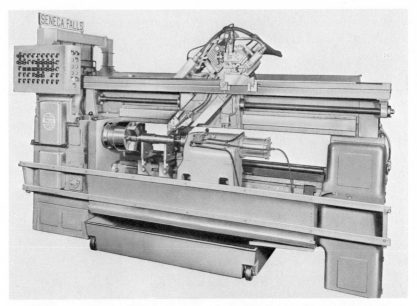

**Fig. 19-20.** Single-spindle tracer lathe (courtesy Seneca Falls Machine Co.).

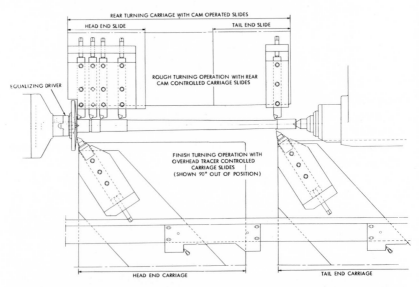

**Fig. 19-21.** Tool slides at rear of lathe are cam-operated; those on overhead-carriage slides are template-controlled (courtesy Seneca Falls Machine Co.).

## Automatic Tracer Lathes

The automatic tracer lathe may be compared to an engine lathe with a tracer attachment. It is, however, much larger, and is capable of considerably higher production. The one shown in Fig. 19-20 is the single-spindle type, which is equipped with both a vertical and a horizontal bed. Several tool slides may be engaged at one time with one or more tools in a block (Fig. 19-21).

Automatic tracer lathes are also of the multiple-spindle type (Fig. 19–22). Long, multiple-diameter parts are easily handled on a machine of this type. A support arm, shown in the top spindle position, maintains accuracy against the forces of the cutting tool.

**Fig. 19-22.** Multiple-spindle tracer lathe (courtesy The New Britain Machine Co.).

The four-spindle automatic tracer machine provides three work stations and one loading and unloading station. After the work is machined at one station, all four spindles are made to index, or move up to the next position. Template-controlled hydraulic slides perform the tracing operations. Forgings or castings can provide for a relatively uniform cut, since they are of the general shape required in the finished product. When parts are started from bar stock, it is necessary to take one or more roughing cuts in order that the last finishing cut will be accurate. On some machines of this type, provision is made to dial in one or more roughing cuts and a final finish cut, as shown in Fig. 19-23.

## Automatic Cross-Slide Lathe

The automatic cross-slide lathe was built to provide multiple tooling on both the front and the rear sides of the stock (Fig. 19-24).

Turning multiple diameters on long stock is difficult unless the stock is properly supported. Cutting tools located on both sides of the

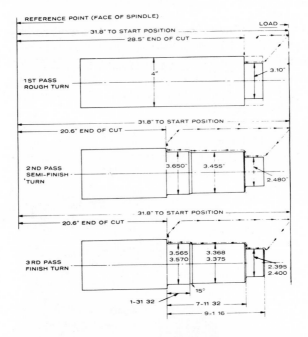

REFERENCE POINT (FACE OF SPINDLE)

LOAD →

31.8" TO START POSITION
28.5" END OF CUT

1ST PASS
ROUGH TURN

4"

3.10"

31.8" TO START POSITION
20.6" END OF CUT

2ND PASS
SEMI-FINISH
TURN

3.650"    3.455"

2.480"

31.8" TO START POSITION
20.6" END OF CUT

3RD PASS
FINISH TURN

3.565    3.368
3.570    3.375

2.395
2.400

15°

1-31 32    7-11 32
9-1 16

**Fig. 19-23.** Roughing and finishing cuts required to produce a part from bar stock on a tracer lathe (courtesy The Seneca Falls Machine Co.).

**Fig. 19-24.** Automatic cross-slide lathe equipped for machining long bar stock to several diameters within close tolerances (courtesy Seneca Falls Machine Co.).

stock at one time will balance thrust and minimize the deflection caused by tool forces. In addition to the supporting effect of opposing tools, auxiliary rollers are used (shown supporting the stock). The tooling layout (Fig. 19-25) shows the arrangement of tools for a common production part.

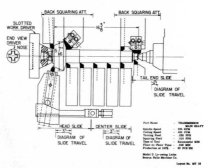

**Fig. 19-25.** Tooling layout for automatic cross-slide lathe.

Notice that the amount of travel for each tool slide is also shown. The various tool slides can be made to cut simultaneously or in sequence. This type of lathe is not limited to between-center work but may be used for facing and boring operations, as shown by the tooling layout in Fig. 19-26. Some parts require more than one layout and setup, since it is not possible to reach all surfaces in one operation.

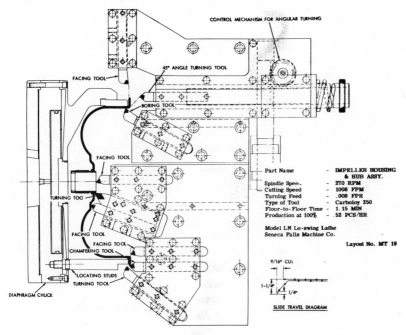

**Fig. 19-26.** Tooling layout for facing and boring with an automatic lathe.

### Turret Lathes

Turret lathes are an outgrowth of a demand for a variety of repetitive turning operations on one machine. Although the engine lathe is versatile, it requires time to change the tool for each different operation. Also, some repetitive accuracy is lost. The turret lathe derives its name from the fact that the tailstock has been converted into an indexing turret with five or six stations. On the front side of the cross slide is mounted a square turret, which is indexed or turned by hand. On the back of the cross slide is a single toolholder. Once the tools have been properly placed on these tooling stations, they need not be removed, other than for sharpening, for the entire run of parts. This makes for a high degree of repetitive accuracy and for parts that can be used in interchangeable manufacture.

**Types of Turret Lathes.** The turret lathe is manufactured in a wide variety of types which may be broadly classified as horizontal, including ram type (bar or chucking) and saddle type (bar or chucking); and vertical, with single- or multistation models.

HORIZONTAL TURRET LATHES.

*Ram type.* Turret lathes have been developed to handle efficiently, several types of work. The ram-type bar machine (Fig. 19-27) is made to handle bar stock which is fed through the collet-type chuck either by feed fingers actuated by a hand lever or by hydraulic or airdraulic arrangements.

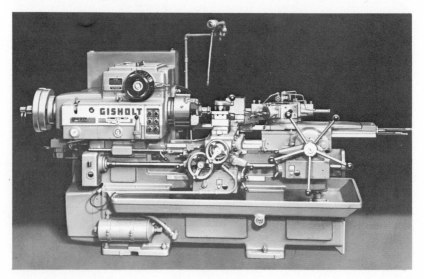

**Fig. 19-27.** Ram-type turret lathe (courtesy Gisholt Machine Co.).

The principal difference between a bar and a chucking machine is in the way the stock is held, whether this is by collet chuck for bar stock or by the larger two-, three-, or 4-jaw chucks for individual parts. Some machines are made so that they may be quickly adapted to either type of work.

Parts turned out by the ram machine both bar and chucking, are shown in Fig. 19-28.

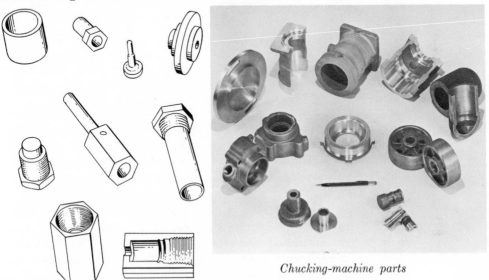

*Chucking-machine parts*

**Fig. 19-28.** Ram-type turret-lathe production parts (courtesy The Warner and Swasey Co.).

*Bar-machine parts*

The distinguishing feature between a ram-type and a saddle-type machine is in the way the hexagon turret is mounted. The ram-type machine is so called because the hexagon turret is mounted on a slide or ram that fits in the saddle bolted to the bed of the machine. This arrangement makes for ease of operation, since only the ram and the turret move back and forth, and the heavier saddle can remain in one position for the entire run of parts.

*Saddle type.* In the saddle-type turret lathe, the hexagon turret is mounted directly on the saddle of the machine (Fig. 19-29). This arrangement, although slower and more cumbersome to operate, provides for a heavy-duty setup and is able to handle larger parts than the ram-type machine.

*Size.* The size of a turret lathe is given by a number. The ram-type machines, numbered from 2 through 5, give an indication of the bar capacity. The number corresponds to twice the diameter of the

**Fig. 19-29.** The hexagon turret of the saddle-type machine is mounted directly on the saddle (courtesy The Gisholt Machine Co.).

bar, in inches, that can be inserted through the spindle. The number also bears a relationship to the overall size of the machine. The saddle-type-machine size numbers are followed by a letter, and range from 1A through 4A. The number corresponds roughly to one half the bar-diameter capacity through the spindle, in inches, and the overall size of the machine.

*Tooling.* Special tooling has been developed for the turret lathe to make for higher production and ease of handling. Some of these tools are now associated with other machines, but they remain essentially turret-lathe tools. Figure 19-30 shows turret-lathe tools, with an explanation of their use and typical applications. Study the tooling carefully to gain an understanding of the type of work that can be done without difficulty on the turret lathe.

*Tooling principles.* Efficient use of the turret lathe requires as many tools cutting at one time as is feasible. More than one tool may be used to cut from one face or station of the hexagon turret; for example, on the multiple turning head shown in Fig. 19-30, an outside diameter is being turned, the end of the part is being chamfered, and two inside diameters are being bored. In turret-lathe terminology, this is known as *multiple tooling.*

Tools may be made to cut from both turrets at one time; that is, a hole may be bored by a tool on the hexagon turret at the same time that a tool on the square turret is being used to cut the outside diameter. This is known as a *combined cut.* Careful planning in the tooling layout is necessary to take advantage of these principles. The lot size will also decide how much time can be spent on making the setup and if any special tooling is warranted. As an example, compare the tooling layout for small-lot production on a given item with a high-production lot of the same item (Fig. 19-31 on page 529). Notice how the principle of multiple tooling is being used in part (*b*). In this case the

(a) Collet pads

Round, square, and hexagonal collets are used to hold the bar stock.

(b) Combination stockstop and starting drill

The combination stockstop and starting drill is used to let the stock extend a designated distance from the chuck. The drill is then brought out to make a start for a drilled hole.

(c) Chamfering tool

The chamfering tool is used to bevel the end of the bar stock. This operation is always used before the box tool and the self-opening die head, (d), (e), (g).

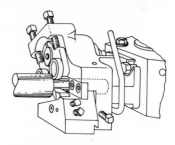

(d) Single-roller turner or box tool

The box tool furnishes support for the bar stock as it is being cut, maintaining accuracy of the machined surface.

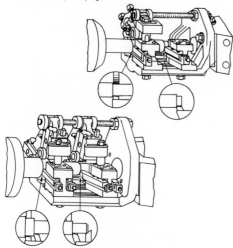

(e) Multiple-roller turner

The multiple-roller turner has positions for several tools to turn several diameters at one time.

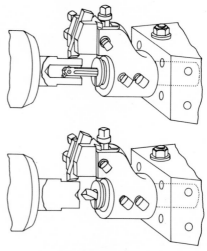

(f) Adjustable knee tool

The adjustable knee tool can be used for both internal and external machining. The vertical external tool can be adjusted to turn different diameters.

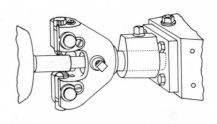

(*g*) Self-opening die head

The self-opening die head is used for making threads. The finished thread can be produced in one or two passes.

(*h*) Knurling tool

The knurling tool is used to make a diamond-shaped or a serrated surface.

**Fig. 19-30A.** Tooling used in machining bar stock on a turret lathe.

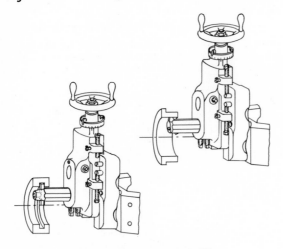

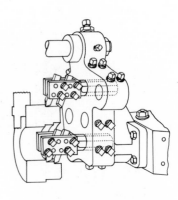

(*a*) The adjustable vertical slide

The adjustable vertical slide allows the tool mounted on the hexagon turret to be raised and lowered. Adjustable stops are also provided for ease of tool resetting. Boring, recessing, and external turning may be done with this type of tooling.

(*b*) The multiple turning head

The multiple turning head provides mounting holes for several tools to cut at one time from one tooling station or one face of the hexagon turret. The bar at the top is an overarm support which slides into a bearing on the headstock to give rigidity to the setup.

**Fig. 19-30B.** Turret lathe tooling commonly used for chucking work on the saddle-type machine.

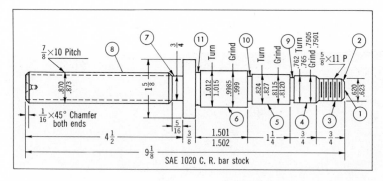

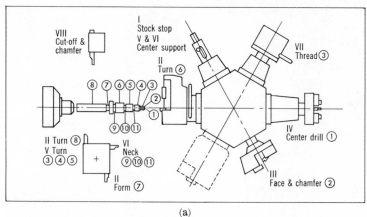

(a)

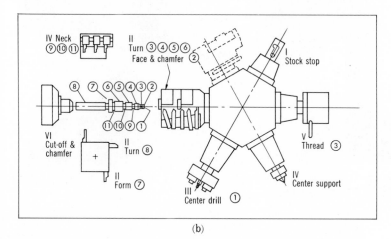

(b)

**Fig. 19-31.** Comparison of (*a*) small-lot and (*b*) high-production tooling layouts (courtesy The Warner Swasey Co.).

**Fig. 19-32.** The vertical turret lathe, with a part being machined (courtesy Giddings and Lewis Machine Tool Co.).

production time per piece for the small-lot setup was 5.3 min, but this was reduced to 3.8 min for the high-production setup. The additional setup time for the multiple tooling required in (b) was only 57 min.

### VERTICAL TURRET LATHES.

*Single-station vertical lathes.* Large castings, forgings, and other parts are difficult to mount and hold in chucks or between centers for machining on the horizontal turret lathe. The vertical turret lathe (Fig. 19-32) was developed to overcome some of the difficulties encountered in mounting and holding large workpieces. The tabletop is a combination three-jaw chuck and faceplate. The size of this lathe is given by the diameter of the table, in inches, which usually ranges from 30 to 46 in. The main structure of the machine, in addition to the table, consists of a column which supports a crossrail and a side rail. On the horizontal crossrail are mounted one or two vertical slides, one with a turret toolholder, the other with a square toolholder. The side rail supports a square turret used for holding tools to cut the outside diameter of parts mounted on the table. As with the horizontal turret lathe, combined cuts and multiple tooling are possible.

*Multistation vertical lathes.* The six- or eight-station vertical lathe or chucking machine is designed for high production. The six or eight independently driven spindles are mounted on a carrier around a stationary column. This is somewhat similar to the multispindle tracer lathe described previously, but it is now in a vertical position. As the machining operations are completed, the tools retract and the spindle carrier indexes one station. Thus one part is completed with each indexing cycle. These machines have the advantage of requiring only the minimum amount of floor space (Fig. 19-33).

## HIGH-PRODUCTION LATHES

The border line between medium- and high-production lathes is not well defined, but the distinction is made here to help the reader consider the machines in terms of relative quantity production. Generally, high-production machines are those that run continuously, with very little operator attention. The amount of production depends on the difficulty of the job, the degree of automation, and the number of tooling stations available. Lathes placed in this category are: automatic turret lathes (including electric, hydraulic, and tape-controlled lathes, and single-spindle, automatic-chucking-type lathes), and single- and multi-spindle automatic screw machines.

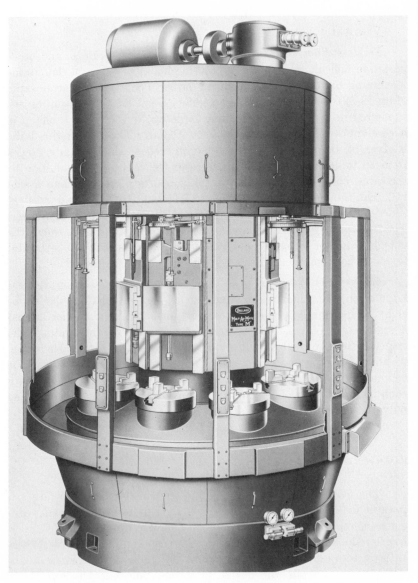

**Fig. 19-33.** Multistation vertical turret lathe (courtesy The Bullard Co.).

## Automatic Turret Lathes

**Electric, Hydraulic, and Tape-Controlled Lathes.** Many turret lathes are now equipped with automatic indexing devices for the hexagon turret which minimize the machine- and work-handling responsibilities of the operator (Fig. 19-34). Automatic controls can be set up to take care of spindle speed changes, spindle reverse, start and stop, feed changes, and indexing.

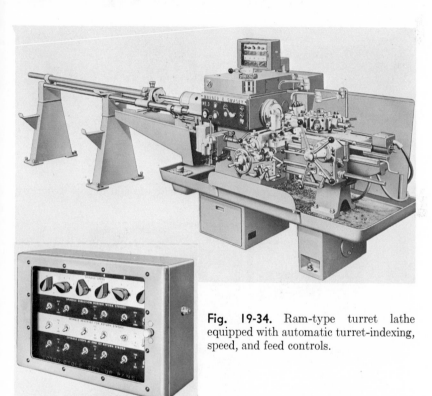

**Fig. 19-34.** Ram-type turret lathe equipped with automatic turret-indexing, speed, and feed controls.

Both electric and hydraulic drives have been used to make these machines automatic. Punched cards and tape are also used to provide a wider variety of operations, including contour turning (Fig. 19-35).

**Single-Spindle, Automatic-Chucking Lathes.** Automatic turret lathes have long been referred to as single-spindle automatic-chucking machines. These machines are of two distinct types, depending on the position of the turret. They may be automatic ram or saddle machines, with the turret conventionally mounted as just described, or they may

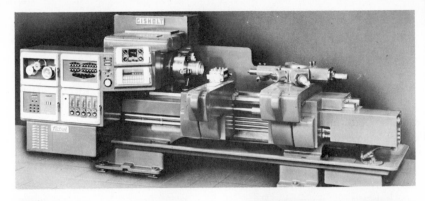

**Fig. 19-35.** Tape-control-type turret lathe, with machined part (courtesy Gisholt Machine Co.).

**Fig. 19-36.** Single-spindle automatic-chucking machine (courtesy The Warner & Swasey Co.).

have the turret vertically mounted (Fig. 19-36). Both the front and back cross slides can be used simultaneously, and they can be combined with cutting from any one of the turret faces. Speeds, feeds, and cutting distances are set by adjustable trips (Fig. 19-37) on the selector drum.

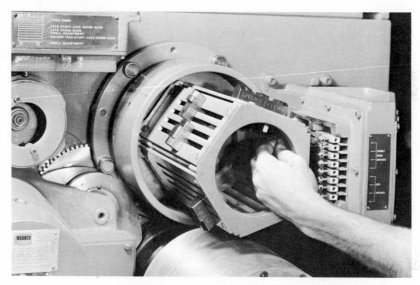

**Fig. 19-37.** Setting the stops of a selector-drum switch of the single-spindle automatic (courtesy The Warner & Swasey Co.).

On this machine, the larger the diameter of the work, the greater the rigidity, since the tools need not be extended so far from the overhead mounting. Also, chips, coolant, and dirt tend to fall free of the machined surfaces.

Single-spindle automatics of this type may be obtained with $8\frac{1}{2}$- and $10\frac{1}{2}$-in. swing over the cross slides; these are designated for size as No.1 and No. 2, respectively.

The tooling used is identical with that of the other turret lathes. The tooling layout sheet (Fig. 19-38) indicates the type, position, and sequence of operations to produce a given part. The layout includes standard machine times for cutting and indexing, which are important in keeping the machine supplied with stock and for cost estimating. Note that this 8-in. flange may be entirely machined inside and out in less than 8 min.

### Automatic Screw Machines

**Single-Spindle Automatic.** Screw machines of the single-spindle type may be thought of as small cam-operated turret lathes. The dis-

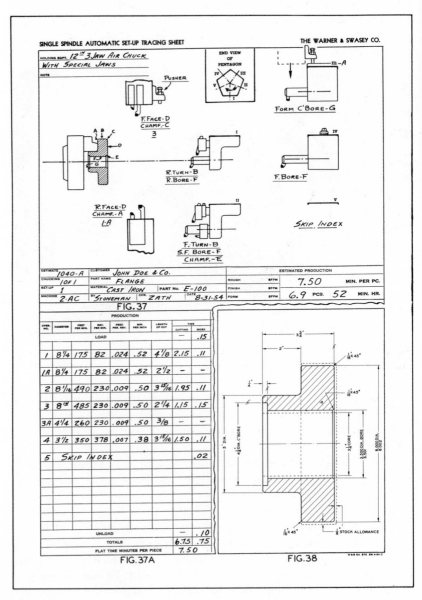

**Fig. 19-38.** Tooling layout and production sheet for a flange on a single-spindle automatic.

tinguishing features of these machines are the position of the turret and the tool mountings. The automatic screw machine (Fig. 19-39) has the turret mounted on a horizontal pin so that it may rotate on a vertical axis.

**Fig. 19-39.** Single-spindle automatic screw machine, showing turret and front, rear, and vertical cross slides (courtesy Aluminum Co. of America).

The front, top, and rear slides are fed at predetermined rates by means of disk cams. The three superimposed cams needed to perform the four operations of rough turn, finish turn, form the head, and cut-off are shown in Fig. 19-40. You will note that the cam perimeter is divided into 100 parts. Each part is assigned a certain number of seconds, depending on the speed of the camshaft.

**Fig. 19-40.** Various cams required to make a part automatically on a Brown and Sharpe automatic screw machine.

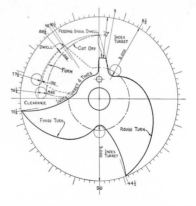

Although single-spindle screw machines are generally associated with small parts, the bar capacity through the headstock may range from 5/16 in. on a No. 00 Brown and Sharpe machine to 2 in. on a No. 6 machine. The tolerance that can be maintained ranges from 0.0005 in. on small diameters to 0.002 in. on the larger diameters. This machine provides for rapid production of a wide variety of identical parts from rod, bar, or tube stock (Fig. 19-41).

AUTOMATIC-SCREW-MACHINE ATTACHMENTS. Many attachments are available for automatic screw machines that can extend its usefulness

**Fig. 19-41.** Types of work performed on an automatic screw machine (courtesy the Brown & Sharpe Mfg. Co.).

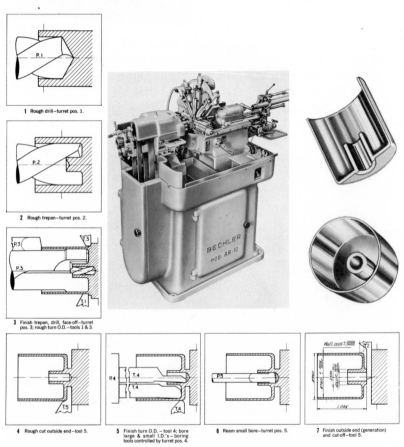

1  Rough drill—turret pos. 1.

2  Rough trepan—turret pos. 2.

3  Finish trepan, drill, face-off—turret pos. 3; rough turn O.D.—tools 1 & 3.

4  Rough cut outside end—tool 5.

5  Finish turn O.D. — tool 4; bore large & small I.D.'s – boring tools controlled by turret pos. 4.

6  Ream small bore—turret pos. 5.

7  Finish outside end (generation) and cut-off—tool 5.

**Fig. 19-42.** The Swiss automatic-type screw machine. The part and the tooling layout illustrate the type of work that can be done with a single-spindle drilling attachment on an inclinable slide mounted on the front end of the machine (courtesy Bechler Service Corporation).

and eliminate second machining operations. Some of them are for screw slotting, burring, nut tapping, rear-end threading, and cross drilling. Most of these attachments operate automatically at the same time that another piece is being produced in the machine spindle, thus reducing overall production time.

SWISS-TYPE SCREW MACHINE. The Swiss-type screw machine has five radially mounted tools (Fig. 19-42) that are cam-controlled. The single-point tools mounted at each of these five stations operate close to a carbide-lined guide bushing that supports the work. By coordinating the forward movement of the stock with the single-point cam-controlled tool, the desired shape may be generated. Accuracy can be maintained, on small diameters, to 0.0005 in. The part shown in the figure indicates the variety of operations that can be done on this type of machine.

Attachments may be mounted in front of the spindle for internal operations. American-made machines of this kind range in size from a 3/32- to ½-in. maximum bar capacity; Swiss makes, as large as 1¼-in.

**Multispindle Automatic.** The principle of the tooling arrangement of the single-spindle automatic has been broadened to include four, six, eight, and nine spindles, with corresponding cross slides (Fig. 19-43),

**Fig. 19-43.** Multispindle automatic (courtesy The National Acme Co.).

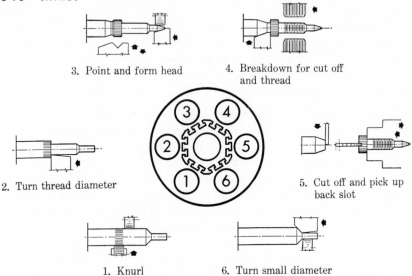

3. Point and form head

4. Breakdown for cut off and thread

2. Turn thread diameter

5. Cut off and pick up back slot

1. Knurl

6. Turn small diameter

**Fig. 19-44.** Tooling for six-spindle automatic lathe used to complete a part in nine operations (courtesy The National Acme Co.).

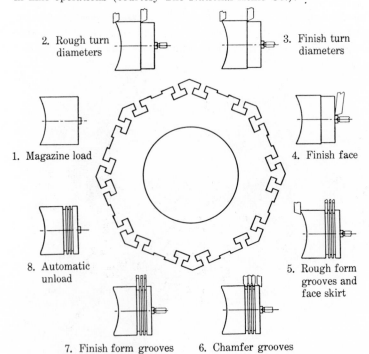

2. Rough turn diameters

3. Finish turn diameters

1. Magazine load

4. Finish face

8. Automatic unload

5. Rough form grooves and face skirt

7. Finish form grooves

6. Chamfer grooves

**Fig. 19-45.** An example of tooling used on a chucking-type multispindle automatic screw machine. Castings are conveyed to the magazine which loads the machine. After machining (16 operations in 8 sec) is completed, the piston is automatically unloaded, and the castings are carried on to assembly (courtesy The National Acme Co.).

to make a high-production lathe. This lathe may be of either the bar or the chucking type. In the bar-type machine, the stock moves up by cam arrangement; in the chucking machine, the stock may be either hand- or magazine-loaded.

The tooling needed for nine operations performed automatically in 3 sec on a carburetor adjusting screw is shown in Fig. 19-44. An example of automatic magazine-load chucking work is shown as a tooling layout in Fig. 19-45.

Typical bar-production parts (Fig. 19-46) give some idea of the wide variety of work performed on these versatile machines. Note that many of the parts have milling, cross drilling, and slotting operations. This covers only a few of the attachments that may be used to avoid second-step machining operations; another part is shown in Fig. 19-47.

The operation of a multispindle automatic may be best understood by following closely the tooling layout shown previously in Fig. 19-44. The work is actually started at tooling station No. 6, where the small

**Fig. 19-46.** Typical parts for multispindle bar-type automatic (courtesy The National Acme Co.).

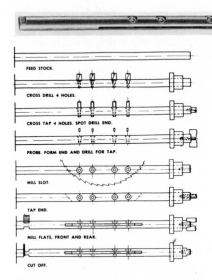

**Fig. 19-47.** This part, turned out on an eight-spindle machine, shows the use of attachments to eliminate secondary machining operations. All 16 operations are performed on the same machine to complete the shaft at a production rate of 200 shafts per hour (courtesy The National Acme Co.).

diameter is turned. At station No. 1 a straight-type knurl is applied with a roller, shown on the back side, for support. Tools with roller supports are similar to the roller turner tools of the turret lathe. At station No. 2 the thread diameter is turned. This may be done from either the cross slide or the end tool slide. At station No. 3 a form tool cuts in back of the knurl, and another points the end. At station No. 4 a preparation cut is made for cutoff, and the thread is rolled. At station No. 5 the part is cut off and taken by a pickup over for slotting, which completes the cycle.

The time to complete a part is the length of time required for the longest operation. If one operation is excessively long compared to the others, it may be divided up between two or more stations, thus substantially reducing the overall time. Bar stock may be fed in at two stations to permit the completion of two pieces in one cycle.

In order to justify the investment required for a multiple-spindle machine, long-run jobs are necessary. The information needed to determine whether or not a job is to be assigned to a multiple-spindle machine is based on the complexity of the part, the size, and the quantity. A rule-of-thumb judgment requires a minimum 4-day run to justify tool planning and setup.

The size of a multiple-spindle automatic bar machine is given by the maximum-diameter bar that the machine can handle. The size of the multiple-spindle chucking machine is given by the outside diameter of the chuck. A 6-in. chucking automatic lathe has a maximum chucking capacity of 4⅝ in.

## MACHINE TIME

The time required to make a cut on a lathe is based on the speed in revolutions per minute and the feed used. Use the following procedure:

1. Find the cutting speed of the material for the type of tool used.
2. Use this formula for finding the speed:

$$\text{Rpm} = \frac{S \times 12}{D \times \pi} \text{ or, simplified, rpm} = \frac{S \times 4}{D}$$

where $S$ = surface feet per minute, or cutting speed

$D$ = diameter of the material being turned

$\pi = 3.1416$

3. Select a feed rate. This is based on the type of cut made and on experience. For average work, it may range from 0.001 in. for the feed of a cutoff tool to 0.020 in. for a roughing cut.

4. After the speed is known and the feed rate is established, calculate the time for machining.

$$\text{Time in minutes} = \frac{\text{length of cut}}{\text{feed in thousandths} \times \text{rpm}}$$

### QUESTIONS

1. Why are engine lathes called by that name?
2. Name, and tell the function of, the five main parts of an engine lathe.
3. How is the size of an engine lathe designated?
4. Compare the uses of the three-jaw universal chuck and the four-jaw independent chuck.
5. What is the advantage of the rubber, flex-type collet?
6. What is the purpose of a mandrel?
7. What is the difference between a follower rest and a center rest?
8. Why is the automatic cross-slide lathe particularly adapted to turning long, multiple-diameter shafts?
9. Why is the turret lathe well suited to repetitive manufacture of complex cylindrical parts?
10. What is the main difference between the ram-type turret lathe and the saddle type?
11. What special tooling is associated with the turret lathe?
12. Explain the difference between multiple tooling and combined cuts.
13. For what type of work is the vertical turret lathe suited?
14. Describe a single-spindle, automatic chucking lathe.

15. Why would it be better to assign a small-diameter, close-tolerance instrument part to a Swiss-type screw machine rather than to a conventional (Brown and Sharpe) type lathe?

16. What are the two main types of multi-spindle automatic lathes?

17. What types of secondary machining operations can be performed on the multi-spindle automatic lathe?

18. What is the controlling factor in the relative length of time required to turn out a part on the multi-spindle automatic lathe?

19. How is the size of a multi-spindle automatic lathe designated?

## PROBLEMS

1. Find the rpm that would be used in turning a 8-in.-diameter piece of 1020 steel 10 in. long with (a) a high-speed tool, (b) a carbide tool. Assume a cutting speed of 100 fpm for the HSS tool and 300 fpm. for carbide.

2. Find the time required to make one cut over the stock described in (a) and (b) of Prob. 1 if the feed used is 0.005 in. per revolution.

3. What would be the time required to machine 100 shafts of 4130 steel 3 in. in diameter and 8 in. long. A carbide tool is used. The cutting speed is 300 fpm and the feed is 0.010 in. Allow 1 min for center drilling each piece and 2 min for handling.

4. What would the cost of the previous job be if the material cost is 20 cents per lb. The time required for sawing each piece to length is 15 sec. Allow $\frac{1}{8}$ in. of length for each saw cut. The labor and overhead charge is $9 per hr. Steel weighs 0.2816 lbs per cu in. Lathe set-up time is 10 min.

5. It takes 20 minutes to turn out a bolt on an engine lathe. The same bolt can be turned out on a turret lathe in 3 min. The set-up time for the turret lathe is 45 min. The engine has to have all tools changed each time a bolt is made, so the set-up time is included in the time for the part. How many pieces would have to be made before it would pay to set up on the turret lathe?

6. Compare the production obtainable between a brazed-type carbide tool (A) and a throw-away insert-type tool (B). Tools A and B are of comparable cost. After 1 hr and 100 pieces both tools have a 0.030 wear land. It takes 15 min to regrind tool A and 3 min to reset it in the machine. It requires only 30 sec to reindex tool B. (a) How many more pieces can be turned out using tool B than A in an eight-hour day? (b) If labor and overhead are charged at the rate of $12 per hr, what would be the savings with tool B in fulfilling a contract for 1,000 pieces?

## REFERENCES

*How To Run a Lathe*, South Bend Lathe Works, South Bend, Ind., 1947.

*Production Handbook for Warner and Swasey Turret Lathes*, The Warner and Swasey Co., Cleveland, 1956.

# 20

# SHAPERS AND PLANERS

BOTH SHAPERS AND PLANERS employ single-point tools for metal removal. A reciprocating action is used on the shaper cutting tool, whereas the work reciprocates on the planer. The other main differences in the two machines are size and the number of tools employed. Comparatively small workpieces are cut on a shaper. Large workpieces are handled on the planer because of its capacity and number of tool-holding stations. The planer may be used for smaller parts when they can be set up in quantity to take advantage of the long table travel.

## SHAPERS

The shaper makes use of a single-point tool that traverses the work and feeds over at the end of each stroke. The types of surfaces it is best able to produce are shown in Fig. 20-1.

Contour work may also be done by coordinating the tool hand feed to a layout line, or by a duplicating attachment placed on the machine (Fig. 20-2). Thus contours can be formed with inexpensive single-point tools for short runs where the cost of form tools for milling the work would be prohibitive.

A shaper is usually not considered a production machine; however, it is widely used in machine shops and toolrooms, since it is easy to set up and operate. The cutters are low in cost and are easily sharpened. Because the amount of metal removed at one time is relatively small

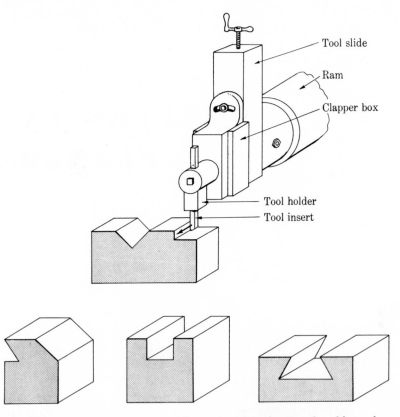

Tool slide

Ram

Clapper box

Tool holder

Tool insert

**Fig. 20-1.** Types of external and internal surfaces best produced by a shaper.

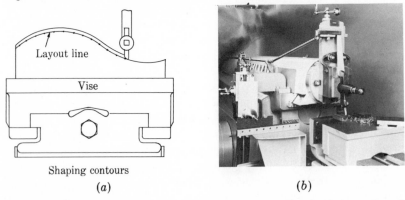

Layout line

Vise

Shaping contours

(a)

(b)

**Fig. 20-2.** Contour cutting (a) to a layout line by hand feed of the tools, and (b) by use of a hydraulic duplicating attachment and template (courtesy Cincinnati Shaper Co.).

in area, little pressure is imposed upon the work, and elaborate holding fixtures are not needed. Although many shaper operations can be more rapidly performed by other machining processes, usually more costly tooling and setups are involved. These alternate methods are economical where the number of parts to be machined is large enough to justify a greater initial investment.

### Shaper Parts

The principle parts of a shaper are shown in Fig. 20-3. The vertical slide, base, table, and ram make up the large structural elements.

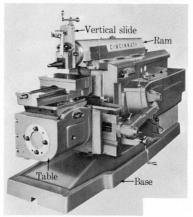

**Fig. 20-3.** Principle parts of a shaper (courtesy The Cincinnati Shaper Co.).

The toolhead assembly is fastened to the front of the ram and consists of a tool slide, tool post, and clapper box. The slide movement can be measured by means of a micrometer dial near the handle. The toolholder rests in a clapper box which is a means of hinging the tool. If no provision were made for allowing the tool to swing up on the return stroke, the work surface would be badly gouged and the tool quickly damaged. The clapper box is provided with a slotted arc which permits it to be swiveled away from the work surface. This is particularly important when vertical and angular cuts are made.

### Ram Drives

Ram movement is obtained either mechanically or hydraulically. The mechanical quick-return crank mechanism is shown in Fig. 20-4. The ram is reciprocated by means of a pivoted rocker arm which is fastened through linkage to the ram. The forward stroke requires a

220 deg of arc and the backstroke 140 deg, which gives a cutting-time ratio of approximately **2:1** and a return-time ratio of **1:2**.

Hydraulic drives consist of a variable-delivery pump, reservoir, and control valves.

Both types of ram drives have their advantages and limitations. Hydraulic-ram speeds and table feeds are quickly set and are infinitely variable within the design limitations of the machine. A more nearly constant stroke velocity can be obtained hydraulically with more efficient shock-free action. The return time for hydraulic shapers is about **1:2**. Mechanical-type drives are less expensive and less complicated.

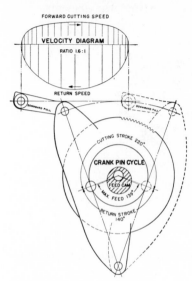

**Fig. 20-4.** The quick-return crank-type mechanism of the shaper (courtesy The Cincinnati Shaper Co.).

### Shaper Size

The size of a shaper is given by the maximum length of the stroke or ram movement, in inches. Shapers are built in a wide range of sizes, from **7** to **36** in. The planer is used where longer cuts are required.

### Shaper Classification

Shapers are classified with respect to the plane of the ram—*vertical* or *horizontal*. The horizontal machines are further classified, according to the action of the cutting strokes, as *pushcut* or *drawcut*. The push-cut horizontal shaper is by far the most common type. Unless otherwise qualified, the term *shaper* refers to this class of machine. A further breakdown of the horizontal-shaper classification is *plain* or *universal*. The universal machine is so designed that the table may be tilted for angular cutting. The vertical shaper (Fig. 20-5) is very much the same

**Fig. 20-5.** A vertical shaper being used to cut a keyway (courtesy Rockford Machine Tool Co.).

as a slotter except for size. The slotter is the larger machine and was so named because it was originally designed for slotting operations.

The vertical shaper has several advantages over a push-type horizontal shaper. The cutting thrust is directed against the table bed, and there is no possibility of deflection of the table. Since the cut tends to force the work onto the table, only the simplest holding devices are needed. The table can be moved in three directions—longitudinally, laterally, and with a rotary motion. This makes for accurate positioning of the work, because more than one surface may be cut without disturbing the initial work setting. The rotary table may be indexed through 360 deg by a worm and worm-wheel arrangement. The vertical shaper is best for short-run cutting of splines, slots, and keyways.

### Shaper Operation

A vise mounted on the shaper table furnishes a quick and easy method for holding the work. To be certain the vise alignment is true with the ram, the fixed jaw of the vise is checked with an indicator (Fig. 20-6).

Truing the vise with the ram does not always give the accuracy desired. Greater precision may sometimes be obtained by having the indicator move along the work after it has been properly seated in the vise. Work is usually placed on parallels resting on the vise base. Since the vise is quite deep, various sizes of parallels are used to lift the work high enough above the vise top for convenient machining. Rough and irregular work can be clamped in the vise with the help of equalizers or with shim stock.

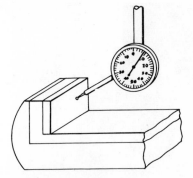

**Fig. 20-6.** The fixed jaw of the vise is checked for true alignment with the ram.

### Estimation of Machine Time

To calculate the time necessary to remove a given amount of material with a shaper, the following formulas are used:

$$S = \frac{sfpm \times 7}{L}$$

$$Tm = \frac{W}{F \times S}$$

where: $S$ = strokes per minute
$sfpm$ = surface feet per minute
$7$ = constant
$L$ = length of stroke
$Tm$ = time, in minutes
$W$ = width of stock
$F$ = feed, in inches per stroke

The constant 7, used in finding the number of strokes per minute, is based on an approximate ratio of the cutting time to the return stroke. The cutting-stroke time on mechanical shapers is about 60 percent of the total stroke time.

The length of the stroke allows for overtravel to both the front and the rear of the work. The tool must travel forward enough to break the chip off and come back far enough to allow the tool to swing into position for the next cut. The total allowance is approximately 1 in.

The time calculation is based on the total number of strokes needed to traverse the work at a given feed. Some allowance may be made for the tool to approach the work and for overtravel. Since this amount of time is so small, it may be neglected, unless very accurate time computations are required.

The feed on a shaper is designated in thousandths of an inch per stroke. The finish desired or the cubic-inch removal rate will help determine the proper amount of feed. A broadnosed tool with a feed setting of 0.010 in. per stroke can produce a finish of approximately 50 rms or better. Where metal removal is the primary consideration, cuts in the range of 0.250- to 0.500-in. depth with feeds of 0.040 to 0.060 in. are used. The higher cubic-inch removal rates must be related to the horsepower of the machine.

### Shaper Accuracy

Dial feeds on both the table cross-feed and the vertical tool slide are graduated in .001-in. increments. The tolerance expected is approximately 0.002 in. However, accuracy depends primarily on the condition of the machine and on the operating variables.

### Keyseaters

Keyseating machines are not so well known as vertical shapers, but, they fulfill a need similar to that of the slotter. Although it is called a keyseater, which implies that its primary function is to make keyways, it can also be used for a variety of external or internal cuts (Fig. 20-7). The serrations, grooves, slots, etc., are cut by a single-point tool held in the cutter bar shown in the inset picture.

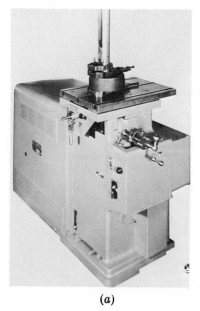
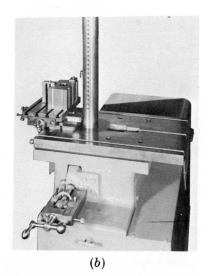

(a)                              (b)

**Fig. 20-7.** A hydraulic keyseater is used for both internal (a) and external (b) keyways. The combination tilting table allows positioning of the work for splines and keyway cutting on tapered surfaces (courtesy Mitts & Merrill).

The keyseater is a rather specialized machine and has several advantages for the type of work it can perform. The initial cost is comparatively low, so it can be used to free more expensive machines for other operations. The work is chucked or located from the bore rather than from the outside diameter, as in the case of shapers and slotters. In this way, keyways can be made that are more nearly true to the bore. The combination tilting and indexing table makes possible straight or tapered keyways and accurately spaced multiple keyways or splines.

## PLANERS

Planers are used for much the same type of surface cutting as shapers are, but on a larger scale. On the planer the tool remains stationary, and the work reciprocates back and forth. At the end of each cutting stroke, the tools are fed a small distance across the work so as to give a fresh bite in the work. The work is fastened to the table which, in turn, rides over the bed of the machine.

Three or four tooling stations are available, depending on the type of planer. Two toolheads are mounted on the overhead crossrail and one on each of the columns. When more than one surface is to be cut, three or four cutting stations can be engaged at one time (Fig. 20-8).

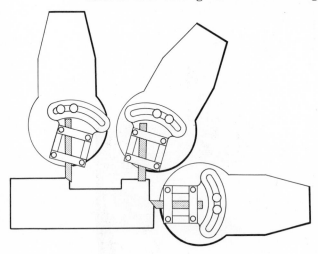

**Fig. 20-8.** Three or four tooling stations may be used at one time on a planer.

### Planer Action

The single-point tool used in the planer imposes relatively little pressure on the work, and only a small amount of heat is generated. This is important when producing large, accurate, distortion-free sur-

**Fig. 20-9.** String planing of duplicate pieces (courtesy Giddings & Lewis).

faces. Modern planers are able to move carbide cutting tools in semi-steel at the rate of 400 fpm. Large heavy castings usually receive their first cuts on a planer. A roughing cut used to true the casting surface will be approximately ¾ in. deep, with a feed of 1/16 to 1/8 in. per cut. Two or three finishing cuts are taken to obtain accuracy on large surfaces. As little as a 0.001- or 0.002-in. depth may be left for the last finishing cut. Although planers are most often associated with the machining of large parts, such as machine tables, beds, rams, and columns, they may be used economically on many similar parts. The practice of setting up duplicate pieces in tandem is known as *string planing* (Fig. 20-9).

### Planer Classification

Planers are classified according to their main structures—*openside, double-housing, pit* and *edge* or *plate* type. The double-housing type shown in Fig. 20-10 is of extremely solid construction. The support furnished the tool by the two columns and heavy crossrail allows heavy cuts to be taken even far above the table.

The openside planer (Fig. 20-11), is made with only one supporting column. Its main advantage is that work may be extended out over the bed. It is also somewhat easier to get at for setup work.

The pit-type planer is more massive in construction than the double-housing planer. It differs also in that the tool is moved over the work by means of a gantry-type superstructure which rides over the ways on either side of the table. The clapper boxes, which are of the double-block type, allow planing in both directions. Since the pit-type planer has its bed recessed in the floor, loading and unloading are facilitated.

Another more specialized planer is the *plate planer,* used for squaring or beveling the edges of heavy plate stock.

**Fig. 20-10.** Double-housing planer (courtesy Giddings & Lewis).

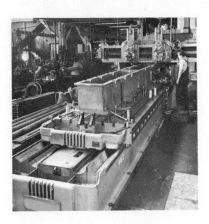

**Fig. 20-11.** Openside planer (courtesy Giddings & Lewis).

### Profile Planing

The hydraulic tracing attachment shown in Fig. 20-12 allows this planer to do three-dimensional work. Simple tracing jobs that do not change in their right-angle relationship to the table motion are done with templates. Where the contour of the part changes in both directions, a model is necessary. The model or pattern may be wood, plaster, metal, or plastic. The tracer rides over the pattern lightly, so softer inexpensive materials may be used.

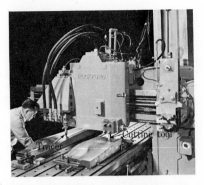

**Fig. 20-12.** Hydraulic tracer attachment being used on an openside planer to facilitate contour cutting (courtesy Rockford Machine Tool Co.).

### Planer Size

Planer capacity is expressed by the maximum width, height, and length of stock that can be planed on the machine. Thus a 62-in. planer refers to a 62-in. width and height capacity, with various lengths of table in feet. Planers have been made that can accomodate work more than 40 ft in length, but half of this figure would be nearer the average size. The openside planer width is given by the distance from the column to the cutter in the extreme outboard position on the crossrail.

### Table Drives

As with shapers, the driving mechanism may be either mechanical or hydraulic. The most common arrangement for the mechanical-drive systems is a d-c variable-voltage reversing motor. Motor-generator sets are needed where direct current is not available. Motion is transmitted from the motor to the table through a series of gears. The gear train driven by the motor is made to mesh with the gear rack on the underside of the table.

The hydraulic-drive system consists of a constant-speed motor to operate the hydraulic pump. Oil pressure is directed through valves to a long cylinder located under the table between the bedways. A rod is attached from the piston in the cylinder to the table. Valves direct oil pressure to either end of the cylinder, which, in turn, forces the piston back and forth. Table speeds are regulated by means of control valves which meter the oil flow. Trip dogs fastened to the table are used to regulate the stroke length.

### Planer Control

Central control of planer operations can be realized by means of a pendant (Fig. 20-13). The pendant consists of a number of remote push-

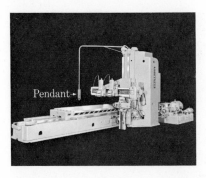

Pendant

**Fig. 20-13.** A pendant makes possible the central control of planer operation (courtesy Rockford Machine Tool Co.).

button switches for motor control. From this central location the operator is able to obtain very close control of all cutting tools. As an example, the "automatic-cut" button will cause the table to start in the cut direction; the "inch-cut" button will move the table slowly toward the columns, stopping when the button is released. Other buttons are used to "inch" the cutters into position, so important in setup work. Rheostats may also be provided on the pendant for controlling the table speed.

### Work Layout

Before the workpiece is placed on the planer table, it may be necessary to make various guidelines on the part. This is done on a layout table. The layout man establishes surface lines in relation to cored holes, pads, and webs. He shims the work on the layout table until it is level in regard to the reference points he has chosen. Scribed lines are then made on the painted surfaces for the machine operator to follow. It is important that the layout be reasonably accurate, since planing is often the first operation on a rough surface. Once the rough surface has been removed, all other machine operations, such as drilling, boring, and milling, use the planed surface as the reference point.

### Work-Clamping Methods

The planer table is made with evenly spaced T-slots and holes. Use of the T-slot is the most common method of holding work against the surface of a machine. Shown in Fig. 20-14 are various T-slot clamp-

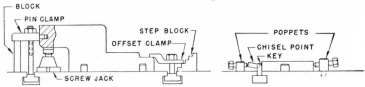

**Fig. 20-14.** Various methods used in clamping work to the planer table.

ing methods. Blocking materials are used to support the heel of the clamp at the proper height. These may be any scrap materials or more conveniently, step blocks, parallels, and jack screws. Flat work is held on the table by means of toe dogs, chisel points, and poppets.

Other methods of holding work to the planer table include electro-magnetism and hydraulic and vacuum clamping. Owing to large inertial forces and intermittent cutting action, these methods usually must be aided by mechanical blocking methods at each end.

### Speeds and Feeds

It is difficult to make definite speed and feed recommendations for planers, since cutting conditions vary widely. Some of the considerations involved in setting speeds and feeds are the size of the workpiece, clamping facilities, ability of the workpiece to withstand the pressure of the cut, and the type and number of tools used at one time.

### QUESTIONS

1. What are the main differences between a shaper and a planer?
2. How may contour work be done on a shaper?
3. What advantages does the shaper have for limited production?
4. What are the advantages of a hydraulic-type driving mechanism for a shaper?
5. How does a plain shaper differ from a universal shaper?
6. What is a slotter used for?
7. How much longer than the workpiece is the shaper stroke? Why?
8. What types of work are performed on a keyseating machine?
9. Why is there comparatively little heat and pressure imposed on the work during a planing operation?
10. How can a planer be economically used on many small, similar parts?
11. Describe the main types of planers and their particular applications.
12. How can three-dimensional contour work be done on a planer?
13. How is the size of a planer designated?
14. What is the purpose of a pendant as used on large machines?
15. What does the set-up man use as reference points when he aligns a casting on a planer for the first cut?
16. What are some of the ways the work material is held on the planer table?

### PROBLEMS

1. Find the correct number of strokes per minute to use on a shaper cutting 1020 steel 10 in. long and 5 in. wide. The cutting speed is 100 fpm for a HSS tool.

2. What would the machining time be for the material in Prob. 1 if a 0.040 feed were used? What is the machine time if a carbide tool is used at 325 fpm?

3. A large, medium-hard, cast-iron casting is machined on a planer. It is 20 ft long and 48 in. wide. Two roughing and two finishing cuts are required. Find the machine time needed if carbide tools are used at 250 fpm. Both of the cross-rail tools are used at the same time in tandem, set at different depths with the cutting edges 8 in. apart. The roughing feed is 0.060 in. and the finish feed is 0.020 in. The return stroke is made at two times the speed of the cutting stroke.

4. The horsepower for planing can be estimated using the cubic-inch removal rate per min as the basis. Thus the depth of the cut in in. $\times$ feed in in. $\times$ (speed in fpm $\times$ 12) $\times$ a constant = the approximate horsepower required. The constant for free cutting steel is 0.6 and for medium cast iron is 0.3. Find the approximate horsepower required for a roughing cut on the casting described in Prob. 3. The depth of cut for roughing is $\frac{1}{2}$ in.

5. If the number of shaper strokes per min is 100 for B1112, what will it be for each of the following: 4150, 8650 cast steel, 1020 annealed, malleable cast iron (standard), and 303Se stainless steel? (See Chap. 3 for ratings.)

REFERENCE

*Tool Engineers Handbook*, The American Society of Tool and Manufacturing Engineers, McGraw-Hill Book Company, Inc., New York, 1959.

# 21

# MILLING
# MACHINES

A NEW CONCEPT in machines was born when the first multipoint cutters were introduced. Just when this came about, however, is somewhat uncertain. The first milling-type cutters are known to have been used in France well before 1800. These cutters resembled our present-day rotary files. Eli Whitney is believed to have built the first milling machine, in 1818, to aid in the manufacture of interchangeable gun parts.

The introduction of the multitooth rotary cutter made possible many new machining operations, such as slab milling, face milling, gear cutting, and keyway cutting.

The modern-day milling machine, with all its attachments, is thought of as the most versatile machine of the metalworking industry.

## MILLING-MACHINE CLASSIFICATION

Many machine-tool builders are engaged in the manufacture of milling machines. Each one has a special purpose, requirement, or condition. As a result, we have a wide variety of milling-machine types. These can be classified, depending on their use, in three general groups—low-production, high-production, and special types. In the first category are the column-and-knee machines. Fixed-bed machines comprise the second group. Special types include duplicating or profiling machines, pantograph mills, rotary-table mills, and others especially adapted for certain jobs.

### Column-and-Knee Milling Machines

The column-and-knee mills are so named because of their two main structural elements (Fig. 21-1).

The column-and-knee mill is classified as plain or universal, depending on whether or not the table can be swiveled in a horizontal plane. The table on the universal machine can be swiveled up to 45 deg to the right or left, making possible angular and helical milling.

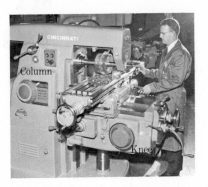

**Fig. 21-1.** A plain, horizontal, column-and-knee milling machine (courtesy Cincinnati Milling Machine Co.).

**Horizontal and Vertical Mills.** The table of a column-and-knee milling machine has a wide range of feeds that can be applied in all three directions—vertically, longitudinally, and laterally. The table can also be quickly positioned by means of a rapid traverse mechanism, and some incorporate automatic table movements. Graduated dials allow the operator to set the table within 0.001 in. accuracy. The rigid overarm and bearing support used on horizontal machines also increase accuracy.

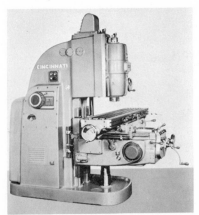

**Fig. 21-2.** A column-and-knee milling machine of the vertical type.

The vertical milling machine is so called because the spindle extends in a vertical position (Fig. 21-2). Some vertical spindles are adjustable only vertically; others can swivel through 360 deg across the face of the machine.

A variation is a combination vertical and horizontal machine (Fig. 21-3). Some machines of this type have an independently driven head mounted on the overarm ram. This head is of the universal type and can be swiveled for cuts at any angle between the cutter and a horizontal plane.

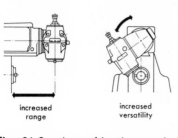

increased
range

increased
versatility

**Fig. 21-3.** A combination vertical and horizontal column-and-knee milling machine. The Universal ram-mounted head adds range and versatility to the machine (courtesy The Cincinnati Milling Machine Co.).

To gain a better understanding of the use of both the vertical and the horizontal milling machines, study the types of work done by each as shown in Fig. 21-4. You may see that there is some overlapping in the type of work performed; however, each kind has its own advantages.

**Hand Mill.** The simplest form of milling machine is the hand mill (Fig. 21-5). On this mill, the feed movements are accomplished by the operator. By using the hand levers, he can "feel" if the work is advancing at the proper speed for the machine. This arrangement is often termed *sensitive-type feed*. The hand mill is ideally suited to small parts and short-run production. It is made in two basic types, depending on whether the vertical feed is accomplished by raising and lowering the table or the spindle. If the table is fixed, it is classified as a fixed-bed machine; otherwise, it is column-and-knee type.

### Fixed-Bed Milling Machines

Fixed-bed milling machines are made, as the name implies, with a stationary bed. All vertical movements for depth of cut and lateral

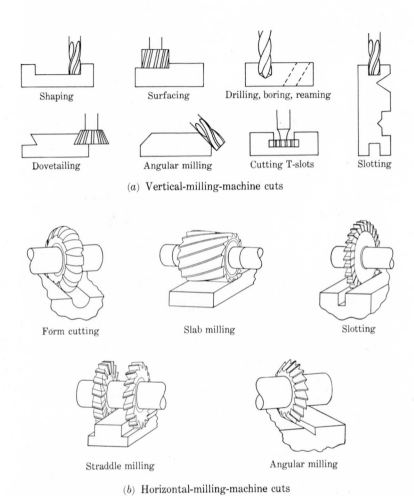

Shaping

Surfacing

Drilling, boring, reaming

Slotting

Dovetailing

Angular milling

Cutting T-slots

Slotting

(a) Vertical-milling-machine cuts

Form cutting

Slab milling

Slotting

Straddle milling

Angular milling

(b) Horizontal-milling-machine cuts

**Fig. 21-4.** Applications of vertical and horizontal milling machines.

**Fig. 21-5.** Hand mill (courtesy Barker Engineering Co.).

cutter positioning are made on the spindle. This arrangement makes for more rigidity and accuracy in the heavy-production cutting required of these machines.

The main components of the fixed-bed machine are shown in Fig. 21-6. An inset view shows how the machine may have either one, two, or three independently driven spindles. The machines, according to the number of spindles, are classified as simplex, duplex, and triplex. Some machines of this type have more than one spindle in line, to provide roughing and finishing cuts in one pass.

The distinctive feature of fixed-bed machines is the automatic cycle. The work may be set to approach the cutter at rapid traverse, make the cut at a predetermined feed, and then automatically return to the starting position. Thus, once the machine is set up, the operator is only required to clamp the part in the milling fixture and start the automatic cycle. If continuous operation is desired, a workpiece is placed in a fixture on one end of the table while cutting is taking place on the workpiece at the other end. This is known as *continuous reciprocal milling* (Fig. 21-7).

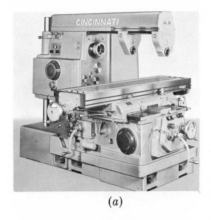

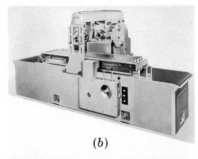

(b)

(a)

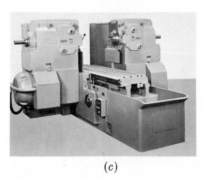

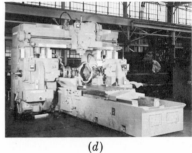

(d)

(c)

**Fig. 21-6.** Various types of fixed bed milling machines, (a) all purpose, (b) simplex, (c) duplex, (d) triplex (courtesy The Cincinnati Milling Machine Co.).

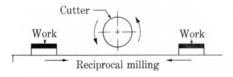

**Fig. 21-7.** Reciprocal milling.

**Rise-and-Fall Milling Machine.** A variation of the single-spindle or simplex fixed-bed machine is a rise-and-fall arrangement. Rise and fall can be accomplished either by a power-feed arrangement or as shown in Fig. 21-8, the spindle is made to rise and fall as the outline of the cam dictates. The rise-and-fall arrangement is suited to such work as cutting keyways and other slots that require both longitudinal and vertical movement.

The automatic fixed-bed machine may incorporate a variable-feed attachment to take into account the variation in the depth of the cut (Fig. 21-9). These machines have hydraulically controlled vertical movement on the spindle carrier and are termed *tracer-controlled* machines. Tracer-type mills are widely used in production milling of both straight and irregular surfaces.

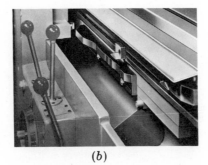

(a)

(b)

**Fig. 21-8.** (*a*) Template and tracer of tracer-controlled mill for rise-and-fall milling. (*b*) Variable-feed attachment and cam automatically vary the feed rate for cutting conditions (courtesy The Cincinnati Milling Machine Co.).

**Fig. 21-9.** Rise-and-fall milling machine. Note that cam section is bolted in place to control movement of the head (courtesy Cincinnati Milling Machine Co.).

**Planer Mill.**   A planer mill is very similar in structure to the double-housing planer discussed in Chap. 20. On the planer mill, the single-point tools are replaced by rotary milling heads (Fig. 21-10).

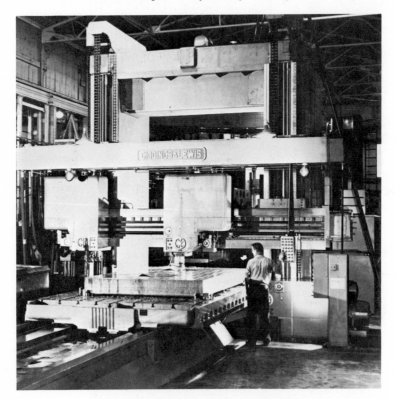

**Fig. 21-10.**   Planer-type mill (courtesy Giddings & Lewis Machine Tool Co.).

This mill is usually equipped with two cutting heads on the overhead crossrail and one on each of the columns. The overhead units can be positioned for angular cuts. When several cutting heads are employed at one time, the metal-removal rate is high. This is necessary on a machine of this type in order to justify the large initial investment, the cost of operation, and the special tooling.

## Special Types

Many special types of milling machines are made to accomplish specific kinds of work more easily than present standard machines. In this category are the duplicating mills, die sinkers, profiling machines, and pantographs. Most of these machines are vertical mills that have been adapted to reproduce accurately by means of a tracer, the forms and contours from a master pattern.

**Fig. 21-11.** Mechanical-type duplicating mill with twin spindles profiling 15 blades on two impeller rings from a single-blade master (courtesy George Gorton Machine Co.).

**Duplicating Mills.** In the hand-type duplicating mill, the operator must guide the tool back and forth across the pattern (Fig. 21-11). Automatic machines are made to traverse the pattern either electrically or hydraulically. Once the cycle is started, the tracer will automatically follow the master pattern until it is completed. The pattern may be of easily formed material such as wood or plaster. Large electrically controlled machines of this type, used extensively in making sheet metal dies for aircraft and automotive bodies (Fig. 21-12), are better known by their trade name of Kellering machines.

**Pantograph Mills.** The pantograph, or engraver, is generally considered a two-dimensional tracer, but it can also be used in three

(a)                                    (b)

**Fig. 21-12.** (a) The Keller mill being used to finish a propeller forging, using a finished propeller as a master; (b) a steel mold for a precision aluminum casting being cut using a wood model (courtesy Pratt & Whitney Co., Inc.).

dimensions. It can be made to trace on either an enlarged or a reduced scale. The tracer is guided by hand, and this, in turn, through a pantograph linkage, controls the cutter. The larger-sized pantographs are made for three-dimensional machining (Fig. 21-13). These machines are used to reproduce models, dies, etc.

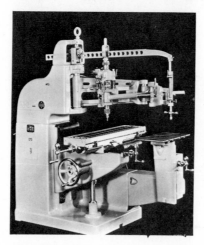

**Fig. 21-13.** Large-sized three-dimensional pantograph used for engraving, milling, and duplicating in two or three dimensions on flat or curved surfaces from enlarged masters, for making of punches, stamps, hobs, and rolls; dies and molds for plastics, rubber, and glass; engraving of complex designs; short-run research and development work; and long-run production work with toolroom accuracy (courtesy George Gorton Machine Co.).

**Rotary-Table Mills.** To facilitate the loading and unloading of a large number of parts while the machine is cutting, a rotary-type table is used for holding the work. Figure 21-14 shows a view of a rotary-table machine. These individual fixtures are being used to hold the work. Each fixture locates and holds one block, which is clamped automatically as it approaches the cutters. After the cut is completed, the part is automatically unclamped. The table may be made to travel continuously or on a cycle of alternate feed, dwell, and rapid traverse.

**Fig. 21-14.** Rotary-table mill (courtesy Ingersoll Milling Machine Co.).

The same kind of operation is accomplished on a smaller scale by equipping a standard horizontal mill with an automatic indexing table, shown in Fig. 21-15.

**Fig. 21-15.** An automatic indexing base mounted on standard milling-machine table. Table cycling and indexing are automatic. This allows the operator to load and unload two parts while two others are being machined. Production rate—800 per hr.

Small parts may be milled at rather high rates, since loading and unloading can be done during the machining time. Two parts are loaded while two are being machined. Clamping and unclamping are done automatically during the table cycle.

**Other Special Machines.** Oftentimes, the machine-tool builder is called on to make a special machine to fulfill a particular machining requirement. The part shown in Fig. 21-16 is being straddle-milled on a

**Fig. 21-16.** Special-type milling machine with an example of the work done (courtesy Sundstrand Machine Tool Co.).

special machine so that all three lugs may be done in one pass. This same part could be done with no special equipment on a standard milling machine, or it could be done somewhat more rapidly with a standard machine and an automatic indexing table, described previously. In one case, 15 parts per hour are produced, whereas the specialized machine can turn out 12 times that many.

## MILLING-MACHINE ATTACHMENTS

There are a number of attachments that contribute greatly to the versatility of the milling machine. By means of attachments, rotary motion is turned into reciprocating motion, accurate indexing is accomplished, spirals and helixes may be cut, and compound angles are made, to mention but a few of the operations that are made faster and easier.

### Dividing Head

The dividing head (Fig. 21-17) is one of the most interesting and most-used milling attachments. It is used for many different operations but, basically, is designed to divide a circle into any desired number of parts. To accomplish this one widely used type of dividing head makes use of a worm and wheel reduction with a ratio of 40:1. That is, it takes 40 turns on the crank to make the work revolve through 1 revolution. Thus, by taking less than 40 turns, the work may be indexed through any required portion of a revolution. Accurate fractional turns may be obtained by using the hole circles in the front of the indexing head. An example of its use will serve to illustrate the point, as follows:

Let 6 equal the desired number of circle divisions or cuts to be made. The formula used is

$$\text{Plain indexing} = \frac{40}{N} \quad (N) = \text{desired number of cuts}$$

$$\frac{40}{6} = 6\frac{2}{3} \text{ turns on the indexing crank per cut}$$

The $\frac{2}{3}$ fraction is increased to make it usable on a hole circle as

$$\frac{5 \times 2}{5 \times 3} = \frac{10 \text{ holes}}{15\text{-hole circle}}$$

Complete indexing per cut = 6 complete turns plus 10 holes on a 15-hole circle.

Several indexing plates are available with hole circles ranging from 15 to 49, which will take care of all numbers through 50 and many

**Fig. 21-17.** A universal dividing head (courtesy Kearney & Trecker Corp.).

above 50. Other forms of indexing, designed to handle more complex problems, are differential, wide-range, and astronomical. As many as 1,296,000 divisions of a circle may be obtained with an astronomical attachment (Fig. 21-18). Simple degree indexing is based on one turn of the crank being equal to 1/40 of 360 deg or 9 deg. The formula is $N/9°$. Smaller parts of a degree are obtained by changing the 9 deg into minutes or seconds, thus 9 deg equals 540 min.

**Fig. 21-18.** Astronomical dividing-head attachment (courtesy Kearney & Trecker Corp.).

The dividing head is sometimes used to rotate the work by means of a gear train to produce helical cuts, as in making milling cutters, helical gears, or tapered spirals (Fig. 21-19). Helical cuts, as used

**Fig. 21-19.** The gear train used to drive the indexing head, powered by the machine lead screw (courtesy Kearney & Trecker Corp.).

in making the milling cutters (Fig. 21-20), are made by gearing the lead screw to the indexing head which is used to turn the work as it is being cut.

**Fig. 21-20.** Milling the helix of a high-speed-steel milling cutter, using the indexing head, powered by a gear train from the lead screw, to turn the work as it is being cut (courtesy Kearney & Trecker Corp.).

### Slotting Attachment

The slotting attachment is designed to change the rotary motion of the spindle into a reciprocating action similar to that of a shaper. This attachment (Fig. 21-21) is clamped to the machine column and receives its drive from the machine spindle. It is usually used when single-piece parts require keyways, splines, and slots.

**Fig. 21-21.** Milling machine slotting attachment machining serrations in workpiece (courtesy Kearney & Trecker Corp.).

## Universal Head

The horizontal-style milling machine is considered the most versatile type, although there are times when a vertical arrangement would be more advantageous. The universal head is made to adapt a horizontal spindle for vertical or angular milling (Fig. 21-22).

**Fig. 21-22.** A universal milling attachment (courtesy Kearney & Trecker Corp.).

A universal head is made to swivel 360 deg on either of its two axes. This attachment, because of the ease of setting compound angles, is very useful in making dies, jigs, and fixtures.

## Other Attachments

Many other attachments are available, such as a cam-and-rack milling attachment, a universal chuck that can be mounted on the machine spindle or indexing head, and micrometer spindles for table adjustments.

## MILLING CUTTERS

As mentioned previously, the versatility of the milling machine is due in part to the wide variety of cutters available. Although this variety may at first appear confusing, it is simplified if we classify them in seven main groups, as shown in Fig. 21-23. These include plain, side, slitting saws, form, angle, end, and special. By studying Fig. 21-23, you will become familiar with the type of work each cutter is capable of doing, since each is pictured in a typical work situation.

In choosing a cutter for a particular job, the shape and size of the cutter are of first importance. Though the type of cutter may be selected from these shown, one must bear in mind that many variations

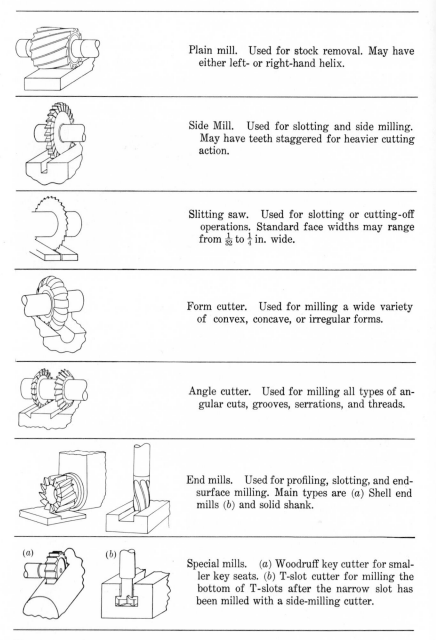

Plain mill. Used for stock removal. May have either left- or right-hand helix.

Side Mill. Used for slotting and side milling. May have teeth staggered for heavier cutting action.

Slitting saw. Used for slotting or cutting-off operations. Standard face widths may range from $\frac{1}{32}$ to $\frac{1}{4}$ in. wide.

Form cutter. Used for milling a wide variety of convex, concave, or irregular forms.

Angle cutter. Used for milling all types of angular cuts, grooves, serrations, and threads.

End mills. Used for profiling, slotting, and end-surface milling. Main types are (a) Shell end mills (b) and solid shank.

Special mills. (a) Woodruff key cutter for smaller key seats. (b) T-slot cutter for milling the bottom of T-slots after the narrow slot has been milled with a side-milling cutter.

**Fig. 21-23.** Milling-cutter types and applications.

of each kind are made to suit special situations. A complete listing may be found in manufacturers' catalogs.

### Design Considerations

Side-milling cutters are made with regular of staggered-tooth spacing. Staggered-tooth cutters are designed so that each alternate tooth is offset. This type is best for heavy cutting, as it allows for greater chip room. The relationship of the metal removal to the tooth spacing is shown in Fig. 21-24.

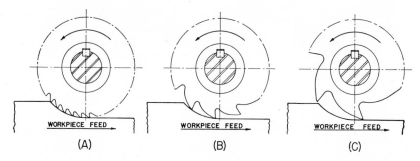

**Fig. 21-24.** The relationship of the number of teeth in milling cutters to the work material. (*a*) Too many teeth—limited chip space. (*b*) Cutter has one or two teeth in contact with the workpiece—gives smooth operation. (*c*) Too few teeth—causes cutter to lose workpiece contact, resulting in shock and damage.

High-helix-angle cutters are chosen primarily for finishing cuts in the softer, more ductile materials (Fig. 21-25).

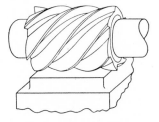

**Fig. 21-25.** A high-helix-angle cutter used for finishing cuts on soft material.

As was pointed out in the study of single-point tools, more rake angle, both side and back, was required for the soft ductile materials. Milling-cutter angles are much the same as those of single-point tools; in fact, each tooth on the cutter may be considered a single-point tool in which the same rake and clearance angles are applicable (Fig. 21-26).

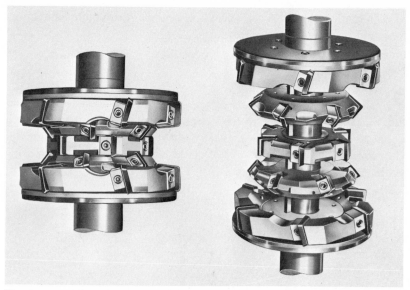

**Fig. 21-26.** The milling cutter is like a number of single-point tools fastened together, the same rake and clearance angles being applicable (courtesy Futurmill Inc.).

## THE MILLING PROCESS

### Milling-Cutter Rotation.

Milling cutters may be mounted on the arbor so that the cutting action will bring the cutting forces down into the work (called *climb milling*), or the forces may be directed up as in *up,* or *conventional, milling* (Fig. 21-27). The advantage of climb milling is that the downward action of the cutter helps hold the material in place. Thus the fixture can be less rugged and of simpler design. This is especially helpful in milling thin materials that are hard to clamp. Higher feed rates may be used, with a corresponding increase in production, increased cutter life, and lower horsepower per cubic inch of metal re-

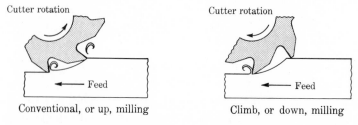

Conventional, or up, milling          Climb, or down, milling

**Fig. 21-27.** Cutter relationship to work in conventional and climb milling.

moved. However, as the name implies, there is a tendency for the cutter to climb over the work. This imposes undue strain on both cutter and arbor. The climbing action may be eliminated if the work can be made to feed into the cutter at a steady pace. On production machines, this is taken care of by a hydraulic backlash eliminator.

Up milling tends to pull the work up away from the fixture. However, where no provision has been made to eliminate the lead-screw backlash, this method is used exclusively.

## MILLING METHODS

The methods used to mill a part or a number of parts may vary widely. Wherever possible, ways of increasing production are given prime consideration. The practice of placing more than one cutter on the arbor at one time or more than one workpiece on the milling-machine table may be the deciding factor as to whether or not a job will prove profitable.

### Straddle Milling

When two cutters are mounted on an arbor and are spaced so as to cut on each side of the material (Fig. 21-28), the term applied is straddle milling. The cutters are spaced very accurately and are held rigidly. Therefore, the parts produced are uniform.

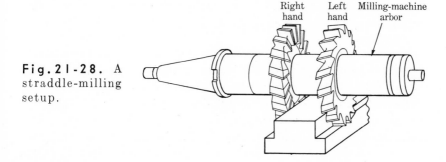

Right hand    Left hand    Milling-machine arbor

**Fig. 21-28.** A straddle-milling setup.

### Gang Milling

Many cutters may be placed on the same arbor to make an entire surface or contour change in one pass (Fig. 21-29). A combination of gang and straddle milling cutter arrangement is also shown.

**Fig. 21-29.** Gang-milling setups used to machine a combination of surfaces simultaneously (courtesy Ingersoll Milling Machine Co.).

## Multiple Piece-Part Milling

When more than one piece part is to be machined at one time, the parts may be arranged in various ways on the milling-machine table. These are identified briefly, as follows: *Progressive milling* means that two or more operations are performed successively on identical parts. In *reciprocal milling* the parts are loaded at each end of the table. While one part is being cut, the other station is being unloaded and loaded. In *abreast milling* the parts are placed side by side on the milling-machine table for simultaneous milling. For *string milling* the parts are placed in line on the table and are milled successively.

### PLANNING FOR PRODUCTION MILLING

After a preliminary study of the part prints, it is necessary to specify the most suitable type of milling-machine fixture, tools, cutters, speeds, and feeds to produce the part at the lowest unit cost. The following outline may aid in accomplishing this.

1. Determine the type of machine to be used. Keep in mind, when selecting a machine, that the column-and-knee machines are easily set up and operated. They can be changed quickly and are therefore ideal for short-run jobs. The bed-type machines require more setup time, since feeds and speeds are set by change gears; therefore, longer runs are desirable. Specialized machines are considered only for parts not conveniently handled on a regular machine and where the quantity is large enough to warrant the extra cost.

2. Determine the type of milling to be done—whether straddle, contour, etc. Also, decide on the method of mounting the work—whether several parts can be placed on the table for abreast milling, string milling, or reciprocal milling, or if indexing or other fixtures are to be used.

3. Check the Brinell hardness of the part in several places to obtain a basis for cutting speed.

4. Choose the type of cutters needed, including the style, size, and material. Milling-cutter dimensions are given by outside diameter, width, and inside diameter. The cutter diameter is based on the depth of cut plus the clearance between the arbor collars and the work. Too large a cutter adds to the time of the job and to the horsepower requirements. Heavy cutting requires rigid cutter mounting. A 2-in.-diameter arbor is 16 times as rigid as a 1-in. arbor. Face mills mounted on stub arbors (Fig. 21-30), have minimum overhang and can be counted on for heavy roughing cuts as well as for accuracy in the finished cut. The cutting-tool material, whether high-speed steel, carbide, or ceramic, will be governed by the rigidity of the machine and the setup. Carbides and ceramics demand rigid setup of both the cutter and the work, or chipping of the tool will occur.

**Fig. 21-30.** A face mill mounted on a stub arbor (courtesy Kearney & Trecker Corp.).

5. Determine proper speeds and feeds. The speed at which the cutter rotates is based on the formula

$$\text{Rpm} = \frac{S \times 12}{D\pi}$$

where
$S$ = surface feet per minute
$D$ = cutter diameter
$\pi$ = 3.1416

The Brinell hardness and the cutting-tool material may be used to determine $S$, as mentioned previously.

The feed, in inches per minute of table travel, will be based on the machine horsepower, the finish desired, and the chip clearance of the cutter. The feed rate will be calculated by the formula

$$Fr = F_t N_t R$$

where $Fr$ = feed rate of milling-machine table, inches per minute
$N_t$ = number of teeth in cutter
$R$ = rpm of cutter
$F_t$ = feed per tooth in inches

6. The time required to make a cut with a plain milling cutter can now be obtained by the formula

$$Tm = \frac{L + A + O}{F}$$

where $Tm$ = time, in minutes
$L$ = length of material being cut, in inches
$A$ = approach. [This includes the distance before the cutter actually touches the work and until it is cutting at full depth.]
$O$ = overtravel, in inches
$F$ = feed in inches per minute

Thus

$$A = \sqrt{d(Cd - d)} + CL$$

where $A$ = approach
$d$ = depth of cut
$Cd$ = cutter diameter
$CL$ = clearance (distance cutter is from work)

Cutter approach time for face milling cuts may be calculated by the formula

$$A = \frac{D}{2} - \sqrt{1 - \left(\frac{W}{D}\right)^2}$$

where $D$ = cutter diameter
$W$ = width of cut

A roughing cut is finished when the forward edge of the cutter reaches the end of the material. However, for a finishing cut, the entire cutter must pass over the work; therefore, the approach for a finishing cut is equal to the diameter of the cutter.

7. The horsepower of the machine should be considered, since it is economical to take advantage of the amount available, but it is not wise to run the machine continuously over its rated capacity. Milling-

machine horsepower is based on the cubic-inch removal rate, which, in turn, must be based on the proper cutting speed for the material and cutter. The cubic-inch removal rate is determined by the formula cim = depth × width × feed in inches per minute, and

$$hp_c = \frac{cim}{K}$$

where $hp_c$ = horsepower at cutter
$K$ = a factor based on the material and the feed rate used

Tables giving these values may be found in the *Tool Engineer's Handbook*. A few are given here for some common materials:

| | |
|---|---|
| Alloy steel: 300–400 Bhn.......................... | 0.5 |
| Aluminum....................................... | 2.5–4.0 |
| Cast iron, soft.................................. | 1.5 |
| Stainless steel, austenitic free-machining.............. | 0.83 |

When all the above factors have been considered, a reasonable estimate as to the type of equipment needed for a given production rate can be made. For the overall time of a given item, other factors should be included, such as start, rapid traverse time, rapid return indexing, etc. Much of these data may be obtained from books on standard times.

### QUESTIONS

1. Why is a column-and-knee classification appropriate for several kinds of milling machines?
2. How does a vertical milling machine differ from a horizontal?
3. In what ways is a universal column-and-knee milling machine more versatile than a single-spindle fixed-bed machine?
4. Why is a fixed-bed milling machine better for production work than a plain column-and-knee mill?
5. What type of milling machine would be used to make a mold cavity for a shovel?
6. For what type of work is a pantograph mill most often used?
7. Explain how an indexing table is able to speed up production on an ordinary fixed-bed machine.
8. What is the function of the indexing head as a milling-machine attachment?
9. Explain the uses of a slotting attachment and a universal head.
10. Name the main types of milling cutters and their uses.
11. Explain the difference between *climb* and *up* milling.
12. What is meant by straddle milling and gang milling?
13. What is meant by reciprocal milling?

14. How do you determine the type, material, and size of the milling cutter to use for a given operation?

15. What is the basis for calculating the power required for a given milling-machine operation?

## PROBLEMS

1. Calculate the rpm of the following diameter milling-machine cutters. The cutting speed is 120 sfpm. (*a*) 4-in.-shell end mill, (*b*) 8-in., staggered-tooth, side-milling cutter.

2. Calculate the cutting speed in sfpm of the cutter of Prob. 1(*a*) if the rpm is 90.

3. A ¾-in.-diameter end mill runs at 210 rpm, and the table feed is 4½ in. per min. Find the cutting speed. Find the feed per tooth if the end mill has four teeth.

4. The information for a given milling operation is as follows: feed, 0.015 inch per tooth; C. S., 120 sfpm; diameter, 6 in.; number of teeth, 14. Calculate the following: (*a*) cutter rpm, (*b*) feed in in. per min.

5. For a given vertical milling operation it was decided to switch from high-speed steel cutters to carbide cutters changing the cutting speed from 100 sfpm to 340 sfpm.

|  | Carbide cutters | High-speed steel cutters |
|---|---|---|
| Diameter | 6 in. | 5 in. |
| Feed | 0.017 in. per tooth | 0.015 in. per tooth |
| Number of teeth | 12 | 10 |

Calculate the following for each of the cutting tools: (*a*) cutter rpm, (*b*) feed in in. per min, (*c*) time required to take a cut 7 in. long, (*d*) percent savings in time by changing to a carbide cutter.

6. Calculate the actual approach required of a milling cutter 6 in. in diameter making a cut ½ in. deep on a horizontal mill.

7. Calculate the correct indexing for the following equally spaced divisions: (*a*) 4, (*b*) 60, (*c*) 93.
Standard change gears: 24, 28, 32, 40, 44, 48, 56, 64, 76, 86, and 100; Plate 1. 15, 16, 17, 18, 19, and 20-hole circles

8. Calculate the correct indexing for a 30-deg angle.

9. What is the gearing required to machine a 14-in. helix on a standard milling machine?

## REFERENCES

*Tool Engineers Handbook*, The American Society of Tool and Manufacturing Engineers, McGraw-Hill Book Company, Inc., New York, 1959.

*Treatise on Milling and Milling Machines*, Cincinnati Milling Machine Company, Cincinnati, 1951.

# 22

# DRILLING, REAMING,
# AND BORING
# OPERATIONS

**DRILLING**

The most common method of originating a hole in metal and many
other materials is by drilling. For precise hole location and size, drilling
is often followed by boring and reaming operations.

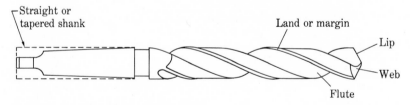

**Fig. 22-1.** The cutting action of the
drill can be compared to a single-point
tool used in a vertical position. The
helix angle of the flute becomes the back
rake, and the lip angle becomes the end
cutting-edge angle.

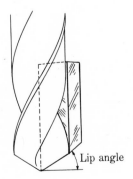

583

## Theory of Drill Action

The cutting action of a drill can be compared to that of two tools. The main cutting action is along the lip of the drill, which is like a single-point tool, as shown in Fig. 22-1.

The closer the cutting action gets to center, the less efficient it is. The action under the web of the drill is a combination of chisel action and of the metal being forced away by extrusion.

## Hole-Locating Methods

In a simple small-quantity production, a layout is first made on the part to be drilled. At the intersection of two layout lines, a prick-punch mark is made, which, if well centered, is enlarged with a center punch (Fig. 22-2). The drill is carefully positioned over the center-

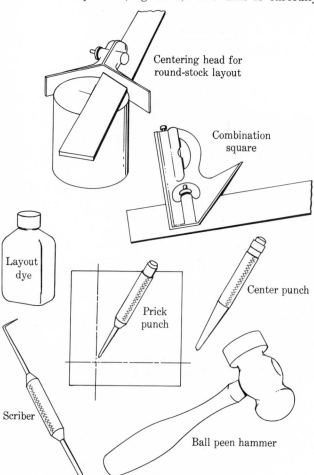

Centering head for round-stock layout

Combination square

Layout dye

Prick punch

Center punch

Scriber

Ball peen hammer

**Fig. 22-2.**   Tools and materials needed to properly lay out and center-punch a hole for drilling.

punch mark, and the hole is drilled. Although this method is slow, for small-quantity production the tool cost is low.

Large-quantity production requires quick and accurate hole location. One method of accomplishing this is by means of a drill jig (Fig. 22-3). The part to be machined is placed in the drill jig against a number of locating pins. Clamping holds the part tightly against these pins to maintain constant location of the holes. Notice that the work does not rest against a flat surface. A well-designed drill jig makes provision for chip clearance, chip removal, and quick and easy loading and unloading of the piece parts. The hardened and ground drill bushing is accurately located in the jig and acts as a guide for the drill. Drill bushings are pressed in for a semipermanent arrangement, or they may be of the slip-renewable type held in place by a screw, as shown in Fig. 22-3. A slight turn of the bushing allows the slot on the bushing head to clear the screw and be removed. This type of bushing is used if another operation, such as tapping or reaming, follows drilling.

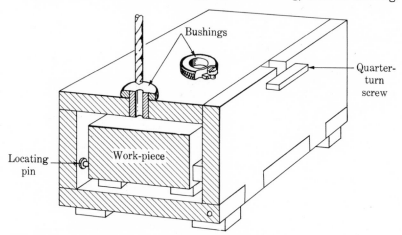

**Fig. 22-3.** The drill jig is used for accurate hole location.

A drill-template sheet is quite similar to a drill jig except that it has a number of accurately located drill bushings on a piece of sheet metal (Fig. 22-4). The template sheet is clamped over the part to be drilled, and a portable drill is used to make the holes.

A newer method of automatic location of the part for each hole to be drilled makes use of punched or magnetic tape. The table of the drill press is made to move along $X-Y$-coordinates according to a previously programmed tape (Fig. 22-5). The drill is automatically fed down and retracted after each table movement. A more complete description of the tape-control process is given in Chap. 29.

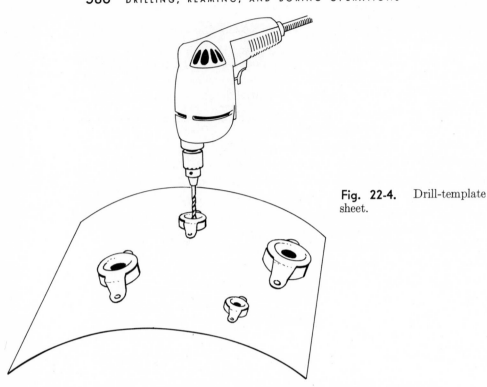

**Fig. 22-4.** Drill-template sheet.

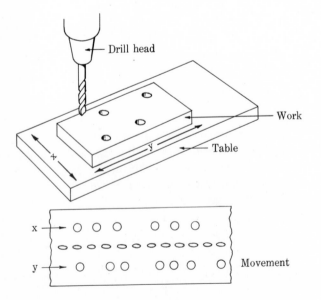

**Fig. 22-5.** Tape control used for automatic hole location in the drilling operation.

A new development in drill points, called the *spiral tip* (Fig. 22-6), simplifies hole location. A drill can be started accurately without center punching or drill bushings, even on a curved surface. The drill is of a standard type, but it requires a special grinding operation to obtain the spiral tip.

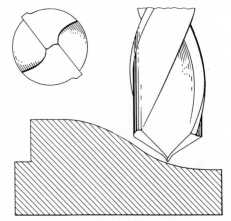

**Fig. 22-6.** The spiral-point drill is used to accurately start a hole, without previous preparation

## Common Drill Types

A wide variety of twist drills are made so as to gain peak performance under many conditions. The standard drill point included angle is 118 deg, with a lip clearance angle of 12 deg. These angles will vary with the type of material being cut. A general rule is to increase the included angle for very hard materials and decrease it for the softer ones.

**Straight-Flute Drills.** On some soft materials such as the purer grades of the nonferrous metals, too sharp a point combined with drill lip angle will cause the drill to "hog in," or take too deep a cut and break. This condition is overcome by the straight-flute drill (Fig. 22-7). This drill is also recommended for sheet metal work.

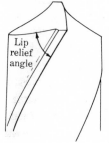
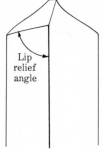

**Fig. 22-7.** The included lip relief angle of a straight-flute drill is increased to reduce "hogging" tendencies on soft metals.

**Core Drills.** Cored holes in casting are often rough and out of round. A special heavy-duty core drill with several cutting edges is needed to act as a combination drill and reamer for these holes (Fig. 22-8).

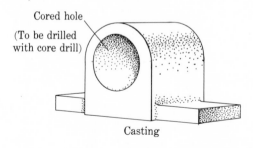

Cored hole
(To be drilled
with core drill)

Casting

**Fig. 22-8.** Four-flute core drill and casting.

**Multiple-Diameter Drills.** Multiple-diameter drills are used to cut down on secondary operations which are time-consuming and less accurate. Figure 22-9 shows a multiple-diameter drill and some typical applications. Multiple-diameter drills may be of the step type or sub-

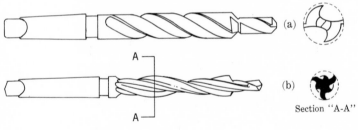

(a)

(b)

Section "A-A"

**Fig. 22-9.** Multiple-diameter drills may be of (a) the step type or (b) the sub-land type (courtesy Morse Twist Drill & Machine Co.).

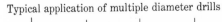

Typical application of multiple diameter drills

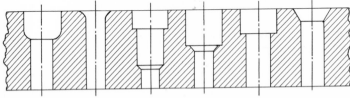

land type. A sub-land drill provides a flute and land for each diameter up to a maximum of four. A step drill is a standard drill that has been ground down to provide the various diameters needed. The sub-land tools are more complex than the ordinary step tools, but they offer a much better chip passageway, since each cutting edge has a flute. A sub-land drill is never sharpened on the diameter; therefore, good concentricity can be maintained for the life of the tool.

**Oilhole Drills.**    Drilling poses a problem in that it is difficult to maintain cooling action at the cutting tip. Oilhole drills provide a means of flowing the coolant through the body of the drill (Fig. 22-10). These drills are made for drilling deep holes and are used in drill presses, lathes, and special deep-hole drilling machines.

**Fig. 22-10.**    Oilhole drill (courtesy Morse Twist Drill & Machine Co.).

**Variations in Standard Drills.**    In addition to the types of drills mentioned, variations may be obtained in standard drills. A change in the helix angle of the flutes makes a difference in the ease with which the chips are removed from a hole and in the rake of the cutting edge or lip of the drill. For materials of low tensile strength that tend to pack and do not climb out easily, such as some aluminum, magnesium, copper, and thermoplastics, a low-helix angle is recommended. The slow helix is used for materials that break into very fine bits or powder, as is true in drilling hard rubber, bakelite, and plastic laminates (Fig. 22-11).

### Special Drills

**Gun Drills.**    Gun drills (Fig. 22-12) differ from conventional drills in that they are usually made with a single flute [Fig. 22-12(a)] or a tubular shape. The hole in the single-flute type provides a passageway for the pressurized cutting fluid, which serves to keep the cutting edge cool as well as flush out the chips. Single-flute gun drills form a wedge-shaped chip that tends to curl and break easily. Because of this chip-generating action, single-flute gun drills are effective in drilling holes in low-carbon steels or other tough, stringy materials where two-flute designs tend to clog.

The two-flute pin-cutting type [Fig. 22-12(b)] has an off-center coolant through-hole in the molded carbide tip which generates a pin (Fig 22-13). The two cutting edges provide a balanced cutting action which allows extremely high feed rates and excellent size control.

Gun drills are used to produce true holes to depths and tolerances not obtainable with ordinary drills. Depths from 6 diameters to 130 in. are possible in a single uninterrupted operation. Even though the drill is made to advance rapidly—from 15 to 60 in. per min—good tolerance and finish are maintained. This is due, in part, to the high (60 to 1,500 psi) cutting-fluid pressure. The efficient metal-cutting operation is due

**Fig. 22-11.** Difference in chip-removal action between a low-helix angle drill used for material that does not climb out easily, and a regular drill (courtesy Greenfield Tap & Die).

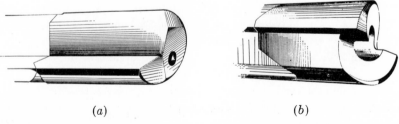

(a)                                              (b)

**Fig. 22-12.** (a) Single-flute gun drill and (b) two-flute pin-cutting gun drill.

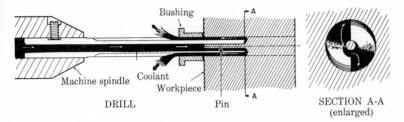

**Fig. 22-13.** Coolant flow and pin generation of a two-flute pin-cutting gun drill (courtesy Star Cutter Company).

to the thorough cooling of the drill point and to the continuous scavenging of the chips by the high-pressure cutting fluid. A general rule for the maximum depth that may be attained by deep-hole drills is 100 times the drill diameter. Some parts that require deep-hole drilling include gun barrels, camshafts, crankshafts, machine-tool spindles, and connecting rods. Deep-hole drills may develop a runout of as much as 0.0005 in. per in. of depth. The general hole tolerance, however, is 0.002 in. for most materials. Fairly good finishes are obtained, usually in the range of 65 rms.

**Trepanning Drills.** Trepanning is a method of producing holes, ordinarily more than 2 in. in diameter, by cutting a narrow annular ring of material from the work so as to leave a center core or plug. The drill is similar to the two-lip gun drill mentioned previously. A trepanning drill, however, is made for larger holes and has a separate head keyed or threaded to the end of a tube (Fig. 22-14).

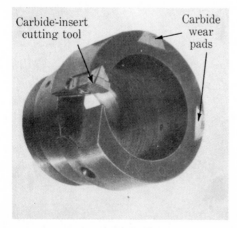

**Fig. 22-14.** A trepanning head used with inserted wear pads. It is threaded on the end for inserting into a drive tube (courtesy The Tool and Manufacturing Engineer).

On large holes, trepanning offers considerable advantage. A 6-in.-diameter hole 10 in. deep requires the removal of 282.6 cu in. of metal as chips with a conventional drill. A trepanning drill, using a ¾-in.-wide cutter, calls for removing only 126.6 cu in. of metal as chips. Normally, the tolerance may be held to ±0.003 in. on the hole diameter. A comparison of trepanning time and regular or spade-drill time is given in Fig. 22-15.

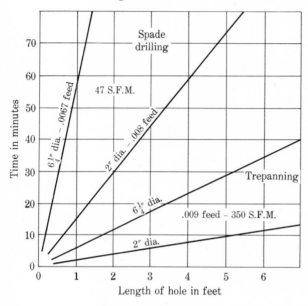

**Fig. 22-15.** A comparison of times for spade drilling and trepanning (courtesy *American Machinist/Metalworking Manufacturing*).

### Drill Sizes and Materials

**Sizes.** As with other gradual developments, no one standard method of designating sizes was used. The small-sized drills are known as number or wire size and range in numbers from 80 to 1, or 0.0135 to 0.228 in. The letter-size drills are larger, with a range of *A* to *Z*, or 0.234 to 0.413 in. Fraction-size drills cover the whole range from 1/64 to 3 in., by 64ths of an inch. Metric sizes range from 3 to 13 mm. Both larger and smaller drills may be obtained, but they are not in the standard series.

**Materials.** Comparatively few metal-cutting drills are now made from low-capacity carbon steel. Production demands have made high-speed steel, carbide-tipped, and solid-carbide drills imperative. Solid-carbide drills may now be obtained as small as 0.015 in. in diameter.

## REAMING

Reamers are multipoint cutting tools designed to finish a previously drilled or bored hole. They may be used to finish a hole to very
close tolerance or to produce a better surface finish, or both.

### Reamer Types

As with most cutting tools, many kinds gradually developed to
meet the demands of industry. Reamers may be classified into three
main types (Fig. 22-16)—solid (including straight, rose-chucking, and
tapered), shell, and adjustable. Additional kinds are expansion reamers
and multiple-diameter piloted reamers.

**Solid Reamers.** The solid reamers are made from high-speed steel
bar stock or they may be made from high-carbon steel and have brazed-
carbide cutting edges. A straight reamer (*a* in the figure) is tapered
about one third of its cutting length for ease of starting. It next has
a straight portion for the sizing and finishing operation, and then tapers
off again. The rose-chucking reamer (*b*) is quite similar to the straight
reamer except that it is used for roughing rather than finishing cuts.
Most of the cutting is performed on the forward beveled end of the tool.
Tapered reamers (*c*) are used to produce a specified taper such as
Morse or Brown and Sharp. A hole is drilled to the small diameter of
the taper, followed by the roughing reamer and then either a straight
or a spiral-flute finishing reamer. Spiral flutes are especially good on
surfaces that are interrupted by a longitudinal slot or keyway. Tapered
reamers (*d*) are used in reaming holes for standard taper pins used in
assembly operations.

**Shell Reamers.** Shell reamers (*e*) are essentially the same as solid
reamers except for a mounting hole in the center. This serves two purposes—to conserve expensive cutting materials and for ease of changing
the tool.

**Adjustable Reamers.** Adjustable reamers are made to cover an infinite number of sizes over a small range. The type shown in Fig.
22-16(*f*) can be obtained in a range of sizes from $\frac{3}{8}$ to $2\frac{1}{2}$ in. The
$\frac{1}{2}$-in. size, for example, ranges from 15/32 to 17/32 in., and others have
similar variations.

**Expansion Hand Reamers.** Expansion hand reamers are often used
where it is necessary to enlarge a hole slightly in order to secure the

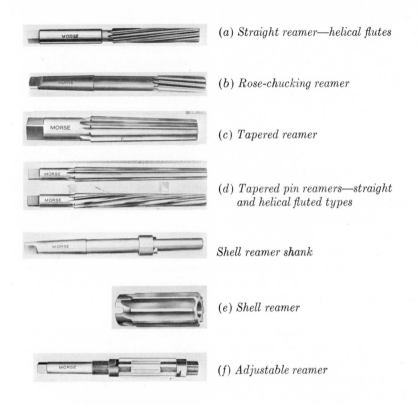

(a) *Straight reamer—helical flutes*

(b) *Rose-chucking reamer*

(c) *Tapered reamer*

(d) *Tapered pin reamers—straight and helical fluted types*

*Shell reamer shank*

(e) *Shell reamer*

(f) *Adjustable reamer*

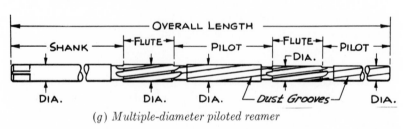

(g) *Multiple-diameter piloted reamer*

**Fig. 22-16.** The main types of reamers (courtesy Morse Twist Drill & Machine Co.).

necessary fit. Such an operation is common in assembly work and maintenance operations.

**Multiple-Diameter Piloted Reamers.** Several diameters can be finished at one time with the multiple-diameter reamer (g). A pilot, which may ride in the work but preferably in the fixture, is necessary to avoid chatter and maintain accuracy.

## Hand and Machine Reaming

Hand reamers are recognized by their square shank, whereas machine reamers have a tapered shank to fit into a drill or lathe spindle. The amount of stock left for reaming varies with the type of operation and the material being cut. A general rule allows 0.005 to 0.010 in. for hand reaming and 0.010 to 0.015 in. for machine reaming.

## Reaming Speeds and Feeds

High-speed reamers should be run at two thirds to three fourths of the speed of drills. Too high a speed causes the material to cling to the cutting edges, resulting in premature dulling and rough hole diameters. The feed is generally two or three times that used for a drill of corresponding diameter. As with other machining operations, feed is related to the finish desired. Too fine a feed, however, will cause the tool to idle in the cut and produce undue wear.

## Counterboring, Countersinking, and Spot-Facing

Closely associated with the operations of drilling and reaming are those of counterboring, countersinking, and spot-facing, as shown in Fig. 22-17. Counterboring is done so that a bolt head will be flush with

**Fig. 22-17.** (*a*) The application of countersinking and counterboring to obtain a flush surface for a bolt or screw. (*b*) Spot-facing produces a smooth seat for a bolt head.

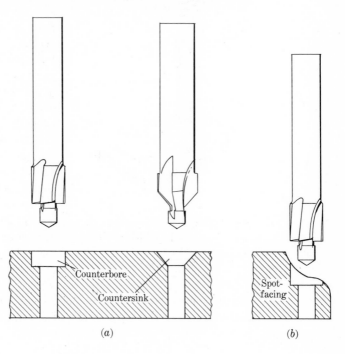

(*a*)          (*b*)

the surface. Countersinking provides a tapered recess for flathead screws and bolts. Spot-facing is used to smooth the surface around a hole so that the washer and bolt head may have a level surface.

### Drilling Equipment

Drilling equipment ranges from the portable hand drill to the large multispindle machines able to drive hundreds of drills at one time. The main types are sensitive, upright, radial, gang, turret, multispindle, special drilling and tapping machines, self-contained drilling heads, and deep-hole drilling equipment.

**Sensitive Drill Press.** The most common type of drill press (Fig. 22-18) is known as the sensitive, or hand-feed, type. The operator is sensitive to the rate at which the drill is cutting and can regulate it according to the cutting conditions. The careful operator will watch for excess drill deflection and correct it before the drill breaks or inaccuracies result. Machines of this type have a speed range from 300 to 30,000 rpm. The size is designated by twice the distance from the center line of the spindle to the column. Thus, a 16-in. drill press would be able to drill to the center of an 8-in. plate.

Bench drill presses are very similar to the sensitive drill presses but are of lighter construction and are made to be fastened on a table or bench. The work is usually held on the drill-press table by means of a vise. If the work is large and the holes to be made are also large, it is necessary to bolt the work to the table, making use of the T-slots

**Fig. 22-18.** Sensitive-type drill press shown with production table (courtesy Power Tool division, Rockwell Manufacturing Co.).

and holes provided. Drill jigs and fixtures are used for accurate hole placement when the work is of sufficient quantity to warrant the cost of such tooling.

**Upright Drill Press.** The upright drill press is quite similar to the sensitive drill press in appearance. It is equipped with power feed and a speed-change gearbox. The feeds may range from 0.004 to 0.025 in. per revolution. This machine is of heavier construction and is better suited to a wide range of jobs than is the sensitive type. A universal table may be used in place of the standard T-slot table, providing accurate lateral and longitudinal movement.

**Radial Drill Press.** Work that is large and requires several holes is difficult to position for each operation. The radial drill press (Fig. 22-19) is equipped with a radial arm that can be swung through an arc of 180 deg or more. On the radial arm, which is power-driven for vertical movement, is an independently driven drilling head equipped with power feed. The drilling head may be moved along the arm by hand or power on a gear and rack arrangement. To drill a hole, the following procedure is used: The arm is raised or lowered as needed, the drill head is positioned and locked on the arm, the column is locked, the spindle speed and feed are adjusted, and the depth is set. The drill will then feed down and retract when the proper depth has been reached. The arm and column may then be unlocked and the drilling head moved to a new position without disturbing the work.

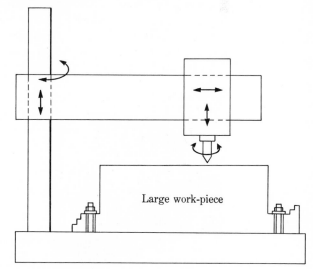

**Fig. 22-19.** Components and movements of a radial drill press.

Large work-piece

Universal radial drills allow the radial arm to be rotated on a horizontal axis, providing for angular-hole drilling.

The size of a radial drill is designated by the radius, in feet, of the largest plate in which a center hole can be drilled, and the diameter of the supporting column, in inches. Sizes range from **3** to **12** ft for arm capacity and 4- to 34-in. column diameters. Spindle speeds ranging from 20 to 1,600 rpm and feeds from 0.003 to 0.125 in. per revolution are available.

Large work is clamped to the table by means of T-slot bolts, step blocks, clamp straps, and angle plates. Angle plates are used to hold work in the vertical position (Fig. 22-20). Some angle plates are of the adjustable type and can be used to hold work at any desired angle.

**Fig. 22-20.** An angle plate is used for vertical and angular mounting of parts to be drilled.

**Gang Drill Press.** The gang drill press is made up of a number of upright drill presses placed side by side, with a common table and base (Fig. 22-21). The parts being drilled, reamed, counterbored, tapped, etc. can be easily transferred from one spindle to the next with no lost time for tool changing.

**Fig. 22-21.** A gang drill press (courtesy Boice-Crane Co.).

**Turret-Type Drill Presses.** When a number of drill sizes or other tools are needed to complete a part, the turret-type drill is very useful. Any one of the six tools can be quickly indexed into place and used (Fig. 22-22).

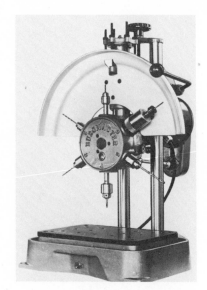

**Fig. 22-22.** An autoindexing turret drill and tap machine (courtesy Burgmaster Corp.).

**Multispindle Drilling Heads.** Multispindle drilling heads can be attached to a single-spindle machine to provide a means of drilling several holes at one time. These heads are of two main types—adjustable, for intermediate production, and fixed, for long high-production runs.

The adjustable head [Fig. 22-23(a)] is driven by a gear from the spindle through a universal-joint linkage to each drill. This arrangement allows maximum variation in drill placement with minimum center distances ranging from 5 to 12 in. As many as 15 drills can be held at one time in a head of this type. Previously drilled and bored templates are used to position the drills for accurate center distances.

Single and double eccentric heads (b) and (c) allow drill positioning anywhere within the radius of the eccentric circle. Locating and locking templates, shown at (c), are necessary to ensure constant drill location. Three to eight spindles are standard for this type of drilling head.

Fixed multispindle drilling heads are usually of the geared type, taking their drive from a central geared spindle through gear trains direct to the working spindle (d). All gears are in the same plane, except where ratios must be established. Gearless-type heads (Fig. 22-24 on page 601) may employ a wobble plate and crankpins to drive the drills. This arrangement provides for many more spindles and closer center distances.

Fixed-head drills are engineered for a specific job. When the production run for that pattern is over, the heads are torn down and rebuilt

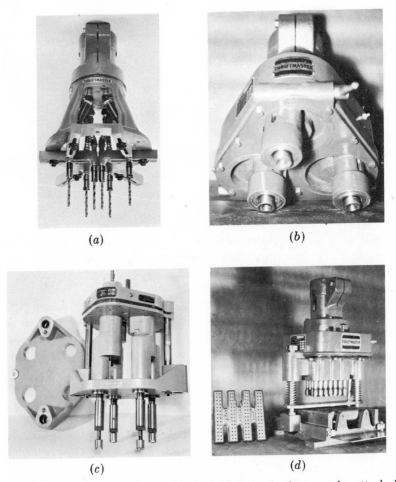

**Fig. 22-23.** Various types of multispindle drill heads that may be attached to a single-spindle drill press. (*a*) Multispindle adjustable drill head, (*b*) single eccentric head, (*c*) double eccentric head, (*d*) geared multispindle drilling head (courtesy Thriftmaster Products Corp.).

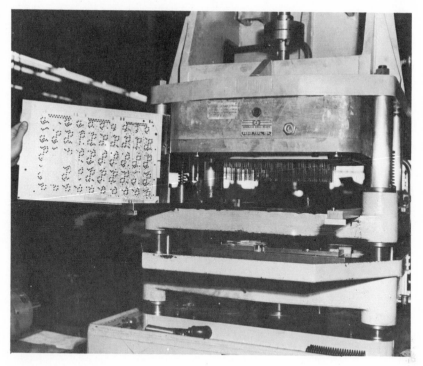

**Fig. 22-24.** A gearless-type multiple drill head allows a large number of spindles with close center distance (courtesy Zagar Tool Inc.).

to suit the new requirements. Each job requires a jig-bored bushing plate and gearing or wobble plates to suit.

Whether a fixed- or an adjustable-type head is used is determined by the length of the run or the cutting load. Adjustable heads are, theoretically, subject to more wear and may require more maintenance. One approach to the problem of selecting the proper type of production-drilling equipment is to temporarily substitute an adjustable head for individual or gang drilling. If it proves satisfactory, the more expensive fixed-type head can be made up.

**Special Drilling and Tapping Machines.** The next step beyond the multispindle head for higher production is the multispindle automatic-indexing machine built to suit the customer. Automatic indexing of a piece part is usually done with a rotating table that indexes in either the vertical or the horizontal position. Individual motor-driven spindles equipped with automatic feed are positioned to work on parts as they are indexed on the work-holding table (Fig. 22-25).

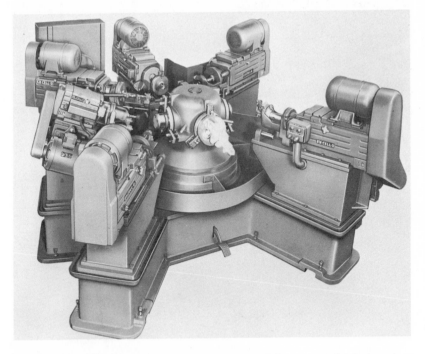

**Fig. 22-25.** Self-contained drilling units grouped for a special job (courtesy Ex-cell-o Corporation).

**Self-Contained Drilling Heads.** A self-contained drilling head has an electric motor which originates both the spindle drive and the automatic feed. Power feed is obtained either by a cam drive from the motor or through a hydraulic system. The feed cycle can be adjusted to advance the spindle at rapid traverse, change to slow feed, have a short dwell interval, and provide a rapid return stroke. Manufacturers use these self-contained drilling units, together with air or hydraulic clamping devices and indexing heads, to fabricate automated setups for small items.

### Deep-Hole Drilling Equipment

Deep holes, exceeding three times the drill diameter, may be drilled on modified precision boring machines, on special gun-drilling machines, or on modified lathes (Fig. 22-26).

### BORING

James Watt and others tried to produce more efficient steam engines but were unsuccessful until John Wilkinson improved a boring machine

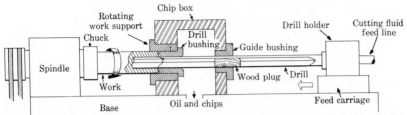

In this setup, the gun drill is supported at the back end by a drill holder and a guide bushing far forward. The work is supported by a rotating bushing. Cutting fluids are fed directly through the drill from the back end.

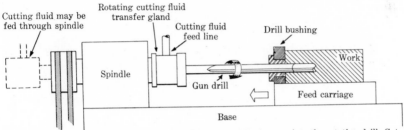

The work in this setup is mounted on the feed carriage which advances into the rotating drill. Cutting fluids are fed through a rotating oil gland which takes the fluid directly from the feed line or through the machine spindle.

**Fig. 22-26.** A modified lathe used as gun-drilling equipment (courtesy Metalworking).

to such an extent that it could make large bores (48 to 72 in. in diameter) with a degree of accuracy described as "true within the thickness of an old shilling." Up until 1774, there had not been much demand for accurately bored holes. Early cannons were made of bronze with carefully cored cylinders which were gradually cleaned out. Accuracy was not considered the greatest factor, since the cannonballs were used in the "as-cast" condition. After seeing James Watt's early attempts to build a steam engine, an English civil engineer by the name of John Smeaton reported to the Society of Engineers, "Neither the tools nor the workmen exist that can build so complex a machine with sufficient precision."

Fortunately, Wilkinson, Watt, Smeaton, and the others were not dismayed by this statement but continued to design and build machines of increasing accuracy. Today's boring machines are able to work with an accuracy of a few ten thousandths of an inch on production work.

Boring is used to enlarge and locate accurately a previously drilled or cored hole. Drills tend to wander or drift, making hole placement inaccurate. Also, if the lips of the drill are not equal, the hole will be oversized. When accurately positioned holes are needed, they are first drilled and then bored. Boring a previously drilled hole has the advantage of accurate location, since the tool does not follow the hole but bores on its own center or axis (Fig. 22-27).

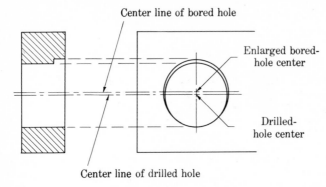

Center line of bored hole

Enlarged bored-hole center

Drilled-hole center

Center line of drilled hole

**Fig. 22-27.** A boring tool is used to correct the location of a drilled hole.

Boring tools are single-point, high-speed, carbide or ceramic tools held in a supported or nonsupported bar. The single-point tool shown in Fig. 22-28 is mounted in a nonsupported bar and is of the adjustable type. The vernier adjustment allows the tool to be set within 0.0001 in.

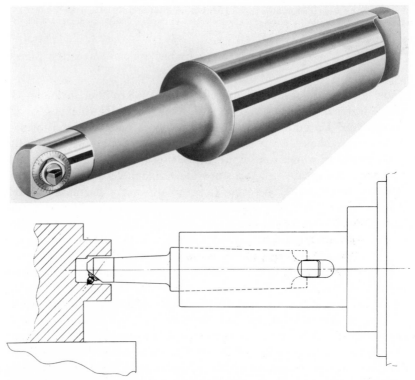

**Fig. 22-28.** Boring bar with vernier adjustment on tool setting (courtesy Microbore).

These tools may also be arranged to make a multiple-type boring head to machine several surfaces at one time (Fig. 22-29).

An adjustable-slide arrangement can be obtained that will extend the boring tool's usefulness to other operations of facing, turning, grooving, and undercutting, as shown in Fig. 22-30.

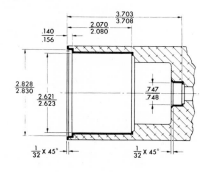

**Fig. 22-29.** Multiple-tool-type boring head with part to be machined (courtesy Microbore).

**Fig. 22-30.** Boring head and job applications (courtesy Chandler Tool Co.).

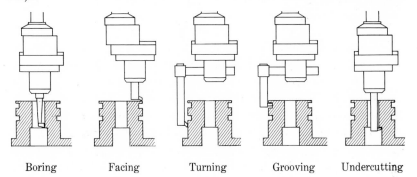

| Boring | Facing | Turning | Grooving | Undercutting |

The supported bar with a tool-block insert, as shown in Fig. 22-31, is also made with micrometer adjustment. Several cutters are placed on one bar. Tools placed on opposite sides of the bar balance the cutting forces, resulting in a smoother, more accurate cut.

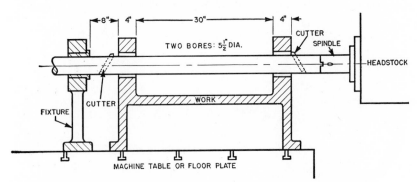

**Fig. 22-31.** The supported boring bar used to machine two diameters.

### Boring Machines

The main types of boring machines are the horizontal and vertical mills, and the precision and jig boring machines. In addition to these, boring operations are often performed on a lathe and milling machine.

**Horizontal Boring Mill.** The horizontal boring mill, shown in Fig. 22-32(a), is a versatile machine used for milling, drilling, and boring. It is especially well adapted for in-line boring, as shown in the figure. The boring bar can be supported either in a fixture or, on long work, in the support column at the end of the machine. The boring-bar extension is removed when closeup operations of milling and drilling are performed, as shown in Fig. 22-32(b) and (c). Mills of this type are used extensively in machining diesel-engine bearing seats, cylinder bores, and block surfaces. The size of the horizontal boring mill is designated by the diameter of the spindle, in inches, which ranges from 3 to 11 in.

**Vertical Boring Mill.** The vertical boring mill (Fig. 22-33) is designed to handle large outside turning and inside boring applications.

Large parts are rather difficult to mount in a lathe chuck for machining. With the vertical boring mill the task is simplified, since the table becomes the chuck, and the weight of the part is not critical. The parts to be machined are put on the faceplate table surface and centered according to the bore or outside diameter. T-slot bolts and clamps are then used to hold the part in place for machining. Cutting

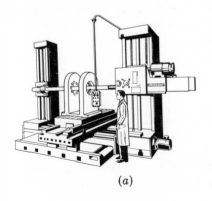

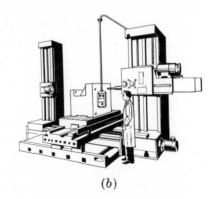

(a)

(b)

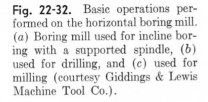

**Fig. 22-32.** Basic operations performed on the horizontal boring mill. (*a*) Boring mill used for incline boring with a supported spindle, (*b*) used for drilling, and (*c*) used for milling (courtesy Giddings & Lewis Machine Tool Co.).

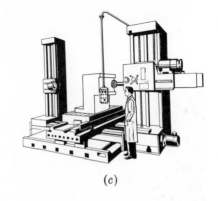

(c)

**Fig. 22-33.** Vertical boring and turning mill (courtesy Giddings & Lewis Machine Tool Co.).

is done from either of the two vertical heads or the horizontal cross slide. Angular cuts up to 30 deg can be made on one of the vertical slides. These machines may be equipped with tracer controls operating from a template, to speed production of the contour cuts. The size of the vertical boring mill is designated by the diameter of the table, which ranges from 54 in. to 40 ft.

**Precision Boring Machines.** Precision boring machines have comparatively small high-speed spindles (Fig. 22-34). These machines vary in design, depending upon the way the spindles are mounted and the number of them. Basically, all the machines are equipped with a number of fixed spindles and a reciprocating table.

**Jig Boring Machines.** Because of its accuracy and versatility, the jig boring machine (Fig. 22-35) is generally considered a toolroom rather

**Fig. 22-34.** Precision boring machine with part ready to be bored (courtesy The Heald Machine Co.).

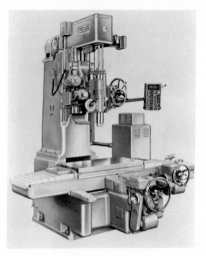

**Fig. 22-35.** A size-2 jig boring machine, table size 22 by 44 in. (courtesy Pratt & Whitney Co., Inc.).

than a production-line piece of equipment. Whereas, the average milling machine is capable of an 0.002-in. accuracy, the jig boring machine works to accuracies of 0.0001 in. or less.

As the name implies, this machine is often used for making drill jigs, as shown in various steps in Fig. 22-36. Drill jigs and templates are usually made at one tenth the tolerance allowed on the parts they will be used to produce. This, plus the fact the jigs and templates will control the accuracy of thousands of parts, accounts for the painstaking care with which they are machined. Jig boring machines are used whenever close tolerances are required in drilling and boring operations.

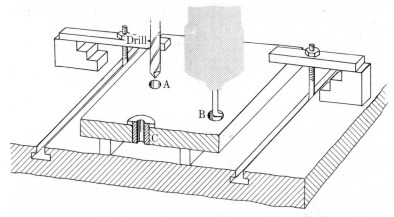

**Fig. 22-36.**  Drill jig, in sequence of construction and use. (*a*) drilled hole, (*b*) drilled and bored hole, (*c*) drilled hole with hardened bushing pressed in place.

Several methods are used to obtain accurate table settings. One system employs precision-length rods supplemented with vernier micrometers and dial indicators. Another system uses an electromagnetic head with a magnetic center, together with a master bar. Still another system makes use of a photoelectric optical centering device which guarantees repeat table movement within 0.00015 in.

## QUESTIONS

1. What are the two cutting actions associated with drilling?
2. What is the advantage of using a drill jig when production quantities are large?
3. Why is the spiral-point drill particularly adaptable to tape-control drilling?
4. What is the general rule regarding the included angle of the drill point and the hardness of the material being drilled?
5. Why are straight-flute drills used for nonferrous materials and sheet metal?
6. What is the difference between an ordinary step drill and a sub-land drill?

7. What is meant by an oilhole drill?

8. What is a general limitation on the depth that can be attained with a given gun drill?

9. What is meant by trepanning a hole?

10. How are drill sizes designated?

11. Generally, how much material is left for hand reaming? Machine reaming?

12. What is the meaning of the term, sensitive drill press?

13. For what type of work is the radial drill press best suited?

14. What are the two main types of multispindle drilling heads?

15. What is meant by a self-contained drilling head?

16. Why is it often necessary to bore a drilled hole, even though it is of accurate dimension?

17. What type of work can be done on the horizontal boring mill?

18. How is the size of a vertical boring machine designated?

19. Why is the jig boring machine generally a more accurate machine than the milling machine?

## PROBLEMS

1. Drilling speed is 60 to 80 percent of the regular surface-foot speed listed for the type metal being cut and the tool material. Using B1112 as a base, with a regular cutting speed of 100, what will the rpm be for a $\frac{1}{2}$-in. drill in the following materials: 4150, 4340, 8650, 1330 normalized and tempered, meehanite and 416 Se stainless steel? (See Chap. 3 for machinability ratings.)

2. The approach and overtravel in drilling a hole may be roughly calculated at $\frac{1}{2}$ the diameter of the drill. How long will it take to drill two 1-in.-diameter holes in 4130 steel if the feed used is 0.005 in. per revolution and the material is $\frac{1}{2}$ in. thick? The machinability of 4130 is 67 percent of B1112 as given in Prob. 1.

3. What size drill would be used for a hole that is to be hand reamed to $\frac{1}{2}$-in.-diameter?

4. It takes 5 min to lay out and center-punch 5 holes on a bolt circle. A jig can be built for $125. If the labor and overhead rate is $8 per hr, how many parts must be made before the jig is paid for?

5. A part with eight holes can be drilled in nine minutes with the use of a drill jig. A multispindle head and drills can do the same job in $1\frac{1}{2}$ min. The multispindle head costs $800 more than the drill jig. If the labor and overhead rate is $10 per hour, how many parts would have to be made to justify the use of the multispindle head?

## REFERENCE

*Handbook for Horizontal Boring, Drilling and Milling Machines*, Giddings and Lewis Machine Tool Company, Fond du Lac, Wis., 1947.

# 23

# BROACHING, SAWING, AND FILING

Broaching is a method of removing metal by a tool that has successively higher cutting edges in a fixed path. Each tooth removes a predetermined amount of material. The broach is used equally well on straight or irregular surfaces, either externally or internally, and it can perform many of the operations that are done more laboriously on milling, drilling, boring, shaping, planing, or keyway-cutting machines.

## Broaching Tools

**Internal Broaching.** Internal broaching tools are designed to enlarge and cut various contours in holes already made by drilling, punching, casting, forging, etc. This tool (Fig. 23-1) has the essential elements found in most broaches. The first teeth are designed to do the heaviest cutting and are called the *roughing teeth*. The next portion has the *semifinishing teeth*, followed by the *finishing teeth* with progressively lighter cuts. Some broaches are made so that the last few teeth do no cutting at all but have rounded edges for a burnishing action.

The amount of stock that each tooth can remove varies with the type of operation and the material. A general average is 0.002 or 0.004 in. per tooth for high-speed-steel broaches. The space between the teeth must be sufficient to provide ample chip room, since the chip is carried by each tooth until it clears the stock. On ductile materials, it

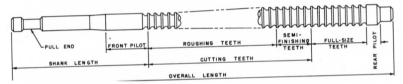

Fig. 23-1. Internal broach with sample workpieces (courtesy Sundstrand Machine Tool Co.).

is necessary to have staggered grooves in the cutting teeth to act as chip breakers.

The internal forms shown in Fig. 23-2 represent only a few of the shapes that have become standard. Special broach shapes are built by manufacturers for odd and difficult contours.

Fig. 23-2. A variety of forms produced by internal broaches (courtesy Colonial Broach Co.).

SPLINE AND GEAR BROACHING. The involute type of spline, shown in the center sample of Fig. 23-3, is an improvement over the regular straight-sided spline in that it is much stronger and tends to centralize under a turning load. When there is an endwise movement under load, the spline acts as a gear, transferring the load uniformly from tooth to tooth.

The broaching of internal gears is similar to that of internal splines. Usually, however, involute form, tooth spacing, runout, and finish must be held to closer limits. Broaching of internal gears may be applied to

Fig. 23-3. Internal gears and splines cut with internal broaches, some to extremely close tolerances (courtesy Colonial Broach Co.).

either straight or helical gears (Fig. 23-3). If the helix angle is less than 15 deg, the broach will turn as it cuts its own path. Angles greater than 15 deg require a spiral-lead-type drive head to turn the broach as it is pulled through the work.

**External Broaching.** External surface broaching competes with milling, shaping, planing, and similar operations. It offers a combination of a high degree of accuracy and excellent surface finishes, combined with high output rates and low downtime.

Automobile manufacturers have replaced many milling operations with surface broaching because of the combined speed and accuracy. An example of this kind of work is shown in Fig. 23-4. A maximum of 3/16 in. of stock is removed in a single pass. The broach consists of carbide-tipped inserts made up of five sections in combinations of half-round and facing broaches. As many as 22,000 cast-iron engine blocks can be run before the tool needs resharpening. Some broaches of this type are made on the same principle as the single-point lathe tool with throwaway inserts. As the carbide tips become dull, they can be unclamped and indexed 90 deg; they will then be ready to cut again. By incorporating negative rake into the toolholder, six or eight cutting edges can be utilized before the insert is discarded.

**Fig. 23-4.** A large carbide-tipped sectional broach used to machine several surfaces of a V-8 engine block in one pass (courtesy Ex-cell-o Corporation).

Broaching speeds have increased tremendously with this kind of tooling. Formerly, 20 to 40 fpm was considered average; now, speeds in excess of 200 fpm are used on cast iron. A further timesaving is made on large surface broaches by mounting them in pairs. With this arrangement, cutting can be done on both the forward and the return strokes. The top broach on a horizontal machine may be cutting on the forward stroke and the lower broach on the return stroke.

Some idea of the wide variety of surface broaching operations can be gained by referring to Fig. 23-5.

| | | | |
|---|---|---|---|
| TRANSMISSION PART | CAM | GEAR | CARRIAGE RACK |
| BOTTLE MOLD | CYLINDER HEAD | MOTOR FRAME | CARRIER |
| CYLINDER LOCK PLUG | GEAR SECTOR | HEAD-COMPRESSOR | PAWL |

**Fig. 23-5.** A variety of surfaces prepared by broaching (courtesy Cincinnati Milling *Report*).

**Broach Pullers.** Many kinds of pullers, which grip the broach as it is pulled through the material are available (Fig. 23-6). Key-type pullers are simple, low in cost, and particularly good for low production. The key is inserted manually and detached after each broaching operation. Pin-type pullers are good for the small-diameter broaches, since very little material need be removed from the small shank. Threaded pullers are used primarily for keyway broaches. For high production, automatic sleeve-type pullers are used.

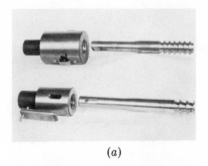

*(a)*

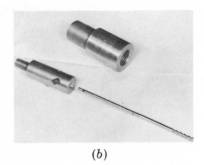

*(b)*

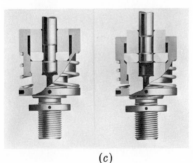

*(c)*

**Fig. 23-6.** Various types of broach pullers: (*a*) key type, (*b*) pin type, and (*c*) automatic sleeve (courtesy Colonial Broach).

## Broaching Machines

The main types of broaching machines are vertical ones, including pull-up, pulldown, and ram; and horizontal ones, both plain and the continuous-chain-type surface broach. These operate primarily as a means of either pushing or pulling the tools through or over the work.

**Vertical Broaches.** The various vertical machines are similar in appearance. In fact, one broach builder makes a convertible machine that can perform all four of the basic operations—push down, surface, pull down, and pull up (Fig. 23-7).

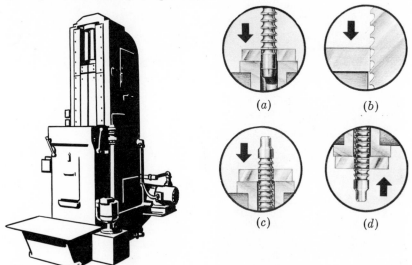

**Fig. 23-7.** Vertical broaching machine convertible to four basic operations. (*a*) Push down, (*b*) surface, (*c*) pull down, (*d*) pull up (courtesy Sundstrand Machine Tool Co.).

Aside from the convertible machines, each machine mentioned above, as well as the keyway broach, will be discussed briefly. (See also Fig. 23-8.)

VERTICAL PULL-UP. This machine is adapted for handling parts in high production. Parts can be gravity-fed to the lower part of the machine and placed in position for broaching. The broaches can also be handled automatically.

VERTICAL PULL-DOWN. In the vertical pulldown machine, the workpiece rests on the platen of the machine. Therefore, it is suited to larger, heavy parts. Automatic broach handling can be incorporated into these machines also.

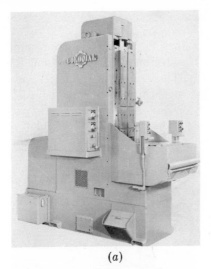

(a)

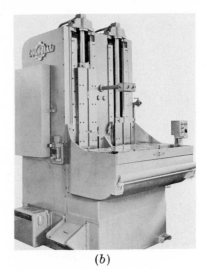

(b)

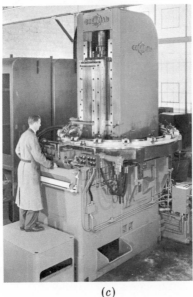

(c)

**Fig. 23-8.** (*a*) Single-ram, (*b*) dual-ram, and (*c*) indexing-table broaching machines (courtesy Colonial Broach Co.).

VERTICAL SINGLE AND DUAL RAM. Ram-type broaching machines are so called because the hydraulic cylinder is used to operate a vertical ram. Dual-ram machines are made so the operator can load one fixture while that ram returns and the other is cutting. Receding tables or fixtures provide work clearance during the return stroke and simplify the loading.

Rotary indexing tables can be set up around or in front of the machine to eliminate any manual material-handling time.

KEYWAY BROACHING. Small broaching jobs of limited quantity are often done on hand-operated arbor presses (Fig. 23-9). If the quantity is larger or the amount of metal to be removed is of sufficient quantity, small hydraulic presses are used. Keyseat broaches may be of the type (shown in the figure) that make use of bushings to guide them, or they may be the solid combination type. The combination keyway broach sizes the hole and then cuts the keyway.

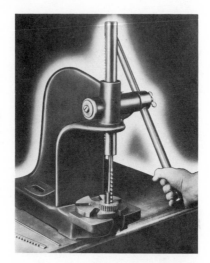

**Fig. 23-9.** Hand-operated arbor press used to push a keyway broach through a gear (courtesy The duMont Corporation).

**Horizontal Broaches.** PLAIN MACHINES. Horizontal broaching machines (Fig. 23-10) are used primarily for broaching keyways, splines, slots, round holes, and other internal shapes or contours. They have the disadvantage of taking more floor space than do the vertical machines. However, long broaches and heavy workpieces are easily handled on the horizontal machine.

CONTINUOUS-CHAIN-TYPE SURFACE BROACH. The continuous-chain-type surface broach (Fig. 23-11) is used where extremely high production is desired. This machine consists mainly of a base, driving unit, and several work-holding fixtures mounted on an endless chain. The work is pulled through the tunnel where it passes under the broach. The operator has only to place the work in the fixture as it passes the loading station. Work is automatically clamped, machined, and unloaded.

**Broaching-Machine Sizes.** The size of a broaching machine is expressed by the total ram travel, in inches, and the maximum pressure exerted on the ram, in tons.

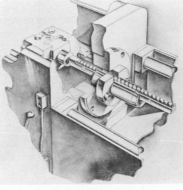

**Fig. 23-10.** Horizontal broaching machine and operation (courtesy Colonial Broach Co.).

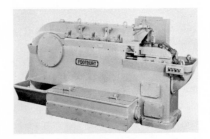

**Fig. 23-11.** Continuous-chain surface-broaching machine.

### Broaching Fixtures

Most internal broaching operations require no fixtures, as the work is pulled against the platen, and the cutting forces normal to the surface being cut oppose each other.

In surface broaching, on the other hand, all or most of the cutting is on one side of the part, and these forces must be countered by the work-holding fixtures; thus their design will depend on part contour, broaching force, quantity of parts, etc. Clamping for surface broaching is often done pneumatically or hydraulically (Fig. 23-12). Indexing arrangements are built into the fixture if more than one surface is to be machined with the same broach.

**Fig. 23-12.** Hydraulically operated surface-broaching fixture (courtesy Colonial Broach Co.).

### Finish and Accuracy

A 30-$\mu$in. finish can be consistently held when broaching steel of uniform microstructure. Better finishes are available, but costs are higher. Irregular and intricate shapes can be broached to tolerances of ± 0.001 in. from a location established on the part. Tolerances of ± 0.0005 in. can be held between surfaces cut simultaneously.

### Broach Length and Machining Time

The length of a broach will determine the cutting cycle. Also, the length of the broach must be suited to the machine on which it is to be used. By way of example, if the average amount of stock removed per tooth is 0.003 in., the pitch (or tooth spacing) is ½ in., and the material to be removed is ⅛ in., the *effective length* of the broach can be calculated. By effective length is meant the area containing the broach teeth.

$$E_l = \frac{C_d}{C_t} \times p \quad \text{or} \quad E_l = \frac{0.125}{0.003} \times 0.500 = 20.8 \text{ in.}$$

where
$E_l$ = effective length of broach
$C_d$ = depth of cut to be made
$C_t$ = cut per tooth (average)
$p$ = pitch

The length of the broach will change with the cut per tooth and the pitch. On internal operations the amount of metal to be removed from the diameter will be divided in half.

The pitch of the broach varies with the length of the cut to be made, for example, a cut only 3/32 in. long would require a 3/64-in. pitch, whereas a cut 1 in. long should have a pitch of 3/8 in.

### Economic Considerations

Broaching tools are usually more costly than milling cutters. However, this initial outlay can be offset by other factors. The machine time for broaching is generally less, and the piece part is often completed in one pass. Further timesavings per piece are realized when more than one part is broached at a time, by stacking. Stack broaching generally is best adapted to internal operations.

The relatively low speed and small cut per tooth give broaches a long life. Contour broaches can be resharpened by grinding on the face of the teeth. Generally, special fixtures are needed for sharpening the broach, making it a rather expensive operation. Surface broaches are often made in sections so that, as the teeth are reground and become shorter, they can be moved forward. The last section will be all that has to be replaced. The cost of broaching tools runs high because of the care needed in forging and grinding. Generally, a high quantity of production is necessary to justify the cost of the tool.

### SAWING

Many machining operations start with the sawing of the stock to length or size. Improvements in the speed, accuracy, and the variety of operations that can be performed on sawing machines give this process an important place in the field of manufacturing.

### Basic Types of Sawing Equipment

Sawing equipment may be classified by the motion used for the cutting action. These are reciprocating saws, represented by the power hacksaw; band saws, including cutoff and contour (traditional types and other applications); and circular saws, such as the cold saw and those with friction disks or abrasive disks.

**Reciprocating Saws.** The reciprocating motion in sawing is familiar to all who have used the hand hacksaw. Although it is hardly a production process, its usefulness is appreciated in many toolroom and maintenance situations.

POWER HACKSAWING. The power hacksaw is probably the simplest of the metal-cutting machines. It consists of a vise for clamping the work and a means of reciprocating the saw frame. Either spring or hydraulic pressure is used to regulate the downward feed force on the blade. A hydraulic or mechanical arrangement is also incorporated for lifting the blade on the return stroke. This prevents the teeth from being dragged backward over the work, which would cause them to become prematurely dull.

The stock to be cut is held between the clamping jaws. Several pieces of bar stock can be clamped together and cut at the same time. Both square and angular cuts can be made. Some of the larger heavy-duty hacksaws have hydraulic feeding and clamping devices which automatically move the bar forward to the correct length, and clamp it. After the cut, the stock is automatically unclamped, and the cycle repeats as long as the stock lasts (Fig. 23-13).

**Fig. 23-13.** Power saw, showing hydraulic bar feed (courtesy The DoAll Company).

### Band Saws.

CUTOFF TYPE. Band saws have a continuous cutting action in contrast to the intermittent action of the power hacksaw. This makes for shorter cutting time—up to 10 sq in. per min on some steels. Another advantage of the cutoff band saw is the narrow *kerf*, or cut, that it makes. This results in material savings, as shown in Fig. 23-14. The cut made by a circular cold saw is ¼ in. wide; with a power hacksaw, ⅛ in. wide; with a band saw, 1/16 in. wide.

Larger machines can be equipped with bar-feeding attachments similar to that described for power hacksaws.

Saws of this type usually have a 12-in.-diameter cutting capacity.

 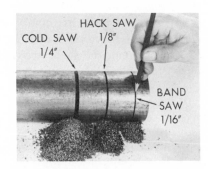

**Fig. 23-14.** The cutoff-type band saw, showing the saving in material because of the narrow cut (courtesy The DoAll Company).

CONTOUR TYPE. The metal-cutting contour band saw is an outgrowth of the woodworking band saw. One of the first models was produced in 1935. It provided the advantage of being able to remove large pieces of unwanted metal without reducing them to chips, and thus an immediate market for this machine (Fig. 23-15) was created.

Many developments followed the early models. First among these improvements was a variable-speed control. A wide choice of speeds resulted in greater accuracy, faster cutting, and increased tool life. Other refinements were added gradually, such as the flash butt resistance welder used to join the saw bands right on the machine for internal cutting. A grinder mounted on the column of the machine is used to smooth the weld joints, permitting them to pass through the saw guides.

Numerous attachments added to the versatility of the machine. Among these are the circle-cutting attachment, ripping fence, and magnifying lens. Power feeds and coolant systems have also been added. On some of the larger machines, the work can be bolted directly to the power-fed table (Fig. 23-16). This reduces operator fatigue and increases accuracy.

Other operations performed on the regular contour band saw are filing and polishing. These are discussed later in the section on filing.

*Friction contour-sawing machines.* Special contour-cutting band saws are those that are capable of doing operations beyond the scope of the regular machine. For example, friction sawing is a comparatively

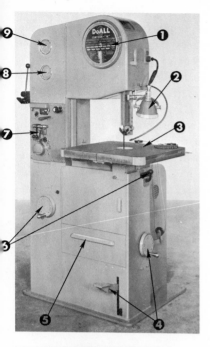

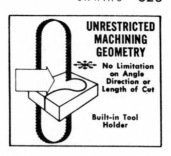

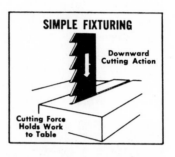

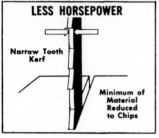

**Fig. 23-15.** A standard metal-cutting contour band saw and some advantages of the sawing process. (1) Job selector dial, (2) reflector flood lamp, (3) tilt table—45 deg right, 10 deg left, (4) work feed controls, (5) chip drawer, (6) speed control and indicator, (7) saw blade welder, (8) band tension indicator (courtesy the DoAll Company).

**Fig. 23-16.** A clevis yoke being slotted with the use of a standard holding fixture. The power-fed worktable helps maintain consistently straight cuts so that little or no machining is required for further finishing (courtesy the DoAll Company).

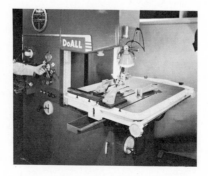

new term when applied to contour-sawing machines. The process consists of a fast-moving blade that produces enough friction to heat the material to the softening point. The heat of friction is confined to a small area just ahead, and a little to each side of, the blade. When the material becomes soft and loses its strength, it is removed by the saw-teeth.

The right blade for friction sawing is more critical than in ordinary sawing. Too few teeth for the material thickness will tend to remove more material than is softened, and will ruin the blade. Too many teeth, on the other hand, will tend to clog, and will not remove the material at all. Specially made blades are required for most friction-sawing operations. Saw velocities range from 6,000 fpm on ¼-in.-thick carbon steel to 13,500 fpm on 1-in.-thick armor plate. The latter can be cut at the rate of 5 in. per min.

The chief advantage of friction sawing is that it can cut many times faster than conventional methods on hard materials (Fig. 23-17).

**Fig. 23-17.** This fast-action photo stops the saw blade traveling 9,000 fpm in a high-speed milling cutter. Heat penetration is at the immediate saw point (courtesy The DoAll Company).

The contour band saw used for friction sawing has an infinitely variable speed up to 15,000 sfpm (surface feet per minute). The motor supplied ranges from 7 to 10 hp, depending on requirements.

*Articulated contour-cutting machines.* Where large, heavy work is to be accurately contour-cut, it may be more practical to move the machine than the work (Fig. 23-18).

From the picture and diagram, you will notice that the articulated band saw consists of a pedestal which forms the anchor unit and the cutting yoke that is fastened to a swinging arm, making it possible to rotate the saw through 180 deg in either direction. The saw is guided through the cut by the manual operation of a steering wheel just above the material.

The articulated machine shown has a throat depth of 60 in. and is capable of sawing material 21 in. thick. Heavy work requires no clamping; the operator has only to guide the power-fed saw.

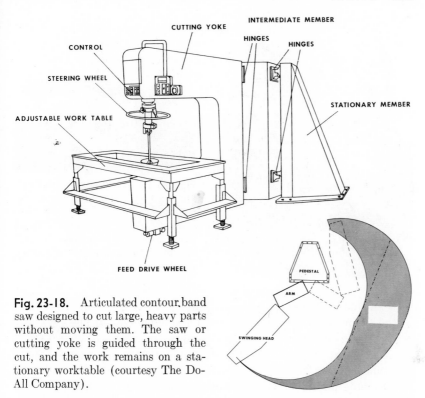

**Fig. 23-18.** Articulated contour band saw designed to cut large, heavy parts without moving them. The saw or cutting yoke is guided through the cut, and the work remains on a stationary worktable (courtesy The Do-All Company).

**Circular Saws.** Circular saws cut by means of a revolving disk. The disk may have rather large teeth, as in the case of cold saws, or almost no teeth, as in the friction disk.

COLD SAWING. Cold sawing would imply that no heat is generated in the cutting operation. Since this is not true, the term is used only to distinguish it from friction-disk cutting, which heats the metal to nearly the melting temperature at the point of metal removal. Also the blades are usually large which allows cooling time for the tooth after leaving the cut until reentering.

Cold saws (Fig. 23-19) cut very rapidly because of the large-diameter blades, with correspondingly large teeth. Mild steel can be cut at the rate of 25 sq in. per min. The cut made is comparable, in smoothness and accuracy, to surfaces produced by slitting saws in milling operations or by the parting tool in lathe operations.

These machines can be equipped with automatic bar-feeding mechanisms. The stock is held in a vise capable of handling one or a number of parts at the same time.

FRICTION SAWS. Circular friction saws operate on the same principle as the friction band saw. However, since the saw friction heat is

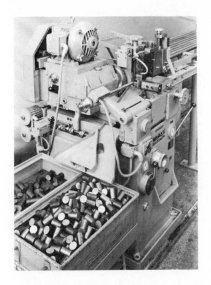

**Fig. 23-19.** Cold-sawing machines are used as automatic cutoff machines for both small and large stock. Cuts may vary from 150 per hr on 1½-in.-diameter steel to 1800 per hr on ⅝-in.-diameter aluminum alloy.

high and natural cooling is insufficient, an auxiliary coolant must be forced against the blade to keep it from becoming red hot. The saws may be as large as 6 ft in diameter, operating at speeds up to 25,000 sfpm.

Steels that are the most satisfactory for friction sawing are those in the annealed, normalized, or hardened condition. Cast iron and nonferrous materials do not possess the characteristics of maintaining grain structure while losing tensile strength. Some thermoplastic materials are satisfactory for friction sawing, since they can lose sufficient strength without melting.

ABRASIVE-DISK CUTTING. Abrasive-disk cutting, frequently used in cutoff operations, is not a true sawing technique, but, since it serves the same purpose, it is frequently classified with the cutoff sawing operations.

Thin resinoid or rubber-bonded wheels rotating at 12,000 to 14,000 sfpm are used. The cutting action is fast and accurate. Various structural shapes are shown, with cutting times, in Fig. 23-20. The finish maintained on the cut end is approximately 65 rms.

Machines for abrasive-disk cutting are fairly simple and usually feature a powerful drive motor with a belt-driven wheel head. Most of the machines use a swing frame and are fed into the work manually.

To speed cutting action and handle diameters from 2 to 12 in. an oscillating wheel is used, Fig. 23-21. The wheel is power-fed and made to travel back and forth across the material. Cutting capacities are high. Wheels range from 16 to 34 in. in diameter, with corresponding motors of 7½ to 30 hp.

**Fig. 23-20.** The abrasive cutting times for five parts are shown. The cut surface is approximately a 34$\mu$ finish (courtesy Wallace Supplies Mfg. Co.).

**Fig. 23-21.** A swing-frame-type cut-off machine that is designed to move in and out as well as up and down. Units of this type are available that can travel up to 12 feet for cutting off plate and other special applications (courtesy Wallace Supplies Mfg. Co.).

### Saw Blades

**Band Saws.**   Improvement in materials and heat treatment has changed the band saw from an exclusively soft-material cutting tool to an all-purpose cutting tool. Most of the blades are made with hardened teeth and a tough, flexible back. More recently, a high-speed-steel band blade has been introduced. Although the blades cannot be welded on the ordinary resistance flash butt-welding attachment, they are able to cut up to 10 times faster and last up to 30 times as long as conventional metal-cutting blades.

The important characteristics to keep in mind when choosing a saw blade for a particular job are tooth set, tooth form, blade width, and saw pitch.

TOOTH SET.   The set refers to the way the teeth are offset on each side of center (Fig. 23-22). This offset provides clearance for the back of the blade. The path made by the saw is referred to as the *kerf*. If the blade becomes worn, the set is reduced, causing the blade to bind in the work.

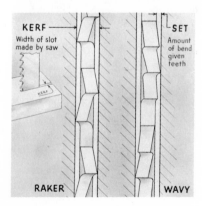

**Fig. 23-22.** Saw-set patterns—raker and wavy. The kerf and saw set are also shown (courtesy Nicholson File Co.).

The two types of saw-set patterns are raker and wavy, as shown in the figure. Raker set is recommended for all-around heavy cutting operations. The wavy-set pattern is used on materials that vary in thickness. It is especially good in cutting extremely thin sections.

TOOTH FORM.   The main sawtooth forms, shown in Fig. 23-23, are buttress, claw-tooth, friction, knife, scallop, and spiral. The diamond-tooth band is also described in the text.

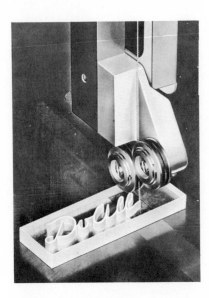

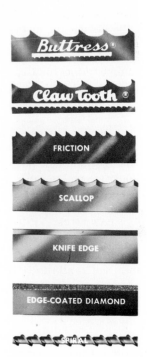

**Fig. 23-23.** Standard sawtooth forms. The spiral blade can be used to cut in any direction (courtesy The DoAll Company).

*Buttress form.*   The buttress or skip-tooth design is used in cutting heavy sections of wood, metal, or plastics. The wide gullet area allows ample chip room in front of each tooth.

*Claw-tooth form.*   The claw-tooth blade has positive rake teeth that can penetrate the material more easily than can be done with the full contact of the buttress tooth. It has more bite under light feed pressures. This blade is especially recommended for the softer materials, and it can be used effectively on thicker sections of the ferrous metals.

*Friction form.*   The friction blade is intended for high-velocity and friction sawing of ferrous metals. A blade similar in appearance is made for very fine cutting of any material on standard contour-sawing machines.

*Knife and scallop forms.* The knife and scallop blades are used for cutting soft fibrous materials. They are used in stack cutting all types of fabrics, since they can cut without tearing, shredding, or producing dust.

*Spiral form.* The spiral blade was designed to permit sawing in any direction without the necessity of swinging the work. These blades are made in four diameters, ranging from 0.020 to 0.074 in. There are two types—one for cutting wood and plastics, and another hard-edge type for cutting metal.

DIAMOND-TOOTH BAND. The diamond-tooth band consists of a number of cylindrical segments with diamonds tightly bonded in a sintered tungsten-alloy matrix. These bands are used in sawing stone, glass, and other vitreous materials.

BLADE WIDTHS. Band saws vary in width from 1/16 to 1 in. Generally, it is best to use the widest blade allowable for the radius to be cut. A wide blade has greater beam strength and so can take a heavier load. Allowable radii for each blade width are usually posted on the front of the machine.

SAW PITCH. Pitch refers to the number of teeth per inch. The pitch of the saw chosen will be governed by the thickness of the material to be cut. A general rule is that there shall be at least two teeth in the material at all times. Too fine a pitch will slow the sawing operation excessively, and too coarse a pitch will tend to tear the teeth out of the blade.

**Circular Saws.** Circular or cold saws are made in four main types—solid, segmental, carbide-tipped, and inserted-tooth. These saws can be roughly divided into two groups—those used for ferrous materials and those used for nonferrous materials (Fig. 23-24).

The solid saws are made of high-speed steel or semihigh-speed steel.

The segmental saws are made by riveting segments of high-speed steel to a tough alloy saw plate. This combines the cutting qualities of high-speed steel with the tougher shock-resisting steel plate.

The carbide-tipped saws are recommended for the nonferrous metals. Excellent wearing qualities can be expected of this type of saw, even in abrasive materials such as plastics. They are not recommended on harder materials where shock is likely to be a factor.

The inserted-tooth saws make use of high-speed or carbide inserts in a tough alloy plate. Worn or damaged teeth can easily be replaced.

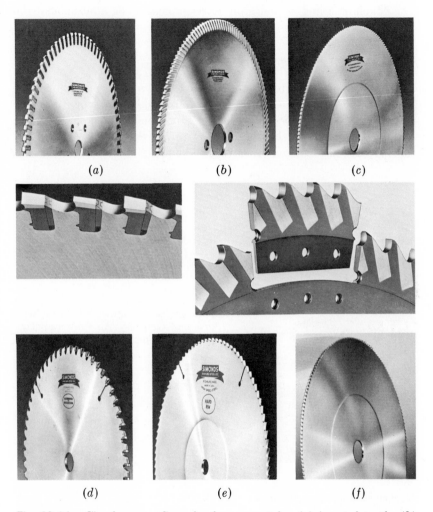

**Fig. 23-24.** Circular saws. Saws for ferrous metals—(*a*) inserted tooth, (*b*) segmental, (*c*) solid type. Saws for nonferrous metals—(*d*) carbide tipped, (*e*) high-speed steel, hard rim, (*f*) solid steel (courtesy Simonds Saw and Steel Co.).

### FILING

Machine filing is done on a reciprocating or continuous-band machine.

### Reciprocating, or Jig-Type, Filing Machines

A short reciprocating motion is used on the filing machine shown in Fig. 23-25. These machines are used in model building and tool-and-die work. They are especially good for filing die clearances. A uniform angular clearance can be obtained by tilting the table. Machines of this type can also be used for sawing and honing.

**Fig. 23-25.** Reciprocating-type filing machine (courtesy All American Tool and Mfg. Company).

### Continuous-Band Filing Machines

Contour-cutting band saws can be made to handle other operations such as filing, polishing, and line grinding. The various types of blades are shown in Fig. 23-26.

**Continuous-Band Filing.** File bands are made up of short file segments riveted to a flexible steel band. The files are made to interlock and present an even surface before they come in contact with the work. The band can be unlocked for internal filing operations.

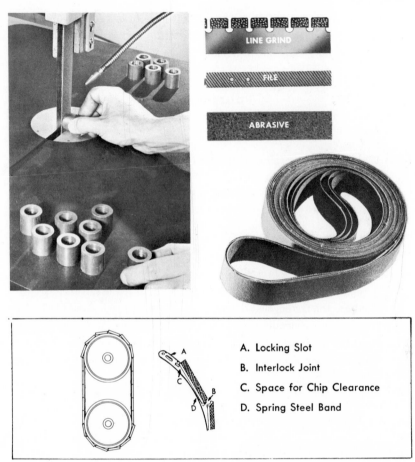

*Precision files linked together in a continuous band for external and internal finishing of tools, dies, castings, parts, ferrous and nonferrous metals.*
*File bands provide a method for continuous filing that is nine times as fast as hand filing and almost four times as fast as machine jig filing.*

**Fig. 23-26.** Band types used for filing, polishing, and grinding (courtesy The DoAll Co.).

Band files are obtainable in flat, half-round, and oval shapes. The file cuts are coarse, medium coarse, medium cut, and bastard.

Filing by this method is rated nine times faster than by hand and four times faster than the jig filing machine.

**Band-Saw Polishing and Line Grinding.** Filing is often followed by a polishing operation. Three grits—150, 80, and 50 grain size—are available. The amount of material to be removed, the finish desired, and the type of material will determine which abrasive band to use.

Line grinding is done with a band that has abrasive inserts mounted for the cutting edges. They are used in cutting and grinding many different alloys and geological materials.

## QUESTIONS

1. About how much stock is the average tooth on a broach expected to remove?
2. What is necessary to broach internal helical gears when the helix angle is greater than 15 deg.
3. What is one of the big advantages of broaching?
4. What are two factors that have led to increased production rates for broaching?
5. What are the principal types of broaching machines?
6. Describe the continuous-type broaching machine.
7. How is the size of a broaching machine designated?
8. Why do parts to be surface broached require rugged fixtures?
9. What are the factors that determine how long a broach should be?
10. Why is it not generally feasible to specify broaching for a few odd parts?
11. What are the three primary types of action involved in sawing machines?
12. What are some advantages of a horizontal band saw over an ordinary reciprocating hack saw?
13. What are some of the features of a modern vertical band saw that have made it quite versatile?
14. Explain what is meant by friction sawing.
15. For what type of work is the articulated band saw applicable?
16. Why are cold saws given this name?
17. Why are cast irons and nonferrous materials not recommended for friction sawing?
18. What type of abrasive disk machine is used when large-diameter pieces of stock are to be cut off?
19. What is meant by a claw-tooth blade?
20. What determines the pitch of the saw that should be used?
21. Where does a jig-type filing machine find its best application?
22. How much faster is band filing than jig filing?

## PROBLEMS

1. A hole in a 1-in.-thick casting is ⅞ in. in diameter and is to have a 3/16-in.-deep, ⅛-in.-wide keyway broached in it. If the average amount of material removed by each tooth is 0.003 in. and the pitch of the broach teeth is ½ in., how long will the cutting portion of the broach have to be? How

long will it take to broach 1,000 parts if the broaching speed is 30 fpm and a total of 1 min is allowed for the return stroke, handling each part, and placing the broach in position for the cut.

2. A cylinder head 8 in. wide and 20 in. long with ¼ in. of material to be removed can be surface broached or milled. Milling is done with a 10-in.-diameter face mill in one pass. The carbide mill has 25 teeth with a chip load per tooth of 0.009. The cutting speed is 300 fpm. The carbide broach has an average chip load of 0.005 in. per tooth with a pitch of ⅝ in. and moves over the surface at 150 fpm. The return stroke is made in one-third the cutting-stroke time. Which method will be faster? If labor and overhead at $10 per hr are the same for each machine, how long will it take to pay for the broach which costs $1,000 more than the milling cutter?

3. What would the correct pitch of saw blade be for the following material thicknesses: 1/16 in., ¼ in., ½ in., and 4 in.?

4. Standard pipe 4 in. in diameter can be cut off in 16 sec with an abrasive wheel. How long will it take to cut the same pipe on a horizontal band saw if the blade feeds down at 6 in. per min?

## REFERENCES

*Broaching Practice*, National Broach and Machine Co., Detroit, 1953.

*Manual of Broaching*, Detroit Broach Co., Detroit, 1948.

*Sawology*, a Nicholson Handbook, Nicholson File Co., Providence, 1960.

*The DoAll Friction Sawing Manual*, The DoAll Company, Des Plaines, 1953.

Warner, J. H., "Broaching Saves Time in Small Part Production," *The Tool and Manufacturing Engineer*, July, 1958.

# 24

# GRINDING AND
# RELATED
# ABRASIVE-FINISHING
# PROCESSES

THE USE OF abrasive minerals originated in ancient times. Precious stones and metals were polished with abrasives to bring out their true value. As man began to use steel, the problem of sharpening it was solved with abrasive stones found in nature.

The first manufactured grinding wheel was made in a pottery shop of the Norton Company. A patent was issued to Mr. Norton in 1876 for a ceramic or vitrified bonded wheel, with emery as the abrasive.

It is with the abrasive wheel that precision has been brought to the metalworking industry. Tolerances on machine parts have become continually smaller, until we are no longer satisfied with one thousandth or one ten-thousandth, but, in many cases, hundred thousandths and millionths of an inch are required. These exacting tolerances are not achieved by grinding alone, but with the related processes of lapping, honing, and superfinishing.

Abrasives are also used to improve product appearance. These processes are barrel finishing, vibration finishing, polishing, and buffing.

## ABRASIVES

Abrasives are of two main types—natural and manufactured.

### Natural Abrasives

Abrasive stones found in nature are emery, sandstone, corundum, and diamonds.

636

Emery was first discovered in Turkey, Greece, and Asia Minor. Later, deposits of it were found in the southern part of the United States. Corundum first came from India. Both of these stones are often called by the name of the place from which they are obtained, as "Arkansas stone" for emery and "India stone" for corundum.

The large sandstone wheels used to grind hand tools have now almost passed out of existence. Emery and corundum, however, are still being used. Though these two products are found in nature and have different characteristics, they both contain aluminum oxide. The main difference is that corundum crystals are much larger, which makes it more suitable for fast, rough cutting or *snagging* on soft-steel and annealed malleable castings.

## Manufactured Abrasives

**Silicon Carbide.** The search for a means of making precious stones by artificial methods led Edward Acheson to some experiments. In 1891, by means of a very crude carbon-arc furnace, he developed the first silicon carbide crystals. Although the industry is now large, the same basic method of mixing pure white quartz sand, petroleum, coke, salt, and sawdust is still used. Huge electric furnaces are used to drive off the impurities and fuse the silicon and carbide.

**Aluminum Oxide.** At the time silicon carbide was being discovered, work was being done on aluminum oxide. Aluminum ore was mixed with coke and iron filings and subjected to a high temperature. This resulted in a glassy mass which, when cooled and crushed, became the most widely used abrasive in industry today—aluminum oxide.

**Diamonds.** Diamonds can be classified as both natural and artificial. The natural stones unsuitable for gems are crushed down into a series of sizes known as *bort*.

The General Electric Company was the first to manufacture diamonds on a commercial scale. In 1955 they announced a successful commercial diamond that could sustain pressures up to 470,000 psi for long periods of time and extremely high temperatures.

Shortly after GE's successful manufacture of diamonds, the Carborundum Company fabricated the first man-made diamond wheel.

## Abrasive Properties

Certain desirable properties inherent in abrasives are hardness, toughness, and fracture qualities.

Hardness allows the abrasive to enter the material, toughness keeps it from fracturing with the impact of the cut, and fracture allows part of the grain to leave so as to present a new cutting surface.

If the abrasive and the material holding it are too tough, the grains become dull and glazed. Under these conditions the work heats up, and very little material is removed. For this reason, silicon carbide, the harder abrasive, is considered the best for hard and brittle materials. Aluminum oxide is best for the tough, high-strength materials.

The natural diamond does not fracture to present new cutting faces, but becomes dull and tends to glaze after continued use. There are, however, applications where the diamond is superior to all other abrasives. An example of this is the finish grinding done on carbide tools. There is some controversy over the comparative qualities of natural and artificial diamonds. Artificial diamonds are now being made in greater quantities, and the price is approaching that of natural diamonds. Man-made diamonds have greater *friability,* or breakdown, for cooler cutting action.

### GRINDING

### Grinding Wheels

**Cutting Action.** The cutting action of a grinding wheel is dependent on the abrasive type, grain size, bonding materials, wheel grades, and wheel structure.

ABRASIVE TYPE. Industrial use of abrasives is largely limited to emery, aluminum oxide, silicon carbide, and diamonds.

GRAIN SIZE. After fusing the necessary ingredients in a furnace, the manufactured abrasive is taken out, cooled, and crushed. The grains are then cleaned and screened into many different size groups. Grit sizes

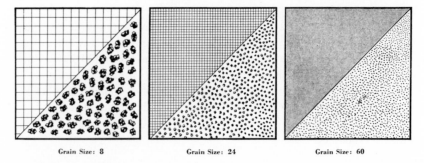

Grain Size: 8  Grain Size: 24  Grain Size: 60

**Fig. 24-1.** Typical screens through which have been sifted grain sizes 8, 24, and 60. Screens shown represent 2-in. squares (courtesy The Carborundum Co.).

are standard throughout industry. They are based on the number of openings per linear inch of screen (Fig. 24-1). A 60 grit size, for example, is approximately 1/60 of an inch square.

BONDING MATERIALS.   The abrasive grains are held together in the grinding wheel by what is known as the bonding material. This material is of six main types. The four most extensively used kinds—vitrified clay, resinoid materials, rubber, and shellac—will be discussed here.

*Vitrified clay.*   Vitrified clay is the most common abrasive bonding material and is used in about 75 percent of the wheels manufactured. Good strength, with porosity, allows a high metal-removal rate.

*Resinoid materials.*   The resin bond is made from synthetic organic materials. Wheels can vary from the hard, dense, coarse type to the soft, open, fine type. Resinoid-bonded wheels are designated as cool cutting, with high rates of stock removal.

*Rubber.*   Rubber-bonded wheels are used where good finish is required. Because of its strength, rubber is often used in making thin cutoff wheels.

*Shellac.*   Shellac-bonded wheels are used for cool cutting with good finish.

WHEEL GRADES.   The grade of a grinding wheel refers to its strength in holding the abrasive grains in the wheel. This is largely dependent on the amount of bonding material used (Fig. 24-2). As the amount of bonding material is increased the linking structure between grains becomes larger which makes the wheel act harder.

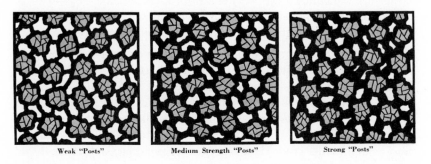

Weak "Posts"          Medium Strength "Posts"          Strong "Posts"

**Fig. 24-2.**   The grade of the grinding wheel is based on the strength of the bond posts (courtesy The Carborundum Co.).

WHEEL STRUCTURE.   Grinding should not be thought of as a rubbing action. The grinding wheel is more like a milling cutter with hundreds of teeth. You will notice that the wheel must have voids to allow space for the chips and for proper cutting action (Fig. 24-3). This space must not be too small or the chip will stay in the wheel, causing it to "load up." A loaded cutting wheel heats up and is not efficient in cutting action. Too large a space is also inefficient, as there will be too few cutting edges.

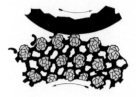

**Fig. 24-3.**  Voids in the wheel provide chip room.

**Grinding-Wheel Selection.**  From the foregoing discussion, you can see that there are many factors which must be taken into consideration in choosing a wheel for a given job.

Grinding-wheel manufacturers developed codes for putting on the particular wheel all the information for its identification. Each company had its own system, and this was very confusing. However, in 1944, a standard code of seven main parts, as shown in Fig. 24-4, was adopted by all the grinding-wheel manufacturers.

Among the factors that help decide what type of wheel to use are the material to be ground, the type of operation, and the machine condition.

MATERIAL TO BE GROUND.  If the material to be ground is hard, the bond or grade of the wheel must be relatively soft to ensure that the abrasive grains will be able to break away before they become dull and glazed. If the material is soft, the grade of the wheel can be relatively hard, since the abrasive will stay sharp for a longer time. High-tensile-strength material should be ground with aluminum oxide abrasive. For most low-tensile-strength materials, silicon carbide should be used.

TYPE OF OPERATION.  The type of operation will determine the wheel contact area. A straight, or plain, wheel, used to grind the outside diameter of a cylinder, has only a small contact area. Under these conditions the wheel breaks down much faster than when it has a larger contact area, as in grinding flat or internal surfaces. Since the relative pressure on the wheel is high for a small contact area, the structure must be of a harder grade than is needed for grinding the same material with a larger surface contact.

MACHINE CONDITION.  The type and condition of the machine will determine the size of wheel that can be used, the work speed, the feed, etc.

JOB SPECIFICATIONS.  Since so many varying conditions exist in grinding, manufacturers often urge their customers to send in the exact job specifications. As with many other processes where variables are

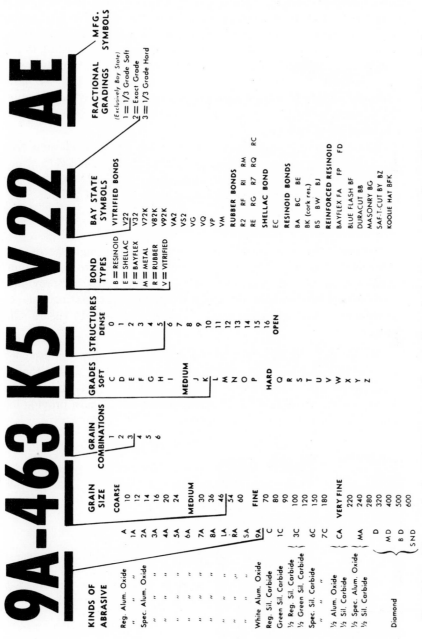

**Fig. 24-4.** The standard marking system for grinding wheels (courtesy Bay State Abrasive Products Co.).

numerous, grinding-wheel manufacturers have turned to punched cards for help. The five main grinding-wheel elements—abrasive type, grain size, grade, structure, and bond—make up the main code. With these five main elements, over 150 variables can be matched according to the customer's job specifications. One change in any of these variables will make a totally different wheel. A computer is used to relate the basic information to the variables, thus producing a grinding-wheel formula. This formula is then used in weighing out and mixing the ingredients that make up the wheel.

Examples of grinding-wheel manufacturers' recommendations are:

General-purpose surface-grinding aluminum     37C24J8
General-purpose surface-grinding steel     32A60G12
General-purpose surface-grinding brass     37C24L5B

### Wheel Care and Use.

SAFETY. Grinding wheels run at comparatively high speeds, the recommended speed for most operations being 5,000 to 6,000 sfpm. Grinding-machine manufacturers follow safety codes in providing proper guards. Wheel manufacturers' specifications as to testing, balancing, mounting, and operating must be followed closely to ensure safe practice.

BALANCING. Wheels that are out of balance not only produce poor work but may put undue strains on the machine. Large wheels should be placed on a balancing stand (Fig. 24-5) and balanced by moving weights around a recessed flange. Some manufacturers now provide for dynamic balancing right in the machine.

**Fig. 24-5.** The weights in the flange are shifted until the wheel is in balance, as shown (courtesy The Carborundum Co.).

Dᴿᴇssɪɴɢ ᴀɴᴅ ᴛʀᴜɪɴɢ ᴛʜᴇ ɢʀɪɴᴅɪɴɢ ᴡʜᴇᴇʟ.

*Dressing.* After use, the wheel becomes dull; that is, the individual abrasive grains become rounded over. The wheel may also become loaded. It is then necessary to cut a portion of the face off the grinding wheel. This is done with various types of dressers, as shown in Fig. 24-6.

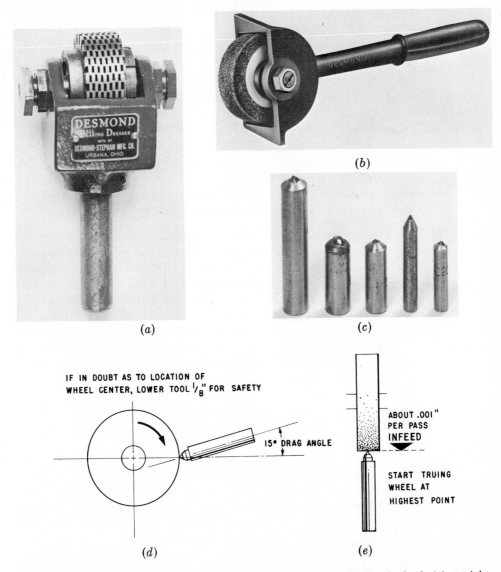

**Fig. 24-6.** Dressing and truing tools. (*a*) Multiple-disc type, (*b*) hand wheel, (*c*) straight-shank diamond nibs, (*d*) diamond position, and (*e*) recommended infeed per pass (courtesy The Desmond-Stephan Mfg. Co.).

The multiple-disc dresser is used for coarse wheels. It serves to cut down the wheel a small amount, which helps restore a true surface and free any metal embedded in the wheel.

Abrasive sticks and wheels are used for dressing purposes. The abrasive stick does not cut the wheel as fast as the multiple-disc dresser, but it works well on softer wheels, and it is lower in cost. Relatively small abrasive wheels are also used as dressing tools. Their use requires a quick plunge infeed of 0.002 to 0.005 in. and a rather fast traverse speed.

Diamonds set into the end of a rod are used for dressing and truing purposes also. The diamond should be kept pointed, since only the point can be used for cutting. This is accomplished by slanting the holder down at a 15-deg angle and using a new surface each time the wheel is dressed. A good supply of coolant should be used when dressing with a diamond, as overheating can cause the diamond to fracture or drop out of its setting. Cluster or multipoint diamonds are used on larger wheels.

*Truing.*   Truing is the process of changing the shape of the grinding wheel. This is done to make the wheel true and concentric with the bore, or to change the face contour for form grinding. Truing and dressing are done with the same tools but not for the same purpose.

DIAMOND-WHEEL USE.   Diamond wheels are made with three different types of bonds: resinoid, vitrified, and metallic. Each has particular applications, with some overlapping. Vitrified wheels cut well but tend to be brittle. Resinoid wheels can take a lot of abuse and are good for heavier metal removal, as in cutting chip breakers in carbide tools. The metallic-bonded diamond wheels will outlast, by 10 times, the resinoid-bonded wheels, but they are more apt to cause heat checks.

Diamond, and other wheels are made in a variety of standard shapes (Fig. 24-7). In order to conserve diamonds, wheels larger than 1 in. in diameter are produced with a bonded diamond layer at the cutting surface.

All diamond wheels operate at greater efficiency when used wet. Either flood- or mist-coolant applications are effective. Plain water is

Face wheel

Straight wheel    Flared cup

**Fig. 24-7.**   Standard diamond grinding-wheel types (courtesy The Carborundum Co.).

an effective coolant. However, if rusting is a problem, water-soluble oils or mineral-seal oils are used. They also provide a better finish.

Diamond wheels can be cleaned with a lump of pumice or a stick of fine soft silicon carbide. A diamond wheel should not be dressed with a diamond tool.

Only hard materials should be ground on diamond wheels. Soft materials tend to load the wheel quickly. For this reason, carbide tools are often ground with three wheels: (1) aluminum oxide for the secondary clearance on the tool shank, (2) silicon carbide wheels for rough-grinding the carbide, and (3) diamond wheels for the finish grind of the carbide tip.

Ceramic cutting tools are similar to carbide cutting tools in grinding characteristics. Either silicon carbide or diamonds are used as the abrasive. The moderately hard ceramic materials, such as porcelain, can be satisfactorily ground with silicon carbide, but ceramics of high aluminum oxide content should be ground with metal-bonded diamond wheels.

### Grinding Operations and Equipment

The wide variety of grinding operations can be classified as to the main types of surfaces to be ground. These include cylindrical external, cylindrical internal, flat, cutoff, and formed and crushed. Various surfaces are shown in Fig. 24-8.

Also to be discussed are tool and cutter grinding and snag grinding.

**Cylindrical Surfaces.** Cylindrical surfaces are ground on a number of different machines. Both external and internal surfaces can be ground on a universal grinder. A chuck is mounted on the headstock to hold the work, and a motor-driven spindle is used in place of the tailstock. Most cylindrical grinding that is not of high volume is done on a center-type grinder. The work is mounted between centers and driven with a dog (Fig. 24-9).

To ensure accuracy on longer pieces where the wheel pressure would tend to spring the work, steady rests are used. They are mounted on the grinding-machine table and adjusted to provide bearing surfaces for the back and bottom sides of the work.

The general range of work speeds for cylindrical grinding is from 60 to 100 sfpm. The traverse speed is generally one half of the wheel width per work revolution. The amount of traverse feed governs the finish obtained. Feeds greater than three fourths of the wheel width are not recommended, even in rough grinding. The best surface finishes are obtained with slower traverse feeds and by using at least two wheels.

**A. On Cylindrical Pieces**

1. Straight        2. Tapered        3. Formed

**B. On Flat Pieces**

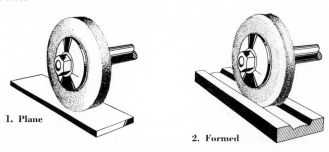

1. Plane

2. Formed

**C. In Holes**

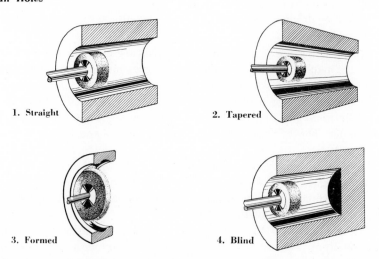

1. Straight        2. Tapered

3. Formed        4. Blind

**Fig. 24-8.** Main types of surfaces to be ground (courtesy The Carborundum Co.).

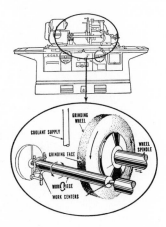

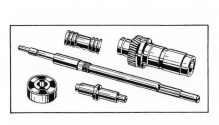

**Fig. 24-9.** Center-type cylindrical grinder with work examples (courtesy The Carborundum Co.).

To avoid wheel changes, rough and finish grinds are generally done on two different machines.

Surfaces that are the width of the wheel, such as shoulders and recesses, are ground with no table traverse movement. The wheel is fed straight into the work. This is known as "plunge-cut" grinding (Fig. 24-10). The wheel face may be formed or straight as shown.

**Fig. 24-10.** Plunge-cut grinding (courtesy Landis Tool Co.).

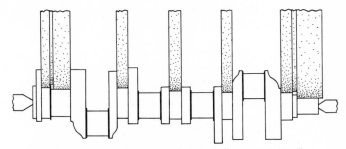

Crankshaft line bearings specified size tolerances: 0.0005″

CENTERLESS GRINDING. Cylindrical grinding that does not have to have a definite relationship to the center holes can be done on a centerless grinder. The work is supported between the grinding wheel, a regulating wheel, and a work-rest blade (Fig. 24-11).

The regulating wheel controls the work speed and traverse feed. On *through-feed* centerless grinders, the work is made to pass between the grinding and the regulating wheels. This is accomplished by setting the regulating wheel at an angle (Fig. 24-12).

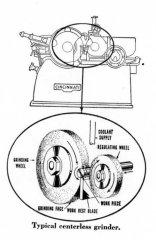

Typical centerless grinder.

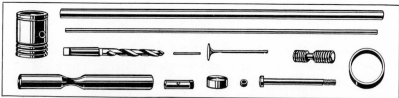

Examples of cylindrical pieces ground on centerless type grinders.

**Fig. 24-11.** Centerless grinding, with examples of work performed (courtesy The Carborundum Co.).

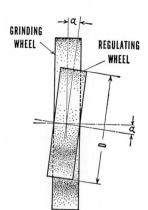

**Fig. 24-12.** The regulating wheel is set at an angle to control the through-feed rate of the work.

The best correction for out-of-roundness is obtained by raising the work above the center line of the wheels. Rods that need some lengthwise straightening effect are ground below the center line of the wheels. After straightening, subsequent normal grinding is done.

When work cannot feed through because of a change in diameter, it can be ground on an *infeed* arrangement. There is no traverse feed. The wheel is moved forward as in plunge grinding. The length of the workpiece is limited to the width of the wheel. The regulating wheel is set at only a slight angle to keep the workpiece up against the stop.

Special applications of centerless grinding are shown in Fig. 24-13.

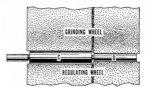

Multiple diameter centerless grinding.

**Fig. 24-13.** Special centerless-grinder applications (courtesy The Carborundum Co.).

Centerless profile (formed) grinding.

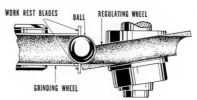

Spherical centerless grinding.

**Surface Grinding.** All grinding could be construed to be surface grinding. However, it refers specifically to flat or plain surfaces.

The two main types of machines are classified, by the position of the spindle, as horizontal or vertical (Fig. 24-14).

The horizontal-type surface grinder uses a plain wheel. Special shapes of wheels, such as the cup and cylinder type, are used on the vertical surface grinder. The tables shown in Fig. 24-14 are of the reciprocating kind, but both types of grinders are also built with rotary work-tables. Ferrous materials are usually held on the table by electromagnetic action. Nonferrous materials can be held by a vacuum chuck, a vise, or a fixture.

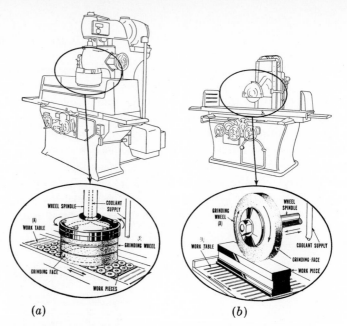

**Fig. 24-14.** (*a*) Vertical, and (*b*) horizontal surface grinders (courtesy The Carborundum Co.).

MATERIAL: High chrome, high-carbon tool steel, annealed

WHEEL: 9A30HI8V — $11'' \times 5'' \times 9''$K. Blanchard cylinder wheel

BLANCHARD GRINDER: Standard No 11, 16″ chuck, 15 hp

THE JOB: Grind 2 sides. Flat and parallel $\pm .002''$. Commercial finish

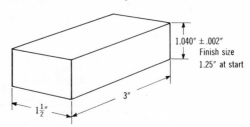

HOW LOADED: 24 pieces center of chuck, appropriate blocking

TABLE SPEED: 24 rpm

FEED: 0.016″/minute

DRESSED WHEEL: Once very lightly going through scale

STOCK REMOVED PER PIECE, CU. IN.: 0.945″ (average)

GRINDING TIME PER PIECE: 51.5 seconds

RATE OF STOCK REMOVAL, CU. IN. PER MIN.: 1.1

WHEEL WEAR PER PIECE, CU. IN.: 0.157

ABRASIVE COST PER PIECE: $.014

FLOOR-TO-FLOOR TIME PER PIECE: 1.2 minutes

**Fig. 24-15.** Surface-grinding job specifications with machine data (courtesy The Blanchard Machine Co.).

To get some idea of the metal-removal rate on a vertical surface grinder using a cylinder wheel and a rotating table, a manufacturer's specifications are cited in Fig. 24-15.

You will note that the cubic-inch removal rate is over 1 cubic in. per min on high-chrome–high-carbon tool steel.

**Form and Crush Grinding.** Threads and other formed surfaces can be ground with a grinding wheel that is dressed to the proper form. The wheel face may be formed with a diamond, as in the case of a simple V thread. For more complicated forms and faster grinding, the wheels are crush-formed with a hardened roller (Fig. 24-16).

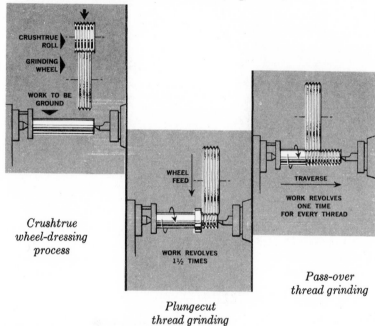

**Fig. 24-16.** The grinding wheel is crushed to the desired form with a steel roll. The wheel is then used to grind the form in the material (courtesy The Sheffield Corp.).

A hardened-steel or carbide roller of the same profile as the desired workpiece is fed into the abrasive wheel until the wheel takes on the reverse form of the roll.

Either of the wheels may be rotated at approximately 300 fpm, with an infeed of a few thousandths per revolution. Forming the wheel takes only a few minutes, and redressing it only a few seconds.

The best wheels for crush forming are the vitrified bonded ones, although resinoid wheels are also used for this purpose.

Crush forming of the grinding wheel has many advantages. It is not only faster than diamond dressing, but it is possible to make forms that are impossible by any other method. It has been found that the wheel dressed by crushing cuts better, since many more sharp cutting points are left than by conventional dressing. Close tolerances can be maintained, and grooves as narrow as 0.020 in. can be cut. Surface finishes as low as 8 μin. are obtainable.

Figure 24-17 shows a thread that was ground from the solid 0.180 in. deep. The tolerance maintained was ± .001 in. on the diameter. The wheel is able to grind 60 to 65 parts before recrushing is needed.

**Fig. 24-17.** Thread ground with a crush-formed wheel (courtesy The Sheffield Corp.).

**Tool and Cutter Grinding.** Tool and cutter grinding refers to sharpening all types of metal-cutting tools. Single-point tools used in lathe work are often sharpened by hand on a bench- or pedestal-type grinder. This is called *offhand* grinding. Carbide and ceramic throwaway inserts have eliminated a large amount of this type of grinding.

Cutter grinding refers more specifically to the sharpening of milling cutters, hobbing cutters, drills, reamers, etc. It is considered economical to grind a metal-cutting tool *before* it gets very dull. Sharpening at the proper time will give longer tool life, better finish, and closer tolerances. The horsepower required will also be less.

Cutters are ground on special tool and cutter grinders or universal grinders. The wide variety of attachments available for these machines makes it possible to hold the work either between centers, in a chuck, in a vise, or directly in the headstock spindle. Figure 24-18 shows a few of the setups used for cutter grinding.

**Snag Grinding.** Snag grinding is done where a considerable amount of metal is removed without regard to the accuracy of the finished surface. Examples of snag grinding are trimming the surface left by sprues

*Helical-flute grinding*

*Form-cutter grinding*

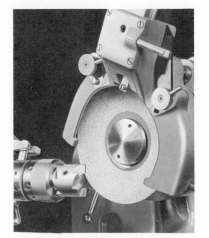

*End-mill grinding*

**Fig. 24-18.** Setups for grinding various milling cutters (courtesy Barber-Colman Co.).

and risers on castings, removing the excess metal on a weld, or grinding the parting line left on a casting.

Three types of machines are used for snag grinding; these are stand or bench grinders, portable grinders, and swing-frame grinders (Fig. 24-19).

Castings and rough workpieces that can be handled are brought to the stand grinder. The wheels may be as large as 36 in. in diameter on these solidly built machines.

Castings that are too large for the operator to hold up to the wheel are ground with a swing-frame grinder. This machine is moved around with a jib crane suspended from columns, or by mobile units.

Portable grinders are self-contained or flexible units used for miscellaneous grinding operations such as removing excess weld material,

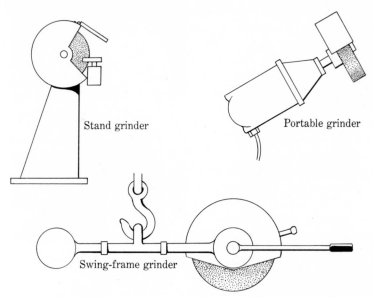

Stand grinder

Portable grinder

Swing-frame grinder

**Fig. 24-19.**   Types of machines used for snag grinding.

defective spots needing repair, parting lines, and fins. They are easily moved about and are used to the best advantage in removing comparatively small amounts of stock from widely separated areas.

## LAPPING, HONING, AND SUPERFINISHING

Grinding is considered an accurate method of producing surface finishes. However, it is not always possible or economical to achieve the degree of accuracy and finish desired. The more refined methods of lapping, honing, and superfinishing are used to obtain the ultimate in finishes.

### Lapping

Lapping is an abrading process done with either abrasive compounds or solid bonded abrasives. Lapping is performed primarily to increase accuracy, improve the surface finish, and match mating surfaces. Gage blocks are lapped to $\pm$ 0.000002 in. per in. of length, and they are also parallel within this dimension. Surface finishes obtained are within 1 or 2 rms. The reason lapping is more accurate than grinding and some other finishing operations is that very little heat and pressure, which induce strains in the finished part, are involved.

**Lapping Abrasives.**   Abrasives used in lapping are of either the natural or the artificial types used in grinding. Very hard surfaces, such as carbides, require diamond or silicon carbide grit. Softer materials, including steel, can be lapped with aluminum oxide, emery, or corundum. Grits for lapping are sold as compounds which are made with a suitable oil and other ingredients that act as a vehicle or carrier.

**Lapping Processes.**

HAND LAPPING.   Hand lapping, shown in Fig. 24-20, illustrates the main principles of this process. The lapping compound is spread out on the lapping plate. One of the most-used materials for the plate is soft gray cast iron. Being porous and soft, it is able to pick up and hold the lapping medium. The part is then rubbed over the lapping compound on the plate with a figure-eight or irregular motion. This motion is designed to use all of the plate so as to keep the surface true. Shallow grooves are cut into the plate to provide space for any excess lapping compound.

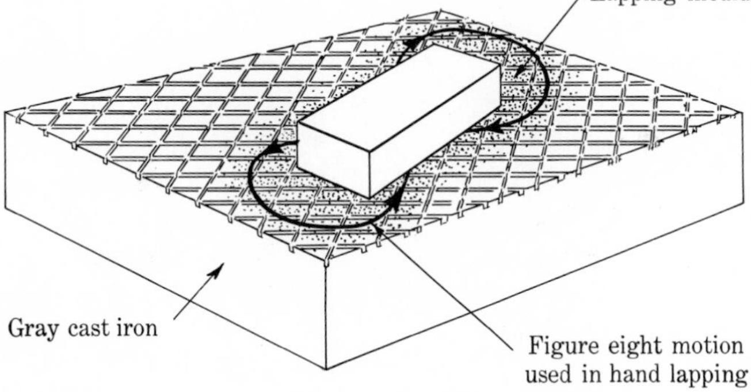

Lapping medium

**Fig. 24-20.**
hand-lapping.

Gray cast iron

Figure eight motion
used in hand lapping

MACHINE LAPPING.   In machine lapping, the lapping plate becomes a rotating table (Fig. 24-21). The parts to be lapped are confined to cages that impart a rotary and gyratory motion at the same time, covering the entire surface of the lapping table. Parallelism is maintained by having a stationary lapping plate on top of the workpieces. Cylindrical piece-part lapping is done by a cage arrangement as shown in Fig. 24-22.

A newer type of lapping machine uses vibratory rather than rotary motion. In this case the lapping plate, or pan, as it is called, is covered with an abrasive cloth that is cemented down. Light oil is used as a lubricant. Parts are held down on the abrasive paper by means of one or more pressure plates. There are no rotating parts. An electromagnet is used to furnish 3,600 vibrations per minute. A combination of drive components causes the parts to flow around the bottom of the pan.

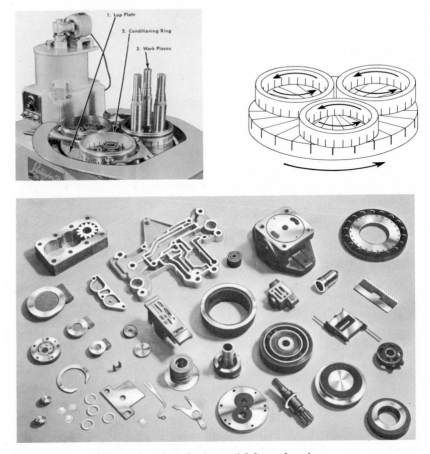

*Examples of work pieces with lapped surfaces*

**Fig. 24-21.** Work to be lapped is placed within the conditioning rings on two of the rotating lap plates. The conditioning rings are held in place but are free to rotate. The work tends to wear the lap plate, but the rotating action of the conditioning rings causes the lap plate to wear evenly, maintaining a flat surface. A wide variety of shapes and surfaces can be lapped. Standard machines handle parts from ⅛ in. to 32 in. Steel, tool steel, bronze, cast iron, stainless steel, aluminum, magnesium, brass, quartz, ceramics, plastics, and glass can be lapped by the same lap plate (courtesy Crane Packing Co.).

**Fig. 24-22.** A cage arrangement used for lapping cylindrical parts (courtesy Norton Co.).

BONDED-ABRASIVE LAPPING. Lapping compounds tend to leave a dark, dull surface that is hard to remove. Solid bonded abrasives are used on machines, similar to the vertical type shown, to remove the lapping compound and improve the finish.

MATING SURFACES. Oftentimes, it is desirable to have two surfaces match within extremely close tolerances, as in valves to valve seats. The lapping compound is placed between the two parts, after which one of the members is rotated. Gears and threads are also corrected in this manner.

### Honing

Honing deals primarily with internal surfaces. It is designed to correct the geometry of holes and impart a prescribed finish. Fine abrasive stones or sticks are used for the cutting action. Rotary and reciprocating motions are used simultaneously.

**Equipment.** For internal honing, the abrasive stick is mounted on what may be termed an adjustable mandrel [Fig. 24-23(a)]. By spring or wedge action, the stone can be fed out a predetermined distance during the honing operation. The desired honing pressure is also set. When the hole reaches the prescribed preset limits, the cutting action stops and the part is removed for gaging.

Either the workpiece or the hone is placed in a free-floating position. The hone shown at (b) is of the rigid type, and the work is held in a floating fixture or by hand for small workpieces. The hone at (a) is portable and is allowed to float in the hole; that is, the hone seeks the natural axis of the hole.

Honing can also be done externally, as shown in Fig. 24-24.

**Tolerance and Finish.** Honing, unlike grinding, is done at low speeds. Very little heat is generated. Therefore there is no submicro-

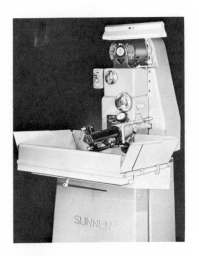

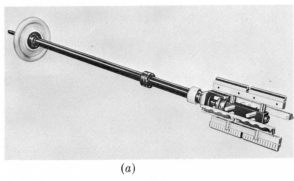

(a)

*Work example*

(b)

*Part:* Comparator column
*Use:* Gage
*Material:* Cast iron
*Hole Diameter:* .813″ ± .0002″, tandem
*Length:* 1″, 3″ between centers
*Finish:* Smooth base metal
*Stock Removal:* .0015″ to .002″
*Gage:* Ames Comparator
*Prev. Operation:* Grind
*Production Rate:* 50 per hr

**Fig. 24-23.** Honing equipment for internal surfaces (courtesy Sunnen Products Co.).

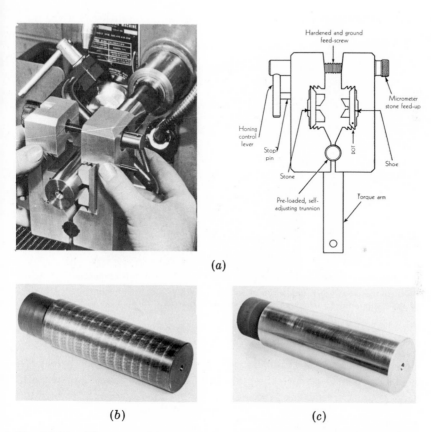

(a)

(b)                              (c)

**Fig. 24-24.** The external hone (a) is used to correct geometric defects left
by other processes. It is able to produce parts within 0.0001-in. tolerance or
less and surface finishes up to 2 μin. in hardened steel. Shown at (b) are
spiral marks left by grinding that can be eliminated by external honing. The
surface has been treated with a black oxide and then rubbed with a fine-grit
stone. A surface analyzer indicated a 30 μin. finish. Shown at (c) is the same
surface after honing. The wave contours have been eliminated (courtesy Sunnen
Products Company).

scopic damage to the workpiece surface. Tolerances are easily maintained within 0.0001 in.

The surface finish produced can be very smooth (1 $\mu$in.) or rough (100 $\mu$in.). A crosshatch pattern of varying angles is imparted to the work surface to enhance the lubrication-holding qualities (Fig. 24-25).

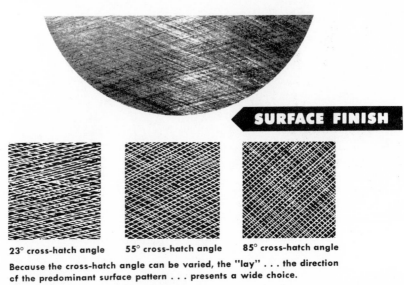

23° cross-hatch angle  55° cross-hatch angle  85° cross-hatch angle

**Because the cross-hatch angle can be varied, the "lay" . . . the direction of the predominant surface pattern . . . presents a wide choice.**

**Fig. 24-25.** Crosshatch pattern obtained by honing (courtesy Micromatic Hone Corp.).

In repair work, cylinder walls are honed not only to correct the geometry but to replace the glazed surface with a crosshatch pattern. Hole geometry that can be corrected by honing is shown in Fig. 24-26.

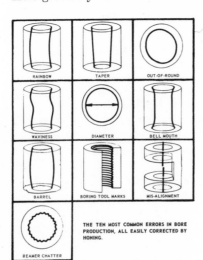

**Fig. 24-26.** Hole geometry that can be corrected by honing (courtesy Sunnen Products Co.).

**Stock Removal.** The rate of stock removal varies with the material and the size of the work. A hone that would be used for a ¾-in.-diameter hole 2½ in. long could be expected to remove metal at the following rates: hardened tool steel, 0.0015 in. per min; annealed steel SAE 1020, 0.004 in. per min; 3004 ST aluminum, 0.010 in. per min.

## Superfinishing

Superfinishing is somewhat similar to honing but is applied primarily to external surfaces. The process was first conceived in 1936 in answer to the age-old problem of obtaining maximum wear on mating parts. Extensive studies indicated that the more closely the bore and shaft diameters approximate each other, the greater will be the load-carrying capacity of the bearing. The oil film between the mating members is in danger of being punctured by any sharp points left by the finishing process (Fig. 24-27). As these sharp points penetrate the oil film, the concentration of weight and friction causes the two

**Fig. 24-27.** A smooth surface does not have high load-concentration points that puncture the oil film (courtesy Gisholt Machine Co.).

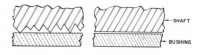

metals momentarily to weld and tear apart, causing rapid wear conditions. Wear will help break down the high points and correct some of the out-of-roundness. The difficulty lies in the foreign particles scoring the smooth surfaces. For this reason, hardened rotating shafts should have the smoothest surface possible. Owing to the difficulty in maintaining an oil film on reciprocating parts, a crosshatch pattern is recommended. Scratches at a substantial angle to the motion of the two bearing surfaces will break up minute weldments from one part to the other. It is also easier for the oil contained in the valleys to move across the angular ridges than if they were in the lengthwise direction. The depth of the crosshatch pattern will depend on the severity of conditions that tend to produce welding, but the depth should seldom exceed 10 to 12 $\mu$in.

**Equipment.** The superfinishing equipment for cylindrical surfaces consists of an abrasive stone mounted on the end of a spring-loaded quill (Fig. 24-28). The assembly has an oscillating mechanism by which the stone can move back and forth a maximum distance of 3/16 in. at 425 cycles per min. The assembly can be mounted on the cross slide of a lathe or on a machine especially designed for the purpose. If the part to be superfinished is not longer than the stone, traverse motion will not be necessary.

The stone is formed to the radius of the work by putting emery cloth over the workpiece, face out. As the stone contacts the emery

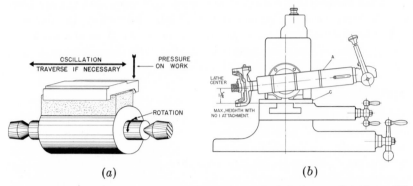

(a)                              (b)

**Fig. 24-28.** (a) Basic equipment used for cylindrical superfinishing. (b) Superfinishing attachment for a lathe (courtesy Gisholt Machine Co.).

cloth, it is soon worn in to the approximate radius needed. The rest is taken care of during the operation.

After the stone is dressed, it is brought in contact with the work at about 20 or 30 psi pressure. The part is rotated at a speed equal to 50 or 60 fpm. The oscillation motion is started, and coolant is allowed to flood the area. If traverse is not needed, the part can be finished in less than a minute.

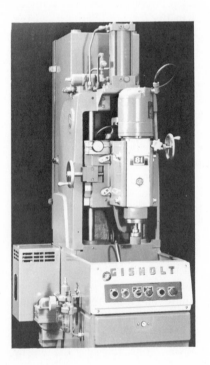

**Fig. 24-29.** The type of superfinishing machine used for flat surfaces (courtesy Gisholt Machine Co.).

Flat surfaces are superfinished with a machine containing both an upper and a lower spindle (Fig. 24-29). The upper spindle is a spring-loaded quill on which a stone is mounted. The lower spindle carries the work. Both spindles are parallel so that, when they rotate, the result is a very flat smooth surface.

**Tolerance and Finish.** The superfinishing process is not designed to remove material or correct part geometry. The amount of material removed from the part may range from 0.0001 to 0.0004 in. on the diameter. The surface finish produced ranges from less than 1 to 80 $\mu$-in., with the average around 3. When a surface smoother than 3 $\mu$in. is desired, the time needed to produce it goes up rapidly. As an example, a part that can be brought to a 3-$\mu$in. finish in 1 min may require 3 min more to bring it to a 2-$\mu$in. finish or better. Figure 24-30 shows a range of finishes that can be produced by this process.

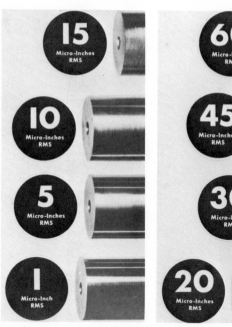

**Fig. 24-30.** Superfinishing can be used to produce a pre-selected surface finish from 1 to 80 $\mu$in. (courtesy Gisholt Machine Co.).

## BARREL FINISHING

Basically, barrel finishing consists of putting a number of work-pieces in a six- or eight-sided barrel together with an abrasive medium. The barrel is rotated so that superfluous stock can be removed by the abrading action of the medium used.

## Applications

Barrel finishing is used for economical deflashing, deburring, descaling, chamfering holes, generating controlled radii, and improving surface finish. The process has been successfully used on ferrous and nonferrous metals, plastics, rubber, and wood. Barrel finishing is usually associated with small parts, but the size of the parts tumbled is limited only by the size of the equipment used. Parts range in size from sewing needles to 400-lb castings.

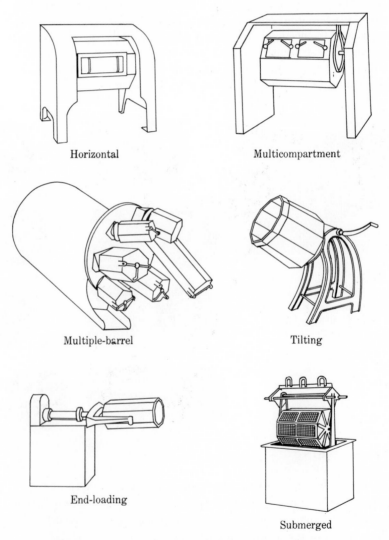

Horizontal

Multicompartment

Multiple-barrel

Tilting

End-loading

Submerged

**Fig. 24-31.** Various kinds of barrel-finishing equipment.

One important aspect of barrel finishing is that it can replace hand-filing, wire-brushing, polishing, and buffing operations. Parts may be finished by the dozen or by the thousand, with practically no increase in labor cost. Another important factor is uniformity; barrel finishing makes the parts completely uniform, whereas with hand finishing this is impossible.

### Equipment

Six- or eight-sided horizontal barrels, either with or without baffles, are the most common type of equipment (Fig. 24-31). These barrels may have vertical dividers, making possible several operations at once.

### Barrel-Finishing Media

Figure 24-32 shows a number of different media used in barrel finishing.

| Natural stones | Man-made stones | Bonded shapes | Abrasive grains |

FINISHING SHAPES

| Balls | Diagonals | Pins | Cones | Oval balls |

**Fig. 24-32.** Some barrel finishing media.

**Balls, Diagonals, and Cones.** Hardened steel balls are used for burnishing. Hardened and unhardened steel and zinc are used for an abrasive action. Diagonal steel and zinc pieces are good for getting at inside corners. Balls and cones are often used together for workpieces that have flat and curved surfaces that meet.

**Natural and Man-Made Stones.** Natural and artificial stones are also called *nuggets* or *chips*. The natural stones consist of granite, limestone, gravel, and sand. Aluminum oxide is the principal artificial stone. It has considerable cutting ability, as, with the grinding wheel, it can be made constantly self-sharpening.

**Bonded Shapes.** Small abrasive particles are difficult to reclaim. To overcome this and to furnish an all-around media, the aluminum oxide abrasive is made in triangles, pellets, and diamonds. Both vitrified and rubber bonds are used. Vitrified shapes are extremely fast for deburring or descaling operations.

**Special Media.** Considerable ingenuity is often used by engineers in finding media to fulfill a specific purpose. Wooden pegs, for example, are excellent for plastic finishing. Sawdust and corncob meal are nonabrasive mediums used for drying and polishing.

## Compounds

In addition to the above media, abrasive compounds are used. They may be used with or without media. They may be acid, alkaline, or neutral, and they usually contain soaps or detergents. Compounds have many and diverse functions. They prevent loading and glazing of nuggets, increase metal-removal rate, saponify and emulsify oils and greases, soften water, improve color and, in some cases, act as lubricants for improved surface finish. The alkaline- and acid-type compounds are designed for fast chemical action and are particularly good in aiding descaling of heat-treated parts.

## Basic Operating Conditions

There are several basic operating conditions that control barrel finishing.

**Size and Type of Media.** The nuggets used must be free to pass to all surfaces of the workpiece. Large nuggets cut faster than small ones. Combinations are used in certain given ratios to obtain the benefits of both.

**Ratio of Parts to Media.** The normal average ratio is 3 parts of nuggets to 1 of workpieces. This will vary with the size of the parts, large parts needing more nuggets to prevent damage to other parts.

**Load Height.** The principal abrasive action is caused by the sliding of the upper layer of the work load. More than 90 percent of the abrasive action takes place in the sliding action of this top layer. The ideal load height for the fastest grinding rate is when the barrel is 50 percent full. The length of the slide, under these conditions, is maximum.

**Water.** The amount of water used influences the grinding speed, finish, and color, and also helps control damage. The amount of water varies from 4 to 6 in. under the load level for modest grinding, to 3 to 6 in. above load level for burnishing and cushioning of larger parts.

**Compounds.** By choosing the proper compound, it is possible to achieve optimum results in descaling, rust removal, grinding, polishing, cleaning, and many other operations.

**Barrel Speed.** The barrel speed controls the movement of the parts, from a cascading effect at high speed to a gentle turnover at low speeds (Fig. 24-33). Too high a speed may cause scratching and peeling of the parts. A general recommendation is 130 sfpm.

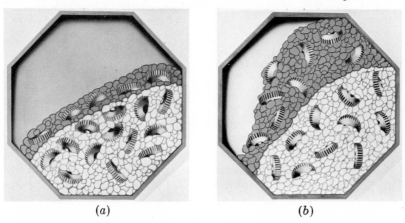

$(a)$          $(b)$

**Fig. 24-33.** The effect of speed on workpieces in the barrel. $(a)$ Speed—10 to 12 rpm produces gentle action. $(b)$ Speed—26 rpm produces violent action (courtesy The Carborundum Co.).

**Time.** Cycle time must be determined from preliminary test runs. Generally, a 2-hr cycle will perform most operations satisfactorily. However, simple descaling jobs may be accomplished in a matter of 15 to 30 min. Workpieces containing holes and requiring large radii may have to run 6 to 12 hr.

### Applications

As mentioned previously, barrel finishing is limited only by the size of the equipment available. Small parts are shown here with data to give the reader an idea of some of the most important factors involved (Fig. 24-34).

Part: Machine gear
Operation: Remove burrs caused in hobbing operation
Medium: ⅜-in.-diameter pellets. 2 hr
Compound: Carbofast No. 4
Former method: Remove burrs with hand file. 10 min required per gear
Cost savings: 24¢ each (approx.)

Part: Hydraulic-press shims
Operation: Removal of heat-treat scale and surface roughness. Original at left
Medium and compounds: 1 hr in No. 3 Nuggets and Carboscaler No. 61. Step 2—1 hr combination neutralizing and polishing
Former method: Clean with hand file and coated abrasive. Time—2 min each
Cost savings: 1.3¢ per piece

**Fig. 24-34.** Examples of barrel finishing with time cost data (courtesy The Carborundum Co.).

### VIBRATION FINISHING

Barrel finishing does not work well where blind holes are encountered and in the inside of narrow slots.

A newer concept of finishing that depends on vibrated rather than tumbled abrasive is shown in Fig. 24-35, with an aluminum casting and data. This method also has the advantage of continuous abrading action, and less danger of the workpieces colliding.

**Fig. 24-35.** Vibratory abrasive-finishing equipment and examples of finished parts (courtesy Pangborn Corporation).

**POLISHING**

Coated abrasive cloths are used to remove material and improve the finish of a wide variety of products. The abrasive applied to the cloth or paper backing can be either natural or manufactured. Natural abrasives used are flint, emery, and garnet. Garnet is usually thought of as a precious stone; however, common garnets, as used in polishing, are found in many kinds of silicate rocks. Manufactured abrasives are aluminum oxide and silicon carbide. The mesh size ranges from 12 to 400.

Many kinds of machines have been built to bring the coated abrasive in contact with the workpiece. They may be broadly classified in two groups—the endless-belt machines and the coated abrasive wheels.

### Endless-Belt Machines

The five main types of belt machines—platen, contact wheel, formed wheel, centerless, and flexible belt—are shown in Fig. 24-36.

**Platen Grinder.** The platen machine provides a support or platen for part of the belt surface. It is designed for light cuts, with stock removal seldom exceeding 1/32 to 1/16 in. on ferrous metals and twice this on nonferrous metals. Platen grinders permit semiautomatic operations, with pressure, depth of cut, and rate of feed all constant.

**Contact Wheel.** There are many variations of the contact-wheel or wheel-and-idler machine as it is sometimes called. An adaptation of this machine is the swing grinder shown schematically in Fig. 24-36. Swing-frame grinders are used to advantage when the workpiece is difficult to move. They may also be used above or beside conveyor lines. Stand-mounted arrangements provide for greater movement of the part around the contact wheel. A typical machine of this kind uses a 1½-hp motor for driving and a 2½- by 72-in. belt over a 6- by 2½-in. contact wheel.

**Formed Wheel.** The formed wheel acts as a special platen. By forming the fiber-backing wheel, it is possible to direct the abrasive belt into the irregular surface, as shown.

**Centerless Machine.** Several arrangements are made for centerless grinding with the abrasive belt. One setup uses a resilient contact wheel with a conventional regulating wheel. Through-feeds of 35 fpm

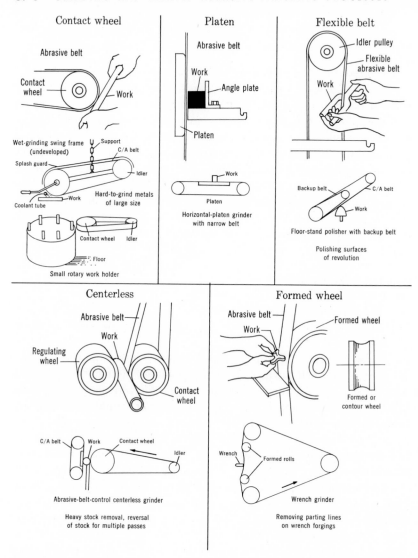

**Fig. 24-36.** The five main types of endless-belt polishing machines. Variations of each kind are also shown.

are available, with tolerances of 0.001 in. on small diameters. The maximum diameter reduction on steel is about 0.005 in. per pass at 2 fpm.

**Flexible Belt.** Flexible-belt machines are made in several ways, but they usually consist of a wheel-and-idler arrangement. These machines are often used for polishing difficult inside and outside contours. Large abrasive-belt machines are now available which are capable of handling stock up to 80 in. wide and 10 ft long. They are used to remove surface defects, and produce fine finishes, often to close tolerances.

### Coated Abrasive Wheels

A comparative newcomer to the field of industrial polishing equipment is the soft abrasive type of wheel [Fig. 24-37 (a)]. This is made up of hundreds of small abrasive strips mounted on a hub. It has the advantage of conforming to a wide variety of contours without having to be made to any special form. The abrasive-coated leaves form a resilient surface, cushioned by their own flexibility.

**Fig. 24-37.** An abrasive-type wheel that presents a resilient surface allowing it to follow the contour of the work piece. Abrasive polishing wheels are also made as flat discs that can be used on the end of portable drills (courtesy Merit Products Inc.).

Abrasive discs are considered among the best tools for removing and blending welds. They are also used in many other sanding applications.

Closely associated with abrasive wheels are wire-wheel brushes. They are used on both stationary and portable tools. Brushes of this type are used with very fine abrasives to impart a brushed-satin finish.

### BUFFING

Buffing wheels are usually made from muslin or canvas. They are designated by the way in which they are sewed—concentric, radial, radial arc, parallel, and square. Some loose wheels have only a row of stitching around the hub (Fig. 24-38).

Buffing is used to give a much higher, lustrous, reflective finish than can be obtained by polishing. For a mirrorlike finish, the surface must be free of defects and deep scratches. Abrasives embedded in wax are applied directly to the rotating wheel. The cutting action, whereby a small amount of metal is removed, is accomplished with an aluminum

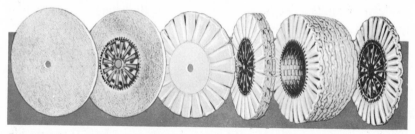

**Fig. 24-38.** A variety of buffing wheels, ranging from the hard-stitched wheel to the soft-pleated wheel (courtesy American Buff Company).

oxide abrasive. A "coloring" operation, that brings out the best color and luster of the metal, is done by using a white compound of levigated-alumina-type abrasive.

Cutting is done at approximately 10,000 sfpm. Speeds higher than this are hazardous for handwork. Surface speeds of 9,000 fpm should not be exceeded for color buffing.

### QUESTIONS

1. What are the most used abrasives in industry today?
2. What are the various kinds of bonding materials used in making grinding wheels?
3. What is meant by the grade and structure of a grinding wheel?
4. Why is a soft-type wheel used on hard materials and vice versa?
5. What is a modern method of getting the specified ingredients in a grinding wheel?
6. What is the difference between dressing and truing a grinding wheel?
7. Compare the advantages and disadvantages of the various bonds used in diamond wheels.
8. What three wheels are often used in grinding carbide tools?
9. What are the main differences between cylindrical, or center-type, grinders and centerless grinders?
10. What are the two main types of centerless grinders?
11. Describe the process of crush forming a grinding wheel.
12. What are some examples of snag grinding?
13. What accuracy can be achieved by lapping?
14. What types of corrections can be made on internal surfaces by honing?
15. What tolerance and surface finish can be obtained by honing?
16. What is the purpose of superfinishing a machined surface?
17. What are some applications of barrel finishing?
18. Describe and give the applications of some of the tumbling mediums and compounds used in barrel finishing.

19.  Why are tumbling barrels only loaded to about fifty percent of capacity?

20.  What are some of the advantages of vibratory action over tumbling action in abrasive finishing?

21.  What are the main types of polishing machines?

22.  What is meant by *color* buffing?

### PROBLEMS

1.  A shaft 2 in. in diameter and 10 in. long is to have 8 in. of the length ground on a cylindrical grinder. The wheel is 1 in. wide and 12 in. in diameter. (*a*) What should the rpm of the wheel be? (*b*) What should the rpm of the shaft be? What is the feed rate?

2.  How long would it take to grind 30 shafts as described in Prob. 1?

3.  How long would it take to mill the part shown in Fig. 24-15 lengthwise if a 2-in.-diameter carbide cutter were used with 6 teeth at a cutting speed of 450 fpm and 0.010 chip load per tooth? How does this compare with the grinding time? What would you expect the surface-finish range to be for each operation?

4.  What would the approximate production rate be for honing a ¾-in.-diameter hole 2½ in. long in hardened tool steel if the amount of metal to be removed were 0.003 in.?

5.  If a pin 4 in. long and 1 in. in diameter can be superfinished to about 3 $\mu$in. in 1 min, how long will it take to bring it to 2 $\mu$in. or better?

6.  What would be the proper rpm to run a 24-in.-diameter tumbling barrel?

7.  What would the maximum production rate be in pieces per hour for steel pins 3 in. long and 1 in. in diameter on a centerless abrasive belt machine?

### REFERENCES

Black, T. W., "Fundamentals of Barrel Finishing," *The Tool and Manufacturing Engineer*, April, 1957.

McLaughlin, J. K., "The Abrasive Belt and Its Use in Machine Tools," *The Tool and Manufacturing Engineer*, May, 1956.

# 25

# GEARS AND
# GEAR MANUFACTURE

**T**HE PURPOSE OF gearing is to transmit motion from one machine part to another at a uniform ratio of speeds. Cylinders are sometimes used to transmit motion by rolling one on the other; however, owing to a certain amount of slippage, the speed ratio of the two cylinders will not be constant. Properly formed teeth allow gears to roll together without slipping, giving a constant-speed ratio and the capacity for transmitting large amounts of power.

## GEARS

### Gear Classification

Gears are classified by their tooth form or by the plane of the surface on which they are cut. For example, when straight gear teeth are cut on the outside or inside of a cylindrical surface, they are referred to as *spur gears*. When teeth are cut on a conical cylindrical surface, they are called *bevel gears*. Gear teeth cut on a straight surface make a *rack gear*. When a pair of gears are of unequal size, the smaller one is known as the *pinion* and the larger one as the *gear*.

Gears may also be classified in pairs by the geometric orientation of their intersecting shafts (shown in Fig. 25-1), as follows: parallel-shaft gears, intersecting-shaft gears, and nonintersecting-shaft gears.

674

Spur-gear set*          Double helical-gear set*          Zerate gear pair*

(*a*) *Parallel-shaft gears*

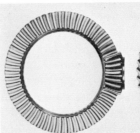

Zerol*                    Spiral bevel*

Straight bevel gear†

(*b*) *Intersecting-shaft gears*

Worm-gear set*          Hypoid*          Skewed-axis
                                          helical gear*

(*c*) *Nonintersecting-shaft gears*

* Courtesy Gleason Works

† Courtesy Philadelphia Gear Works, Inc.

**Fig. 25-1.**   Gears classified by shaft relationship.

**Parallel-Shaft Gears.**

SPUR GEARS. One of the principal advantages of spur gears is their ability to transmit power without end thrust and without axial displacement. Spur gears are generally used on drives of moderate speeds, such as marine equipment, hoisting equipment, feed-change gears, etc. However, when the gears are finished by a shaving process and proper heat treatment, they can be used for high-speed applica-tions.

The fact that spur gears are relatively simple to manufacture and economical to maintain accounts for their wide usage.

HELICAL GEARS. Helical gears have their teeth cut at a helix angle. Mating gears have the identical angle, but of opposite hand. Properly designed helical gears provide for an overlapping of the gear teeth. Thus, when the gears are in mesh, there is always more than one tooth in contact. Compared to spur gears, they are quieter in operation and run with less vibration.

Helical gears produce an end thrust which is a function of the helix angle. The larger the helix angle, the larger the axial thrust. Mounting assemblies must be built to absorb this thrust load.

These gears, when finished by shaving and heat treatment, are available for speeds in excess of 9,000 fpm.

*Double helical gears.* Double helical gears have two sets of opposed helical teeth. End thrust such as occurs in single helical gears is eliminated, because the two sets of teeth counterbalance each other. Because there is no thrust, it is possible to cut the teeth with a greater helix angle than is generally used in single helical gears, and thus obtain greater overlap with smoother tooth action.

Double helical gears are sometimes cut staggered, the teeth in one row being in advance of the opposite row. Staggered teeth add extra smoothness to the tooth action, since the teeth in the opposing rows do not pick up their loads at the same instant.

When shaved, heat-treated, and dynamically balanced, these gears can be run at speeds in excess of 9,000 sfpm.

HERRINGBONE GEARS. A gear similar to the double helical gear is the herringbone gear. This gear does not have a parting groove in the middle. The method of cutting the herringbone gear without the central groove was developed by W. E. Sykes and has made possible optimum gear capacity. These gears are used for the transmission of heavy loads at high speeds, where continuous service is required, where shock and vibration are present, or where a high reduction ratio is necessary in a single train.

ZERATE GEARS. The Zerate gear is the trade name given to the curved-tooth-type spur gear shown in part *a* of Fig. 25-1. The curved tooth provides for some overlap and a self-centering action eliminating end thrust.

### Intersecting-Shaft Gears.

BEVEL GEARS.

*Straight bevel.* Straight bevel gears are used to transmit motion to shafts that intersect, usually at 90 deg to each other. When the shafts are at right angles and the gears are of the same size, they are referred to as *miter gears.* Straight bevel gears are considered satisfactory for velocities up to 1,000 sfpm.

*Spiral bevel.* The spiral bevel gear differs from the straight bevel gear in that the teeth are not straight but are cut on an arc. Spiral bevel gears are superior to straight bevel gears because the load is distributed over two or more teeth at any given instant. Spiral bevel gears are quieter and smoother in action because the teeth mesh together gradually. These gears are satisfactory for velocities up to 8,000 sfpm.

*Zerol gears.* Zerol bevel gears get their name from the fact they have curved teeth with zero degrees of spiral angle. These gears are superior to straight bevel gears in that their operation is smoother and quieter owing to the curvature and slight overlap of the teeth. Zerol gears are replacing straight bevel gears, in many applications, because of their superior operating characteristics.

### Nonintersecting Gears.

WORM GEARS. In worm-wheel gearing, the small gear is referred to as the *worm gear* and the large gear as the *worm wheel.* Because of their screw action, worm-gear drives are quiet and vibration-free. This type of gear is extremely compact. Much higher reduction ratios can be attained through a worm-gear set on a given center distance than with any other type of gearing. Thus, the number of moving parts in a speed-reduction system is lowered to the absolute minimum. Worm gearing of the higher ratios cannot be driven backward through the worm gear. When this condition occurs, the worm-gear set is said to be "self-locking."

HYPOID GEARS. Hypoid gears resemble spiral bevel gears, but they differ in that they do not have intersecting axes. The pinion and the gear are cut on a hyperboloid of revolution, this term being shortened to "hypoid." Hypoid gearing is widely used in the automotive industry as a rear-axle drive. These gears are also used in steel mills, in paper mills, and in the printing industry.

SKEWED-AXIS HELICAL GEARS (SPIRAL GEARS). Skewed-axis helical gears, sometimes referred to as *spiral gears*, resemble regular helical gears. They are used, however, to transmit motion to shafts that are not parallel and do not intersect. They are principally gears of convenience, in that they can transmit motion at any angle on nonintersecting shafts. Also, ratios can be altered without change of pitch or center distance. Spiral gears are not used to transmit heavy loads.

### Gear Nomenclature

Gear nomenclature and formulas comprise a rather long and involved subject. This limited presentation is for the purpose of clarifying some of the more pertinent terms; no attempt to cover the whole field will be made.

As stated previously, some slippage is encountered when one cylinder is used to roll another cylinder. If a tooth is raised on one of the cylinders and a matching depression is cut on the opposite cylinder, it is the beginning of a positive drive. The distance from the top of the tooth to the middle is termed the *addendum*. The bottom half of the tooth, plus some clearance for the mating tooth, is known as the *dedendum*. A circle drawn on the gear at the mid-point of the tooth, less the clearance, is the *pitch-line circle*. The diameter of this circle is the *pitch diameter*. Diametral pitch is the number of teeth per inch of pitch diameter, expressed as

$$DP = \frac{N}{PD}$$

or the number of teeth divided by the pitch diameter of the gear. Figure 25-2 shows sections of 4 and 8 diametral-pitch gears.

4

**Fig. 25-2.** Comparison of gear-teeth sizes for 4 and 8 diametral-pitch gears.

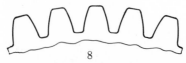

8

You will notice that the tooth profile is curved outward. This curve is known as the *involute* curve, and it is the best tooth form for smooth, continuous action. It also has the important feature of being able to maintain a constant-speed ratio with a change in center distance between two gears. The *pressure angle,* as the name implies, is the angle at which the tooth pressure is applied and distributed. As shown in Fig. 25-3, it is the angle between the line of action and the common tangent to the pitch circle of the gears. A 20-deg pressure angle is now the accepted standard for gears of heavy loading, because they are quieter running and have greater wear resistance than the 14 ½-deg pressure angles of the same size. The 20-deg gear teeth are wider at the base and are thus stronger. There is also a disadvantage in increasing the pressure angle, as it increases the forces tending to push the mating gears apart. A *stub-tooth* gear is a 20-deg-pressure-angle gear whose tooth depth equals 1.8 divided by the diametral pitch. Although this shorter tooth is stronger, the time of contact of the mating teeth is shortened, and there is an increase in noise unless the gears are very accurately cut, finished, and mounted. A stub-tooth gear is used to eliminate the interference that sometimes occurs when there are many teeth on the gear and few on the pinion.

*Gear ratio* is equal to the ratio of the number of teeth in one gear to the number of teeth in the mating gear. For example, if a pair of gears have pitch diameters of 2 and 4 in., respectively, the ratio is 2:1. Likewise, if a pair of gears have 24 teeth and 48 teeth, respectively, the ratio is 2:1.

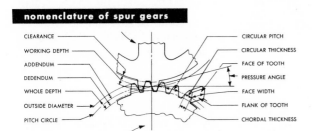

**nomenclature of spur gears**

| | |
|---|---|
| CLEARANCE | CIRCULAR PITCH |
| WORKING DEPTH | CIRCULAR THICKNESS |
| ADDENDUM | FACE OF TOOTH |
| DEDENDUM | PRESSURE ANGLE |
| WHOLE DEPTH | FACE WIDTH |
| OUTSIDE DIAMETER | FLANK OF TOOTH |
| PITCH CIRCLE | CHORDAL THICKNESS |

**Fig. 25-3.** Common spur-gear nomenclature (courtesy Philadelphia Gear Works, Inc.).

### Gear Materials

Innovations in manufacturing processes have made it possible to use satisfactorily materials that formerly could not have been employed. Material selection is based primarily on the service conditions that will be encountered by the gear, but consideration is also given to the machinability of the material, production-rate factors, and cost.

Desirable properties for gear materials include resistance to wear, shock, static compression, shear, and fatigue. Gear-tooth design is such that it tends to minimize the rubbing, wearing action of one tooth on the other. It provides, rather, a rolling contact action that minimizes frictional wear.

**Ferrous Gear Materials.** Because of its great strength and toughness, steel is widely used for gears. The blank may be forged, cast, or cut from bar stock, but most gears that will encounter heavy loads or shock are made from forgings. Plain carbon steel is not used extensively owing to the distortion encountered in quenching. Nickel-, chromium-, and molybdenum-alloy steels are used either for full hardening or for carburizing, depending on the percent of alloying elements present. Carburized gears have a minimum of distortion, extremely hard surfaces free from soft spots, and tough cores.

The higher-carbon gears may be fully hardened, flame-hardened, or induction-hardened to develop desirable physical properties (Fig. 25-4).

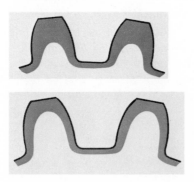

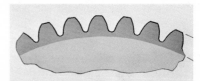

**Fig. 25-4.** The amount of flame or induction hardening varies with the pitch of the gear and the treatment (courtesy National Broach and Machine Co.).

Forged gear blanks are cooled from the forging heat in a furnace or by burying each forging individually in ashes or mica. After cooling, they are annealed to develop a uniformly machinable microstructure. If higher strength is desired, they may be cooled in still air or normalized.

Cast iron is a good gear material for general machinery because of its relatively low cost and good resistance to wear. In addition, it can easily be molded into any desired form.

**Nonferrous Gear Materials.** Nonferrous materials, such as aluminum and brass, are often used in the finer-pitch gears because of the increased machinability and good wearing qualities under light loads. Aluminum bronze is used in all types of gears, especially where the mating gears are of hardened steel.

Die-cast gears which require no machine finishing are usually made of a zinc-aluminum alloy. As with powdered-metal gears, they are generally classed from good commercial to low-precision types by the American Gear Manufacturers' Association (AGMA).

**Plastic Gears.** Plastic materials are widely used for gears because of the comparative ease of manufacture, good wear qualities (if starting loads are not too heavy), and noiseless operation. Nylon is a popular injection-molding material for gears, since it has good bearing characteristics (operation without lubricant), can be produced at high rates, and is light in weight.

Thermosetting plastics are used for making gears either by molding or by machining from canvas-base laminated sheets.

## GEAR MANUFACTURE

There are many ways by which a gear can be made. The process used will depend on the type of material, size, accuracy, and quantity. The main manufacturing methods can be broadly classified as cutting, casting, molding, powder metallurgy, and rolling.

### Gear-Cutting Processes

The principal method of producing gears is by cutting the teeth in a cast, forged, or machined blank. The teeth may be cut with a *form cutter,* which is a cutter that has the profile of the space to be cut between the teeth. The tooth form may also be *generated* by following a template or by rotating a cutter in such a way as to generate the shape of the gear tooth. *Generate,* when used in gear cutting, indicates that the cutter produces tooth profiles differing from the form of the cutter itself. Generating gear teeth is done with hobbing cutters or by gear-shaper cutters (Fig. 25-5).

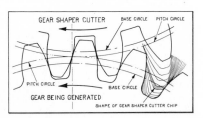

**Fig. 25-5.** Generating a tooth profile with a shaper cutter (courtesy Fellows Gear Shaper Co.).

**Form-Cutting Gear Teeth.** When a limited number of gears are needed, they can be cut on a milling machine. Straight spur and bevel gears can be cut on a plain horizontal column-and-knee-type mill. Helical gear teeth require a universal milling machine with the indexing head geared to the table lead screw (Fig. 25-6).

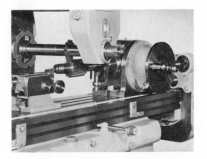

**Fig. 25-6.** Milling a helical gear requires a universal milling machine with the indexing table geared to the table lead screw (courtesy Cincinnati Milling Machine Co.).

**Gear Hobbing.**   A gear-hobbing cutter is somewhat similar to having several form cutters ganged together, but arranged so as to give a continuously helical path like a worm thread. The hob has teeth with straight sides, and the tooth form is generated as the hob passes over the gear blank. Both the gear blank and the hob revolve in a continuously timed relationship. All the teeth are cut by the hob as it gradually feeds across the blank (Fig. 25-7).

**Fig. 25-7.** The gear-hobbing cutter cuts a portion of each tooth with each revolution. Either straight or helical teeth can be cut (courtesy Barber Coleman Co.).

On large gears several feet in diameter, the hob is run across the face at least twice. The first cut is a rough cut for removing most of the metal. The second cut, usually made with a different cutter, is a finishing cut which is run at higher speed and feed to clean up the tooth to size. A third cut may be taken if the size is not within limits. For gears that require a very accurate profile, as many as four or five cuts may be taken. The teeth are checked after each cut with a gear-tooth caliper on which the size of the addendum is set and the width of the tooth at the pitch line is read off on the vernier scale in thousandths of an inch.

Herringbone gears can be hobbed in two half sections and bolted together afterward, or they can be cut in one solid piece. In the one-piece gears, the teeth are finished on one side and then on the other.

Small gears are usually hobbed on the horizontal-type machine, as shown in Fig. 25-7, and larger gears on the vertical hobbing machine.

Gears in the range of 200 in. in diameter are often fabricated as a weldment from either a forged rim or a rolled and welded steel rim. Connecting webs are welded in place, after which the whole structure is normalized. After normalizing, the gear is assembled on a shaft, and the rim and face are machined on a vertical boring mill. A fabricated gear of this type with a face width of 88 in. will weigh as much as 72 tons. Despite their size, concentricity and tooth spacing may be controlled to within ±0.0002 in.

**Gear Shaping.**    Cutting gears with a gear shaper is also a generating process. A gear-shaped cutter held on a vertical reciprocating spindle is made to feed into the gear blank until it reaches full depth. The cutter and the gear blank then rotate slowly and continuously, as though they were two gears in mesh. Since the cutting action starts at one definite point on the gear periphery, it continues around to the starting point with a slight amount of overlap.

The gear shaper is not limited to making spur gears or even to involute forms. As shown in Fig. 25-8, many external and internal forms can be cut. Odd-shaped parts require odd-shaped cutters.

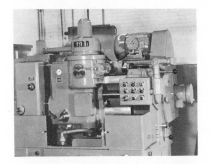

**Fig. 25-8.** The gear shaper is not limited to the production of gears. Both involute and noninvolute forms can be developed (courtesy Fellows Gear Shaper Co.).

To cut helical gears on a gear shaper, a right- or left-hand helical cutter is required. This cutter must then be given a twisting or turning motion in a helical path as it travels up and down past the face of the gear blank. The turning motion, which corresponds to the helical teeth of the gear, is controlled by means of helical guides on the cutter spindle.

**Planing Herringbone Gears.** The Farrel Sykes gear generator can be used for cutting spur gears, internal gears, and helical gears, but it is especially adapted to the duplex planing of continuous herringbone gears. As shown in Fig. 25-9, the cutters in the background are made to reciprocate back and forth. One cutter is in action in one stroke and the opposite one the next time. The helical guide, to the far left, produces the proper motion as the cutter advances through the tooth. There is a partial rotation of the cutters in unison with the helical reciprocating motion.

**Fig. 25-9.** The Farrel Sykes machine used to cut a herringbone gear. A reciprocating motion is applied to the cutters in the background, and the helical motion is obtained by the guide on the left (courtesy Sykes Machine and Gear Corporation).

**Bevel-Gear Generator.** Shown in Fig. 25-10 is a closeup view of the Gleason bevel-gear generator. The cutters are spaced apart a distance equal to the thickness of the tooth to be cut and are reciprocated horizontally while being swung with the turret on its axis. The swing of the turret carries the tool or tools alternately above and below a horizontal position, but only enough to generate a single tooth during each roll.

Spiral bevel gears are cut on a special machine manufactured by the Gleason Works. It has a rotary cutter into which the gear blank is fed. The cutter cuts one tooth at a time, and then the blank is automatically moved out and indexed to the next tooth. The gear blank is twisted as it is moved into the rotary cutter, and this produces a spiral (Fig. 25-11).

Hypoid gears are cut in much the same manner as spiral bevel gears, the main difference being that the pinion is cut with its axis

**Fig. 25-10.** The bevel gear tooth is generated by two reciprocating cutters (courtesy Gleason Works).

**Fig. 25-11.** A spiral bevel gear being cut on a hypoid gear-cutting machine (courtesy Gleason Works).

offset an amount equal to the offset of the shafts on which the gears are to operate.

**Gear Broaching.** One of the more recent achievements of broaching lies in the field of machining internal high-speed gears, both spur and helical. The process formerly consisted of rough broaching of the gear teeth, followed by a gear-shaping operation, and finally a gear-shaving operation. The new method consists of rough and finish broaching. With these two operations, high production and high accuracy can be maintained. Accuracy of ±0.0002-in. tolerance on tooth characteristics, including spacing, lead, and involute form, is a production accomplishment.

It was found that one broach could produce 38,000 gears before it was discarded. A gear and the broaches of the type used to produce it are shown in Fig. 25-12.

**Fig. 25-12.** Broaches are used to produce precision internal gears at high-production rates. Broaching is also used to make relatively small external gears (courtesy National Broach and Machine Co.).

**Stamped Gears.** Inexpensive lightweight gears for light- to medium-duty applications can be designed for stamping from sheet metal. The initial cost of tooling for stamped gears may be rather high; however, if high production is required, the unit cost will be low. Stamped gearing allows for much latitude in design, such as tabs, stops, bosses, holes, nontoothed portions, etc. The stamped accuracy is generally within 0.002 in. of the required tooth profile. If greater accuracy is required, the stamped teeth can be die-shaved to within 0.0005 in. of the desired profile.

Typical stamped flat gears are found in low-cost gear trains in nonprecision instruments, toys, clocks, timers, etc. The possible size range is wide enough to fulfill almost any low-load requirement. Pitch diameters may range up to 10 in. and material thickness up to ¼ in.

### Casting of Gears

Conventional practice is to sand-cast gray iron, steel, or semisteel to make a gear blank. However, with improved casting methods such as shell molding, it is practical to cast nonprecision gears complete with teeth. The recommended tolerances for steel and nonferrous alloys are ±0.020 in. per inch. Eccentricity can be held to ±0.020 in. also. When closer tolerances are needed, a minimum of machining can be used.

Die-cast gears are popular, lightweight, small gears used in toys and small household appliances.

## Molding of Gears

Nylon has become a popular material for molded gears, the reason being that it can be economically injection-molded to finished size in one simple operation. These gears are quiet in operation and have a very low wear rate, even though little or no lubricant is used.

The pitch diameter of the plastic mold must be made larger to compensate for radial shrinkage of the entire gear. Effects on the tooth profile are so small they can be ignored. Molded plastic gears will increase in importance as materials with improved properties become available.

## Powdered-Metal Gears

Heat-treated powdered-metal gears have high strength and good wear qualities. Copper-steel alloys of medium density are used when extreme impact conditions will not be encountered. For very rugged applications, as in hydraulic pump gears, a steel similar to AISI 4630 is made by combining manganese, silicon, carbon, and ferrite.

## Gear Rolling

Gear teeth can also be rolled on a shaft or gear blank. Since this method is somewhat newer than the conventional methods presented here, it is discussed in Chapter **30**.

## Gear-Finishing Methods

Gear-finishing methods have been developed to produce greater accuracy in the gear than can be obtained by the conventional methods discussed thus far. However, before any finishing cuts are taken, large gears are often *shot-peened*. Metallic shot about 0.011 in. in diameter is discharged at high velocity and large volume on the gear surfaces. This is done to provide a greater factor of safety against tooth breakage. Tests indicate that as much as 60 percent gain in fatigue strength of the teeth is obtained in this way.

There are three main gear-finishing processes—shaving, grinding, and lapping.

### Gear Shaving

ROTARY GEAR SHAVING. The rotary gear-shaving process consists of rotating a gear at high speeds with a shaving cutter. The shaving cutter is a hardened, precision-ground cutter having the same diametral pitch as the gear. Gashes cut in the teeth of the shaver extend the full length of the tooth. Being razor sharp, the cutting edges produced by the gashes on the teeth cut the gear as they turn in mesh. The shaver is on a power shaft and drives the gear. For helical gears, the shaver has a helix angle opposite that of the gear.

CROWN SHAVING. In crown shaving the thickness of the gear teeth is reduced slightly on the ends. There is a difference of only a few thousandths of an inch between the ends and the center; however, this will make the teeth bear only in the middle portion of the gear, even though there may be slight misalignments of the shafts. This crown will eventually wear off, but by that time the gears will be in nearly perfect mesh. Crowned gears are produced by rocking the table that holds the work while the cutter head remains stationary (Fig. 25-13). This process may be reversed on some machines.

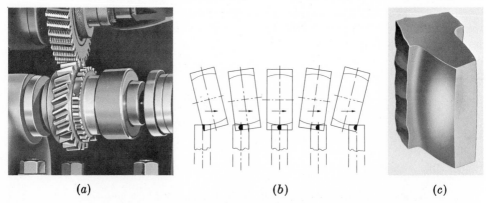

(a)  (b)  (c)

**Fig. 25-13.** (a) A gear-shaving cutter used to finish a gear; (b) the crowning action of a gear-shaving cutter; (c) the exaggerated shape of a crowned gear tooth (courtesy National Broach and Machine Co.).

TAPER SHAVING. In taper shaving, the teeth are shaved smaller on one end. This is a correction measure and is used where the gears have a tendency to burnish. The process consists of setting the table at an angle to the horizontal. This will make the shaver take a greater amount of material off one end.

RACK SHAVING. Gear shaving is also done by making the cutter in a rack form. The gear to be finished is mounted on live centers and the tool is driven across it. When shaving helical gears, the head and arbor on which the gear is mounted are swiveled at an angle equal to the helix. The rack is made to reciprocate back and forth until the required shaving action is complete. The number of strokes needed to finish the gear will depend on the amount of material left for the operation. As an example, an automobile-transmission gear would require 15 strokes if 0.008 in. were left for finishing.

**Gear Grinding.** Grinding is generally used as a finishing process for gears that have been hardened and are to be used at high speeds in machine-tool equipment, turbines, aircraft engines, etc. The amount left for grinding is about 0.003 in., which eliminates the need for a finish cut in hobbing or shaping.

As with gear cutting, there are two basic methods of grinding gears—*generating* and *form grinding*. Spiral bevel and hypoid gears may be ground by either method, but their pinions are always generated.

FORM GRINDING. Form grinding is done with a wheel that is accurately trued to the negative form of the tooth. This can be accomplished by means of diamond fixtures controlled by a pantograph mechanism six times the gear tooth size, or by crushing the grinding-wheel face with a hardened roller of the desired form (Fig. 25-14).

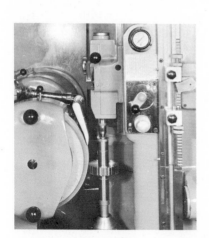

**Fig. 25-14.** Finishing gear teeth by grinding. The grinding wheel is used in form-cutting the involute curve (courtesy Fellows Gear Shaper Co.).

GENERATING-TYPE GEAR GRINDING. The involute form of the gear tooth is generated as a grinding wheel rotates in harmony with the work (Fig. 25-15). Only a small portion of the wheel contacts the work along the line of involute action at one time.

The universal-type diamond truing device will true the wheel so that it will produce true involute teeth. Crown grinding can also be

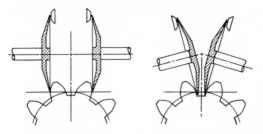

**Fig. 25-15.** A two-wheel gear-grinding setup. The tooth form is generated by the rolling action of the gear as the wheels pass over it. The diamond truing device is shown at the top.

incorporated into the operation. The facts that only a small portion of the wheel touches the work at any one time and that the work can be manually repositioned along different portions of the face of the wheel make it possible to grind a large number of teeth before retruing. This machine uses a relative rolling motion of the work as the wheels traverse lengthwise along the tooth. Grinding is done on two involute surfaces, generating one side of every other tooth per pass.

**Gear Lapping.** Gear lapping is sometimes used as the final finishing process for hardened and ground gears. It is used more to improve the finish than to correct tooth errors. However, errors up to 0.002 in. in tooth spacing, profile, and lead may be corrected by lapping.

Single gear lapping consists of running the gear with a cast-iron master and providing fine abrasive for the cutting action. The lapping gear is rotated rapidly and drives the gear, which is also subjected to a reciprocating motion, back and forth across the face of the lap.

Multiple-spindle lapping machines consist of three lap gears mounted around the gears to be lapped. Effective lapping is provided by running one gear parallel, one offset 3 to 5 deg, and the third offset 3 to 5 deg in the opposite direction. Brakes are used to prevent acceleration and to give a better, faster lapping action. A crowning action can be easily worked in by setting the lap gears at the proper angle in opposite directions. Crowning by lapping the hardened gear is often preferable to crowning by shaving on the unhardened gear.

The average time for lapping a gear should not be more than 1 to 4 min. When longer times are needed, the cause should be determined and corrected in the previous finishing operations. Lapped gears usually wear longer and are quieter in operation than ground gears.

### Gear Inspection

Gear inspection is both functional and analytical. A functional check is quickly made to tell how the gear will operate. The analytical check goes into more detail as to tooth spacing, profile, etc., to determine the cause of the error.

**Functional Gear Inspection.** Functional gear checking is done on the production floor, either with a simple gear-rolling fixture (Fig. 25-16) or with one that may be completely automated, as described in Chapter 27.

**Fig. 25-16.** A gear-rolling fixture and mechanical-recorder attachment (courtesy Illinois Tool Works).

The variable-center-distance gear-rolling fixture shown in Fig. 25-16 can check errors of eccentricity, composite tooth errors, tooth pressure, and the total composite error.

Since the gear to be checked is rolled with a master gear, any errors present are charged exclusively to the gear being inspected.

A mechanical recorder may be attached to the basic rolling fixture to provide a permanent record of the gear runout on a graphed chart, as shown in Fig. 25-16.

**Analytical Gear Inspection.** Analytical inspection equipment in the gear laboratory determines the reasons why gears are outside of tolerance limits and permits the foreman to make corrective adjustments in tooling, machine setup, etc.

Analytical checks are made for tooth spacing, tooth profile, pressure angle, and lead. The Red Liner, made by the Fellows Gear Shaper Company, is designed to measure and record simultaneously several gear errors. The master gear is flexibly mounted so that errors in the gear being tested affect the center-distance relation between the fixed work holder and the master gear. Movements of this flexibly mounted trunnion are enlarged 200 times and transferred to a pen which traces a red line on a constantly moving chart. The chart has parallel ruled lines 0.200 in. apart, and, since the errors are magnified 200 times, the distance between lines represents an error of 0.001 in.

All errors are recorded in combination. However, it is easy to identify errors such as eccentricity, tooth spacing, tooth shape, etc., and to determine their magnitude. Each error causes a characteristic deviation from the straight line, Fig. 25-17.

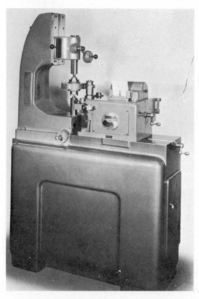

**Fig. 25-17.** The Red Liner is used for analytical gear inspection. A tape is used to record variations in circular pitch, eccentricity, and pressure angle (courtesy Fellows Gear Shaper Company).

Fig. 25-18 shows a Red Liner chart before and after shaving. The upper charted line is of the finish-cut gear, and the lower line is of the same gear after shaving. The shaving operation has reduced many of the inaccuracies and has also smoothed the contacting surfaces.

A comparatively recent device for analyzing gear errors is the optical spur-gear analyzer (Fig. 25-19). The principle of this device

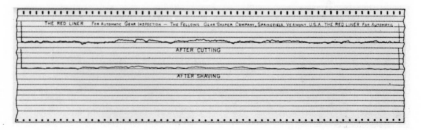

**Fig. 25-18.** The Red Liner chart used to show gear accuracy before and after shaving (courtesy Illinois Tool Works).

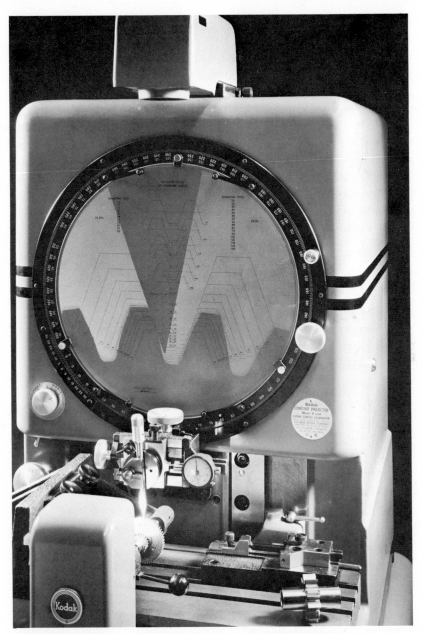

**Fig. 25-19.** An optical spur-gear analyzer used to check gear action (courtesy Optical Gaging Products Co.).

is analogous to the motion of a basic rack and gear, in mesh and operating without slippage.

The correct conjugate action can be determined and deviations limited to changes in pressure angle. Tooth-thickness variations from a specified size can also be determined, as can circular-pitch errors.

Gear inspection is seldom 100 percent complete unless it is done on an automatic basis. It is usually based on statistical studies that take into account the laws of random distribution of errors. The cost of inspection should be compatible with the cost of the finished product. Except in rare cases, where safety of personnel is a factor, it should be based on three things: first, the cost of the part; second, the replacement cost of that part in the mechanism; and third, the selling price of the item.

## QUESTIONS

1. What are some systems of classifying gears?
2. Name some desirable and less desirable features of the helical gear.
3. What type of gear is recommended for heavy loads at high speeds?
4. How are spiral-bevel gears superior to straight-bevel gears?
5. How do Zerol gears differ from spiral-bevel gears?
6. Name some applications of worm gearing.
7. Why can't hypoid gears and spiral-bevel gears be used interchangeably, even though they may be the same size?
8. How is the size of a gear tooth expressed?
9. What is meant by the pressure angle of the gear?
10. What methods are used to impart high wear resistance to gears?
11. Why is nylon considered a good gear material for some purposes?
12. What are two methods by which the gear tooth form may be cut?
13. How does gear shaping differ from gear hobbing?
14. How can stamped gears be made to an accuracy of 0.0005 in.?
15. When is it practical to produce gears by stamping?
16. Why are some gears shot-peened after they have been cut?
17. What is the purpose of crown shaving a gear?
18. What are the two main methods of grinding gear teeth?
19. How can crowning of the gear tooth be accomplished in the lapping process?
20. What are the various checks made on a gear during inspection?
21. What instrument is used to make several analytical checks of the gear at one time?

## PROBLEMS

1. What would be the maximum recommended rpm for (*a*) a 4-in.-diameter straight-bevel gear, (*b*) a 6-in.-diameter spiral-bevel gear?

2. What is the diametral pitch of a gear that has a pitch diameter of 3 in., and 21 teeth?

3. A 4-in.-diameter 32-tooth helical gear can be made on a universal mill or a hobbing machine. It takes 30 min to set up the universal mill and 1.32 min to cut each tooth. The time required for backing the gear away from the cutter and indexing is 0.45 min. The gear can be hobbed in 4.5 min. The set-up time on the hob is 20 min. Assuming labor and overhead rates to be $10 per hr for either machine, how long would it take to pay for the hobbing cutter which costs $80 more than the milling cutter?

4. What would the indexing be per tooth for the gear in Prob. 3? If the milling-machine table is set at the tangent angle of the gear with $\pi d$ as the opposite side and an 8-in. lead as the adjacent side, what angle will it be set at?

## REFERENCES

Cheany, E. S., C. L. Paullus, and W. C. Raridan, "Belt, Chain and Gear Drives," *Machine Design*, August, 1959.

Martin, L. D., "The Challenge of Instrument Gears," *The Tool and Manufacturing Engineer*, April, 1956.

Stasser, F., "Design for Stamped Gears," *Machine Design*, December, 1957.

# 26

# METAL CLEANING
# AND PROTECTIVE
# SURFACE TREATMENT

**P**RESENT-DAY MANUFACTURERS are becoming more and more finish conscious. Pleasing, durable finishes have an important effect on final sales appeal. One of the essentials needed to ensure lasting qualities for most finishes is a thorough preparation of the base metal.

## METAL CLEANING

During the process of manufacture, many different types of soiling are encountered. Residues left on the product, as it reaches the final stages of manufacture, include cutting oils, grease, wax, flux, chips, dust, original and heat-treat scale, thick oxide films, buffing and drawing compounds, and plain dirt.

### Chemical Cleaning

Contaminants cannot be removed by one easy-cleaning detergent. The complexity of the problem must be met with a knowledge of the contaminant involved, the cleaning compound needed, and the best method of applying it. For example, a thick coat of cutting oil will require a cleaner and application method entirely different from those used to remove dry dirt or light rust. Also, the effect of the cleaner on the base metal must be considered.

**Basic Metal-Cleaning Considerations.** The selection of chemical cleaning agents is based on a number of factors, two of which—the difficulty of removal of the contaminant and the physical aspects of the soil—have already been mentioned. Other considerations are the degree of cleanliness required and the composition of the workpiece.

Chemical surface cleaning may vary from manually brushing an item with solvent to multistage cleaning systems that are completely automated. In the more complex systems, where considerable soil has to be removed, such methods as vapor degreasing, solvents, and emulsion cleaning are considered preliminary. Alkaline cleaning is an intermediate step. Final cleaning for "chemically clean" surfaces is accomplished by one of the electrolytic processes in combination with an alkaline cleaning solution.

**Cleaning Solutions.** The chemical cleaning compounds are many and varied, however, they can be broadly classified into three groups—solvents, alkalines, and acids.

SOLVENT CLEANING. When heavy oils, grease, and dirt are to be removed, either straight or emulsifiable solvents are used. Straight solvents may be either of the petroleum-base or the chlorinated types.

*Petroleum solvents.* Petroleum solvents are distillates having sufficiently high flash points (100° to 200°F) to permit use at room temperatures. They are less expensive than the chlorinated hydrocarbons, but they are a fire hazard and must be handled accordingly. The equipment used can consist simply of a tank for dipping the part, a brush for removing the soil, and a cloth for wiping it dry. Solvents are quickly contaminated and, when this occurs, they do not produce a high degree of surface cleanliness.

*Chlorinated solvents.* Chlorinated solvents do not have the fire-hazard disadvantage of the petroleum solvents. They are usually used in vapor degreasers. The parts are generally placed in a wire basket and suspended in vapors of the boiling solvent. Trichloroethylene boils at 188°F and perchloroethylene at 250°F. A cooling jacket in the upper portion of the tank causes the vapors to condense on the metal surfaces and carry off the grease and soil. This method has the advantage of making the most effective use of the solvent over the entire surface of the part. Good penetration is obtained in even the deepest recesses.

Solvents can become contaminated with water, cyanides, or other reactive materials that have lodged in the recesses of the part as a result of preceding processes. The designer can prevent some of this by including provisions for drainage without functional interference.

*Emulsifiable solvents.* The emulsifiable solvents are compounded to be diluted with water; thus they are less toxic than the chlorinated solvents and less of a fire hazard than the petroleum solvents.

One type of emulsifiable solvent loosens the oil and grease as the part is immersed in the hot agitated solution of the dip tank. Another kind consists of a compound, mixed with kerosine, which can be used at room temperature. The solution is used to loosen the oil and grease, and emulsification takes place when the parts are removed from the tank and given a hot-water spray. Both methods usually require an alkaline spray rinse, before final finishing, to remove the remaining oil film.

ALKALINE CLEANING. Alkaline cleaning consists mainly of detergents dissolved in water at the time of use. The process is often used as a follow-up for other cleaning processes, or, if the contaminants are not too difficult to remove, an alkaline cleaner may be sufficient in itself. The solution concentration may range from 10 to 25 percent by volume in the dip-tank method to 1 oz of cleaner per gallon in the pressure-spray method. In most cases, the solution is used hot. For every 20°F above the usual 140°F cleaning temperature, the time required is reduced 50 percent.

ACID CLEANERS. Acid solutions are used for pickling, deoxidizing, and bright dipping. These operations are performed after oil, grease, and other substances not soluble in acids have been removed from the metal surfaces.

*Pickling.* Pickling refers to the removal of oxidation mill scale, flux residues, etc., by solutions of sulfuric or hydrochloric acid. Sulfuric acid is cheaper, and its rate of scale removal can be stepped up when heated to 150°F. Hydrochloric acid is used at room temperature. Inhibitors have been developed to reduce the harmful action of the acid fumes on plant equipment. The pickling process must be followed by a neutralizing dip and rinse.

Alkaline pickling solutions that are less severe in nature have been developed to remove oxide, scale, oil, and paint. They are also recommended for combined cleaning and deoxidizing of steel before electroplating or other finishes.

*Deoxidizing.* The deoxidizing process is used on aluminum more than on other metals because of the rapidity with which the oxide film forms on it. A 5 percent caustic soda solution is used to remove the film. A subsequent dip in 20 to 50 percent nitric acid solution is used to remove the dark smut formed in the caustic bath and to neutralize any alkali remaining on the surface.

*Bright Dipping.* To produce a highly reflective surface on nonferrous metals, bright-dip acids are used. Copper, for example, is first dipped in sulfuric acid, which acts to oxidize the surface. This is followed by a nitric acid dip to dissolve the newly formed oxides. By this process the microscopic hills and valleys on the surface are leveled off, increasing the reflectivity of the metal. The bright-dip process is followed by a thorough rinsing and rapid drying to avoid tarnishing.

Proprietary solutions are obtainable for both copper and aluminum. The solutions used for aluminum consist basically of phosphoric and nitric acids.

**Cleaning Equipment.** Most metal cleaning is accomplished by dipping or spraying. Neither method is universal; most parts can be dipped, but not all can be effectively sprayed. The important thing is that the cleaning be *intimate* and *turbulent*.

DIP TANKS. Much of the metal-cleaning process is accomplished in metal, plastic, or rubber tanks. Some parts require only one tank, but others must go through a sequence of soaking and rinsing operations.

Oakite Products, Inc., recommends a series of tanks as a basic arrangement for handling any cleaning problem from washing away a light film of oil to removing a heavy mixture of grease, scale, and burned-on solid particles of dirt. A basic series of tanks may be as follows:

| Tank Number | Operation |
|---|---|
| 1 | Tank of self-emulsifying solvent cleaner for removing most of the heavy dirt |
| 2 | Rinse tanks with pressure sprays |
| 3 | Tank of hot alkaline solution for removing moderate amounts of oil, grease, and other dirts (separate tanks for ferrous and nonferrous metals) |
| 4 | Running rinse tank |
| 5 | Tank or crock of acid solution for removing scale, rust, tarnish, and other corrosion |
| 6 | Running rinse tank |

Sample cleaning-tank sequences are:

For moderate soil with no scale or corrosion, use Tanks 3 and 4.

For heavy soil with grease and oil but no scale or corrosion, use Tanks 1, 2, 3, and 4.

For heavy soil plus scale or corrosion, use Tanks 1, 2, 3, 4, 5, and 6.

MACHINE CLEANING. Most machines used in cleaning metals are combination types. The monorail degreaser, shown in Fig. 26-1, uses solvent vapors as the initial step in removing grease. The parts then move on to the next station, where they are sprayed with warm solvent. The last station consists of a pure vapor rinse to ensure complete removal of all soil. The cost of equipment similar to that shown ranges from $5,500 to $9,500.

**Fig. 26-1.** A conveyorized degreaser used for both vapor- and spray-type cleaning (courtesy Detrex Chemical Industries, Inc.).

Other machines are made to handle parts in baskets (Fig. 26-2). The baskets, suspended from crossbars, can be made to rise and fall alternately, or to advance longitudinally in steps from one end of the machine to the other and back again. The baskets may be exposed to vapor rinsing, immersion in solvent, spraying from nozzles, or combinations of these cleaning cycles.

**Fig. 26-2.** Automatically operated crossbar containers used in both dip and vapor degreasing applications (courtesy Detrex Chemical Industries, Inc.).

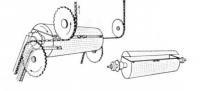

ULTRASONIC CLEANING.   It is often necessary to remove insoluble particles left on work from grinding, polishing, lapping, honing, buffing, and drawing. Much of this material is deposited in hard-to-reach cavities, indentations, slots, and small holes. Precision parts such as hypodermic needles, automatic transmissions, carburetors, fuel-injector parts, and hydraulic needle valves must be perfectly clean. One of the newer, more efficient, ways of cleaning such pieces is with an ultrasonically produced scrubbing action.

The principal parts needed for ultrasonic cleaning are shown schematically in Fig. 26-3. The generator produces the high-frequency electrical energy. A transducer changes the electrical impulses into high-frequency sound waves that vibrate the cleaning agent and parts to be cleaned.

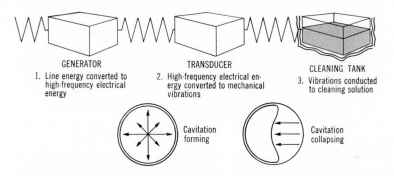

GENERATOR
1. Line energy converted to high-frequency electrical energy

TRANSDUCER
2. High-frequency electrical energy converted to mechanical vibrations

CLEANING TANK
3. Vibrations conducted to cleaning solution

Cavitation forming

Cavitation collapsing

**Fig. 26-3.** Schematic diagram to illustrate the principles of ultrasonic cleaning (courtesy Turco Products Inc.).

When sound passes through an elastic medium such as metal, both the sound energy and the medium vibrate at the same rate. When sound passes through a liquid, it, being inelastic, ruptures or *cavitates;* that is, small vacuum pockets are created, which almost immediately collapse or *implode.* The rapid action results in scrubbing of a speed and vigor impossible by conventional means.

Ultrasonic cleaning may be used wherever the soil is not a part of the metallic surface, as are scale, rust, and tarnish. The cleaning agent may be either solvent or detergent solutions. The extremely fast cleaning action makes up, in part, for the higher cost of the equipment.

ELECTROCLEANING. Before steel is electroplated, it is electrocleaned. This is done by making it the anode in a hot alkaline solution. As the current passes through the metal, thousands of tiny oxygen bubbles are formed on the surface. As these bubbles burst, they perform a scrubbing, scouring, agitating motion over the entire surface of the metal. Thus the dirt can be said to be "unplated" from the steel.

Direct current is usually supplied by a generator or rectifier. The current used ranges from 25 to 150 amp per sq ft of surface.

STEAM CLEANING. Parts that are too large to be placed in tanks or conveyed through washing machines can be cleaned with the aid of steam guns. These guns are used to apply a detergent solution along with the steam pressure. The heat and impact of the solution rapidly removes heavy oils and greases.

### Mechanical Cleaning

Mechanical methods of metal cleaning consist of dry, wet, and centrifugal abrasive blasting; power brushing; and barrel finishing.

#### Abrasive Blasting.

DRY ABRASIVE BLASTING. Dry abrasive-blasting equipment consists of a cleaning cabinet, an abrasive reservoir, and an air nozzle. The abrasive is drawn up through the hose to join the high-velocity airstream at the nozzle and impinge on the metal surface. The used abrasive slides down the centrally sloped bottom of the cabinet and returns to the reservoir.

The abrasive used may be shot, steel grit, or coarse sand. Fine sands are not used, since they do not have so rapid a cutting action and they present more of a feeding problem.

WET ABRASIVE BLASTING. Wet abrasive-blasting machines are quite similar in appearance to dry abrasive-blasting machines. The main difference is that the wet machines use an abrasive slurry that is kept in suspension by an agitator. The abrasive is fed to the blasting gun by a centrifugal pump. Once at the gun, the abrasive is forced out at extremely high velocities with compressed air.

The abrasives usually used are silica, quartz, garnet, aluminum oxide, and novaculite (a soft type of silicon dioxide).

The abrasive-blasting machines is used for both cleaning and finishing metals. The action obtained depends on the size and type of abrasive. In addition to the ordinary purposes such as removing scale, paint, carbon deposits, buffing and drawing compounds, etc., it is used to impart very fine finishes. In fact, this machine is referred to by the manufacturer as a Liquid Honing machine. It has been successfully used to hone metal-cutting tools such as milling cutters and carbide-tipped single-point tools. More than 100 percent increase in tool life has been attributed to this honing method. The machine with examples of surfaces produced are shown in Fig. 26-4.

CENTRIFUGAL BLASTING MACHINES. Centrifugal blasting machines make use of a rotating bladed wheel to throw the abrasive particles (Fig. 26-5).

These machines are recommended for high-volume blasting of parts that do not have small crevices and holes to clean. A machine having a 19½-in.-diameter wheel 2½ in. wide is capable of throwing 300 lb of abrasive a minute. This is the equivalent of five ⅜-in. nozzles being used on sandblasting machines.

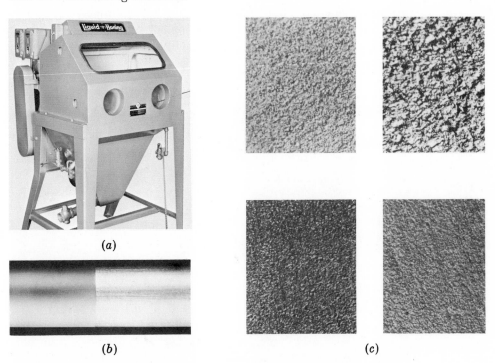

(a)

(b)

(c)

**Fig. 26-4.** (a) The liquid honing machine. (b) A comparison of conventionally honed and liquid-honed surfaces on a drill rod. (c) Photomicrographs showing effect of various abrasives on metallic surface (courtesy Vapor Blast Mfg. Co.).

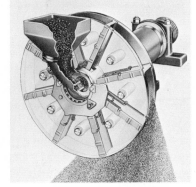

**Fig. 26-5.** Centrifugal-type blasting equipment (courtesy Wheelabrator Corporation).

Centrifugal blasting machines are used to remove forging scale and molding sand, and to produce a brighter surface. A peened surface (one with small identations) can be obtained by using the proper-sized shot as the abrasive material.

**Power Brushing.** Rotary wire and fiber brushes are used to remove heat-treat scale, weld flux, and machining burrs. They can also impart fine microfinishes to metal parts. Some applications of wire brushing are shown in Fig. 26-6.

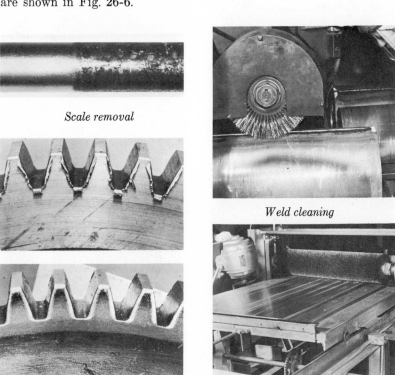

*Scale removal*

*Weld cleaning*

*Burr removal*

*Satin finishing*

**Fig. 26-6.** Some applications of power brushing (courtesy Osborn Manufacturing Co.).

POWER-BRUSH TYPES. The principle kinds of power brushes, as shown in Fig. 26-7, are wheel brushes, cup brushes, end brushes, side-action brushes, and wide-faced brushes. The wheel brushes range in size from 1 to 18 in. in diameter, with wheel widths from $\frac{1}{8}$ to $2\frac{3}{4}$ in. The fill material may consist of a variety of natural fibers, including Tampico (treated and untreated), horsehair, and cord. Various syn-

**Fig. 26-7.** The main types of power brushes are wheel, cup, end, side-action, and wide-faced (courtesy Osborn Manufacturing Co.).

thetic fibers are also used. Wire wheels are made of steel, stainless steel, or brass.

Wire-wheel or radial brushes are usually made with crimped or knot-type wires (Fig. 26-8). The crimped-wire brushes were the first to be used and, as a result, are still the most popular, even though types more suited to a particular application are available. These wheels are good for deburring, cleaning, and producing a satin finish on parts held by the operator. The larger-sized brushes operate at 4,500 to 6,000 sfpm. When used with abrasive compounds, they can improve the microinch finish of metal surfaces.

**Fig. 26-8.** The left picture shows the more common crimped-wire brushes and the right picture the knot-type wire brushes for stronger brushing action (courtesy Osborn Manufacturing Co.).

The twisted-knot brush is very versatile. At low surface foot speeds it is very flexible, but at high speeds it becomes very hard and fast cutting.

At higher speeds, it is used with excellent results in weld cleaning, paint removal, and imparting a deep satin orange-peel finish.

The nonmetallic wheel brushes, made of such materials as Tampico or cord, are used primarily for improving the microfinish or to improve the surface for plating. Power brushing blends the sharp hills and valleys left by grinding, so that uniform plating can result. Polishing marks, draw marks, and scratches can also be blended.

Skin surfaces of aircraft and missile parts that are highly stressed and subject to vibration can benefit by power brushing. Sharp edges and microscopic cracks may go undetected. Even a few seconds of power brushing can reduce the V-notch effect of small cracks, and greatly increase the fatigue life.

Cup brushes (Fig. 26-9) are used for extremely fast cleaning of welds, scale, rust, and other oxides. Cup brushes can also be used to produce a uniform blended radius on machined edges, such as gear teeth and boiler-tube ends. These brushes cover quite a large area at one time and can be operated by relatively inexpensive portable power tools.

**Fig. 26-9.** Crimped-wire and knot-type-wire cup brushes (courtesy Osborn Manufacturing Co.).

The wheels on centerless grinders may be taken off and replaced with brushes. They are used, in this capacity, not to remove any metal but to improve the finish. A part can be brushed rapidly, automatically improving the surface finish from a 25- or 30-$\mu$ to a 10- or 15-$\mu$ finish in a matter of a few seconds. Likewise, parts that have a 10-$\mu$ finish after grinding may have a 4- to 6-$\mu$ finish after brushing.

Wide-faced brushes are used in strip mills to scrub and clean metal, as well as to impart a satin finish as the metal moves along opposite to the rotation of the brush.

Small side-action brushes are used for internal cleaning and finishing operations.

POWER-BRUSHING EQUIPMENT. Standard machines, such as polishing and buffing lathes, are made for power brushing. Semiautomatic and automatic programmed machines are also available. An example is shown in Fig. 26-10. As many as 800 parts per hr can be finished on a machine of this type.

**Fig. 26-10.** A standard semiautomatic finishing machine with rotary indexing table and three brushing heads (courtesy Osborn Manufacturing Co.).

**Barrel Finishing.** Barrel finishing is used for both metal cleaning and metal finishing. However, since it is primarily an abrasive process, it was described Chap. 24.

## PROTECTIVE AND DECORATIVE METAL FINISHES

Protective and decorative coatings applied to metal surfaces may be broadly classified as metallic, organic, and conversion coatings.

### Metallic Coatings

Protective metallic coatings are applied by four different methods —hot dipping, electroplating, metal spraying, and vacuum metallizing.

**Hot Dipping.** In the hot-dip method, the plating material is first heated to the molten state. The item to be plated is cleaned and immersed in the molten bath.

To obtain an even coating on small objects such as nuts, bolts, pins, and washers, the objects are centrifuged, after being taken from the bath, until the coating is hard.

Some applications of the dip-coating process are aluminum to steel and tin, and lead alloys and zinc to nonferrous metals.

Zinc dipping, or hot galvanizing, is widely used on steel as an effective protection against corrosion.

**Electroplating.** Electroplating is the most popular means of applying metallic coatings. The controlled thickness of the deposit and its uniformity are the method's greatest assets. In practice, coatings of 0.0002 to 0.0003 in. are not uncommon.

Surfaces to be plated must be buffed smooth to eliminate scratches and unevenness, as the quality of the plated surface depends, to a great extent, on the preparation of the bare metal. The work is then cleaned in suitable cleaning solutions to remove all grease, dirt, buffing compound, etc. After rinsing, the part is ready for plating.

The four essential elements of a plating process are the cathode, anode, electrolyte, and direct current. Current leaves the anode, which is a bar of the plating material, and migrates through the electrolyte (salts of the plating metal in solution) to the cathode, or part to be plated. As the ions are deposited on the cathode, they give up their charge and are deposited as metal on the cathode. The current density largely determines the rate at which the metal is deposited.

Common plating metals are chromium, nickel, copper, zinc, cadmium, and tin. The more precious metals—silver, gold, platinum, and rhodium—are also applied by plating.

Chromium plating is widely used because of its pleasing appearance and its resistance to corrosion and wear. It is seldom used by itself, for it stands up much better if a layer of copper is put on for a base coat, followed by a layer of nickel, and then the chromium coat. The final chromium coat may be only 0.0001 in. thick.

Parts to be plated should be designed with generous fillets and radii instead of sharp corners, since current concentrations occur at sharp points, resulting in excessive deposits. Plating thickness should be taken into consideration when designating design tolerances on mating parts.

**Metal Spraying.**   Although this method is used to furnish a protective coating for some metals, it is more commonly associated with welding equipment and is discussed in Chapter 10.

**Vacuum Metallizing.**   Vacuum metallizing is a process whereby a reflective, mirrorlike and chromelike surface is applied to plastic, metal, glass, paper, textile, or other materials. It is a low-cost mass-production process used for both decorative and functional purposes.

Briefly, the process consists of first applying a lacquer or resin base coat. This coating is then baked. A metallic film (aluminum is most widely used) is then condensed directly on the base coat in a chamber under high vacuum. Finally, a protective surface coat of clear lacquer or enamel is applied over the thin (4- or 5-$\mu$in.) coating. The surface coating may be pigmented with transparent colorants to simulate gold, brass, copper, or other highly reflective metallic colors.

## Organic Coatings

**Coating Materials.**   Organic coatings may be oil-base paint, shellac, lacquer, varnish, enamel, bituminous paints, or rubber-base coatings.

OIL-BASE PAINT. This paint consists of linseed oil, pigment, and turpentine or some other solvent to thin the mixture to brushing consistency. Some important pigments are titanium dioxide, white lead, red lead, Prussian blue, and lampblack. Drying takes place partially by evaporation of the solvent, but mainly by oxidation of the vehicle —linseed oil. Tung oil is also very desirable as a vehicle because it is fast drying. Oil-base paint makes an excellent coating for wood and is sometimes used on exterior steel structures, but it is not used extensively in production finishing.

SHELLAC. Shellac is a solution of lac and alcohol. Lac is a secretion of small bugs found in India. Dissolved in alcohol, lac produces orange shellac. When orange shellac is bleached and further treated, it becomes white shellac. There are numerous industrial uses for shellac, but as a sealer or coating it is used only on wood.

LACQUER. By definition, lacquer is "a film-forming material which dries by the evaporation of a solvent." Since it dries very quickly, it was given a warm welcome, many years ago, by a young auto industry that was looking for a means of eliminating production bottlenecks. For the same reason, it is still one of the favorite metal finishes. Most lacquers are made of nitrocellulose dissolved in solvent, with pigment added for color. Lacquers can be modified to develop desired characteristics, as shown in Table 26-1.

**TABLE 26-1.**

**Characteristics of Modified Lacquers Compared with Basic Lacquer\***

| Modified Lacquer | Characteristics Improved |
|---|---|
| Ethyl cellulose | Alkali resistance |
| Cellulose acetate butyrate | Weather resistance |
| Styrene butadiene | Adhesion, chemical, and water resistance |
| Cellulose acetate | Heat and oil resistance |
| Vinyl | Toughness, abrasion, and oil resistance |
| Acrylic | Acid, alkali, and water resistance |

\* Courtesy *Machine Design.*

VARNISH. Varnish is a resin dissolved in and cooked with a drying oil. The resin may be natural or synthetic. Among the natural resins are Kauri gum, Congo gum, batu, dammar, and amber. Synthetic resins include alkyd, phenolic, epoxy, silicone, urea, and melamine. The resin is cooked in combination with a drying oil such as castor, soybean, fish, cottonseed, or corn oil.

Varnish characteristics can be changed or modified by changing ratios of resin and oil or by using other resins. An example of this is alkyd modified with silicone.

ENAMEL.   When pigments are added to varnish, an enamel results. Drying may take place at room temperature or by baking anywhere from 180° to 400°F, depending on the *vehicle* or base.

The characteristics of various enamels are shown in Table 26-2.

**TABLE 26-2.**

**Characteristics of Enamels***

| Enamel | General Characteristics |
|---|---|
| Alkyd | Excellent resistance to weathering, water, and chemicals. Excellent color and gloss retention. Modified by changing resin-to-oil ratio. |
| Alkyd phenolic | Improved water and chemical resistance over straight alkyd. Reduced flexibility, and color and gloss retention. |
| Alkyd styrene | Decreased air-drying time over straight alkyd. Decreased abrasion resistance. |
| Alkyd silicone | Increased resistance to heat. |
| Epoxy esters | Approximately equal to straight alkyd. |
| Epoxy | Excellent chemical resistance, flexibility, and adhesion (including adhesion to plastics) modified with amine resins. Less gloss retention than alkyds. Baking required unless a suitable catalyst has been included. |
| Phenolic | Excellent chemical, water, and oil resistance. Baked finish can be submerged in water. Coating is brittle — modifiers improving brittleness can decrease other good characteristics. |
| Silicone | Outstanding heat resistance. |
| Urethane | Good dielectric properties. Abrasion resistant. |
| Vinyl | Excellent water resistance. |
| Acrylic | Resists discoloration at high temperatures. High temperature required for curing. |

* Courtesy *Machine Design.*

BITUMINOUS PAINTS.   A solution of coal-tar bituminous paint is that in which coal tar is dissolved. The solvent evaporates, leaving a bituminous film. Fillers are added when heavier applications are needed for thermal insulation or sound deadening, as in automobile undercoating.

Coal-tar paints have extremely low permeability and a consequent high resistance to water. They afford excellent protection for items that are submerged constantly. However, when exposed to the sun, the film buckles and cracks. This is called *alligatoring*.

RUBBER-BASE COATINGS. The three important types of rubber-base coatings are chlorinated rubber, neoprene and Hypalon.

*Chlorinated rubber.* The outstanding characteristic of good chlorinated-rubber materials is resistance to water. These materials are often used on metals that are subject to splash or spillage, or on submerged metals. Chlorinated-rubber paints also resist acids, alkalies, salts, alcohol, gasoline, and mineral oil. They are not resistant to animal or vegetable oils and greases. Because of a limited range of colors, chlorinated-rubber paints are used for protective reasons rather than decorative ones.

*Neoprene.* Neoprene coatings consist of neoprene dissolved in a solvent. They dry by evaporation of the solvent, leaving a film that is outstanding in its chemical resistance to alkalies, many acids, alcohol, salts, and natural oils.

*Hypalon.* Hypalon is a chlorosulfonated polyethylene whose outstanding characteristic is resistance to oxidizing agents. It has good temperature resistance from $-80°$ to $300°F$. The available colors are almost unlimited.

PRIMERS. Primers are required on most metal surfaces to produce a good bond, filling characteristics, and corrosion resistance right at the surface. Generally, undercoat materials are of the enamel type. In addition to bonding to the metal, forming close corrosion control, the primer must "hold out" or support, but not absorb, the topcoat materials. To accomplish this a complete finish system of the highest quality might consist of a primer, a surfacer, and one or more topcoats.

**Finish Specifications.** Many methods are used in writing finish specifications. The simplest specification puts the greatest responsibility on the shop foreman. Such a specification might read: "Finish blue, color number 87." This leaves the selection of primer, thinners, coating thickness, and method of application in the hands of the foreman. For a few stock materials being applied on a few items, such a specification might be sufficient; however, it will leave the inspection department at a loss unless inspection includes only final color and appearance.

At the other extreme, the specification would list everything, leaving nothing to the shop foreman.

Perhaps the best specification for most industries is one which fixes the type and color of the topcoat, specifies a final grade of appearance for a prepared standard, and provides optional primer surfacers for a compatible system.

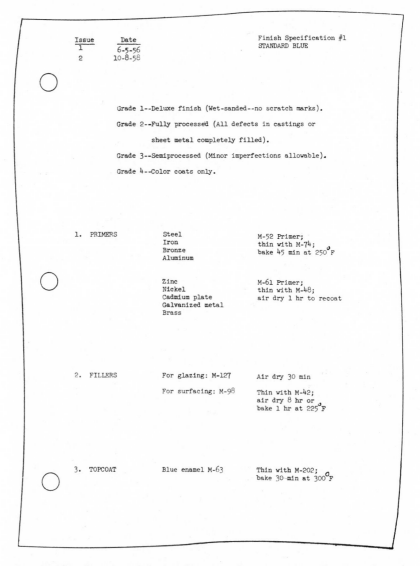

```
Issue    Date                                    Finish Specification #1
  1      6-5-56                                   STANDARD BLUE
  2     10-8-58


        Grade 1--Deluxe finish (Wet-sanded--no scratch marks).

        Grade 2--Fully processed (All defects in castings or

                 sheet metal completely filled).

        Grade 3--Semiprocessed (Minor imperfections allowable).

        Grade 4--Color coats only.



1.  PRIMERS              Steel            M-52 Primer;
                         Iron             thin with M-74;
                         Bronze           bake 45 min at 250°F
                         Aluminum


                         Zinc             M-61 Primer;
                         Nickel           thin with M-48;
                         Cadmium plate    air dry 1 hr to recoat
                         Galvanized metal
                         Brass


2.  FILLERS              For glazing: M-127   Air dry 30 min

                         For surfacing: M-98  Thin with M-42;
                                              air dry 8 hr or
                                              bake 1 hr at 225°F


3.  TOPCOAT              Blue enamel M-63     Thin with M-202;
                                              bake 30 min at 300°F
```

**Fig. 26-11.** Sample finish-specification record (courtesy *Machine Design*).

A specific but still flexible instruction can be prepared as shown in Fig. 26-11. Permanent standards can be prepared for the design department, finishing shop, and inspection departments. These standards represent minimum requirements.

**Finishing Costs.** The cost of an organic finish is not what the material costs per gallon; it is computed from the coverage obtained from the material, the amount of thinner required to reduce the viscosity to a point where the finish can be conveniently applied, and other factors. The coverage is expressed in square feet per gallon at a specified thickness. Thickness is specified in mils (thousandths of an inch). The major costs in a finishing system are those of application, handling, sanding, etc., and not of the material itself.

**Application Methods.** Since the cost of applying a coating is normally a good deal more than the cost of the coating material, much consideration should be given to selecting the means of application. General methods consist of spraying, dip coating, flow coating, and roller coating.

SPRAY PAINTING. This is the most common method of industrial finishing. A number of adaptations of the basic principle have been developed, including airless, electrostatic, steam, and hot spraying.

*Airless spraying.* In this process, high pressure (300 to 2,000 psi) is used to force the finishing liquid to the nozzle, where it is atomized in the high-velocity discharge. To assist the flow of material, it may be previously heated to decrease the viscosity. This system decreases the overspray common to normal spray painting.

*Electrostatic spraying.* This method is based on the principle of the attraction of unlike electrical charges. As shown in the diagram in Fig. 26-12, an electrostatic charge is supplied to the atomizer by a voltage pack. The items to be painted are electrically grounded through the hanger, as shown. The paint is delivered to the atomizer by a special metering pump unit. As the atomizer turns, it feeds the paint to the outer edge of the disk or bell. Atomization occurs owing to the electrostatic field built up between the atomizer and the workpiece. No air pressure is required. This system results in almost all of the spray, or guided mist, being deposited.

*Steam spraying.* Superheated steam, instead of compressed air, is used in this method. The process provides good coverage in closed areas. The superheated-steam volume decreases as it leaves the nozzle, preventing blowback and overspray. The principle is the opposite of compressed air, which expands as it leaves the spray nozzle. The steam escaping from the nozzle will not burn the operator, although insulation is required on the gun.

*Hot spraying.* This process substitutes heat for solvent to reduce the viscosity of the sprayed material. This method is more economical, since solvents are expensive and must later be evaporated.

DIP COATING. With this method, the article is immersed in a tank of the finishing material, it is removed, and the excess material is allowed to drip off. To prevent droplets from forming on the lower

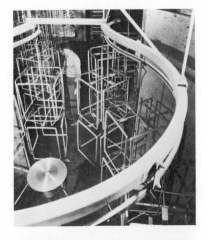

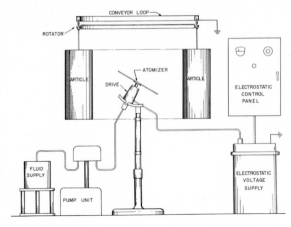

**Fig. 26-12.** Electrostatic spray equipment and examples of its use (courtesy Ransburg Electrocoating Corp.).

edges, the parts can be passed over an electrostatically charged grill. The strong attraction of the charge will pull off any excess material.

The dip tank requires such a large volume of material that use of the process will be limited unless high production rates are involved.

If the dip process is to be used in a plant, the product must be designed with this in mind. The article should be free of pockets that trap air and prevent coating. The design must also permit free flow of the excess finish during the dripping cycle.

Lacquers can be used for dipping, but, because of their high volatility, the process is usually limited to enamels.

FLOW COATING. The flow-coat process is used in conjunction with a conveyorized finishing line. Parts hanging from the conveyor are passed into a tunnel, where the finishing material is flowed on. The flow nozzles apply it to the article in streams. The excess runs off, returns to a sump, and is pumped back to the nozzles. A combination vapor degreaser and flow-coating machine is shown in Fig. 26-13. A machine

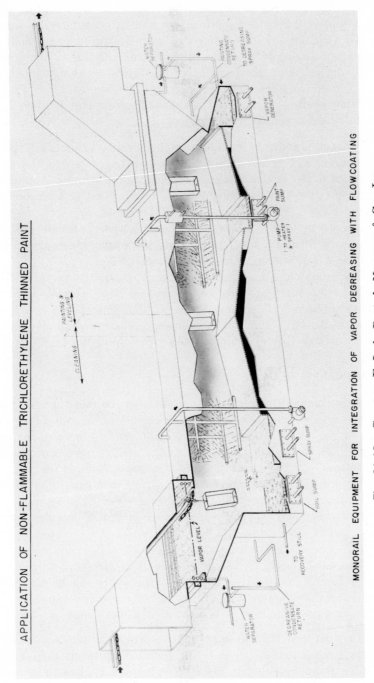

APPLICATION OF NON-FLAMMABLE TRICHLORETHYLENE THINNED PAINT

CLEANING

PAINTING & LEVELING

WATER SEPARATOR

HEATING CONDENSATE RETURN

TO DEGREASING SPRAY SUMP

VAPOR GENERATOR

PAINT SUMP

PUMP ( TO HEATER SPRAY )

SPRAY SUMP

BOIL SUMP

VAPOR LEVEL

TO RECOVERY STILL

WATER SEPARATOR

DEGREASING CONDENSATE RETURN

MONORAIL EQUIPMENT FOR INTEGRATION OF VAPOR DEGREASING WITH FLOWCOATING

**Fig. 26-13.** Courtesy E. I. du Pont de Nemours & Co., Inc.

of this type presents savings in floor space and in operating costs. Heat applied during cleaning can be used to evaporate the volatile thinner (trichlorethylene) before the finished parts leave the machine, thus permitting recovery of the thinner at no added cost. When using an air-drying paint, the part leaves the machine clean, painted, dry to the touch, and ready for packaging.

Flow coating of enamels is most common because of their lower volatility as compared with lacquers.

ROLLER COATING. The roller-coating process is used for coating sheet metal and is not applicable to odd-shaped parts. The finish is applied to the sheet by means of rollers, before forming. Application is similar to the homeowners' process of rolling paint on a plaster wall.

### Coating Selection.

In selecting a coating, whether for an individual item or for items in mass production, the primary consideration is the type of material on which it will be used.

For example, a cast-iron machine base must be carefully filled and primed before the finish coat is applied. It is essential, of course, that the finish coat be chemically compatible with the primer. A machine tool must also be virtually immune to penetration by oil or water. Other surfaces require flexibility and wearing qualities.

### Conversion Coatings

A conversion coating gets its name from the fact that the metal surface is chemically converted to a corrosion-resistant film. Most of these are not durable and are used primarily to increase the bond between the metal and an organic finish. Briefly, these coatings provide "tooth" for anchoring coatings, are good retainers for wax and oil rust preventives, and prevent undercutting of organic films if they are ruptured.

The four main types of conversion coatings are phosphate, chromate, anodic, and oxide.

### Phosphate Coating.

Phosphatizing is the treatment of a metal part with a heated solution that contains a phosphate salt or phosphoric acid and an accelerator. These salts can be of several types, such as iron phosphate, zinc-iron phosphate, or manganese-iron phosphate.

IRON PHOSPHATES. Iron phosphates provide a light crystal coating for steel. A detergent can be incorporated to permit simultaneous cleaning and phosphatizing. The coating is spray-applied and provides a paint bonding surface and temporary protection against rust.

ZINC-IRON PHOSPHATES. Zinc-iron phosphate not only provides a corrosion-resistant paint base, but it can also act as a retainer for nondrying oils and waxes. With the lubricant, these coatings reduce friction and minimize the galling of mating surfaces.

MANGANESE-IRON PHOSPHATES. Manganese-iron phosphate produces a heavy black coating that is used on frictional surfaces to prevent galling, scoring, or seizing of parts, as exemplified in run-in of pistons, piston rings, camshafts, and tappets.

In brief summary, the outstanding properties of phosphate coatings are the ability to retain paint, also lubrication when necessary, and to provide corrosion resistance. Machines are made that can accomplish vapor degreasing, phosphatizing, and painting (Fig. 26-14) in a single pass.

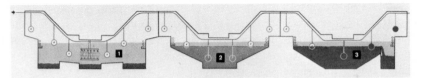

**Fig. 26-14.** (1) Vapor degreasing, (2) phosphatizing, and (3) painting being done completely in one machine. If baking enamels are used, a fourth but shortened baking step is required (courtesy E. I. du Pont de Nemours & Co., Inc.).

**Chromate Coatings.** Chromate coatings are used on zinc, cadmium, aluminum, copper, silver, magnesium, and alloys of these metals. These coatings provide for corrosion protection either as a final finish or as a base for an organic coating.

Dye, when desired, is introduced in an immersion treatment following the chromating process. The dye colors, however, are neither as brilliant nor as lightfast as those obtained with anodic solutions. Dyed components are usually limited to indoor applications.

Chromate coatings for copper, brass, and bronze perform the dual purpose of chemically polishing the surface and providing a thin film of moderately protective value.

**Anodic Coatings.** Anodized films are produced by electrochemical reaction. They are harder, more resistant to corrosion and abrasion, and more expensive than the chromate films. Anodized films are used on aluminum and magnesium both for decorative appeal and for protection of the base metal.

The aluminum becomes the anode instead of the cathode, as it would be in electroplating. An electrolyte capable of yielding oxygen on electrolysis is used. As current is passed, oxygen is liberated at the surface, forming an oxide film. Following the anodic treatment, the oxide film may be sealed with boiling water. This closes the pores and destroys the absorptive characteristics of the coating. Of the many treatments available for anodizing aluminum alloys, the sulfuric and chromate are the most widely used.

The sulfuric acid process is used extensively for decorative finishes, as it produces a surface that can be readily dyed.

The chromic acid process produces a film that is darker in color than the sulfuric coating and is generally softer.

Hard-coat anodizing uses the same basic process, but a higher voltage produces a harder surface. Thus items made from a light metal can still have a hard, wear-resistant surface. Some of the parts which are now successfully treated with hard-coat anodizing are gears, pinions, bearing races, pistons, cams, and cylinders.

The properties of the anodized aluminum surface depend largely on the thickness and porosity of the oxide coating. The smaller the holes, the greater the hardness and wear resistance. Higher current densities and a lower-temperature electrolyte tend to decrease the hole size or porosity.

Alumilite is a type of hard-coat anodizing that has the superior qualities attributed to this denser, thicker coating. Ordinary anodized surfaces are 0.0001 to 0.0006 in. thick. An Alumilite coating may be 0.001 or 0.002 in.

**Oxide Coatings.** Black oxide films used on ferrous metals are produced by alkaline oxidizing solutions, by fused nitrate baths, or by heating. Oxide coatings are satisfactory for good indoor-storage corrosion protection, but they must be supplemented with a protective coating of wax, oil, or lacquer if outdoor storage is contemplated.

**Conversion-Coating Summary.** A summary of the various conversion coatings, the material coated, and their effectiveness is shown in Table 26-3.

### QUESTIONS

1. What are the three stages of metal cleaning in a complex system?
2. Why are chlorinated solvents preferred to petroleum solvents for some applications?
3. What must the designer keep in mind if the part manufactured is to be solvent cleaned?
4. Why are emulsifiable solvents easier to use than the petroleum or chlorinated types?
5. What does alkaline cleaning of metal consist of?

**TABLE 26-3.**

Summary of Conversion Coatings and Uses*

| Coating | Material Coated | Remarks |
|---|---|---|
| *Paint bonding* | | |
| Phosphate | Aluminum, zinc, cadmium, iron, and steel. Sometimes used on magnesium and tin. | Excellent paint-bonding ability attributed to rough, crystalline structure which aids mechanical adhesion. When paint film is damaged, corrosion is confined to that area. |
| Chromate | Aluminum, cadmium, magnesium and zinc. Sometimes used on copper, tin, titanium, iron, and steel. | Fair paint-bonding ability. Nonporous structure affords high corrosion protection. |
| *Corrosion resistance* | | |
| Anodic | Aluminum and magnesium. | Rated as best within the conversion-coating field. Highest cost. |
| Chromate | Aluminum, zinc, cadmium, magnesium, and copper. Sometimes used on tin, silver, iron, and steel. | Nonporous structure acts as a moisture barrier and affords excellent corrosion resistance. Soluble chromate in coating retards corrosion at damaged areas. |
| Phosphate | Aluminum, zinc, iron, and steel. Sometimes used on cadmium and tin. | Coating is most effective when treated with oils, waxes, or stains. Provides short-term protection of iron and steel. |
| Oxide and similar | Occasionally used on zinc, copper, cadmium, aluminum, iron, and steel. | Least effective. Used on short-term protection. |

* Courtesy *Machine Design.*

**TABLE 26-3** (continued)

| Coating | Material Coated | Remarks |
|---|---|---|
| *Decorative effect* | | |
| Anodic | Aluminum and magnesium. Occasionally used on zinc. | Excellent when sealed. May be colored with a variety of dyes. Underlying metal imparts metallic sheen. |
| Chromate | Aluminum, cadmium, copper, magnesium, and zinc. Occasionally used on tin, iron, and steel. | Offers a wide variety of natural and dyed colors. Colors are not as lightfast as those obtained from anodic coatings. |
| Oxide and similar | Aluminum, zinc, copper, cadmium, iron, and steel. | Produces black and blue-black coatings on zinc, cadmium, iron, and steel. A variety of colors can be obtained on copper and aluminum. |
| *Wear resistance* | | |
| Anodic | Aluminum and magnesium. | Heavy coatings afford excellent wear and abrasion resistance. |
| Phosphate | Iron and steel. | Prevents welding between bearing surfaces under load when coating is supplemented by oil film. |
| *Cold-forming aid* | | |
| Phosphate | Titanium, iron, and steel. | Excellent, especially when used with a lubricant to minimize metal-to-metal contact. |
| Oxide and similar | Titanium. | Special coatings are available for this use. |

6. Explain what is meant by bright dipping?

7. What are some applications of ultrasonic metal cleaning?

8. In what respect are ultrasonic cleaning and electrocleaning alike?

9. Why are the wet-abrasive blasting machines considered more versatile than the dry type?

10. What is the advantage of the twisted-knot wire brush?

11. What materials other than wire can be used in power brushes?

12. What beneficial effect other than cleaning may power brushing have?

13. What are the main classifications of protective and decorative metal coating?

14. How is the rate of metal deposit controlled in the electroplating process?

15. What are some design considerations for products that will be plated?

16. How thick is the coating produced by vacuum metallizing?

17. What are the main types of organic coatings?

18. Why are lacquers a favorite organic finishing material?

19. What is the difference between varnish and enamel?

20. Explain the principle of electrostatic spraying.

21. What is the meaning of the term conversion coating?

22. What are the main types of conversion coatings and their applications?


### PROBLEMS


1. A fabricated structure has 5.2 sq ft of unmachined surface to be given a protective coating. Fabricating costs total $32.15. The total cleaning cost per sq ft. is 0.005 cents per sq ft. It can be enameled for $1.75 cents a sq ft. Two coats of enamel are required. What percent of the total cost are the finishing costs?

2. After fabrication a part was found to have heavy soil plus scale and corrosion. Dip-tank cleaning was recommended. The time required in each cleaning tank was approximately 15 min. The running-rinse tanks require only 3 min. How much time must be allowed for cleaning each part?

3. A monorail degreaser costs $15,000 installed and ready to operate. Parts are processed through it at the average rate of one every 3 min. If the machine is in operation 60 percent of the time and the plant operates on a 40-hr week, how much must be added to the cost of each item to allow for depreciation of this equipment in 10 years?

4. How much paint would be required to paint 7,000 snow saucers stamped from 3-ft-diameter blanks that are to be painted on both sides? The enamel thickness required is 0.003 in., and a thickness of 0.0015 in. can be obtained in each application. Since electrostatic spraying is used, only 5 percent need be allowed for waste.

5. A part can be either brass plated, gold plated, or silver plated. The relative costs can be rated as 5, 6, and 1, respectively. What would the cost be of plating 20 sq ft with each metal if silver plating is figured at 0.15 cents a square foot? How much would it cost for rhodium plating with a rating of 20?

## REFERENCES

Linsley, H. E., "Vapor Degreasing," *American Machinist / Metalworking Manufacturing*, April, 1961.

Murphy, R. G., "A Guide to Selecting and Specifying Organic Finishes for Metal Surfaces," *Machine Design*, June, 1960.

Spencer, L. F., "Selecting Conversion Coatings for Metal Surfaces," Part I, *Machine Design*, September, 1960.

Spencer, L. F., "Chemical Cleaning of Metal Parts," *Machine Design*, July, 1961.

# 27

# MEASUREMENT AND GAGING

MEASUREMENT HAS played an important role in man's scientific advancement. Early attempts at standardization of length measurements were based on the human body. The width of a finger, for example, was termed a digit, and a cubit was the length of the forearm from the end of the elbow to the tip of the longest finger.

From these simple beginnings, man progressed gradually toward standardization of basic measurements. The most significant advancements were made in the metric system. It not only provided an easily usable scale of linear measurements, but volume and weight measurements as well. All units are in multiples of 10. Some comparisons of the English system of measurement with the metric system are shown in Fig. 27-1.

The metric system is based on the earth's measurements, the meter determined astronomically as being 1 ten-millionth part of the distance from the North Pole to the equator, measured on a line running along the earth's surface through the City of Paris. At the Convention of the Meter in Paris in 1875, several platinum-iridium bars of modified X cross section were made. Fine lines were etched on these bars to represent the standard meter length when measured at 0°C. Most nations have accepted this as the national standard of measurement. (Recently, a new standard for the inch was issued, making it 41,929.399 wavelengths of krypton light.) Although these standards were necessary, they were not available to the average manufacturer. The task of bringing a workable standard of length to industry still remained.

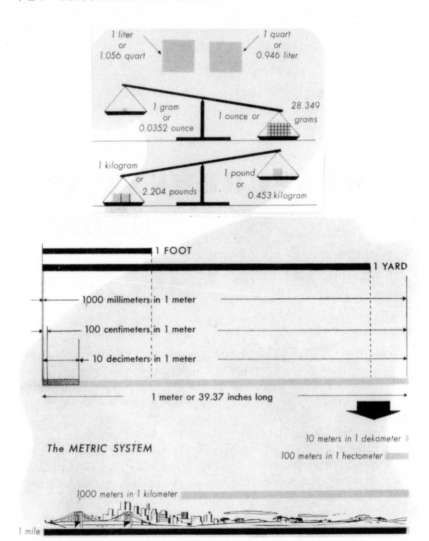

**Fig. 27-1.** A comparison of the English and metric systems of measurement (courtesy General Motors).

### THE DEVELOPMENT OF GAGE BLOCKS

Toward the close of the 19th century, Carl Johansson of Sweden decided to make measurement standards that would be available to industry. These were to duplicate the government standards as nearly as possible. To accomplish this, he painstakingly made a set of steel blocks that were accurate to within a few millionths of an inch. This was an unheard of tolerance, and how it was achieved remained a secret with Johansson for many years. Since these blocks were so accurate, they could be used to check the manufacturers' gages and other measuring instruments.

Modern gage blocks are made of a medium-carbon-alloy steel, hardened to a Rockwell C65, stabilized, ground, and lapped to exact size. Stabilization is a carefully controlled heat treatment performed to relieve internal stresses so that the blocks will retain their exact size over a long period of time. More recently, case hardened stainless-steel gage blocks have been placed on the market. These have the added advantage of corrosion resistance, an ever-present problem with steel gage blocks and much greater stability. Solid carbide blocks are made for use where wear is likely to be an important factor.

### Gage-Block Classification

Gage blocks are classified by the National Bureau of Standards according to accuracy, as follows:

| Letter | Meaning |
|---|---|
| AA | Laboratory gage blocks are within plus or minus two millionths of an inch per inch of length; they are also flat and parallel within this tolerance |
| A | Inspection gage blocks are similarly accurate to +6 millionths − 2 millionths of an inch |
| B | Working gage blocks are similarly accurate to +10 millionths − 6 millionths |

### Gage-Block Use

Gage blocks are sold in sets of from 5 to 103 pieces (Fig. 27-2). The predetermined selection of sizes in the set makes it possible to arrive at any one of thousands of reference dimensions by using combinations of blocks. The blocks may be used singly or in combinations to check micrometers, vernier calipers, vernier height gages, and fixed gages, and to set comparators, snap gages, and other adjustable gages. (Fig. 27-3), to mention a few of their uses. Thus we see that gage blocks are the connecting link between the international standard of measurement and the manufacturers' measuring and gaging equipment.

Gage blocks maintain accuracy even though several have to be used in combination to give a specified dimension. Plus and minus dimensions of blocks tend to balance out. The air can be eliminated from between the blocks by what is known as a *wringing-in process*. The procedure used is to clean the blocks thoroughly and then slide them into full contact while pressing them firmly together (Fig. 27-4).

Precision gaging is done in an air-conditioned room kept at 68°F. This was the temperature specified at the Convention of the

**Fig. 27-2.** Gage blocks may be either square or rectangular. There are usually 88 blocks in a set (courtesy Dearborn Gage Company).

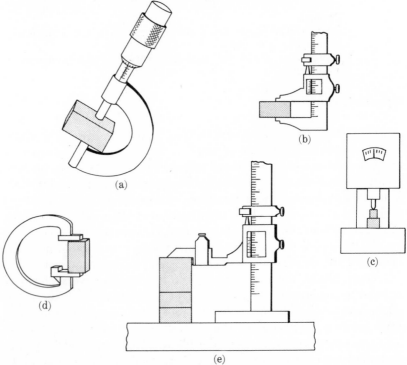

**Fig. 27-3.** Gage blocks are used as a standard for comparison in many ways. Gages shown are (a) micrometer, (b) vernier calipers, (c) comparator, (d) snap gage, and (e) vernier height gage.

A. Be sure gaging surfaces are clean.

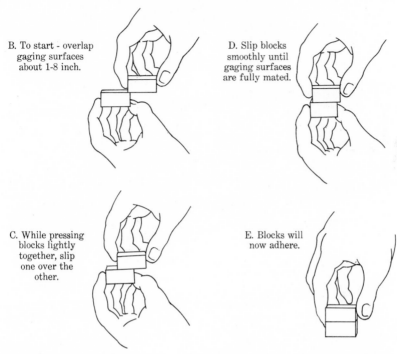

B. To start - overlap gaging surfaces about 1-8 inch.

D. Slip blocks smoothly until gaging surfaces are fully mated.

C. While pressing blocks lightly together, slip one over the other.

E. Blocks will now adhere.

**Fig. 27-4.** The procedure used in wringing gage blocks together (courtesy DoAll Company).

Meter in Paris, and it has since been adopted internationally. By using 68°F as a standard, materials other than steel can be checked with gage blocks, even though they may have a different coefficient of expansion.

Oftentimes, it is desirable to have an accurate reference in a shop which is not kept at 68°F. Because the coefficients of expansion of steel parts are so nearly alike, the gage blocks will correspond to the material in the measuring instruments so that accurate measurements and setups will result.

### Gage-Block Calibration

We have seen how gage blocks are the usable measurement standard for industry. The question arises as to just how the gage blocks are measured by light waves to a high degree of accuracy. Professor A. A. Michelson, of the United States, developed the optical arrangement, shown in Fig. 27-5, for studying the various phenomena in the interference of light. A monochromatic light emanating from a source, as shown, is passed through a condenser lens so that the light rays are parallel. A sodium light having a wavelength of 0.00002 in. is usually

Principle of the interferometer

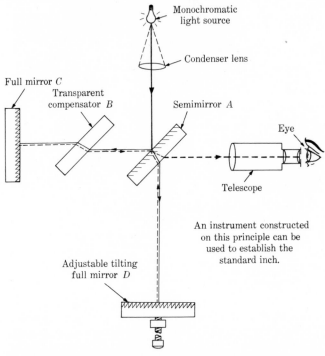

**Fig. 27-5.** Schematic diagram showing the principle of the interferometer (courtesy DoAll Company).

used. The light waves fall at 45 deg on a semimirror $A$, where they are partly reflected and partly transmitted. The transmitted rays are reflected normally from the full mirror $D$, and, after a second reflection at the mirror $A$, pass into the telescope and eyepiece. The reflected portion of the original rays traverses an inclined transparent compensating quartz plate $B$, which is exactly the same thickness as mirror $A$, and is reflected normally at the fully silvered mirror $C$. The rays returning from mirror $C$, after passing through $B$ and $A$, enter the telescope, and thence pass to the eye.

The two sets of rays, one reflected from $D$ and the other from $C$, when united, produce interference effects, or fringe lines.

Fringe lines may be understood more easily by studying the optical flats shown in Fig. 27-6. The monochromatic light goes through a quartz flat $A$, to the surface of the work, and is reflected back through the quartz flat. If the wave from the bottom of the flat and the wave reflected from the work surface are exactly out of phase, they cancel each other, so that they appear as dark bands. Such interference will occur at every point where the distance from the flat to the work is in odd multiples of one half the wavelength of the light used.

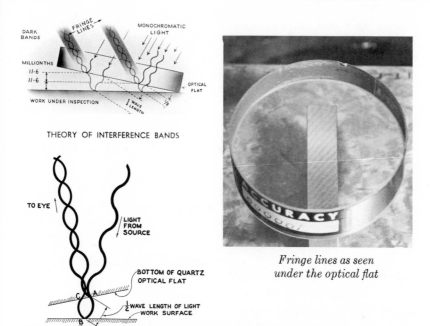

THEORY OF INTERFERENCE BANDS

*Fringe lines as seen
under the optical flat*

**Fig. 27-6.** Monochromatic light passing through an optical flat is partly reflected by the lower surface of the flat, while the remainder passes through. As the two reflected light rays travel different distances they create a series of alternating bright and dark bands (courtesy DoAll Company).

The picture at the right of Fig. 27-6 shows the top view of a gage block under the optical flat.

In the interferometer these fringe lines are picked up in the telescope by wringing a gage block to mirror *D* Fig. 27-5. As one of the mirrors is slowly displaced to cover the surface of the gage block, the observer counts the lines as they pass.

This procedure will give the length to within one half wavelength of light, but still further accuracy can be obtained. The spectrum colors of red, yellow, green, blue-green, blue, and violet from the helium light in the interferometer have definite relations with one another at various distances from the source. Constellations of fractional divisions or pattern arrangements of the spectrum recur at uniform intervals. Since the recurrence of constellations is absolutely known, lengths may be determined to a very high degree of accuracy.

## MEASUREMENT

Measuring tools and instruments are of two broad types—direct and indirect. Direct measuring instruments obtain the measurement without the aid of other equipment. Indirect measuring tools transfer the given size to a measuring instrument for the actual size reading. Measurement may be further divided into four main areas—linear, angular, roundness, and surface. Each of the four areas will be discussed in the order given, with direct measurement first in each case.

### Linear Measurement

**Direct Measurement.** The following hand-operated measuring tools are used for linear measurement.

STEEL RULE. The simplest measuring device is the steel rule. It is divided into fractions of an inch, usually by 64ths, but sometimes in 1/100ths of an inch. Rules are made with various attachments so that they can be used as depth gages and hook rules.

MICROMETER CALIPERS. As mentioned, the steel rule is used successfully for measurements to within 1/100th of an inch. In most machine-tool work this is far from satisfactory, as the work must be held to a few thousandths or even 1/10,000 of an inch. In 1638 an astronomer by the name of William Gascoigne was interested in measuring the size of the sun and moon. To do this he chose the screw-thread principle (Fig. 27-7), which became the forerunner of the present-day micrometer caliper. The micrometer screw has 40 threads to the inch. This means that each revolution of the screw moves the spindle 1/40 of an inch toward the anvil or away from it. Therefore 1/40 of a

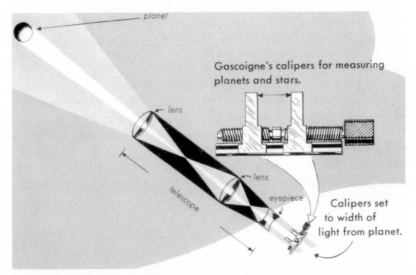

**Fig. 27-7.** Gascoigne's calipers for measuring planets and stars (courtesy General Motors).

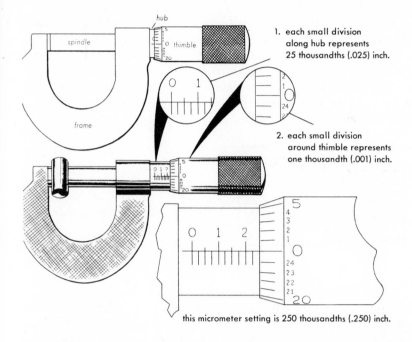

1. each small division along hub represents 25 thousandths (.025) inch.

2. each small division around thimble represents one thousandth (.001) inch.

this micrometer setting is 250 thousandths (.250) inch.

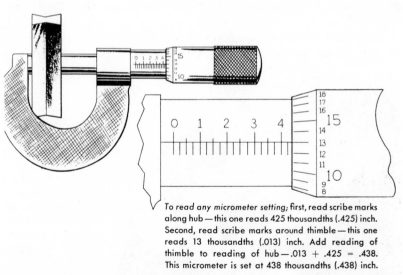

To read any micrometer setting; first, read scribe marks along hub — this one reads 425 thousandths (.425) inch. Second, read scribe marks around thimble — this one reads 13 thousandths (.013) inch. Add reading of thimble to reading of hub — .013 + .425 = .438. This micrometer is set at 438 thousandths (.438) inch.

**Fig. 27-8.** Micrometer-caliper readings (courtesy General Motors).

revolution will move the spindle $\dfrac{1}{40} = 0.025$. Rather than move one

revolution, the distance may be changed to 1/25; this amount may be accomplished by having the sleeve graduated into 25 parts (Fig. 27-8).

The 0.001 reading may be further refined by adding a vernier scale. The vernier in this case consists of 10 divisions marked on the barrel which equal, in overall dimension, 9 divisions on the thimble (Fig. 27-9). Notice that the fourth-place number is obtained by observing which of the vernier lines coincides with a line on the thimble. This number is added to the thousandths reading in the example: 0.369 + 0.0005 = 0.3695.

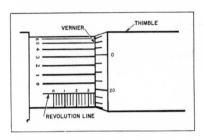

**Fig. 27-9.** The vernier micrometer caliper is read to 0.0001, as shown.

*Indicating micrometer comparator.* The fact that the micrometer is made to measure to 0.001 or 0.0001 in. does not mean that it will guarantee this accuracy to every user. There is a difference in the amount of pressure used in closing the micrometer on the workpiece. To overcome this objection, an indicating micrometer (Fig. 27-10) was developed.

*Standard measuring machine.* A still more advanced step, using the micrometer principle, is the standard measuring machine (Fig.

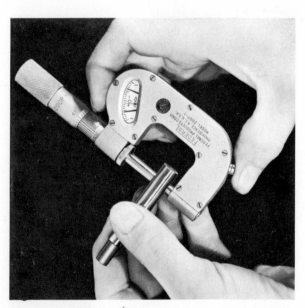

**Fig. 27-10.** The indicating micrometer is used to a high degree of uniform pressure (courtesy Federal Products Corporation).

27-11). This machine is equipped with an electrolimit pressure tailstock. The desired pressure, from 1 to 2½ lb, for measuring a workpiece is determined and then set into the tailstock. When the part being measured has the set pressure exerted on it, the pointer of the milliammeter dial, located on the tailstock, will be in the center of its scale range. The measurement reading is then determined on three scales beneath a magnifier on the head. The first scale indicates in tenths and hundredths of an inch, the second scale indicates in thousandths and ten-thousandths, and the third, or vernier scale, indicates hundred-thousandths of an inch.

**Fig. 27-11.** A standard measuring machine being used to measure a plug gage to within 0.00001 in. (courtesy Pratt & Whitney Co. Inc.).

*Special anvil micrometers.* Micrometers are adapted to special purposes by changing the contacting surfaces on the anvil. The special types shown in Fig. 27-12 are *screw-thread micrometer,* used to measure the pitch diameter of threads; *rounded anvil micrometer,* useful for measuring tubing wall thickness. Another micrometer, called a *tube micrometer,* may be used for tubing wall thickness or checking the distance of a hole to an edge, as shown in the figure. Extra large anvil and spindle faces permit accurate measurements of paper, rubber, plastics, etc., also shown in Fig. 27-12.

*Inside micrometers.* Inside micrometer calipers are of several types, two of which are shown in Fig. 27-13. One kind of inside micrometer, *a,* has measuring rods that may be inserted, making a range of 2 to 32 in. possible. Another type, *b* is made in two sizes, covering a range from 0.200 to 2 in.

*Depth micrometer.* Depth micrometers (Fig. 27-14) have the same calibrations as outside micrometers, but the reading is in reverse. For example, the 1-in. reading is with barrel screwed down and the rod fully extended. Gaging depths of more than 1 in. may be obtained with measuring rods of even inch lengths inserted into the head.

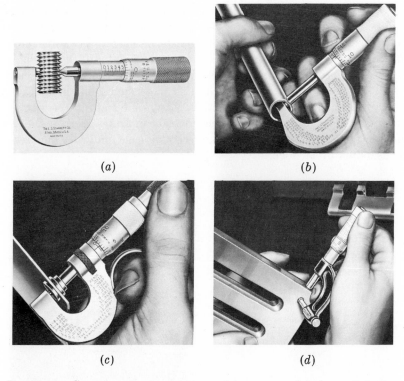

**Fig. 27-12.** Special anvil micrometers used to measure (*a*) screw-pitch diameter, (*b*) tubing wall thickness, (*c*) paper thickness, and (*d*) hole-edge distance (courtesy The L. S. Starrett Co.).

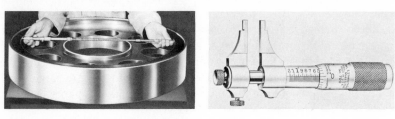

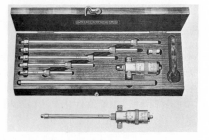

**Fig. 27-13.** Inside micrometers (courtesy The L. S. Starrett Co.).

**Fig. 27-14.** Depth micrometer used to measure the depth of the milled slot (courtesy The L. S. Starrett Co.).

*Vernier calipers.* Another instrument that is capable of measuring to 0.001 in. accuracy is the vernier caliper. The inset picture of the vernier scale (Fig. 27-15) is used as an example of how the total vernier

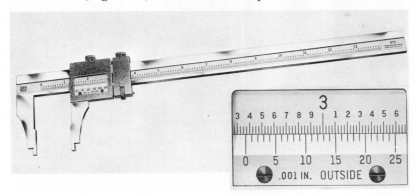

**Fig. 27-15.** The vernier caliper, with enlarged scale inset (courtesy Brown & Sharpe Mfg. Co.).

reading is obtained. Notice that the zero on the vernier is past the 2-in. mark on the scale, thus we have:

|       |       |                                                    |
|-------|-------|----------------------------------------------------|
|       | 2.000 |                                                    |
|       | 0.300 | hundred-thousandths on scale                       |
|       | 0.050 | two twenty-five thousandths lines                  |
|       | 0.018 | the line on vernier that coincides with a line on scale |
| Total | 2.368 |                                                    |

Both inside and outside diameters may be measured with a vernier caliper.

*Vernier height gage.* The vernier height gage uses the same principle as the vernier caliper. It is, however, mounted on a base and is used to measure and scribe accurately layout lines of a given height from a plane (Fig. 27-16).

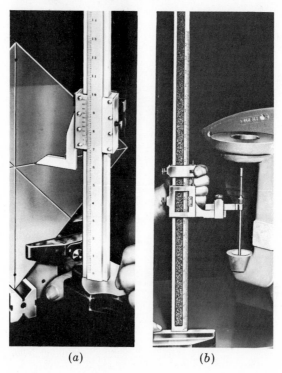

(a)                    (b)

**Fig. 27-16.** (*a*) Vernier height gage used in making layout lines on a steel plate and (*b*) Measuring the depth of a recess (courtesy The L. S. Starrett Co.).

**Indirect Measurement.** Indirect measuring tools are used to transfer or compare distances and sizes.

CALIPERS. Some of the uses of the common types of calipers—inside, outside, and hermaphrodite—are shown in Fig. 27-17. The caliper setting is obtained when the points bear lightly on the surface of the work. After the adjustment has been made, the diameter can be read from a rule, as shown, or, in the case of inside calipers, by a micrometer.

SMALL-HOLE GAGES. It is often difficult to check small-hole diameters accurately with either an inside micrometer or inside calipers and micrometer. The best combination for this purpose is the small-hole gage (Fig. 27-18). The ball contacts are made to spread apart to the diameter of the hole, by means of adjusting the knurled handle. A micrometer is then used to measure the distance over the split curved

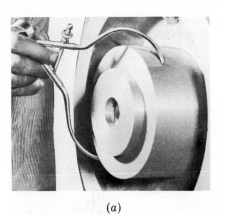

(a)

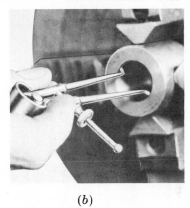

(b)

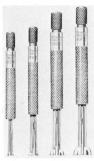

(c)

**Fig. 27-17.** Using (a) outside, (b) inside and (c) hermaphrodite calipers.

**Fig. 27-18.** Small-hole gages are used to check small holes, slots, and recesses in the range of 0.125 to 0.500 in. (courtesy The L. S. Starrett Co.).

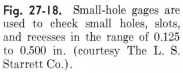

surfaces. As shown in the figure, the small-hole gage is also used for gaging slots and recesses.

TELESCOPING GAGES. The telescoping gage is used for the same type of work as the small-hole gage, but the size range is enlarged to cover ½ in. through 6 in. (Fig. 27-19).

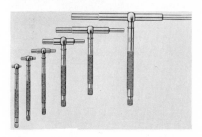

**Fig. 27-19.** Internal slots, holes and recesses ranging from ½ to 6 in. may be checked with a telescoping gage and micrometers (courtesy The L. S. Starrett Co.).

DIAL INDICATORS. Dial indicators are used to compare a part with a master setting. The master setting may be a combination of gage blocks (Fig. 27-20). By means of rack-and-pinion arrangement, the

**Fig. 27-20.** A dial indicator used to check the height of a ground ring against a gage block (courtesy The L. S. Starrett Co.).

movement of the contact pointer is greatly amplified so that dimensional variations are easily read on a dial. The value of each graduation on the face of the dial may vary from 0.00005 to 0.005 in. In addition to comparing parts with a master setting, dial indicators are used extensively in making machine-tool setups (Fig. 27-21). Notice the variety of methods used to hold the indicator. Dial indicators are used as standard mechanical-type comparators and in other gages discussed later in this chapter.

(a)

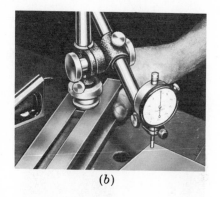

(b)

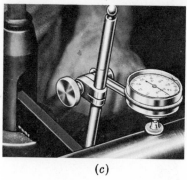

(c)

**Fig. 27-21.** The dial indicator is used in making accurate machine setups. At (a) a part is being checked for center location in a three-jaw chuck. (b) The indicator is used to check the depth of a cut. (c) Checking the runout of work mounted between centers on a lathe (courtesy The L. S. Starrett Co.).

## Angular Measurement

**Direct Measurement.** Angular measurements can be made in a variety of ways ranging from the use of a simple protractor to that of an angle-calibrating interferometer.

PROTRACTORS. Angular measurements are made with an ordinary bevel protractor (Fig. 27-22).

**Fig. 27-22.** A protractor head and 12-in. rule (courtesy The L. S. Starrett Co.).

**Fig. 27-23.** A universal bevel protractor being used to measure an acute 10-deg angle. The enlarged dial shows the reading of the vernier scale at 50 deg 20 min (courtesy The L. S. Starrett Co.).

**Fig. 27-24.** A sine bar used to check the 45-deg angle of a squaring head.

A more precise measurement can be obtained with a vernier bevel protractor which can be accurately read to within 5 min, or 1/12 deg. Reading the inset vernier of Fig. 27-23, we notice that the zero on the vernier scale lies between 50 and 51 on the protractor dial, or 50 whole deg. The line from the vernier scale that coincides with the protractor scale is 20. Therefore the reading is 50 deg and 20 min (50° 20′).

### Indirect Measurement.

SINE BARS. A sine bar is a very accurate straightedge to which two plugs have been attached (Fig. 27-24). These two plugs are very accurate in diameter, and the center distance is within 0.00002 in. or less per inch of length. The length between centers is given in multiples of 5 in. from 5 to 20 in.

The sine bar makes use of the known relationships between the sides of a right triangle and its angles. Measurements are made by using the principle of the sine of a given angle or the ratio of the opposite side of the right triangle to the hypotenuse. To check the accuracy of the 45-deg angle of a squaring head, using a 10-in. sine bar (Fig. 27-24), the following procedure would be used:

1. Find the sine of 45 deg from the tables (0.70711).

2. Use the procedure given earlier for selecting and wringing in the proper gage blocks to obtain this height.

$$
\begin{array}{r}
0.121 \\
0.950 \\
2.000 \\
4.000 \\
\hline
7.071
\end{array}
$$

3. Use a dial indicator, as shown, to check if the 45 deg is now parallel to the top of the surface plate. Any change in the dial reading would indicate an error in the angle. The amount would be according to the change necessary in the gage block height.

A variety of sine-bar fixtures have been made to make the setting up and checking of angles easier. Shown in Fig. 27-25 are two sine-plate fixtures and a magnetic table.

ANGULAR GAGE BLOCKS. With a set of angle gages consisting of 10 pieces, it is possible to make any angle between 0 and 180 deg

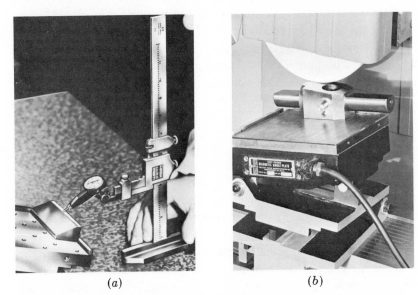

(a)                              (b)

**Fig. 27-25.** (a) A universal sine-bar fixture and (b) a magnetic sine-bar table being used for accurate checking and machining of angular surfaces (courtesy The Taft-Peirce Manufacturing Co.).

**Fig. 27-26.** The precision microptic clinometer is used to check angular settings to within 1 sec of arc direct-reading, and ½ sec by interpolation (courtesy Engis Equipment Co.).

by 5-min intervals. These blocks may be set up in combination and used as a standard to check a given part, with the aid of a dial indicator.

MICROPTIC CLINOMETER. The precision microptic clinometer (Fig. 27-26) is used for angular measurement direct to 1 sec of arc and estimation to ½ sec. The clinometer is fitted with a circular glass scale that is divided into 10-min intervals, figured at each degree. Subdivisions of the graduation are made by an optical micrometer, the scale of which is divided at 1-sec intervals. A coarse scale on the outside of the body is used for approximate angular readings.

A spirit level in which the bubble is split down the center is used to tell when the clinometer is precisely level.

The two ends of the bubble are optically viewed side by side, and therefore any movement appears doubled. The bubble becomes a null-setting device many times more accurate than the value of a graduation.

### Roundness Measurement

Roundness may be measured indirectly. For example, the Talyrond* instrument (Fig. 27-27) is used for measuring the roundness of parts such as balls, roller races, pistons, and cylinders. Both external and internal diameters can be checked. Diameters range from 1/16 to 14 in., with the maximum height of the specimen being 10 in.

**Fig. 27-27.** The Talyrond used for precision roundness measurement (courtesy Engis Equipment Co.).

An electric displacement indicator, in operation, is carried on an optically guided precision spindle of extreme accuracy, which is rotated around the outside or inside of the part to be examined; the part itself

* Talyrond is a trademark of Taylor, Taylor and Hobson.

remains stationary on the table. The signal from the indicator is amplified and then applied to a polar-coordinate recorder.

In Fig. 27-28 are various graphs showing the degree of amplification that can be obtained on one surface. The one on the left shows only major errors; the one in the center shows all the errors; the one on the right shows an average between the two.

**Fig. 27-28.** Talyrond trace charts can be used to record either major or minor errors, depending upon the amplification used, and can also record the average of these two records (courtesy Engis Equipment Co.).

### Surface Measurement

The quality of the surface finish of running or sliding parts has a great deal to do with how long these items will last. A smoother finish than required is costly to produce. Instrument and surface-finish comparison blocks have been made to help designate this measurement of "how smooth is smooth?" in millionths of an inch. After the design engineer has specified the proper surface finish, the methods department can determine the type of machine and the tools that will be required to produce it.

**Surface-Finish Characteristics.** The American Standards Association has defined surface-roughness characteristics in ASA B461-1955. These characteristics, shown in Fig. 27-29, may be described as follows:

ROUGHNESS. This term refers to the finely spaced irregularities, the height, width, and direction of which establish the predominant pattern. These irregularities are produced by the cutting tool and the machine feed. The height is measured in microinches, using an arithmetical average. The width is rated in inches.

WAVINESS. Irregularities of greater spacing than roughness are called waviness. They may result from machine or work deflection, vibration, heat treatment, etc. The height is rated in inches as the peak-to-valley distance. The width is rated in inches as the spacing of adjacent waves.

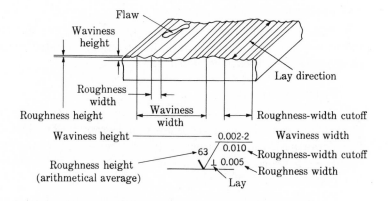

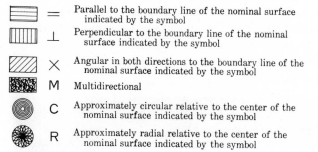

Symbols indicating direction of lay

| | = | Parallel to the boundary line of the nominal surface indicated by the symbol |
| | ⊥ | Perpendicular to the boundary line of the nominal surface indicated by the symbol |
| | × | Angular in both directions to the boundary line of the nominal surface indicated by the symbol |
| | M | Multidirectional |
| | C | Approximately circular relative to the center of the nominal surface indicated by the symbol |
| | R | Approximately radial relative to the center of the nominal surface indicated by the symbol |

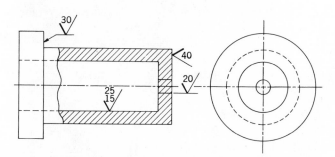

How surface roughness is specified on working drawings. Figures in V-shaped symbols show roughness in microinches

**Fig. 27-29.** Surface-finish characteristics and symbols as defined by the American Standards Association.

LAY. Lay is the predominant direction of the surface pattern. This is normally determined from the method by which the material was produced.

FLAWS. Irregularities that occur at one place, or at relatively infrequent intervals on the surface, for example, a scratch, ridge, hole, peak, crack, or check, are called flaws.

### Indirect Measurement.

VISUAL INSPECTION. An unscientific but often satisfactory method of checking surface roughness is by visual examination. The sense of feel—drawing a thumbnail across the surface—is also sometimes enlisted as an added check. This method gives a rough approximation but requires considerable skill.

CALIBRATED BLOCKS. An improvement over the above-method is to have a set of blocks of known surface finish with which a close comparison can be made (Fig. 27-30). The surface roughness of each block is specified by a number representing the arithmetic average deviation from the mean surface, in microinches (Fig. 27-31). Various methods have been used to improve and refine this technique, including microscopic comparison, illumination comparison, and the use of photo-electric cells.

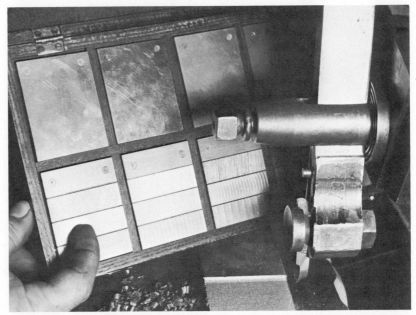

**Fig. 27-30.** Comparing a machined surface finish with calibrated blocks to determine approximate rms finish.

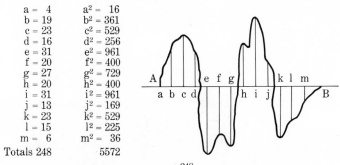

| | |
|---|---|
| a = 4 | $a^2$ = 16 |
| b = 19 | $b^2$ = 361 |
| c = 23 | $c^2$ = 529 |
| d = 16 | $d^2$ = 256 |
| e = 31 | $e^2$ = 961 |
| f = 20 | $f^2$ = 400 |
| g = 27 | $g^2$ = 729 |
| h = 20 | $h^2$ = 400 |
| i = 31 | $i^2$ = 961 |
| j = 13 | $j^2$ = 169 |
| k = 23 | $k^2$ = 529 |
| l = 15 | $l^2$ = 225 |
| m = 6 | $m^2$ = 36 |
| Totals 248 | 5572 |

Arithmetical average = $\frac{248}{13}$ = 19.1 $\mu$ in.

Root-mean-square average = $\sqrt{\frac{5572}{13}}$ = 20.7 $\mu$ in.

**Fig. 27-31.** Arithmetical average roughness and rms average roughness can be calculated from profile charts of the surface. Calculations are simple but time-consuming. Direct-reading stylus instruments are preferred for mass inspection of ferrous parts (courtesy *American Machinist/Metalworking Manufacturing*).

### Direct Measurement.

TRACE-TYPE SURFACE MEASUREMENT. A number of instruments have been made that operate on the principle of a fine (0.0005-in.-radius tip) stylus that is moved over the surface to be checked. The vertical movements of this tracer point are transmitted to a coil inside the tracer body. The coil moves in a field of a permanent magnet, and this produces a small fluctuating voltage that is related to the height of the surface irregularities (Fig. 27-32).

The trace may be moved either manually or mechanically over the surface of the work. Mechanical movement gives a more consistent and dependable roughness measurement. Manual operations, however, make for convenience and timesaving setups. The surfaces measured may range from 1 $\mu$in. or less up to 1,000 $\mu$in. of roughness. Figure 27-33 shows the profile of a machined surface with both roughness and waviness.

Other trace-type instruments are the Surfindicator, with a range of 0 to 1,000 $\mu$in., and the Talysurf, with a range of 0 to 200 $\mu$in.

These instruments do not give a total surface indication. Flaws, waviness, or some scratches too minute to measure will not show up on the record.

OPTICAL SURFACE MEASUREMENT. Visual methods of surface inspection were mentioned previously, but they did not include means of actual surface-roughness measurement. An optical-surface-roughness measuring instrument, such as the surface finish micro-interferometer,

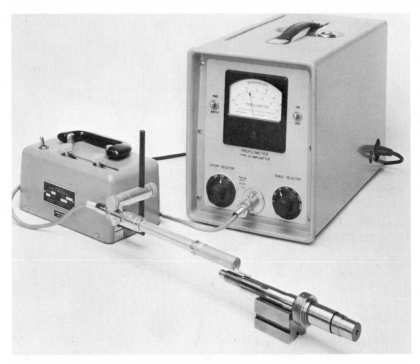

**Fig. 27-32.** The profilometer being used manually to check the roughness of a cylindrical surface. The meter on the panel shows roughness directly in microinches as the tracer is moved along the work (courtesy Micrometrical Mfg. Co.).

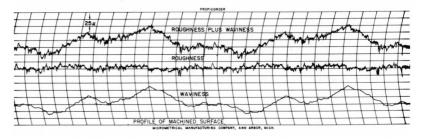

**Fig. 27-33.** The recorded profile of a machined surface, showing both roughness and waviness (courtesy Micrometrical Mfg. Co.).

makes use of light-wave-interference principles and provides a quantitative measurement. A similar instrument, capable of measuring roughness depths between 1.2 and 400 $\mu$ in., is the interference microscope shown schematically in Figure 27-34. This instrument is often referred to as the 45-deg microscope or the light-section microscope. The light is permitted to shine through a slit, falling on the work in the form of a fine band. This band of light traces out the profile of the surface,

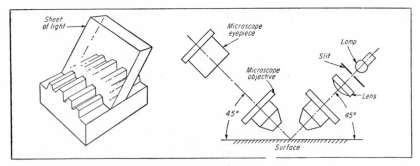

**Fig. 27-34.** Schematic view of the interference microscope which provides a sheet of light upon which the section of the surface pattern is viewed. The height and width of the irregularities can be measured.

that is, its peaks and valleys. A reticle in the microscope can be shifted within the field of view to measure the height (or the width) of the surface irregularities. Both roughness and waviness may be determined.

Two advantages of using optical instruments in measuring surface roughness are that they do not mar the work and they can be used to measure more than one parameter at a time. They also can measure surface roughness, waviness, and flaws.

**Machined-Surface Characteristics.** There are so many factors, within one machining area, affecting surface finish that it is difficult to make a conclusive statement of what to expect. On a lathe, for example, the feed, depth of cut, condition of the tool, and other factors beyond the operator's control will influence the surface finish. The American Standards Association recognized the need of a guide, and established a surface-finish range for each type of machine operation, as shown in Figure 27-35.

### Optical Tooling

When large, accurate, machine-tool surfaces or jig and fixture points and alignment have to be checked, optical methods are used; that is, a line of sight is established and used somewhat as a surveyor uses a theodolite. There are other ways of checking large flat surfaces or points of alignment, such as with stretched wires or large block levels, but they are more cumbersome.

The basic instruments needed in optical tooling are a theodolite, a microalignment telescope, and an autocollimator. The theodolite is used for measuring horizontal and vertical angles. The microalignment telescope is an internally focusing telescope with an erecting eyepiece that is used in conjunction with a target. Built-in micrometers enable the operator to observe both horizontal and vertical displacement of the target and make readings as close as 0.0002 in. The autocollimator combines a collimator (an instrument for projecting parallel light rays) and a telescope.

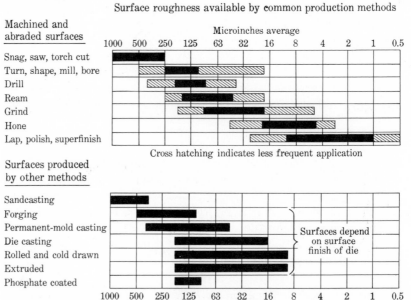

Surface roughness available by common production methods

Cross hatching indicates less frequent application

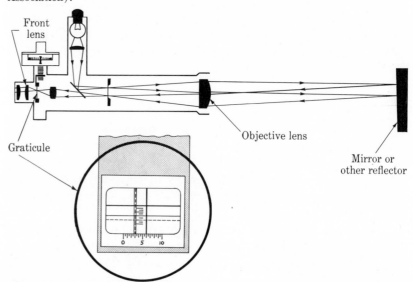

**Fig. 27-35.** The general range of surface finishes that can be obtained by various machining, casting, and other methods (courtesy American Standards Association).

**Fig. 27-36.** The principle of the autocollimator (courtesy Engis Equipment Co.).

The principle of the autocollimator can best be explained with the aid of the diagram in Fig. 27-36. Light projected from the front lens, in the form of parallel rays, is reflected from a front-surface mirror or other reflector. After reentering the objective lens, the light forms an image of target wires in the same plane as the wires in the graticule. The microscope eyepiece enables the observer to measure any angular displacement caused by misalignment at the point where the mirror is stationed.

The autocollimator can also be used to measure the flatness of surfaces or the accuracy with which locating points lie within a straight line. High accuracy is possible because the autocollimator can measure angles as small as 1 sec of arc.

An example of the use of the autocollimator is shown in Fig. 27-37. The autocollimator is mounted on the surface plate. A line across the plate is calibrated by moving a reflector carriage across the table

**Fig. 27-37.** The autocollimator is used to calibrate a surface plate (courtesy Engis Equipment Co.).

in lengths equal to the carriage base. A straightedge clamped to the surface plate is used in guiding the reflector carriage. Tilts of the carriage indicate a variation in the surface. Several tracks are made across the surface plate to determine its overall accuracy. A corner mirror is used when the line of sighting is changed. The results are correlated, and the deviation from the mean true plane is established.

An example of the use of the microalignment telescope is shown in Fig. 27-38. Two alignment telescopes are mounted on the tooling fixtures with targets located in the templates. The targets may be of the cross-hair type for alignment only, or they have scales that allow measurement of displacement. Mirrored targets make it possible to determine the tilt.

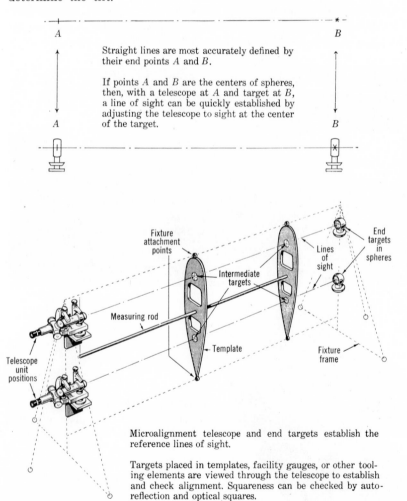

Straight lines are most accurately defined by their end points A and B.

If points A and B are the centers of spheres, then, with a telescope at A and target at B, a line of sight can be quickly established by adjusting the telescope to sight at the center of the target.

Microalignment telescope and end targets establish the reference lines of sight.

Targets placed in templates, facility gauges, or other tooling elements are viewed through the telescope to establish and check alignment. Squareness can be checked by autoreflection and optical squares.

**Fig. 27-38.** Optical tooling used for alignment of aircraft-wing templates.

The telescopes are removed from the tool upon its completion, but the telescope mounting and the targets remain an integral part of the tool. These mountings allow replacement of the telescopes for rechecking the tooling as needed.

## GAGING

Most of the tools and instruments discussed thus far are used for fine accurate work on an individual basis. Even though more and more accuracy is being called for and some of the tools mentioned are moving into the work areas, it remains for specially built gages to handle the bulk of production inspection.

A gage is a device used by a machine operator or inspector to determine whether the manufactured part is within the prescribed dimensions. In mass production, gages provide the best means of securing interchangeability. Gaging is done as much to *prevent* unsatisfactory parts from being made as to sort out the correct from the incorrect.

Gages are built on a system of *fits* which, in turn, have prescribed limits, tolerances, and allowances. These and related terms are identified as follows:

*Tolerance* — the amount of size variation which is permitted on a part without interfering with its functional operation
*Limits* — the extreme dimensions of the tolerance
*Clearance* — the difference in size between mating parts when the critical dimension of the male part is smaller than the corresponding internal dimension of the female part [Fig. 27-39a]

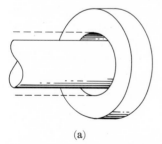 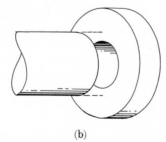

(a)                              (b)

**Fig. 27-39.** (a) Clearance fit and (b) interference fit.

*Interference* — the difference in size between mating parts when the critical dimension of the male part is greater than the corresponding internal dimension of the female part [Fig. 27-39(b)]
*Allowance* — the prescribed difference (minimum clearance or maximum interference) between mating parts to attain a specific class of fit

*Basic size* — the size from which the limits of size are derived by the application of allowances and tolerances

*Unilateral tolerance* — tolerance in which the variation is permitted in one direction only

*Bilateral tolerance* — tolerance in which the variation is permitted in both directions from the design size

## Classification of Fits

Fits are of three general types—running, locational, and force.

**Running or Sliding Fits.** Running or sliding fits are broken down into seven gradations, starting with the designation RC1 and running through RC7, each with an increasing clearance. The first classification in this series is intended for accurate location of parts without perceptible play; the last in the series is for a free-running fit where accuracy is not important.

**Locational Fits.** The locational fits are designated by letters, as follows: LC for locational clearance, LT for locational-transition fits, and LN for locational-interference fits. This group of fits, intended to determine the location of mating parts, varies from the clearance type with free assembly to the interference type used to provide rigid or accurate location.

**Force Fits.** Force fits are designated by the letters FN, followed by a number indicating the degree of force needed to assemble the parts. FN1 indicates a light drive fit, whereas FN5 is a force fit used for parts able to take a high degree of stress, or for shrink fits when heavy pressing forces are impractical.

The design engineers, along with the various draftsmen, are responsible for selecting the limits or tolerances according to the functioning of the equipment. There are no set rules for establishing limits and tolerances for all phases of mechanical design, so careful judgment must be exercised in specifying the proper amounts. The greater the permissible limits or tolerances, the less costly the part is to produce; there will be less scrap and lower labor costs, and less expensive tools will be needed.

## Gage Types

The designer may specify the proper tolerances and allowances, but it remains for the production department to see that they are maintained. To ensure production standards, gages used to inspect the work are made to very rigid tolerances, usually about 10 percent of the workpiece tolerance, Fig. 27-40.

Gages may be divided into mechanical and comparator types.

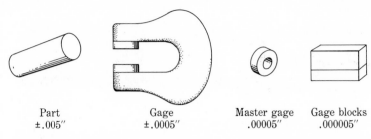

|          |          |              |             |
|:--------:|:--------:|:------------:|:-----------:|
| Part     | Gage     | Master gage  | Gage blocks |
| ±.005″   | ±.0005″  | .00005″      | .000005″    |

**Fig. 27-40.**  A gage must be ten times more accurate than the dimension being checked for reliable quality control (courtesy DoAll Company).

**Mechanical Gages.**   Mechanical gages are often termed *fixed-limit gages*. These gage by attributes, meaning that the part is either passed or is not passed by a single gage setting; there is no variation. These gages may be subdivided into groups, according to the purpose for which they are used.

PLUG GAGES.   Plug gages are used to check internal diameters. A go–not-go plug gage is a double-ended gage used to control minimum looseness or maximum tightness of mating parts. Plug gages may also be tapered or threaded, as shown in Fig. 27-41.

RING GAGES.   Ring gages are used to check external diameters. They may be used to check straight, tapered, or threaded external diameters.

SNAP GAGES.   A snap gage is used to check the outside diameter of a part, somewhat like the action of a caliper. It may be made adjustable within small limits. With two pairs of anvils, it also becomes a go–not-go snap gage, as shown in Fig. 27-42.

**Comparator Gages.**   Comparators are instrument-type gages that make use of a standard, such as a template or gage blocks, for a reference. They differ from the fixed-limit or attribute gages in that they are able to show the amount of variation from the standard. For this reason they are also called *variable* gages.

The four main types of comparators, based on the amplification mechanism, are mechanical, electrical, air, and optical.

Many special gages have been made using the dial indicator to measure directly in thousandths or ten-thousandths of an inch. Some of these are thickness gages, caliper gages, adjustable snap gages, automatic grinding gages, depth gages, and dial bore gages, as shown in Fig. 27-43.

Among the advantages set forth for the grinding gage, is that it can be put on the work while the machine is running; thus the work may be ground right down to the desired size without stopping

*A go–not-go progressive plug gage*

*A go–not-go double-ended-thread plug gage*

*A not-go ring gage*          *A go ring gage*

**Fig. 27-41.** Various plug and ring gages (courtesy The Taft-Peirce Manufacturing Co.).

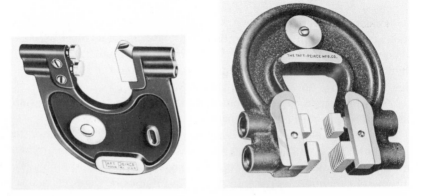

**Fig. 27-42.** Go–not-go snap gages of the adjustable type, used to check plain and threaded outside diameters (courtesy The Taft-Peirce Manufacturing Co.).

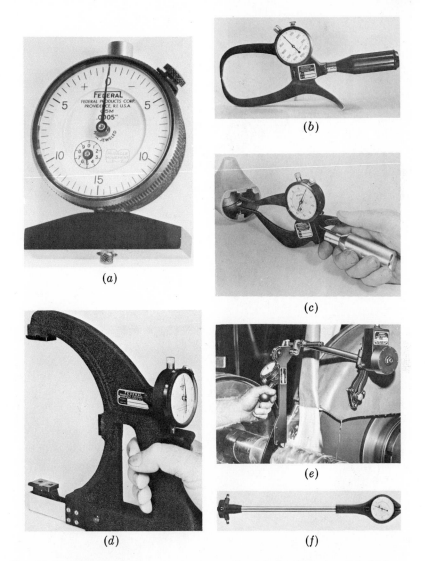

**Fig. 27-43.** Dial indicators are used to make (*a*) depth gages, (*b*) thickness gage, (*c*) caliper gage, (*d*) adjustable snap gage, (*e*) grinding gage, and (*f*) dial bore gage (courtesy Federal Products Corp.).

the machine. Out-of-round and chatter may also be observed directly on the dial while the machine is running.

*Visual gage.*    Closely associated with the dial indicator or mechanical comparator is the visual gage (Fig. 27-44). The magnification on this type of comparator ranges from 500 to 1 to 20,000 to 1. The

**Fig. 27-44.** Visual gage with sine bar and wire being used to check tapered threads (courtesy The Sheffield Corp.).

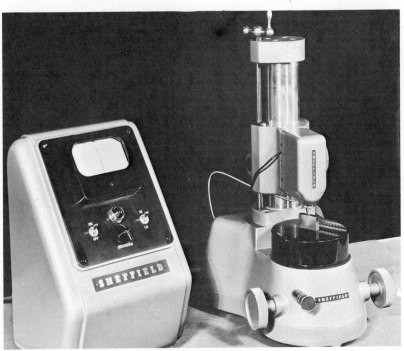

**Fig. 27-45.** An electrical comparator used to check a gage block (courtesy The Sheffield Corp.).

highest magnification has a scale on which each graduation represents 0.000002 in.

ELECTRICAL COMPARATORS. The Electrichek (Fig. 27-45) uses signal lights to show whether or not the part being checked is within tolerance. The tolerance range may be set between 0.000050 and 0.060 in. As with the dial-type grinding gage, the head of the Electrichek can be mounted directly on a machine to tell the operator when the part being ground has been brought to size.

A variation of the Electrichek is the Multichek. A battery of Electricheks is set up to indicate simultaneously all the critical dimensions of the workpart (Fig. 27-46). A red master light at the top will

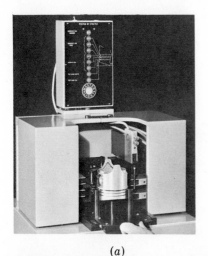

**Fig. 27-46.** (*a*) A Multichek used to check the grooves in a piston. (*b*) A bank of Multichek machines checking parts with the outlines shown above the machines (courtesy The Sheffield Corp.).

(*a*)

(*b*)

automatically go on if any one of the dimensions is out of tolerance. A quick check of the small lights on the panel will indicate exactly which dimensions or dimensions are wrong.

Other electrical comparators are made that are used for the same type of work just described, but they embody different principles of design in the amplification mechanism.

AIR COMPARATORS. Air comparators are gaging devices that utilize the effect of minute dimensional changes on metered air. The air gage (Fig. 27-47) consists principally of an air plug with small orifices, a gage to register the rate of the escaping air, and pressure regulators.

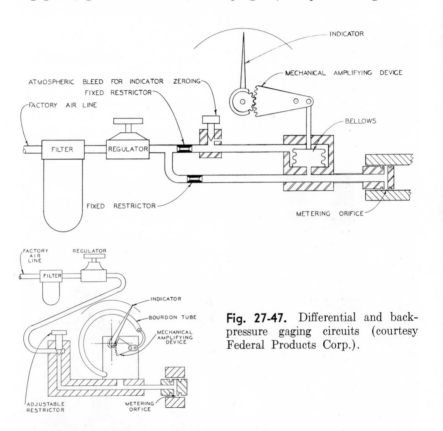

**Fig. 27-47.** Differential and back-pressure gaging circuits (courtesy Federal Products Corp.).

The gaging plug is first placed in a master ring gage, at which time the pointer is set to zero on the dial. The difference in size of the workpiece and the master will then show up as an amplified reading on the dial indicating the clearance between the plug and the work. The air gage is useful in showing out-of-round, taper, irregularity, and concentricity of a bored hole (Fig. 27-48). Magnifications ranging from 1,250 to 1 and 20,000 to 1 may be obtained, with a full-scale

**Fig. 27-48.** The air gage can be used to indicate various conditions of the hole. (*a*) Taper, (*b*) concentricity, (*c*) out of round, (*d*) waviness (courtesy The Sheffield Corp.).

(*a*)

(*b*)

(*c*)

(*d*)

range of 0.006 to 0.0003 in., respectively. Measurement is in 0.0001- and 0.000005-in. increments. Air-gaging principles are also used on snap gages, depth gages, and in multiple-diameter checking.

OPTICAL COMPARATORS. With the aid of lenses and mirrors, an enlarged "picture image" of an object may be projected on a screen and measured, as shown both schematically and pictorially in Fig. 27-49.

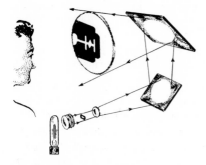

**Fig. 27-49.** The principle of the optical comparator is shown schematically, and as ordinarily used to check contours (courtesy Jones and Lamson Machine Co.).

A master chart of the magnified image, usually containing tolerance limits, is superimposed over the image on the viewing screen. By visually comparing the chart lines, an operator can quickly determine if the part meets prescribed tolerance standards. Direct measurements may also be made with accuracy in the order of 0.0001 in. The optical comparator is particularly useful in checking contours and a number of dimensions at one time. A tracing attachment makes it possible to check optically hidden surfaces, as shown in Fig. 27-50.

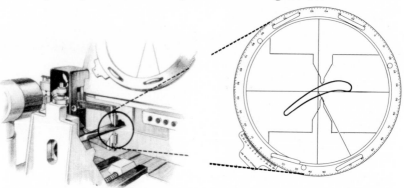

Inspecting optically-hidden surfaces which cannot be projected or reflected (such as the contours of dies, molds, airfoils, etc.) can be done with the Universal Tracing Attachment.

Adjustable carbide styli are fastened to tracing arms which are mounted on a coordinate slide. The styli of one arm are in contact with the object surface, the others lie in the focal plane of the comparator. The movement of the tracing styli over the object surface is duplicated by the projected styli. The magnified shadow of the projected styli appears on the viewing screen, where its path of travel can be compared to a master outline chart.

**Fig. 27-50.**   Optically hidden surfaces can be inspected by means of a tracing stylus. The magnified shadow appears as shown on the viewing screen (courtesy Jones and Lamson Machine Co.).

*The toolmaker's microscope.*   The toolmaker's microscope (Fig. 27-51) may be thought of as both a direct and a comparative measuring instrument. It is principally a microscope that is equipped with a protractor head and a stage or table that can be moved in increments of 0.0001 in., either longitudinally or laterally. A part to be checked may be mounted in a fixture on the table and viewed in magnifications of from 10X to 100X. Typical applications are also shown in Fig. 27-51.

### Automatic Gaging

Automatic gaging provides a means of checking each part, as it is being made or immediately afterward. Automatic gaging has

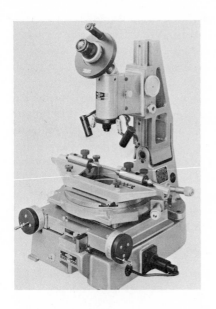

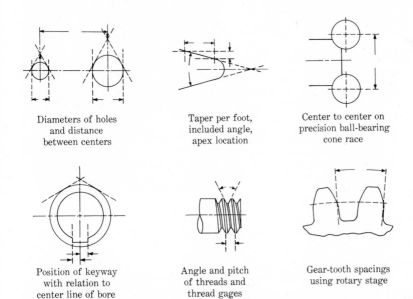

Diameters of holes
and distance
between centers

Taper per foot,
included angle,
apex location

Center to center on
precision ball-bearing
cone race

Position of keyway
with relation to
center line of bore

Angle and pitch
of threads and
thread gages

Gear-tooth spacings
using rotary stage

**Fig. 27-51.** A toolmaker's microscope and typical applications for measurement (courtesy The Gaertner Scientific Corporation).

come into being through a series of progressive steps aimed at reducing inspection costs, as well as tying the inspection process more closely to the operator and machine. It is estimated that, since World War II, 85 percent of measurement has changed from mechanical to air and electrical-electronic gaging.

The first step gave the operator some of the standard inspection equipment, such as mechanical comparators. With this equipment near his machine, he could check quickly and accurately the parts produced.

A second step was to place the gage directly on the machine (Fig. 27-52), which was termed *in-process* control. By this method, the size of the part is shown continuously as the metal is being removed. The cutting tool is directed automatically to retract when the part is finished to size. The control circuit may be made to adjust the tool automatically when the size is toward either limit of tolerance.

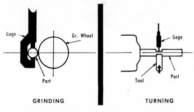

GRINDING        TURNING

"In-process" control or gaging during machining provides the machine or cutting tool with signals to:

- **Automatically stop or change the tooling from a roughing to a finishing cut.**
- **Automatically retract the cutting tool when the part is to finished size.**
- **Automatically indicate and adjust the tool when the size trend is toward either limit of tolerance.**
- **Automatically stop the machine after the tools become worn and parts no longer can be machined within limits.**

"In-process" control prevents faulty parts from being made by initiating signals for tool correction or replacement before part size is out of control.

**Fig. 27-52.** The gage is placed right on the machine for continuous measurement, or *in-process* control (courtesy The Sheffield Corp.).

A third step for closer product control made use of charts to plot the results of the operator's inspection. By watching the process, with respect to control limits, the operator could follow the trend toward the upper or lower tolerance limit. Before limits were exceeded, the necessary machine adjustments could be made and scrap parts avoided.

**Postprocess Control.** A fourth step was postprocess control. In this method, the parts move out of the chucking or holding device into the gaging station to be inspected before being transferred to the next operation. The postprocess inspection makes use of a *feedback* control that can automatically warn the operator or adjust the tool when the part size is approaching the extreme limits of control (Fig. 27-53). Feedback means that the information from the gage is given to the machine control center, which, in turn, can bring about the necessary tool adjustments.

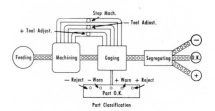

In "Post-process" Control, signals are initiated to:

- Automatically warn and/or adjust the tool when part size is approaching the extreme limits of control.
- Automatically stop the machine in event of tool failure.
- Automatically stop the machine if a specified number of consecutive parts is beyond tolerance.
- Automatically actuate segregating mechanism so that faulty parts are rejected before reaching the next operation.

With "Post-process" control or gaging, the part is machined, moved out of the chucking or holding device (leaving the machining station open for another part) and into the gaging station where it is inspected before being transferred to the next operation.

A major advantage of "Post-process" Control over "In-process" Control is that the parts are gaged in a free state—without influence from chuck or machine.

"Post-process" Control means on-the-spot inspection and rejection of faulty parts.

With this type of control, the gaging station is generally located adjacent to the machining operation. Or, it may be remotely located and the parts from several machines channeled to it in sequence, so that the machine that produced the faulty part is indicated and shut down after a specified number of consecutive parts has been rejected.

**Fig. 27-53.** Postprocess gaging. Parts have passed from the immediate vicinity of the machine (courtesy The Sheffield Corp.).

An example of how automatic postprocess gaging works will serve to illustrate this method. The part being made by the machine is a bushing (Fig. 27-54), which is to be checked for length, outside diameter, taper, inside diameter, and out-of-roundness.

The parts are received directly from the machine equipped with automatic controls. The gaging equipment is timed at a practical rate for the machine's capacity. Parts pass from the machine on an endless

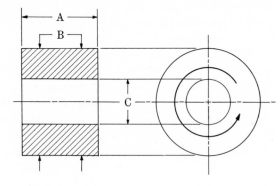

**Fig. 27-54.** Bushing, showing dimensions to be checked by automatic gaging (courtesy The Sheffield Corp.).

belt, as shown in Fig. 27-55. At the gaging station, a part enters a specially prepared tooling to hold it while it is being checked. In this case, air gages are used to check all the parameters mentioned (shown in the inset view of figure 27-55).

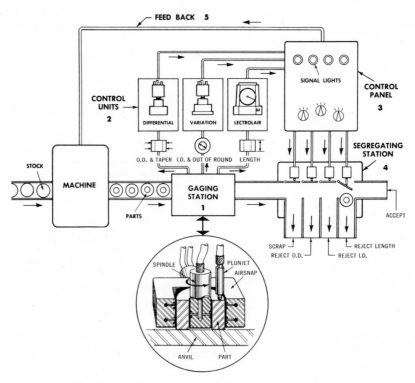

**Fig. 27-55.** Components of an automatic gaging system (courtesy The Sheffield Corp.).

Air lines from each of the tooling elements are connected to respective control units which sense size by the escape of air from the tooling jets. The pneumatic measurements are transferred into electrical signals for the control panel. Pressure changes as small as 0.05 psi can initiate the operation of size-indication lights, set off relay feedback signals to the machining operations, and energize the part-segregation elements. The segregating mechanisms eject the parts into their respective classification chutes.

Automatic postprocess gaging stations are generally located adjacent to the machining operation, but they may be placed remotely so that parts from several machines can be channeled into them. If one of the machines produces faulty parts, it will automatically be shut down after a specified number of parts have been rejected. One bad piece can be caused by some minor trouble, such as chip interference, which will correct itself in the next cycle. It is unlikely that this condition would repeat itself a second time in succession, therefore, needless machine shutdown is avoided.

A pedestal-mounted unit (Fig. 27-56) is an example of postprocess control used to check parts immediately after a forming operation. This unit can be placed at any point near a machine tool and, from there, automatically change machine feeds and speeds to prevent the continued production of bad parts. This type of gage also segregates parts into various size classifications and rejects those that are out of tolerance before they can be passed to the next operation.

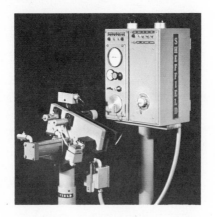

**Fig. 27-56.** A portable pedestal-mounted package control unit used for postprocess machine control (courtesy The Sheffield Corp.).

Other automatic postprocess inspection systems have been worked out to check several parameters at one time. The automatic gear-gaging equipment shown in Fig. 27-57 is used to check the outside diameter, eccentricity, helix angle, full tooth, and tooth thickness. Gear noise may also be checked electronically as the manufactured gear is made to run with a master gear. Sound-discriminating devices reject the noisy gears.

In the automatic gear-checking equipment shown, the manufactured gear passes between two master gears. One of the gears is motor-driven and rotates, while the other one does not. The size is checked by noting the distance that the nonrotating gear moves. The helix angle is checked by measuring how much the nonrotating gear is made to pivot. Solenoid-operated trapdoors are made to open and close according to the movement of the nonrotating gear.

Rejects are further sorted as to type and separated as to their salvageability and nonsalvageability.

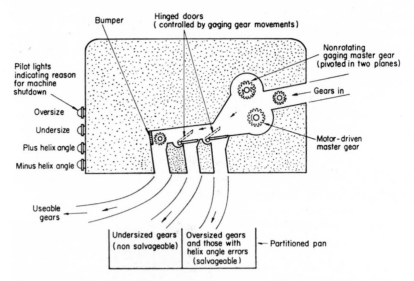

**Fig. 27-57.** Schematic drawing showing automatic gear-checking arrangement. Both size and helix angle of the gear are checked (courtesy *The Tool and Manufacturing Engineer*).

**Automatic Electronic Gaging.** Electronic gages make use of displacement transducers for automatically checking parts. The most commonly used types are the differential transformers and the variable capacitors. In the variable-capacitor type, any movement of the gage tip is transformed into a usable signal for deflecting the pointer of a meter which shows a visual interpretation of the size reading. The same signal may also be used to operate electronic limit switches. Thus, specific electrical signals initiated by the gaging tips can be used to operate limit switches through the gaging unit to sort parts into undersize, acceptable, and oversize categories. This is done by setting one limit switch to energize a relay at the low-tolerance limit and another at the high-tolerance limit. A part that does not cause either switch to operate is undersize. If only one switch is actuated, the part is within tolerance range. If both switches are actuated, the part would be oversize.

Other elements in the decision-making portion of electronic inspection systems are computers. The sum-type computer is used for adding the output signals for two gage circuits and the difference computer is used for subtracting the output signals of two gage circuits.

The computer elements may be combined in a variety of ways to determine almost any measurable dimension, and even some physical properties. For example, the overall length of one cross member of a universal joint cross (Fig. 27-58) and the length of each of its segments relative to the centerline can be determined by the use of two gage circuits and a sum computer. A gage unit is used to measure the length of each of the two segments, and a sum computer adds these values to obtain the overall length.

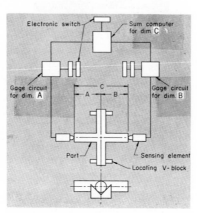

**Fig. 27-58.** Automatic inspection of three critical dimensions on a universal joint cross. The gage units measure lengths *A* and *B* and the sum computer adds these values to obtain the total length.

Physical properties such as hardness of metal parts, which are measured by the indentation of a penetrator under a specified load, may be interpreted electronically. By means of a sensing element to measure the travel of the penetrator, a gage circuit, two electronic switches, and appropriate sorting mechanism, parts may be automatically segregated into categories of too soft, acceptable, and too hard.

Electronic gaging systems are used on automatic-production machines for accurately checking and sorting parts having dimensional tolerances as small as 0.000020 in.

A distinct advantage of electronic gaging is the speed at which it can operate. Examples of sorting rates are: diameter inspection of bearing rollers, 15,000 parts per hr; hardness inspection, 4,000 parts per hr; weighing, 6,000 parts per hr.

### Other Automatic-Gaging Functions.

SALVAGE CORRECTIONS. Automatic-gaging units are used not only to separate parts into their various categories but also to salvage parts that have been rejected. The schematic diagram (Fig. 27-59) shows how distorted connecting rods are checked for parallelism between the crank and pin bores. Two air spindles determine the amount and direction of the "out-of-parallelism" through a differential head. The resulting signal actuates a ram that exerts predetermined increments of force on the part. Other heads may be brought in for further corrective action if required.

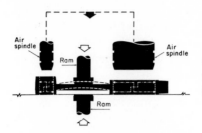

**Fig. 27-59.** Automatic salvaging operation of distorted connecting rods (courtesy *The Tool and Manufacturing Engineer*).

SELECTIVE FITTING.    Although all the parts made may be of such tolerance as to make them interchangeable, selective assembly adds quality to the product. To illustrate, if a pulley of maximum allowable diameter were to be assembled with a shaft representing the minimum allowable diameter, the fit would be loose. The opposite condition would give a tight fit. Selective assembly would narrow this margin. In some assemblies the tolerance limit can mean the difference between a long or short life.

The automatic gage shown in Fig. 27-60 checks glass medical syringes. The glass plungers are gaged and classified into seven size ranges at the rate of 3,600 per hr. A companion unit is utilized to find matching glass cylinders for selective assembly.

**Fig. 27-60.** This gaging machine automatically classifies glass plungers in seven sizes. They can then be given to an assembly unit for close-tolerance fitting (courtesy The Sheffield Corp.).

**Future Automatic Gaging.**    Pneumatic-electronic gaging systems will continue to be made in the decision-making field. These will accurately control high-speed production lines, or they may be used to control entire plants through a centralized system.

**Measurement Comparison.**    The chart shown in Fig. 27-61 will serve to summarize and compare the measuring characteristics of some of the tools and gages presented in this chapter.

## Gage Comparison

| Instrument | Type | Reliability (Degree of Accuracy[1]) | | | | |
|---|---|---|---|---|---|---|
| | | Discrim-ination | Repeat-ability[2] | Observa-tional error[3] | Measuring Range[4] | Practical Tolerance |
| *Scales* | | | | | | |
| to 12 in. | direct reading | 1/64 | 1/64 | 1/64 | 1/64–12 | ±1/32 |
| over 12 in. | " " | 1/64 | 1/32 | 1/64 | 1/64–50 | ±1/16 |
| *Vernier Gages* | | | | | | |
| to 12 in. | direct reading | .025 | .002 | ±.001 | .001–12 | ±.003 |
| 12 to 24 in. | " " | .025 | .003 | ±.001 | .001–24 | ±.005 |
| *Micrometers*, plain | | | | | | |
| to 6 in. | direct reading | .001 | .001 | .0005 | .001–1.000 | ±.002 |
| 6 to 12 in. | " " | .001 | .002 | .0005 | .001–1.000 | ±.003 |
| over 12 in. | " " | .001 | .003 max. | .0005 | .001–1.000 | ±.005 |
| *Micrometers* with vernier and ratchet | | | | | | |
| 1 in. | direct reading | .0001 | .0003 | .0001 | .0001–1.0000 | ±.0005 |
| 1 to 6 in. | " " | .0001 | .001 | .0001 | .0001–1.0000 | ±.001 |
| *Dial Indicators* | | | | | | |
| thousandths | transfer | .001 | ±.0004 | .0003 | ±.010 | ±.003 |
| tenths | " | .0001 | ±.00004 | .00003 | ±.001 | ±.0003 |
| half-tenths | " | .00005 | ±.00002 | .00002 | ±.0005 | ±.0004 |
| *Electronic Compara-tors (Trans-Chek)* | | | | | | |
| .001 scale | transfer | .001 | set-up scale | .00025 | ±.030 | set-up etc. |
| .0005 scale | " | .0005 | .00005 | .00013 | ±.016 | ±.001 |
| .0001 scale | " | .0001 | .00001 | .000025 | ±.0024 | ±.0005 |
| .00005 scale | " | .00005 | limited by | .000013 | ±.0016 | ±.0001 |
| .00001 scale | " | .00001 | other factors | .000003 | ±.00024 | ±.00005 |
| *Optical Comparators 50X* | | | | | | |
| screen (linear measure) | direct reading | .001 | .001 | .0005 | entire screen | ±.003 |
| protractor ring (angle meas.) | " " | 1° | 7' | 1' | 360° | ±.5' |
| micrometer stage (linear meas.) | " " | .0001 | .0005 | .0005 | .0001–1.0000 | ±.001 |
| *Gage Blocks,* quarter-tenth series | | | | | | |
| inspection blocks (.000006) | end standards | .000025 | .00002/block | minimum | .010–16.6 | |
| master blocks (.000004) | " " | .000025 | .00002/block | minimum | .010–20.0 | |

[1] The best combination of these factors is the standard of accuracy with which specific examples may be evaluated.
[2] Repeatability is stated bilaterally for instruments that can be zero set and have balanced scales.
[3] Observational error, one component of repeatability, is isolated for separate control.
[4] The range shown is the range within which the other data apply. Generally longer dimensions will have cumulative linearity errors that exceed the discrimination. Overtravel is not included.

**Fig. 27-61.** The purpose of the chart is to show characteristics of basic gaging equipment, not to show definitive data. All dimensions are given in inches (courtesy DoAll Company).

## QUESTIONS

1. What is used to measure gage blocks? What is the accuracy of the measurement?

2. What is the difference between direct and indirect measuring instruments?

3. What is the principle of the micrometer?

4. What advantage is offered by the indicating micrometer?

5. Why is a special anvil micrometer needed to measure the wall thickness of tubing?

6. What advantage does a vernier caliper have over a micrometer? What advantage does the micrometer have over the vernier caliper?

7. Name some instruments that can be used to check both large and small inside diameters.

8. Explain how a dial indicator can be used in centering stock in a lathe chuck.

9. Compare the accuracy of the bevel protractor and the vernier bevel protractor.

10. What instrument could be used to check the roundness of a cylinder wall?

11. Explain the difference between roughness and waviness.

12. What instrument is commonly used to check surface roughness?

13. Name two advantages of optical methods of checking surface roughness.

14. What are some applications of optical tooling?

15. What is the difference between tolerance and allowance?

16. Name the three main types of fits?

17. What standard type of gage can be used to check outside diameters?

18. How do comparator-type gages differ from attribute gages?

19. What type of gage is useful in checking several dimensions at one time?

20. Name some parts you are familiar with that can be accurately checked on the toolmaker's microscope?

21. Explain the principle of automatic post-process gaging.

22. What principles are utilized in building electronic gaging?

23. Give some examples of speed that can be attained in electronic gaging systems.

24. What are some auxiliary tasks performed by automatic gaging systems?

## PROBLEMS

1. In making gage block combinations the right hand numbers are eliminated first, working progressively to the left. Assume you have the following set of blocks:

   9 blocks   0.1001 in. to 0.1009 in.
   49 blocks   0.101  in. to 0.149  in.
   19 blocks   0.500  in. to 0.950  in.
   4 blocks   1.000  in. to 4.000  in.

   Choose the minimum number of blocks that will make the following dimensions: 2.5489, 1.8541, 3.2737, 2.1875.

2. If a micrometer is received in the closed position and opened 3½ revolutions what would the reading be? What would the vernier reading be?

3. A 10-in. sine-bar fixture is used to check a bevel gear whose face angle should be 37 deg 5 min. What should the combination of gage blocks be that make up the opposite side? Use the blocks as listed in Prob. 1.

4. A shaft is to be machined for a nominal 1-in.-diameter hole. The maximum and minimum clearances are specified as 0.005 in. and 0.003 in., respectively. Set up tolerances for the hole and shaft. What is the allowance?

5. What would be the size and the tolerance prescribed for a snap gage used to check the shaft of Prob. 4?

## REFERENCES

Boppel, H., "Present Metrology Spearheads Future Automation Growth," *The Tool and Manufacturing Engineer*, March, 1958.

Gates, T. S., "Gear Gaging Goes Automatic," *The Tool and Manufacturing Engineer*, May, 1956.

Houck, D. R., "Inspection and Decision by Electronics," *The Tool and Manufacturing Engineer*, November, 1959.

Michelon, L. C., *Industrial Inspection Methods*, Harper & Row, Publishers, New York, 1950.

Parsons, S. A. J., *Metrology and Gauging*, Macdonald & Evans, Ltd., London, 1957.

"Surface Finish Measurements on Non-Ferrous Materials," *American Machinist/-Metalworking Manufacturing*, Special Report No. 476, August, 1959.

Witske, F. W., "Putting Electronic Gages to Work," *The Tool and Manufacturing Engineer*, May, 1960.

# 28

# INSPECTION AND QUALITY CONTROL

T HE MANUFACTURER must watch each step of the production process from the time the raw material enters the plant until the final finishing operations and assembly. It is false economy to let any faulty material or poor workmanship "get by." Inspection becomes increasingly more difficult and expensive as the products progress toward completion. A satisfactory means of inspection and quality control must be carefully planned for each stage of production.

The terms *inspection* and *quality control* may, at first, seem somewhat synonymous. They are, however, quite different in application. Inspection is concerned with *how well* the physical specifications for a product are being met. Quality control is not concerned with physical aspects, as such, but rather with the *amount* of inspection that will be necessary to produce a good product.

### INSPECTION

Inspection has two broad and equally important tasks. One of these is to detect errors in workmanship and defects in materials so that the item will meet specifications; the other is to help minimize future errors. It is the latter which occasionally leads the inspection function to go beyond workmanship and materials into design specifications. For example, inspection may reveal tolerances that are impractical or materials that are inferior, etc.

774

## Inspection Methods

In repetitive manufacture there are several points at which inspection may take place. These are process inspection, including first-piece inspection, sampling inspection, and batch sampling; and final inspection.

**Process Inspection.** Inspection of the parts as they are being made is known as process inspection. It is also referred to as *line, floor, patrol,* or *roving* inspection. The purposes of process inspection are to prevent scrap and rework, reduce operating losses, save fitting repairs at assembly, detect hidden defects, and assure a higher quality of the finished product. Process inspection may be performed at the machine, on the manufacturing floor, or in the assembly line. The inspector not only checks the finished parts but watches the manner in which they are produced to detect possible causes of defects.

FIRST-PIECE INSPECTION. Before an inspector can check an item that has been produced, he must have certain specifications and standards for reference. The specifications are usually obtained from the part print. Not all the dimensions listed on the print are checked. Except for the first piece, critical dimensions are selected and are used thereafter as the basis of inspection.

Specifications may be abbreviated on the print by a reference to a standard. An example of a standard reference for a thread may be ¾-16 NC.-3. The inspector knows that this refers to the American National Coarse Thread 16 pitch series, Class 3 fit, as found in the National Bureau of Standards *Screw Thread Handbook*. The size in this standard is specified as 0.7500 maximum diameter, 0.7410 minimum diameter, tolerance 0.0090. Many other standards are established by engineering societies and by plant usage. These standards are necessary so that the inspector can be sure that items conform to specifications; they also prevent much duplication of effort.

First-piece inspection refers to the first good part that is turned out after a new setup has been made. The inspector may be called for a first-piece check after a new tool has been installed, after a new shift has started, or at any time when there is a change of operator.

SAMPLING INSPECTION. A roving inspector is called by the setup man when he has finished the first production part. After that, the inspector may return at regular set intervals to check a sample number of parts. The sample is taken to show what the machine is doing. This method is useful not only to show what is being produced at that time, but also to predict any trouble in the near future.

Since so much depends on the inspector's measuring tools, they too must be checked at set intervals or whenever there is any doubt as to their accuracy. Gage departments or laboratories are established in the plant to collect and check regularly the various measuring instruments and tools. After calibration and repair, they are returned to the job.

BATCH SAMPLING. Batch sampling generally concerns parts that are removed from the manufacturing floor and sampled according to statistical methods (to be discussed later in this chapter).

### Final Inspection.

Inspection of parts and assemblies just before they are prepared for packaging is called final inspection. It is vitally important to the reputation and goodwill accorded to the producer. With many products, the inspection will be visual—a check for flaws, defects, and missing or damaged parts. Products such as engines and motors may be given a brief operational test. Some products, such as ammunition, require destructive tests. Destructive testing or inspection points up the need for the proper use of sampling plans as developed in statistical quality control.

### Inspection Requirements

The inspection department must have a broad knowledge of the products being manufactured and of their use. The principal functions of the inspection department are to be familiar with the product design and specifications; to know the relationship of each component part of an assembly and how it functions in respect to the completed assembly; to set up a sequence of inspection operations, designating the type and the point in the manufacturing process at which each is to take place; and to determine the equipment needed for inspection.

### Product Design.

It is advantageous for the inspection department to learn as much about the product as possible. Advanced planning can be done by checking both the prints and the product in the early stages of manufacture.

### Relationship of Components to Function of the Product.

It is necessary to understand the relationship of each component to the proper functioning of the completed assembly. The performance of the assembled end product will be governed by the type and amount of inspection carried out on the various components.

### Inspection Sequence.

The manufacturing process is analyzed to establish the best sequence of inspection operations. It must be determined whether one of the in-process types of inspection can be used, or whether the product should be checked in the final assembly.

**Equipment Needed.**　The type and amount of equipment needed will depend on the manufacturing process, the production schedule, the amount of labor involved, the cost of the equipment, and whether the inspection tests made of finished items will be destructive or nondestructive.

Destructive tests were discussed in connection with welding. Equipment used for inspecting machined parts was also described in the preceding chapter; therefore, to complete the picture, nondestructive testing is presented here.

### Principles of Nondestructive Testing

Nondestructive testing usually refers to an evaluation of quality characteristics and reliability that are beyond the scope of the visual inspection. The characteristics inspected are those that affect product performance and safety. Therefore, to avoid failure of the finished product, certain standards must be set for each type of test. These standards will be discussed later.

Nondestructive tests are those that do not impair the function of the part or the material. They are used to reveal imperfections or faults in the material or in the fabrication of the product. Imperfections are classified, according to origin, as: *inherent*, resulting from melting and solidification of the materials; *processing*, resulting from fabrication of the finished product, as in forging, drawing, welding, grinding, heat treatment, rolling, and plating; or *service*, cracks resulting from use, the most common being fatigue cracks.

The methods usually employed to reveal these imperfections include radiography (X rays and gamma rays), sonic and ultrasonic imperfection, magnetic tests (magnetic particles and eddy currents), penetrant inspection (dye and fluorescent penetrants), and leak tests (oil and kerosine, soap bubbles, freon, halide, mass spectrometer).

**Radiography.**　Radiography is basically a method of taking pictures. Instead of using visible light rays, the radiographer uses invisible short-wavelength rays developed by X-ray machines, radioactive isotopes (gamma rays), and variations of these methods. These rays penetrate solid materials—metals, glass, wood, plastic, leather, and ceramics—and reveal their defects on a film or screen. Flaws show up on films as dark areas against a lighter background (Fig. 28-1).

Four main types of film, based on grain size and speed, are used in radiographic recording. Fine grain offers high quality with excellent

RADIOGRAPHIC EXAMINATION

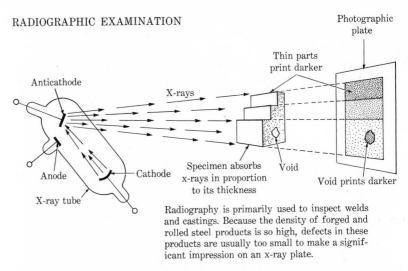

Radiography is primarily used to inspect welds and castings. Because the density of forged and rolled steel products is so high, defects in these products are usually too small to make a significant impression on an x-ray plate.

**Fig. 28-1.** Principles of industrial radiographic examination (courtesy of *Steelways,* published by American Iron and Steel Institute).

contrast. High-speed films are used for the examination of steel, brass, etc., with machines of limited kilovoltage.

X-RAY MACHINES. The X-ray machine is used mainly to inspect the interior soundness of various materials. On welds, it is used to detect gas porosity, slag inclusions, incomplete penetrations, cracks, and burn-through. It is used, to a lesser extent, on castings, forgings, and cold-formed parts.

The unit consists basically of a high-voltage transformer, an X-ray tube, and controls. These machines are classified according to their maximum voltage (designated as kvp or kilovolt peak) which may range from 50 kvp (50,000 volts) to 15 to 24 mev (15 to 24 million electron volts). They will handle up to 20 in. of steel, or its equivalent.

Selection of the proper machine size will depend on the thickness and density of the material, its absorption characteristics, the time available for inspection, and the location of the parts to be inspected.

A 50-kvp unit can be used on very thin sections. A 150-kvp unit can be used on 5-in. aluminum or its equivalent in light alloys, and on 1-in. steel or its equivalent. A lead-foil intensifying screen is sometimes used with a fluorescent (calcium tungstate) intensifying screen. With this setup the strength of a 150-kvp unit is stepped up enough to check steel 1½ in. thick. Other sizes include 250, 400, 1,000, and 2,000 kvp and 15 to 24 mev, the largest being capable of penetrating 16-in.-thick steel with a lead-foil screen, and 20 in. with a fluorescent screen.

The size and weight of these machines increase rapidly as the voltage increases. A 120-kvp X-ray unit and accessories weighs around 75 lb with carrying case, and costs about $2,500. A 120-kvp stationary unit will cost between $12,000 and $14,000. A large 2,000,000-volt X-ray machine is shown in Fig. 28-2.

**Fig. 28-2.** A 2,000,000-volt X-ray machine used in penetrating a steel casting 8 in. thick (courtesy Lebanon Steel Foundry).

GAMMA RADIOGRAPHY. Gamma rays are used for the same industrial purposes as X rays, but there are two main advantages—portability and low cost. Gamma-ray machines are more portable because of their smaller size, and they do not require an outside source of power, or water or oil cooling. Thus they are available for smaller and more complex jobs. They can also cover a wider range of metal thickness with the same radiograph.

This does not mean that gamma rays are preferable to X rays for every application. X rays are generally better for the thinner materials. Also, the radiation source can be turned off when not in use. Trained technicians are needed to operate either type of equipment.

Up until 1942 the only source of gamma rays was radium, however, with the advent of nuclear fission, the door was opened to several types of man-made isotopes. Gamma rays have various wavelengths, which may be compared to X rays generated at different voltages. The source of the radioactive rays is, however, constantly decaying. The period in which the energy of the isotope decays to half its original value is called its *half-life*. Radium, for example, has a half-life of 1,620 years.

There are five radioactive materials commonly used as gamma-ray sources. These are radium, cobalt 60, iridium 192, thulium 170, and cesium 137. Each of these materials has particular applications. Cobalt 60, for example, is equivalent to X rays of about 1.3 mev, with a half-life of 5.3 years. Its capacity range on steel is from 1 to 6 in. Its advantages include high specific gravity, low cost, and a wide range of applications.

RELATED X-RAY TECHNIQUES. Related X-ray techniques include fluoroscopy, X-ray television systems, and xeroradiography.

*Fluoroscopy.* Fluoroscopy differs from radiography in that the image is viewed directly on a fluorescent screen rather than on a film record (Fig. 28-3). This technique offers fast, low-cost, reasonably sensitive inspection. Because the part can be viewed from all directions, the overall quality level may be equal to that of radiography. The initial cost of the equipment may exceed the cost of a radiographic setup.

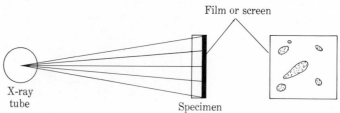

**Fig. 28-3.** Principles of industrial radiography and fluoroscopy.

*Televised X ray.* Televised X ray is a direct-viewing, remote, instantaneous system. Materials to be inspected are X-rayed and viewed simultaneously on a remote monitor screen. No film is used. Images can be viewed in normal light. The image size can vary from one half to three times the original object.

*Xeroradiography.* Xeroradiography is a rapid method for dry-processing X-ray images. It will frequently disclose discontinuities that cannot be seen on film. Images can be viewed in less than 1 min after exposure.

### Sonic and Ultrasonic Inspection.

SONIC INSPECTION. Sonic inspection consists of tapping the specimen with a hammer and listening to the sound waves through a stethoscope. The blow by the hammer sets up both natural and forced vibrations. Sounds will be similar in good sections, but a high-pitched, reedy sound will occur if a defect is present. The disadvantage of this method is that the defective area is not located exactly, and the findings depend largely on the operator's skill.

ULTRASONIC INSPECTION. Ultrasonic flaw-detection equipment makes it possible to locate very small checks, cracks, and voids too small to be seen with X rays. Variations of the technique permit inspection of sheets, forgings, shafts, and even bars up to 42 ft long.

Many new applications of ultrasonic inspection are being developed. The object here is only to present some of the basic operating principles. There are two principal inspection techniques: *reflection testing,* in which the echoes of the pulse are used to detect discontinuities, and *through-transmission testing,* in which two transducers are used to indicate the presence and extent of discontinuities.

*Reflection testing.* The ultrasonic inspection unit consists of a pulse generator or transducer which sends out high-frequency electrical pulses to a crystal. The crystal sends a pulse and receives an echo that is then amplified to show up either as a straight line or as a pip on the cathode-ray oscilloscope screen. A pip indicates a defect (Fig. 28-4).

ULTRASONIC EXAMINATION

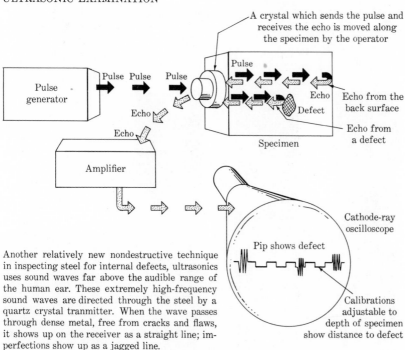

Another relatively new nondestructive technique in inspecting steel for internal defects, ultrasonics uses sound waves far above the audible range of the human ear. These extremely high-frequency sound waves are directed through the steel by a quartz crystal tranmitter. When the wave passes through dense metal, free from cracks and flaws, it shows up on the receiver as a straight line; imperfections show up as a jagged line.

**Fig. 28-4.** The ultrasonic inspection unit consists of a pulse generator or transducer, a transmitter, amplifier, and cathode-ray oscilloscope (courtesy *Steelways,* published by American Iron and Steel Institute).

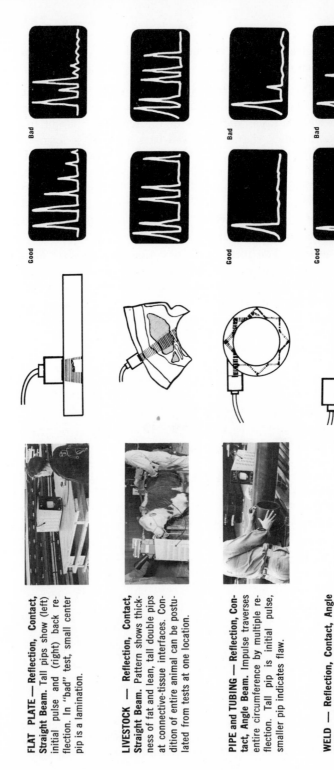

**FLAT PLATE — Reflection, Contact, Straight Beam.** Tall pips show (left) initial pulse and (right) back reflection. In "bad" test, small center pip is a lamination.

**LIVESTOCK — Reflection, Contact, Straight Beam.** Pattern shows thickness of fat and lean, tall double pips at connective-tissue interfaces. Condition of entire animal can be postulated from tests at one location.

**PIPE and TUBING — Reflection, Contact, Angle Beam.** Impulse traverses entire circumference by multiple reflection. Tall pip is initial pulse, smaller pip indicates flaw.

**WELD — Reflection, Contact, Angle Beam.** Two-dimensional scanning covers entire weld-bead.

**Fig. 28-5.** Ultrasonic inspection is applicable to discontinuities of all types, such as voids and cracks. It can indicate metallurgical variations such as flaking and density. It is even used on livestock to show thicknesses of fat and lean (courtesy Magnaflux Corp.).

Ultrasonic waves are not transmitted through air, so a suitable coupler must be used to couple the searching unit to the work. Oil, grease, glycerin, water, or other similar liquids are suitable for this purpose.

Ultrasonic inspection is used to examine many kinds of materials, from the raw stock to the fabricated assembly. Figure 28-5 shows a variety of applications, with good and bad screen indications.

As higher frequencies are approached, the problem of crystal coupling and wear becomes more severe. To overcome this, the part should be immersed in a liquid, usually water, and the searching unit suspended in the liquid over the part (Fig. 28-6).

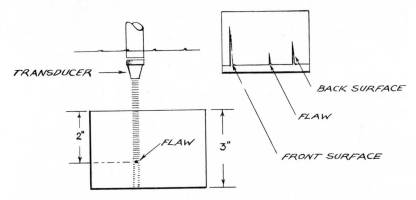

**Fig. 28-6.** The immersion crystal is focused on a test block and indication to be expected is shown on the screen (courtesy Branson Ultrasonic Corp.).

Ultrasonic inspection is set up for continuous automatic operation, as shown schematically in Fig. 28-7. Units of this type have been used to inspect tubing that has a continuous weld. The unit not only detects the flaw but also marks it. Poor welds, caused by improper adjustment, laminations, etc., are brought to the attention of the operator by a signaling horn. Immediate detection makes possible prompt adjustment, reducing scrap loss. Instantaneous marking assures 100 percent inspection even at speeds up to 100 fpm.

**Fig. 28-7.** A schematic view of continuous-type ultrasonic testing used on seam-welded pipe at rates up to 100 fpm.

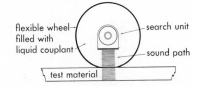

*Through-transmission testing.* In through-transmission testing, the transducers are arranged coaxially facing each other on opposite sides of the test piece. Pulses are received by the second transducer. A

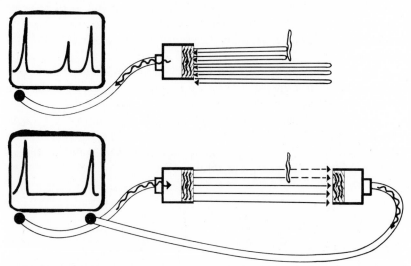

**Fig. 28-8.** Schematic diagrams to show both *reflected* (top diagram) and *through* ultrasonic-testing techniques (courtesy Branson Ultrasonic Corp.).

reduction in amplitude of the received signal indicates the presence and size on discontinuities, but not their location in depth (Fig. 28-8).

A portable ultrasonic thickness tester is shown in Fig. 28-9. It measures the thickness from one side by determining the resonant frequency of vibration in the thickness direction.

A transducer probe, vibrating at ultrasonic frequencies, is placed in contact with one side of the material to be tested. The sound waves travel through the material and are reflected back by the opposite surface. When the transmitted and reflected waves are in phase, "resonance conditions" are established. Since the velocity is a known constant, the fundamental frequency required to produce resonance is an ac-

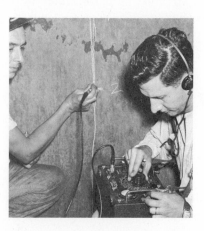

**Fig. 28-9.** An ultrasonic thickness tester used to inspect the extent of corrosion on a paper-pulp digester (courtesy Branson Ultrasonic Corp.).

curate and reliable measure of unknown thickness. The signal produced is heard on a headset, and on some models the thickness of the material is indicated directly in inches.

Reflections will occur at any discontinuity, and the resonance pattern will change when the Audigage is tuned for the thickness of a laminated section. Voids may also be detected in bonded material by the same method.

In summary, ultrasonics can be used on a variety of materials, with only negligible loss in great thicknesses. Angular cracks can be readily found. The initial equipment is considered low in cost, as is the cost of necessary supplies.

Work is in progress to develop scanning and recording techniques aimed at reducing reliance on the human element, and to provide permanent records where desired or needed.

## Magnetic Tests.

MAGNETIC-PARTICLE INSPECTION. Magnetic-particle inspection is used to find nonvisible cracks at or near the surface on ferrous materials. The method utilizes magnetized particles (usually iron powder), in *dry* or *wet suspension*, applied to a workpiece in which an intense magnetic field has been formed. Breaks or flaws in the magnetized part set up local magnetic fields. These local fields, and the flaws that cause them, can be revealed by the way in which the iron powder is attracted to them.

The parts can be magnetized by either direct or alternating current. The former finds subsurface defects and is commonly used for inspecting castings and welds. Alternating current is usually used to check finished machined parts.

*Wet-suspension method.* The wet-suspension method uses a paste or iron powder and oil or water. The part is dipped into this magnetic-particle paste to show tiny surface defects. Fluorescent paste is often used with this method. An ultraviolet light causes the defect to stand out brightly. Figure 28-10 shows a part as it appears before inspection, after treatment with a wet suspension, and, lastly, with a fluorescent paste.

*Dry-suspension method.* The dry method is more sensitive to subsurface defects. Magnetic powder is dusted or blown over the part to be inspected.

*Equipment.* Magnetic-particle inspection is done with either stationary or portable equipment. Stationary equipment is used on smaller parts for hand or automatic inspection. Portable equipment ranges from small hand-held magnetic yokes to large 6,000-amp heavy-duty power units. Some equipment is specially designed for automatic conveyorized production lines.

**Fig. 28-10.** A kingpin immediately after grinding, treated with a wet magnetic paste and a fluorescent paste, and brought out with an ultraviolet light. Excessive heat during grinding had caused dangerous cracks (courtesy Magnaflux Corp.).

Magnetic-particle inspection does not show cracks that are parallel to the magnetic field, so magnetism in two directions is needed to show all discontinuities.

EDDY-CURRENT TESTING. Eddy currents are used to detect cracks and porous or embrittled areas, and to locate welds and sudden changes in both ferrous and nonferrous metals.

Simply stated, eddy currents are composed of free electrons, made to drift through metal under the influence of an induced electromagnetic field. The minute eddy currents explore the part and give back information as to cracks, porosity, or any discontinuity in the metal. The eddy currents act as compressible fluids; thus, when they encounter a discontinuity, they detour around it and, as a result, are compressed, delayed, and weakened (Fig. 28-11 at *A*). This causes a relatively large electrical reaction in the coil, which can be amplified and reflected on a cathode-ray tube or by other means.

Some instruments use a hand detector pickup (Fig. 28-11 at *B*) to determine electrical conductivity in absolute units, with a readout on a meter scale. Since other properties, such as hardness, alloy proportions, thermal conductivity, etc., are related to electrical conductivity, these instruments have a wide variety of uses.

**Penetrant Inspection.** Penetrant inspection is usually used to examine nonporous materials for defects that are open to the surface.

Surface defects that can be located include all types of cracks (connected with welding, forging, grinding, shrinkage, and fatigue) porosity, seams, laps, cold shuts, and lack of bond between two metals.

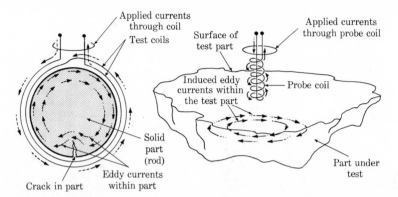

Applied currents through coil

Test coils

Surface of test part

Applied currents through probe coil

Induced eddy currents within the test part

Probe coil

Solid part (rod)

Crack in part

Eddy currents within part

Part under test

(a)  A part is passed through a test coil. The applied current in the coil induces eddy currents within the part. These are affected by a crack, or other change in the part.

(b) Electric currents in the probe coil induce eddy currents within the test part. These react back on the applied current, for "readout."

**Fig. 28-11.**  Two methods of using eddy currents to inspect a part for flaws or other characteristics (courtesy Magnaflux Corp.).

There are two kinds of penetrant inspection—*dye* and *fluorescent*. In both, the penetrant is applied by brushing, spraying, or dipping.

DYE PENETRANTS.  In dye-penetrant inspection, the penetrant is applied to a clean, dry surface and allowed to soak for awhile. The dye penetrates surface defects. Excess dye is wiped off, and a thin coating of developer chemical is applied. The developer acts like a blotter, drawing the dye to the surface. Contrast between the color of the developer (usually white) and the dye penetrant (usually red) outlines the surface flaws. The red area will indicate the extent of the crack or defect. It is very important that the part being inspected be thoroughly cleaned before the dye penetrant is applied; not *wiped* clean, but cleaned with the best method available, preferably one such as vapor degreasing. The dye-penetrant process is shown in Fig. 28-12.

Commercial dye-penetrant kits are made up in pressurized cans. This makes it a very portable inspection tool that can be used anywhere in the plant or field.

Both dye and developers have been made in water-wash formulas. This aids in removal and reduces cost in moderate- to high-volume inspection.

FLUORESCENT PENETRANTS.  In the fluorescent method the solution is applied just like the regular dye penetrant, but the surface is inspected under a black light. Cracks or flaws glow brightly under this light. A black light is one that is near the ultraviolet range in the spectrum.

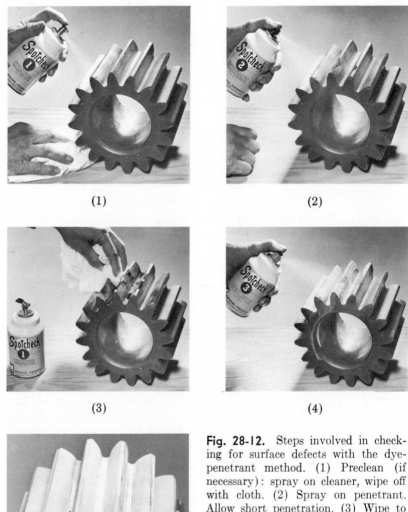

(1)

(2)

(3)

(4)

(5)

**Fig. 28-12.** Steps involved in checking for surface defects with the dye-penetrant method. (1) Preclean (if necessary): spray on cleaner, wipe off with cloth. (2) Spray on penetrant. Allow short penetration. (3) Wipe to remove penetrant from surface. Use cleaner if surface is very rough. (4) Spray on developer. (5) Inspect. Cracks will show as red lines in white developer area (courtesy Magnaflux Corporation).

The black-light source is normally a 100-watt mercury-vapor bulb of the sealed-reflector type, used with a suitable transformer. The transformer unit allows the black light lamp to be plugged into ordinary 110-volt 60 cycle per second circuits. The complete kit, with examples of its use on tools, castings, forgings, and maintenance, is shown in Fig. 28-13.

(a)

(b)

**Fig. 28-13.** (a) Fluorescent-penetrant inspection kit. (b) Crack in aircraft aluminum landing-gear cap. (c) Fatigue cracks in aluminum piston. In critical wrist-pin boss these would probably have caused failure (courtesy Magnaflux Corporation).

(c)

**Leak Tests.** A number of techniques are used for leak checking, depending on the degree to which the leaks are tolerated. All methods involve the passage of a "tracer" medium from one side of a pressurized leak to the other, and the subsequent detection of the medium on the latter side.

OIL AND KEROSINE. Oil and kerosine are often used to check leaks in cast iron. Inhibitors or fluorescent substances are placed in the oils to make any penetration show up brightly when examined with an ultraviolet light.

SOAP BUBBLES. Small vessels may be pressurized and submerged to detect leaks. Larger vessels can be coated with a mixture of glycerin and soap in the area to be tested. Air pressure from the inside will cause bubbles to form in the area of the leak. Air testing can be very hazardous and should not be attempted without careful safety precautions.

FREON. Extremely small leaks are checked with an inert gas, usually Freon 12. The areas to be checked are "sniffed" or probed with a sensitive sampling device. The presence of a leak is indicated on a meter or by an audible alarm. It is possible to measure leaks quantitatively by using set standards.

HALIDE. A variation of the preceding method is to have the areas "sniffed" with a halide torch. The presence of a leak shows up in the change of color in the torch flame.

MASS SPECTROMETER. The most sensitive leak-test detection method devised is by the use of the mass spectrometer. It measures the rate of tracer gas, usually helium, through leaks. This sensitive instrument is used to convert any helium gas coming through the leak into an electrical signal. The location and size of the leaks are determined on the basis of the signal received.

### Nondestructive Inspection Standards

In nondestructive testing, it is necessary to correlate the quality of the part with the results of the test. Where these correlations have not been worked out, evaluations are based on experience and judgment. The development of nondestructive inspection specifications does much to reduce the need for operator decisions.

A proper standard is one which sets the acceptable quality level at a point where the part serves its function as required. A supply of suitable inspection equipment is necessary for the development of such standards. It is also necessary to know how the part is produced, what materials are used in it, and what type of service it will be required to perform.

Some nondestructive testing is done by visual examination. This type of inspection, to be effective, presupposes a thorough knowledge of the manufacturing process and the service expected by the customer. Weld inspection, for example, should be done only by trained, qualified welders. The training will enable the inspector to know what to look for and what tests are necessary.

## QUALITY CONTROL

As stated previously, quality control is concerned with *how much* inspection is necessary to achieve the desired product standards agreed upon by engineering and management. By statistical means, quality control is able to set up sampling plans which will assure that the process quality is being controlled and, at the same time, that inspection costs are being kept at an economical level. The brief description given here is intended only to present an overview of some of the tools and methods available. For a more complete discussion of the subject, consult the references at the end of this chapter.

### The Normal Frequency-Distribution Curve

To understand why sampling plans are not a hit-or-miss proposition but, rather, a carefully worked out mathematical approach, one should know something about a normal frequency distribution. To illustrate, suppose that 50 parts were turned out on a lathe and measured with a micrometer. It is probable that most of the parts would fall close to the size the operator was trying to obtain. A few parts might be larger and a few smaller, as shown in Fig. 28-14.

The normal frequency-distribution curve may be divided into six zones that are mathematically equal in width. Each part is represented by the Greek letter sigma ($\sigma$). By referring to Fig. 28-15, we can see that plus or minus two sigma ($\pm 2\sigma$) from the center will include 95.5 percent of the parts. Likewise, $\pm 3\sigma$ will include 99.75 percent of the parts. The $3\sigma$ limit is usually referred to as the *natural tolerance* limit. The peak of the curve shows where the process tends to center itself. The shape and spread of the curve give useful information to the engineering department in helping them decide the limitations of a process.

These facts can be applied in establishing realistic quality concepts. When a designer asks for achievements beyond the capabilities of the available manufacturing equipment, three alternatives arise: The designer can revise his demands to a level at which the manufacturing equipment will satisfy them; the production process can be refined to satisfy the designer's demands; or more costly individual piece-part inspection can be undertaken.

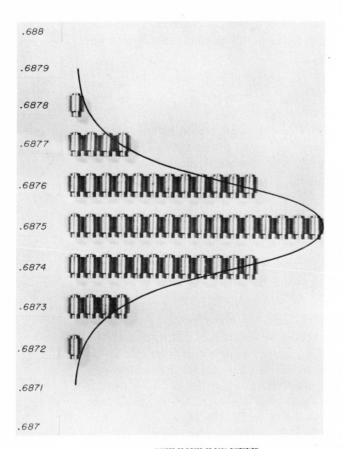

**Fig. 28-14.** Shafts turned out on a lathe, showing normal size variation (courtesy Federal Products Corp.).

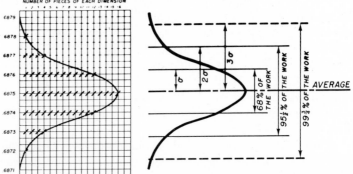

**Fig. 28-15.** The normal curve, showing six mathematical divisions. This breakdown applies to Fig. 28-14 (courtesy Federal Products Corp.).

A designer has to recommend certain limits; however, in meeting them, oftentimes only the second and third alternatives have been followed. The result is higher costs, either through additional capital purchases or through inspection procedures.

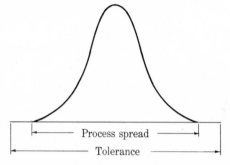

**Fig. 28-16.** The process is shown as being within tolerance, or design changes have been made to help the process stay within tolerance.

Many manufacturing processes will be found to follow the pattern of the normal curve. If, however, the original design requirements happen to lie outside the spread of the process, all of the products will be acceptable, and only accidental deviations need be inspected; if the process was not within tolerance but the designer revised his demands, the first alternative has been followed. Figure 28-16 illustrates these situations.

The second alternative—that of refining the process—is represented in Fig. 28-17.

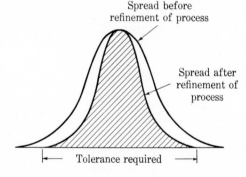

**Fig. 28-17.** The process has been refined to bring it within the acceptable tolerance zone.

The least desirable alternative, in which individual inspection is needed, is represented graphically in Fig. 28-18.

The above simplification assumed that, even though the spread was incorrect, at least the *mean* or average was correct. This is not necessarily true; in Fig. 28-19, for example, neither the spread nor the mean is satisfactory. This illustration can be applied to the previous ones to help one realize the complications that can exist.

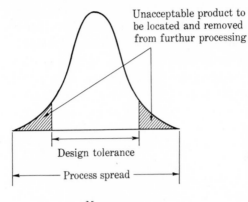

Unacceptable product to
be located and removed
from furthur processing

**Fig. 28-18.** Parts manufactured are falling outside the acceptable tolerance zone and therefore require a greater amount of inspection.

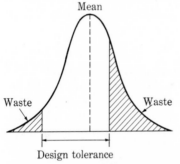

**Fig. 28-19.** The process spread is excessive, and the mean is to one side of the design tolerance.

Thus we see that design and production engineers need to keep the capabilities of their plant constantly in mind. The production engineer must also know the tolerance capabilities of equipment being purchased. If special equipment must be built, it would be advisable to have tolerance-capability specifications clearly defined.

### Methods of Quality Control

Quality control is concerned with establishing a certain quality level both for the incoming materials and for the manufactured product. Two broad aspects are involved: establishing a reasonable number of defective parts for a given quantity (acceptance sampling), and watching the manufacturing process and recording the results (control charts). Acceptance sampling may be further subdivided into the various plans that have been formulated, such as single sampling, double sampling, multiple sampling, and sequential sampling.

### Sampling Plans.

BATCH OR LOT SAMPLING. Batch or lot sampling usually refers to large quantities of parts that have left the machining area, have gone through the necessary cleaning, and have been brought to the inspection room. Sampling plans are based on the premise that a number of parts taken from a lot will be representative of this lot. Since 100 percent inspection of all parts is not practical, except on an automatic basis, a certain small percentage of defectives is allowable. This is referred to as the acceptable quality level (AQL). From past experience and trial runs, the AQL can be determined. For example, the AQL for small parts made on an automatic screw machine may be 1.2 to 2.2 percent defective. The average outgoing quality limit (AOQL) for the same lot will be from 1.5 to 2.5 percent defective. This means that the parts leaving the inspection station will average no more than a certain percentage of defects, either because all the lots met the sampling requirements or because any lots that did fail at sampling were reinspected and sorted before they were allowed beyond the inspection station.

A typical problem will serve to illustrate the principles used in various sampling plans. Table 28-1 is for a batch or inspection lot of 800 to 1,300 pieces with an AQL of 1.2 to 2.2. You will note that in the single-sampling plan a sample size of 55 is required, and that 3 defective parts are acceptable but 4 will cause the lot to be rejected. A rejected lot is not scrapped, it is screened; that is, each part of the sample is examined, and the defective parts are replaced. You will notice the data for double and sequential sampling in the same table.

### TABLE 28-1.

### Sampling Plans for Various Lot Sizes Ranging from 800 to 1,300

| Type of Sampling | Sample | Sample Size | Combined Samples Size | Acceptance Number | Rejection Number |
|---|---|---|---|---|---|
| Single | First | 55 | 55 | 3 | 4 |
| Double | First | 35 | 35 | 1 | 5 |
| | Second | 70 | 105 | 4 | 5 |
| Sequential | First | 14 | 14 | * | 2 |
| | Second | 14 | 28 | 0 | 3 |
| | Third | 14 | 42 | 1 | 4 |
| | Fourth | 14 | 56 | 3 | 5 |
| | Fifth | 14 | 70 | 3 | 5 |
| | Sixth | 14 | 84 | 3 | 5 |
| | Seventh | 14 | 98 | 4 | 5 |

* Acceptance not permitted until two samples have been inspected.

These plans operate in much the same way, the main difference being in the size of the first sample. In the double-sampling plan the first sample size is 35. The acceptance number is 1 and the rejection number is 5. If more than 1 but less than 5 defectives are found, we neither accept nor reject the lot. In this case a second sample of 70 must be taken, making the total number of parts checked 105. There is now no spread between the acceptance and the rejection numbers. If there are 4 or less defective, we accept the lot; if there are 5 or more, it is rejected and subjected to screening.

FACTORS AFFECTING THE CHOICE OF A SAMPLING PLAN. One ever-present consideration is cost. Sampling plans always add expense and man-hours for the user but nothing to the price received for the product. Incoming parts such as small machine screws are standard items that need little if any inspection. On the other hand, precision parts such as crankshafts will need a close check. Single-sampling plans are the easiest to use. Double- and sequential-sampling plans are more involved.

Single sampling makes use of a larger original sample. It has been shown that where a single sample would require 100 pieces to be inspected, double sampling will provide the same protection with 74 pieces, and sequential with 55.

Where parts are of rather homogeneous large lots and a relatively quick, inexpensive check on them is needed, sequential sampling will fill the bill. If the parts need rather close checking, as for the crankshafts mentioned, the larger single-sampling plan will be necessary.

**Control Charts.** While there are many kinds of control charts, they all provide a graphical representation of the process undergoing inspection. Commonly used control charts are p-charts which show the percent defective in a sample, c-charts that are used in plotting the number of defects in one piece, $\overline{X}$-charts used in plotting the variations in the averages of samples, and R-charts which show variations in the ranges of samples. The last two are usually used together and are referred to as $\overline{X}$- and R-charts, or average and range charts. Since these two are the most common, they will be discussed briefly.

Samples of a part being manufactured are taken at regular intervals. The size of the sample is usually four or five items. The average of the sample is plotted for the given time interval on the chart as shown in Fig. 28-20. Care must be exercised to get samples of the same size each time and to get a random sample. At the same time, the range (the largest dimension minus the smallest dimension) is plotted as shown in Fig. 28-20.

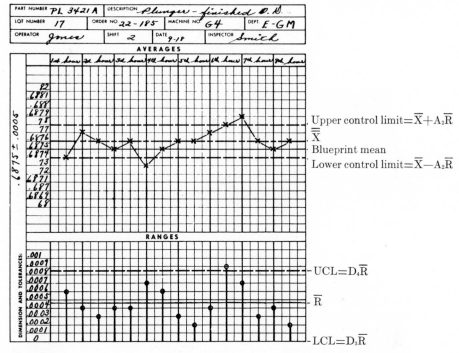

**Fig. 28-20.** An average and range chart with sample averages posted each half hour. The range of each sample is also shown (courtesy Federal Products Corp.).

After all the samples have been plotted, the grand average $\overline{\overline{X}}$ is computed and marked on the chart as a red dashed line. The ranges are averaged and the $\overline{R}$ line is drawn on the chart. The upper and lower control limits are obtained by multiplying the average range $\overline{R}$ by an $A_2$ constant based on the sample size, as shown in Table 28-2. If our sample size were 5 and the average range turned out to be 0.006 in., the upper control limit would be $0.006 \times 0.577 = 0.003462$. This figure is added to the grand average and becomes the upper control limit. The lower control limit is obtained in the same way, except that the resulting number is subtracted from the grand average.

The range-control limits are obtained by multiplying the average range $\overline{R}$ by the $D_4$ constant (found in Table 28-2) for the upper limit, and by the $D_3$ constant for the lower limit.

The blueprint mean is drawn on the chart as the solid zero line. Control limits can be established after a reasonable number of samples have been taken, say 20 to 25. Too few samples will not give a true picture, and too many will add to the cost.

**TABLE 28-2.**

**Control-Chart Constants for Small Samples\***

| Number of Observations in Sample, $n$ | Chart for Averages | | | | Chart for Ranges | | | |
|---|---|---|---|---|---|---|---|---|
| | Factors for Control Limits | | | Factor for Central Line | Factors for Control Limits | | | |
| | $A$ | $A_1$ | $A_2$ | $d_2$ | $D_1$ | $D_2$ | $D_3$ | $D_4$ |
| 2.............. | 2.121 | 3.759 | 1.880 | 1.128 | 0 | 3.686 | 0 | 3.268 |
| 3.............. | 1.732 | 2.394 | 1.023 | 1.693 | 0 | 4.358 | 0 | 2.574 |
| 4.............. | 1.500 | 1.880 | 0.729 | 2.059 | 0 | 4.698 | 0 | 2.282 |
| 5.............. | 1.342 | 1.596 | 0.577 | 2.326 | 0 | 4.918 | 0 | 2.114 |

\* Courtesy American Society for Testing Materials.

USING THE CHARTS. The information plotted on the control chart forms the basis for action not only by the inspector, operator, and foreman, but also by engineering and management. Inspectors can watch the chart and notice if the process is erratic and needs close attention, or they can shut down a machine before too much scrap occurs.

The engineering department can use the information to specify tolerance limits more favorably. This does not mean that engineering will set its specifications in accordance with the process-control chart. If a process constantly goes beyond tolerance limits, perhaps another method will be used for its manufacture, or perhaps a better machine can be substituted. On the other hand, parts may be made that are within the control limits but outside the tolerance limits. This may call for a reexamination of the specifications. A process that does not come near either tolerance limit may be speeded up.

**QUESTIONS**

1. What is the basic difference between quality control and inspection?
2. What are the two important functions of inspection?
3. Explain the difference between sampling inspection and batch sampling?
4. Explain the difference between radiography and X rays?
5. What is the principle of ultrasonic inspection?
6. Name some applications of ultrasonic testing?
7. Explain the principle of magnetic testing?

8. Compare the use of dry and wet-suspension methods.
9. Explain the principle of eddy-current flaw detection in metals.
10. What are the two main types of penetrant inspection?
11. Name some recommended methods for checking pressure vessels for leaks.
12. What is meant by a normal distribution?
13. Upon what premise are sampling plans built?
14. In what respect may a double sampling plan be better than a single?
15. What purpose do control charts serve?

## PROBLEMS

1. What would the rating of a cobolt-60 machine after 5.3 years of use?
2. After inspecting 750 manufactured parts it is found they fall into a normal distribution. How many parts will be within plus or minus three sigma?
3. How many parts would have to be inspected out of a lot of 1,000 pieces if a single-sampling plan were used?
4. How many parts would have to be inspected out of a lot of 1,000 pieces if a double-sampling plan were used? How many parts would have to be inspected if five defective parts were found?
5. If a sequential sampling plan were used, what would the sample size be? How many parts would be inspected if three samples had to be taken?
6. In constructing an $\overline{X}$- and R-chart the $\overline{\overline{X}}$ was computed to be 8.502 in. and $\overline{R}$ 0.008 in. What would the upper and lower control limits be if the sample size were 4? What would the upper limit be on the range chart?

## REFERENCES

Bowker, A. H., and G. J. Lieberman, *Engineering Statistics*, Prentice-Hall, Inc., Englewood Cliffs, N.J., 1959.

Burr, I. W., *Engineering Statistics and Quality Control*, McGraw-Hill Book Company, Inc., New York, 1953.

*Dimensional Quality Control Primer*, Federal Products Corporation, 11th Printing, Providence, 1959.

Duncan, A. J., *Quality Control and Industrial Statistics*, Richard D. Irwin, Inc., Homewood, Ill., 1959.

Grant, E. L., *Statistical Quality Control*, 2nd ed., McGraw-Hill Book Company, Inc., New York, 1952.

McDermott, G. W., "Applying Non-Destructive Test Standards to Improve Product Quality and Reliability," *General Motors Engineering Journal*, April, May, June, 1960.

"Nondestructive Testing of Welded Fabrications," *Industry and Welding*, Special Report, March, 1959.

Schrock, E. M., *Quality Control and Statistical Methods*, 2nd ed., Reinhold, New York, 1957.

# 29

# AUTOMATION AND NUMERICAL CONTROL

AUTOMATION IS A relatively new word, coined in 1935 by D. S. Harder, then vice president in charge of manufacturing for the Ford Motor Company. The word did not receive popular acceptance until 1947. Automation is a substitute word for "automatization," which means to make something operate automatically. This definition, when applied to manufacturing, refers not only to individual machines but also to the linking of automatic machines together until a continuous process emerges.

## AUTOMATION

Automatic machines and production lines are a reality, but the automatic factory does *not yet* exist. Process industries such as food preparation, oil refinement, and chemical extraction come nearer to fulfilling the dream of automation than does the metal-fabricating industry.

The limitations imposed on the metalworking industry are constant. No manufacturer can produce an item of any consequence without knowing that it may be obsolete tomorrow, through a competitor's ingenuity. Therefore, the metalworking industry has been content to take automation in smaller steps, employing individual-machine automation and multiple-machine automation. In the former, individual machines may be cam-, electric-, air-, hydraulic-, or tape-controlled.

Circular-indexing automation also is included in this category. Multiple-machine automation is described by the kinds of lines that are used to connect the machines.

### Individual-Machine Automation

**Cam-Operated Machines.** Some automatic screw machines, the multispindle automatic lathe, and gear-cutting machines are examples of individual-machine automation. In a true sense of the word, unless machines have automatic stock loading and unloading, they should be classified as semiautomatic. Magazine-type feeders are now used to supply lathes with bar stock, and gear blanks to the gear-cutting machines, etc., to make them fully automatic.

**Electric, Air, and Hydraulic Controls.** The basic machine movements are linear, as in the travel of a drill, or rotary, as in the case of an indexing table. The power used to accomplish these movements can be furnished by electricity, air, or hydraulic fluid. The selection of the power source will depend on what is readily available, the relative cost, amount of power required, space available for actuation, and speed requirements.

Space does not permit an explanation here of each of these systems, but, because of its relative simplicity, compactness, versatility, low initial cost, and wide acceptance, the principles of pneumatic automation will be discussed briefly.

Rotary motion is produced by air motors, and linear motion by air cylinders. This motion is controlled by valves which, with air lines, filters, and lubricators, make up the pneumatic circuit.

The successful application of pneumatic power depends on good circuit design. Despite their complex appearance, all pneumatic circuits are essentially simple. In fact, the simpler the circuit, the better the results. A pictorial sketch of an automatic electric circuit is shown in Fig. 29-1. This simple pneumatic system serves to illustrate how a variety of automatic operations, such as drilling, assembly, packaging, stamping, etc., can be accomplished. A gravity conveyor is used to feed the parts. When toggle switch (1) is placed in the *on* position, current flows through switches (2) and (3), advancing the piston of cylinder (4), which trips switch (5) advancing the punch. The clamping piston returns automatically and does not advance again until cylinder (6) has completed its work and returned to trip switch (2). The operation is continuous until the toggle switch (1) is thrown to the *off* position.

Pneumatic power is becoming an important item in helping manufacturers automate many operations, but, because air is compressible,

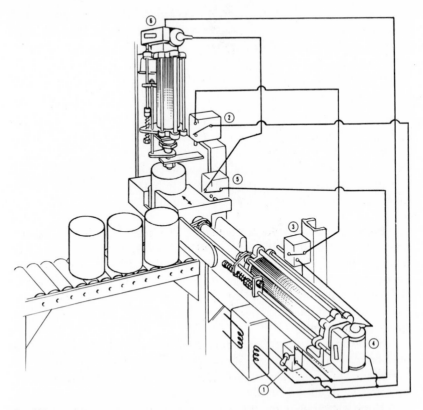

**Fig. 29-1.** A pneumatic electric circuit used to automate a simple operation of stamping, assembly, punching, etc. (courtesy The Bellows Co.).

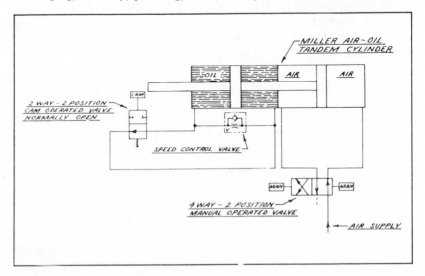

**Fig. 29-2.** A combination air-hydraulic circuit (courtesy Miller Fluid Power Division).

it is generally impractical to use it for the smooth, even movement of machine feeds with varying loads. Air and hydraulic circuits can be combined for this purpose. In the sample circuit shown in Fig. 29-2, air alternately enters the ends of the air cylinder through the four-way valve. The piston used to feed the work or tool is attached to the rod that extends through the hydraulic cylinder. A pipeline connects the two ends of the hydraulic cylinder. When the air cylinder cycles back and forth, it drives the hydraulic piston, forcing oil through the connecting pipeline from one end of the hydraulic cylinder to the other. This arrangement incorporates some of the advantages of both systems, namely the lower-cost air circuit with the smoother-acting hydraulic system needed for machining operations.

**Tape Control.** Although numerical control will be discussed in more detail in the latter half of this chapter, it is introduced here to show how it fits into individual-machine automation. An individual machine of this type is versatile and is referred to as a combination-operation machine.

In combination-operation machines, all operations are performed with the part held in a single fixture. Tolerance build-up due to varying fixture locations is eliminated, and piece-part handling is minimized.

The machine shown in Fig. 29-3 is equipped with a pallet shuttle and a tool-selector magazine. The machine has automatic tape-con-

**Fig. 29-3.** A combination-operation drilling, milling, and boring machine (courtesy Kearney & Trecker).

trolled movements in three axes, *X, Y,* and *Z.* The table can be automatically rotated in increments of 5 deg. Examples of work done on this machine are shown in Fig. 29-4.

**Fig. 29-4.** Examples of parts that can be handled on a combination-operation machine (courtesy Kearney & Trecker).

Fixturing for the part is designed to provide maximum accessibility consistent with good rigidity (Fig. 29-5).

The operations performed on the switch bracket are shown in Fig. 29-6. The time needed to complete each surface is also shown. Each of the operations requires a number of machine movements which are directed by the tape. Operation 1, for example, calls for rough and finish milling of two surfaces. The steps involved are:

1. Select the required face mill from the tool magazine.

2. Transfer the selected tool into the spindle.

3. Bring the tool into position at rapid traverse rate. Mill the surface at 15 in. per min.

4. Turn the coolant on, and preselect the tool for operation 2.

5. Rapid traverse to the next surface.

6. Mill the surface at 15 in. per min.

This sequence, or similar ones, is repeated for each of the surfaces until all surfaces are completed. With the machining finished, the fixture and pallet shuttle to the empty bed, and the next part moves to the

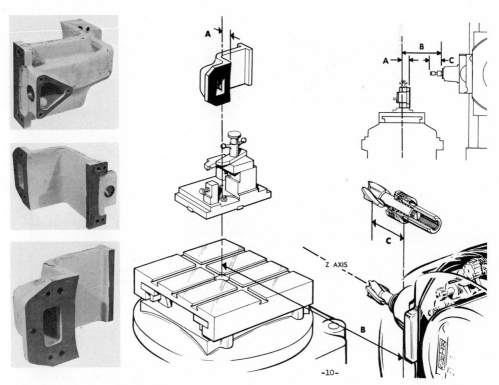

**Fig. 29-5.** The fixture is designed to complete as many operations in one setting as possible. *A* dimension is established by the holding fixture. *B* dimension is 20¾ in. when spindle is fully retracted. *C* dimension is specified by programmer, and tools are set to correspond (courtesy Kearney & Trecker).

AN EXAMPLE OF A MILWAUKEE-MATIC FLOOR-TO-FLOOR
TIME ANALYSIS

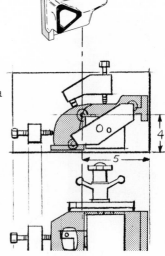

ESTABLISH PART ORIENTATION--Orientating this part
horizontally as illustrated exposes all the
machining operations to the spindle when the part
is properly indexed. When the part must be held
more than once for completion, all critical
surfaces should be machined on the final holding
if possible. The sequence of operations is
established at this time.

SKETCH HOLDING FIXTURE--A rough layout is prepared
of the fixture or holding device. This layout
serves useful purposes:

1.  It is used for estimating the MILWAUKEE-MATIC
    tooling cost.

2.  It serves as a check for validity of the
    machining process--most tool access or
    interference problems will be apparent on
    the layout.

3.  It establishes the reference dimensions used
    in estimating the cycle time.

**Fig. 29-6.** Operations, tools, and times needed to complete the switch bracket
on the combination-operation machine (courtesy Kearney & Trecker).

index table. Thus, very little machine time is lost in changing from
the finished to the incoming piece.

Figures given for the machining of the switch bracket, comparing
the tape-controlled combination machine with conventional machining
methods, are as follows:

| | |
|---|---:|
| Number required per year | 90 |
| Conventional tooling cost | $1,890.00 |
| Conventional manufacturing time | 85.38 min. |
| Combination-machine tooling cost | $260.00 |
| Combination manufacturing time | 19.18 min. |

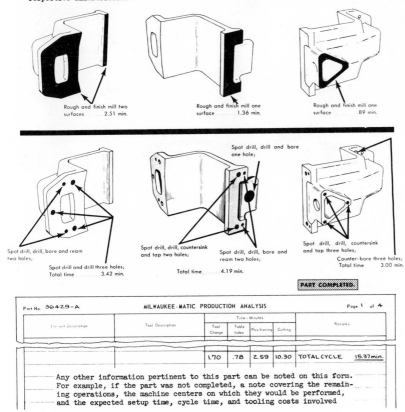

This procedure is followed in accounting for all elements involved in the machine cycle. The elemental times required to machine this bracket are shown beneath the respective illustrations.

Rough and finish mill two surfaces ... 2.51 min.

Rough and finish mill one surface ... 1.36 min.

Rough and finish mill one surface ... .89 min.

Spot drill, drill and bore one hole;

Spot drill, drill, bore and ream two holes;

Spot drill and drill three holes; Total time ... 3.42 min.

Spot drill, drill, countersink and tap two holes;

Spot drill, drill, bore and ream two holes;

Total time ... 4.19 min.

Spot drill, drill, countersink and tap three holes;

Counter-bore three holes; Total time ... 3.00 min.

PART COMPLETED.

| Part No. 36429-A | MILWAUKEE-MATIC PRODUCTION ANALYSIS | | | | | | Page 1 of 4 |
|---|---|---|---|---|---|---|---|
| | | | Time - Minutes | | | | |
| Element Description | Tool Description | Tool Change | Table Index | Positioning | Cutting | Remarks | |
| | | 1.70 | .78 | 2.59 | 10.30 | TOTAL CYCLE 15.37 min. | |

Any other information pertinent to this part can be noted on this form. For example, if the part was not completed, a note covering the remaining operations, the machine centers on which they would be performed, and the expected setup time, cycle time, and tooling costs involved

**Fig. 29-6.** (*cont.*)

**Circular-Indexing Automation.** Circular-indexing automation consists of intermittently moving the work from one station to the next in a circular path, Fig. 29-7.

Among the favorable factors of circular-indexing automation are the following: floor-space requirements are lessened; holding fixtures always return to their starting position; the work is clamped only once; loading and unloading are accomplished during the machine-cycle time; and a finished part is produced with each index.

Less favorable aspects include the need for balancing operation times, the practical size limit of the indexing table, the vibration trans-

**Fig. 29-7.** Circular-indexing automation (courtesy The Cross Co.).

mitted between stations, and the difficulty of power clamping. The production rate of the machine is established by the longest operation, plus indexing. It is therefore necessary to plan operations carefully to avoid one of long duration. Tool changes idle the entire machine, cutting down on overall efficiency.

Similar automatic indexing systems have been worked out in which the work is moved in a vertical plane. These are referred to as *trunnion-type machines*. Machine heads are mounted on each side of the vertical table, permitting simultaneous machining of opposite sides of the work.

### Multiple-Machine Automation

The discussion thus far has been concerned with circular- and linear-movement controls applied to individual machines. The next step is the integration of a number of machines performing a wide variety of operations on a given product.

**Integrated Lines.**  The first major step in the integration of individual machines into an automatic line was in 1940. At that time, some modifications were made on existing machines, and a means of connecting them by suitable conveyors was worked out. The grouping consisted essentially of drilling, reaming, tapping, and milling, arranged along both sides of an automatic conveyor. The workpiece was attached to a special locating plate and was pushed along a section of roller conveyors until it was engaged by a catch on a reciprocating transfer bar. The bar pulled the work into its approximate position at the first machine station, and hydraulically operated pins were raised to engage with the locating holes for exact positioning. Hydraulic clamps locked the plate, and the first set of tools performed the first machining operation. When the operation was completed, the tools withdrew, the clamps released, and the work was pulled into the next position by the transfer bar. At the same time, a new workpiece was pulled into the first position.

In spite of its tremendous potential, this transfer device had inherent weaknesses. If a tool became worn or broken, there was no

**Fig. 29-8.** Tool board and gaging equipment used to maintain an automatic line (courtesy Scully, Jones & Co.).

way to detect this until inaccurate pieces were discovered by inspection at the end of the line.

Improved transfer-line designs incorporated automatic inspection stations at various places. After drilling operations, a jet of compressed air blew out the chips, and metal fingers probed to make sure that proper depths had been reached and that no broken tool or tightly packed chips remained. Only as all intermediate checks were completed and found satisfactory was the machine able to index and repeat the sequence of operations.

Tool life expectancy can now be predicted, based on past experience and statistical data. This information is incorporated into a special control board (Fig. 29-8) that is used to maintain a cumulative record of each tool. Rather than wait for a tool to wear excessively or to break, a predetermined number of revolutions is set for a given tool. When this amount of cutting has been done, the board signals the machine to stop. Preset tools are then taken from the board and used to replace tools that have run their predetermined number of cycles. Gages are kept near the tool board so that all tools can be accurately set before they are placed in the machine.

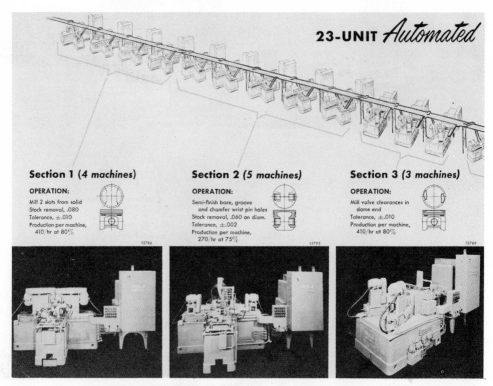

**23-UNIT** *Automated*

**Section 1 (4 machines)**

OPERATION:

Mill 2 slots from solid
Stock removal, .080
Tolerance, ±.010
Production per machine,
410/hr at 80%

15786

**Section 2 (5 machines)**

OPERATION:

Semi-finish bore, groove
and chamfer wrist pin holes
Stock removal, .060 on diam.
Tolerance, ±.002
Production per machine,
270/hr at 75%

15795

**Section 3 (3 machines)**

OPERATION:

Mill valve clearances in
dome end
Tolerance, ±.010
Production per machine,
410/hr at 80%

15789

**Fig. 29-9.** The sketch shows a part of a unitized type of transfer line. Note

The integrated line is still used. It has a great deal of flexibility, since machines can be taken out and substitutions made when the part changes design.

**Unitized Lines.** Several improvements have been made in the integrated line. Special handling equipment, such as chutes, conveyors, and elevators, have been added, as shown in the partial line of Fig. 29-9.

Work starts at one end of the main conveyor and flows along to takeoff stations which supply parts to the machine units. The work is processed automatically through these independent machines, and then goes back up to the conveyor line by means of elevators. In the unitized system, one group of machines does the first operation, another group does the second operation, the third group does the third operation, etc.

A number of favorable factors influence the choice of the unitized system. It provides a truly continuous work flow, as the individual units are releasing work to the main conveyor at different times, and the conveyor itself is moving the work along at all times. One can have complete freedom in planning the number of stations required.

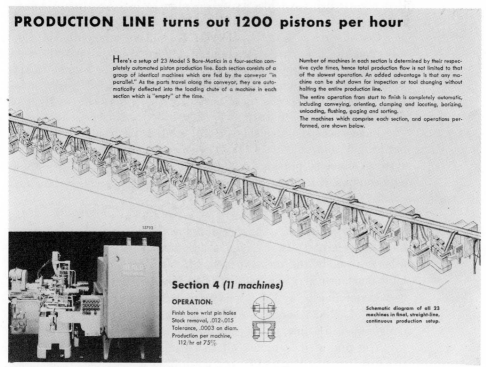

## PRODUCTION LINE turns out 1200 pistons per hour

Here's a setup of 23 Model S Bore-Matics in a four-section completely automated piston production line. Each section consists of a group of identical machines which are fed by the conveyor "in parallel." As the parts travel along the conveyor, they are automatically deflected into the loading chute of a machine in each section which is "empty" at the time.

Number of machines in each section is determined by their respective cycle times, hence total production flow is not limited to that of the slowest operation. An added advantage is that any machine can be shut down for inspection or tool changing without halting the entire production line.

The entire operation from start to finish is completely automatic, including conveying, orienting, clamping and locating, borizing, unloading, flushing, gaging and sorting.

The machines which comprise each section, and operations performed, are shown below.

### Section 4 (11 machines)

OPERATION:

Finish bore wrist pin holes
Stock removal, .012-.015
Tolerance, .0003 on diam.
Production per machine,
112/hr at 75%

Schematic diagram of all 23 machines in final, straight-line, continuous production setup.

the machines are arranged in groups or units (courtesy The Heald Machine Co.).

Opportunities to reorient the part are practically unlimited, since these can be varied from machine to machine. Consequently, the approach to the workpiece is unrestricted. The machine units can readily be designed for automatic loading and unloading. The most suitable type of loading can be used for each unit in the line.

The use of separate machines makes for easier application of a variety of machine types, including standard models. If suitable units are available, it is possible to fit them into this system. Furthermore, the unitized arrangement gives the user an opportunity to employ specialized machines made by different manufacturers, thus taking full advantage of their particular abilities. Aftergaging and feedback can be fully utilized to increase efficiency and improve quality by making corrections in successive cycles.

Banking of parts between operations is provided automatically and allows one group of machine units to continue functioning even though machines on prior operations are stopped temporarily.

It is entirely possible to operate this system efficiently at production rates below the normal maximum. In this case, a portion of the units performing each operation can be made inoperative, the remaining units being allowed to perform normally. This is the only system that allows such flexibility in adding or removing operations, increasing production, or accommodating part changes.

Considerations affecting the use of unitized automation are not all favorable. There are restrictions on the workpiece sizes and design. As an example, it would be rather inefficient to handle a large casting such as an automotive engine block. In general, small parts create fewer problems, and the ideal parts are those that can easily pass through the simple chutes.

Floor-space requirements present another problem, since a number of independent units will not be so compact as some of the other systems discussed previously. There is also the need for making duplicate equipment to orient the part, for gaging, and for other functions needed owing to part design.

**Transfer Machines.**    The specialized in-line transfer machines probably come nearer the average conception of automation than any other system in the metalworking industry. It is in these specially built machines that hundreds of operations are performed on rough-cast engine blocks, and they emerge as a finished component without the aid of human hands. To illustrate some of the steps involved in designing such a line, let us examine the casting shown in Fig. 29-10.

The first step is to list all the machining operations which, in this case, are 8 milling, 30 boring, 40 drilling, 4 recessing, 24 chamfering, 24 tapping, and 32 checking operations. The second step involves

**Fig. 29-10.** Casting considered for automatic transfer-line machining (courtesy Greenlee Bros. & Co.).

the design of work-holding fixtures and pallets (Fig. 29-11) so that as many operations as possible can be done with one clamping. This helps preserve accuracy and prevents marring the machined surfaces.

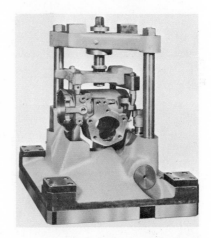

**Fig. 29-11.** Casting fixtured and palletized in preparation for placing it on the line (courtesy Greenlee Bros. & Co.).

The actual machine units may then be chosen from basic "building-block" units such as the vertical and horizontal bases, slide units, and boring heads used for drilling, reaming, chamfering, spot facing, and counterboring (Fig. 29-12).

The number of stations necessary is determined. The transfer mechanism to be used will help decide the line layout (Fig. 29-13).

You will note that provision is made for probing, rotating the part, and inspection. Other considerations are cleaning, deburring the casting, chip removal, coolant distribution, and safety interlocks. The manual operation consists of removing the finished parts and placing the rough castings on the pallet. Locating of the part in the pallet, clamping, and unclamping are automatic.

**Fig. 29-12.** Some basic "building-block" units used to make up circular automation and transfer lines as shown in the assembled views (courtesy The Heald Co.).

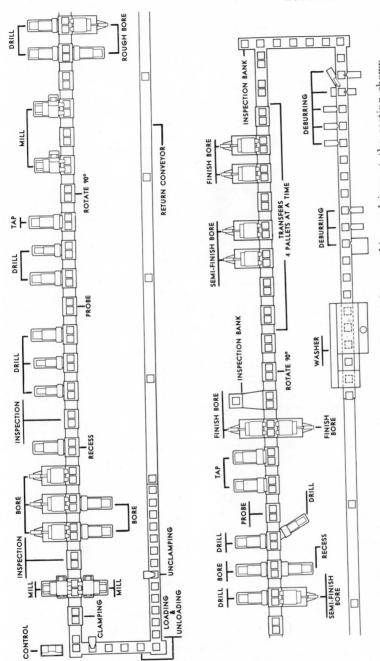

**Fig. 29-13.** Plan view of the completed transfer line used to machine and inspect the casting shown in Fig. 29-12 (courtesy Greenlee Bros. & Co.).

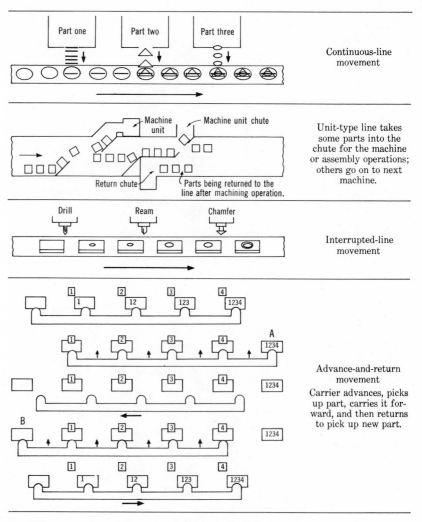

**Fig. 29-14.** Four types of transfer-line movements.

Transfer-line movements are of three types—continuous, intermittent, and advance-and-return (Fig. 29-14).

CONTINUOUS LINE. The continuous conveyor is the simplest of the three basic types of line movements. The cost is generally lower, and the cycle speed is higher. Some assembly and machining operations, such as milling and broaching, are done on a continuous-type line. The continuous movement of parts limits the kinds of operations that can be performed. Since clamping and locating are done only once, not all surfaces can be reached. Loading and unloading must be done "on the fly" or during movement of the line.

A unitized line may be considered a continuous-line operation, but the parts leave the conveyor for the machining operations via outlet chutes and return by means of elevators. The part banks at each station ensure continuous machine utilization.

INTERMITTENT LINE. The intermittent line is the conventional movement used where a time interval is required at specific stations to perform an operation. This type is usually expensive from the standpoint of the number of pallets and fixtures required.

ADVANCE-AND-RETURN LINES. The advance-and-return movement is used in many large press-working operations. The part is moved through the sequence of operations by means of transfer bars and fingers which grasp the part during the transfer movement. This type of moving arrangement is generally more economical than the interrupted- or indexing-type movement.

**In-Line-Automation Evaluation.** Floor-space requirements and operating efficiency are the two principal limiting factors of in-line automation. Some lines allow considerable flexibility in the number and type of stations used. With the proper equipment, work may be reoriented and repositioned so that all surfaces can be machined and inspected. Continuous chip removal is relatively easy to incorporate, since the chips can be dropped on straight-line chutes and conveyors. The effect of vibration between stations is slight, because machine units are separated. The in-line machine is easy to load and unload by automatic means; it can also be adapted to manual handling at the beginning or end of the line. Heat and distortion are greatly minimized owing to unclamping of the workpiece and the time interval needed to progress from station to station.

## Workpiece Orientation and Movement for Automation

Many devices have been developed to make piece-part orientation and movement automatic. Best known among these for part orientation are the vibratory and rotary hoppers.

**Vibratory Hopper.** Bowl feeders are used to orient, and feed in a straight line, pieces from $\frac{1}{8}$ to 11 in. long. The pieces may be either metal or plastic and of almost any conceivable shape. Vibration, induced by electromagnetic action, causes the parts to feed up a spiral ramp around the inside of the bowl.

Orienting devices (sweeps) are placed at various points on the spiral ramp to reject parts that are not in the desired position. For example, the simple sweep shown in Fig. 29-15 is used to wipe off excess parts and those whose minor diameter is down. A part can usually be turned 90 to 180 deg, laid down, stood up, or flipped around, as required.

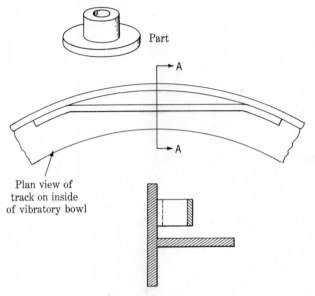

Part

A

A

Plan view of track on inside of vibratory bowl

**Fig. 29-15.** Part to be oriented and type of sweep used to perform the task. Parts that are perpendicular or whose smaller diameter is down will be wiped off.

Feeds of 10 to 15 fpm are considered normal. However, this does not mean that all the parts are oriented at this rate. A part takes several positions as it travels along the track. Therefore, the desired feed rate is set at the number of correctly oriented parts needed per minute.

Vibratory-hopper feeders, combined with air cylinders, are widely used for assembly as well as for small machining operations. A bowl feeder is used to load gear blanks into the machine in Fig. 29-16 where they are automatically bored and gaged.

**Rotary Hopper.** Many parts that are not difficult to orient can be fed by a rotary centrifugal-hopper feeder. Examples of these parts are bearing balls, needle bearings, bearing races, gears, and screw-machine parts. Fragile parts that do not tangle readily and parts that have a high surface finish are also suitable for rotary feeding. The bowl of the hopper has a revolving plate in the bottom, and, as each piece is spun out, it passes through a controlled orifice onto a track, and then on into the production line. Orienting devices are provided when the pieces must be positioned so that they all face in the same direction. The parts are urged up the spiral ramp by a crowding action of the mass of parts in the bowl. As the part leaves the ramp, it enters a gravity chute leading to the machine being fed.

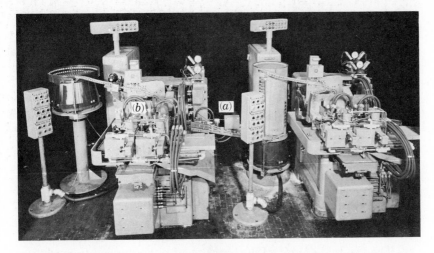

**Fig. 29-16.** Parts are fed from a vibrating hopper into a loading chute where they are gaged and bored. At (*a*) they are gaged and data are fed back to tool block (*b*) which automatically corrects. Correct-sized parts go to the vibrating loader of No. 2 machine, where the gear blank is completed (courtesy The Heald Machine Co.).

### Further Development and Use of Automation

The incentive behind automation has been the desire to make things faster and more cheaply. However, the greatest benefit has been in doing jobs that are beyond the power of human workers. Instrumentation, mechanical gaging, and perception have made possible closer tolerances than human hands can achieve. The blessing of automation is that it eliminates many of the tedious, monotonous jobs formerly done by hand.

Automation requires engineers of broad background who can encompass the various technologies needed to design, build, and maintain the automatic factory. More highly trained technicians will also be needed to maintain the automatic lines.

Plants become obsolete not by the age of the equipment but when they can no longer produce in competition with the prevailing market. Competition is the driving force that will make the automatic factory a reality. With the progress already attained, and with new concepts available to industrial planners, the possibility of great increases in productivity by automation will be difficult to resist.

### NUMERICAL CONTROL

Numerical control, or control by numbers, is not new in the sense that numbers have always been used for accurate tool-table movements. However, numerical control as it is spoken of today is a much more complex control based on electronic computations. These computations are used in giving physical movement, continuous or intermittent, through servomotors to the tool, machine table, or auxiliary functions.

Many other industries have shared with the machine-tool industry in the development of numerical control. Wherever equipment is instructed to perform a function now done by an operator, there is a potential application of numerical control.

Table and tool movements may be made by electrical, hydraulic, or mechanical means, as long as the input signal represents a numerical value.

### Types of Numerical-Control Systems

The two main forms of numerical control, as applied to machines, are point-to-point positioning and continuous-path control.

**Point-to-Point Positioning.** Point-to-point, or *discreet*, positioning is a relatively simple method of moving the tool or work on the $X$- and $Y$-coordinates to a desired position. This type of control is applicable to a wide variety of machine tools, such as drill presses, boring mills, punch presses, and jig boring machines. Point-to-point positioning, as used in drilling or boring holes, requires a high degree of accuracy as to location of the coordinates, but it places no restriction on the path used in achieving the location.

**Continuous-Path or Contouring System.** Contouring is by far the most complicated system of numerical control. In milling a profile of a three-dimensional surface, the entire path must be described by the data input medium. The tool path may be for any shape, whether it is a parabola, arc, sphere, square, or any combination of these in three dimensions. In reality, this system is an advanced stage of the point-to-point system. The controls are such that the tool can move only in a straight line. The straight-line distances can be made so short (0.0005 in.) and so well blended that they will appear as a continuous smooth cut.

Of the two systems, point-to-point positioning is the most commonly used. Contouring was first developed in cooperation with the aircraft industry for complex machining jobs (Fig. 29-17), and this is still one of its best applications. As the industry grows and more technical help becomes available, it is likely that tool-and-die shops may become the biggest users.

Computers are rarely needed to prepare data for positioning systems, but the thousands of points needed for continuous-path control provide a complex problem not practical to solve except with a com-

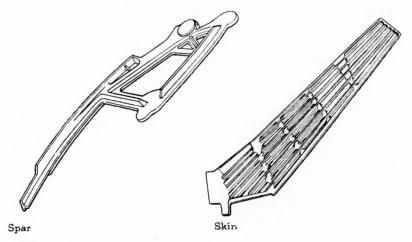

Spar                          Skin

**Fig. 29-17.** Complicated aircraft members milled with continuous-path numerically controlled machine.

puter. The fact that a computer could be used to calculate the thousands of physical points needed for any mathematical shape had a marked influence on the development of numerically controlled machines.

The three axes of movement, termed $X$, $Y$, and $Z$, are normal to each other. More movements are available. There is an axis of rotation about each of the basic axes, making six in all. Numerically controlled machining often calls for extra maneuverability (Fig. 29-18).

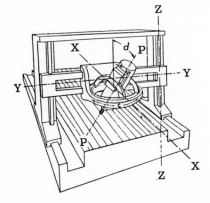

**Fig. 29-18.** Positioning axes X, Y, Z, and P.

### Numerical-Control Programming

Numerical control may best be understood by following the various steps from the time the design is conceived until the finished part is completed. The steps involved for point-to-point and continuous-path control are shown in Fig. 29-19. The steps in continuous-path control concern design and numerical drawing; process-sheet preparation (programming); process card or tape preparation; making the control tape with the computer; and machine controls.

**Design and Numerical Drawing.** The engineer who has become familiar with numerical control adapts his designs so as to facilitate machining and handling. After the design has been made, it is given numerical dimensions; that is, all dimensions are in the form of coordinates referenced to a common axis (Fig. 29-20). Much of the conventional dimensioning is omitted.

After the drawing is complete, it goes to a methods engineer or a methods group. It is at this point that decisions are made as to the best way of making the item. Weaknesses of the design may also be detected, and more suitable materials selected. Cutters are chosen, and speeds and feeds are set for each cut.

**Process Sheet.** After the methods and tools have been selected, a process sheet is made up in which dimensions from the numerical

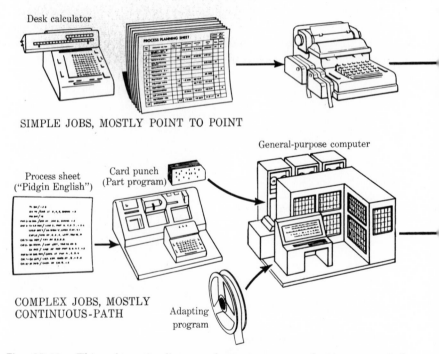

SIMPLE JOBS, MOSTLY POINT TO POINT

COMPLEX JOBS, MOSTLY CONTINUOUS-PATH

**Fig. 29-19.** This schematic diagram shows two ways of using numerical control. On simple jobs the process sheet is worked out by a human programmer. His instructions to the machine are then coded on a tape by means of a

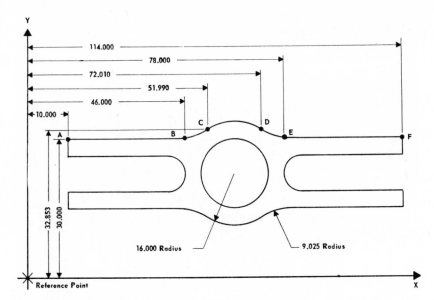

**Fig. 29-20.** Numerical drawing.

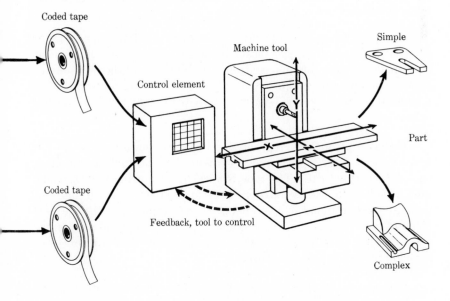

key-punch typewriter. For complex jobs a computer is needed. The process is then comparatively simple because the burden is shifted to the computer (courtesy *Fortune,* March 1962).

drawing, along with other information including machining sequences, cutter diameters, machine speeds, and feeds, are shown in preparation for coding on the tape (Fig. 29-21).

| | | Cutter Radius (in.) | Feed Rate (in./min.) | Cutter L.(1) R(2) | Tolerance (mils) | End Point Of Section | | | Circle Radius (in.) | Center L.(1) R(2) |
|---|---|---|---|---|---|---|---|---|---|---|
| Section | | | | | | X | Y | Z | | |
| Start | | | | | | 10.000 | 30.000 | 12.000 | | |
| A | B | 1.50 | 40.0 | 1 | .3 | 46.000 | 30.000 | 12.000 | | |
| B | C | 1.50 | 25.0 | 1 | .3 | 51.990 | 32.853 | 12.000 | 9.025 | 1 |
| C | D | 1.50 | 25.0 | 1 | .3 | 72.010 | 32.853 | 12.000 | 16.000 | 2 |
| D | E | 1.50 | 25.0 | 1 | .3 | 78.000 | 30.000 | 12.000 | 9.025 | 1 |
| E | F | 1.50 | 40.0 | 1 | .3 | 114.000 | 30.000 | 12.000 | | |

WORK ORDER NO. 10389    DWG. NO. 32B447    DATE 5-20-57

**Fig. 29-21.** Process sheet showing tool-size information, dimensions in each axis, and tolerance.

There are many ways of conveying numerical information from the drawing to the machine. The most common are punched cards, punched tape, magnetic tape, and dial controls. Combinations of these are offered by some manufacturers. For point-to-point positioning control, there is a trend to standardize on 1-in.-wide tape with eight rows of punched holes.

**Process Tape or Card Preparation.** From the information on the process sheet, a series of punched cards or a perforated tape is made on a special typewriter. The tape is verified by putting it in a reader unit attached to the typewriter. If a mistake is punched into the original tape, a signal can be given to the verifier to skip the next block of perforations. Thus, the second tape is mechanically proofread and is error-free. If punched cards are made first, they are processed through a card-to-tape converter.

**Computer Preparation of Control Tape.** The computer automatically carries out detailed process calculations and punches the control tape. The computer makes its calculations based on data received from the process tape and on information stored on magnetic tape in auxiliary storage units; these are fed to the computer for calculations as needed.

The computer automatically converts the process-tape information to a binary, two-number 0—1 code, and also offsets the tool center from the actual part. The control tape (Fig. 29-22) is punched in blocks. Each block controls the machine in a straight-line path from one point to the next. Only one block of information is required for any straight-line cut.

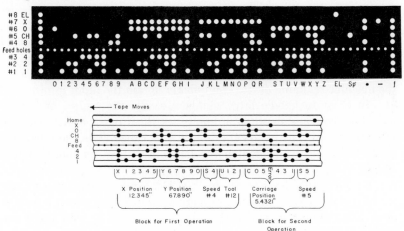

**Fig. 29-22.** A punched-tape program.

Curves are cut by the straight-line approximation method to any desired accuracy. A series of arcs and tangent lines such as those shown in Fig. 29-20, need be defined only by giving the radii and center coordinates of each arc. The interpolation of curves is performed by the computer.

Command information on tape consists of binary numbers corresponding to the number of command pulses that must be delivered to each axis in order to drive the cutting tool along a straight line from one point to the next specified point. Other information for full numerical control consists of instructions to the machine, such as direction of motion, start, stop, reverse, rapid traverse, etc.; numerical values, such as dimensions or length of travel and speeds, feeds, number of pieces, etc.; and auxiliary functions, such as tool changing, coolant on or off, chuck open or closed, end-of-cycle signal, operate lubricator, etc.

In semiautomatic systems, signals from the tape can tell the operator when to perform auxiliary functions manually.

**Machine Control Unit.** The tape is mounted on a photoelectric reader in the machine control unit which senses the holes in the tape. One block of information from the control tape is received by the electronic buffer unit immediately, and is stored. The storage unit supplies information to the decoder as required. The coded digital information is changed to command pulses by the decoder. Each pulse commands an increment of travel, which may be as small as 0.0005 in. These pulses serve as input to the servos for the machine lead-screw motors.

**Machine Interpretation of Numbers.** A machine is not able to understand Arabic numbers, so they must be changed to a two-number, or *binary*, system. In this system only two numbers are used, 0 and 1. A circuit is either open (0), or closed (1). The machine has only to sense this difference. So, if a hole is punched for 1 and none for 0, the machine scanning device can quickly obtain the input information.

In order to handle large numbers easily, the figures are spread over four columns in what is known as the *Binary Coded Decimal* (BCD) system. The binary digits 1, 2, 4, 8, called "bits," are arranged in vertical lines which match the horizontal lines, as shown in Fig. 29-23.

By following the example in Fig. 29-23, we see that, in any row, we have four distinct locations where we can either punch a hole or do nothing. You will notice that, in order to get 5, both the 1 and the 4 were punched. Likewise, 6 was obtained by punching the 4 and the 2. The tape reader can, where desired, read each decimal digit or read the integer separately from the decimal fraction, which is useful in coarse and fine positioning.

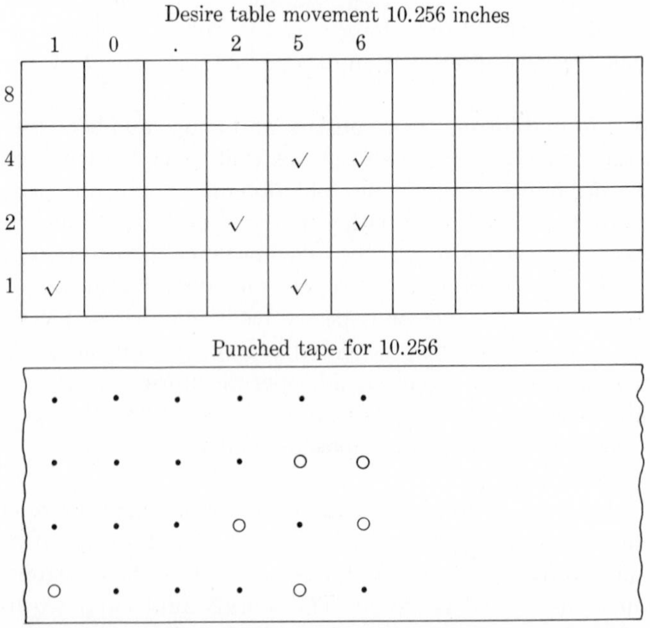

Desire table movement 10.256 inches

| | 1 | 0 | . | 2 | 5 | 6 | | | | |
|---|---|---|---|---|---|---|---|---|---|---|
| 8 | | | | | | | | | | |
| 4 | | | | | √ | √ | | | | |
| 2 | | | | √ | | √ | | | | |
| 1 | √ | | | | √ | | | | | |

Punched tape for 10.256

**Fig. 29-23.** Binary-coded decimal system of writing Arabic numbers, and punched tape for corresponding number.

**Manual Position Selectors.**    Provision is made, on some numerically controlled machines, for manually feeding the information for the desired coordinates into the system (Fig. 29-24). The manual arrangement consists of a number of 10-position rotary switches, each of which provides 1 digit of numerical position information. This information is converted within the machine to the binary-coded decimal

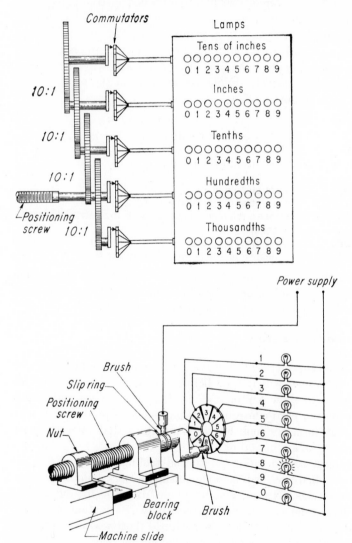

**Fig. 29-24.**   An analog-to-digital converter is shown schematically. Any degree of fineness can be provided through the dial settings (courtesy *American Machinist/Metalworking Manufacturing*).

form and is fed to the servomotors by means of impulses from the decoded punched tape.

**Newer Developments.** A newer system of tape programming being developed is known as APT, or automatic programmed tool. The aim of the developers of this system is to make input information as close to human language as possible.

APT consists of over 30,000 preprogrammed instructions to the computer. Thus it adapts a general-purpose computer to a special-purpose computer for programming machine tools. The computer, when given instructions, can, with lightning speed, find the preprogrammed information and apply it to the job at hand. This is why the process sheet becomes comparatively simple. An example of the process-sheet information is as follows:

| *Part Program* | *Explanation* |
| --- | --- |
| CUTTER/1 | Use 1-in.-diameter cutter |
| TOLER/.005 | Tolerance: 0.005 in. |
| FEDRAT/80 | Feed rate: 80 in. per min |
| HEAD/1 | Use head 1 |
| SPINDL/2400 | Turn on spindle at 2,400 rpm |
| COOLNT/FLOOD | Turn on coolant, flood setting |
| PT1 = POINT/4,5 | Define a reference point, PT1, as the point with coordinates 4,5 |
| FROM/(SETPT = POINT/1,1) | Start the tool from the point called SETPT, which is defined as the point with coordinates 1,1 |

This simplified programming points the way to the production of parts merely by feeding design information directly into the computer, thereby eliminating even the part drawings.

## Advantages and Considerations

**Costs.** Cost considerations always loom foremost in obtaining new equipment. How long will it take before the equipment will pay for itself and begin to show a profit? Some fantastic savings have been reported, such as a card-controlled milling machine producing a part in 25 min that formerly took 60 hr. Wing skins that formerly took 750 hr are being made in 200 hr.

Another cost consideration is reduced tooling. Much of the numerically controlled work can be done on simple work-holding devices, replacing costly jigs, fixtures, and templates. Because tooling can be simplified, lead time can be cut substantially. Parts that normally require weeks for tooling can now be machined shortly after the tape is prepared, with the aid of conventional holding devices.

Since less tooling is required, a secondary benefit may be realized in less tool-storage space. Storing tape or punched cards requires very little space. Right- and left-hand parts require double tooling, but one tape can be programmed to take care of both.

Replacement parts can be machined cheaply, even one at a time, with numerical control. This will relieve many companies of carrying large inventories of spare parts. A manufacturer may even rent the control tape to a customer.

**Conventional versus Tape-Control Manufacture.** Perhaps the easiest way to see how tape control compares with conventional methods is to take one job and follow it through.

The part under consideration is the die mold shown in Fig. 29-25. The conventional method of manufacture is to transform the data from the drawing into templates. These templates, made out of sheet metal, are set up and spaced at proper intervals to make the male model. Plaster is put in between the templates and smoothed down to make a solid form. This male is then used as the pattern to make a

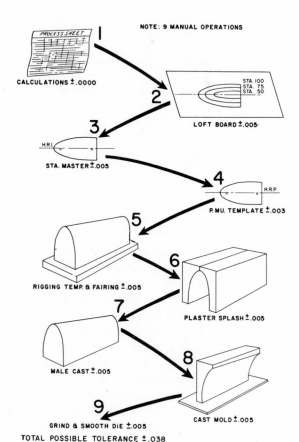

**Fig. 29-25.** Conventional die-mold operations required for producing a honeycomb die cavity (courtesy *The Tool and Manufacturing Engineer*).

casting which must be hand-ground and smoothed to the proper contour. In this process there are nine basic steps, resulting in a possible tolerance on the final die of $\pm$ 0.038 in.

When producing the same die by the numerical process, the information is retained in its original numerical form until the final machining operation, which results in a very small accumulated tolerance. The basic steps involved are planning, calculating, tape preparation, and machining the finished part. More detailed data are given in Table 29-1.

**TABLE 29-1.**

**Comparison of Numerical and Conventional-Method Times to Make the Die Mold Shown in Fig. 29-25\***

|  | Numerical Control (hr) | Conventional (hr) |
|---|---|---|
| Planning | 16 | 8 |
| Calculating | 40 | 20 |
| Tape preparation | 12 | 0 |
| Loft drawing | 0 | 40 |
| Station master template | 0 | 30 |
| Plaster-mold template | 0 | 42 |
| Rigging template and fairing | 0 | 80 |
| Plaster splash | 0 | 80 |
| Male casting from plaster splash | 0 | 100 |
| Cast metal die | 0 | 110 |
| Machining die | 24 | 0 |
| Finish grind die | 30 | 60 |
|  | 122 hours | 550 hours |
| Lead time | 3 days | 7 weeks |

\* Courtesy *The Tool and Manufacturing Engineer.*

The cost of numerically controlled tools should not be looked on entirely from the standpoint of capital investment, but rather from the amount of savings that can be realized through advantages already given, and others such as the following: Human error is greatly reduced—hence greater accuracy, fewer inspections, and less scrap result. The method is versatile, with the ability to handle a wide range of jobs. Control information is easily changed.

Numerical control is not built for mass production. Existing machines, discussed in the section on automation, can be built that will take care of these jobs faster and more economically.

Point-to-point positioning can be added to conventional drill presses and mill and jig borers through packaged kits that consist of the necessary tables, servos, and control elements. The tape preparation for point-to-point positioning does not require the complex and expensive equipment needed for continuous-path control. For this reason it is believed that discreet numerically controlled machines will be widely used before the more complex continuous-path-control machines become common.

Already, a completely automatic point-to-point tape-controlled drill press is being marketed for less than $9,000. This opens up a market for numerical control in thousands of small shops throughout the industry.

## QUESTIONS

1. Why is automation used less in metal working than in some of the processing industries?

2. How can pneumatic circuits be made to deliver the smooth, even movement needed for machining operations?

3. What are some advantages of circular-type automation?

4. Why is the integrated line considered quite flexible?

5. How does a unitized line differ from an integrated line?

6. What are some standard building-block units that can be used to make up an automated line?

7. Can drilling operations be done on a continuous-type line?

8. What are some advantages in-line automation has that circular automation does not have?

9. What is the function of a *sweep* in the vibratory hopper?

10. What are some of the human demands of a successful automation program?

11. Explain the difference between continuous-path control and point-to-point positioning.

12. How does a numerical-control drawing differ from a conventional drawing?

13. How can errors be eliminated in a punched tape?

14. What information is needed for the computer to calculate the movements needed to cut an arc or a circle?

15. Explain how binary information is fed to the machine?

16. Why is APT programming much simpler than conventional programming?

17. What are some of the cost-cutting advantages of numerical control?

18. Why can numerical control be economically set up to make one particular part?

## PROBLEMS

1. Show by means of a *bits* chart how 13.209 in. would be arranged before placing it on the tape.

2. Make a chart similar to that of the lamps in Fig. 29-24. Show how 13.209 in. would appear in the light.

3. Assuming a cutting speed of 60 fpm for drilling cast iron and a feed of 0.008 in. per revolution, how long would it take to drill the three ½-in.-diameter holes through the flange and spot-drill two ⅜-in.-diameter holes halfway through the flange of the casting shown in lower left corner of Fig. 29-5. The flange is ½ in. thick. Use half the largest drill diameter for approach and overtravel. A drill jig will be used. How does the time needed to drill the holes shown compare with the time given in Fig. 29-6? How would it compare if a multi-spindle drilling head were used?

4. Write in APT language what you would consider the instructions to be for the operations needed on the casting in the lower left corner of Fig. 29-6. Use Prob. 3 for other information needed.

## REFERENCES

Booth, F., "Production Experience on Numerically Controlled Machine Tools," paper given at 26th Annual Conference of ASTME, May, 1958.

Gorham, J. C., *Potentialities and Problems of Numerical Control*, Bendix Aviation Corporation, Industrial Controls Section, Detroit.

Solow, H., "How to Talk to Machine Tools," *Fortune*, March, 1962.

Stocker, W. M., "ABC's of Numerical Control," *American Machinist/Metalworking Manufacturing*. Special Report No. 494, August, 1960.

# 30

# NEWER METHODS
# OF MANUFACTURE

**N**EW AND EXOTIC materials often present difficult fabricating problems. These have sparked man's creative genius into providing new concepts of material removal and metal forming. The aircraft and missile industry has had to pioneer some of these new processes because of the demand for minimum weight, high strength, and high-temperature-resistant materials. Competition also serves to spur the search for newer, faster methods that will bring reduced manufacturing costs.

The newer methods and techniques discussed briefly in this chapter are chipless machining, ultrasonic machining, electric-discharge machining, ultrahigh-speed machining, hot and cold machining, forming, chemical milling, high-energy-rate forming and lasers.

## CHIPLESS MACHINING

Chipless machining is based on the theory that it is better to move the metal than to remove it. Processes that employ a form of this chipless machining are casting and some hot-working methods such as forging, rolling, and extrusion. These are older, better-known processes of moving metal around, and have been discussed previously. Chipless machining, in this chapter, refers to those operations more closely associated with metal cutting, such as thread rolling, spline and gear rolling, internal contour forming, cold heading, and cold impact extrusion.

### Machining Principles

Material savings, improved surface finish, and higher production rates are advantages claimed for chipless machining. In addition, there is some indication that tensile strength is improved up to a point. This point depends on the cold-working deformation of the crystalline structure. Too much cold working will set up residual stresses that will ultimately weaken the structure of the metal. A relatively small amount of cold working tends to produce a large increase in tensile and yield strength, with only small losses in ductility. When it becomes necessary to move relatively large amounts of metal, undue stress is prevented by an annealing process. This allows the deformed crystals to be replaced by new crystals formed from the nuclei at the recrystallization temperature, as discussed in Chapter 2. The temperature at which the recrystallization takes place will depend on the amount of cold working and the kind of metal used. Cold-worked steel will recrystallize between 950° and 1300°F. The steel can be quenched after this heat without fear of hardening, since it is below the critical temperature.

### Thread Rolling

Thread rolling has been placed in the category of newer processes, even though records indicate that it was known early in the 19th century. However, it was not used until the latter part of that century, and until 1940 it was used only in the smaller-type fasteners. The industry did not progress rapidly, and for a long time the cold-forged thread made with wrought iron was an inferior product. For accuracy and fine quality, the "cut thread" label was much preferred over the "rolled thread."

Now the picture has changed, owing first to an improvement in the quality of rolling or forging steels; second, to the improvement of dies in making the raw stock more uniform; and third, to the thread-rolling dies and machines themselves.

**Equipment.** The most common method of making cut threads is with a die, as shown in Fig. 30-1. The thread-cutting tool, called a chaser, gradually cuts to full depth, as shown in Fig. 30-1(b). This type of die is also known as *self-opening*. When the machine part on which it is mounted, such as a lathe turret, comes to the end of its travel, the die springs open. This allows the tool to be backed off without touching the thread.

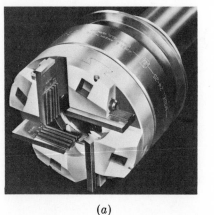

(a)                                    (b)

**Fig. 30-1.** (a) Self-opening die used to cut threads. (b) Cutting action of the die (courtesy Jones and Lamson Machine Co.).

Thread-rolling dies can be very similar to the thread-chasing dies (Fig. 30-2). Instead of the cutting edges on the dies, there are two or three rolls that form the material to the desired shape as it passes between them.

**Fig. 30-2.** Thread rolling can be done from the cross-slide position of a turret lathe or an automatic screw machine (courtesy Reed Rolled Thread Die Co.).

High production requires special machines which are of three basic types—reciprocating die machines, through-feed rolling machines, and the continuous die machines.

Reciprocating die machines utilize two flat dies, one stationary and one moving [Fig. 30-3(a)]. These machines are widely used for making bolts.

A more recent development is the through-feed die machine [Fig. 30-3(d)], that provides the highest rate of production for headed workpieces ¾ in. or less in diameter and less than 7 in. in overall

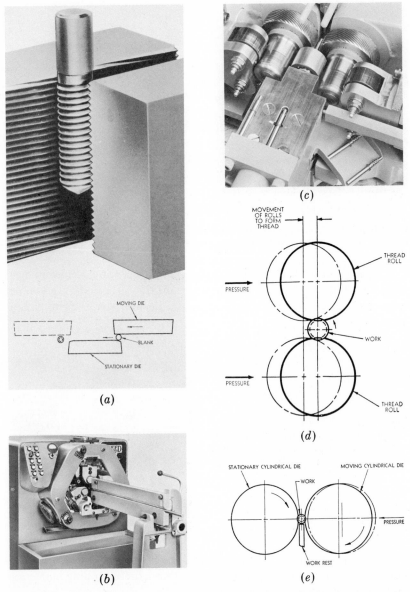

**Fig. 30-3.** Several types of thread-rolling machines. (*a*) Flat reciprocating dies. (*b*) Three-roll machine for continuous through-rolling of long bars. (*c*) Infeed rolling machine. (*d*) Through-feed die machine. A high-production setup for headed short pieces. (*e*) An infeed plunge-rolling setup for threading comparatively large diameters and shouldered parts (courtesy Reed Rolled Thread Die Company).

length. The rolls are maintained at a predetermined fixed center distance as required to produce the desired pitch diameter. Continuous rolling of threads is done on the three die machine shown in Fig. 30-3(*b*). This is also referred to as through-feed rolling.

Infeed (plunge rolling) of threads is accomplished by supporting the work on a work-rest blade between the two cylindrical dies [Fig. 30-3(*e*)]. As the machine cycle starts, the right-hand roll advances a predetermined distance toward the left-hand roll, which has a stationary spindle. Upon completion of the roll, the right-hand wheel is backed off and the work is unloaded. This type of rolling is done on large diameters and shouldered parts.

**Accuracy and Surface Finish.** Since rolling does not remove any material, the size and condition of the blank are very important. In general, the blank diameters are somewhat smaller than the pitch diameter of the thread. Bolts, cap screws, and machine screws are cold-forged in heading machines. Some blanks are given a light shaving cut, and others may be centerless-ground before threading. The end of the blank is normally given a 30-deg bevel to prevent chipping the rolling dies.

In cold forming, surface finish is a close approximation of the surface finish of the dies. This holds true for thread rolling, except that the finish is usually smoother than the dies, owing to a burnishing action. Average finish values of cut, milled, ground, and rolled threads are given in Fig. 30-4.

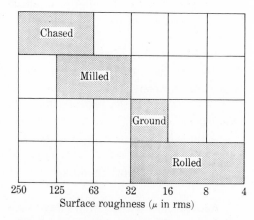

**Fig. 30-4.** Comparison of screw-thread surface finishes produced by various processes (courtesy *Machine Design*).

**Economics.** Rolling is considered the fastest method of producing threads. The fully automatic reciprocating machines used by the fastener industry are commonly operated in batteries, one operator being responsible for several machines. Production rates vary with the size of the machine; for example, a ⅛-in. machine can produce 175 pieces per min, and a ¾-in. machine 50 pieces per min.

The savings of material over the cut thread vary from 27 percent on a ⅜-in.–16 bolt to 16 percent on the 1½-in.–6 thread.

**Properties.**    Rolled threads increase in hardness at the root by as much as 30 percent. This improves fatigue strength from 50 to 75 percent. Because the longitudinal fibers (Fig. 30-5) are re-formed rather than cut, the shear strength of the material is improved. The smooth dies leave no cutter marks or tears, which often act as stress concentrators and starting points for fatigue cracks.

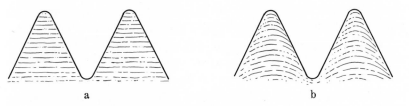

a                                                                          b

**Fig. 30-5.**    (*a*) Cut thread. (*b*) Rolled thread.

**Internal Threads.**    The most common way of making internal threads is with a tap. The hole is drilled slightly larger than the minor diameter of the thread. This produces a 75 percent thread, as shown in Fig. 30-6. Calculations show that when 75 percent of the external thread form, measured radially, is engaged with the internal thread, the shear strength of these threads will be equal to the tensile strength of the bolt.

Internal rolling of threads is done in much the same way except that the tap has no cutting edges. [Fig. 30-6(c)]. A hole somewhat larger than for conventional tapping is required because of the material flow. As a result of the material flow, the thread has a concave crest (Fig. 30-7).

Although the taps appear round, they are ground with both pitch and major diameter relief. This reduces the torque requirements and permits the use of cutting oil.

**Applications.**    Good results have been obtained on nonferrous materials, particularly aluminum, zinc, copper, and brass. Tap life varies greatly with size, fit, and material. Case studies show the range to be between 10,000 holes on seamed copper tubing to 300,000 holes per tap on a ½-hard brass screw-machine parts.

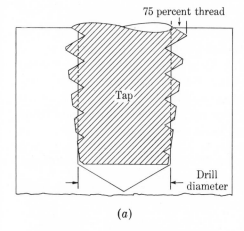

(a)

**Fig. 30-6.** (a) Tapped hole showing usual 75 percent thread. (b) Fluted tap. (c) Nonfluted thread-rolling tap.

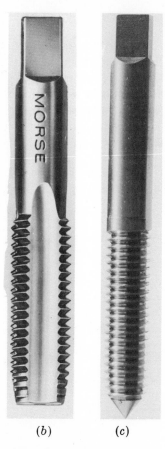

(b)  (c)

**Fig. 30-7.** Internal thread-rolling action (courtesy Besley-Welles Corp.).

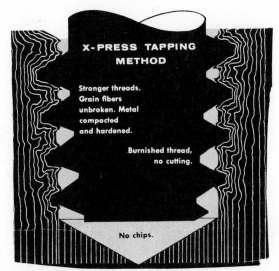

X-PRESS TAPPING METHOD

Stronger threads. Grain fibers unbroken. Metal compacted and hardened.

Burnished thread, no cutting.

No chips.

### Spline and Gear Rolling

Closely associated with thread rolling is spline, gear, and ser-ration rolling. A spline is an involute profile raised on the surface of a shaft. The major differences between splines, gears, and serrations are the pressure angles and their use. The pressure angle for a spline is 30 deg; for a gear, 20 deg; and for serrations, 45 deg. Splines are used for axial movement with rotation, gears are usually for fixed rotation, and serrations are for fixed-position fastening.

**Principles and Equipment.**   A machine used to roll splines, serrations, and gear teeth on a shaft is shown in Fig. 30-8.

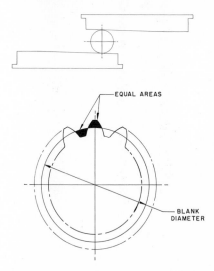

**Fig. 30-8.**  The method and princi-ples of rolling gear-teeth, splines, and serrations (courtesy Michigan Tool Co.).

Figure 30-9 shows how splines or gear teeth can be rolled with two planetary rollers that contact the workpiece simultaneously and repeatedly. The forming rolls are held on rotor carriers that take them to and from the work. The blank is either continuously rotating in synchronization with the forming-roll contact or is indexed to ex-pose all grooves to the rolling operation. The stock is fed axially past the intermittently contacting rollers. Forming is completed in one pass.

Gears are made in bar form and cut to desired widths. Gears as large as 10 in. in diameter have been produced by this method.

**Production Rate, Accuracy, and Finish.**   Ordinarily, gears and splines of this type are cut with a gear hob. A comparison of the time for hobbing 16 splines on a shaft 4 in. long, similar to the one shown in Fig. 30-9 was 3 min and 45 sec. Rolling time for the same operation was 40 sec. As with thread rolling, accuracy and surface finish are generally better by the rolling process than by cutting.

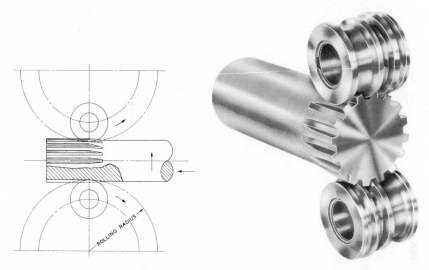

**Fig. 30-9.** A two-roller planetary-type gear machine (courtesy Grob Inc.).

### Internal Contour Forming

**Forming Operations.** Internal forming operations can be performed on hollow cylindrical stock by placing it over a mandrel and squeezing it by rapidly pulsating dies. Parts that are difficult and time-consuming to machine are formed quickly and with the metallurgical advantages inherent in the chipless process.

The hollow workpiece is placed on the mandrel and moved up between the dies (Fig. 30-10). The dies, mounted on cams, are made to pulsate as they come in contact with steel rollers located in the machine's headstock (Fig. 30-11). The sine curve results in a smooth, continuous squeezing action with no hammering effect. The squeezing action takes place at more than 1,000 times per min.

The action of the dies is gradually to draw the workpiece forward while the mandrel remains in one position. As the operation is completed the mandrel retracts. The incoming piece serves to eject the previous piece from the dies. Because of the forward movement of the stock, long pieces may be formed over a short mandrel.

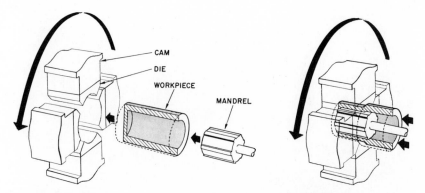

(a) Workpiece before Intraform operation.

(c) Workpiece feeds over mandrel. Reduction in workpiece diameter is evident in formed area.

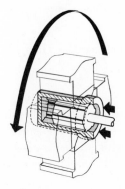

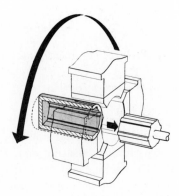

(b) Workpiece and mandrel between dies. Contact with rotating dies causes free-wheeling workpiece (and mandrel) to revolve at about 80% of die rpm.

(d) Operation completed, mandrel retracted. Next piece ejects completed part into discharge chute.

**Fig. 30-10.** The hollow cylindrical piece is mounted on the mandrel and moved up between the dies. As the mandrel retracts, the part is left between the dies and the next part pushes it into the discharge chute (courtesy Cincinnati Milling Machine Co.).

(a)

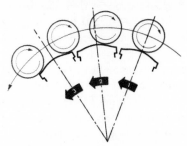

*Sketches show how the cam of one of the four Intraform dies moves without interruption from one roller to the next. Sine curve form in contact with roller results in smooth, vibrationless squeezing action.*

(b)

**Fig. 30-11.** (a) Part ready to be placed on mandrel. (b) The action of the cam on one of the four dies, which makes for rapid, smooth squeezing action (courtesy The Cincinnati Milling Machine Co.).

**Applications.**    A part formed by the Intraform process, as it is termed by the Cincinnati Milling Machine Company, is shown in Fig. 30-12.

**Fig 30-12.** Internal helical splines made on the Intraform machine (courtesy The Cincinnati Milling Machine Co.).

**Finish and Accuracy.**    The finish produced depends to a large extent upon the surface preparation, the finish on the mandrel, and the type of metal used. Generally, finish is considerably improved by rolling; for example, rifle barrels (AISI 4140) after drilling and reaming had a 32-rms reading and after internal forming of the rifling a 7- to 8-rms reading. Another example is a AISI 8640 sleeve with a bored finish of 125 rms that was improved to an 8-rms finish while forming the internal taper. Tensile-strength improvements are as much as 30 percent higher. Many operations that require a 0.0002 inside-diameter tolerance can be done by this process.

The machining cycle of the Intraform can be made fully automatic with loading and unloading chutes.

## Cold Heading

Cold heading is a comparatively old process that has been used on nails and rivets for many years. However, it is only in more recent years that the process has been looked upon as a chipless-machining operation.

The greatest factor in the recent advancement of cold heading has been the development of high-impact carbide header tools that are able to maintain very close tolerances. Impact forces range from 3 tons on the small header to 100 tons on the very large headers. Cold heading is seldom done on wire diameters larger than 1 in.

**Cold-Heading Process.**    Cold heading is basically cold forging or cold upsetting. It is done on two types of cold-heading machines— the open die and the solid die (Fig. 30-13). The wire is fed through

SPLIT OR OPEN DIES

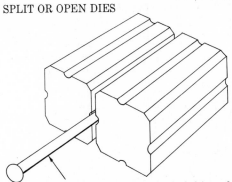

The dies open as the wire is fed in and
the finished part is ejected. The lateral
motion of the dies shears the wire.

Knockout pin

SOLID DIES

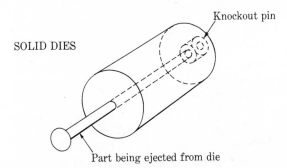

Part being ejected from die

The wire is cut off and then driven into
the solid die against a steel pin which
also serves to eject the finished part.

**Fig. 30-13.** Split and solid dies used to hold the
wire for cold heading.

the open dies and against a stop which measures the correct amount
for cold heading. The dies close on the wire and move laterally to
shear the wire. At the same time, the heading punch moves forward to
form the head. As the heading punch moves off, the dies open, and
the incoming wire ejects the finished part (Fig. 30-14). The whole
operation can be performed at the rate of 400 parts per min on small
machines. Speeds are considerably reduced on the very large cold
headers, ranging down to 50 blanks per min.

**Advantages and Limitations.**   As with other chipless-machining operations, there is a gain in tensile strength and in fatigue and shock
resistance because the material flow lines follow the contour of the
upset section. Better properties also result because fillets are required
for all inside corners.

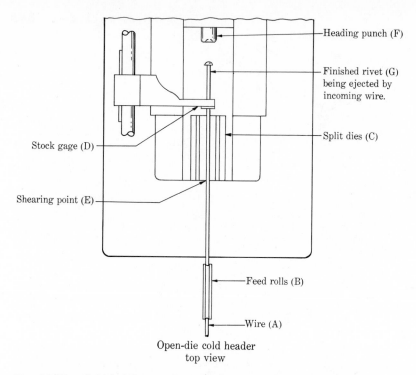

Heading punch (F)

Finished rivet (G)
being ejected by
incoming wire.

Split dies (C)

Stock gage (D)

Shearing point (E)

Feed rolls (B)

Wire (A)

Open-die cold header
top view

**Fig. 30-14.** Cold-heading-machine operation.

Cold-headed parts can take a wide variety of shapes (Fig. 30-15) and need not be symmetrical, as they must be in most regularly machined parts.

When volume is large, production costs are relatively low because of the high speed and very small scrap factor. The material used must be ductile and highly resistant to cracking.

**Fig. 30-15.** A variety of cold-headed parts (courtesy Industrial Fasteners Institute).

846

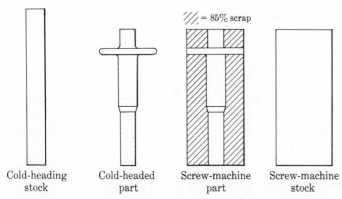

= 85% scrap

Cold-heading stock    Cold-headed part    Screw-machine part    Screw-machine stock

**Fig. 30-16.** Comparison between lathe and cold heading as to material savings and design limitations (courtesy Townsend Co.).

The maximum amount of material that can be upset in a single blow is 2¼ times the diameter of the wire. If two blows are used, 4½ times the wire diameter may be upset. Extending the wire too far out of the die will cause folds or laps.

A comparison of the amount of material needed to make a part on a lathe and by cold heading is shown in Fig. 30-16. Some design limitations are also indicated by the rounded corners and fillets.

Cold-headed parts can sometimes replace several pieces of an assembly, as shown in Fig. 30-17. The part was redesigned to in-

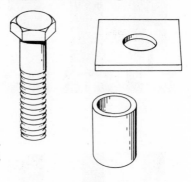

**Fig. 30-17.** A three-piece assembly redesigned for a one-piece cold-headed part (courtesy Townsend Co.).

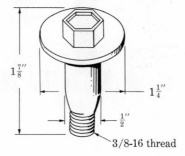

$1\frac{7}{8}''$    $1\frac{1}{4}''$    $\frac{1}{2}''$    3/8-16 thread

corporate the bolt, washer, and spacer in one cold-formed part which reduced the cost over 50 percent.

### Cold Impact Extrusion

Cold impact extrusion is a combination forging and extruding operation. Although the process is nearly 40 years old, it has not had significant development in the ferrous-metals field until fairly recently.

**Process.** Cold impact extrusion consists of making unheated metal speed through an orifice or up around a punch in a fraction of a second. Although the blank is loaded cold, the severity of the operation may cause the temperature to rise 500°F. The formed blank has a forged base and extruded sidewalls. The process can be classified as reverse, forward, or combination impact extrusion. The terms *forward* and *reverse* refer to the direction of metal flow. When the metal flows in the same direction as the movement of the punch, it is termed forward; when it moves opposite to that of the punch, it is known as reverse extrusion.

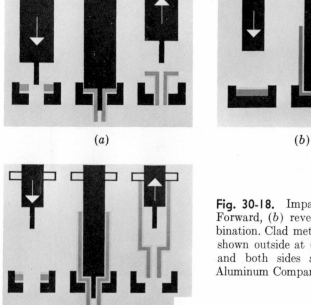

(a)

(b)

**Fig. 30-18.** Impact extrusion. (*a*) Forward, (*b*) reverse, and (*c*) combination. Clad metals are used here, shown outside at (*a*), inside at (*b*), and both sides at (*c*) (courtesy Aluminum Company of America).

(c)

FORWARD. In this case the opening or orifice for the metal is between the extension on the punch and an opening through the die [Fig. 30-18(a)]. The body of the punch seals off the top of the die, preventing reverse flow.

REVERSE. A slug is placed in the die, and high impact pressure is exerted against it by the rapidly moving punch [Fig. 30-18(b)]. The metal flows up around the punch, making the sidewalls of the vessel.

COMBINATION. A double-orifice die makes possible forming in both directions—forward and reverse [Fig. 30-18(c)].

**Advantages and Limitations.** Metals particularly adapted to impact extrusion are the softer, more ductile ones, such as aluminum, copper, and brass. However, low-carbon steels 1010 and 1012 have been used successfully. Higher alloys such as 4130 have been worked only experimentally. The harder metals present tooling difficulties, since the process is the most severe of all forming operations.

Lubrication of the workpiece, especially in the case of steel, tends to eliminate galling and welding between the die and the work. One of the best methods of providing lubrication is by surface coating the blank with zinc phosphate and then adding a reactive soap-type lubricant to the treated surface.

Generally, steel impacts are limited to $2\frac{1}{2}$ times the punch diameter on reverse extrusions. Approximate limits for aluminum extrusions are 14 in. in diameter and 60 in. in length. These limitations are due largely to present demand and the equipment available. Mechanical presses are used where they can provide sufficient capacity. For loads over 2,000 tons, hydraulic presses are used because of longer stroke and economic advantages.

Tolerances will vary with materials and design, but production runs calling for 0.002 to 0.005-in. tolerance are regularly made.

**Applications.** Impact extrusion competes with other press-working operations and with metal machining. Several examples are shown in Fig. 30-19 to give an idea of the variety of parts that can be made by this process. Common products are aerosol cans, cocktail shakers, coffee makers, fire extinguishers, flashlight cases, lipstick cases, pen and pencil shells, and vacuum bottles. Secondary operations, such as beading, thread rolling, dimpling, and machining, are sometimes needed to make the completed item.

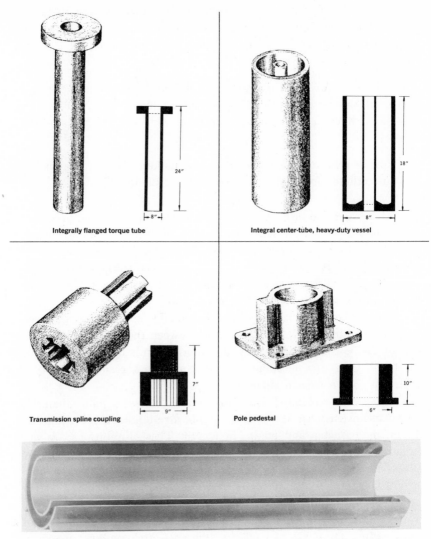

**Integrally flanged torque tube**

**Integral center-tube, heavy-duty vessel**

**Transmission spline coupling**

**Pole pedestal**

**Fig. 30-19.** A variety of parts made by impact extrusion (courtesy Aluminum Company of America).

### ULTRASONIC MACHINING

More extensive use of hard, brittle materials has led to the search for better methods to machine them. Carbides have excellent wearing qualities, but to make a drawing die out of this material may present a problem, since the material is considered unmachinable. Scientific advancements have specified such things as a 0.004-in-wide slot in a stainless-steel valve or a 1-mil hole in a piece of glass. These and many other difficult machining problems have been handled by a comparatively new development known as ultrasonic machining.

### Machining Principles

Ultrasonic machining uses a tool that is made to vibrate at a frequency beyond audible sound. An abrasive is circulated between the tool and the work. One's first impression may be that this is a stepped-up lapping process; however, this is not true. The small abrasive particles are made to strike the work with impact forces as high as 15,000 times their own weight, yet cutting forces seldom exceed 10 lb. The ultrasonic toolholder held in a transducer has a maximum amplitude of $\pm0.002$ in. Although this is not large, the fact that it occurs at 25,000 cycles per second makes it effective.

### Equipment

The principal elements needed for ultrasonic machining are ultrasonic coils, a transducer, a velocity transformer, a circulating system for the abrasive, and a cutting tool, as shown in Fig. 30-20.

The cutting tool can be made out of cold-rolled steel or other materials, such as brass and copper, that can be easily machined to the desired shape for the cut. The tool should not be tapered, because this will change the cut as material wears off the end. Tool wear takes place only on the face or end. Wear on the tool is at the rate of 1:1 when cutting carbide, and 200:1 when cutting glass.

The abrasives used are silicon carbide, boron carbide, or aluminum oxide. The grit size ranges from 180 to 800, or 0.002 to 0.00014-in. diameters, respectively. The larger size gives faster cutting action but poorer accuracy. Concentration of the abrasive and water mixture is important; a thick slurry will not distribute itself well under a large tool, and, therefore, it is limited to thin mixtures and slower cutting. A continuous supply of abrasive must be maintained at the work surface. This is accomplished by a pump which recirculates the slurry.

### Cutting Speed and Accuracy

Best machinability can be obtained on brittle materials, with cutting rates being highest on glass and certain ceramics. Glass can be cut at a rate of 0.250 in. per min, whereas tool steel, under similar conditions, would be only 0.015 in. per min.

Ultrasonic cutting is not intended for heavy stock removal, and every effort should be made to keep it to a minimum by coring holes in carbide or by rough machining before hardening.

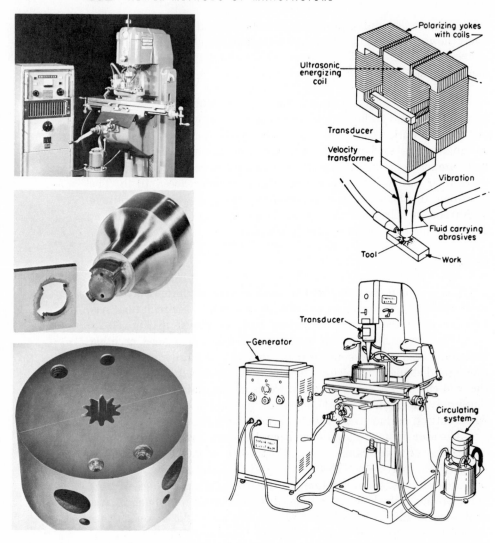

The labels visible in the diagram include: Polarizing yokes with coils, Ultrasonic energizing coil, Transducer, Velocity transformer, Vibration, Fluid carrying abrasives, Tool, Work, Transducer, Generator, Circulating system.

**Fig. 30-20.** Ultrasonic-machining equipment showing work setup and dies machined in carbide (courtesy The Sheffield Corp.).

The cavity made by an ultrasonically driven tool will be larger than the tool, since the abrasive must go down the sides to get to the bottom. The amount of enlargement can be calculated by taking into consideration the abrasive size and the depth of the hole. The over-size will correspond closely to the upper limit of the grit dimension. Some taper also is encountered in drilling holes, the top of the hole being oversize on each side by the diameter of the largest abrasive, and the bottom of the hole by the diameter of the smallest abrasive.

Great accuracy can be obtained by using several tools, the last or finishing operation being done with a close-tolerance tool and a polishing abrasive of about 2,000 grit. Dimensional accuracy of ±0.0005 in. is obtainable in two-stage drilling of glass with a recirculating 800-mesh abrasive.

## Surface Finish

Surface finish depends on the size of the abrasive grains and the cutting time. A 10-rms finish can be produced with an 800-grit boron carbide.

## Applications

Although it appears that ultrasonic machining fills a real gap in our present machining methods, it does have limitations. It is not well adapted to working softer materials, nor is it suitable for heavy stock removal. Its principal field is machining hard materials such as carbides and ceramics, and in jobs requiring detail and accuracy impossible to obtain by other machining methods. No elaborate setups or skilled operators are required, and this helps to lower the production costs.

The science of ultrasonics has been put to work in the fields of food processing, inspection and quality control, altering and mixing applications in the chemical industry, medical therapy, in industrial cleaning and degreasing, oil-well drilling, soldering and welding, and heat-transfer improvement. Other processes are currently under development. Most impressive among the newer applications is descaling steel strips without acid. The strip is first shot-blasted and then ultrasonically cleaned. Operating costs are about half the usual acid-pickling setup. This process also solves the acid-disposal problem that plagues many mills.

## ELECTRIC-DISCHARGE MACHINING

Electric-discharge machining (EDM) is closely associated with ultrasonic machining since it has some of the same uses, principally that of machining intricate shapes and contours on hard, brittle materials.

A high-frequency intermittent spark is used to erode the work-piece. The work acts as the anode and the tool as the cathode. Three closely related processes that can be classified as EDM are contact-initiated discharge, spark-initiated discharge, and electrolytic discharge.

### Contact-Initiated Discharge

In contact-initiated discharge the electrode is made to contact the workpiece and is then withdrawn to form an arc. The arc causes the temperature to rise on the workpiece, which, in turn, is cooled by a coolant. The thermal shock that occurs causes small particles to break away from the work. This type of equipment is most often used to remove broken taps and reamers.

### Spark-Initiated Discharge

Spark-initiated discharge does not require that the tool or the electrode be in contact with the work. You may have noticed at some time or other, when checking to see if all spark plugs in your car were firing, that the spark caused pit marks in the screwdriver. The same principle applies here, only on a more concentrated scientific basis. Anywhere from 10,000 to 250,000 sparks per second go across a 0.001-in gap. A dielectric fluid, usually kerosine, helps control the spark, carry away heat, and wash away the debris.

The intensity of the current flowing through the spark is very high— as much as 1,000 amp. The spark diameter, however, is small— between a few ten-thousandths and one hundredth of an inch. Its life is short, lasting between 0.1 and 10 $\mu$ sec or between 1 ten-millionth and 1 hundred-thousandth sec, depending upon the energy of the spark. A tiny portion of the workpiece is converted to metallic vapor which has a positive charge and starts back to the negative electrode, but is washed out by the coolant. Instantaneous voltages range from 40 to 60 volts in some systems and from 400 to 600 volts in others.

**Equipment.** The equipment shown in Fig. 30-21 consists of a machine similar in appearance to a vertical milling machine, with base, column, and head. The vertical feeding head may have a ram arrangement for extra-large plunging cuts. The electrodes consist of copper, molybdenum, copper-tungsten, or other conducting materials.

**Metal-Removal Rate.** The rate at which metal is removed depends on the amount of current used, the length of each pulse, and the frequency. The cubic-inch removal rate ranges from 0.02 cu in. per min in sintered carbide to 0.03 cu in. in hardened steel to as much as 0.15 cu in. per min in aluminum.

**Surface Finish and Accuracy.** A 10- to 20-rms finish may be obtained on extremely hard, brittle materials. Hole diameters, slot widths, and hole spacing can be held to a tolerance of $\pm0.0005$ in.

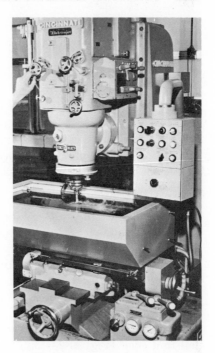

**Fig. 30-21.** The electric-discharge machine. The part being cut is a ⅞-in.-diameter beryllium missile component with 12 cutouts being machined simultaneously in 5 min (courtesy Cincinnati Milling Machine Co.).

## Electrolytic Discharge

The electrolytic-discharge process uses an electrolyte as the conducting medium. The process may be considered as the reverse of electroplating. It is generally applied to grinding and cutoff operations. The workpiece, which must be metallic, is the anode, and the metal-bonded abrasive wheel is the cathode (Fig. 30-22). Short circuiting is prevented by the protrusion of abrasive particles (diamonds) from the surface of the wheel. An electrolyte (water-base fluid) flows across the surface of the wheel, passing current from the work to the wheel. This causes the anode to dissolve.

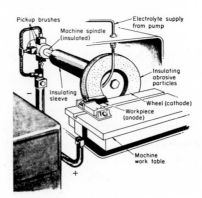

**Fig. 30-22.** Setup for electrolytic grinding (courtesy Anocut Engineering Co.).

**Metal-Removal Rate.** The rate at which the metal is removed is directly proportional to the amount of current passing through the electrolyte. The current used is determined largely by the area of contact between the wheel and the work. Hardness and tensile strength are not important. As a general rule, about 0.100 cu in. of material can be removed per minute with each 1,000 amp of current.

The diamond particles in the wheel, in addition to being insulators, help to scour the metal being cut, making it more receptive to the "unplating" action of the electrolyte. Since cutting, or making chips, is not the main function of the diamonds, the life of the wheel is increased many times.

**Finish and Accuracy.** Carbides, hardened tool steels, cermets, germanium, cobalt, nickel, and titanium, to mention some of the more difficult machining materials, may be cut with tolerances of ±0.0002 in. Cutting time is reduced by about 30 percent over conventional grinding. A 10- to 20-rms finish can be maintained.

Since this is essentially a "cold" grinding process, there is no minute softening of heat-treated surfaces. Also, very thin parts, such as stainless-steel honeycomb, can be cut without leaving a burr on the foil-thin edge (Fig. 30-23).

**Fig. 30-23.** Electrolytic grinding performed on stainless-steel honeycomb leaves a burr-free edge (courtesy Anocut Engineering Co.).

## ULTRAHIGH-SPEED MACHINING

There has long been a theory, in the field of metalworking, that materials have a critical impact velocity which, if exceeded, causes instantaneous failure. Less than the critical value merely causes plastic deformation. With the critical speeds, normal wear would not occur. Some basis for this belief was found in the experiments of Salomon, of Germany, who was issued a patent in 1931 for work in which he plotted speed against temperature. The results indicated that in trial milling runs using 55,000 sfpm on nonferrous metals, the heat generated followed a peak curve. Both the tool and the work were able to go beyond this peak. From these data, estimated curves for steel and cast iron were made, showing 148,000 and 128,000 sfpm, respectively. The conclusion was that temperatures rise to the critical cutting speed and then decrease as the critical speed is exceeded.

The questions arise: Why must the theory be proved, and will it ever be practical? The incentive to find the answers is the difficulty being experienced in machining space-age materials. Aluminum, which can be machined at 15,000 sfpm, is giving way to materials such as titanium and stainless steel, whose cutting speeds may range from 50 to 300 fpm. If the same amount of machining should be necessary on these harder metals, it would mean a considerable outlay in plants and equipment. This does not mean, should the facts back up the theory, that whole plants would be changed over. It would, however, have a profound influence on all metalworking, and those operations that could receive the most benefit would be done at ultrahigh speeds.

### Equipment

Two early approaches consisted of projectiles fired past a stationary cutting tool (Fig. 30-24) and high-speed air motors.

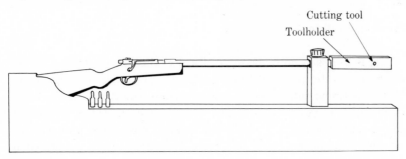

**Fig. 30-24.** Early equipment used to test the theory of ultrahigh-speed machining.

The first projectiles were fired with rifles, using a 30-06-caliber Mauser bored out to accept a 0.3-in.-diameter slug 2 in. long. The rifle was later changed to a 20-mm cannon which fired a supersonic sled at Edwards Air Force Base. With this equipment, speeds as high as 240,000 sfpm were obtained. Also, tool contact time was increased as cuts 4 ft long were made. Conventional single-point tools were used. These were made from high-speed steel, stellite, and ceramic. It was found that there was a decrease in tool wear at the higher speeds. This may be accounted for, in part, by the difference in chip formation

(Fig. 30-25). Conventional metal cutting results in a chip thicker than the depth of the cut, but in ultrahigh-speed machining, the reverse was found to be true. The favorable shear angle makes less work for the tool.

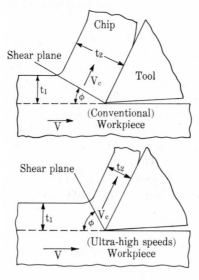

**Fig. 30-25.** Comparison of chip formation between conventional and ultrahigh-speed machining. Note the difference in chip thickness and shear plane (courtesy *American Machinist/Metalworking Manufacturing*).

**Future Applications**

It is too early to make any critical evaluation of the test results obtained in ultrahigh-speed machining. Further work is being carried on to determine cutting forces under various conditions and to relate these to horsepower requirements. The types of machine design best suited for this work are also being studied. Associated problems are vibration dampening, bearings, drives, operator safety, acceleration, deceleration, and centrifugal and dynamic forces.

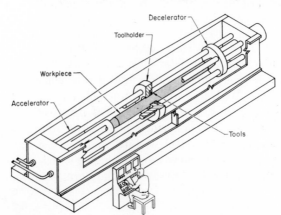

**Fig. 30-26.** Machine tools of the future may look something like this. A cutting tool is fired so that it grazes a workpiece with rifle-bullet speeds (courtesy *The Tool and Manufacturing Engineer*).

The machine shown in Fig. 30-26 may answer some of these problems. Electromagnetic, explosive, pneumatic, or hydraulic forces may be used to actuate the cutting tool. Air cushions or electromagnetic brakes could be used for deceleration.

Another approach to high-speed machining, and one that is already a small-scale-production reality, is the use of small air motors and carbide burrs. These motors have spindle speeds as high as 300,000 to 400,000 rpm. At this speed, it is possible to machine materials as hard as $R_c$ 62. Even carbides are machined, using diamond-mounted points.

The tool (Fig. 30-27) can be mounted in various machines such as the lathe, jig, borer, and milling machine, or it may be used by hand.

**Fig. 30-27.** Setup for enlarging a hole in a die block. The airotor is in position for machining. The offset boring head carries it around the periphery of the hole. The unit at the left houses the pressure regulator and filters for the air supply. These units are capable of spindle speeds as high as 300,000 to 400,000 rpm (courtesy *The Tool and Manufacturing Engineer*).

## HOT AND COLD MACHINING AND FORMING

### Hot Machining

Another approach to the difficult task of efficiently machining high-strength, high-temperature-resistant materials is to machine them at elevated temperatures. This is a radical departure from conventional machining, where every effort is directed toward keeping both tool and material temperatures as low as possible.

The theory of hot machining is that the strength of alloy steels is less at elevated temperatures. This reduces the needed cutting force; as the metal acquires a plastic character, it eliminates chip formation in the accepted sense.

The heat used must be less than the amount that would change the physical properties of the materials: Hardened steels must not be heated above the tempering temperature, and other steels must remain below the annealing temperature. To be safe, in both cases the temperatures are kept 100°F below the upper limit.

Although the tool forces are less, the fact that the work is hot causes the tool to heat up, especially on larger sections, where milling-cutter teeth are engaged for longer periods of time. Jobs done with short tool-contact time have shown that tough metal can be successfully hot-machined. This method has proved particularly effective on metals that tend to work-harden rapidly.

Solid-carbide and clamp-on tools are the best for this type of work. Brazed-type carbide-tipped tools tend to loosen up at the higher operating temperatures. High-speed steel tools are not used, as they are not able to withstand the temperatures encountered. Using the same technique, stretch presses and forming tools have successfully applied heating to make titanium alloys form more easily, reduce residual stress, and cut down warpage and springback.

### Cold Machining

At the opposite extreme of machining theory is the method of keeping the metal at a very low temperature, which, in turn, reduces tool-tip temperatures. Ways to accomplish this include surrounding the area with a cold mist (−109°F), using dry-ice coolant (−76°F), or deep-freezing the part itself.

Temperatures at the tool-and-work interface may sometimes reach 2000°F when machining tough, high-alloy materials. Problems arising from this much heat include galling, seizing, work hardening, low-temperature oxidation, and short tool life. Conventional practice has been to reduce the surface foot speed to prolong the tool life but the resulting reduced output has spurred the search for a better way.

Extensive research on subzero machining has been done by Convair for the Air Materiel Command. Some of the results indicate that mist cooling and flooding are superior to having the part cooled. Tool life improved, on some alloys, from 100 to 300 percent over conventional machining. Still further research is necessary; the information gained thus far indicates only that subzero-temperature machining may have merit and needs further study.

## CHEMICAL MILLING

Chemical milling is a method of removing metal with the aid of chemicals. Basically, it is an etching process that holds some advantages over the conventional machining methods.

### Process

The process consists of first thoroughly cleaning the metal so that the masking material, a thin, opaque, plastic film, will adhere well. Cleaning is accomplished by degreasing, acid or alkali dips, and rinsing. A good clean surface is essential to ensure uniform adhesion of the masking material. Several layers of masking material are sprayed on the part to avoid pinholes that may ruin the work.

Templates, representing the areas to be cut, are placed on the masked surface and scribed around with a knife. The cutout area of masking is removed, and the part is placed in the etchant tank (Fig. 30-28). The time in the etching bath is determined by the desired depth of cut, the acid concentration, and the temperature of the bath. The approximate rate of metal removal is 0.001 cu. in. per min. After the required amount of metal has been removed, the part is taken from the etching bath and placed in a deoxidizing bath to remove the black

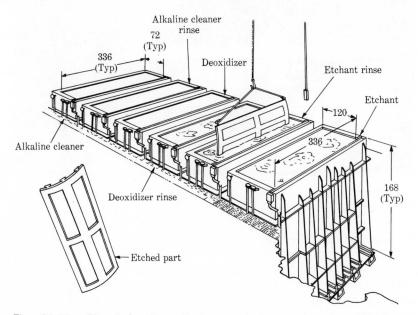

**Fig. 30-28.** Chemical-milling equipment (courtesy *American Machinist/ Metalworking Manufacturing*).

surface smut. The parts are then rinsed, and the masking is removed from the finished part.

### Applications

Chemical milling is particularly advantageous when metal must be removed from a curved surface. It is used also on surfaces too thin to machine, surface areas that have intricate outlines, and for making tapers on sheet metal parts (Fig. 30-29). By lowering the sheet into the etchant and taking it out at a predetermined rate, tapers can be milled to exceptional accuracy. A relatively rapid withdrawal produces a small taper angle, and a slow withdrawal, a large taper angle. Conical and semispherical tapers may be milled on cylindrical stock in much the same way.

**Fig. 30-29.** Examples of chemically milled parts (courtesy Chemical Milling Division, Turco Products Inc.).

### Surface Finish and Tolerances

Surface finish is dependent on the condition of the original surface. However, on deep cuts the original surface defects tend to be accentuated. The range lies generally between 30 and 125 rms. Tolerances that can be obtained are shown in Fig. 30-30.

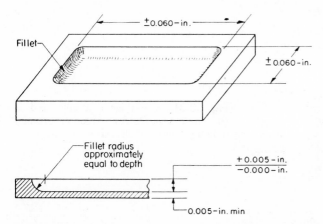

**Fig. 30-30.** Tolerances shown can be readily produced by chemical milling (courtesy *Machine Design*).

## HIGH-ENERGY-RATE FORMING METHODS

### Explosive Forming

Explosive forming is an outgrowth of drop-hammer forming. Several years ago, "trapped rubber" was used to form sheet metal blanks. The method was similar to the Guerin process except that, instead of the slow squeezing action, the rubber was made to strike the part. In this instance the rubber was encased in steel, which made a total free-falling weight of 8,970 lb. The results were so successful, in that there was no springback in the formed parts, that it was decided to extend the process to include much greater forces.

One of the first explosive-forming models used a 12-gauge shotgun shell without the shot. From this model, it was found that relatively high instantaneous forming pressures could be obtained. The 12-gauge shotgun shell developed forces equivalent to 4,500 tons in a conventional press. Figure 30-31 shows how a cartridge explosion drives a ram, forcing trapped hydraulic fluid to bulge the blank held in the forming die.

**Explosive Action.** Explosive forming is the application of extremely high pressures—from 100,000 to over 1,000,000 psi—during a very short (microsecond) interval. Metal displacements are 100 times those obtained by conventional presses. During this extremely short ultra-rapid stress-loading period, the metal passes through its elastic range into the plastic range, where it assumes a permanent set. It has not yet been determined why metals behave differently under this ultrahigh stress loading, although it has been known for years that metals can

**Cartridge**

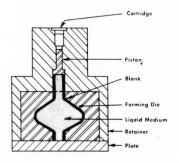

**Fig. 30-31.** Cartridge explosive used as the energy source for explosive cylinder bulging (courtesy *Metal Working*).

Explosion drives ram, forcing trapped hydraulic fluid to bulge blank into forming die.

momentarily withstand stresses and undergo elongations that would cause failure by the usual forming methods. How these phenomena relate to the improved metallurgical properties and highly uniform metal distribution in the part formed, without effect on grain structure, is also unknown. It can only be theorized that, under high stress-strain rates associated with explosive forming, the atoms go through a series of slip, break, and heal events very rapidly. Failure occurs when cohesive forces between the atom of the metal are insufficient to cope with continued slipping. This happens when the stress duration has been applied for too long a period. Explosive-forming stress duration is very short, which accounts for its success.

**Equipment.** The basic setup for explosive forming consists of the energy source, transfer medium, blank, die, and some type of retainer.

**Energy Sources.** The energy source may be one of four types— low-explosive, high-explosive, pneumatic, or electric.

Low EXPLOSIVES. Low-explosive powders do not actually explode but burn at a rate of several hundred feet per second, with rapid evolution of gas. The pressure generated by the expansion of these gases, when transferred through the air or hydraulic pressure, forces the blank to conform to the die. Low explosives are used in a closed chamber [Fig. 30-32(a)].

HIGH EXPLOSIVES. High explosives detonate in a few millionths of a second and produce shock waves whose magnitudes are in millions of pounds per square inch. The charge is suspended over the workpiece in either air or water [Fig. 30-32 (b) and (c)]. The charges may be shaped to direct the shock waves to specific areas of the blank. The

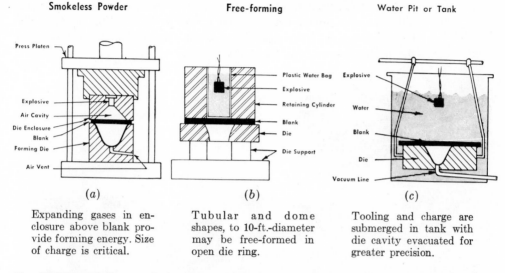

Smokeless Powder     Free-forming     Water Pit or Tank

(a)     (b)     (c)

Expanding gases in enclosure above blank provide forming energy. Size of charge is critical.

Tubular and dome shapes, to 10-ft.-diameter may be free-formed in open die ring.

Tooling and charge are submerged in tank with die cavity evacuated for greater precision.

**Fig. 30-32.** (a) Low explosives are used in a closed chamber. (b), (c) High explosives use either air or a liquid to transfer the shock waves to the workpiece. Either free or bulkhead forming is done by this method (courtesy *Metal Working*).

medium used to conduct the shock wave is usually water, but oil, plastics, talcum powder, and clay are also used.

COMPRESSED GAS. The Hyge machine, built by Convair, is actuated by 2,000 psi of nitrogen. The high pressure of the gas is instantly released from its storage chamber, driving a piston-column assembly at high velocity into a liquid medium which acts against the blank in the die (Fig. 30-33). The machine is able to sustain working pressures up to 300,000 psi for 2 to 10 msec. The machine

Gas Actuation

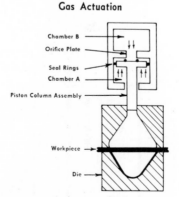

**Fig. 30-33.** Compressed gas is instantaneously released against the piston, which transfers the force to a liquid medium and then to the blank (courtesy *Metal Working*).

Hyge machine drives ram by sudden surge of 2000 psi gas through orifice between chambers.

has also been used to extrude tungsten, forge ferrous and nonferrous alloys, and compact ceramic and metal powders (Fig. 30-34). The big advantages of this machine are the elimination of explosives as the power source, and high repeatability.

**Fig. 30-34.** Parts formed by the compressed-gas method (courtesy General Dynamics Corporation).

HYDROSPARK FORMING. The discharge of an electric spark under water produces a shock wave with energy sufficient to form metal parts (Fig. 30-35). Forces equal to 6,000 hp within 40 millionths of a second are possible at present, with larger capacities being built.

*Equipment.* The equipment consists basically of a high-voltage power supply, capacitors for storing the charge, a discharge switch, and a coaxial electrode. The applied force needed can be varied by varying the voltage. Energy increases as the square of the voltage.

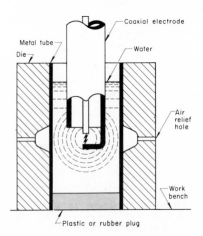

**Fig. 30-35.** Hydrospark forming used to bulge a cylinder (courtesy *The Tool and Manufacturing Engineer*).

*Advantages.* The advantages of hydrospark forming are greater safety, more precise control, and lower cost. It is estimated that this tool can be constructed at one tenth the cost of a conventional hydraulic press used to do the same work, and it occupies only a fraction of the floor space.

**Advantages of Explosive Forming.** The benefits of explosive forming may be summarized briefly as follows:

1. It is possible to obtain high working energies (up to several million pounds per square inch). This is higher than is economically or physically possible with mechanical or hydraulic presses.

2. Springback is virtually eliminated. Parts may be formed to finished size. Close tolerances—within 0.005 in.—are possible. This means better mating between interchangeable parts.

3. Greater deformation (up to 2.5 times the elongations normal with usual forming methods) can be obtained without failure of the part. Many parts that formerly required multiple draws or spinning steps, with intermediate anneals, can now be formed with a single draw.

4. Physical properties are improved. The hardness of ductile and non heat-treatable metals can be increased for greater strength. Yield strength can also be increased.

5. Economic benefits can be obtained through less expensive capital equipment. Simpler setups require only a well or an underground tank large enough to accommodate the die. Die costs are reduced, since explosive forming requires only one die, usually a female. Die materials can be relatively inexpensive, such as cast epoxy and epoxy-faced dies, Kirksite, and aluminum. Standard tool steels are preferred for long runs.

6. Excellent repeatability can be obtained where the quantity and placement of the charge are carefully controlled. Even greater repeatability is evidenced by compressed-gas and hydrospark forming.

**Limitations of Explosive Forming.** 1. The formability of brittle metals or metals with 1 to 2 percent elongation is not improved.

2. Proper selection of the type, quantity, and shape of the explosive charge is an art. Too little energy will not form the part; too much will destroy it. In designing the charge, small models are used, and the results are extrapolated for full-scale workpieces with almost 100 percent accuracy.

**Future Applications.** Good progress is being made in adapting explosive forming to extruding, forging, shearing, and blanking. Metal and ceramic powders have been successfully compacted with explosive forming. New techniques in welding dissimilar metals (aluminum to steel) at room temperatures have been done successfully, and this, in turn, suggests a new cladding technique.

### Magnetic Forming

The newest concept in high-energy forming is magnetic forming. Electric energy in the form of magnetism acts as the forming force. The magnetic pulses last only 6 millionths of a second and exert pressures up to 560,000 psi.

Magnetic pressures of this magnitude require a 1-megagauss field. (The gauss is used to indicate the density of the magnetic flux.)

The commercial magnetic forming-machine shown in Fig. 30-38 is capable of forming pressures up to 50,000 psi in pulses with durations of 10 to 20 millionths of a second. Electrical energy is stored in a capacitor and discharged rapidly through the coil, as shown in the schematic diagram. The current is induced from the coil to the conducting workpiece. The induced field in the workpiece interacts with the coil field and produces the necessary forming force.

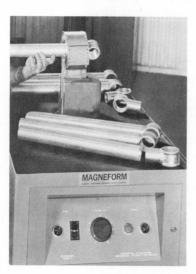

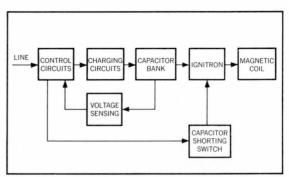

**Fig. 30-36.** The type of machine used for magnetic forming, showing parts being placed in the coil and a schematic diagram of the circuit used (courtesy General Dynamics Corporation).

**Principal Methods.** Magnetic forming can be classified in three basic arrangements—compression forming, expansion forming, and hammer forming.

COMPRESSION FORMING. The principle of compression forming is shown in Fig. 30-37. The tube is formed against a mandrel. The pulsed forming time is so short that the depth of penetration of the field is small compared to the thickness of the tube. Therefore, there is no magnetic leak to the inside of the tube.

When insulated mandrels are used, the collapse rate is retarded. The magnetic flux must leak through the tube to fill the entire cross-sectional area before a significant back pressure develops.

**Fig. 30-37.** Compression forming causes the metal to shrink,
compress, or collapse against the
mandrel (courtesy General Atomic Division, General Dynamics
Corporation).

EXPANSION FORMING. In expansion forming, the work coil is
placed inside the material to be formed (Fig. 30-38). A slowly rising
magnetic field is established in the coil and the tube to be expanded.
Then the field outside the tube is reduced to zero in less time than
the field penetration. The trapped magnetic field presses the tube
outward.

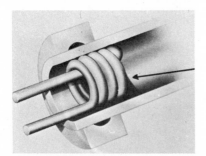

**Fig. 30-38.** Expansion forming is done by placing the coil on the inside and
using the forming force to expand the workpiece (courtesy General Atomic
Division, General Dynamics Corporation).

HAMMER FORMING. Flat materials can be formed by placing them
between an insulated die and the coil (Fig. 30-39). The same principles
used in tube forming apply.

**Advantages.** This new forming method has several distinct advantages that facilitate production operations.

1. It does not mar nor scratch the work surface, and thus eliminates further finishing operations.

2. The operation can be used to produce quantities—as many as
600 forming operations per hour.

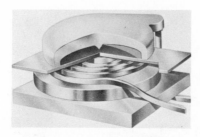

**Fig. 30-39.** Hammer forming can be used to form dimples or blanks, or to emboss by pressing the workpiece against a die form (courtesy General Atomic Division, General Dynamics Corporation).

3. The fact that there is no moving part minimizes maintenance and provides for quiet operation.

4. The process can be used on refractory metals when covered by an inert atmosphere or a vacuum.

5. Coils can be easily changed for different applications, minimizing downtime.

6. The exact amount of force needed can be adjusted and set so there will be no variance from part to part.

7. Forming operations that are impractical or are inaccessible by other means can often be formed by this method.

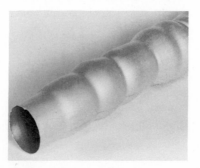

**Fig. 30-40.** Examples of the different types of work performed by magnetic forming (courtesy General Atomic Division, General Dynamics Corporation).

**Applications.** Some general applications in use at the present time (Fig. 30-40) are forming tubing into precise and difficult shapes; expanding tubing into bushings, hubs, and split dies; swaging inserts, fittings, and terminals into many diverse parts, including rope, control cables, etc.; and rapid coining, shearing, and blanking.

## CUTTING, WELDING, AND MEASURING WITH LASERS

### Laser Light Beams

The laser light beam is one of the newer tools being examined for industrial applications in welding machining and measurement. The term laser stands for *light amplification by stimulated emission of radiation*. It was first demonstrated in 1960 and since that time has had a great deal of development. Briefly, it is a device that amplifies light to phenomenal energy intensities, emits it as coherent light and focusses it on a pinpoint. The result is that the hardest and most refractory material can be pierced. Molybdenum can be vaporized instantly, and even diamonds can have holes drilled in them by this method.

The laser, like the electron beam used in welding, has a very high depth-to-width ratio resulting in a minimum of grain growth and distortion in the weld area. Electron-beam welding requires a vacuum chamber, but the laser can be used out in the open with simple inert-gas shielding.

The interferometer, as explained in Chapter 27, uses light that is only partially coherent, permitting only short-distance measurement. Since laser beams are nearly coherent, measurements can be performed over an extremely long distance, possibly a mile. This measurement may be too accurate for many applications, but as lasers with differing wave lengths are developed, the accuracy of measurement can be reduced to a more workable range of 0.0002 in. between the interference fringes rather than 10 microinches. The helium light used in connection with optical flats discussed in Chapter 27 has a wave length of 23.2 microinches.

The first lasers were of a intermittent or pulsed output type. In 1962 the first gas laser was announced. This laser used a neon–helium mixture and was capable of producing a continuous-wave (c-w).

The laser is undergoing continual development. Researchers are on the trail of still more types and are studying such systems as glass fibers, liquids, semi-conductors, and organic molecules. Laser action in organic molecules is of particular interest, since it would permit generating light of virtually any frequency.

## QUESTIONS

1. What is meant by the term chipless machining?

2. What harmful effect may chipless machining have? How can this be overcome?

3. Why are rolled threads considered to be of higher quality than cut threads?

4. How does the average roughness of a cut thread compare with that of a rolled thread?

5. What is meant by a 75-percent thread?

6. Explain what is meant by in-feed thread rolling.

7. What is the big advantage of internal forming?

8. What are some limitations of cold heading?

9. Name two advantages of the impact extrusion process?

10. What is the main application of ultrasonic machining?

11. Why can very hard materials be cut better by the ultrasonic process than soft ones?

12. In what respect are EDM and ultrasonic machining alike?

13. What is the difference in application between contact-initiated discharge cutting and spark-initiated discharge cutting?

14. Why is EDM more applicable for cutting nonferrous materials than ultrasonic machining?

15. What is the main application of electrolytic grinding?

16. What is the theory behind ultrahigh-speed machining?

17. What is meant by a favorable shear angle?

18. What is the theory behind hot machining?

19. What are some practical applications of chemical milling?

20. What is the theory behind explosive forming?

21. What is the principle of hydrospark forming?

22. Name two distinct advantages of explosive forming. Name two limitations.

23. What is the principle of expansion magnetic forming?

24. Name two advantages of magnetic forming?

25. What are some applications of magnetic forming?

## PROBLEMS

1. At what rpm would a 4-in.-diameter shaft have to turn to attain the high-speed machining range of 150,000 sfpm?

2. What is the approximate shear angle of the material shown in (a) conventional cutting, (b) high-speed machining in Fig. 30-25.

3. If the cutter used in Fig. 30-27 is a boring tool set at a ¼-in. radius, what will the sfpm be at 400,000 rpm?

4. Approximately how long will it take to chemically mill an aluminum-alloy material to a $\frac{1}{2}$-in. depth? What would the tolerance of the etched surface be if the original surface tolerance were $\pm 0.005$ in.?

5. Approximately how long would it take to drill a $\frac{1}{2}$-in.-diameter hole through 1 $\frac{5}{8}$-in.-thick glass by the ultrasonic method? What tolerance and surface finish could be attained?

6. What would the feed rate be for an electric-discharge drill $\frac{3}{4}$ in. in diameter cutting solid carbide? How would this compare with doing the same work ultrasonically?

## REFERENCES

Beckim, R. W., and H. H. Muller, "Designing for Chemical Milling," *Machine Design*, June, 1957.

Birdsall, F. C., H. P. Ford, and R. E. Riley, "Magnetic Forming," *American Machinist/Metalworking Manufacturing*, March, 1961.

Cadwell, G., "Spark Forming Goes to Work," *American Machinist/Metalworking Manufacturing*, November, 1961.

*Cold Forming Design Data*, Townsend Company, Ellwood City, Pa., 1956.

*Cold and Hot Heading*, The Industrial Fasteners Institute, Terminal Tower, Cleveland, 1958.

Degroat, G., "Ultra High Speed Machining," *American Machinist/Metalworking Manufacturing*, February, 1960.

Lemmond, C. Q., "Industrial Uses Loom for Lasers," *Machine Design*, October 25, 1962.

Parr, J., "Hydro-Spark Forming," *The Tool and Manufacturing Engineer*, March, 1960.

Rose, C. N., "Chemical Milling Today," *The Tool and Manufacturing Engineer*, October, 1961.

Watts, F. W., and D. C. Harleman, "Why Form Explosively?" *The Tool and Manufacturing Engineer*, April, 1960.

Wood, W., "High Energy Forming Methods," *The Tool and Manufacturing Engineer*, June, 1960.

# INDEX